HEBRAIC INFLUENCES ON GREEK CIVILIZATION

WAS ACHILLES A JEW?

LARRY S. MILNER, MD, JD, MLS

Mazo Publishers

Hebraic Influences on Greek Civilization: Was Achilles a Jew?

Paper: ISBN 978-1-936778-47-8
Cloth: ISBN 978-1-936778-18-8

Published by

■■■

Mazo Publishers
P.O. Box 10474
Jacksonville, FL 32247 USA

www.mazopublishers.com
Email: mazopublishers@gmail.com
Tel: 1-815-301-3559

Note: Portions of this book were originally published in "Was Achilles A Jew? Hebraic Contributions to Greek Civilization", 2008.

"Does that mean, Professor Gordon, that Achilles was Jewish?"* **"**

* In a talk by Cyrus Gordon, the renowned professor emeritus of Brandeis and New York Universities, who suggested that the ancient Hebrew and Greek civilizations both developed from a common societal heritage in Ugarit, explaining the similarity between Achilles and King David, an elderly lady intrigued with his proposal, boldly asked, "Does that mean, Professor Gordon, that Achilles was Jewish?" Marblestone, Howard, "A 'Mediterranean Synthesis.'" *Biblical Archaeologist* 59 (1996): 22.

CONTENTS

The Author

Dr. Larry S. Milner, MD, JD, MLS is a retired physician, board-certified in Internal Medicine, Hematology and Oncology. He trained at the University of Illinois, Massachusetts General Hospital, University of Pennsylvania Hospital, and the National Institutes of Health. He is also an attorney trained at Loyola Law School in Chicago, and has a Master of Liberal Studies degree from Lake Forest College.

In addition to being recognized as a biblical historian, he is an expert in the field of infanticide, and the author of *Hardness of Heart, Hardness of Life: the Stain of Human Infanticide*.

His other books published in 2015 include *Tainted Hands: An Encounter With The Mosiac Code* and *Your Name Is Achilles, Son Of Daniel*.

Dr. Milner has been married to his wife, Marlene, for fifty-one years, and has three daughters, Kimberly Seiden, Wendy LaVarre, and Jodi Morton, and eight wonderful grandchildren. He divides his time between Lincolnshire, Illinois and Boynton Beach, Florida.

INTRODUCTION

Cyrus Gordon, the renowned professor emeritus of Brandeis and New York Universities, compared Achilles, as portrayed by Homer in the *Iliad*, with the young King David of Israel, from the Old Testament[1] book of *Samuel*, in a lecture he entitled "The Common Background of Greek and Hebrew Civilizations."[2] Gordon had elaborated on the many similarities between the plots and characters in the writings of Homer and the Old Testament in previous publications, concluding that this resemblance was due to the ancient Hebrew and Greek civilizations having both developed from a common societal heritage in Ugarit, the ancient Syrian city a few miles north of Laodicea that functioned as a center for international trade in the second millennium BCE. He created much controversy among biblical scholars with this view, and his findings, outlined in numerous papers and books, have been hotly debated for years. His conclusion that the similitude between the Hebrew and Greek accounts indicate that the two societies "are parallel structures built upon the same East Mediterranean foundation,"[3] is not accepted by the majority of historians, although most scholars agree that unique similarities of structure and form do exist between passages in the Homeric epics and the tales of the Old Testament.[4] Following this particular well-received talk, an elderly lady, intrigued with the implications of his theory, came up to Gordon and boldly asked: "Does that mean, Professor Gordon, that Achilles was Jewish?"[5] Gordon's response is not recorded, but I believe it is likely that those around him smiled at the frivolity of the question, quickly brushed the woman's remark aside, and turned their attention to other, more important, matters.

I surmise that the participants did not give serious consideration to the

---

1 I will refer to the Hebrew Bible, or *TaNaKh*, which is composed of the *Torah* (Instruction or Law), *Nevi'im* (*Nebi'im*) (Prophets), and *Ketuvim* (*Ketubim*) (Writings), as either the Bible or the Old Testament in this book, since it is generally recognized under these terms in modern times. The Torah, which is the first five books of the Bible including *Genesis*, *Exodus*, *Numbers*, *Leviticus*, and *Deuteronomy*, is also sometimes simply referred to as "the Book," but I will use the term Torah in this book.

2 Marblestone, Howard, "A 'Mediterranean Synthesis.'" *Biblical Archaeologist* 59 (1996): 22.

3 Gordon, Before the Bible: The Common Background of Greek and Hebrew Civilizations, 9.

4 The similarities have led William G. Pollard (1911-1989 CE), the well-known nuclear physicist and Episcopal priest, to refer to the biblical tales as the "Hebrew Iliad," and the "Hebrew Odyssey." Pollard, The Hebrew Iliad: The History of the Rise of Israel Under Saul and David, 8.

5 Marblestone, "A 'Mediterranean Synthesis'," 22.

suggestion because few modern scholars have postulated that the ancient Greeks and Hebrews had any connection whatsoever, despite the intriguing correlation between their ancient texts. Although many articles have identified similar styles and literary motifs between the writings of Homer and the Old Testament, no one has actually suggested that Homer was influenced by encountering biblical texts, or that the Greeks owed any of their remarkable development to ancient Hebrew infiltration during the Late Bronze Age (1600-1200 BCE).[6] This attitude is typified by H. D. F. Kitto (1897-1982 CE), the late professor of Greek at Bristol University, who noted that "here were two races, each very conscious of being different from its neighbors, living not very far apart, yet for the most part in complete ignorance of each other and influencing each other not at all until the period following Alexander's conquests."[7] Even Cyrus Gordon, while postulating a common origin for the two cultures, recognized their disparity, and admitted that Israel and Greece (*Hellas*) were basically "two water-tight

---

6 The three-age system of dating Old World archaeology into the Stone Age, Bronze Age, and Iron Age was first developed by the Danish archaeologist Christian Jurgensen Thomsen (1788-1865 CE) of the National Museum of Denmark in Copenhagen in 1819 CE, and published in 1836 CE. It is still accepted as the standard measure today, although there is disagreement on the exact dates applied to each era. Freeman, Egypt, Greece and Rome: Civilizations of the Ancient Mediterranean, 27. Although there are differences in estimates of the standard chronology of the Bronze Age, the generally accepted divisions include the Early (3000-2000 BCE), Middle (2000-1600 BCE), and Late (1600-1200 BCE) Bronze Ages. Kenyon, Royal Cities of the Old Testament, 13. The Iron Age, which follows, is frequently divided into Iron Age I (1200-1000 BCE), the period of the Israelite Judges and United Monarchy, and Iron Age II (1000-587 BCE), the period of the Israelite Divided Monarchy. Soggin, A History of Ancient Israel, 360. Recent suggestions have been made by various scholars to radically revise the dates of the Bronze Age, making my assumptions in this study subject to change. Dr. Donovan Courville (1901-1996 CE), Professor of Biochemistry at the Loma Linda School of Medicine, has suggested that the end of the Early Bronze Age should be moved forward from 2000 BCE to c. 1400 BCE, a point coincident with his timing of the conquest of Canaan under Joshua. Courville, The Exodus Problem and Its Ramifications, I.100. Dr. Immanuel Velikovsky (1895-1979 CE), a Russian-born Jewish psychiatrist who helped found the Hebrew University of Jerusalem, on the other hand, claimed that the battle pictures at Medinet Habu depicting the victory of Ramesses III (1184-1153 BCE) over the Peoples of the Sea, were not from the twelfth century BCE, as is generally believed, but rather from 525-390 BCE. Velikovsky, Peoples of the Sea, 34. If either of these extreme alterations is proven correct, my present analysis will obviously have to undergo major modification, but I will not attempt to disprove their claims in this book.

7 Kitto, The Greeks, 8. This conviction is buttressed by John Van Seters, Professor of Biblical Literature at the University of North Carolina, Chapel Hill, who noted that it is "doubtful that there was much direct cultural contact between the Greeks and the Hebrews before the fourth century B.C." Van Seters, In Search of History: Historiography in the Ancient World and the Origins of Biblical History, 53-54.

compartments, totally different from each other."[8] Gordon never suggested that a direct connection between the two societies ever took place, and provided only a cursory explanation of how the Ugaritic culture influenced both the Hebrews and Greeks by postulating that it was transmitted by human agency, either by tribal units seeking grass and water for their flocks of sheep, or by transplantation of colonies or enclaves.[9] Since there were continuous migrations of many diverse people throughout the ancient Near East during the second millennium BCE, such an affirmation adds little to our knowledge of how Homer and the compilers of the Old Testament happened to develop such intricate correlations in their literary style.

This conclusion that the ancient Hebrews and Greeks were isolated entities, having little chance to interact on a social or intellectual level is not supported, in my opinion, by a close investigation of the historical data that is available from a variety of sources. The primary problem with all the analytic determinations disputing a similarity between the ancient Hebrews and Greeks is that they refer to the lifestyle and beliefs of Judaism following the return of the Israelites from the Babylonian Exile (587-538 BCE), rather than to what is known about the attributes of the Hebrew people both before and following the Exodus, when Moses began to impose the modifications demanded by the Ten Commandments (Decalogue). Although modern Judaism is recognized as the first monotheistic religion, and is thereby clearly the antithesis of the Classical Greek culture (500-323 BCE), which was polytheistic, worshiping multiple deities that had their origin in adjacent contemporary civilizations, most ancient cultures from the Middle and Late Bronze Ages, including the Patriarchs and the Hebrews who began the Exodus following their sojourn in Egypt, did not restrict their faith to a single God alone.[10] Moses may have required that the Hebrews change their religious practices and worship only YHWH,[11] but there was so much opposition to his attempt to force the Hebrews into a monotheistic mode that over 42,000

---

8 Gordon, Before The Bible: The Common Background of Greek and Hebrew Civilizations, 11.

9 Ibid., 22, 26.

10 Rabbinic tradition refers to Abraham, Isaac, and Jacob as the "Patriarchs." I will refer to the participants of the Exodus as Hebrews, rather than Israelites (literally "sons of Israel" or "descendants of Israel"), as the latter description does not properly apply until after Jacob had migrated to Egypt with his entire family (Gen 32:33). The name of "Israel" was not actually given to the sacral alliance of the Hebrew tribes until after the Settlement, when Joshua led the Hebrews into the land of Canaan. von Rad, Old Testament Theology, I.6.

11 Although most academic texts refer to the primary God of Israel as Yahweh, or Jehovah, I will follow the use of the Tetragrammaton YHWH throughout this book, as a sign of respect to the prohibition of the more common term by Orthodox Jews.

participants were killed when they failed to follow his radical demand.[12]   In my opinion, this parricidal reprisal caused many other dissident Hebrews to flee the Exodus and emigrate to Mycenae (Mykene) because they wished to remain faithful to the polytheistic tenets of their ancestors, and were not willing to change, just because Moses claimed that God demanded they forgo the faith of their forefathers.[13]

When these dissident Hebrews arrived in Mycenae, they carried with them the traditions of the Patriarchs that eventually would carry over into the writing of the Torah by the later generations of Jews who followed Moses into the Promised Land. The dissidents knew much of this story firsthand, even though they may have left the conclave before the Jordan River was crossed, and their recollections of what it meant to practice the Hebrew faith before its modification in a monotheistic belief would have been very compatible with the religion of the early Greek civilization, as I will detail in the chapters which follow. One oral tradition I believe they were most certainly aware, and the one which clearly indicates to me that the early Greeks were influenced by Hebrew legends, was the story of the attempted sacrifice of Isaac by Abraham in order to obey the directives of God.[14]   Known as the Akeda (*Akedah*), this tale highlighted the overwhelming faith of Abraham in God's commands, and rabbinic writings over the centuries have extolled Abraham for his willingness to sacrifice his only son in

---

12 After returning from the top of Mt. Sinai with the Ten Commandments and finding the Hebrews worshiping the golden calf-idol, Moses ordered 3,000 men killed. Exod 32:28. In response to the rebellion of Korah, a plague was sent to kill his impudent supporters, and in the conflagration which followed, 14,700 people died. Num 16:49. After the orgy at Acacia, Moses ordered those who worshiped Baal to be executed, and 24,000 people died. Num 25:9. This total of almost 42,000 does not include the unnumbered people who died when God sent venomous snakes as punishment when they complained about the lack of food and water on their way to Edom (Num 21:6), the ones killed by a plague at Kibroth-hattaavah (Num 11:33-34), or the objectors who were burned in a fire sent by God at Taberah (Num 11:1-3).

13 Moses knew that the Hebrews were adamantly loyal to ancestral teaching, for just before he died, he told the Hebrews in the *Ha'azinu* (Song of Moses) to: "Remember the days of old, Consider the years of ages past; Ask your father, he will inform you, Your elders, they will tell you." Deut 32:7. Levinson, "Deuteronomy," 441.

14 It is generally accepted that oral traditions were passed from one generation to another throughout the Bronze Age, as will be discussed in more detail throughout this book. Homer included many instances in the *Odyssey* where the participants eagerly took part in prolonged story-telling (*Odyssey* 1:325ff; 4.594ff; 8.62ff; 8:266ff; 11.373ff; 13:27; 15.391ff). According to Susan Niditch, Samuel Green Professor of Religion at Amherst College: "While biblical works cannot be proven in any instance to have been orally composed, the written works of the Hebrew Bible evidence traits typically associated with ascertainably orally composed works." Niditch, Oral World and Written Word: Ancient Israelite Literature, 8-10.

fulfillment of the request made by God that he prove himself worthy of becoming the ancestor of the Chosen People. Abraham's capacity to put the commandment of God above the life of his own son proved to faithful adherents that his piety to the Lord was more important than attachment to another human being, and his unselfish devotion to God became the hallmark act of monotheism, as ultimately defined in the Ten Commandments of the Mosaic Code.[15]

While the Akeda remains the most famous story of child-sacrifice, or more accurately attempted child-sacrifice, a similar obedience to a divine infanticidal directive was seen in ancient Greek lore, where Agamemnon finally agreed to sacrifice his daughter, Iphigenia, when told by the seer Calchas that the goddess Artemis was preventing the Greek armada from sailing to the Trojan War because homage had not been given by a proper sacrifice. This action was used by Classical Greek philosophers and playwrights to demonstrate that the survival of the Greek State was more important than the survival of any cherished individual, even if that person was the leader's own child. The choice Agamemnon made has survived to the present day as a model of how far a leader may have to go to assure fulfillment of a valid political aim.[16]

Both of these stories emphasized the mandate that the instructions given by a God were to be carefully and literally followed. In the Jewish faith, the requirement was based upon the covenant made between Abraham and YHWH, thereby identifying the Hebrew descendants as the Chosen People; while with the Greeks, the need was based on the overriding importance of the survival of the Greek state over the survival of any individual person. Both stories were handed down within each culture from generation to generation as evidence of morally appropriate behavior, and every member of society was taught to accept the actions of Abraham and Agamemnon as models for their own future conduct. Although many individuals were applauded by other societies for their willingness to immolate themselves, or their loved ones, for the sake of a higher authority, no other culture on earth, except for the ancient Hebrews and Greeks, elevated the sacrifice of a child by its parent to the level of a laudable parable which was

---

15 The Ten Commandments are listed at Exod 20:1-17 and Deut 5:6-21. The list includes (1) Thou shalt have no other gods before me; (2) You shall not make yourself an idol; (3) You shall not lift up the name of YHWH in vain; (4) Observe the Sabbath day and keep it holy; (5) Honor your mother and father; (6) You shall not murder; (7) You shall not commit adultery; (8) You shall not steal; (9) You shall not give false witness; and (10) You shall not covet. The two listings differ on the reason why the Sabbath day is to be kept holy, with the one in *Exodus* saying that it was because God rested on the seventh day of Creation, and the one in *Deuteronomy* concluding it was because God led them out of Egypt during the Exodus on the Sabbath.

16 Soren Kierkegaard (1813-1855 CE), the Danish philosopher and theologian, labeled Agamemnon's action as indicative of the tragic hero where "the father will turn his face away, but the hero will raise the knife." Kierkegaard, Fear and Trembling, 68.

divinely approved or demanded. The story of the infanticide was not only part of their traditional lore, it was told with few comments to suggest that the act was not acceptable under the circumstances presented. The similarity between the two legends is so great that I believe it strongly suggests – as Jean-Pierre Vernant, the well-known literary critic and scholar of Greek myths, has pointed out about Hellenic legends in general – that congruence can be used to conclude that there was an established kinship between them.[17] The fact that these two widely separated societies could independently develop this concept, at exactly the same time in history, in almost the same region of the earth, cannot, in my opinion, be due to chance alone.

Supporting my thesis that there was a direct transference of attributes from the ancient Hebrews to the Greeks are many other congruencies, including the political framework of amphictyony, the nature of religious worship in both cultures, and other heroic legendary themes. In addition, there are many attributes of Classical Greek philosophical and theatrical works which I believe represents the continued influence of Hebraic thought on the evolving Greek view of the world. I realize that this claim is likely to be met with resistance because scholars generally view the Golden Age of Greece as the primary generator of Western civilization, creating an aura of uniqueness to the Classical Greek Age that interferes with any consideration that its success was due to contemporary sources which were not inherently Greek. Werner Jaeger (1888-1961 CE), the illustrious twentieth century Classicist, grouped the Western nations as "Hellenocentric," given his belief that our history begins with the Greeks, adding that "the law and the prophets of the Israelites, the Confucion System of the Chinese, the Dharma of the Indians are in their whole intellectual structure fundamentally and essentially different from the Greek ideal of culture."[18] But Jaeger, like many other western intellects, was so fascinated by the glory that was ancient Greece that he failed to imagine that the Greek advancements were suggested by any of the ancient cultures that preceded them. He reacted like the English poet Percy Shelley, who romantically noted: "We are all Greeks ... our laws, our literature, our religion, our arts, have their root in Greece."[19]

It is easy to see where this impressive characterization of the ancient Greeks came from, even if it has resulted in a biased view of history. The origins of Western architecture, sculpture, philosophy, literature, ethics, and even the democratic form of government, have all had their germination in the attributes of the ancient Greek civilization. The truly remarkable era of Homer (c. ninth century BCE) and Hesiod (c. eighth century BCE), of the famous Greek tragedists, Aeschylus (c. 525-426 BCE), Euripides (c. 480-406 BCE), and Sophocles (495-406 BCE),

---

17 Vernant, The Universe, the Gods, and Men: Ancient Greek Myths, ix.
18 Jaeger, Padeia: The Ideals of Greek Culture, vol. I, xv, xvii.
19 Shelley, Selected Poetry and Prose, 71.

of the celebrated philosophical schools of Plato (427-347 BCE) and Aristotle (384-322 BCE), and of the founder of historical writing, Herodotus (c. 490-420 BCE) – to name just a few seminal figures – are filled with scholarship that truly seems to be at the very beginnings of modern Western thought.[20] This incredible epoch of Greek history, primarily from the seventh to the fourth centuries BCE, spawned the dawn of free speech, independent thought, and a vision of life that promoted the virtuous elements of courage and justice.

But what has never been answered in all the accolades which have been placed on the innovations of the Greek thinkers, from the philosophers to the playwrights, from Homer to Herodotus, is how they first developed their creative, ingenious thoughts in the first place. Was Herodotus truly the world's first historian, or are we simply ignoring his predecessors? Was Thales truly the world's first philosopher, or do we want to ignore the advancements made by authors for centuries before? Many of the Greek concepts, I believe, did not originate for the first time with these famous men, but were first formulated in early biblical texts, which predated the writings of all these literary giants, and were available in either early written form, or in the oral prophecies in Israel and the adjacent countries of Egypt and Babylon, by the Hebrew prophets who were contemporary with the Greek intellectuals. While it has generally been assumed that some of the Greek originality came from the Egyptians, Babylonians, and Phoenicians, a possible Hebrew contribution has been totally ignored. This is especially surprising when one realizes that the writings of the Old Testament, and the eventual recording of the Homeric epics, both appeared in the same era, from the ninth to seventh centuries BCE, and that the lives of the philosophers followed, rather than preceded, their Hebrew predecessors. While it is true that the Greeks were reluctant to apply much involvement of the gods in their new theories of cosmogony, they nevertheless were so similar to the biblical concepts that many historians have labeled them as "monists," and it is my belief that they were convinced of this unity in nature by the teachings of the Old Testament, which highlighted the role of YHWH as the single Creator, rather than in utilizing concepts of the scientific method that did not truly appear on the scientific scene until centuries later. While the Greeks, until the time of Plato, struggled to deny the role of "God" in this process, and stick to rational, scientific accounts, it is clear that their entire cosmogony resembled the format presented in the book of *Genesis*.

It must be remembered that the stories of the biblical text were carried on in an oral tradition, much like what has been generally accepted for the transmission of the legend of the Trojan War. Homer's text was passed in an oral format for many generations before it was finally memorialized in a written text, and in a

---

20 Although Herodotus is generally acknowledged as the "father of history," the first Greek historian was actually Hecataeus of Miletus, who lived c. 550-475 BCE, but whose books are not extant.

similar fashion, at a contemporary period of time for a similar length of time, the biblical information was eventually collected into the biblical text. The oral traditions would have been known to all of the participants in the Exodus, and when the dissident Hebrews fled the Exodus they would have brought these stories with them into Mycenae, thereby introducing concepts which I believe were reintroduced to the Greeks during the Archaic Age (850-480 BCE), the dynamic era of Greek intellectual advancement between the time of Homer and the Persian Wars. I will explain this contribution throughout the chapters of this book in great detail, but by positing a significant Hebraic influence upon the development of the Classical Greek culture, I expected the first edition of my book to be received with an air of incredulity, and I was not surprised. Despite the fact that all other attempts to explain the heritage of the Greeks have been woefully barren of any credible evidence, to date no academic scholar has been willing to either refute or support my proposal, leaving me standing at the starting gate with no one to contend against. When Martin Bernal, Professor of Government and Near Eastern Studies at Cornell University, first suggested in *Black Athena* that the Classical Greek culture owed its development to dark-skinned emigrants from ancient Egypt, rather than to white-skinned pioneers from Europe, he created a storm of controversy, almost all of it negative.[21] My proposal, perhaps because I lack the university academic credentials enjoyed by Bernal, fell like a tree in an uninhabited forest. The Scottish diplomat and author, Sir William Drummond (1770-1828 CE), appears to have been correct when he noted that "to instruct Pride is to affront it."[22] I seem to have affronted, rather than instructed, my audience

21 Bernal claimed that the reluctance of scholars to accept his alternate evolutionary theory of the Classical Greek culture was due to racism, which he believed characterized academic debate in the nineteenth and twentieth centuries CE, causing the dark-skinned Egyptians to be seen as fundamentally alien to Western Man. Bernal, Black Athena, I.441. This accusation created such a heated debate among academicians, that his critics soon published their response to his charges in a rebuttal book labeled Black Athena Revisited. The public press also responded excitedly to this claim, with the cover of Newsweek magazine asking boldly "WAS CLEOPATRA BLACK?" on its September 23, 1991 issue. Bernal was not the first to make this claim, as evidenced by the views of Cheikh Anta Diop (1923-1986 CE), director of the radiocarbon laboratory at I.F.A.N. (Institut Fondamental d'Afrique Noire) at the University of Dakar, who claimed in 1973 CE that the ancient Egyptians were Negroes, and were responsible for the development of "Pythagorean mathematics, the theory of the four elements of Tales of Miletus, Epicurean materialism, Platonic idealism, Judaism, Islam, and modern science." Diop, The African Origin of Civilization: Myth or Reality, xiv.

22 Drummond, Oedipus Judaicus: Allegory in the Old Testament, ii. Drummond sagely explained that what we are taught to credit as children, we are seldom disposed to question as men, and as a result a powerful prejudice ensures conviction without the trouble of thinking. The multitude, he notes, "is not very likely to applaud an author, who calls upon it to consider what it had hitherto neglected." Ibid., iii.

by pointing out the similarities between the ancient Hebrews and Greeks, and so I now have expanded my argument in this book to include a detailed analysis of where I believe the writings of the Greek philosophers and playwrights directly reflect the teachings of the Old Testament, in order to buttress my original thesis. The Eastern influence in Greece, in my opinion, did not come from Phoenicians, Babylonians, or Egyptians, as is claimed by almost all historians, but rather, was a reflection of the explanations offered by early biblical manuscripts. By combining a credible chain of intellectual evolution, with a credible avenue of cultural contacts, beginning in Mycenae with the emigration of dissident Hebrews who fled the Exodus, and then continuing through the dissemination of thought during the Babylonian Exile, I believe my argument of Hebraic influence best answers how the Classical Greek culture imbibed ancient Eastern concepts, and in the process closely resembled ancient Hebrew teachings.

It is not as if there are any better explanations about where the early Greeks originated, for all that can be said of the early Greek population today is that it was composed of those citizens "who used the Greek language," based upon documents written in a syllabic script known as Linear B.[23] Linear B documents, along with those in the related Linear A script, have been found in ancient sites on Crete and the Greek mainland from 1750-1400 BCE, and are accepted by most scholars as the precursor language of the Classical Greek alphabet. Linear A is primarily the alphabet used by the ancient Cretin populace, while Linear B was the alphabet of the Mycenaeans, who dominated the Greek mainland during the Mycenaean Age (1650-1200 BCE). Since it is the Mycenaeans who are believed to have initiated the Linear B script, it is generally accepted that they functioned as the earliest ancestors of the Classical Greek culture. Although few scholars deny this close relationship, details of this remarkable society are incredibly sparse indeed. Who these Mycenaeans were, where they came from, and how they formulated their magnificent culture is entirely unknown.

The reason for this informational gap is that the Mycenaean society suddenly disappeared from the geopolitical scene shortly after the Trojan War (c. 1183 BCE), and the Greek mainland then entered into an unknown era, known as the Dark Age (c. 1000-850 BCE).[24] A few centuries later, the Archaic Age emerged, to be followed by the Classical Greek civilization. Both the Mycenaean

---

23 Smith, <u>The Ancient Greeks</u>, 6-7. The Linear B script was very cumbersome, using 60 ideograms and at least 89 signs, and was probably only utilized by a small number of scribes. Hall, <u>A History of the Archaic Greek World, ca. 1200-479 BCE</u>, 56.

24 Scholars generally dislike the use of the term "Dark Age," and utilize instead the Submycenaean phase (c. 1070-1000 BCE), Protogeometric period (c. 1000-900 BCE), and Geometric period (c. 900-700 BCE). Ibid., 59. Because this book is written for both scholars and the general public, I am going to risk academic scorn and continue to utilize the term "Dark Age" throughout this book to refer to the era following the Trojan War and preceding the Archaic Age.

civilization, and the society that remained on the Greek mainland during the Dark Age, left very little archaeologic data defining the details of their philosophy and heritage, and so historians have had to look elsewhere to try and determine who acted as the progenitors of the Classical Greeks. Although the linear B text has been deciphered, all of the records are simply simple lists of commercial products, and do not contain details of the activities of the state, either with descriptions of social life, legal records, or military victories or defeats. Unlike the Egyptians, who left a veritable storehouse of their history on hieroglyphic recordings, written material uncovered at Mycenaean archaeologic sites has been restricted to simple commercial lists, and no detailed historical records have yet been found to explain the pathway from Mycenae to Classical Greece. Evidence of their culture shows up in pottery ware and architectural designs all along the trade routes throughout the Levant, but the written historical slate is so far blank with respect to the development of their legendary traditions.[25]

Many modern historians of the Neo-Assyrian (911-627 BCE) and Neo-Babylonian (612-539 BCE) Empires have tried to promote the importance of their ancestors by claiming that the Assyrian provincial administration provided the primary conduit by which Babylonian culture affected the ancestors of the Classical Greek culture.[26] Aramaic was made the official language of the Assyrian Empire in 752 BCE, and it rapidly became the *lingua franca* of much of the ancient Near East.[27] Since many of the Greek scholars would also have known the language, these pundits argue that the Greeks would have ready access to the Babylonian material, and once introduced to the legends, would have readily incorporated their teachings. Aramaic was also spoken among the populace of the Hebrews during this very same era, however, and the speeches of the prophets were often translated into Aramaic so that the entire audience could understand the lessons being disseminated. There is therefore no reason to claim that the Babylonians were any more likely to have been the source of the knowledge to the Greeks, especially since there are so many similarities between the teachings of the Hebrews and the Greeks during this critical Archaic and Classical Age, as I will point out throughout this book.

Although there is little documentation of Mycenaean culture in the

---

25 The Levant is a term coined in the fifteenth century CE to refer to the lands which run along the coast of the eastern Mediterranean, today encompassing the countries of Lebanon, Israel, Jordan, the Palestinian territories, Syria, and Iraq. It comes from the Middle French Word *levant*, meaning "the Orient."

26 See The Heirs of Assyria: Proceeding of the Opening Symposium of the Assyrian and Babylonian Intellectual Heritage Project Held in Tvarminne, Finland, October 8-11, 1998, edit. Sannaa Aro & R. M. Whiting, Helsinki: The Neo-Assyrian Text Corpus Project, 2000.

27 It became the *lingua franca* of the region even though it was the language of the conquered, rather than the conqueror.

archaeologic record, stories of the Mycenaean civilization nevertheless abound in the traditions of the Classical Greeks, and I believe that this material holds the key to understanding how the stories of the Old Testament directly affected the writings of Homer and the mythology which developed in Classical Greece. As I have already explained, it is remarkable that the Greeks and Jews both highlight a single event in the legends of their ancestors that is not only unique in the history of mankind, but is generally condemned as an act of murder in every known legal code.[28] It does not matter that we cannot prove that either of these acts actually took place, but it is clear that the legend of the sacrifice was seen as a seminal event to each civilization. The incredibly unique nature of these stories, and the fact that only the Hebrews and Greeks highlighted the honor accorded to each father, makes it mandatory, in my opinion, that one culture brought their tale to the other, and, as I will show throughout this book, I believe it was the dissident Hebrews who took the story with them when they left the Exodus and migrated to Mycenae, allowing the tale to evolve into the memory of the Trojan War.

Mycenae was the logical final destination for this group of dissident Hebrews, since remaining in Canaan would have been far too dangerous, given the fact that they were despised by almost every inhabitant of Canaan at that time, including the Egyptians, from whom they fled as part of the congregation led by Moses. Rather than search for safety on the eastern shore of the Mediterranean Basin, the Hebrews, in my opinion, looked toward Mycenae, on the western shore, where stories of religious freedom and economic opportunities would have been supplied by the many commercial contacts which had developed throughout the ancient Near East by the time of the Exodus. The Mycenaeans were known throughout the Levant during the Late Bronze Age, and, as noted by Cyrus Gordon, they "differed from the Hebrews less than either did from the Upper Egyptians."[29] Recommending a migration to Mycenae would not have been seen as an unreasonable move by the leaders who directed the Hebrew dissidents away from the ravages of Moses. Booking passage to the Aegean shore would also have been relatively easy, since the Mycenaeans distributed their goods to the international market through Ugarit at the time, using the island of Cyprus as a primary market base. Once the Hebrews reached their destination, they would have found work as either mercenaries or construction workers, given their vast experience as slaves building large brick and stone projects in Egypt. The city of Mycenae, as well as

---

28 In my study of infanticide, *Hardness of Heart/Hardness of Life, the Stain of Human Infanticide,* I pointed out that although infanticide was very common throughout human society during the Late Bronze and Iron Ages (1200-587 BCE), no other society or tribe ever made infanticide as prominent a part of their tradition as did the ancient Hebrews and Greeks. Milner, Hardness of Heart/Hardness of Life, The Stain of Human Infanticide, 341, 353.

29 Gordon, Before the Bible: The Common Background of Greek and Hebrew Civilizations, 222.

other cities in Greece, was undergoing extensive development at that time, and archaeologic finds have shown evidence of fortified walls built with large stones, called Cyclopean because of their size, with which the Hebrews would have been very familiar. Although most scholars have theorized that it was the Phoenicians who were instrumental in engineering these projects, I believe it is much more likely that it was the Hebrews who suggested the technique to the Mycenaeans, and then provided the necessary manpower and experience to successfully carry out the complex construction plan.

The Hebrews also could have supplied much needed assistance as military conscripts, becoming an integral part of the Mycenaean military machine. Expanding their influence into the ancient Near East, and eventually participating in an extended military conflict on foreign shores, took its toll on the available manpower in Mycenae, and the Hebrews were a force to be reckoned with, as evidenced by their numerous victories in the accounts of the Old Testament. Herbert C. Alleman (1868-1953 CE), the Lutheran biblical commentator, aptly noted how the ancient Hebrews "could pray and they could fight."[30] Their victories showed an impressive degree of fortitude and strength, and the Mycenaeans would have seen this as a cause for admiration and reward, rather than the censure which Moses reaped on those who were in disagreement with his commandments and rules. If the dissident Hebrews arrived in Mycenae before the thirteenth century BCE, it is likely that they would have fought as advisers and soldiers at the side of King Agamemnon during the ten-year Trojan War, and the traditions and stories they brought would have been incorporated into the Greek heritage, as were many other aspects of their knowledge and training, including the amphictyony political organization. Through this valuable assistance, the Hebrew legacy would have easily become an integral part of the Greek heritage, helping to formulate the storylines which later became famous in Homer's the *Iliad* and the *Odyssey*. In addition to providing a much-needed infusion of manpower, the Hebrews were very familiar with the topography of the region from their years of travel during the Sinai wanderings, and this knowledge would have made them invaluable as translators and advisers to the Mycenaean expeditionary forces.

That the Mycenaeans would have incorporated Hebrew traditions into their own set of beliefs once the dissidents became a settled part of their community is supported by evidence which shows that Mycenae generally welcomed, rather than shunned, external influences in their heyday during the Late Bronze Age. Unlike the Egyptians, who never assimilated the religious tenets of Semitic inhabitants, the Mycenaeans readily adapted to foreign peoples in everything – from their social structure to the nature of their religious beliefs. John Chadwick (1920-1998), the well-known Mycenaean historian and late Professor Emeritus of Cambridge University, has noted that they almost always "took over and absorbed

---

30 Alleman, "Why We Study the Old Testament," 2.

into their own system other religious systems with which they came into contact."[31] Like a dry sponge placed in a pan of water, they imbibed new data and modified the information to fit the growing nature of their own creed. This may be why they were able to advance to a position of power in such a relatively short period of time, for rather than ostracize those they confronted, they expanded their own base of knowledge through mutual understanding, and modified their views to include the beneficial social, military and religious offerings of the foreigners.

While eccentric at first glance, this somewhat heretical conception of the early Greek civilization is clearly supported by social conditions that were present throughout the Mediterranean Basin during the Late Bronze Age. Mercenary forces were very commonly utilized by many countries during that era, and successful empires like Mycenae incorporated warriors from adjoining lands to supplement their own limited supplies. It was not possible to provide enough manpower at home to continue an adequate production of food supply, while at the same time gathering a large enough military force to assure victory and conquest of new lands. War brought about cultural interchange, not only through invasion and conquest, which led to exportation of slaves and development of colonization, but also by the importation of mercenary forces during the many armed conflicts. One of the ways in which soldiers were paid was to promise them land when their time of service was completed. The Hittite army, for example, depended upon charioteers and full-time soldiers who were paid for their services by land grants from the king.[32] For the Hebrews, such an offering in Mycenae would have been warmly welcomed after many years of wandering in the desert under the command of Moses. Finally, before they died, they could lay roots for their sons to inherit, while at the same time continuing to follow the faith of their forefathers.

Once the legends and practices of the Hebrews were incorporated into the Mycenaean society, the succeeding generations of Greeks that arose during the Archaic Age continued to be influenced by what they read of the Hebrew Bible in manuscripts which were circulating throughout the Levant at that time, as well as the oral word of God that was being disseminated by the Hebrew Prophets during the Babylonian Exile, and following their eventual return to Jerusalem after being liberated by the Persian King Cyrus the Great (c. 600-529 BCE). Very few historians have remarked upon the influence of such factors on early Greek philosophic and dramatic thought, but the lives of the Greek philosophers and playwrights were congruent with the development of the Hebrew Bible, and it is clear that Greek scholars traveled widely throughout the ancient Near East, gathering wisdom from the Egyptians and Babylonians and, in my opinion, from the Hebrew sources as well. I will discuss this in more detail in chapter 14, but the

---

31 Chadwick, The Mycenaean World, 85.

32 Sandars, The Sea Peoples: Warriors of the Ancient Mediterranean 1250-1150 B.C., 32.

influence of biblical thought can be found in Greece from the time of the Trojan War through the entire Classical Greek and Archaic Ages.

As mentioned above, the key to connecting the dissident Hebrews to Greece is Ugarit, the city to which I believe the Hebrews fled, and which Cyrus Gordon has championed as the forerunner of the Hebrew and Greek civilizations. Gordon never suggested, as I have, that Hebrews actually came to Ugarit and then traveled to Mycenae, bringing with them their similar cultural characteristics, but rather pointed out how the unique position of this city as the meeting place for international trade between Egypt, the Aegean, and the countries of the Near East during the second millennium BCE, allowed various cultures to intermingle in a peacetime atmosphere that eventually led to a coalescing not only of ideas, but of migrations of inhabitants who became an integral part of the societies we know today. Cyrus Gordon was correct in emphasizing the importance of Ugarit in the development of many societies during the Late Bronze Age, but rather than being the primary generator of the ancient Greek and Hebraic worlds directly, as he has championed in his many articles and books, the city simply functioned, in my opinion, to bridge the two societies by providing an easy access route for the Hebrews to take after they fled the Exodus and the parricidal actions of Moses.

Ugarit was the natural place for the outcast Hebrew conclave to make this initial contact with the Mycenaeans, for it was the meeting place of Semite and Indo-European Aryans in many commercial endeavors. Ugarit acted as a bridge because of its vital placement as a sea port situated at the juncture between Anatolia (Roman Asia Minor), on the northern edge of the Mediterranean Sea, and Syria-Palestine on the eastern edge. If one studies a map of the countries which surrounded the Mediterranean Sea during the second millennium BCE, it is easy to recognize why sea travel was the most effective means of communication. Travel by land was seriously impeded: to the north were the Taurus mountains of the Anatolian Plateau which prevented the migration of large numbers of people over short periods of time due to the uneven terrain; to the east, caravan routes were able to effectively move material goods and people, but could not provide an outlet to the Aegean Sea; and to the south, Egypt was a formidable obstacle to traffic over the northern coast of Africa, and no ports-of-call were available in Egypt, or along the southern Canaanite coast. Sea travel from Phoenicia and Ugarit, however, was readily available as many islands with safe harbors dotted the sea route between Greece and the Levant, and ships were generally able to sail within sight of land, providing a relatively safe passage during intervals of unstable weather. It is for this reason that civilizations prospered on the islands of Crete, Rhodes and Cyprus, since they were the links which bound the economies of the countries which bordered the Mediterranean Sea. Ugarit lay at the point where ships traveling north up the coast from Egypt would then turn west toward Cyprus and the Aegean Sea, and for that reason almost every country had offices in Ugarit in order to provide contacts to multiple nationalities. In Ugarit, the Hebrews could find agents who spoke a multitude of languages, and offered a ready supply of opportunities, either to work the land or hire on as mercenaries in distant countries.

To see why my theory of Hebrew migration to Mycenae explains better than any other theory to date the origin of many aspects of the Classical Greek culture, we have to look to the Late Bronze Age, a period of chaos and cultural change throughout the ancient world. Interaction between the civilized states was intensified because of the differentiated distribution of vital resources. Fibers for the production of clothing came from western Asia and Egypt, oil from olives in Anatolia and the Levant, copper from Cyprus, tin from Afghanistan, silver from Anatolia, gold from Egypt and Nubia, and semiprecious stones from even more distant locations. The political upheavals which shook the international community during this pivotal era involved the entire Mediterranean Basin, and the results of those violent struggles helped shape the social structure of our modern society. Robert Drews, Professor of Classics and History at Vanderbilt University, has referred to this epoch as the "dawn time" in which the ancient people of Israel, Greece, and Rome sought their origins.[33] What seems evident to me, is that those origins are more intimately entwined than has heretofore been realized.

My analysis in this book will center on two specific Late Bronze Age events which are of particular interest to the Western world: the Trojan War, made famous by Homer, the man who instituted the fictional heritage of Western civilization, said to have taken place in the thirteenth or twelfth century BCE; and the Exodus of the Jews from Egypt, as chronicled in the Old Testament, the backbone of the Jewish, Christian and Moslem religions, the date of which is generally placed between the fifteenth and thirteenth centuries BCE. Both of these incidents have no extant historical accounts to prove that either one actually took place, but the fictional narratives have become so ingrained in academic historical circles, that a majority of scholars have accepted the fact that both are based on factual events, even though those facts are hotly contested. A third incident, closely intertwined with both of these narratives, is the invasion of the People of the Sea into Syria, Palestine and Egypt at the end of the thirteenth century BCE. This conflict is generally thought to be responsible for the great alterations which drastically modified the status of world powers at the end of the Late Bronze Age leading into the Iron Age, and may have helped camouflage the migration of the Hebrews out of Egypt, explaining why the Exodus is absent from contemporary chronicles. It is very likely that both the Mycenaeans and the Hebrews were part of this mix of marauders, and it is possible, in my opinion, to garner some understanding of how the ancient Hebrews may have had contact with Mycenae before the Trojan

---

33 Drews, The End of the Bronze Age, 4.

War by looking into the composition of the People of the Sea in more detail. This will particularly involve the historical origins of the Philistines, since the migration of these invaders from Crete into Canaan during the Late Bronze Age provides assistance in analyzing my postulate of a similar migration of the Hebrews in the opposite direction to Mycenae a few generations earlier.

As to when the Exodus took place, I intend to show that the historical data of the Mediterranean Basin during the Late Bronze Age supports the contention that Joseph invited Jacob and his family to enter Egypt during the rule of the Hyksos, a group of shepherd kings who invaded and controlled Egypt 1648-1550 BCE, and that the Exodus occurred at some time thereafter, in the fifteenth or fourteenth century BCE. This sequence fits well with the presumed dates of the emigration of Abraham from Mesopotamia to the Levant, and the period of time the Hebrews lived in Canaan and Egypt before the Exodus, although it is earlier than estimates which place the Exodus during the reign of Ramesses II (1279-1213 BCE). The forty-year wandering in the Sinai would then have taken place during the Amarna Age (1353-1336 BCE), when the Habiru (Apiru, Hapiru, Hab/piru) were ravaging the countryside in a fashion similar to the movements of Moses and the Hebrew contingent.

In the chapters which follow, I will expand upon the evidence supporting my theory of Hebrew immigration and assimilation into Mycenaean society in great detail. While no sole piece of the puzzle is thoroughly convincing, I believe that no other theory of Greek heritage fits the facts so completely, and that consideration of Hebrew influence on the development of Classical Greek culture must be given serious consideration. We cannot know with certainty how the Greeks evolved into the flowering of their civilizations during the illustrious Classical Age, but as Martin Bernal has argued, one cannot and should not require proof or certainty, but merely "competitive plausibility" when considering the murky regions of Mediterranean prehistory.[34] Despite the criticism of scholars such as Thomas Thompson, from the Biblical Studies program of the University of Copenhagen, who has cautioned against accepting as "enough evidence" the "accumulation of sufficient coincidence to bring about a judgment of 'historical probability,'"[35] it is unlikely that we will ever uncover more direct evidence of Hebrew life during the era of the Patriarchs and the Exodus, and we must therefore evaluate the data we have in the most critical way we can, and draw conclusions which at least fulfill the test of reasonable interpretation. John H. Walton, Professor of Old Testament at Wheaton College, has set forth ten principles which are necessary for comparative studies, and two of these require proximity in time and geography, as well as a likely channel of transmission, both of which I believe are fulfilled by

---

34 Bernal, Black Athena Writes Back, 383-384, 388.

35 Thompson, The Historicity of the Patriarchal Narratives: The Quest for the Historical Abraham, 53.

the arguments presented in this book.[36]

I want to emphasize at the outset of this book that I am not making this claim of an Hebraic influence on the ancient Greek civilization in order to rewrite history from a Jewish perspective. Following her negative response to the claims of Martin Bernal in *Black Athena* that the Greeks owed their origin to black Egyptians, Mary Lefkowitz, Professor Emeritus of Classical Studies at Wellesley College, encountered such antagonism from academic black proponents of the theory that she was labeled as a racist for her views. She responded to this outrageous claim by noting that "there is a current tendency, at least among academics, to regard history as a form of fiction that can be and should be written differently by each nation or ethnic group."[37] I am not rewriting history here, or claiming that the Jews were the primary founders of the Mycenaean race. I am, however, asserting that the early Jews were the primary source for the Eastern influence in ancient Greece, rather than the Phoenician or Egyptian cultures.

Should my theories be given credence, given the fact that I do not have academic credentials in the field of biblical or ancient history? While many sceptics will scoff at my presumptions, I agree with Norman K. Gottwald, Professor of Old Testament Emeritus at New York Theological Seminary, who complained that one problem today is "the myopia of academic overspecialization."[38] Each scholar focuses on their own particular skill and interest, focusing on it with a single, highly refined methodology. Few bother to stand back and attempt to synthesize the whole, both from a present, and an historical perspective. I believe in this book I can connect the dots of data discovered by centuries of talented academicians and theologians, and present a well-documented support of my thesis that can stand up to the arguments of the most illustrious academicians.

Was Achilles a Jew? Perhaps not, but in this book I hope to show that the Classical Greek culture incorporated much ancient Hebrew tradition, and this amalgam of Late Bronze Age legendary material formed the society which became the backbone of our modern Western World. I want to make one final comment before proceeding with the detailed account I plan to present about why I believe the ancient Hebrew teachings profoundly influenced the Classical Greek civilization. We read history and attempt to interpret today with the foreknowledge of the modern mind. We know the geography of the world; we know, in great detail, the timelines developed through the benefit of hindsight; we know what modern science and education has taught us about the evolution of our entire world; but the one thing we must remember about attempting to understand what happened

---

36 Walton, Ancient Near Eastern Thought and the Old Testament: Introducing the Conceptual World of the Hebrew Bible, 26-27.

37 Lefkowitz, Not Out of Africa: How Afrocentrism Became an Excuse to Teach Myth as History, xiv.

38 Gottwald, The Tribes of Yahweh: A Sociology of the Religion of Liberated Israel, 1250-1050 BCE, 5.

in the Late Bronze Age, is that we *must* somehow forget all we "know" when we attempt to analyze the thought patterns of our ancestors, and try to put ourselves back into the mind-set of what inquisitive people thought about themselves, and the world they lived in, almost thirty-five hundred years ago. If you do that, and if you pay attention to the citations I present to you in this book, I believe that you will see that there is no question that the Classical Greek civilization was incredibly influenced by a group of staunch Hebrew emigrants, who believed in the teachings of their ancestors, and transmitted that faith to their neighbors and descendants straight through into the Classical Greek Age.

HEBRAIC INFLUENCES ON GREEK CIVILIZATION

WAS ACHILLES A JEW?

Chapter 1
ANCIENT NEAR EAST

As I previously discussed, the two events which are of primary importance to my thesis that ancient Hebrew legendary material was incorporated into the Classical Greek culture by dissident Hebrews who traveled to Mycenae during the Late Bronze Age (1600-1200 BCE) are the Exodus of the Hebrews from Egypt, as described in the Old Testament, and the Trojan War, as recorded in the *Iliad* and the *Odyssey* by Homer. Both of these events have not been verified by extant archaeologic records, making it impossible to establish exactly when each event may have taken place, but it is generally believed by those who accept the veracity of the legendary accounts that the Exodus took place somewhere between the fifteenth and thirteenth centuries BCE, as will be discussed in chapter 6, and that the Trojan War was fought in the twelfth century BCE, c. 1183 BCE, as will be discussed in chapter 8. Since my hypothesis assumes that each account is based on factual events, I will now begin to analyze the history of the Mediterranean Basin, in order to set the groundwork for why I believe the ancient Hebrew and Greek cultures interacted during the Late Bronze Age, based upon both legendary and archaeologic evidence. To this end, I will summarize the history of the ancient Near East in this chapter, and the history of Egypt in Chapter 2, in order to provide a geographical background for the era of the Hebrew Patriarchs, and then discuss the patriarchal background of the Hebrews in Chapter 3, and the Exodus of the Hebrews from Egypt in Chapters 4-6, pointing out in each chapter the attributes of the Hebrews which I believe are apparent in the Greek civilization. In Chapter 7, I will present the history of Greece, emphasizing Mycenae and Crete, and in Chapter 8, the Trojan War, once again highlighting the areas which likely indicate a Hebrew contribution. I will then analyze specific aspects of the ancient Hebrew and Classical Greek cultures which I believe support the theory that the Greeks derived many of their characteristic features from traditions eventually recorded in the Old Testament in Chapters 9-14. Although this undertaking is quite extensive, I believe it is necessary to support my unique thesis, given the virtual exclusion of consideration of Hebrew contributions to ancient Greek civilization by the academic community.

A. *Mesopotamia*

I will begin my analysis in the region generally accepted as the cradle of civilization – Mesopotamia. In the Early (3000-2000 BCE) and Middle (2000-1600) Bronze Ages, the regions which dominated the ancient Near East included Mesopotamia, which gave birth to the Sumerian, Babylonian, and Assyrian kingdoms;[1] the Levant, which was the land that abutted the eastern coastline

---

1 Assyria corresponds to the northern half of Mesopotamia, and Babylon to the southern half. The capital city of Assyria was Ashur. After about 2000 BCE, the Assyrians were made up of a mixture of Amorites and older Akkadians (Accadians) who both spoke a

of the Mediterranean Sea between Egypt and Mesopotamia, including Canaan and Syria; and Egypt, which included the region of the Sinai wilderness, the land link between Asia and Africa. All of these regions played a prominent role in the stories of the Torah, as Abraham was born in Mesopotamia, left his homeland to live in Canaan, briefly immigrated to Egypt during a period of famine, and then returned to Canaan, where the Lord promised that his descendants would have dominion over the Promised Land. Since Mesopotamia was the birthplace of Abraham, I will begin my discussion with the history of that region.

The name "Mesopotamia" is derived from the Greek words *mesos*, or "middle," and *potamoi*, or "river," referring to the land between the Tigris and Euphrates rivers, which in contemporary usage included the regions of modern Iraq, eastern Syria, and southeastern Turkey. Although most anthropologists now point to East Africa as the location where humanoids first evolved from the apes, Mesopotamia has generally been accepted as the figurative birthplace of mankind, for it was there that civilization made the greatest strides toward the complex systems of language and economy which characterize our modern societies. One reason for the rapid progress made in this region was the ability to provide an adequate food supply through agricultural methods, first evidenced by the cultivation of wild cereals in the Fertile Crescent c. 9000-8000 BCE, followed shortly thereafter by the domestication of wheat and barley. Because early hunter-gatherers could only stay in camps for a short time, given the seasonal nature of their food supply, reliable plantings allowed for the formation of permanent communities, so that by 7500 BCE, in the Neolithic or "New Stone Age" period (8800-4700 BCE), dense farming settlements of a few hundred inhabitants began to appear in the uplands of the Levant, southern Anatolia, and the Zagros mountains. Soon thereafter, other aspects of civilized metropolises began to appear in rapid fashion, as evidenced by archaeologic remains at Catal Huyuk in Turkey, where a town-sized settlement of over six thousand people has been uncovered from c. 7000 BCE, making it the largest Neolithic collective yet found. This transformation has frequently been referred to as "the urban revolution," since from that time forward, people tended to gather in collective communities, rather than remain in mobile, transitory abodes.[2]

A number of cultures have been identified in Mesopotamia during this Neolithic era, including the Hassuna, which was centered in northern Mesopotamia from 6500-6000 BCE; the Halafian, named after the site of Tell Halaf, which succeeded shortly thereafter, c. 5200-4800 BCE; and the Ubaid, which controlled southern Mesopotamia from c. 5500-4000 BCE., and laid the foundations for

---

Semitic language. About 1200 BCE, Arameans, who were Semitic-speaking seminomads from the Syro-Arabian desert, also began to make incursions into Assyria. The Oxford Encyclopedia of Archaeology in the Near East, I.228.

2 Lerner, The Creation of Patriarchy, 54.

the Sumerian civilization, the direct ancestors of our modern age.[3] With the invention of the plow in the fifth millennium BCE, and the discovery of artificial watering techniques in the fourth millennium BCE, the ability to maintain a secure food supply strengthened, allowing for the formation of large city-states during the fourth millennium BCE, an era known as the Uruk period (4000-3000 BCE).[4]

By this time, most of the population of Mesopotamia lived in cities, the majority of which had a population of between two and eight thousand people, although the capital city of Uruk (biblical Erech, modern Warka) is estimated to have had over 10,000 inhabitants, reaching a level of 50,000 by 2900 BCE.[5] Such an intense concentration of people in so small an area required a strong political structure to maintain a hierarchy of legal and economic authority. Tribal cohesiveness was no longer reliable with such an expanded populace, and to assure a stable transfer of command, most cities chose to form a monarchal government, whereby jurisdiction was invested in a single autocratic ruler, thereby redirecting loyalties from "kin to kings."[6] These monarchs were at first appointed by a governing council and then, to solidify their power base and legitimize their autocratic control, a concept of divine dominion was invoked whereby the authority of the king was assimilated into the power of a god. Since each region had its own interpretation of which deity was more powerful, a continuous struggle for domination ensued that has lasted until modern times. The ability to rule over a neighboring territory was a powerful economic asset that paid dividends for years to come, but with fortune and fame came jealousy and retaliation, and many societies quickly faded after brief periods of colonial success. As I will discuss in more detail in the next chapter, Egypt had also evolved in a similar fashion, but in contrast to Mesopotamia, the control of the monarchy generally remained under a single ruler, the Pharaoh.

As the Early Bronze Age began, the competition for control of the region intensified, and southern Mesopotamia became politically divided between cities which coalesced into the Akkadian Dynasty in the northern region of Akkad

---

3   The Akkadian word for this area of the world was *Sumerum,* leading to the designation of the name Sumer. Freeman, Egypt, Greece and Rome: Civilizations of the Ancient Mediterranean, 23.

4   Some historians label the Uruk era, when major population growth took place, as the Chalcolithic Age (c. 4500-3300 BCE), because of the combined use of both copper and stone. The Bronze Age refers to the combination of copper with tin, arsenic, or antimony to produce the bronze alloy which was more easy to cast, and more resistant to destruction, than copper alone. Roaf, Cultural Atlas of Mesopotamia and the Ancient Near East, 58.

5 Uruk is generally considered as the first city in human history. Van De Mieroop, A History of the Ancient Near East, ca. 3000-323 BC, 23.

6 Knapp, The History and Culture of Ancient Western Asia and Egypt, 62.

(Agade), and those which united into the Sumerian Dynasty in the southern region of Sumer.[7] For the next one thousand years, these two empires vied for control of the region, and historians have generally categorized the sequence of events into the Sumerian Early Dynastic period (c. 3000-2300 BCE), which ended with the accession of Sargon I of Akkad (Sargon the Great, c. 2334-2279 BCE); the Sargonid Era (c. 2300-2150 BCE), named for Sargon I and his followers; the Sumerian Third Dynasty of Ur (c. 2150-1950 BCE), founded by Ur-Nammu (2112-2095 BCE);[8] and finally, the Old Babylonian Era (1950-1600 BCE), which included the reign of Hammurabi (1848-1806 BCE), the Amorite king of Babylon, known for his famous Hammurabi Law Code.[9]

The first of these eras, the Sumerian Early Dynastic Period, offers our first opportunity to obtain clear details of the historical record, since Sumeria was the initial culture to introduce writing, thereby leading to its designation as the Protoliterate Period. Although the Sumerian language has no known surviving close relatives, the information provided by their archaeologic records confirms the advanced level of their civilization. The name "Sumeria" comes from the ancient name of the southern part of Iraq, *Sumer* or *Shumer*, an area which would later be referred to as Babylonia. Political unity in the region was maintained by the cooperation of about a dozen city-states, each ruled by a king who was nominated to his position by the leading deity of the city.[10] Although comprising an area less

---

7 The principal city-states in Sumer were Ur, Uruk, Eridu, Larsa, Shuruppak, Kish, Sippar, Adab, Isin, Umma, Girsu, and Lagash. Tetlow, Women, Crime, and Punishment in Ancient Law and Society, vol. 1, The Ancient Near East, 6. Ur is the biblical birthplace of Abraham.

8 King Ur-Nammu was believed to have built the impressive ziggurat found at the ancient city of Nippur, which was the most important religious center of the Sumerians. Roaf, Cultural Atlas of Mesopotamia and the Ancient Near East, 81. The ziggurat was an enormous stepped pyramid that served as the base for a temple, and was the model for the biblical Tower of Babel. The law code of Ur-Nammu is the oldest surviving legal document in the world, and appears to have set the stage for many of the legal treatises which followed. Some believe the code was actually that of Shulgi (2094-2047 BCE), rather than Ur-Nammu. Matthews & Benjamin, Old Testament Parallels: Laws and Stories From the Ancient Near East, Third Edition, 101.

9 Hammurabi is particularly known today for his law code, which was a new formulation of a legal tradition that reached as far back as the third millennium BCE, including the codes of King Ur-Nammu, King Lipit-Ishtar of Isin (1934-1924 BCE), and King Dadusha of Eshnunna (c. 1770 BCE), a small Amorite kingdom in the Diyala valley of Old Babylonia. Roaf, Cultural Atlas of Mesopotamia and the Ancient Near East, 59, 78. The structure of these case-laws "is identical with that of the Book of the Covenant," and in some cases the laws are identical. Albright, Yahweh and the Gods of Canaan, 102. This suggests that the Old Testament may have drawn some of its legal tradition from the Babylonian sources, since no formal compilation of laws has ever been found in Egypt.

10 The names of these kings survive in the Sumerian King List, which is known only from manuscripts dated to the first centuries of the second millennium BCE. It

than the size of Belgium, and devoid of many natural resources, Sumer became the dominant force in Mesopotamia during the Early Bronze Age. It was in the important Sumerian city-state of Ur (Tell Muqqayar) that Abraham was born, so the culture of the region obviously played an important part in his childhood and early adult training. This is reflected in the fact that aspects of Sumerian mythology appear in the biblical story of Noah and the Great Flood, which is very akin to the Sumerian legend of Gilgamesh, as well as in multiple other legendary motifs.[11] Although the Bible never actually mentioned the Sumerians by name, the Hebrew word *sin'ar*, which represents the Sumerian term for "Sumer-Akkad," occurs eight times in the Old Testament, supporting the proposition that the biblical compilers were aware of the Sumerian civilization.[12]

The Sumerians solidified their position of power by building massive walls around many of their the cities to protect the populace from invasion by neighboring forces. This imposing defensive technique, which came to characterize much of Early Bronze Age architecture, was necessitated by the introduction of bronze weapons, which enabled armies to quickly conquer an unprotected city and convert the entire populace into slaves for the first time in the historical record. Importing nonmilitary prisoners-of-war to provide a readily available labor force at home allowed these early city-states to free up their own adult male population to join mobile military maneuvers abroad, and the resultant institution of slavery became a characteristic of the entire civilized world. As we will see in the next chapter, Egypt also imported a large number of Semitic captives during this era to assist in the building of the pyramids, a process which continued into the Late Bronze Age, eventually resulting in the enslavement of the entire Hebrew population. The Sumerian fortifications worked quite well at first, and their culture became so widespread that by the end of the third millennium BCE their influence had penetrated as far east as India, south to Ethiopia, and north to the Caspian Sea.

As the second half of the third millennium BCE neared, the dominance of the Sumerians began to wane, and their northern neighbors, the Akkadians, gradually expanded their authority over the Sumerian provinces. The Akkadians were a Semitic people who first began to aggregate from their original homeland

---

divided human history into divisions before and after the Great Flood, again suggesting a contribution to biblical theology. The Illustrated Family Encyclopedia of the Living Bible, I.28.

11 Other themes or motifs that occurred in both the Bible and Sumerian literature include the Creation theme, with mankind fashioned out of clay; the paradise stories; the Great Flood legend; rivalry motifs, like that of Cain and Abel; the story of the Tower of Babel; the trait of divine retribution by the gods; the plague motif; the suffering of the righteous; and the bleakness of the nether world. Averbeck, "Sumer, the Bible, and Comparative Method: Historiography and Temple Building," 90.

12 Gen 10:10; 11:2; 14:1, 9; Josh 7:21; Isa 11:11; Dan 1:2; Zech 5:11. Bodine, "Sumerians," 19.

in the Arabian Desert on the northern fringes of Sumer around 2900 BCE. Their language was written in cuneiform and syllabic, and is the first Semitic language on record. Eventually, they coalesced into the region's mightiest military force under the leadership of their first king, Sargon I, who overthrew his former master in a palace revolt and ruled the Akkadian realm, incorporating both the Sumerian and Akkadian city-states into a vast kingdom which extended as far away as Egypt, Ethiopia and India. He was the world's first empire builder, and his capital city at Agade flowed with great wealth. His influence during his lifetime was spread over the entire Near East, but his empire soon began to fall apart after his death, and by 2200 BCE, the Gutians invaded Agade from the northeast, and literally wiped the city from the face of the earth.[13] No archaeologic remains of the Akkadian capital have ever been discovered, and the richness of Sargon I's realm appears to have been lost forever.

Although the lifespan of the Akkadian reign was relatively short when compared to other Bronze Age dynasties, they were nevertheless influential on the evolution of Hebrew tradition, for the legends of their kings, like those of the Sumerians, shows up in the folktale motif of many biblical tales, as well as in the literature of the surrounding cultures. This can particularly be seen in the legend of the birth of Sargon I, whose mother was said to have set him adrift on the Euphrates River in a watertight wicker basket soon after his birth. He eventually was saved by Aqqi, who raised him as his adopted son, a storyline so similar to that of Moses that most biblical scholars believe that the authors of the Torah directly incorporated the material from the ancient Akkadian sources into the legend of Moses's birth.

In addition to legendary material, the effect of the Akkadians on the future development of the region was prodigious because the Semitic Akkadian language became the dominant dialect in the ancient Near East for the next two thousand years, gradually becoming modified into separate and distinct tongues by the cultures which they engendered.[14] Today, the Semitic languages are generally divided into three categories: the East Semitic, which includes the Akkadians, Assyrians, and Babylonians; the Northwest (West) Semitic, which includes the Canaanites, Hebrews, Aramaeans,[15] Amorites, and Phoenicians; and the

---

13 The Gutians were nomadic pastoralists from the Zagros Mountains, who held sway in the land for about a hundred years. Bright, A History of Israel, 42.

14 Akkadian was written in cuneiform, and was a logo-syllabic script that consisted of a combination of logograms and syllables, which retained the standard Semitic consonants. Marcus, "Akkadian," 20, 23. The Akkadian language was the first Semitic tongue on record, followed by Aramaic, in the late second millennium BCE, and then Phoenician and Hebrew, which had their origins in the local language of ancient Ugarit. Healey, "The Early Alphabet," 204-205.

15 Moses told the people before they crossed the Jordan River that when they arrive in the Promised Land they were to bring gifts for the Lord from each annual harvest, and

Southwest (South) Semitic, which includes the Arabs and Ethiopians. Although the modern dialects of descendants of these groups are not often intelligible from one subgroup to another, intercourse between diverse peoples in ancient times was possible since the early modifications were not of major proportions. This is evident in the biblical patriarchal tales, where the Hebrews interacted quite extensively with other people in the region who spoke the Northwest Semitic tongue.[16] It is likely that a similar situation existed generations later when Moses communicated with various Canaanite kings as he tried to obtain passage through their lands on the way to the Promised Land. This ability to converse with foreign dignitaries would have also enabled the dissident Hebrews to make their wishes known as they migrated north to Ugarit, as will be discussed in chapter 5.

As the second millennium BCE began, initiating the Middle Bronze Age and the era of the Hebrew Patriarch according to most biblical scholars, the Sumerian and Akkadian cultures disappeared from the political scene, and various Semitic and Indo-European tribes began to infiltrate throughout Mesopotamia, gaining control of local city-states and dividing the resources of the region into feuding empires. In the north, the Assyrians took control of the territory which was originally part of the Akkadian empire, while in the south, the Babylonians gathered enough strength to dominate the former political scene of Sumer. The Babylonians are particularly pertinent to biblical historicity since Hammurabi, who was the sixth in line of the Old Babylonian Dynasty, ascending the Babylonian throne during the Hyksos era, was the author of a law code which is believed to have influenced the development of the Mosaic Code.[17] The biblical *lex talionis*

---

say to Him that "my ancestors were migrant Arameans who went to Egypt for refuge." Deut 26:5. The Living Bible, 170. The Bible relates the patriarchs to the Aramaeans by originating the patriarchs in Aram-Naharaim (Paddan-Aram), and by calling Laban an Aramaean. Gen 25:20; 28:5; 31:20, 24. de Vaux, The Early History of Israel, 200.

16 The ancient Hebrew language was a distinct dialect of Canaanite, and fully comprehensible to their neighbors. Brown, Ancient Israel and Ancient Greece: Religion, Politics, and Culture, 8. The Old Testament does not mention the tongue as Hebrew, and the book of *Isaiah* referred to it as "the speech of Canaan." Isa 19:18. Huehnergard, & Hackett, "The Hebrew and Aramaic Languages," 7. Even today, remnants of their writings so closely overlap that the ability to distinguish them is usually based on historical information, rather than on linguistic criteria. Smith, The Early History of God: Yahweh and the Other Deities in Ancient Israel, 20.

17 The chronology of the Old Babylonian Dynasty is inexact because the dates are calculated from the astronomical periods in the "Venus Tablets," which are not agreed upon by scholars. This has led to the calculation of three separate Babylonian chronologies during the second millennium BCE: the so-called high, middle and low chronologies. Knapp, The History and Culture of Ancient Western Asia and Egypt, 8. Most scholars today favor the middle chronology which places Hammurabi at 1792-1750 BCE, but recent restudy of the Ammisaduqa Venus Tablets of Babylon have revised his dates of reign to 1848-1806 BCE. Tadmor, "Chronology of the Ancient Near East in the Second

punishment of "an eye for an eye and a tooth for a tooth," is literally taken verbatim from the Hammurabi text, and it is likely that the biblical compilers were aware of this treatise when the Torah underwent its final collation.[18]

It is at this juncture, when mass migrations took place across the entire Mediterranean Basin, that the beginnings of both the early Greek and Hebrew civilizations first appeared on the geopolitical scene. The Greeks are believed to have been derived from Indo-Europeans who moved onto the Greek mainland and Anatolia from the north and east, while the Hebrews were one of a number of Semitic tribes who spread into the Levant in a movement commonly called the "Amorite Invasion," as will be discussed in chapter 3. Although the Indo-European ancestors of the Greeks are related to the invaders who generated the Akkadian civilization, their heritage is quite different, and will be discussed in chapter 7. In this section, I will discuss the history of the people who gradually transformed the civilizations of the ancient Near East, and evolved into the cultures with which the Hebrew Patriarchs and Moses interacted.

1. Indo-European Hittites and Hurrians

It is not known from exactly which region the Indo-European immigrants first began to spread into the Fertile Crescent and Greece around 2000 BCE, with scholars favoring such diverse areas as Europe, the region around the Caucasus mountains, and the distant district of Russia.[19] But wherever they began their trek, the settlers eventually populated an extensive area across the entire Fertile Crescent, concentrating their strength in a powerful kingdom known as Anatolia, in present-day Turkey. This mineral-rich region was part of the great mountain system which extended from the Himalayas to the Atlantic seaboard of France, Spain and North Africa. It formed a huge peninsula between the Black Sea and the Mediterranean Sea, creating a land bridge between Asia and Europe, much as the Levant connected Asia and Egypt. Nestled in between the Pontus Mountains on the north and the Taurus Mountains to the south, the fertile

---

Millennium BCE," 65-66).

18 The law of "an eye for an eye," also called the law of retribution, is found at Exod 21:23-24; Lev 24:17-20; and Deut 19:21. Earlier law codes had exacted financial penalties for injury, but Hammurabi was the first to require physical injury for physical injury. The Bible also applied the *lex talionis* to one accused of false witness, so if he was found guilty, he would bear the same punishment as the person whom he attempted to injure. Deut 19:17.

19 The Indo-European homeland most favored by scholars is the northern Pontic (Black Sea), from the Dniepr River to the Caspian Sea, with the formative period taking place in the Late Neolithic/Eneolithic (4500-3500 BCE), and the common phase ending about 2500 BCE. The Oxford Encyclopedia of Archaeology in the Near East, vol. III, 155.

Anatolian highland plateau was rich in timber and agricultural products, as well as in abundant mineral wealth, such as copper, silver, tin, and iron. During the Middle Bronze Age, these resources were particularly valuable, and the migrating Indo-Europeans took advantage of the productivity of the land to gain a reliable foothold in their struggle for economic power and survival.

The autochthonous population which inhabited central Anatolia before the Indo-Europeans appeared were referred to as Hattians, so when the new immigrants settled in the land and gradually took control of the region, the surrounding cultures referred to them as Hittites, which meant from the "land of Hatti."[20] In time, they built their capital city at Bogazkoy (Hattusas, Kushshar), a vast fortification which stretched for three miles, a site as large as classical Athens. A cache of thousands of tablets written in a script known as Arzawan have been uncovered in the remains, providing historians with a wealth of information on the workings of the city.[21] One reason why the Hittites were able to so successively expand their authority throughout Anatolia in such a short period of time was that after they defeated the State of Arzawa, they were able to utilize the established Arzawan language and have access to the Aegean Sea at Apasas, which later became Ephesus. In addition, they were the first army in the region to use chariots, which enabled them both to defend their capital city, and to make successful long-distance raids.

The first known Hittite King was Labarna I, who is believed to have ruled from c. 1680-1650 BCE, according to the Middle Chronology. This was the same era that the Hyksos ruled in Egypt, and because Egyptian influence in the Levant was significantly reduced during that period of time, a power vacuum was created which was quickly filled by the Hittites. Little is known of Labarna I, and many scholars have therefore regarded his nephew and successor Hattusilis I (c. 1650-1620 BCE), or "man of Khattusha," as the first true Hittite king, since he was able to establish a program of territorial expansion by defeating the states of Arzawa and Yamhad, which was aimed at controlling the trade route running from Babylonia to the Mediterranean coastlands. He died before he could completely subdue the city of Aleppo (Halab), which was the capital city of Yamhad, however, and it was his grandson, Mursilis I (c. 1620-1590 BCE),

20 Schwantes, A Short History of the Ancient Near East, 44. The term "Hittite" was applied to at least four distinct groups in the ancient Near East: Hattians who occupied Anatolia before 2000 BCE; the Indo-European invaders of Anatolia, after 2000 BCE, who developed the great Hittite Empire; Neo-Hittites who lived in Syria after 1200 BCE; and the Hittites who were mentioned in the Old Testament. Mayer, "Hittite and Israelite Celtic Practices: A Selected Comparison," 19.

21 Arzawa was the name given to a group of states that formed the principal power of western Anatolia during the early years of the Hittite dynasty, and their language was distributed as the official script throughout the Hittite realm. Macqueen, The Hittites, and Their Contemporaries in Asia Minor, 24-25.

who finally destroyed the city c. 1595 BCE, overthrowing the dynasty which Hammurabi had extended in Babylon, and putting an end to the celebrated First Dynasty of Babylon. As I will discuss in more detail in Chapter 3, many scholars believe that Joseph was sold into slavery in Egypt during the rule of the Hyksos, so this era comports with the beginning of Hebrew life in Egypt, eventually to end with the Exodus under the leadership of Moses.

As a result of these victories, the Hittites were elevated to supremacy in the ancient Near East, but their reign of glory did not last very long. Mursilis I did not have the force to control such a vast area of land, and upon his return to Bogazkoy, his kinsmen revolted and he was assassinated by his son-in-law. Hantili I (1590-1550 BCE), a co-conspirator, ascended the throne, but Hittite influence quickly began to ebb, and by the time Telepinus (1525-1500 BCE) reigned, the Hittite kingdom was once again confined to central Anatolia. They would not recover domination of the region again until the rise of Suppiluliuma I (1380-1340 BCE).

With the withdrawal of the Hittites from Canaan, and the eviction of the Hyksos from Egypt, the Eighteenth Dynasty Pharaohs took advantage of their military superiority and quickly extended their authority once again into the Levant. Almost immediately after sacking the Hyksos capital of Avaris (*Hwt-W'rt*, Tell el-Dab`a), Ahmose (Amosis) I (1539-1514 BCE) pursued the enemy along the *Via Maris* into Palestine and captured the city of Sharuhen, which was then under Hyksos control.[22] The succeeding line of Thutmoside kings maintained this process of expansion, and impelled Egypt into her most glorious period, accompanied by great material prosperity. By the time of Thutmose III (1479-1425 BCE), Egypt controlled most of Syria-Palestine, and turned the region into an Egyptian province, which they referred to as *Retenu*. This change in military superiority in the Levant is important to my theory of dissident Hebrew migration to Mycenae, for if the Hebrew Exodus took place during this era, it would have been difficult for the Hebrew dissidents to remain in the region, given the combined presence of the Egyptians and the rest of the Hebrew congregation led by Moses, so migration to Mycenae would have been the logical course to take.

With the withdrawal of the Hittites, the only remaining force which could oppose the Egyptians were the Hurrians, a non-Semitic people who had earlier begun to infiltrate Syria and Mesopotamia during the first few centuries of the second millennium BCE. They are believed to have originated in the mountains

---

22 The *Via Maris* was the land route which connected Egypt to Palestine through the Sinai Peninsula. It was also known over the years as the "Way of the Sea," the "Sea Route," the "Great Trunk Road," and the "Coastal Highway," although what it was actually called in ancient days is not certain. Beitzel, "The *Via Maris* in Literary and Cartographic Sources," 65; Dorsey, The Roads and Highways of Ancient Israel, 57.

of eastern Anatolia, and then spread both to the east and south, occupying the land between the Hittites and Assyria. Their movements were very diverse, and they often fractured into many groups, joining other migratory forces to inhabit regions throughout the Levant. Although the Hurrian kingdom was primarily based in Mesopotamia, many Hurrian names also appeared among the Hyksos, indicating that some of their numbers accompanied the migration of Semites into Egypt. With time, the Hurrians consolidated their forces into a large kingdom centered in northwestern Mesopotamia, near Asia Minor with its capital at Alalakh (modern Tell Atchana), which the Assyrians called Mitanni, or the "land of the Hurrians."[23] Around 1480 BCE, they advanced a united force under Parrattarna (c. 1480-1450 BCE), and from that point forward their growth was so impressive that the Egyptians referred to the inhabitants of Syria-Palestine as *Hurru*, because of the predominant presence of the Hurrian population.

Despite their significant numbers, the Hurrians were simply not strong enough to withstand the expansive Egyptian military power of the Eighteenth Dynasty Pharaohs, and Amenhotep (Amenophis) II (1427-1392 BCE) followed up the success of Thutmose III by taking over 36,000 Hurrians captive in one campaign alone. During the reign of Thutmose IV (1392-1382 BCE), just before the period of the Amarna Age (1353-1336 BCE), enough Hurrian prisoners were taken at Gezer to form a colony at Thebes. It was clear to the Hurrians that they could not survive as enemies of Egypt, and to protect their waning interests, they sealed a treaty of peace with the Egyptians by agreeing to a marriage alliance between Tuthmosis IV and the daughter of King Artatama I (c. 1410-1400 BCE). This enabled the Egyptians to buttress their position as the primary military force in the region, and to administer their realm they set up a framework of districts which included the southern Phoenician coast, the northern coast along with the district of Amurru, and the district of Apu, which covered the inland regions. Although this dominance during the fifteenth and early fourteenth centuries BCE has prompted some scholars to doubt whether the Exodus could have been expected to succeed when Egyptian control of the area was strong, it must be remembered that the main focus of the Egyptians was in the populated areas near the *Via Maris*, and they did not exert as much control in the Sinai and the hill country of Palestine, where most of the Hebrew movement took place. In addition, much of the Egyptian military force was busy expanding their supremacy in the Levant, so the number of soldiers in the homefront would have been reduced, thereby allowing for a successful Exodus of Hebrew slaves.

While the Egyptians appeared to be invincible during this early phase of the Late Bronze Age, their power base began to wane as Egypt entered the Amarna Age. As will be discussed in more detail in the next chapter, the Amarna Age

---

23 Roaf, Cultural Atlas of Mesopotamia and the Ancient Near East, 132. The Assyrians, Hittites, and Babylonians also referred to the region as Hanigalbat, while the Egyptians called it Nahrina. Evans, "The Mitanni State," 194.

refers to the time when Amenhotep III (1382-1344 BCE) and Amenhotep IV (Akhenaten)(1352-1336 BCE) sat on the throne of Egypt. The name came from the capital city which Amenhotep IV built at Tell el-Amarna, midway between Cairo and Luxor, and during this period Egyptian control of the region began to ebb as pharaonic support for local regimes diminished under Amenhotep IV, the Pharaoh who attempted to radically change the religious nature of his country by promoting the worship of only one god, the sun-god Aten. As he concentrated his efforts at home on social change, he diverted his attention away from the regional princes in Canaan who were loyal to the Egyptian monarchs, isolating himself from their desperate pleas for assistance. This shifted the balance of power in Palestine away from Egypt and toward the Hittite realm.

It was not only Egyptian laxity in the affairs of the region which led to a resurgence of Hittite power, but also the exceptional military and organizational skills of Suppiluliuma I (1380-1340 BCE), the Hittite king who parlayed his squadrons into such a mighty military force that victories once again assured his taking control of much of Syria and the northern Levantine region. His first undertaking after ascension to the throne was to consolidate the Anatolian realm by successfully campaigning against the provinces of Azzi, Arzawa, and the Kashka lands. He then took advantage of the fact that Amenhotep IV was neglecting his Hurrian Syrian allies, and made an alliance with a rival claimant to the Mitannian throne, moving against the forces of the Mitanni King Tushratta (c. 1450 BCE). After finding that his capital city of Wasshukkani was captured, Tushratta withdrew and Suppiluliuma I then brought the important Syrian states of Halab, Allakh, Qadesh, Nukhasshe, and Amurru within the Hittite sphere of influence. Eventually, he subdued Mitanni completely, including the allied state of Carchemish (Jerablus), and after his death, Hittite power continued to thrive as his son Mursilis II (1339-1306 BCE) defeated the troublesome Anatolian state of Arzawa, which had been allied with the distant power of Ahhiyawa.

The rivalry between Egypt and the Hittites for control of Syria was to culminate decades later in a great battle at Kadesh-on-Orontes, where the Hittite army under Hattusilis III (1275-1250 BCE), the son of Mursilis II, clashed with Ramesses II (1279-1213 BCE) in a battle that matched numerically equal forces of over 20,000 men. I will discuss this engagement in more detail in chapter 2, but the peace treaty which was eventually concluded gave control of Syria to the Hittites, while the Egyptians ruled over Palestine. Although a century of peace between Egypt and the Hittites followed, both countries entered an era of severe decline that was precipitated by invasions of the People of the Sea, a band of marauders who invaded the Levant at the end of the Late Bronze Age. As the Iron Age emerged, the Hittites disappeared from the geopolitical scene, to be replaced by the Assyrians and Babylonians.

Although the Old Testament does not describe any event which relates to the military intrusion of the Hittites into the Levant, there are numerous references to contacts between the Hittites and patriarchal families which indicate that the relationship between the two culturally diverse peoples was congenial. The book of *Genesis* described how Abraham bought the cave of Machpelah for 400 silver shekels from Ephron the Hittite for the burial of Sarah after she died in Hebron (Arabic *El-Khalil*) in a transaction that followed Hittite law.[24] Since Abraham is generally believed to have lived well before Labarna I or Hattusilis I, it is uncertain if the biblical compilers were applying what they understood Hittite law to have been in the patriarchal era, or whether they simply applied principles which were contemporary in their own time. In either case, despite the fact that the early Hebrews interacted peaceably with the Hittites, intermarriage between the two cultures was strictly forbidden by the patriarchal families. This intolerance of intermarriage carried over into the Mosaic Code.[25] When Abraham sent his servant to find a Hebrew wife for Isaac, he made him swear not to let Isaac marry one of the local Canaanite girls. Esau did not obey this tradition, and after his birthright was stolen by Jacob, he married two Hittite women, so disturbing Rebekah by his choice of wives that she sent Jacob to her relatives in Paddan-Aram (Padan-Aram, the "field of Aram") to find a wife, fearing he might do the same.[26]

The Hurrians were also mentioned in the Old Testament, but there is little evidence that they cooperated with the Hebrews in a manner akin to the Hittites. The Hurrians were usually referred to as Horites or Hivites in the Bible, and were connected with two of the seven nations of Canaan which the Lord promised to destroy when the Hebrews entered the Promised Land: the Hivites and the Jebusites.[27] When Abraham's family left Ur and settled in Haran in northwest Mesopotamia, they were living in what was then the major region of Hurrian

24 Gen 23:2, 9-10, 16. Matthews & Benjamin, Old Testament Parallels: Laws and Stories From the Ancient Near East, Third Edition, 115.

25 Gen 26:34-35. In the book of *Deuteronomy*, Moses warned the Hebrews that they must not intermarry with the nations they destroyed, "nor let your sons and daughters marry their sons and daughters," for that would result in your children worshiping their gods. Deut 7:3-4. The Living Bible, 155. After the Babylonian Exile, in the fifth century BCE, when Cyrus the Great allowed the Jews to return to Jerusalem, many Jews married Gentile women, not taken as captives in war, and were condemned for this practice by the prophets Ezra and Nehemiah. Ezra 9:2; Neh 13:23.

26 Gen 24:3-4; 26:34-35; 28:9. Esau's wives are listed differently at Gen 36:2-4.

27 Deut 7.1. Moses told the Hebrews before they crossed the Jordan River to completely wipe out the Hittites, Amorites, Canaanites, Perizites, Hivites and Yebusites. Deut 20:17. Hivite may be a corruption of the name Horite, for Zibeon the Hivite is said to have had an Horite father. Gen 36:2, 20. Kaiser, "Exodus," 318. The Jebusites were first mentioned as descendants of Canaan (Gen 10:16), and were a non-Semitic people who later inhabited the hill country along the southern border with Benjamin. Walton, Matthews, & Chavalas, The IVP Bible Background Commentary: Old Testament, 327.

influence, but biblical tradition does not reflect any fertilization of patriarchal life with known Hurrian practices, although the concern of Laban for the possible theft of his household idols by Jacob, as will be discussed in chapter 3, reflected Hurrian customs.

2. *The Amorite Invasion*

At the same time the Indo-Europeans were migrating into Anatolia and Mesopotamia, engendering the Hittite and Hurrian civilizations, Semitic tribes from the Arabian Desert were beginning to expand eastward into Mesopotamia and the Levant in a process which has often been referred to as the "Amorite movement," a term which is derived from the Akkadian word "*Amurru*," which means "West," referring to the direction from which they came.[28] The Sumerians as early as 2600 BCE had referred to them as "*MAR.TU*," but in the course of time the term Amorite gradually replaced this designation, as well as the term *Amurru*. Their precise place of origin is not known, but their growing numbers rearranged the political order in the Near East, turning Mesopotamia into a virtual Amorite land. By the last year of the Third Dynasty of Ur, their strength was so renowned that a structure to keep out the marauding Amorites became known as the "wall of Amurru."[29] The collapse of the Ur III dynasty initiated the Middle Bronze Age, and by 1900-1800 BCE, virtually every Mesopotamian city-state had a king with an Amorite name, including the founder of the Old Babylonian Dynasty, Sumu-Abu (c. 1667-1653 BCE), an Amorite who was the great-great-grandfather of Hammurabi, as well as of numerous kings of Byblos (Gebal) and Ugarit.[30] As their dominance intensified, the Amorites poured into Syria, speaking Northwest Semitic dialects, and setting up a number of city-states which eventually took over control of the overland trade routes connecting the economies of the ancient Near East. They were a formidable force, frequently described by their neighbors as a hostile and ravaging people, "with canine instincts, like wolves," and when they moved through Canaan, they left a widespread destruction of towns in their wake.[31] In the Bible, they were described as exceptionally tall and strong,

---

28 Redford, Egypt, Canaan, and Israel in Ancient Times, 170. The theory which holds that these immigrants were responsible for the radical cultural changes that characterized the transition from the Early to the Middle Bronze Age is known as "the Amorite Hypothesis." Haldar, Who Were the Amorites?, 27.

29 Roaf, Cultural Atlas of Mesopotamia and the Ancient Near East, 102, 108.

30 Mendenhall, Ancient Israel's Faith and History, 20. Despite the fact that thousands of Amorite personal names appear in records from this era, not a single text has been uncovered written in the Amorite language. Larsen, "The Middle Bronze Age," 14.

31 Haldar, Who Were the Amorites?, 28. This designation was similar to Jacob's forecast for his son: Benjamin is a wolf on the prowl: mornings he devours the prey, and evenings he distributes the spoils." Gen 49:27. Genesis, The Anchor Bible, 364.

and were regarded as the successors, or descendants, of the legendary Rephaim giants.

Since the Hebrew Patriarchs are believed to have lived during this same era, the Amorite movement provides a possible explanation as to why the Hebrews were not cited in extra-biblical chronicles before the Merneptah Stele (c. 1208 BCE). Until the Hebrews coalesced into large enough communities to be recognized as a distinct "people" following their conquest of the Promised Land, they were likely seen by contemporary chroniclers as a band of Amorites, rather than as a group worthy of specific mention. This explanation is quite appealing, for although the Hebrews eventually became isolated from their Semitic neighbors with respect to their religious beliefs, their cultural, linguistic, and lifestyle characteristics were very similar to the Semitic tribes who took part in the Amorite invasion. Some support for this reasoning can be found in documents from the city of Mari, which was the center of Amorite rule during the Mari Age, where biblical names like Ishmael, Levi, Benjamin, Peleg, Serug, and Nahor frequently are cited.[32] In addition, Amorite mythology includes stories of the Creation (*Enuma Elish*) and the flood story (Gilgamesh Epic), and the Tower of Babel in the Bible resembled the ziggurat of the city of Babylon, an indication that the Hebrews may have had contact with other residents of the region.[33] Although the biblical compilers may have been interested in detailing the passage of Abraham through Canaan and Egypt as part of their own ancestral development, it would not be surprising if other observers during that era did not take particular notice of the patriarchal wanderings. I will discuss this in more detail in Chapter 4, when I answer the arguments of those who claim that the Exodus never actually took place.

B. Levant

Although Abraham, if we are to believe the compilers of the Old Testament, clearly developed some of his religious tenets from both the Sumerian and Akkadian cultures during his formative years in Mesopotamia, it was in the Levant, among the thriving Semitic Amorite population, that the Hebrew patriarchal culture formulated the majority of those unique characteristics which eventually culminated in the monotheistic Mosaic Code, following the theophany on Mt. Sinai. The Middle Bronze Age Levant offered the patriarchal families an array of Semitic cultures with which to interact and learn, as well as a broad amalgam of ideas which filtered in from distant regions, such as Anatolia and the northern coast of the Mediterranean Sea. When Moses was growing up in the Egyptian royal court, he also gained first-hand knowledge of these diverse peoples through ambassadors who visited Egypt to promote trade and friendly relations. As he led the Hebrews on their wanderings in the Sinai before crossing

---

32 Anderson, Understanding the Old Testament, 31.
33 Ibid., 32.

the Jordan River into the Levant, these contacts would have provided him with valuable information.

1. Terminology

The term "Levant" is generally used to refer to the southwestern section of the Fertile Crescent, which today comprises the countries of Lebanon, Israel, Jordan, Syria, and parts of Turkey and Iraq. The names associated with the countries of the Levant varied in ancient times, with the Sumerians referring to this area as *Kur Martu-Ki*, the land of the West, and the Akkadians calling it *Amurru*, the land of the Amorites. The Babylonians used the term *Amurru* to refer to the whole of Syria, rather than to parts of Canaan alone, while the Egyptians, particularly during the Middle Kingdom, called the region *Retenu*, a term which included parts of southern Syria, the eastern Delta, and the Palestinian uplands. Other Egyptian names for lands located in the Levant included *Djahy*, *Lotan*, and *Hurru* or *Kharu*. These terms have little meaning today, and in this book I will use the word "Levant" only when I am referring to the general region between Mesopotamia and Egypt, without reference to a specific location.

The names of regions in the Levant which modern readers are more familiar with are those which appear in the Old Testament: "Palestine," "Phoenicia," and "Canaan." The term Syria, or Syro-Palestine, does not appear in the Bible, but was regularly used in contemporary chronicles for the region north of Canaan, including the area south of the Taurus mountains in southeast Turkey, west of the Euphrates River, and east of the Amanus mountains and the Mediterranean Sea. Although specific boundaries are occasionally described in various biblical sections for each of these designations, they are not always consistent, and the same city may fall within the district of any of the names, depending on the chronology under discussion. For the most part, Palestine referred to the southernmost coastal area of the Levant, Phoenicia was used to denote the northern coastal section, while Canaan was often applied to all of the land between Egypt and Syria, west of the Arabian desert. It was in this region, measuring only one hundred fifty miles from north to south, and seventy-five miles from east to west, that most of the stories from the Bible took place. During the Late Bronze Age, these terms were not yet in popular use, but I will refer to them in this work because they are so ingrained in our image of the region that it is advantageous to use them as points of reference when discussing movements of the various military and tribal units at that time. In order to provide a basis for a more detailed research, should the reader desire to expand his or her knowledge in this aspect of Hebrew historical evolution, I will now discuss the terminology of the area in a more thorough fashion.

a. Palestine

In the Bible, the term "Palestine" generally referred to the region occupied by the Philistines at the end of the Late Bronze Age. Scholars do not agree as to exactly when the biblical Philistines first arrived, but most accept that they congregated on the coast of southwest Canaan somewhere between 1180-1150 BCE, following the invasion of the People of the Sea in Year 8 of the reign of Ramesses III (1184-1153 BCE).[34]

The name "Palestine" is generally believed to have been derived from the Greek word *Palastu*, which meant the "Land of the Philistines," as the region was referred to in Assyrian documents from about 800 BCE onwards. The Egyptians referred to these people as *Prst*, and it is generally accepted that they were the Peleset, one of the groups of warriors that comprised the People of the Sea. Most scholars identify the Peleset with the Philistines, not only because of the linguistic similarity in their names, but because the Peleset of the Egyptian texts settled in the areas in which the biblical Philistines were later found.

As they established themselves in the lowlands of Palestine, they set up a political system that was similar to the Canaanite system of city-states, and rapidly expanded their military strength in a wide sphere of influence beyond their immediate area of control. They soon dominated the entire southern coastal plain of the Levant, and became the ruling class in five ancient city kingdoms known as the Pentapolis, that previously had been ruled by the Canaanites: Gaza (Ghazzeh), Ashdod (Esdud), Ashkelon (Askalon), Ekron (Khirbet el-Muqanna), and Gath Tell es-Safi. Unlike the Phoenician cities of Byblos, Sidon and Tyre, the Palestinian coastal cities were all a few miles inland, more accessible to the *Via Maris* than to the Mediterranean Sea itself, which explains why there is little mention of Philistine maritime activity when compared to Phoenicia. Since their era of expansion took place during the time of the Israelite Judges and United Monarchy, the two nations came into frequent conflict, leading to the Philistines being identified in the Bible as the primary adversaries of the Hebrews, from the time of the conquest of the Promised Land up to the Babylonian Exile (587-538 BCE).[35]

The Philistines are important to my analysis of a possible Hebrew migration to

---

34 The entry of the Philistines into Canaan is generally seen as the start of the Iron Age in the Levant, since they are credited in the Bible with the introduction of iron. 1 Sam 13:19-22. Wilson, The Exodus Enigma, 15. The biblical Philistines are believed to have been part of this wave of Philistine migration to Canaan, with some scholars suggesting that an earlier infusion took place in the Middle Bronze Age of people referred to as *Kaptara* or *Caphtorim*. Merrill, Kingdom of Priests: A History of Old Testament Israel, 58-59.

35 The name Philistine appears 288 times in the Bible. Howard, Jr., "Philistines," 231.

Mycenae, for their route of passage from their land of origin in Crete to Canaan was very similar to the one I believe the dissident Hebrews took centuries earlier in the opposite direction. Most scholars accept that the biblical Philistines came from Crete as part of the People of the Sea invasion, although an argument has been made that they traveled by land to Troy, Miletus, Tarsus, and then to Canaan, since maritime travel was costly and had space limitations.[36] If they did travel by sea, it has been estimated that it would have taken 100 penteconter ships, transporting 5,000 people and hundreds of tons of cargo, to accomplish the task of emigration.[37] This origin was accepted by the biblical compilers, who postulated that the Cretans came from *Caphtor* (Egyptian *Keftiu*, or Akkadian *Kaptara*), the Hebrew name for Crete, and that they wiped out the Avvim, who lived in Gaza and settled in their place.[38] Closely identified with the label of Caphtorites, or Caphtorim, as Cretans is the term "Cherethites," which was used to refer to the Philistines in the books of *Ezekiel* and *Zephaniah*.[39] Although most scholars agree that the evidence for a Cretan origin is conclusive, some have placed their origin on the coast of Anatolia, Cyprus, Caria, or Cappadocia, an area in today's eastern Turkey.[40]

Extra-biblical support for a Philistine origin in Crete can be seen in the similarity between the arms and military organization of the Philistines, and the Iron Age peoples from the Achaean world. The Philistines wore distinctive headdresses with a feathered tiara, protected themselves with small round shields, and used broad swords, all of which were very similar to the depiction of Achaean warriors in conflict with the Hattic kings of Anatolia in the early fourteenth century BCE.[41] Pottery motifs are also supportive of a Philistine origin near Mycenae, for the Philistines appear to have evolved their style from the Mycenaean IIIC period (1225-1050 BCE), when the Aegean design reached its greatest height after the settlement of the People of the Sea. The Philistines rejuvenated the Mycenaean pattern with new elements from the adjacent areas of Egypt and Cyprus, which remained for many centuries the dominant form of pottery style in the southern Levant. If indeed the Philistines originated in Crete, and came to the eastern Mediterranean shore as part of the People of the Sea invasion during the thirteenth and twelfth centuries BCE, it is very plausible that Hebrews who left the Exodus a few generations earlier would have taken a similar

---

36 Yasur-Landau, "One if by Sea ... Two if By Land, How Did the Philistines Get to Canaan? Two: By Land," 35, 37.

37 Barako, "One if by Sea ... Two if By Land, How Did the Philistines Get to Canaan? One: By Sea," 64.

38 Gen 10:14; Deut 2:23. See, e.g., Amos 9:7; Jer 47:4.

39 Ezek 25:15-16; Zeph 2:4-5. Howard, Jr., "Philistines," 232.

40 Tigay, Deuteronomy, 30; Dothan & Dothan, People of the Sea, The Search for the Philistines, 94-95.

41 Hindson, The Philistines and the Old Testament, 42-43.

passage in the opposite direction to flee their brethren and other Canaanite forces who opposed their continued presence in the Levant. Stories of their passage may even have permeated the local lore and encouraged the Philistines to travel to the Canaanite region. I will discuss the invasion of the People of the Sea in more detail in chapter 8.

b. Phoenicia

Phoenicia was the name applied to the region of the sea-faring people of the coastal area, north of where the Philistines became entrenched. The district was enclosed by the Litani and Arvad rivers, and corresponded roughly to modern Lebanon, along with parts of Israel and Syria. Included within its borders were the important port-cities of Byblos, Tyre, and Sidon, providing Phoenicia with the most strategic sites of maritime trade in all of Canaan. Since the greatest natural resource of the region was the nearby forestland, which abounded in pines, cypresses, and cedars, the Phoenicians were supplied with an abundant supply of wood to construct magnificent ships, and they took advantage of this bounty to become the foremost purveyors of a sea-faring trade that allowed them to engage in commerce with all the kingdoms that bordered the Mediterranean Sea.[42] Although their land was only five hundred miles long and ninety-five miles wide, they had a virtual monopoly on overseas trade in the entire Levantine region, from the Cilician-Syrian border to Egypt. This success was not simply due to their advantageous natural resources, but also because they advanced the safety and practicality of sea trade by becoming "the first people to navigate by observing the stars; to travel beyond sight of land; to sail at night; and to undertake voyages in winter-time."[43] If you wanted to move goods from one port to another during the Late Bronze Age, you generally hired Phoenician sailors and ships to carry out the appointed task.

In addition to their maritime monopoly, the Phoenicians were also noted for their production of textiles, as well as glass, metal, and ivory work. The very name of Phoenicia (*Phoinike*) was related to the vital textile trade, for the word "Phoenician" is believed to have derived from the Greek word *phoinix* (*phoinos*), or red purple dye, which came from the many *Murex trunculus* or *Murex brandaris* molluscs found off the Phoenician coast during that era.[44] It was the most

---

42 The cedars of Lebanon (Cedrus libani) were renowned in antiquity for their sweet fragrance, beauty, and durable strength. They are slow growing and could live up to three thousand years, attaining heights of 120 feet. They were an expensive item of trade throughout the ancient Near East, used in the construction and paneling of palaces and temples, and also for the construction of merchant ships. Hakimian, "Byblos," 51.

43 Grant, The Ancient Mediterranean, 120.

44 Albright, "Syria, the Philistines, and Phoenicia," 520. Some scholars have denied the derivation of the Phoenician name from this substance, and instead ascribed the word

expensive dye in the ancient world – the color of royalty – and provided a steady flow of income to the Phoenician economy. Its importance could be seen in the Lord's instructions to Moses to have the Hebrew people make fringes on the corners of their garments, and to attach "a cord of blue" at each corner to remind them of the Lord's commandments.[45] The brightly colored fabrics the Phoenicians produced supplied not only the Hebrew people, but also the royal wardrobes throughout the civilized world. Proof of the enormous extent of this industry can be found in the incredible numbers of shells that have been found near the cities of Sidon and Tyre.[46]

The Phoenicians were often referred to as Sidonians, alluding to the city of Sidon which was their primary residence before Tyre, and specified their country as Canaan. References to this nomenclature are present in both Homer and the Bible. Homer referred to the Phoenician inhabitants of Sidon as "dark red men,"[47] and in the *Odyssey*, a Phoenician slave boasted how she was "of Sidon town, smithy of bronze for all of the East."[48] The Bible recognized the primacy of this city, highlighting its importance by referring to Sidon as the firstborn son of Canaan.[49] If the dissident Hebrews who left the Exodus made contact with the Phoenicians to arrange for transportation to Mycenae, they may very well have first contacted them at Sidon, since the city held undisputed sway over southern Phoenicia during the time of the Exodus. Although Tyre would eventually eclipse Sidon during the tenth century BCE as the primary city of the Phoenicians, it was not mentioned in the early biblical narratives, or in Egyptian inscriptions during the campaigns of Thutmose III (1479-1425 BCE) in Canaan and Syria.[50]

The German historian Max Duncker (1811-1886 CE) proposed that in addition to providing the means by which much maritime trade was carried out in the Late Bronze Age, the Phoenicians also arrived in Greece in search of purple shell-fish and metals, and founded many settlements which influenced the early Greeks who

---

phoinix to mean "redskins," referring to the ruddy-brown color of the Semitic people east of the Mediterranean, rather than to the color of the *murex* dye. Godbey, The Lost Tribes - A Myth, Suggestions Toward Rewriting Hebrew History, 60.

45 Num 15:38-39. See e.g., Jer 10:9.

46 In one hill south of Sidon, the shell layer was several meters thick. Moscati, The World of the Phoenicians, 84. Since each *murex* secreted only two drops of yellowish liquid, the process required enormous numbers of shells in order to supply the growing need. Grant, The Ancient Mediterranean, 122.

47 Johnson, Civilizations of the Holy Land, 22.

48 Homer, The Odyssey, XV.425, 281.

49 Gen 10:15.

50 Sarna, Genesis, 75-76. Egyptian documents provide evidence that Tyre had existed in the fifteenth and fourteenth centuries BCE, so that the absence in these records is likely due to some catastrophe, which was then followed by a reorganization of the city. Myres, Who Were the Greeks?, 132-133.

had taken residence there.[51] He believed that the Phoenicians taught the art of building walls to the Greeks, as well as shaft graves and grave-chambers, and that once the Greek tribes grew strong under their tutelage, they "turned against the Carians and Phoenicians on their coasts, and tried to drive them back."[52] Michael Astour, Professor at Southern Illinois University, advanced the case for Phoenician presence in Mycenae by identifying their presence as Western Semites in several parts of Mycenaean Greece and their colonies, including the Danaans of Argolis, the Cadmeians of Boeotia, and the islands of Thera (Santorini), Cos, and Rhodes. He concluded that "the entire Mycenaean civilization was essentially a peripheral culture of the Ancient East, its westernmost extension."[53] As I will discuss in the chapters which follow, I believe that both of these characterizations provide far too much contribution to the Phoenicians, who primarily were maritime traders and transporters rather than colonizers who settled in distant lands and became immersed in local cultures. It is rather the Hebrews, in my opinion, and not the sailors who transported them, who should be given credit for much of what Duncker and Astour ascribe to the Phoenicians. The mere presence of a people in the adjacent geographical location does not support the concept of cultural transferences unless it is accompanied by evidence of other transferrable traits, a condition which I believe is clearly ascribable to the Hebrews, and not the Phoenicians.

c. Canaan

The name most commonly used in the Bible to refer to the area west of the Jordan River, encompassing the modern countries of Lebanon and Israel, as well as the region of Phoenicia, was the land of Canaan.[54] This designation is quite ancient, as testimonials of offerings to the god Dagon, the "lord of Canaan" (*ka-na-na-im*), can be found in numerous clay tablets dating as far back as 2250 BCE, and an eighteenth century BCE letter from Mari made reference to "thieves and Canaanites."[55] During the Tell el-Amarna period, the Egyptians commonly

---

51 Duncker, History of Greece: From the Earliest Times to the End of the Persian War, I.77.

52 Ibid., I.53-55. From 1200-1100 BCE, Duncker believed the Phoenicians were "paramount on the east coast" of Greece. Ibid., I.150. One legendary evidence of their ouster was the defeat of the bull of Marathon by Theseus, and the treaty which he concluded with the Amazons, evidence of the retreat of the Phoenicians from Melite. Ibid., I.152-153. In addition, the expedition of Adrastus of Sicyon, the war of the seven heroes against the seven-gated Thebes, was directed against the Phoenicians of the Cadmea. Ibid. I.154.

53 Astour, Hellenosemitica: An Ethnic and Cultural Study in West Semitic Impact on Mycenaean Greece, 357-358.

54 The words *Canaan* and *Canaanite* appear 160 times in the Bible. Schoville, "Canaanites and Amorites," 157.

55 Ibid., 158. The name "Canaan" first appears in Akkadian texts in the fifteenth

employed the term *Kinahhi* (*Kinahni*) to designate the country south of Carmel, or at times to even embrace the entire area of Phoenicia and Palestine. In many ways, Egypt turned the region into a political province, but most scholars do not believe that Egyptian rule should be equated with a provincial status.[56] Although the name of "Canaan," like that of "Phoenicia," has often been thought to refer to the purple dye (*kinakhna*), modern scholars have generally disregarded this origin, and the exact etiology remains uncertain.[57]

The people who were indigenous to the land of Canaan were not of one ethnic group, but rather were comprised of many clusters of tribes, particularly West Semites and Hurrians who had entered during the Amorite invasion. This included, in all likelihood, Canaanites who had inhabited the land in earlier days as Chalcolithic natives, as well as those who entered the region from elsewhere, such as from the northern Arabian steppe or the Persian gulf during the Amorite Invasion.

Although it is traditional to speak of the Canaanite immigration into Palestine as taking place at the beginning of the historical age c. 3000 BCE, this estimate is based more on a convenient guess, than an historical fact. The geography of the land was interrupted in many areas, creating subregions that did not easily communicate with each other, making unification of the land difficult. In the Old Testament, the Canaanites were often referred to as "Lowlanders," in order to distinguish them from the Amorites, who lived in the hills and were called "Highlanders."[58] Where "Phoenicians" were seen as engaging in the sea-faring trade, the "Canaanites" were typically labeled as traders and merchants.

d. Syria

Although the term Syria does not appear in the Bible, the country played a major role in the political changes which took place in the Promised Land, where the Hebrews eventually settled. It was nearly double the size of Palestine itself, with a coastline that extended from the Ladder of Tyre, which lay at the southern entrance of Phoenicia, up to the protrusion of the Amanus mountains into the sea, a distance of 260 miles. During the Middle Kingdom (2106-1786 BCE),

---

century BCE in the Idrimi inscription, which speaks of a flight to the "land of Kin'ani." de Vaux, The Early History of Israel, 125.

56 Sparks, Ethnicity and Identity in Ancient Israel: Prolegomena to the Study of Ethnic Sentiments and Their Expression in the Hebrew Bible, 101.

57 Kenyon, "Palestine in the Middle Bronze Age," 86.

58 Trumbull, Kadesh-Barnea, Its Importance and Probable Site, 65. The Bible also occasionally used the Amorite designation when referring to the Canaanites in general. See e.g., Gen 15:16, 21; Deut 1:7, 27. Milgrom, Numbers, 105. The "E" and "D" sources used *Amorites* as a general term for the pre-Israelite inhabitants of Canaan, while the "J" source used the term *Canaanites*. Astour, "Place Names," 261.

Egyptians used the term *Retenu* for this region, including all the principalities up to the Euphrates River, while in the New Kingdom (1550-1069 BCE), the names *Djahi*, and the *land of Hurru*, were preferred, referring to the Horite population which had begun to infiltrate the region.

Many ports were built along the bays and promontories of the Syrian coastline, providing access for the importation of necessary construction supplies, such as wood and stone. Northern Syria thereby became a vital component of the southern Mesopotamia culture, much like Phoenicia became the merchants for the entire Mediterranean Basin. The Syrian coastal plain was not as unbroken as that in Phoenicia, however, and there were numerous separations by hills which projected into the sea. This left the city of Ugarit, from which the Hebrews most likely departed for Mycenae, as the most important port city of Syria during the Late Bronze Age. I will return to a more detailed discussion of Ugarit later in this chapter.

Because its location provided ready access into Canaan and Egypt, Mesopotamian leaders began to make military campaigns into Syria as early as 2500 BCE, under the direction of rulers such as Eannatum of Lagash (c. 2500 BCE), Lugal-zaggisi of Uruk (2486-2461 BCE), and Naram-Sin of Akkad (2260-2223 BCE).[59] Archaeologic records from the Middle Bronze Age cities of Ebla (modern Tell Mardikh), Mari (Tell Hariri), and Tell Beidar, have provided many details of life in ancient Syria, and there is evidence that many of the great West Semitic deities were worshiped there, including the god El, who later would be included in biblical texts, as will be discussed in chapter 11. Since Syria was located at the crossroads of traffic between Mesopotamia and Canaan, it was constantly crowded with the movement of caravans crossing the Fertile Crescent in pursuit of economic gain or a better way-of-life, and the dissident Hebrews would not have been seen as a viable threat once they reached this region of relative independence.

2. Geography

Since I believe Ugarit was the most likely destination to have been chosen by the dissident Hebrews after they realized that they could no longer remain with their brethren in the Exodus, I am going to briefly describe the physical lay of the land in the Levant in order to outline a reasonable path that they may have taken to reach Ugarit without encountering significant resistance along the way. If the fracture took place before Joshua led the crossing of the Jordan River into the Promised Land, their departure locale could have been anywhere within the boundaries of Canaan, and so a general summary of the geography of the entire area is in order.

59 Pitard, "Before Israel: Syria-Palestine in the Bronze Age," 42.

The bridge of land in Canaan, between Egypt and Syria, was divided into four longitudinal natural belts that stretched north and south. On the far west, adjacent to the Mediterranean Sea, was the Israeli Coastal Plain, along which the *Via Maris* passed through the Plains of the Negev (Negeb), Judea and Sharon on through Galilee. Abutting the Coastal Plain to the east was the region of the Western Mountains, and then farther to the east was the narrow Jordan Valley, through which the Jordan River flowed for about 150 miles. Finally, on the easternmost edge of Canaan was the Transjordan plateau, an area which stretched from the eastern border of the Jordan Valley to the expansive wastelands of the Arabian desert. Most of the forty-year wandering of the Hebrews before passage into the Promised Land took place within the confines of Canaan, and did not expand into the region of the desert.

A. Coastal Plain

For travelers moving from Egypt northward to Syria, the most direct route was to follow the *Via Maris*, which started in Memphis and ran up the coastline to the Jezreel (or Esdraelon) Valley, and then jogged east at Megiddo, continuing north to Hazor, and then northeast to Damascus, Ebla and Aleppo. Because of the heavy traffic along the *Via Maris*, the fertile Coastal Plain was the most populated section of the Levant, and many walled-cities were constructed in order to provide provisions and commercial support to the multitude of caravans that plied their trade from Egypt to Mesopotamia. In ancient times, the land was lined at the edge of the sea by high sand dunes and ledges, which prevented many of the streams from emptying into the sea, causing the plain to become very swampy during the rainy season. Although the *Via Maris* provided a steady stream of commercial traffic between Egypt and Mesopotamia, the coastline was so unbroken that there were few natural areas for ports to be built in order to support a local maritime industry. The only functional harbor in the southern region was located at Jaffa, but it had a limited ability to handle large number of ships, and this enabled the northern area of Phoenicia to develop the lucrative maritime commercial industry which supplied the entire Mediterranean Basin with goods.

The southern part of the Coastal Plain was referred to as the Shephelah, an undulating region of low rolling hills only a few hundred feet high. Known as the "Lowland," the Shephelah contained the important cities of Beth-Shemesh, Aijalon, Gederoth, and Timnah, and in biblical times the region acted as a staging area for battles between forces which approached from the plains or Judaean plateau. It was a dry land, used mostly for pasturage, and because passage was relatively easy, commercial travelers and Bedouin migrants frequently moved through the region as they passed between Egypt and Syria. Because military traffic was also frequent along this route, most biblical scholars believe that God's advice to shun passage through this location when the Exodus began was due to the presence of Egyptian forces. This danger would also have likely caused the dissident Hebrews who left the Exodus to avoid the Shephelah and move north through the hill country, only returning to the Coastal Plain after passing through the Jezreel Valley.

North of the Shephelah lay an area known as the Plain of Sharon, which incorporated the Plain of Dor. During the Amarna Age, this region was controlled by Labayu, King of Shechem, a Semitic tribal leader whom some scholars have compared to King Saul, as will be discussed in chapter 3. Labayu was part of the Habiru resistance force, and because he commanded Semitic tribes who were antagonistic to the Egyptians, and not allied with the Hebrews who would have remained under the leadership of Moses, he may have provided assistance to the dissident Hebrews if the Exodus occurred in the fifteenth or fourteenth century BCE. Because the Sharon Plain was swampy and interspersed with many thick oak forests, it presented many barriers which restricted easy traffic flow, so the international highway skirted to the west, following the edge of the Ephraimite hills. Although it would have been difficult for the larger force led by Moses to proceed unnoticed along this relatively well-paved route, the smaller contingency of dissident Hebrews would likely have been able to travel without evoking Egyptian resistance from regional military units.

At the northern end of the Coastal Plain was the Carmel ridge, a narrow wedge of land which divided the northern and southern coasts of Palestine, presenting an obstacle to caravans and armies traversing the route on their way northward from Egypt to Syria. Individuals were able to easily pass along the seashore, but the number of people who could travel at any one time was very restricted because the sand generally reached a width of only 65-130 feet. At two points along the coast, the route was not passable at all because small promontories brought the main cliff up to the sea itself, between the rivers Poleg and Alexander, and the rivers Alexander and Hadera. This intrusion made the coastal area mostly impassable to larger groups, and to circumvent this ridge, travelers had to proceed through a variety of roads, or dry river bed channels, known as wadis, which were seasonal streams that dried up in the summer and allowed a relatively easy passage. Two of these wadis led into the Jezreel Valley, and in the Late Bronze Age, the wadis were large enough to be used as roadways. The northernmost one was the Wadi Mileh, which was guarded on the eastern end by the city of Yoqne'am (Jokneam), and to the south was the Wadi `Ara (Arah), a narrow five-mile-long ravine which was guarded on its eastern outlet by the city of Megiddo. This latter path was the one made famous by the attack of Thutmose III (1479-1425 BCE), who disregarded the advice of his generals and marched his army straight through the narrow pass, attacking the city with a full contingent of troops, and capturing it after a prolonged siege.[60] I will discuss this battle in detail in the next chapter.

---

60 Founded around 3300 BCE, Megiddo was destroyed and rebuilt twenty times

Once travelers entered the Jezreel Valley, sometimes called the Plain of Megiddo, they had many directions they could travel to reach the mercantile centers of the Levant. Over 90 percent of the commercial and military traffic of Palestine passed through the Jezreel Valley, making it a vital link in the maintenance of Levantine political hegemony, and one reason for its popularity was the wealth of well-constructed highways which met at its central location. On the western end it reunited with the Coastal Plain near Carmel, and the main branch of the international coastal highway then continued north to the ports of Acco, Tyre and Sidon in Phoenicia, and from there, to Byblos, Ugarit and Kadesh in Syria. To the east, roads led to the Jordan Valley and plain of Beth-shean. If the dissident Hebrews wanted to avoid the main branch of the *Via Maris* journey to Ugarit, they also could take one of at least six capable alternate routes that ran north and south, in addition to an alternate road from Megiddo to Acco through Shim'on and Hannathon.

It was also possible to travel directly north from the Jezreel Valley, traversing through the Lebanon and Anti-Lebanon mountains, which lay on each side of the Beqa' (Biqa') Valley (Coele-Syria). This highway traveled past Lake Kinnereth (Sea of Galilee) to the town of Hazor, which was located in northern Palestine, at the foot of the mountains of Galilee, and was the route that the Patriarchs generally took during their travels throughout the land of Canaan. Hazor lay at the junction of several international trade routes, giving it great strategic importance, and making it the most powerful of the Canaanite cities of the north, from the eighteenth to the fourteenth centuries BCE. Located on a plateau which overlooked the Huleh plain near the modern city of Tell el-Qedah (Kedeh), it was the largest city in the region, measuring 183 acres, and its location allowed it to guard the natural place to cross the Jordan River at the present Bridge of the Daughters of Jacob. According to the book of *Joshua*, King Jabin of Hazor joined forces with other kingdoms in the north to oppose the forces under Joshua, and was defeated, and his city set on fire.[61] Since Hazor and its king, Abdi-Tirshi (mid-fourteenth century BCE), was one of the cities accused in the Amarna letters of allying with the infiltrating Habiru, the dissident Hebrews may have found it to be a place of friendly contact before continuing their travel north to Ugarit. This, of course, would have taken place before Joshua's infiltration of the region. If the Hebrews had indeed allied themselves with Labayu, or any of the

as Egyptian, Hittite, and Mesopotamian armies continuously attempted to control the economic pipeline which the *Via Maris* provided. Walton, Matthews, & Chavalas, The IVP Bible Background Commentary: Old Testament, 231. The repetitive destruction of the city may have been reflected in the biblical battle of Armageddon (Rev 16:6), which literally means the "mountain of Megiddo."

61 Josh 11:1-11. In the book of *Judges*, King Jabin was said to be from Canaan, and reigned in Hazor, oppressing Israel for twenty years, until he was defeated with the assistance of the prophetess Deborah. Judg 4.

other Habiru forces, it is reasonable to believe they would have gone to Hazor for supplies and advice on making further contacts in Ugarit. Roads from Hazor led back to the coastline, and the port cities of Tyre and Sidon, where a large number of ships were engaged in maritime trade with Ugarit, making it relatively easy to then book passage to Mycenae. That the dissident Hebrews may have followed this route is suggested by the fact that the tribe of Dan traveled in this direction after passage into the Promised Land, when they relocated to the region north of Hazor from the area originally allotted them by Joshua.[62]

B. *Western Mountains*

The Western Mountains, which lay to the east of the Coastal Plain, included from south to north the regions of the Negev, Judea (the hill country of Judah), Samaria (the hill country of Ephraim), the hills of Lower and Upper Galilee, and the Lebanon. The mountains in this region are not very high, compared to other mountainous regions of the Near East, but they are very rugged and steep, forming natural frontiers throughout the whole length of the country. Unlike the topography today, during the Late Bronze Age the mountains were densely forested with cypress and cedar trees, and when the Hebrews first entered the Promised Land, there were few permanent settlements, allowing the early Hebrews to build most of their cities in that location. Although passage through the territory was somewhat difficult because of the uncertain terrain, the lack of fortified cities would have provided the band of dissident Hebrews a safer environment in which to travel than if they had been forced to utilize the more congested *Via Maris*.

The Negev, which formed the southern boundary of the Western Mountains, had little rainfall, deriving its name, which meant "dry" or "parched," from the arid soil of the region. Areas which received an annual rainfall of at least ten inches a year were able to support dry farming (cultivation without irrigation), but those regions which received about four inches a year, like the Negev, could support only wild grasses on which animals were able to graze. Despite this limited agricultural resource, the Negev contained twenty-nine cities in biblical days, and formed a land bridge between the mountainous wilderness of Sinai and the hill country of Judah and Samaria. It was into this region that Abraham journeyed following the destruction of Sodom and Gomorrah, and both he and Isaac spent much of their time there tending to their many flocks of sheep and goats. The mountains of the Negev sloped gently into the Plain of Beer-sheba, in the center of which was the city of Beer-sheba, which stood at the intersection of roads from the plain and the Hebron mountains. With its strategic location at the narrowest point of the Negev valley, Beer-sheba guarded the main southern

---

62 Josh 19.47; Judg 18:1.

gateway into the highlands of Israel. The Bible recognized the importance of Beer-sheba, for it was there that God first appeared to Isaac, introducing Himself as the "the God of your father Abraham," and where Jacob offered sacrifices to the God of his father, Isaac.[63]

Directly north of the Negev lay the mountains of Judea, which, unlike Samaria, were protected on all sides, allowing the cities that lay within their protection to be relatively isolated from the rest of Palestine. Three major cities divided the region from south to north: Hebron, in the south;[64] Jerusalem in the center;[65] and Beth-el to the north.[66] Further to the north, the mountains of Samaria were more accessible to penetration from the Coastal Plain, with two ridges branching off the main mass: one leading to Carmel in the northwest, and the other to Gilboa in the northeast.[67] The northern region of Samaria had a relatively moderate topography, making it more amenable to human settlement than was the case for the Judean hills, and this was likely the reason that Samaria was more densely settled than the Judean hills. The Valley of Shechem ran through the Samarian mountains and because of its central position in Palestine, the city of Shechem, today the West Bank city of Nablus, served as a meeting place for the Hebrew tribes after their entry into the Promised Land. Following their settlement in Palestine, Joshua called all the tribes together at Shechem, and made a covenant

---

63 Gen 26:24; 46:1.

64 Hebron is approximately nineteen miles southeast of Jerusalem. The city is mentioned more than sixty times in the Bible, including where Abraham was said to have pitched his tent and built an altar to the Lord; where Abraham pleaded for the innocents of Sodom; where the spies of Moses beheld the richness of the land; and finally where a place of Levitical refuge was founded. The Oxford Encyclopedia of Archaeology in the Near East, III.13.

65 The earliest reference to Jerusalem is in the Egyptian execration texts from the nineteenth century BCE, when the named kings were Yaqirammu and Shayzanu. In the Amarna letters, the king of Jerusalem was Abdi-Heba (c. 1400 BCE). The name does not appear in the Torah, but in the book of *Deuteronomy* a code word is used twenty times as "the place that the Lord your God will choose as a dwelling place for His name." The name of Jerusalem appears about 800 times in other parts of the Hebrew Bible with a number of different spellings, including reference as the city of Zion. Freund, Digging Through the Bible: Modern Archaeology and the Ancient Bible, 134-136.

66 Bethel is usually identified with Beitin, ten miles north of Jerusalem.

67 When king Solomon died in 931 BCE, his kingdom was divided into the kingdom of Judah, populated by the tribes of Judah and Benjamin with its capital in Jerusalem, and the kingdom of Israel, also known as Samaria, populated by the other ten tribes with its capital at Shechem. The term Samaria was used in the Bible to denote both the city that was built by Omri, the King of Israel from 886-875 BCE, and also the territory in which the city was located. It often was used to refer to the entire territory of the northern monarchy of Israel, as distinguished from the southern monarchy of Judah. Courville, The Exodus Problem and Its Ramifications, II.213.

with them to worship only YHWH and forsake all other gods.[68]

The Galilee, which was the northernmost part of the mountain belt, was divided into the Upper and Lower Galilee, a very rugged country with ridges extending in all directions for two hundred and fifty miles. There were no wide valleys in this region and the land was ideally suited for guerrilla warfare. Travel north-south was very difficult in the Lower Galilee, forcing most travelers to move either east or west in order to continue passage to more distant locations. If the dissident Hebrews utilized this direction because of the relative safety from detection, once they reached the northern border of the Western Mountains, they would have been able to travel west to the Coastal Plain without being endangered by frequent Egyptian military excursions.

C. Jordan Valley

To the east of the Western Mountains lay the Jordan Valley, part of the Great Rift Valley that runs for 4,000 miles from Turkey into the great lakes of southeast Africa. This gigantic fracture in the crust of the earth is believed to have been caused by a series of geological spasms, one of which may have resulted in the destruction of the cities of Sodom and Gomorrah.[69] From south to north it included the Dead Sea; the Arabah, which was originally an appellative noun meaning "dry land;" the Beqa' Valley; and the Orontes River Valley. The width of the Jordan Valley did not exceed 6.5 miles, and through its center ran the Jordan River, formed by three head rivulets which emanated in the north, near the foot of Mount Hermon: the Senir (Nahr al-Hasbani), Dan, and Hermon (Baniyas) rivers.[70] On the way south to the Dead Sea, the Jordan first formed the large swamps of Lake Hula, and then Lake Kinnereth, a basin that was about thirteen miles long, and seven miles wide. Fertile flatlands flanked the Jordan River on both sides, and those on the east, where the kingdom of Moab was located, were known as the steppes of Moab.

68 Josh 24:1, 25.

69 Two British geologists, Graham Harris and Anthony Beardow, studied the geology of the Dead Sea, and believed the remains of Sodom and Gomorrah lay on the eastern shore, just north of the Lisan Peninsula, in an area now under water. The region lay on a fault line, and they conjectured that an earthquake c. 1900 BCE ignited the highly flammable bitumen pits, destroying the two cities in flames, similar to what took place in Kansu, China, in 1920 CE. Crawshaw, "Found: The World's Wickedest City," 2. Strabo (63 BCE - 21 CE), the Greek geographer, philosopher, and historian, records a legend that near Massada, the fortress on the south-western shore of the Dead Sea, thirteen cities were once destroyed by an earthquake with similar eruptions of bitumen and sulfur. Graves & Patai, Hebrew Myths, the Book of Genesis, 168.

70 The river ran a very tortuous course, and was about eighty-four miles long, as the crow flies. The depth of the river for most of the year was from three to ten feet. Illustrated Family Encyclopedia of the Living Bible, II.128.

The Jordan Valley lay farther below sea-level than any other valley in the world, and reached its maximum depth at the Dead Sea, almost 2,600 feet below the level of the Mediterranean Sea.[71] The Dead Sea functioned as an evaporation basin for the waters of the Jordan, Arnon (Wadi Mujib), and Zered (Wadi Hasa) rivers, and was also referred to as the "Sea of the 'Arabah," and the "Sea of Salt."[72] During the Israelite period in the Iron Age, few people lived in the Jordan Valley itself, as the river was not navigable except at specific locations. It nevertheless formed an obstacle for the Hebrews to forge before entering the Promised Land, and the eventual crossing became a recognized feat which would forever be identifiable to all followers of the Jewish faith as the moment when the Hebrews fulfilled their destiny as God's Chosen People.

D. Transjordan

The region from the eastern border of the Jordan Valley to the edge of the Arabian desert was known as the Transjordan. It was also called the "Eastern Plateau," because the area consisted of a high plateau in the north that gradually lowered in the middle, and then rose again to several thousand feet in the south. Not considered part of Canaan proper, the Transjordan was home to a number of people in the Late Bronze and Iron Ages, including the Edomites, Amorites, Moabites and Midianites.[73] Archaeologic surveys have revealed that the autochonthous civilization in the region was extinguished c. 1900 BCE, around the time of the Amorite invasion, and that there was then very little evidence of habitation until the fourteenth century BCE, when the Ammonites and Moabites appeared on the scene.[74] Because the region had such a small population density

---

71 This is over 1000 feet lower than Death Valley in California. Merrill, An Historical Survey of the Old Testament, 41.

72 Brawer, "A. The Land of Israel - From 'the Brook of Egypt' to the Litani. 2. Morphology," 21-23. Its salt content today is still six times that of the ocean, and fish which are carried in by the flowing waters of the Jordan River die immediately. Grollenberg, Atlas of the Bible, 16.

73 At the beginning of the first millennium BCE, there were three kingdoms in the Transjordan running from south to north: Edom which included Mount Seir, east of the Arabah and south of the Dead Sea; Moab on both sides of the Arnon River; and Ammon on the upper course of the Jabbok river. de Vaux, The Early History of Israel, 516; Mazar, "The Historical Development," 15. In the Bible, Edom is also called "Hor" (Num 20:23), "Seir" (Gen 36:8-9), and "Esau" (Deut 2:4-5).

74 Roaf, Cultural Atlas of Mesopotamia and the Ancient Near East, 103. In the Table of Nations from the book of *Genesis*, Moab and Ammon are described as descendants of Lot. After Lot lay with his two daughters, the older one bore Moab, whose descendants were the Moabites, and the younger one Ben-ammi, who became the father of the Ammonites. Gen 19:38. See e.g., Deut 2:9, 19. The Ammonites are only known in extra-biblical sources from Late Assyrian annals, c. 733-665 BCE, and scattered local fragmentary epigraphic

before the fourteenth century BCE, many historians believe that the Exodus must have taken place after this date, for if the description of the battles between Moses and the kings of the region are to be accepted as true, a sparse population would not explain the strong resistance against Hebrew passage. As will be discussed in chapter 6, this would favor a thirteenth century BCE Exodus date, rather than a fifteenth century BCE date. Since it is generally agreed that biblical historicity was liberally sprinkled with imagery based on theologic teachings rather than historical facts, however, it is difficult to rely on this data alone to mandate an Exodus date after the fourteenth century BCE, and it remains possible that the biblical compilers simply took advantage of their greater knowledge of these latter people to develop tales which accentuated the tribulations which Moses was forced to face from indigenous rulers.

Most of the highland roads through the Transjordan ran north-south, with few connections to the west. To the east was the Syrian desert, a largely uninhabited region, punctuated by only a few oases. This barren geographic barrier forced traders and armies to remain in the relatively level plateau, utilizing the "King's Highway," which ran along the edge of the Transjordan tableland on the border of the desert, from the eastern arm of the Red Sea (Gulf of Aqaba/Eilat) to the *Via Maris* at Damascus, the capital of Aram (modern Syria).[75] This thoroughfare played a prominent role in the movements of the Exodus as the Hebrews made their way to the crossing of the Jordan River into the region of Jericho, as will be discussed in greater detail in chapter 5. Although passage of the Exodus through this region was difficult because the presiding kings were hostile to large migratory groups, the smaller contingent of dissident Hebrews would not likely have encountered significant resistance as they traveled northward and westward to the Coastal Plain.

C. Ugarit

As discussed earlier, the land of Syria had always been the great junction for overland and sea routes in the ancient Near East, providing an accessible locale where a large variety of people could meet to exchange information and goods. Not only conquering armies, but trade and ideas traveled the roads which transected Syria, and at the center of the region lay the vital port city of Ugarit, or Ras Sharma as it was known in ancient days. Functioning as the primary meeting place for Further Asia, India, Africa and Europe, in addition to Egypt, Mesopotamia and Anatolia, Ugarit was one of the most powerful walled-cities

---

records. Walton, Matthews, & Chavalas, The IVP Bible Background Commentary: Old Testament, 296.

75 This was also the road that the four kings of the North used when they battled the five kings of the South, following the division of land between Abraham and Lot. Gen 14:5-7.

in Syria during the Late Bronze Age. Numerous donkey caravans continuously arrived from Anatolia, Mesopotamia, and Palestine, carrying most of the goods which would be transported to distant destinations around the Mediterranean Basin.[76] Tablets discovered in the palace at Mari in the Middle Euphrates region detailed how Mari merchants in Ugarit, with the service of translators, distributed tin in large amounts throughout the Levant and Anatolia, extending as well to Minoan Crete. This type of activity was duplicated by merchants from many other countries, all taking advantage of the multiple contacts which were available in Ugarit, and nowhere else. Perched on a sixty-foot high coastal bluff, it was strategically placed to supply all the countries which surrounded the Mediterranean Sea, and by the Middle Bronze Age it had grown to become the capital city of a small kingdom.

Ugarit was large by contemporary standards, with massive ramparts enclosing a trapezoidal area of over forty-seven acres. It controlled thirty miles of coastland, including four ports, making it well-placed for the burgeoning sea trade which characterized the Middle Bronze Age. The primary harbor was located a short distance away in the bay of Minet-el-Beidha (White Bay, Leukos Limen), so-named because its mouth was guarded by white limestone rocks. Its vast realm spread for 1350 square miles, and included over 200 surrounding villages, which averaged about one hundred fifty families each.[77] To protect its shore, Ugarit had a naval fleet that was larger than any single Greek state could muster for the siege of Troy. At one time the navy numbered as many as 150 ships, some of which had an estimated displacement of 500 tons. If a general mobilization was necessary, Ugarit was able to recruit about 4000-4600 men to defend its interests. During times of relative peace, such a force was more than adequate to quell local disturbances, but during periods of armed conflicts, a larger supply of troops was necessary, and Ugarit, as was the case with most Late Bronze Age armies, then paid mercenaries to increase the defensive capability of the city. The dissident Hebrews could have fulfilled this requirement if they had wanted to remain in the region, as the need for assistance was frequently present toward the end of the Late Bronze Age, but I believe that their desire to flee to a further distance from their brethren would have encouraged the Hebrews to sail to Mycenae, rather than risk remaining in a region so near the reach of Moses. In this regard, they acted much like their ancestor Jacob when he fled to Mesopotamia after being threatened by Esau for stealing his primogeniture birthright.

A single, unbroken dynasty ruled Ugarit from the time of Hammurabi until the Late Bronze Age. The royal house was founded by King Yaqarum (c. 1825 BCE), a Semite, and from that time forward, the country was dominated by West

---

76 Donkey caravans were common in Palestine in the fourteenth century BCE, and would have been used by the Hebrews until it was superseded by camel caravans about the eleventh century BCE. Albright, Yahweh and the Gods of Canaan, 48-49.

77 Craigie, Ugarit and the Old Testament, 27-28.

Semitic tribes. The palace at Ugarit during the fourteenth and thirteenth centuries BCE was a magnificent structure, twice the size of the palaces of Hattusas and Alalakh and one-third the size of Mycenae, and only the palace at Tyre rivaled it on the eastern Mediterranean coast in size and magnificence. The archaeologic remains are spectacular, covering over two acres, and included two impressive temples, one for Baal, the patron deity of Ugarit, and the other to El (Dagan), the primary god worshiped by Semites throughout the ancient Near East.[78] Many scholars have pointed out similarities between YHWH and the Canaanite gods venerated at Ugarit, suggesting the possibility that the Hebrews may have derived attributes of YHWH from one of these gods. I will discuss this issue in greater detail in chapter 12.

Ugarit had a great commercial advantage over other ports along the eastern Mediterranean shore, not only because it lay at the crossroads of Anatolia and the Levant, but also because of its close proximity to Cyprus, an island which functioned as a base for the storage of large amounts of migratory goods. Cyprus was the third largest island in the Mediterranean Sea, measuring almost 3,700 square miles, and its value was amplified because it was closer to the mainland than any other Cycladic island. Known to the ancient world as *Alashiya (Alashia)* or *Kittim,* because of the name of the Phoenician colony on its southern coast, the island's ability to act as an easy stepping stone to more distant shores enabled it to play an important role in the commercial activity of the entire Near East region.[79] It lay only sixty miles west of the harbor at Minet el-Beida, and also provided easy access to Anatolia, 40 miles to the north; Egypt, 240 miles to the south; and Rhodes, the nearest Aegean island, about 300 miles to the west. From Rhodes, ships then had easy access to the ports of Mycenae and Crete, allowing trading vessels to travel within the sight of land for the entire journey. This may explain why Cyrus Gordon claimed that Ugarit was "closely connected with the Phoenicians," and is the primary reason why I believe the dissident Hebrews chose Ugarit as their departure city after deciding to emigrate to the Grecian shore.[80]

Cyprus excelled as a critical component of the Late Bronze Age commercial industry, not only because of its location near Ugarit, but also because of its ready supply of copper. The discovery of bronze, an alloy of copper and tin which initiated the Bronze Age around 3000 BCE, made production of copper an essential ingredient in the economy of every country that lay in the Mediterranean Basin, and Cyprus possessed the largest supply of copper deposits in the Levant. At the

78 The Ras Shamra tablets provide a list of more than thirty deities who had been included in the pantheon of Ugarit, and this was in no sense exhaustive. Baal is known as the son of El, the father of all the gods, but above all, as the son of Dagan. de Vaux, The Early History of Israel, 146-148.

79 Kittim appeared in the Old Testament Table of Nations as one of the children of Javan, along with Elishah, Tarshish, and Rodanim. Gen 10:4.

80 Gordon, Ugarit and Minoan Crete, 12.

Chapter 1

end of the Early Bronze Age, around 2000 BCE, there was a large population increase on Cyprus because of the development of these copper-mining areas, with people moving in to both mine the valuable metal and develop a growing trade community. By the Middle Bronze Age, Cyprian settlements enlarged even further and began to show signs of substantial military architecture, indicating wealth and power. Foreign relations with neighboring countries appeared for the first time during this prolific period.

The need for copper brought the Minoans to Cyprus in the earliest years of the Middle Bronze Age, although trade with mainland Greece or the Cyclades did not develop until the decline of Crete as a naval power. By 1500 BCE there were Minoan settlements at Salamis, Citium, and Curium. A Cypro-Minoan script has been found at various sites on Cyprus dating to this period of time, and it is believed that the Cypriots borrowed the Minoan language from Cretans living in Syria and Cyprus, and then developed their own alphabet from this model.[81] When Knossos was destroyed in the fifteenth century BCE, Minoan presence was replaced by the Mycenaeans, who began to encroach into the business heretofore provided by the Minoans. By 1420 BCE, the Mycenaeans had occupied Knossos and taken over the trade routes which emanated from there, as well as from their trading colonies. Mycenaean influence, both on Cyprus and across the entire eastern Mediterranean, continued to increase over the next few centuries, and this was accompanied by a marked influx of Mycenaean pottery across the entire island of Cyprus. Evidence of the close relationship between Mycenae and Cyprus can be seen in Homer's the *Iliad*, where the breastplate of Agamemnon, a corselet which had ten circles of cobalt, twelve of gold, and twenty of tin, was the gift of his friend, Kinyras (Cinyras) from Cyprus, who had heard of the Achaian preparation for war against the Trojans.[82] In addition, Homer claimed that Menelaus had visited Cyprus following the Trojan War, and that Odysseus (Ulysses) was forced to live there for a time before reaching home.[83]

It is this advantageous combination of the nearness of Cyprus, along with the vital location of Ugarit at the contact point between Anatolia, Mesopotamia and the Levant, that made Ugarit "a natural link between the Aegean world and the Levant."[84] Evidence of the bristling trade community which developed at the city is demonstrated by a number of half-ton anchors which have been excavated at the harbor. An anchor of that size, weighing more than two hundred tons, would normally have been used on a ship that measured at least seventy feet in length, providing a freight capacity up to five hundred tons. Such ships were clearly used for long range transport, rather than simply for travel up and down

81 Myres, Who Were the Greeks?, 205-206.
82 Homer, The Iliad, 11:20-25, 234-235.
83 Homer, The Odyssey, 17:325, 441-442.
84 Drower, "Ugarit," 131.

‹ 62 ›

the Levantine coast, and were capable of carrying men, as well as cargo. Not only would maritime traders utilize these ships to transport goods, but military and migratory interests would also take advantage of the relative ease in crisscrossing the shores of the Mediterranean Basin.

The international status of Ugarit is attested to by the welter of languages used there, as well as by the presence of embassies from many other kingdoms to provide a trading base for their merchants. Representatives of the Aegean, Hittite, Hurrian, Mesopotamian, Canaanite, Egyptian, and other populations met there "to conduct their affairs in an international order."[85] It became "an important meeting place for Egyptian, Hittite, Mesopotamian, Syrian, Cretan and Mycenaean products and ideas,"[86] and languages spoken in the city included Akkadian, Sumerian, Hurrian, Hittite, Ugaritic, Egyptian, and Cypro-Minoan, while texts found in libraries of the city included cuneiform, alphabetic cuneiform, hieroglyphic and script writings.[87] School texts have been uncovered utilizing a polygot vocabulary with Sumerian, Akkadian, Hurrian, and Ugaritic columns, enabling scribes to learn the most important languages of the day. This multi-lingual capability would be expected from a locale which functioned as a center for international trade, and the dissident Hebrews would have been easily able to take advantage of this protean availability of languages and people to set up terms of passage after they decided to leave the Levant for the Mycenaean shore. The Hebrews also would have been able to communicate directly with the citizens of Ugarit, since their languages were so similar. Although the Ugarit alphabet was a type of cuneiform writing, the letter sequence agreed very closely with the Hebrew sequence, and the consonants in both Ugarit and Hebrew were in the exact order and number (twenty-two) as exists in the present day. According to Gordon, "the Ugaritic ABC gave rise to the Phoenician-Hebrew ABC which in turn was borrowed by the Greeks."[88] Although Gordon has used this linguistic similarity, along with other affinities of religion, literature, and culture, to argue that Ugarit lay among the forerunners of the Classical Greeks and Hebrews, I believe that his postulate goes too far in assessing a primary generative role to Ugarit, and that it is more likely that it was the Hebrews who directly transported much of this information to the Greeks, rather than Ugarit itself. What is clear, however, is that the chronology of early Greek and Hebrew cultural development favors some input from Ugarit during the Late Bronze Age.

---

85 Gordon, Before The Bible: The Common Background of Greek and Hebrew Civilizations, 30.

86 Fine, The Ancient Greeks, A Critical History, 6.

87 Craigie, Ugarit and the Old Testament, 22.

88 Gordon, <u>Before The Bible: The Common Background of Greek and Hebrew Civilizations</u>, 129-130. The Ugaritic style of writing is known as alphabetic cuneiform, which blends an alphabetic script (like Hebrew) with a cuneiform (like Akkadian). "Ugarit and the Bible," 2.

Gordon has attempted to explain the manner of contact between Ugarit and the ancient Hebrews by suggesting that the biblical Hebrews were part of a wave of immigrants who came to Canaan as merchant princes. He argued for this conclusion by pointing out that the terms in a dossier of tablets which were sent by the Hittite emperor Khattushili III (c. 1282-1250 BCE) to King Niqmepa (c. 1291-1236 BCE) of Ugarit to regulate the activities of the merchants of Ur(a) used terminology that was very similar to the terms which the Shechemites offered to Jacob when Shechem sought to marry Leah. This list included details about the right of permanent residence, ownership of real estate, and the ability to conduct business legally throughout the land.[89] In addition, Michael David Coogan, Professor of Religious Studies at Stonehill College in Easton, Massachusetts, has pointed out a similarity between the *Baal* cycle of poems, and the *Psalms* of the Old Testament. Both collections were intended to provide encouragement and comfort in times of crisis or despair, and similar formats were common in Egypt, Mesopotamia, and Syro-Canaanite literature during the Late Bronze Age.

In the Ugarit verse, one reads:

"Behold, your enemy, Baal,
      behold, you will kill your enemy,
      behold, you will annihilate your foes.
You will take your eternal kingship,
      your dominion forever and ever."[90]

In the *Psalms*, there is a remarkably combination:

"Behold, your enemies, Yahweh,
      behold, your enemies have perished,
      all evildoers have been scattered." (Psalm 92:9)
"Your kingdom is an eternal kingdom,
      your rule is forever and ever." (Psalm 145:13)[91]

While this congruence does suggest some intercourse of ideas between Ugarit and the ancient Hebrews, it is not specific enough, in my opinion, to claim a primary role of the city of Ugarit in the generation of Hebrew mythology and theology. While it is certainly plausible that the Ugaritic civilization affected some of the ancient Hebrew myths which later appeared in the Torah, to claim that

89 Gen 34:10. Gordon, "Recovering Canaan and Ancient Israel," 2784.

90 Coogan, Stories From Ancient Canaan, 15.

91 Ibid. Coogan uses data like this to suggest that the Israelite religion should be viewed as a subset of Canaanite religion. Sparks, Ethnicity and Identity in Ancient Israel: Prolegomena to the Study of Ethnic Sentiments and Their Expression in the Hebrew Bible, 12.

Ugarit, rather than the Hebrews, influenced the Greek civilization directly is not consistent with the many Hebraic connections which I believe are overwhelmingly more likely to have generated the resemblance between the ancient Hebrews and Greeks. The Greeks had many opportunities to be impacted by ancient Eastern societies, and Ugarit does not have the type of direct connections which have been shown for societies like the Phoenicians and Hyksos.

Ugarit was clearly an important trading center in the Late Bronze Age, however, and despite the periods of strife between many of its trading partners, it was able to maintain a relatively independent status in the region until the sixteenth century BCE, when its fate was affected by the rise of the Hittite kingdom to the north, the Mitanni (Hurri) kingdom to the east, and the extension of the Egyptian King Thutmose I to the south, which I discussed earlier in this chapter. As these three competing powers grew in strength, each sought to expand its empire and began to apply pressure on Ugarit to supply aid in the form of cooperative alliances. The political pressure became especially acute after Thutmose IV (1426-1417 BCE) and Artatama of Mitanni (c. 1410-1400 BCE) replaced their century old hostility with a friendship pact. Ugarit was not able to remain a neutral entity as Egypt sought to strengthen her position in the area, and signs of vassalage to Egypt began to appear during the reign of Amenhotep III (1417-1379 BCE), the successor to Thutmose IV. Such dependency upon Egypt could have negatively affected the Hebrew dissidents if the Exodus occurred during this era, but most scholars have placed the migration from Egypt during the rule of other Pharaohs, as will be discussed in chapter 6. If the Exodus took place in the fifteenth century BCE, as I believe, and the dissidents traveled to Ugarit to arrange for passage to Mycenae, it is likely that it would have taken place before the reign of Amenhotep III, and so there is little chance that the Hebrews risked expulsion if they sought aid from the Ugarit royal house at this time.

Soon thereafter, in the fourteenth century BCE, Ugarit changed its allegiance from Egypt to the Hittite king, because the nearby Hittite Empire under Suppiluliuma I was too strong to be confronted on an independent basis. From then until the peace treaty between Egypt and the Hittite empire in 1280 BCE, Ugarit vacillated in its loyalties, as evidenced by a letter from Suppiluliuma I to Niqmaddu, the King of Ugarit, c. 1366 BCE, noting how their ancestors were once friends, and that they should continue to act in unison against the enemies of Hatti.[92] When the kingdom of Mitanni was finished as a great power, Ugarit made a formal submission to Suppiliuliuma I and then came under the tutelage of the Hittites. The annual tribute imposed upon Niqmaddu consisted of five hundred shekels of gold, along with a number of gold and silver vessels, pieces of clothing, and quantities of red, blue, and purple wool. This was more than the tribute paid by Amurru, most likely because Ugarit was a much more prosperous

---

92 Astour, "Ugarit and the Great Powers," 10.

country, but in compensation for their support and tribute, Suppiluliuma I increased the borders of Ugarit and provided them with 1245 sq. miles of valuable land. It appears that the terms were satisfactory for Ugarit remained loyal to Hatti "to their common bitter end."[93] This pact of cooperation with the Hittites would have meant that the dissident Hebrews would likely have been welcomed in Ugarit during the late fourteenth and thirteenth centuries BCE, since they were fleeing from Egypt, the country most-hated by the Hittite royal house. They may have even been able to purchase their passage in exchange for information gathered during their years of wandering in the Sinai wilderness.

Although a great fire damaged much of the city of Ugarit during the Amarna Age, c 1365 BCE, the ultimate destruction of Ugarit came with the invasion of the People of the Sea toward the end of the thirteenth century BCE, probably during the reign of Ammurapi (c. 1185 BCE), but there appears to be little evidence that the survivors carried any part of their culture into adjacent lands, as the Mycenaeans did when they emigrated to the coast of Asia Minor.[94] Tribal elements of the People of the Sea established residence throughout the Mediterranean Basin, including the Dannuna, who have been identified by some authorities as connected to the Hebrew tribe of Dan. The possible identification of the Danites as the Hebrew dissidents who traveled to Mycenae before the Trojan War is discussed in more detail in chapter 7, but by this time the Late Bronze Age had come to an end, and the geopolitical scene of the ancient Near East underwent changes which I am not going to cover in this book.

---

93 Ibid., 23.

94 Many scholars have dated the fall of Ugarit to c. 1160 BCE. Lipinski, On the Skirts of Canaan in the Iron Age: Historical and Topographical Research, 35.

Chapter 2
EGYPT

The book of *Exodus* in the Torah tells how the ancient Hebrews, after generations of enslavement following the death of Joseph, left Egypt and traveled to the Promised Land in Canaan in a grand Exodus, during which time Moses transformed Jewish theology from its early polytheistic Semitic beginnings into the world's first lasting monotheistic faith, which eventually gave rise to the kindred covenant communities of Christianity and Islam. Although the first patriarch, Abraham, is generally accepted as the progenitor of the Jews from a genetic perspective, the man who truly determined the nature of modern Judaism was Moses, a reformer whose roots were fed more from the culture of Egypt than from the teachings of his Hebrew ancestors. Moses, we are told, was abandoned as an infant and raised in the royal household of Egypt, where he was educated in the manner of an Egyptian prince, learning the religious and social principles of Egypt, rather than the tradition of his Hebrew brethren. When he was forty years old, Moses was forced to flee his native land, and then lived for another forty years with the Midianites, before finally returning to Egypt to lead the Hebrews out of the land where they had spent four generations of time in an environment of forced labor. At no time during these first eighty years of his life did he receive training in the ways or teachings of the Hebrew Patriarchs.

Despite this foreign background, and limited understanding of the Hebrew ancestral religious customs and practice, Moses set about to convert Judaism from what many consider to have been the polytheistic practice of the Patriarchs into a monotheistic religion, directed by God at each step of the way. Since the Hebrews did not know Moses prior to his sudden appearance as all-powerful liberator and dictator of how the congregation was to behave and believe, it is no wonder that he faced resistance and resentment from dissidents who wished to follow the practices of their ancestors, which they had been taught to obey all of their lives. In order to force obedience to the Divine Law of YHWH, Moses executed more than 40,000 of his brethren, creating a religious schism which I believe caused a group of dissidents to abandon the congregation, and flee to Mycenae in order to maintain the customs of their forefathers.[1]

---

1 After returning from the top of Mt. Sinai with the Ten Commandments and finding the Hebrews worshiping the golden calf-idol, Moses ordered 3,000 men killed. Exod 32:28. In response to the rebellion of Korah, a plague was sent to kill his impudent supporters, and in the conflagration which followed, 14,700 people died. Num 16:49. After the orgy at Acacia, Moses ordered those who worshiped Baal to be executed, and 24,000 people died. Num 25:9. This total of almost 42,000 does not include the unnumbered people who died when God sent venomous snakes as punishment when they complained about

Before analyzing the methods used by Moses to achieve this remarkable transformation of Hebrew theism, I will dissect the history of Egypt in great detail, in order to set the framework for determining when Moses was born, and under which Pharaoh I believe the Exodus took place.[2] These assessments will require correlating known circumstances of Semitic enslavement in Egypt with biblical events and pharaonic activity so that a consistent timeline can be developed between the two sets of historical data. There are five Pharaohs mentioned in the Torah, none of whom were identified by name.[3] These include the Pharaoh who brought Sarah into his harem when Abraham explained that she was his sister, rather than his wife; the Pharaoh who raised Joseph to the position of vizier after he was sold into slavery by his brothers; the Pharaoh "who did not know Joseph," and ordered the killing of newborn Hebrew males at the time of Moses' birth; the Pharaoh who sought to kill Moses, forcing him to flee to Midian; and the Pharaoh who was sitting on the throne at the time of the Exodus.[4] If either of these men or women can be identified with greater certainty, it will then be possible to settle on a more secure date for the Exodus than is presently available.

A. Background

Egypt is one of the most ancient and well-studied civilizations on earth, with the earliest evidence for human existence in the Nile Valley found in fragments from the Upper Paleolithic, Late Stone Age (45,000-10,000 BCE). These early remains are quite sparse and isolated, but by the time of the Neolithic period (8800-

---

the lack of food and water on their way to Edom (Num 21:6), the ones killed by a plague at Kibroth-hattaavah (Num 11:33-34), or the objectors who were burned in a fire sent by God at Taberah (Num 11:1-3).

2 Although the term "Pharaoh" (*per-aa*) is universally used today to designate the Egyptian king, it actually is an Egyptian phrase meaning "great house," and was not used as a title for the king before the reign of Thutmose III (1479-1425 BCE). McCarter, Jr., "The Patriarchal Age, Abraham, Isaac and Jacob," revised by Ronald S. Hendel, 29.

3 The first Pharaoh to be actually named in the Old Testament is Shishak (Shishaq, Shushaq), who is identified as Shoshenq I (945-924 BCE), the founder of the Twenty-Second Dynasty. He attacked Jerusalem during the reign of Rehoboam (931-915 BCE), Solomon's successor as king of Judah, and also harbored Jeroboam I (931-911 BCE), the future king of Israel who had rebelled against Solomon and was forced to leave the country. 1 Kgs 11:40; 14:25-26; 2 Chron 12:2-9. Hendel, Remembering Abraham: Culture, Memory, and History in the Hebrew Bible, 48.

4 I will continue to refer to the Pharaoh who ordered the killing of the newborn male Hebrews as the Pharaoh "who did not know Joseph," since his role provides the best way we can estimate when the Exodus took place. Exod 1:8, Exodus 1-18, 119. Although rabbinic tradition held that the name of this Pharaoh was Malol, the son of Magron, such a determination is not accepted by most biblical scholars. Ginzberg, The Legends of the Jews, II.246.

4700 BCE) a variety of complex cultures are readily identified, with at least three ethnic elements able to be differentiated, including: the Berber-Hamite culture, also known as Merimde or northwest Hamite (5000-4200 BCE); the Badarian culture (4400-4000 BCE), where the earliest attestation of agriculture is found in Upper Egypt; and the Naqada-I (Amratian) (4000-3500 BCE), and Naqada-II (Gerzean) (3500-3200 BCE), which are contemporary with the late Uruk period in Mesopotamia, and are the first Egyptian societies known to contain a Semitic element.

There is no evidence of significant conflict between the Semites and native Egyptians during this early Neolithic era, with the various elements living apart from each other, but in peaceful coexistence. Sometime between 3100-2850 BCE, at the end of the Naqada II period, Upper and Lower Egypt coalesced under the rule of one king, creating the Dynastic Era, which ruled Egypt for the next three thousand years. Unlike the adjacent development of monarchies which came and went relatively quickly in Mesopotamia, this dynastic development was truly the "world's first stable monarchy."[5]

The man generally credited for carrying out this unification of Egypt was King Menes (Meni, Min), sometimes referred to as King Narmer. He was from the southern part of the country, and it is believed that he was able to assimilate the various factions after preliminary moves made by another southern ruler, King Scorpion. His success is memorialized in a pictorial representation of the two aspects of the united Egypt on a palette uncovered at the Temple of Horus in Nekhen, in the ancient town of Hieraconpolis, known as the Narmer Palette, where Menes is shown wearing the Double Crown (*pschent*), with the Red Crown (*deshret*) and papyrus plant of Lower Egypt on one side of the slab, and the White Crown (*hedjet*) and flowering lotus of Upper Egypt on the other side, highlighting the extent of his control over the entire Egyptian topography.

The ability of Menes to create not only a powerful unified country, but also a national consciousness which ran across widely separated regions, each with their own strong local customs, is considered by many Egyptologists to be the greatest achievement of Egypt's early rulers. In a relatively short period of time, from a historical perspective, he was able to assemble a system of government that would be acceptable to the indigenous population for thousands of years to come. One of his first actions, perhaps meant to appease the northern inhabitants who likely viewed him as an outsider, was to create a new capital city at Memphis, the world's first imperial seat of government, which lay at the apex of the Delta, on the northern section of the Nile River, south of present-day Cairo. Because it was situated at the crossroads of Upper and Lower Egypt, it provided excellent communication with both sections of the country, and the site maintained its status as the seat of pharaonic power for many centuries.

---

5 Freeman, Egypt, Greece and Rome: Civilizations of the Ancient Mediterranean, 46.

The changes brought about by King Menes were profound and incredibly long-lasting, but despite the success of his planning there is still little known about the details of his reign. It is not clear, for example, whether his transformation of the country was due to the simultaneous entry of a new people, known as the Dynastic Race, who were then able to gain control over Egypt because of military advancements, or whether the change occurred from within the indigenous population, without outside intervention. There are few archaeologic remains of his capital city at Memphis, and no hieroglyphic recordings of his history have ever been found. While the methods he used to achieve his objectives are unknown, the fruits of his labor proved incredibly durable, and from the time he first rose to prominence and united Egypt into a single political force, the country remained under the command of a king with the authority of a god until the Christian era. The stone images of Menes appear to have distinct Negro features, and the Senegalese historian and Egyptologist Cheikh Anta Diop (1923-1986 CE) has used this representation to buttress his belief that the Egyptians were a Negro civilization.[6] His theory that black Egyptians played a significant role in the development of Greek culture would later be championed by Martin Bernal, as will be discussed shortly.

The capital city of Memphis not only served as the Egyptian seat of government during the early part of the Dynastic era, it also gave Egypt its modern name, as the appellation is derived from the Greek *Aigyptos*, one of the early names of Memphis. The ancient Egyptians did not have a consistent name for their country, and often referred to it as *Kemet* (*Kmt*), "the Black Land," or *Ta-meri*, "the beloved land," both of which referred to the fertile flood plain of the lower Nile Valley. Since much of Egypt was virtually rainless, the periodic rise of the Nile river during the summer months, caused by torrential rains in the Upper Nile Basin being carried down to the Delta by the Blue Nile, was the sole source of irrigation for the flood basins, and the northern section of the country thereby became the only region which could provide enough agricultural output to feed the population.[7] The ability to rely on a secure agricultural base, not dependent on erratic rainfall which often disappeared during prolonged periods of drought, was the primary reason for the political and economic stability of Egypt, when compared to other regions of the ancient Near East.[8]

---

6 Diop, The African Origin of Civilization: Myth or Reality, xiv, 13. Negro features also characterized the depiction of pharaohs during the Third Dynasty. Ibid., 204.

7 The flooding continued into the twentieth century CE, when Egypt's rulers sought to gain control of the intermittent deluge by building the Aswan Dam in 1902 CE, and the Aswan High Dam in 1970 CE, creating Lake Nasser – the world's largest man-made reservoir.

8 Most ancient people acknowledged the advantage of this annual event, but when the Hebrews were about to cross into the Promised Land at the end of the Exodus, Moses told them that the region they were about to enter was favored because it did not require

The Nile River not only functioned as the lifeblood of Egyptian commerce and agriculture, providing secure irrigation for crops on a yearly basis, it also afforded a means of transportation to move men and goods from one part of the country to another. Since no point in the Nile Valley was more than a few miles from the river, it was possible for the waterway to function as a highway, and boats were able to readily connect one habitable area to another. The prevailing winds in Egypt blew from north to south, enabling ships to travel south with the aid of sails, and then return north with the natural flow of water back to the Mediterranean Sea.[9] While this kept the inhabitants of Egypt in contact with each other, it did not allow for distribution of goods to foreign lands, for there were no navigable harbors along the seacoast, as the marshland of the Delta was low-lying and filled with reefs and shallows, which prevented the construction of usable ports for international trade. This meant that the Egyptians had to travel on foot into the Levant to receive goods from distant locations, leading to the development of a land route which connected Egypt to Palestine through the Sinai Peninsula, the so-called *Via Maris*, which was discussed in the previous chapter. The road was well-traveled in ancient times, providing a means of ingress and egress for both commercial travelers and military personnel.

Once travelers left Egypt proper, they entered the Sinai Peninsula which, like the Delta, was triangular in shape, but much larger. It measured 23,500 sq. miles, about the size of the state of West Virginia, and since it lay northeast of the Delta, between the borders of Egypt and Palestine, it functioned not only as an easy means of passage, but also as an effective buffer zone, allowing Egyptian sentries to warn the Pharaoh of approaching danger from the nations of Asia. Travel was primarily carried out on foot with pack animals during the Bronze Age, and progress was slow and easily identifiable.[10] The Egyptians expanded their military advantage by building a string of fortifications along the Sinai border, providing both a first line of defense to the motherland, and also a deterrent to those attempting to flee the country without permission from the Pharaoh. The construction of these fortresses will be discussed later in this chapter, but the distribution of military installations along this border is what most scholars believe was the reason God directed Moses to veer south, away from the *Via Maris*, shortly after the Exodus began in order to avoid being detected by Egyptian sentries.

---

irrigation, as did Egypt, but rather was watered by the rains of heaven. Deut 11:11. This shows that the tasks of maintaining the irrigation canals was probably very labor-intensive, and fell upon the Hebrew slave population.

9 It took about three weeks to a month for a raft to float from the southern end at the First Cataract to the apex of the Delta using current flow alone. Redford, Egypt, Canaan, and Israel in Ancient Times, 13.

10 A rate of 15-19 miles a day was standard for large caravans, but greater speeds could reach 25 miles per day on foot, and 25-37 miles per day by camel caravan. Isserlin, The Israelites, 25.

The power of the Egyptian throne grew rapidly after unification, soon reaching a level where the sitting king became imbued with the authority of a god. From the time of the Old Kingdom, the king was revered as a divine being by his subjects, with sacred attributes that were passed from one generation to another. As aptly stated by John Bright (1909-1995 CE), the former Cyrus H. McCormick Professor of Hebrew and the Interpretation of the Old Testament at Union Theological Seminary in Virginia, the Pharaoh was not just deified, "he *was* god - Horus visible among his people."[11] The extent of his power was summarized by Rekhmire, a vizier (chief minister) of the Eighteenth Dynasty, who referred to the ruler as "the god by whose actions we live, the father and mother of all men, alone by himself without an equal."[12] Although the position was inherited from father to son, the scion was not deified at birth, but rather acquired this status upon his coronation. If a male heir was not available, some other member of the royal court was made king, resulting in a new inheritable sequence that would still pass divine power from father to son. Marriage to the royal heiress, especially the Great Royal Daughter, who was the eldest daughter of the King and Chief Queen, virtually ensured accession to the kingship if no male heir was alive at the time of the Pharaoh's death. Occasionally, a woman was allowed to sit on the throne, although this was usually intended as a temporary measure during the period of time when a future male heir was too young to be made king.

This succession of divine kings who ruled over the next three millennia is primarily known to us today because of an historical text called *Aegyptiaca Upomnemata* (*The History of Egypt*), from the third century BCE (c. 290-260 BCE) by Manetho of Sebennytus, an Egyptian priest who lived in Heliopolis (Biblical On), during the reigns of Ptolemy I Soter (305-283 BCE), Ptolemy II Philadelphos (283-246 BCE), and possibly Ptolemy III Euergetes (246-222 BCE). In this seminal account, written in Greek, Manetho gathered all the information that was then available on the lives of the Pharaohs from contemporary records, including privileged registries in Egyptian temples, and categorized their history into thirty-one Dynasties, which he numbered according to changing social events, or to a discontinuity in the locale or family of the rulers. Manetho's outline of pharaonic rule, which ran from the beginning of the First Dynasty to the conquest of Egypt by Alexander the Great (356-323 BCE) in 332 BCE, was so authoritative that it remains today the label by which the various periods of Egyptian history are known. His original writing has never been uncovered intact, however, and the only references which have survived are preserved in the chronicles of a variety of ancient authors, including the early Christian chronographers Sextus Julius Africanus (c. 180-250 CE), Bishop Eusebius of Caesarea (c. 260-340 CE), and George the Monk (c. 800 CE), also known as

---

11 Bright, John, <u>A History of Israel</u>, 39.
12 Johnson, The Civilization of Ancient Egypt, 46.

Syncellus, as well as the Jewish historian Josephus (fl. 70 CE).[13] The works of these classical authors contain testimonials of the writings of Manetho, but they frequently disagree about details of his classification, indicating that they may not have seen his work firsthand. Despite these limitations, Manetho's work was often accepted by subsequent commentators as true, leaving future scholars little opportunity to research the veracity of his outline.

The reason for the comprehensive acceptance of Manetho's classification is that in addition to knowing of the traditions that were carried down by the priestly caste, Manetho claimed he had access to biographies of people who lived during the reign of the Pharaohs, as well as to primary sources which recorded events in the past, including the Palmero Stone (c. 2400-2300 BCE), which was part of the Old Kingdom Annals;[14] the Turin Papyrus (Royal Canon of Kings), from the thirteenth century BCE;[15] the Abydos Table (Royal List of Abydos), which was inscribed in the temple of Seti I, from c. 1300 BCE;[16] the Karnak Table (Royal List of Karnak), which listed the kings down to Tuthmosis III, from c. 1500 BCE;[17] and the Sakkara (Saqqara) Tablet, which listed the kings to Ramesses II (1279-1213 BCE), from c. 1250 BCE.[18] Using all of these sources, Manetho divided his chronicle of the Egyptian kings into thirty-one Dynasties, but it is clear that he edited some of his primary sources, although how he made

---

13 Schedl, History of the Old Testament I. The Ancient Orient and Ancient Biblical History, 21; David, Handbook to Life in Ancient Egypt, 6. Manetho's original book was destroyed when Julius Caesar captured Alexandria in 47 BCE and burned the Library. Vercoutter, The Search for Ancient Egypt, 14-15.

14 The Old Kingdom Annals were inscribed on a slab of diorite stone, originally almost seven feet long by two feet high, and broken in fragments, of which the Palmero Stone is the largest piece now extant. Verbrugghe & Wickersham. Berossos and Manetho, Introduced and Translated, 103. The Palmero Stone enumerated the annals of the kings of Lower Egypt, beginning with the thousands of years the mythological rulers lived, until the time of the god Horus, who gave the throne to the human king Menes. It then listed the kings who ruled up to the Fifth Dynasty. Shaw, "Introduction: Chronologies and Cultural Change in Egypt," 4.

15 The Turin Papyrus is dated to the time of Ramesses II (1279-1213 BCE), and when it was complete, it contained the names of over three hundred kings, along with the lengths of their reign. Verbrugghe & Wickersham. Berossos and Manetho, Introduced and Translated, 105. It is the most informative of the Egyptian King-lists, stretching back with reasonable accuracy from the Second Intermediate Period to the reign of the First Dynasty ruler Menes. Shaw, "Introduction: Chronologies and Cultural Change in Egypt," 9.

16 The Abydos Table shows Pharaoh Seti I and his son Ramesses I making an offering to their 76 predecessors.

17 This engraving on the vestibule wall of the temple of Tuthmosis III includes the names of 61 rulers from Dynasties XI, XIII, and XVII, unfortunately not placed in chronologic order.

18 Clayton, Chronicle of the Pharaohs, 11-12.

his choices, and why he did not follow the details of every primary source, has never been satisfactorily answered. The Turin Papyrus, for example, listed fifty-two Pharaohs in the first six Dynasties, while Manetho placed the number at forty-nine, giving no reason for the alteration. In addition, if one adds all of the years Manetho ascribed to the reign of Egyptian Pharaohs until the time of Alexander the Great, the total is 5800 years, while modern historians have shown that this sum could only be a maximum of 3200 years. Such discrepancies have caused modern scholars to view Manetho's information as "indispensable but untrustworthy,"[19] and although his Dynastic labels have generally been retained to the modern day, the dates he applied have been mostly put aside, as scholars have uncovered new data which suggests that his designations were arbitrary.

Since the dates each Pharaoh reigned is a vital part of attempting to date the Exodus, and thereby name the Pharaohs delineated in the biblical text, it would be helpful if there was a chronology that was agreed to by all Egyptologists. This is not possible, however, for much controversy still exists among Egyptologists today about when each king actually ascended the throne. One of the reasons underlying this uncertainty is the difficulty in knowing which year is referenced in Egyptian records, since the Egyptians defined both a Civil and Sothic year, which were not precisely equal, and no specification was made as to which one was being recorded. The Civil year was determined by the annual Nile river flooding, which began on a day known as *Hapy*, and because the agricultural output of the entire country was dependent on the advent of irrigation that occurred at this time, the date was the most important event on the Egyptian calendar. The particular day that the flooding began was worshiped as a divine event, depicted with water-plants sprouting from a male head with female breasts below to represent fertility. The Egyptians estimated that it took 365 days for successive inundations of the flooding of the Nile river to begin, and referred to this interval as the Civil year, but the initial flooding did not always take place on the same day each year, so the Civil year could not be directly correlated to a standard astrological time frame.

Because the starting date of the Civil year could not be relied upon year after year, the Egyptians also determined a Sothic New Year date, which was dependent on reproducible astronomical calculations. Ancient astronomers, including the Egyptians, were well aware of the fixed movements of the stars, and often dated specific historical events to a specific astronomical occurrence. The Egyptians chose the rising of the Dog Star (Sirius), which is the brightest light in the Egyptian celestial sphere after Venus on July 21, as the start of their Sothic New Year's Day. The Sothic year corresponded to about 365 1/4 days, rather than the 365 days of the Civil year, and this resulted in one year being lost every 1460 years between the two determinations. This is not a great variation in and of itself,

19 Vercoutter, "The Second Intermediate Period and the Hyksos Invasion of Egypt," 384.

but the Egyptians did not state from which city the observation of the rising was made, and it is now known that the point of reference affected the calculation by up to twenty-five years. There are two instances when the Sothic rising was recorded in ancient hieroglyphic inscriptions of particular Pharaohs: one from an unspecified year of Thutmose II (1492-1479 BCE); and one from year 9 of Amenhotep I (1514-1493 BCE). In 238 CE, the Roman writer Censorinus, in a work entitled *De Die Natali*, determined that in 139 CE the Dog Star rose on the first day of Thoth, which was equivalent to the twelfth day of Kalends in the Roman calendar. This notation thereby related an ancient Egyptian event to a specific modern date, and scholars then began to ascertain the years a Pharaoh ruled by historical references to the rising of the Dog Star during his reign. But because the records did not include the precise site where the sighting was made, scholars differ on which date should be accepted as consistent with the Sothic chronology, as will be discussed later in this chapter.

Other reasons for a disputation among scholars over the exact dates of the reign of each Pharaoh include the indeterminate length of co-regencies; the belief that some Dynasties ran parallel with each other, rather than consecutive as suggested by Manetho; and the occurrence of interregna, when the Egyptian throne was vacant, all of which complicate the determination of the actual date of ascension to the throne of a specific individual. In addition, a king's regnal year was generally judged to begin on *Akhet* I, although his ascension day may have taken place at some other period during the year. This discrepancy in the actual date of ascension was not clarified until the Middle Kingdom (2106-1786 BCE), when it was decided to end the king's first regnal year on *Akhet* 1, rather than to begin at that time.

A final factor which has made it difficult to assign a specific Pharaoh to a particular period of time is the variation in the estimated length of time each Dynasty remained in control. This aspect is particularly evident during the Seventh to the Eleventh Dynasties, and during the Hyksos invasion. Historians date these periods at widely varying intervals, leaving large gaps in time for the estimated dates of rule. Those who have estimated the gaps to be quite short have defined what is referred to as a "Low Chronology," while those who have expanded the gaps produce a "High Chronology," and those who have accepted a compromise in between the two have created a "Middle Chronology." Because the time intervals between these determinations can vary by as much as fifty years, it is not possible to align the reign of a particular Pharaoh to contemporaneous events without an accounting for which chronology is accepted. This makes it very difficult to argue for a specific Exodus date, since the Hebrews are not mentioned in any extant extra-biblical sources. Even if one of the Pharaohs referred to in the Old Testament is identified by activities which are consistent with the biblical descriptions, the date of the Exodus will still be uncertain, since there is so much disagreement on when that particular Pharaoh ascended the throne.

Despite these contentious details, there is a chronology of Dynastic timelines which is accepted by many Egyptologists. This can be summarized as follows:[20]

Old Kingdom	(Dynasties 3-6)	2700-2190 BCE
First Intermediate	(Dynasties 7-10)	2190-2106 BCE
Middle Kingdom	(Dynasties 11-12)	2106-1786 BCE
Second Intermediate	(Dynasties 13-17)	1786-1550 (1539) BCE
The Hyksos Period	(Dynasties 15-16)	1648-1550 (1540) BCE
The New Kingdom	(Dynasties 18-20)	1550 (1539)-1069 BCE

Note that the chronology begins with the Third Dynasty, for very little is known of the first two regimes.[21] Within this broad range of standard chronology, there are differences of opinion among Egyptologists on when each particular Pharaoh ruled. There has recently been extensive discussion about radically modifying these standard chronologies, placing the era in which each Pharaoh ruled in much later periods of time. David Rohl, the Chairman of the Institute for the Study of Interdisciplinary Studies in England, is one of the pioneers of this movement, and in his publications he refers to the standard timeline as the "conventional chronology," and his modifications as the "new chronology."[22] For convenience, I will refer to his determination of the standard timeline for each Pharaoh in this book, and then point out the range used by other Egyptologists, in order to provide some reasonable basis for providing a baseline for determining when the Exodus likely took place, and which Pharaoh was sitting on the throne of Egypt when that seminal event occurred. While I will refer to his radical alterations on occasion, I will not follow his attempt to modify the standard chronology with a new chronology.

B. Dynastic Timelines

1. Old Kingdom (Dynasties 3-6), 2700-2190 BCE

It is easier to understand the details of Egyptian history during the Middle and Late Bronze Ages than it is for any other culture from the ancient Near East

---

20 Dates based on the chronologies of Rolf Krauss, Professor of Egyptology at Humboldt University, Berlin, and Kenneth A. Kitchen, Brunner Professor Emeritus of Egyptology, University of Liverpool. Hoffmeier, Israel in Egypt, The Evidence for the Authenticity of the Exodus Tradition, xiv.

21 The first two Dynasties are generally referred to as the Early Dynastic Period (Thinite), or "Archaic Egypt," and do not appear in most academic classifications. The First Dynasty is often dated from 3100 BCE to 2890 BCE, and the Second Dynasty from 2890-2700 BCE.

22 Rohl, Pharaohs and Kings, A Biblical Quest, 15, 20.

because of the multitude of Egyptian historical hieroglyphic recordings which have withstood the ravages of time. The Sumerians may have arrived on the geopolitical scene around the same time as the early Egyptians, and possessed a written script, but the survival of interpretable Egyptian records in archaeologic remains provides a standard of awareness that is unmatched by any other culture during the third and second millennia BCE. As already mentioned, there was a Semitic presence in Egypt during the Predynastic Period, but it is during the Old Kingdom, when the earliest pyramids first appeared at Sakkara under King Djoser (Zoser) (c. 2630-2611 BCE), that a great infusion of Semites took place as slaves were imported to assist in the building of the massive stone construction projects which characterized that illustrious era.[23] It has been estimated that the population of Egypt during the rule of King Djoser was about 1.5 million people, and that more than 70,000, or almost 5%, were Semitic slaves brought in to build the pyramids.[24] This is more than a millennium before the time of Abraham, and it indicates that the Egyptians were familiar with the cultural characteristics of the Semites from the time of their earliest cultural beginnings.

Although the Third Dynasty was begun under King Zanakht (Sanakhte,) (c.2650-2630 BCE), it was dominated by King Djoser, who reigned during a period of time contemporary with Gilgamesh, the Sumerian King whose legendary story included the earliest known record of a flood mythology. The reign of Djoser was seen as particularly important to the ancient Egyptians, who recognized his lasting value in the Turin Papyrus by recording his accomplishments with red ink, a practice which was reserved for only the most important kings. This honor was almost certainly due to his initiation of the building of pyramids, an engineering feat primarily due to the brilliant calculations of his renowned architect, Imhotep. The most outstanding achievement of Imhotep was the Step Pyramid at Sakkara, the first building in the world known to be constructed entirely of stone. Before the Third Dynasty, the Egyptians had traditionally built structures from unbaked bricks that were fashioned from a compound of mud, sand, and chopped straw in oblong molds. This practice is still in use today for the construction of residences, but the material was not strong enough for the erection of large projects. During the Bronze Age, the availability of sturdier tools made the quarry of large stones from nearby rock beds possible, and a new era of design for the building

---

23 Sakkara has about thirty pyramids, fifteen of which are king's tombs, and the rest for queens or royal children. The Oxford Encyclopedia of Archaeology in the Near East, vol. IV, 479.

24 Kishlansky, Geary, & O'Brien, Civilization in the West, 19. Construction crews included Egyptians who were not slaves, as well as other populations, such as the Nubians, although it is likely that the majority were of Semitic origin. Deportation of local populations from Canaan as slaves became a regular tool of Egyptian imperial policy well into the Late Bronze Age. Hendel, Remembering Abraham: Culture, Memory, and History in the Hebrew Bible, 61.

of structures such as pyramids and temples was suddenly at hand. The first of these projects was the Step Pyramid, overlooking the capital city of Memphis. This edifice was not only an impressive visual manifestation of the presence of divine authority in the person of the Pharaoh, it was an engineering masterpiece that utilized computations and methods of measurement which mimicked the accuracy of modern technology. It contained over 92 million cubic feet of stone, more that was used in the construction of all the other pyramids of the Fifth and Sixth Dynasties combined, and soared to a height of over 200 feet, measuring 467 x 393 feet at its base. Based upon the awesome effect this structure has on visitors today, it is easy to see why ancient travelers recognized the Step Pyramid as one of the true wonders of the world.

During the Fourth Dynasty (2613-2498 BCE) which followed, the building of pyramids continued to expand as each Pharaoh marshaled a great amount of wealth to ensure immortality by the construction of a tomb in an attempt to match, or improve upon, the feats of King Djoser. During the reign of Sneferu (Snefru, Soris) (c. 2575-2551 BCE), the founder of the Fourth Dynasty, the external form of the royal tomb changed from the step-design of Imhotep, to that of a true pyramid with smooth, accurately slanted surfaces. A network of canals was dug off the Nile to transport stone for the pyramids, and cities were built to house and feed the large number of workers who were both imported, and gathered from the local populace, to carry out the ambitious building program. Sneferu also expanded trade with the Levant, sending forty vessels to Byblos to receive cedar logs, and in the centuries which followed, this practice expanded and Byblos grew into a major trading partner, providing Egypt with a port city that allowed her access to the entire Mediterranean domain.

The most impressive edifice from the Fourth Dynasty was the Great Pyramid of King Cheops (Khufu), the son of Sneferu, who ruled from c. 2551-2528 BCE. This impressive structure, which is the largest Egyptian pyramid ever built, remains today as the "perfect image" of the Old Kingdom, standing 481 feet high, and containing over 2,300,000 separate blocks of stone, weighing a total of over six million tons.[25] The engineering genius of its construction is attested to by the fact that it remained the tallest building in the world until the nineteenth century CE, and its base area was larger than the cathedrals of Florence, Milan, St. Paul's in London, Westminster Abbey and St. Peter's in Rome combined. The number of laborers needed to construct this massive complex was enormous, and the Greek historian Herodotus estimated that 100,000 men worked for twenty years in order to complete the task, a figure which did not include the number of men who were employed in other projects elsewhere in Egypt.[26]

---

25 Clayton, Chronicle of the Pharaohs, 42.

26 Johnson, The Civilization of Ancient Egypt, 55. It should be noted that many scholars have claimed that Herodotus made up, or falsified, many of the Egyptian historical

This massive building program which characterized the Old Kingdom required a rapid growth in the Semitic slave population, and while the slaves performed admirably, as witnessed by the impressive array of their constructions, their unchecked proliferation eventually disrupted the political stability of the entire country. Many inscriptions on archaeologic remains indicate that considerable numbers of Asiatics entered the country to take advantage of the ever-increasing need for manual labor during this era, and the foreigners needed little coercion to be persuaded to transfer their place of residence to the banks of the Nile, given the uncertainty of the harvest in the Levant, and the ever-present prospect of starvation. Not all of the immigrants were peaceful, however, and many able-bodied workers created civil unrest by marauding the countryside, forcing Egypt to eventually defend herself from the ever-increasing Bedouin nomadic population. This unrest is chronicled in the *Biography of Weni*, an inscription found on the wall of a chapel at Abydos, which told how Pepi I (2390-2361 BCE), a Sixth Dynasty Pharaoh, gathered an army of tens of thousands in order to inflict punishment on the "Asiatic Sand-dwellers" for their disruption of law and order. Not content with simply being forced into the role of slave, competition between Semites and Egyptians surfaced in an ever more prominent nature, and racial dissension eventually culminated in the invasion and take-over of the country by the Semites during the First Intermediate Period, as will be discussed shortly. This history of tension between the Egyptians and their Semitic neighbors was likely the reason why the Hebrews would later be subjected to the order of the Pharaoh "who did not know Joseph" to slay their newborn male children when their ever-increasing population was seen as a threat to Egyptian security.

Another aspect of Old Kingdom life that was indicative of the growing popularity of maritime travel was the remains of an amazing cedarwood boat found in the tomb of Cheops, known as the "solar boat of King Cheops." This vessel is the world's oldest surviving ship, measuring more than 138 feet in length and 211 feet in width, and although it is likely that it was used for ceremonial purposes rather than for commercial transport, the design was indicative of the type of vessel that was commonly used during this era for transportation along the Mediterranean coast and Nile River. Most of the cargo ships during this era were about fifty feet long, and were built very lightly, allowing the Egyptians to easily sail south to Punt, and north to the Levant.[27] It was not until the fourteenth century BCE, that Egyptian ship builders began to strengthen their boats by using

facts he claimed to have learned from Egyptian priests. Nielsen, The Tragedy in History: Herodotus and the Deuteronomistic History, 41.

27 Vinson, "Ships in the Ancient Mediterranean," 14. Evidence of ships sailing to the land now known as Lebanon in order to obtain cedar and other coniferous woods dates back to the Second Dynasty, and an Egyptian worker left his name on an inscribed ax-head at Byblos during the Fourth Dynasty. Bass, "Sea and River Craft in the Ancient Near East," 1425.

lashings to sew the planks together, and by using wooden pegs to strengthen the mortise and tenon joints. Before that time, travel was limited in both tonnage and atmospheric conditions, but despite the fact that sailing to distant ports was dangerous, archaeologic sites have indicated that Egyptians traded with ports as far away as Crete and Syria during the Old Kingdom.

Further improvement in the technique of ship-building took place during the Fifth Dynasty, allowing King Sahure (c. 2491-2477 BCE) to use a fleet of transports to bring his army to the Levantine coast, rather than march his men for days along the *Via Maris*. Pictures of his boats are carved on the wall of his pyramid in great detail, and show that the capacity of the hull was strengthened by looping an enormous hawser on each end of the ship, with a center pole to tighten the harness. Although the device did not improve the suitability of the craft for long voyages across the sea, the chance of major leakage was reduced, making travel up the Levantine coast, where the ship was never far from land, relatively safe. The ability to move troops quickly from Egypt to the Levant allowed the Old Kingdom Pharaohs to look more intently along the entire Mediterranean coast for further areas of colonial expansion, and as they found they could control the wealthy trade routes which moved goods throughout the ancient Near East, an opportunity to fill their own coffers became evident, although a dramatic increase in military invasions of Canaanite lands would not take place until the Middle Kingdom, a few centuries later.

2. *First Intermediate Period (Dynasties 7-10), 2190-2106 BCE*

About the same time the Akkadian Empire in Mesopotamia collapsed following the invasion of the Guti, and the urban civilization in Palestine was disrupted due to the Amorite Invasion, the power of the Egyptian royal house suddenly disintegrated, leaving political and religious power in the hands of provincial governors (gnomarchs), rather than in the autocratic control of a single ruler. The kings who took control of the country moved their royal residence from Memphis to Herakleopolis, but their rule was not included in the King-list of the temple of Seti I at Abydos, indicating that subsequent royal historians did not view their reign as a continuum of accepted Egyptian monarchs, despite the fact that Manetho listed eighteen or nineteen kings who occupied the throne of Egypt during this period of time. The reasons for this sudden change are not known with certainty, but most scholars believe that the disruption was related to increased Semitic intrusions, reflecting what was taking place during the Amorite Invasion throughout the ancient Near East.[28] These immigrants entered Egypt fully armed, rather than as Semitic prisoners-of-war, and as their numbers grew,

28 Another theory is that the collapse was due to the abrupt change in climate following the cessation of the Neolithic Wet Phase about 2350 BCE, leading to successive waves of famine. Aldred, The Egyptians, 120.

and their strength intensified, they took control of the country, albeit for a short period of time.

This era of anarchy and strife was referred to by Manetho as the First Intermediate Period, an era with historical details more obscure than at any other time in Egyptian history. Disunity and feudalism took control of the country, and as the Old Kingdom came to an end, Asiatics from the Levant overran the Egyptian defenses, setting up autonomous areas under Semitic rule. Their primary base of operation was in the Delta, but despite their superior strength on the border of the country, they were not able to move deeper into the Egyptian countryside. This has led many scholars to argue that the First Intermediate Period was not a full-scale invasion, but rather a succession of border raids and skirmishes which created a chaotic political situation, but not an overall defeat of the Egyptian populace.[29]

While the stability of the unified Egyptian royal house was temporarily dismantled, the Egyptians did not passively accept the Semitic presence in the Delta, as indicted by numerous passages in surviving literary texts which told how a number of Pharaohs attempted to face the growing foreign threat with defensive vigor. In the *Instructions to Merikare*, from the Tenth Dynasty, one of the Herakleopolitan kings told his son how the miserable Asiatic foreigner "is like a thief darting about in a group," and that vigilance was constantly needed to counteract their threat.[30] The *Admonitions of Ipuwer* (*Admonitions of a Prophet*), found in the Papyrus Leiden from c. 2000 BCE, detailed how the frontier of Egypt in the northeast was open to Bedouins and Asiatics, and that their numbers grew to such a proportion that the Egyptians could not prevent a rebellion, which resulted in the Semites achieving independent rule. The misery of the people was profound during this era, as evidenced by the fact that "laughter has disappeared and wailing pervades the land."[31]

Because this era coincides with the chronology most accepted by scholars for the time of Abraham, comparisons have been made with recordings in the biblical book of *Genesis* with the Egyptian *Instructions to Merikare*, the *Prophecy of Neferty*,[32] the *Tale of Sinuhe*, and the painting in tomb 3 at Beni-Hasan.[33] I will discuss

---

29 Thompson, The Historicity of the Patriarchal Narratives: The Quest for the Historical Abraham, 140.

30 Hoffmeier, Israel in Egypt, The Evidence for the Authenticity of the Exodus Tradition, 55.

31 Johnson, The Civilization of Ancient Egypt, 67.

32 This literary composition is often dated to the Middle Kingdom and is set in the court of pharaoh Sneferu, where the lector-priest Neferty is summoned to entertain the king. Neferty tells how Egypt is to be overrun by foreigners (Asiatics) and strife until king Amenemhet I is born. It probably was written during his reign, and has been used to validate the invasions of Egypt during the First Intermediate Period. Thompson, The Historicity of the Patriarchal Narratives: The Quest for the Historical Abraham, 142-143.

33 An Egyptian tomb-painting at Beni-Hasan, from about 1890 BCE, showed a

these similarities in more detail in the next chapter, and will only note here that some scholars categorically deny that the patriarchs ever existed, accusing instead that the biblical tale is a fictional account intended to claim a false inheritance of the Canaanite land. If one wants to search for possible references to biblical patriarchal details in Egyptian records from this era, however, there are many similarities that can be found, if you believe that some parts of the Bible are historically valid.

The resistance effort by the native Egyptians to the intrusions of the First Intermediate Period was effective, however, and the victory of the Semites was short-lived, allowing the Egyptians to eventually regain control of their country after less than a century of political disruption. In order to protect against future invasions, King Khety II (c. 2115 BCE), of the Tenth Dynasty, began to establish an extensive line of fortifications along the Sinai border, a strategy that would later be augmented by Amenemhet I (Ammenemes) (1937-1908 BCE) during the glory days of the Middle Kingdom. These strongholds, built at the eastern end of the Wadi Tumilat where the caravan route through the Negev entered Egypt, became known as the "Prince's Wall" ("Wall of the Prince"), and their presence helped to reinvigorate the strength of the royal government. Although the Egyptians reclaimed authority over their land, confrontations between Semite and Egyptian continued to plague Egyptian history for centuries to come. Since Abraham is believed to have been born sometime after 2000 BCE, during the hey-day of the Amorite Invasion, it is unlikely that Hebrews participated in the incursions of the First Intermediate Period, but the successful passage of Semites into and out of Egypt during this era may have been part of the reason why Abraham decided to travel to Egypt when his food supply in Canaan ran low, as will be discussed in more detail in the next chapter.

3. Middle Kingdom (Dynasties 11-12), 2106-1786 BCE

The Asiatic presence in Egypt during the First Intermediate Period created a political system which had divided the country once again into a northern kingdom, manifested by the Tenth Dynasty based in Herakleopolis, and a southern one that arose in opposition in Thebes (modern Luxor), manifested by the Eleventh Dynasty. The desire of the Egyptians to unite under the rule of one king was never lost in the chaos, however, and reunification eventually came about under the Theban King Mentuhotep I - Nebhepetre (2080-2074 BCE), who abandoned the old capital of Memphis, and made his hometown of Thebes the capital of his resurrected country. Eventually, this vital period in Egyptian

---

Semitic clan of 37 people, with the men and women wearing multicolored tunics draped over one shoulder and reaching below the knees, a fashion similar to Joseph's coat. Sarna, Genesis, 255.

history was glorified with the coronation of Amenemhet I, the founder of the Twelfth Dynasty. The son of a commoner named Senusert, Amenemhet I had been employed as vizier during the short reign of Mentuhotep III, and emerged as the successor of a great new Dynasty, which elevated the god Amun-Re (Amun-Ra) to the forefront of Egyptian religious hierarchy.[34] The Karnak temple near Thebes, which was begun by his son Sesostris I (Senusert, Senwosret) (1917-1872 BCE), would soon grow to become the largest religious complex in the world, and although Semitic presence at the Levantine border of Egypt continued to threaten Egyptian sovereignty, the Pharaohs of the Middle Kingdom remained strong enough to resist any insurrection until the time of the Hyksos onslaught.

Contact between Egypt and the Aegean countries expanded greatly during this era, developing into an atmosphere of friendly relations that would last for centuries to come. Martin Bernal, Professor of Government and Near Eastern Studies at Cornell University, has argued that these connections were significant enough to support the view that the Egyptians were actually instrumental in helping to develop the infant burgeoning Aegean civilization. Pointing to the presence of many archaeologic sites which provide evidence of Egyptian influence, Bernal claimed that the establishment of the Cretan bull-cult, as well as the architectural plans of the palaces on the island of Crete, were both due to the impact of Egyptian domination during the era of the Eleventh and Twelfth Dynasties.[35] He concluded that the ram-cults found around the Aegean locale were derived from devotion to the god Amun, who was associated with ram worship, and that the eventual destruction of the Cretan palaces was due to a "Hyksos-Egypto-Canaanite conquest of Crete."[36]

Few scholars accept Bernal's thesis that Egypt actually colonized the Aegean societies during the Middle Kingdom, even though they may have sent emissaries to that distant shore as part of a general migration of people out of Egypt which may have taken place during the twentieth century BCE. There are numerous findings of fragments of Minoan Kamares pottery from Crete at the city of el-Lahun, which housed the workforce involved in the construction of the pyramid and temple of Sesostris I, indicating the presence of Egyptian influence in that part of the Mediterranean world. I believe that this system of trade between Egypt and the civilization in Crete and Mycenae was known to Moses, and eventually to the congregation under him command during the Exodus, and that this information eventually encouraged the dissident Hebrews who left the Exodus

---

34 The Egyptian God Amun (Amon, Amen), in the form of Amun-Re, was similar to YHWH, in that he was the "God of gods, Lord of lords, King of kings, and King of the gods." Murray, The Splendour That Was Egypt, 94. Amun was originally only the local divinity of Thebes, but became the supreme ruler of the Egyptian pantheon, and official god of the empire, on the accession of the Eighteenth Dynasty.

35 Bernal, Black Athena, I.18, 63.

36 O'Connor, "Egypt and Greece: The Bronze Age Evidence," 51.

generations later to arrange for passage to Mycenae, rather than risk remaining in the unfriendly environs of the Levant.

Amenemhet I ruled from 1937-1908 BCE according to the conventional chronology,[37] although other scholars have favored placing his reign at an earlier date, c. 1991-1962 BCE.[38] He was not descended from a royal line, and it is believed that he took advantage of his position as vizier to Mentuhotep III to assassinate his master and take over the throne. He made a lasting effect on the future of Egyptian autonomy by consolidating the Egyptian defenses and expanding the line of fortifications known as the Prince's Wall, a critical element in deterring Asiatics from invading Egypt through the Sinai peninsula. Although there is no surviving archaeologic evidence of this impressive defensive structure, many literary references attest to its presence. The line of fortresses they described covered the entire eastern frontier, from Heliopolis to Pelusium. They were built on the Egyptian side of the Wadi Tumilat, near cultivated ground so that the soldiers could provide for most of their own provisions instead of depending on supplies from the central government, and journals from the border fortresses, as defined by the term *t3s*, included registers of the names of those who received a permit to enter or leave the country.[39] Caravans were forced to stop and ask for permission to enter, even if only to water their animals outside the Egyptian border, and there are detailed records of Semitic tribes resembling the travels of Abraham and Jacob into Egypt, as described in the Old Testament.

As we now are in the era when most scholars believe Abraham lived, it is possible that Amenemhet I was the Pharaoh with whom Abraham interacted on his entry into Egypt. A popular publication from that era, *The Story of Sinuhe*, may have even provided the biblical compilers with information about the travels of Abraham in Canaan before the birth of Isaac, as the plot involved Sinhue, a nobleman of high rank in the court of Amenemhet I, who overheard a conversation which he believed put his life in danger following the assassination of the king. In response, Sinuhe fled the country by traveling northward, coming up to the "Wall-of-the-Ruler, made to oppose the Asiatics and to crush the Sand-Crossers."[40] This barrier was a reference to the Prince's Wall, and just as God

---

37 Rohl, Pharaohs and Kings, A Biblical Quest, 14.

38 Redford, Akhenaten, The Heretic King, 12.

39 Ahituv, "Sources for the Study of the Egyptian-Canaanite Border Administration," 219, 221-222. One of the most important of the border fortresses was at Sile (*Tjel*, or Tjaru, or Djaru, near modern El-Kantara), a stronghold built on the main pass through the swampland. It was also called *Wst Hr*, or "The Way of Horus," since it stood at the beginning of the military road where the Pharaohs, who were felt to be incarnations of the god Horus, embarked on their Asian campaigns. Nibbi, The Sea Peoples and Egypt, 13.

40 Wilson, "The Story of Sinuhe," 5-7. An astonishing number of copies of this book have been found, an indication that it must have been a best-seller, and gone through many editions. Keller, The Bible as History, 77.

would later order the Hebrews to avoid this direction at the start of the Exodus, Sinuhe crouched down in a bush in order to not be seen by the border guards. He then traveled at night, heading for Peten and the island of Kemur, and continued to move up the coast toward Byblos, stopping first at Qedem, where he married the eldest daughter of Ammi-enshi, a ruler of Upper Retenu.

The *Story of Sinuhe* not only highlighted the dangers of the Prince's Wall to anyone wishing to leave Egypt unnoticed, it also clarified why Abraham was able to move so easily through Canaan following his initial contact with the Egyptian Pharaoh. Despite the fact that Abraham was of Semitic origin, he was in possession of valuable gifts from the Pharaoh, including slaves who would have reflected his favored status. Since Egypt was the major military and political force in the Levant during this era, those who were known to be friends of the Egyptian royal court would have been treated as dignified guests, as was Sinuhe when he stopped at Qedem and was offered the king's daughter in marriage. These similarities suggest that the biblical compilers may have been aware of the story when they recorded the movements of Abraham, and that Amenemhet I may have even been the model for the Pharaoh involved with Sarah, since the timeline would fit quite well if Ahmose I was the Pharaoh "who did not know Joseph," as will be discussed shortly.

After Amenemhet I's assassination, he was succeeded by his son, Sesostris I, who not only continued construction on the Prince's Wall, but also carried out an extensive building program throughout Egypt. In the conventional chronology, Sesostris I ruled from 1917-1872 BCE,[41] although most scholars place his reign from 1971-1926 BCE.[42] Once again, the range of estimated dates is great, and the calculations are complicated, because there is a nine-year overlap in the reigns of Amenemhet I and Sesostris I, due to the practice of co-regencies that was instituted by Amenemhet I. This method of simultaneous rule allowed the Pharaoh's son to accede to the throne while the father was still alive, in order to assure a smooth transition upon his death. The technique worked quite well in this case, and the reign of Amenemhet I and his descendants lasted for over two centuries. Although Martin Bernal claimed that Sesostris I was to be identified with the Sesostris who, according to legend, had made advances into Thrace, Anatolia, and Scythia, most scholars do not accept his conclusion, and restrict the primary influence of Sesostris I to the area along the Levantine coast.

Although the Prince's Wall functioned primarily to prevent the incursion of large numbers of uninvited Bedouin immigrants, purposeful importation of Semitic workers into Egypt continued in an ever-increasing fashion, and the number of Semitic slaves working in the country grew to significant proportions during the era of the Middle Kingdom, as evidenced by a number of extant Egyptian chronicles. An inscription of Amenemhet II (1875-1840 BCE), who followed Sesostris I as

41 Rohl, Pharaohs and Kings, A Biblical Quest, 15.
42 Clayton, Chronicle of the Pharaohs, 78.

Pharaoh, indicates that 1,554 men were captured and brought to Egypt as slaves in one Levantine campaign alone. This practice of enslaving Semites to carry out large construction projects may have been the primary reason why Abraham feared for his life when he first met the Pharaoh and passed himself off as Sarah's brother, rather than as her husband, as will be discussed in the next chapter. In addition to the need for labor on state-run projects, usually satisfied by prisoners of military conquests throughout the Levant, Asiatics were often brought into the country by private individuals to work as cooks, brewers, seamstresses, vine-dressers, and workers of the land. The Papyrus Brooklyn, which dates to c. 1745 BCE, from the late Twelfth or early Thirteenth Dynasty, listed over forty Semites who were servants in one estate in the Thebaid,[43] and when one realizes how many estates of this type existed during that period of time, it is obvious that there were large numbers of Semitic servants across Egypt, especially in the Delta which was close to the entry point along the Prince's Wall. The biblical story of Joseph, where Joseph was sold by his brothers for twenty pieces of silver to an Egyptian, may reflect this type of transaction, once again aligning the biblical story with what is known about Egypt during that period of time.

But adhering to the adage that he who neglects to remember history is doomed to repeat it, as was seen in the years before the First Intermediate Period, the increased Semitic population once again proved to be a danger to the Egyptian government, and by the end of the era the immigrant communities had begun to unite and gain control over the territories immediately adjacent to their base of operation. Asiatics soon entered the Delta in ever-increasing numbers, and quickly began to gain superiority over the local population. Their settlements in the eastern Delta, such as at Avaris, were very successful and provided a secure base for Semitic forces to gather resources and arrange for a formidable invasion. Many scholars believe that the powerful Hyksos invaders who entered the country in the eighteenth century BCE likely originated in fortified urban complexes which were constructed by local Syria-Palestine rulers, who maintained communication with allies living in the Delta.

Evidence of the animosity which developed between Egyptians and Asiatics at the end of the Middle Kingdom is provided by the "Execration texts": clay bowls or figurines which were used for the ceremonial cursing and thwarting of the enemies of the Pharaohs during the nineteenth century BCE. Three sets of texts have been found: the Mirgissa texts from c. 1870 BCE; the Berlin texts from c. 1850 BCE; and the Brussels texts from c. 1800 BCE.[44] The name of a

---

43 Hoffmeier, Israel in Egypt, the Evidence for the Authenticity of the Exodus Tradition, 61.

44 Worschech, "Egypt and Moab," 229. The Berlin texts were inscribed on pottery bowls, while the Brussels texts were mostly inscribed on clay figurines. Seters, The Hyksos: A New Investigation, 78.

foe was written on the clay object, and then ceremonially smashed to break the power of the intended recipient, and to inflict a terrible curse. The texts which have survived include names of Libyans and Asiatics, as well as Egyptians, but the majority appear to have been directed against foreign Semitic adversaries. That the biblical story of Abraham may be set in the conditions that were existent in Canaan in the Middle Bronze Age is apparent in the fact that some of the shards revealed names of cities like Jerusalem, Ashkelon, Tyre, Hazor, Beth Shemesh, Aphek, Achshaph, and Shechem, all biblical names of cities, two of which were visited by Abraham.[45] While the superstition may have allayed the concerns of individuals or small family groups, the relentless drive of the Semites was not assuaged by these attempts of magic, and Egypt was about to enter its most difficult prolonged political era.

4. Second Intermediate Period and the Rule of the Hyksos (Dynasties 13-17), 1786-1550 BCE

Following the successful extension of Egyptian authority into Canaan during the Old Kingdom, and the further expansion toward the Aegean Sea in the Middle Kingdom, the fortunes of Egypt took a drastic turn for the worse as Semitic intruders finally gathered enough strength to overwhelm the border defenses and take over control of the country once again. This period of foreign rule is known as the Second Intermediate Period, and it is generally seen as consisting of three overlapping phases: (a) Egypt before the Hyksos (Thirteenth and Fourteenth Dynasties, 1786-1648 BCE); (b) the reign of the Hyksos (Fifteenth and Sixteenth Dynasties, 1648-1550 BCE); and (c) the Kingdom of Thebes and the expulsion of the Hyksos (Seventeenth Dynasty, 1650-1550 BCE).[46]

The most important period of time during this Second Intermediate Period, with respect to my theory of Hebrew emigration to Mycenae, was the actual reign of the Hyksos, a group of Asiatics made up of Semites, Hittites, and Hurrians who were first given their name by the Egyptian priest, Manetho. The term itself was a Greek rendering of the Egyptian *Hikau Khasut*, which means "Rulers of Foreign Lands."[47] Manetho called them "Shepherd Kings," but today such a designation is seen as only partially correct, for *sos* is not believed to be a transcription of *Shasu*, which means "nomad," or "shepherd," but is rather an abbreviation of *khasut*, or "foreigners," hence the label of "foreign kings," rather than "shepherd kings."[48]

---

45 Keller, The Bible as History, 79.

46 Vercoutter, "The Second Intermediate Period and the Hyksos Invasion of Egypt," 386.

47 Hayes, The Scepter of Egypt, Part II: The Hyksos Period and the New Kingdom (1675-1080 B.C.), 3.

48 Vercoutter, "The Second Intermediate Period and the Hyksos Invasion of Egypt,"

The reason why the Hyksos are so important to my thesis, as well as to the dating of the Exodus, is that their period of rule is believed by many scholars to reflect the era when Joseph was brought to Egypt after being sold into slavery by his brothers. If this is true, then Joseph's rule as vizier can be used to construct a timeline for the entire Old Testament.[49] The rationale for this view is discussed in more detail in chapter 3, but the crux of the argument is that a Semite would more likely be elevated to the position of vizier during the rule of a Semitic Pharaoh, rather than during the reign of an Egyptian, since the vizier acted as the second-in-command in the political system, and Semites were generally distrusted by the Egyptian hierarchy.[50] If Joseph can be dated to the era of the Hyksos Dynasty, then the patriarchal era and the birth of Moses can be more accurately estimated using biblical passages which tell how long each Patriarch lived, and how long the Hebrews sojourned in Egypt before the Exodus.

Manetho described the take-over of the Hyksos as an invasion of people from the East, during the reign of Dudimose (Tutimaios, Timaus) (c. 1654 BCE). He interpreted the process as a violent affair, with the Hyksos overpowering the Egyptian rulers and then razing the Egyptian cities to the ground, ascribing their success to superior military strength based upon the use of the horse and chariot, weaponry which the Egyptians had not yet developed. Because ancient historians often followed Manetho's account without critical dissent, his version of the process was generally accepted as true until the modern age, despite the fact that very little evidence for a significant military engagement was apparent in other historical Egyptian texts. When the data was later scrutinized from a myriad of other sources, however, it became apparent that the conquest was more consistent with a waning of Egyptian political power, followed by an infiltration of a "heterogenous concert of various inhabitants of Western Asia," rather than an outright invasion. Eventually the foreigners overpowered the local Egyptian economy, and took over control of the country as the defensive capabilities of the Pharaohs were unable to stem the Semitic tide. This infiltrative process fits well with what is known about the Hyksos culture, since they are generally believed to

---

391-392.

49 Josephus, the first century CE Jewish historian, believed that the Hyksos were actually "our forefathers." Josephus, "Against Apion," The Complete Works of Josephus, I.16, 612. It is likely that Josephus confused Manetho's description of the Hyksos as an invasion by the Hebrews, for he stated that Manetho claimed that "our people had come into Egypt, many ten thousands in number, and subdued its inhabitants." Ibid., I.26, 617.

50 The vizier was, in essence, the entire cabinet of the pharaoh, receiving embassies as the Secretary of State; directing taxation as the Secretary of the Treasury; supervising the water supply and canals as the Secretary of the Interior and Agriculture; controlling the legal system as the Attorney general; directing the army and navy as the Secretary of War; and inspecting the craftsmen as the Secretary of Labor. Mertz, Temples, Tombs & Hieroglyphs: A Popular History of Ancient Egypt, 181.

have been a mixture of Semitic, Canaanite, Hurrian, Hittite and Aryan elements who followed the penetration of the Hurrians into northern Mesopotamia, and then gradually worked their way southward into Egypt. Although the process of domination may not have been a full-scale war, it is generally agreed that the Hyksos were the first to utilize chariots in Egypt, and this expertise gave them a definite military advantage over the slower moving, and more poorly armed, Egyptian militia.

The date of the Hyksos entry into Egypt is generally placed at 1730-1720 BCE, based upon the Stele of the year 400, a monument erected by Ramesses II, and found at the city of Tanis (Zoan), where it was transported after being originally set up at the city of Ramesses (Pi-Ramesses, Raameses). This structure was constructed by Ramesses II to commemorate the four-hundred year anniversary of the reconstruction of the temple of the god Seth (Set, Semitic Baal-Seth) at Avaris, the city in the northeastern Delta which was initially fostered by the Hyksos, and eventually became their capital. Since the fourth centennial was celebrated around 1330-1320 BCE, the date of the building of the temple is thereby fixed to 1730-1720 BCE.

Once settled into the country, the Hyksos rose to political control of Egypt in two stages. Initially, from 1720-1675 BCE, they occupied Avaris as their primary base of authority, and began to consolidate their position throughout northern Egypt.[51] They gradually extended their control toward Memphis, following the eastern edge of the Delta and establishing centers of authority along the way. During the second stage, the Hyksos secured political control over the rest of the country, and elected kings to rule in the same manner as the Pharaohs. This latter period was labeled by Manetho as the Fifteenth Dynasty, which is commonly dated to c. 1660-1550 BCE, although the recent dating of the volcanic eruption of Thera to 1628 BCE may necessitate a change in this chronology.[52] The succession of six sovereigns during the Fifteenth Dynasty is known as the "Great Hyksos," as distinguished from the series of kings of the Sixteenth Dynasty, who ruled contemporaneously in small city-states in northern Egypt and the Delta, known as the "Lesser Hyksos." As with other periods of pharaonic reign, there is great disputation over the length of time the Hyksos remained in control. According to the Turin Papyrus, the foreign kings ruled for 108 years, a period of time that

51 Avaris was at Tell el-Daba, in the eastern Nile Delta, and contained a large palace and military compound that eventually was overrun by Ahmose I. Thousands of fragments of Minoan wall paintings were found at the site in a later Thumosid period palace, indicating a special relationship with Crete. O'Connor, "Egypt, the Levant, and the Aegean from the Hyksos Period to the Rise of the New Kingdom," 108-112.

52 Coleman, "Did Egypt Shape the Glory that was Greece?" 298. The "High chronology" of Rowton would place the final Hyksos expulsion around 1567 BCE, while if we accept the "Low chronology" of Parker, the date is reduced by about twenty-five years. Seters, The Hyksos: A New Investigation, 160.

is generally accepted for the reign of the Great Hyksos today. This is a much shorter period of time than that ascribed by Manetho, who was said by Africanus to have estimated the rule at 284 years, and by Josephus as 259 years.[53] Josephus also stated that Manetho claimed the combined period of time the Hyksos kept possession of Egypt was 511 years, a total much longer than is generally accepted today.[54]

The foundation of the Great Hyksos Fifteenth Dynasty is generally ascribed to a man called Salitis (Salatis), sometimes referred to as Sheshi, or Sharek. He is believed to have been the warrior who ousted the contemporary Egyptian ruler from the capital city of Memphis in 1675 BCE, and then gradually extended Hyksos control southward, eventually including the whole of Upper Egypt and Nubia under his control. Once he was appointed ruler, he made Memphis his capital seat, and fortified the district to the east in order to protect the border against Assyrian attack. There is disagreement, however, among ancient authors over the sequence of Pharaohs who followed: Josephus listed them as Salatis, Beon (Bnon), Apachnas (Apachnan), Apophis (Apepi, Ipepi), Jonias (Iannas), and Assis;[55] Africanus said that they were Saites, Bnon, Pachnan, Staan (Iannas), Archles (Assis), and Apophis;[56] while Eusebius listed only Saites, Bnon, Archles and Apophis, and assigned them to the Seventeenth rather than the Fifteenth Dynasty.[57] Since both Josephus and Eusebius claim to have taken their information directly from books written by Manetho, it is clear that the differences may never be satisfactorily explained unless heretofore missing texts are uncovered. Despite the uncertainty inherent in ancient sources, most scholars accept that Africanus' version of Manethos, which placed Apophis last on the list, was the correct one.

The end of the Hyksos reign is thought to have begun during the rule of the Egyptian Pharaoh Sekenenre Taa-Ken II (c. 1610-1606 BCE), who died in battle against the foreign enemy leaving his elder son, Kamose (1606-1539 BCE), to continue the assault. Kamose, as well, was killed before victory was assured, and it was his younger son, Ahmose I (1539-1514 BCE), who finally succeeded in driving the foreigners out of Egypt. Ahmose I delivered the final blow by destroying Avaris, and forcing the Hyksos into southern Palestine, inaugurating the era of the New Kingdom.

The fullest description of the expulsion of the Hyksos is found in an autobiography of Ahmose, son of Ibina (Ebana), a captain of a Nile vessel in the time of Ahmose I, who bore no relation to his famous namesake. Ahmose described how the siege of Avaris occurred between Years 7-17 of the reign of Ahmose I, and that he personally carried off four people who he kept as slaves

53 Finegan, Handbook of Biblical Chronology, 218.
54 Josephus, "Against Apion," <u>The Complete Works of Josephus,</u> I.14, 611.
55 Ibid.
56 Redford, History and Chronology of the Eighteenth Dynasty of Egypt, 41.
57 Ibid., 41-42.

when the city was despoiled. Following the fall of Avaris, Ahmose I moved his army north to the city of Sharuhen (Tell Farah), which was besieged for three years before being entered and despoiled in a similar fashion. The history related by Ahmose is consistent with that preferred by most historians.

As I have already alluded to, there are a number of reasons to believe that Joseph may have arrived in Egypt during the rule of the Hyksos, making a careful analysis of this era very important. The fact that Joseph was a Semite, and that the Egyptians were very distrustful of all foreign people, especially Semites, makes it very unlikely that he would have risen to the position of vizier during the reign of an Egyptian Pharaoh. The biblical story of Joseph ascribes the elevation of Joseph to this position as a reward for reading the Pharaoh's dream correctly, when the court magicians were unable to provide an explanation. The Bible relates that Joseph was given a shave before leaving prison to interpret the Pharaoh's dream, and many scholars have pointed to this procedure as evidence against the ruler being of Hyksos descent because only the Egyptians were clean-shaven, and it would not have been needed if the Hyksos were ruling at the time. I do not find the cleansing of a prisoner who had spent a long time in jail, however, to be an unusual precaution, no matter who was sitting on the throne at the time, and the elevation of Joseph to the role of vizier seems to be more consistent with the actions of a Hyksos Pharaoh, than a native Egyptian.

The generally accepted timeline of Patriarchal chronology would also fit nicely with Joseph living during this era, as will be discussed in more detail in chapters 3 and 6, since Abraham is most often placed at the beginning of the second millennium BCE. Joseph was in the fourth generation which followed, and so his living c. 1700 BCE is a plausible assumption.[58] An Hellenistic tradition preserved in Syncellus (ninth century CE), a Greek Orthodox Chronographer, went so far as to claim that the Pharaoh who raised Joseph to the vaulted position of vizier was actually Apophis, the last king of the Fifteenth Dynasty.[59]

It is interesting to note that Martin Bernal in *Black Athena* also placed his theory of Egyptian colonization of Greece during the Hyksos era, when "the amalgam of local Indo-European with Egyptian and Levantine influences that we call Greek civilization was first and lastingly formed."[60] He portrayed the Hyksos as a mixture of Indo-Aryan, Hurrian, and Syria-Palestine elements who were overwhelmingly Semitic speaking. Shortly after securing their authority in Egypt, they invaded Crete c. 1730 BCE, and established themselves as rulers, rebuilding the palaces, and introducing the sphinx and griffin as official emblems.

---

58 The lives of the Patriarchs totaled 307 years. Abraham was 100 years old when Isaac was born, Isaac was 60 years old when Jacob and Esau were born, and Jacob was 147 years old when he died. Gen 21:5; 25:26; 47:28.

59 Redford, History and Chronology of the Eighteenth Dynasty of Egypt, 42.

60 Bernal, Black Athena, II.494.

They then imparted both their own culture, and that of the Cretans, as well as an alphabet; unifying many of the ancient beliefs of Eastern and Cretan influence on Greek civilization. This chronology is somewhat earlier than the common representation of the Mycenaean Age as lasting from 1650-1200 BCE, and his view of Egyptian influence during the Hyksos era is not accepted by most scholars of the era, as evidenced by the fact that the records preserved from the great archive of Mari on the Upper Euphrates, which was destroyed c. 1760 BCE, do not even mention Egypt. But as I mentioned above, the standard timeline for the second phase of Hyksos rule is from 1650-1550 BCE, and while the Exodus could not take place this early if Joseph was in Egypt at this time, it is possible that the Exodus did take place in the fifteenth century BCE, as I will discuss in chapter 6, and if my theory of Hebrew migration to Mycenae is true, and the Exodus took place near the time of the expulsion of the Hyksos from Egypt, then facets of the Egyptian culture which have been ascribed to the Hyksos by Bernal could then be due to Hebrew immigrants who also brought their unique legends, which later became incorporated into the Old Testament.

5. New Kingdom (Dynasties 18-20), 1550-1069 BCE

The New Kingdom is a critical period to the dating of the Exodus for it is during this era that most biblical scholars believe that the departure of the Hebrews from Egypt actually took place. Although no contemporary Egyptian archive ever mentioned that a mass emigration of slaves occurred, the lack of a specific historical reference does not negate the historical certainty of the event, since the movement of Semitic tribes was very common into and out of Egypt during the New Kingdom, and Egyptian chroniclers would not have been expected to single out the Hebrews, particularly if their success was not favorable to Egyptian interests. The Egyptians generally only recorded victories on their temple walls and monuments, and the loss of a large number of Hebrew slaves, associated with an embarrassment to the Egyptian Pharaoh, would not have been seen as worthy of eternal memory on temple inscriptions. It is also not surprising that the Exodus was not mentioned by Levantine archivists at the time, since the majority of the wandering of the Hebrews occurred in the rural landscape, away from the heavily populated *Via Maris*. Caravan trade prospered during the economic boom-days of the New Kingdom, and the connecting thoroughfares were always congested with large numbers of Bedouins, who would have been indistinguishable from the congregation led by Moses. This is particularly true of the group of inhabitants known as the Habiru, and the resemblance between the Hebrews and the Habiru, as will be discussed more thoroughly in the next chapter.

It is also important to note that emigration to Mycenae by the dissident Hebrews would also have been relatively easy during this era, for many merchants from Crete and Mycenae were based in Egypt at this time, as evidenced by the appearance of names such as *Pa-Keftyw* (Cretan/Mycenaean) in Egyptian documents from the New Kingdom. If Moses grew up in the royal household during the Eighteenth Dynasty, he would have had contact with many Mycenaen representatives, and would have likely kept his advisers appraised of their value during the years they wandered through the wilderness before passage into the Promised Land. When the dissident Hebrews decided to flee the parricidal repercussions imposed by the Mosaic Code, they would have certainly seen Mycenae as the most likely location to provide a safe-haven.

A. *The Eighteenth Dynasty, 1550-1295 BCE*

The most likely era for the birth of Moses is during the Eighteenth Dynasty, when Egypt expanded into a world power following the defeat of the Hyksos regime. The Bible mentions that Moses was born when the Pharaoh "who did not know Joseph" came to the throne, and if this was a reference to Joseph's affiliation with the hated Hyksos, then the Pharaoh of the Exodus was likely to have been part of the early Eighteenth Dynasty, since this period directly followed the expulsion of the Hyksos from Egypt. The Eighteenth Dynasty covers parts of four centuries, however, and so it is necessary to look at the details of each ruler to try and identify which one in particular was the man, or woman, whose anger at the Hebrews caused the decree to kill each newborn male child to be disseminated throughout the land.

As described above, the final expulsion of the Hyksos was due to the efforts of Ahmose I, and it is for this reason that Manetho placed him at the beginning of the Eighteenth Dynasty, despite the fact that he and his brother Kamose were the scions of Sekenenre and Ahhotpe, who ruled during the Seventeenth Dynasty. In the conventional chronology, Ahmose I ruled from 1539-1514 BCE,[61] although most scholars, using the observations of the rising of the star Sothis in the ninth year of the reign of his son and successor Amenhotep I (1514-1493 BCE), have dated his reign to an earlier period, c. 1570-1546 BCE.[62] Although this variance of forty years is not great, it still represents a significant interval when attempting

---

61 Rohl, Pharaohs and Kings, A Biblical Quest, 20.

62 Tadmor, "Chronology of the Ancient Near East in the Second Millennium BCE," 84. The placement of this particular astronomical date has been debated since the 1870s CE, when Georg Ebers first acquired a calendar found at Thebes which was datable to the ninth year of Amenhotep I, and recorded the helical rising of Sothis on the ninth day of the third month of Shemu. Rohl, Pharaohs and Kings, A Biblical Quest, 131. This so-called "Ebers Calendar" has been used to calculate an ascension either c. 1575-1573 BCE, the "Higher" date if the rising was observed at Memphis, or c. 1550-1548 BCE, the "Lower" date if the observations was made at Thebes. Tadmor, "Chronology of the Ancient Near East in the Second Millennium BCE," 85.

to delineate a more exact chronology of the Exodus.

As part of the reformation of Egyptian authority, Ahmose I pursued the fleeing Hyksos force into Palestine, and once there he turned the princes of Retenu into puppet governments, thereby solidifying Egyptian control throughout the Levant, and assuring that the Hyksos would not be able to gather their forces and return to Egypt once he left for home. This imperialistic transformation required a significant commitment of troops to a campaign far from home, and the resultant lack of security left the country at risk, possibly explaining why the Pharaoh "who did not know Joseph" was worried about the size of the Hebrew slave population at home. If Ahmose I identified the Hebrew slaves with the hated Hyksos invaders, he may very well have ordered all of the male Hebrew newborns to be killed as part of a defensive strategy to reduce the future military threat against homeland security. Such an aggressive reprisal would have clearly fulfilled criteria for his being labeled as the Pharaoh "who did not know Joseph," referring to the prior favored station initially placed upon Joseph's family. Under this timetable, the Exodus would have taken place eighty years later, in the fifteenth century BCE, two centuries earlier than the majority of scholarly opinions, but within the period of time that many scholars have estimated the Exodus to have taken place, as will be discussed in chapter 6. This scenario, would likely label Thutmose III (1479-1425 BCE) as the Pharaoh of the Exodus, since he ruled about eighty years after Ahmose I.

The next Pharaoh to rule in the Eighteenth Dynasty was Amenhotep I, the eldest of the surviving sons of Ahmose I. In the conventional chronology, he ruled from 1514-1493 BCE,[63] with most scholars favoring an earlier date of 1551-1528 BCE.[64] Like his father, Amenhotep I continued to conduct military expeditions into Palestine and Syria, but he met only minimal resistance from local Palestinian powers, since the decline of Hyksos support left the region without a significant defensive military force. The need to maintain a show of military force, however, continued to leave security at home on a fragile basis, thereby increasing the likely success of a mass emigration of Hebrew slaves. There is little reason to separate Ahmose I and Amenhotep I as fulfilling the designation of the Pharaoh "who did not know Joseph," and I will not attempt to argue for one or the other in this regard. Since Thutmose III ruled for fifty-four years, he would have likely still been the Pharaoh of the Exodus if Amenhotep I, rather than Ahmose I, was the Pharaoh "who did not know Joseph," so it is not necessary to try and argue for one or the other.

Amenhotep I failed to sire a male child, and his successor, Thutmose (Thuthmosis) I, although not from strict royal blood, became the primary claimant to the throne through his marriage to Princess Ahmose, the sister of Amenhotep I. Manetho retained him within the Eighteenth Dynasty, despite

---

63 Rohl, Pharaohs and Kings, A Biblical Quest, 20.
64 Wente & Van Siclen, "A Chronology of the New Kingdom," 218.

the fact that the bloodline was altered, because there was little social change in Egypt which accompanied his appointment. In the conventional chronology, he ruled in the fifteenth century, from 1493-1481 BCE,[65] although most scholars place his reign near the end of the sixteenth century, c. 1528-1516 BCE.[66] He was an adept military man, and his prowess initiated a line of Thutmoside kings who would carry Egypt into her most glorious period, characterized by great military strength, territorial expansion and material prosperity. Like Amenhotep I, Thutmose I continued to campaign actively in the Levant, but he did not face strong opposition until he reached northern Syria, where the kingdom of Mitanni had begun to extend its influence from its center in the Khabur Valley, in north-western Mesopotamia. The strength of the Mitanni forces prevented Thutmose I from taking control of the Syrian region, but jurisdiction over the vital traffic arteries which carried goods throughout the Levant remained under Egyptian control.

Because the Thutmoside kings were so powerful in the region of the Levant, many scholars believe that the Exodus could not have been successful during their reign. This reasoning is flawed, however, for it must be remembered that to control such a vast area, Egyptian patrols were spread over a wide region near the *Via Maris*, and since the Hebrews likely wandered in regions away from this population density, Egyptian strength was not necessarily an impediment to success. The necessity to maintain a show of force along the main highway not only deleted the military presence at home, but left the more desolate areas in the Levant safer for traveling bands of refugees. In addition, since the Egyptians were attempting to extend their authority into Syria, military forces were extended far to the north, and the escape of Hebrew slaves who did not threaten Egyptian interests would not have been likely to cause a change in the deployment of troops back to the Sinai wilderness. Since the reign of Thutmose I was only about forty-five years later than Ahmose I, he does not fit the designation of the Pharaoh of the Exodus, which took place when Moses was eighty years old, but it is still possible that he could have been the Pharaoh "who did not know Joseph," although this extended hiatus from the expulsion of the Hyksos seems too long to consider it likely that he would have retained enough hatred for the Hebrews to order an infanticide of an entire generation of newborn male children. If he was the Pharaoh "who did not know Joseph," then Amenhotep II (1382-1344 BCE), rather than Thutmose III (1479-1425 BCE) would have been the Pharaoh of the Exodus, placing the migration at the beginning of the fourteenth century BCE, which is not a time-frame favored by scholars, but still a possibility, as I will discuss in chapter 6.

Thutmose II, the son of Thutmose I and Mutnofret, acceded to his father's

---

65 Rohl, Pharaohs and Kings, A Biblical Quest, 20.
66 Wente & Van Siclen, "A Chronology of the New Kingdom," 218.

throne after his two older brothers, Wadjmose and Amunmose, died during the father's reign. In the conventional chronology he ruled from 1481-1479 BCE,[67] although other scholars have placed his ascension as early as 1518-1504 BCE.[68] He was married as a boy to his half-sister, Hatshepsut (Hashepsowe), the elder daughter of Thutmose I and Queen Ahmose, in order to strengthen his own right to the throne, and although he did not have any male children with this Great Wife, he did have a son, the future Thutmose III, with one of his lesser wives. Thutmose II did not survive as king for very long, and after his death, Hatshepsut relished the possibility of sitting on the throne of Egypt in the role of Pharaoh, rather than simply as Queen. Her ambitious desire to rule Egypt in this exalted manner was not entirely unique, for there had been two previous Queens who had functioned in a similar manner: Queen Nitocris, who Manethos placed at the end of the Sixth Dynasty (c. 2152 BCE); and Queen Sebeknofru, who ruled at the end of the Twelfth Dynasty (1763-1759 BCE).[69] Not only did Hatshepsut believe that this precedent would favor her elevation to the role of Pharaoh, she also maintained that she had a stronger claim to the throne than Thutmose III, since she was the daughter of a king by his Great Wife, and the Great Wife of a King as well, whereby Thutmose III was only the son of a lesser wife, by a father who himself was only the son of a lesser Queen. Although this argument was logical from the standpoint of bloodline purity, pharaonic succession in ancient Egypt had almost always been patrimonial, with a man who lacked a genetic royal lineage being elected to the role of Pharaoh by marrying the daughter of a king.

Hatshepsut is very interesting, for not only does she provide historical evidence linking her with the Semites, but as a woman she can also be considered as possibly being the Egyptian princess who saved the infant Moses when he was discovered floating at the edge of the Nile river. I will discuss this in more detail shortly. Thutmose II must have been aware of his wife's ambition to try and become Pharaoh, for he appointed the young Thutmose III as his successor while he was still alive, apparently in an attempt to secure his son's future position. Although co-regency was not unusual once an elder son achieved the age of majority, such a move was quite rare in the history of royal succession while the son was still of minor age. As fate would have it, Thutmose II died before his son was considered old enough to rule by himself, and so his attempts to counterbalance his wife's ambition failed, and Hatshepsut was made regent of Egypt until her stepson came of age.

After two or three years of acting as regent to Thutmose III, Hatshepsut threw away her pretext of temporary rule, and crowned herself Pharaoh. This act of ruling as an actual King without the assumption of rule as Queen is unparalleled

---

67 Rohl, Pharaohs and Kings, A Biblical Quest, 20.

68 Wente & Van Siclen, "A Chronology of the New Kingdom," 218.

69 Montet, Lives of the Pharaohs, 81.

in the long history of Egyptian royalty, and since it took place near the time when I believe the Exodus occurred, it is necessary to examine her reign more closely. In the conventional chronology, Hatshepsut ruled from 1473-1458 BCE,[70] although others have placed her reign as early as 1503-1483 BCE.[71] She seems to have been an effective ruler, maintaining Egyptian authority in the Levant and expanding the commercial success of the country through a remarkable expedition she arranged to the Terraces of Incense, in the land of Punt.[72] Egypt had developed extensive trade routes to Punt by the time of her reign, but the standard circuit required a time-consuming and expensive trip down the Nile River, followed by an overland trek to the final destination, where access to the Red Sea (Erythrean Sea) was available. Rather than depending on such an arduous route, she arranged to send a fleet of five *kebenit* ships, built and launched at Byblos by Phoenicians, via the Red Sea, a much shorter route of travel that greatly vitalized the Egyptian economy.[73] It is likely that this achievement was made possible through the support of Semites, since a large number of workers with Semitic names is preserved in records from an Egyptian dockyard near Sakkara during her reign, indicating that many of these ships were likely manned by Semitic sailors from Canaan and Syria.[74]

As I previously mentioned, some scholars have questioned whether Hatshepsut could have been the princess who found the baby Moses floating in the Nile river, but this would have meant that Thutmose II would have had to be the pharaoh "who did not know Joseph," a circumstance quite unlikely since it was many years beyond the expulsion of the Hyksos, and no other data exists to explain elevated concern over the rise in the Hebrew slave population. In addition, the obvious stature of Hatshepsut as both a daughter and wife to a Pharaoh would have made it difficult to hide an adopted son from the court records, so I do not believe that she was the savior of the future Hebrew messiah.

Although the success of Hatshepsut was immortalized in an exceptional temple in the bay of the cliffs at Deir el-Bahari, known as the "Sublime of Sublimes," or *Djeser-Djeseru*, her engraved memory was not of lasting value, for Thutmose III

---

70 Rohl, Pharaohs and Kings, A Biblical Quest, 20.

71 Stiebing, Out of the Desert?: Archaeology and the Exodus/Conquest Narratives, 38.

72 The exact location of the land of Punt is not known, with many placing it along the Somali coast. The products of the country, however, included goods that were highly coveted by the luxury-loving Egyptians, such as apes, ivory, gold, spices, and dwarfs. Mertz, Temples, Tombs & Hieroglyphs: A Popular History of Ancient Egypt, 149.

73 Scenes of the ships sailing to, and returning from, Punt are shown throughout the Deir el Bahri temple, clearly indicating how important Hatshepsut felt the trade was to her overall status. Mertz, Temples, Tombs & Hieroglyphs: A Popular History of Ancient Egypt, 150.

74 Bass, "Sea and River Craft in the Ancient Near East," 1426.

sought retribution in Year 51of his reign for the taking of his rightful throne by expunging her name on all of her monuments throughout Egypt, including the date of her death. His efforts were wasted, however, for modern Egyptologists have resurrected much of her history, and she remains today an amazing example of how far a feminine ancestor could go in managing the affairs of a primarily paternalistic society.

If Ahmose I was the Pharaoh "who did not know Joseph," then Thutmose III was most likely the Pharaoh of the Exodus, based upon the fact that Moses was eighty years old when he returned to Egypt. It is also possible, however, that he could have been the Pharaoh "who did not know Joseph" if he was reacting against Hatshepsut and her possible identity with Semitic supporters. Many Semitic prisoners-of-war were taken by the Pharaohs of the New Kingdom, including Thutmose III, and as their numbers grew to large proportions, concerns over homeland security could have worried Thutmose III as he made repetitive incursions into the Levant. Because Hatshepsut utilized foreign sailors and laborers in many of her expeditions, when Thutmose III retaliated against her memory, he may have included the Semites in his fervor to eliminate everything associated with her success, as well as concern with their growing numbers and the memory of the prior Semitic uprising. This would then mean that either Amenhotep III (1382-1344 BCE) or Amenhotep IV (1352-1336 BCE) would have sat on the throne of Egypt during the Exodus, and I will discuss the arguments for and against these possibilities in more detail in chapter 6. Note that this would clearly mean that Hatshepsut was not the princess who received Moses from the Nile River, since the edict would have taken place after her death.

The aggressiveness of Thutmose III against his stepmother was a reflection of his attitude against all Egyptian foes throughout his reign. In the conventional chronology, he ruled from 1479-1425 BCE,[75] but others have placed his accession at various dates, ranging from 1515-1490 BCE, depending on lunar fixations which were recorded during the reign of Amenhotep I.[76] After ascending the throne, Thutmose III set about to subdue Asia in Year 2 of his independent reign, identifying the princes of Palestine and Syria as having been allied with the rule of his detested stepmother. To oppose his forces, the Asiatics had gathered a force

---

75 Rohl, Pharaohs and Kings, A Biblical Quest, 20.

76 These include May 7, 1515 BCE, the so-called "High Date," which agrees with a Memphis Sothic sighting; May, 4, 1504 BCE, the so-called "Intermediate Date;" and May 1, 1490 BCE, the so-called "Low Date," which agrees with a Theban observation. Tadmor, "Chronology of the Ancient Near East in the Second Millennium BCE," 85. The "High Date" is generally rejected by scholars, since it does not leave enough time for the combined reigns of both Thutmose I and II. The "Intermediate Date" determination has also generally been disregarded, and most scholars who base their estimations on the Sothic dating choose 1490-1436 BCE as the most likely dates of Thutmose III's reign. Ibid., 89.

which included the armies of 330 princes at Megiddo in Palestine. Megiddo stood upon a ridge on the Plain of Jezreel, between the hills of Galilee to the north and those of Samaria and Judaea to the south, guarding the entrance to the Plain and serving as a supply-post for the trading caravans which traversed this route between Egypt and Mesopotamia. Because of its vital position, it was known as the great hinge of the Fertile Crescent, and nations fought over control of the city from the beginning of the second millennium BCE to modern times. The city lay at the end of a narrow pass which forced travelers to proceed in single file, and the military advisers of Thutmose III therefore cautioned him to take a diversionary approach when he marched against the forces gathered there. This would have required the army to circumvent the pass, and attack from a more northerly direction, however, an approach which Thutmose III decided would have been expected by the Asiatic forces, and rigorously defended. He therefore ignored the advice of his generals, and marched his army straight through the narrow pass, placing his fate, as he later claimed, directly in the hands of the god Re. Just as Thutmose III had predicted, the Asiatics had not foreseen this move, and had left the pass undefended. Thutmose III was able to thoroughly rout the forces which surrounded the city, claiming that it was divine intervention that assured his victory, although most historians believe that the incredible stupidity of the Asiatics in leaving the pass unprotected was a more likely reason for his success. Whatever the true explanation, the Egyptian army totally destroyed the Asiatic force which had gathered at Megiddo, and set up a strict siege, encamping outside the city for seven months until the town folk were forced to surrender because their food supplies had run out.

This dramatic victory over the combined enemy forces at Megiddo allowed Thutmose III to break the back of Levantine resistance at the very start of his reign, and for the next twenty years he kept the authority of Egypt in the forefront of Near Eastern politics by an annual show of force. His impressive list of victories is recorded at Karnak (modern-day Luxor), revealing that over 350 Levantine cities fell to his military might. In order to prevent future insurrections by the inhabitants, he organized a political network of administrative centers which were managed by selected native princes, but watched over by resident Egyptian commissioners. Garrisons were stationed in fortified towns, and conscripts from the local inhabitants, as well as foreign mercenaries, were inducted into service, in order to conserve the number of Egyptian troops needed to maintain security. The only regions which Thutmose III did not control during this period of time were those located in central and southern Palestine, areas which were favored by the Hebrews during the Exodus and Conquest.

By Year 33 of his reign, Thutmose III attempted to extend his control northward into Syria, crossing the Euphrates River and ravaging Naharin, the western province of the empire of Mitanni. He defeated the Mitanni forces by Year

35, and seven years later finally conquered Kadesh-on-Orontes. Hostilities were then abated when an agreement was reached with the king of Mitanni whereby Egyptian authority in the region would be recognized, and appropriate gratuities would be paid. By the end of his rule, Egyptian dominance in western Asia, which had been first built up by Thutmose I, was reestablished, and according to many Egyptologists, the extent of his dominion made him "the greatest pharaoh to ever occupy the throne of Egypt."[77] Unlike the fate of the Mycenaeans following their victory in the Trojan War, the Egyptians parlayed their victory at Megiddo into a long-lasting success.

Because Thutmose III was so powerful and active throughout the Levant, many historians believe that the Exodus could not have succeeded during his tenure as Pharaoh. They base this opinion on his firm control of the region, and his eventual domination of the Mitanni, indicating a numerical superiority in forces which would have prevented a successful withdrawal from Egypt. In some ways, however, I believe his exploits make success even more likely, since the bulk of his army would have been busy on maneuvers along the *Via Maris*, the major thoroughfare for trade in the region. His topographical list mentioned 119 towns in Palestine and southern Syria which were conquered by his army, none of which were in the central and southern regions of Palestine, where the Hebrews fled and wandered for the ensuing forty years. In addition, if the Exodus from Egypt occurred while Thutmose III was on a military maneuver deep in the Levant, the defensive force left at home may not have been large enough to offer much resistance to the departure of a large number of Hebrew slaves. This distribution of the army would favor a successful outcome of the Exodus, and would also explain why the Egyptian records were more concerned with the victories of Thutmose III, than with his failure to maintain control over a large contingent of Hebrew slaves. For this reason, in addition to the likelihood that Ahmose I was the Pharaoh "who did not know Joseph," I believe that Thutmose III was the Pharaoh during the Exodus, and I will discuss this in greater detail in Chapter 6.

The death of Thutmose III was followed by another attempt to challenge Egyptian authority across the ancient Near East, much like occurred when he first ascended the throne. His son, Amenhotep II, became king and ruled from 1427-1392 BCE in the conventional chronology,[78] although most historians place his reign from 1453-1426 BCE.[79] Amenhotep II immediately found himself threatened by several Asiatic cities which rose in rebellion following his ascension, hoping to take advantage of the change in political power, but the son quickly showed himself to be the equal of his father, and he subdued all the enemy

77 Hayes, The Scepter of Egypt, Part II: The Hyksos Period and the New Kingdom (1675-1080 B.C.), 114, 116.

78 Rohl, Pharaohs and Kings, A Biblical Quest, 20.

79 Redford, Akhenaten, The Heretic King, 13.

forces he faced in short notice. Continuing his campaign against rebellious cities all along the *Via Maris*, he maintained the strict control which his father had instituted, bringing back over ninety thousand captives in Year 9 alone, including 127 Asiatic princes, 36,300 Hurru, 15,200 Shasu, and 3,600 Habiru warriors.[80] The constant presence of Amenhotep II's forces throughout the Levant created a solid political framework, similar to that of Thutmose III, but his many victories against the rulers of local city-states was not matched by success in Syria, and he could not prevent the resurgence of the Mitannians, who gathered a formidable force in Syria and eventually forced him to make a treaty which gave all of northern Syria back to Mitanni. Once again, since the primary focus of his forays were along the *Via Maris*, an Exodus of Hebrews into the central region of Canaan could have been successful, making it possible that he was the Pharaoh during the Exodus, rather than his father.

The next Pharaoh, Thutmose IV, was the son of Amenhotep II and his chief wife, Ti'a. In the conventional chronology, he ruled from 1392-1382 BCE,[81] although others have placed his reign as early as 1426-1416 BCE.[82] With the rule of Thutmose IV, we enter into the fourteenth century BCE, an era supported by some scholars as the date of the Exodus, although most still favor either the fifteenth or thirteenth centuries BCE. The kingdom Thutmose IV inherited had suffered few losses since the time of his grandfather, Thutmose III, and although Semitic Bedouins continued to pose a constant threat to law and order in distant regions throughout the Sinai and Levant, their effect in Egypt itself was now minimized by the large number of Egyptian garrisons that formed the Prince's Wall across the entire Sinai border. Hostilities between Egypt and Mitanni had been reduced by a marriage between Thutmose IV and a daughter of Artatama I (1410-1400 BCE), and the expansion of Hittite power into the region of Syria was not yet significant enough to threaten the security of Egypt. This allowed Thutmose IV to effectively control Palestine and the coastal region of Syria up to Ugarit, as well as Damascus, the Beqa' Valley of Lebanon, and the lands of Qadesh and Amurru in southern Syria.

The successive reigns of Thutmose III, Amenhotep II, and Thutmose IV were truly the pinnacle of Egyptian power in the Late Bronze Age, but a radical alteration in Egyptian authority was about to take place as the most intriguing era in Egyptian history began at the start of the fourteenth century BCE. The reigns of the next two Pharaohs, Amenhotep III and Amenhotep IV (Akhenaten), are generally labeled as the "Amarna Age," from the name of the capital city which Amenhotep IV built at Tell el-Amarna after he began his religious revolution which was to create instability in the political structure throughout the entire

---

80 Wilson, The Culture of Ancient Egypt, 201.
81 Rohl, Pharaohs and Kings, A Biblical Quest, 20.
82 Redford, Akhenaten, The Heretic King, 13.

Near East. The city lay on the middle Nile river, 200 miles south of Memphis, which at that time was the administrative capital of the country, and 250 miles north of Thebes, the New Kingdom's religious and economic center. By the time of its completion, it enclosed an area of over seventy-seven square miles, and housed a population which has been estimated at between twenty thousand and fifty thousand people. Amenhotep IV maintained the city as his primary place of residence, and when the site was excavated in 1887 CE, nearly 400 clay tablets were discovered that turned out to be letters of exchange between the Egyptian Pharaohs and rulers of the Near East, including city-states in Babylonia, Assyria, Mitanni, Hatti, Arzawa and Cyprus.[83] Although many of the letters are incomplete and undated, and probably only represent a small percentage of the letters actually written, the discovery of this cache of correspondence has provided the best surviving information on the political situation in the Near East during the fourteenth century BCE.

The primary message gleaned from the numerous records found at el-Amarna centers around messages from local Palestinian kings who were loyal to Egyptian administrators that they were being attacked by foes of Egypt and needed military assistance in order to retain control of their land. The complaints painted a picture of instability and strife which stretched across all of Palestine, from the Egyptian border to the city of Ugarit, in Syria. Over fifty of the Amarna letters were written by King Rib-addi of Byblos (mid-fourteenth century BCE), who moaned that he was being besieged by both Suppiluliuma I (1380-1340 BCE), the Hittite king who had begun to expand his forces from their base in Anatolia to Syria and Palestine, and by Abdi-ashirta of Amurru (c. 1300s BCE), the king of the coastal district that extended northward from the level of Lebanon to Aradus. Abdi-ashirta had allied himself not only with the Hittites, but also with the Habiru, a group of Semitic people who ranged throughout Palestine and who many scholars believe may have represented Hebrews who took part in the Exodus, thereby providing a basis for identifying the Hebrews in contemporary historical records prior to the Merneptah Stele. Although Amenhotep III had made an occasional show of force in support of Byblos and other important Levantine cities, Amenhotep IV thoroughly neglected the region of Palestine as he struggled to carry out a religious revolution in Egypt whereby all of the gods, except for the sun-god (Aten), were suppressed. His inattention to foreign matters was reflected in ever-increasing demands for assistance by the loyal Levantine princes

---

83 About 350 of the letters were from the reign of Amenhotep III, and 25 from the reign of Amenhotep IV, although there is dispute on these figures since the recipient Pharaoh is frequently not named. Manley, The Penguin Historical Atlas of Ancient Egypt, 80. In the letters where the Pharaoh was actually identified, there were ten to Amenhotep III and ten to Amenhotep IV. Aldred, Akhenaten, King of Egypt, 191. The archive began somewhere about Year 30 of the reign of Amenhotep III, and continued throughout the reign of Amenhotep IV. Reeves, Ancient Egypt: The Great Discoveries, 75.

who were unable to withstand the pressures of both the Hittite and Habiru forces. Since Egyptian interest in the region was at an all-time low during the reign of Amenhotep IV, many historians look to the Amarna Age as an opportune time for the Exodus of the Hebrews to succeed. For this reason, I will discuss the reign of these two Pharaohs in greater detail.

Amenhotep III, according to the conventional chronology, ruled from 1382-1344 BCE,[84] but most estimates place his reign from as early as 1416-1377 BCE.[85] He was the son of Thutmose IV and Mutemwiya, a woman of whom little is known, although it has been suggested that she may have been a Mitanni princess. In Year 2 of his reign, while still a teenager, he married a woman of non-royal origins, Queen Tiye.[86] This marriage would prove to be quite productive, providing him with two sons, including the future Amenhotep IV, and four daughters. He also wed two Syrian princesses, two Mitanni princesses, two Babylonian princesses, and one Arzawan princess, leaving some scholars to suggest that it was his matrimonial endeavors, rather than his military might, that was responsible for the fact that he never had to personally engage an enemy in war, despite reigning for thirty-eight years.[87] Continuing his policy of wedding prominent princesses, and typifying the Egyptian protocol of royal incest, he later in life married his eldest daughter Sitamun, by whom he also had several children, including two future Pharaohs, Smenkhkare and Tutankhamun. Through his prolific progeny, the scions of Amenhotep III would set the stage for royal intrigues which would upset the balance of power in the Levant for the next fifty years.

Amenhotep III was not only renowned for his marriages, he also proved to be an adept politician, maintaining stability throughout the Levant by dividing his vassal states into three administrative areas, each under the management of an Egyptian governor. One region, which included Palestine and the Phoenician coast up to Beirut, was run from Gaza; another, based in the Beqa' Valley at Lebanon (Kumidu), controlled Apu, which stretched inland to Syria and included

---

84 Rohl, Pharaohs and Kings, A Biblical Quest, 20.

85 Redford, Akhenaten, The Heretic King, 13.

86 She was the daughter of the commoners Yuya and Thuya (Tjuyu). The modern Egyptian author and historian Ahmed Osman has claimed that Yuya was actually the biblical Joseph, whose name in the Koran is Yussuf, thereby explaining why Joseph told his brothers that God had made him a "father to Pharaoh" (Gen 45:8), a term which had only been used to identify Yuya. In addition, Yuya was the first vizier in Egypt, the same position to which Joseph was appointed, and both men had two sons and were Semitic. Osman, The Hebrew Pharaohs of Egypt: The Secret Lineage of the Patriarch Joseph, 2-5. This supposition has not been generally accepted, as Joseph is dated by most authorities to a much earlier period of time.

87 His harem was estimated to number over one thousand women. Tyldesley, Nefertiti: Egypt's Sun Queen, 26-27.

Damascus; and a third, located in Syria (Simurru), was responsible for managing the coastal region of Amurru up to the city of Ugarit. He also increased trade with Mycenae, which became the primary force in the Aegean region following the fall of Minoan Crete. Amenhotep III claimed responsibility for the success of these international endeavors, as evidenced by his temple funerary inscriptions at Kom el-Hetan which claimed that his dominion extended to Mycenae, Troy and Knossos. During his rule, the sea routes around the Aegean were so congested with Egyptian ships that a statute base in his mortuary temple at Kom el-Hetan was inscribed with a series of fourteen name rings from prominent Aegean ports, including Phaistos, Mycenae, Ilios (Troy) and Knossos. The prominence of these commercial channels would have been known to Moses if he grew up in the Egyptian royal court during the Amarna Age, and if the Exodus took place in the thirteenth century BCE, as I will discuss in Chapter 6, this information would certainly have been known to his advisers, including those who would have joined the dissident Hebrews who decided to leave the Exodus during the parricidal reprisals.

Interest in labeling Amenhotep III as the Pharaoh "who did not know Joseph," and thereby naming one of his daughters as the princess who rescued Moses, has also arisen from the fact that his son Amenhotep IV instituted a monotheistic cult of Aten-worship which resembled the modifications Moses made in the patriarchal Hebrew faith. If Amenhotep III was the one to order the drowning of all male newborn Hebrews, then Moses would have lived in the palace complex, either before or during the time Amenhotep IV sat on the throne. This would have allowed the two men to interact and know of the unique feature of monotheism through direct contact, rather than by hearsay recollections of other men. While there is no clear reason to connect Amenhotep III with such a hatred of Hebrews to suggest he would have felt that such an infanticidal mandate was necessary, there is evidence that he abused the slave population in general, since the magnitude of his construction projects was very extensive. He undertook a program of self-glorification that was second to none in the history of Egypt, building many magnificent temples, previously unequaled in size and splendor. He was especially known for the erection of massive limestone shrines which would have required very heavy labor, and foremen given the task of assuring that the work would be completed in time may have used such tyrannical methods that the biblical compilers later identified him as the Pharaoh "who did not know Joseph," not so much because of his fear of a slave uprising, but rather of his dictatorial abuse of power over the slave population.[88] Under this scenario, the

---

88 His Malqata palace at Thebes was constructed largely of sun-dried mud-brick, the type of material the Hebrew slaves in the Bible were forced to make without straw. The full extent of his work is often obscured by the fact that many of the buildings were completed by later Pharaohs, such as Ramesses II, and therefore not ascribed to his hand.

edict to kill the male newborns may have been a result of the need to reduce time lost for maintenance of worthless infants, rather than a means of protective population-control. These projects could also fit his being the Pharaoh of the Exodus, however, a role which is supported by some scholars since he was the first Pharaoh to employ chariotry as a separate section of the army, thereby explaining the Egyptian chariot force which attacked the Hebrews at the Reed Sea.[89]

Egypt was at the pinnacle of her political power and the world was at peace throughout much of Amenhotep III's reign, but by the time of his death, her strength had begun to ebb as political unrest spread throughout the region of Canaan, leaving Amenhotep IV a legacy of chaos rather than strength. Amenhotep IV reigned, according to the conventional chronology, from 1352-1336 BCE,[90] although other scholars estimate his rule as early as 1378-1362 BCE.[91] He was not the eldest son of Amenhotep III, but inherited the throne only because his older brother Tuthmosis, who was named for his grandfather, tragically died a few years earlier. Tuthmosis had been groomed for the position of Pharaoh most of his life, having been given the prestigious role of High Priest of Ptah at the temple in Memphis in preparation for this inevitable event. How much the sudden death of his brother, and his resultant unexpected elevation to power, may have affected Amenhotep IV's actions to radically alter the religious structure of the country will never be known for sure, but shortly after acceding to the throne, he began a systematic breakup of Egyptian religious life that was to dramatically affect the balance of power in the Near East during his reign.

For reasons that are still unclear, Amenhotep IV became a zealous adherent of the cult of the sun-god Aten early in his reign, turning his back on the traditions of the older gods, and upsetting the balance of power which had developed over centuries between the royal court and the priestly caste. Religion was not only a monopoly on homage to the gods in ancient Egypt, it was also a powerful corporate structure which controlled vast sums of money and land, resembling the dominion of the Catholic Church in medieval Europe. Polytheistic beliefs had been long-held in Egypt, and each god had its own hierarchy of priests who managed the property allotted to them, controlling the finances of the region, and employing large numbers of people who were hired and fired at will. The extent of their wealth was dependent upon the prominence of the god they served, and

---

Reeves, Akhenaten, Egypt's False Prophet, 62.

89 Exod 14:9. Fletcher, Chronicle of a Pharaoh, The Intimate Life of Amenhotep III, 106. The first Pharaoh to be portrayed wearing a khepresh, ,or helmet of chariot fighters, was King Kamose, but the widespread use of chariot warfare took time to be perfected.. Luban, The Exodus Chronicles: Beliefs, Legends & Rumors from Antiquity Regarding the Exodus of the Jews from Egypt, 85-86.

90 Rohl, Pharaohs and Kings, A Biblical Quest, 20.

91 Tadmor, "Chronology of the Ancient Near East in the Second Millennium BCE," 89.

any attempt to alter the status quo by reducing the importance of one or another god was vigorously resisted, since the priests who served that deity would find their power reduced.

During the Eighteenth Dynasty, the state god Amun, whose temple was at Karnak, became combined with the ancient sun-god Re (Ra) to create Amun-Re, the most powerful of all the Egyptian gods at the time. Each deity continued to retain their separate identity, however, despite their functional incorporation into a single god, and so as Amun-Re's power increased at Karnak, the priests of Re never permitted his followers to take over their control of the temple at Heliopolis. A bitter struggle was thereby avoided by maintaining the status quo of priestly power within the dominion of each deity. Amenhotep IV, however, did not attempt to placate the priestly regime with his alterations, and in Year 2 of his reign he set out to replace the prominence of the presiding god Amun-Re with Aten in the divine hierarchy, eliminating the priests who were loyal to Amun and Amun-Re in temples throughout Egypt, and replacing them with those who favored Aten. Dissension over his actions spread throughout the religious community, as those in power were reluctant to simply give in to the whimsical intentions of a single Pharaoh, but while he sat on the throne there was little they could do but bide their time and plan for a return to power when times changed. Their patience was rewarded, for when Amenhotep IV died, his reforms were cast aside, and the prominence of Aten quickly fell like the setting sun in the west.

The importance of Aten as a deity did not begin with Amenhotep IV, but dated back to the beginning of the Twelfth Dynasty, when Amenemhet I was said to have flown to heaven to unite with Aten after his death. At that time, Aten was not a fully developed deity, but in the middle of the Eighteenth Dynasty, Aten became identified as the primary sun-god, thereby instituting the need for a priestly caste. The first evidence of an actual cult of Aten based at Heliopolis was seen during the reign of Amenhotep II (1427-1392 BCE), who had promoted joint allegiance to the sun-god and Amun.[92] Thutmose IV (1392-1382 BCE) further advanced the importance of Aten's divinity by identifying himself in his inscriptions as the "lord of what the Aten encircles," and he gave thanks to Aten, rather than to Amun, in the recordings of his military conquests.[93] Amenhotep III also publicly announced his solar allegiance, and promoted himself as "Aten-Tjehen," which literally means "the dazzling sun disk."[94] But although Aten was seen as an important deity to these earlier Eighteenth Dynasty Pharaohs,

92 Fletcher, Chronicle of a Pharaoh, The Intimate Life of Amenhotep III, 61. The walls of Amenhotep II's burial chamber are decorated with a complete version of the *Am Duat*, or "Book of What is in the Underworld," which described the king's nocturnal journey with the sun-god through the Underworld, and his rejuvenation as the sun arose the next day. Oakes & Gahlin, Ancient Egypt, 111.

93 Wilson, The Culture of Ancient Egypt, 210.

94 Fletcher, Chronicle of a Pharaoh: The Intimate Life of Amenhotep III, 61.

it was not until the reign of Amenhotep IV that devotion was limited to Aten alone. Amenhotep IV was so devoted to Aten that he changed his name from *Amen*hotep, which means "Amun is content," to Akhen*aten*, which means "Effective for Aten."[95] He erased the name of the god Amun from all of the monuments, and so avidly carried out his reforms that Egyptologists have labeled his changes as the only revolution in Egyptian history.[96] While this religious reform greatly affected life at the royal court, the population throughout Egyptian society continued to live according to the old religious customs, and Amenhotep IV's monotheistic revolution remained mostly confined to the royal family, and did not affect the polytheistic faith of the Egyptian populace.

Although the reason for Amenhotep IV's fixation on the sun-god has never been fully explained, many historians have hypothesized that his physical attributes made him envious of his predecessors, and rather than ineptly follow in their footsteps, he attempted to entirely alter the image of the country. He was physically weak and passive, and had none of the military prowess that so dominantly portrayed most of the Egyptian rulers. His body was portrayed so effeminately in various statutory reliefs that it was sometimes difficult to separate the figures of the King and Queen. He was generally shown with an elongated neck, broad hips, swelling breasts and plump thighs which have prompted suggestions by some physicians that he was suffering from an endocrine disorder, such as Froehlich's syndrome (adiposogenital syndrome). While the physical manifestations of Froehlich's Syndrome do indeed resemble some of the depictions of Amenhotep IV, patients with this disease are sterile, and if the historical record is true, this would mean than he could not have sired the children attributed to him. Shortly after coming to the throne at age sixteen years, Amenhotep IV married his beautiful cousin Nefertiti, and together they had six daughters: Meritaten, Meketaten, Ankhesenpaaten, Nefernefruaten, Neferneferure, and Sotepenre. For this reason, it is generally thought that his unusual statutory appearance was more likely due to artistic expression, than to a pathologic endocrine disease.[97]

Other historians have suggested that his religious alterations were due to an underlying bisexual nature, where he saw himself as both "the father and mother of mankind," causing him to seek an ever more harmonious relationship with

---

95 Kitchen, Pharaoh Triumphant, The Life and Times of Ramesses II, 11.

96 Hornung, Akhenaten and the Religion of Light, 87-88.

97 Numerous diseases have been suggested over the years to explain his unusual appearance, including Marfan syndrome, Wilson-Turner X-linked mental retardation syndrome, Frohlich syndrome (adiposogenital dystrophy), Klinefelter syndrome, androgen insensitivity syndrome, aromatase excess syndrome in conjunction with sagittal craniosynostosis syndrome, or Antley-Bixler syndrome or a variant form of that syndrome. Hawass, Gad, Ismail, Khairat, Fathalla, Hasan, Ahmed, Elleithy, Ball, Gaballah, Wasef, Fateen, Amer, Gostner, Selim, Zink, and Pusch, "Ancestry and Pathology in King Tutankhamun's Family," 639.

nature, and to concern himself with the matters of the mind and the spirit, rather than the body.[98] Under this theory, the daily cycle of night and day was more natural than any other divine act, and by elevating the sun-god to the level of monotheistic devotion, the Egyptians would be focusing their energy in the most appropriate direction, rather than dispersing their loyalties to hundreds of gods, as was prevalent in the Late Bronze Age. Such affection for the more natural aspects of life, however, would not normally be expected to totally overshadow distant dynastic issues, and Amenhotep IV so completely ignored the needs of the Levantine princes for military assistance during the years he sat on the throne, that the very defensive stability of the country was put at risk.

What seems most likely is that Amenhotep IV simply put the rest of the world out of his mind as he focused on altering Egypt to uplift the worship of Aten above all other gods. In Year 6 of his reign, as part of this religious change, he moved the capital from Thebes, which was dominated by the god Amun, to el-Amarna, which he named Akhetaten, or "the Place of the Effective Glory of the Aten." That Amenhotep IV expected all the nations to worship Aten can be seen in one of the wall paintings from the city which shows successive groups of Egyptians, Semites from Syria, Libyans and Nubians all reverently standing, kneeling, or falling upon their faces before the sun-god. This emulation went beyond the elevation of a single god to a position of authority in a polytheistic hierarchy, and clearly was intended as a form of monotheistic worship. What is even more incredible, is that not only did Amenhotep IV restrict the worship to Aten alone, he also forbade the depiction of Aten in any image or idol worship, something which had never before been part of Egyptian idolatry, and which closely resembled the commandments sent forth in the Mosaic Law. His efforts were short-lived, however, and the city which he hoped would become the central shrine for the worship of Aten was completely abandoned after his death.[99]

This adamant restriction of acceptable worship to a single god is what has suggested to many scholars who place the Exodus in the thirteenth century BCE that Atenism was the inspiration source for the monotheistic modifications made by Moses in the Ten Commandments.[100] Not only did Amenhotep IV make Aten the sole god to worship in the Egyptian religious hierarchy, but the procedure of worship was very similar to what would develop in the Bible for

---

98 Aldred, Akhenaten, King of Egypt, 235.

99 It should not be a surprise that the Egyptian populace and religious hierarchy resisted Amenhotep IV's attempts at the promotion of monotheism since there is good evidence that during the dynasty of his successors, over 1200 gods were worshiped throughout Egypt. Budge, The Gods of the Egyptians, vol. 1, x.

100 Wilson, "Egypt - The Kingdom of the 'Two Lands' 4. The Challenges to Power," 320. Sigmund Freud (1856-1939 CE) went so far as to argue that the Jewish religion which Moses promoted was actually the worship of Aten, which he learned in Egypt. Freud, Moses and Monotheism, 27.

honoring YHWH, with a temple containing a Holy of Holies where the spirit of the God resided, and priests who would attend ceremonies dressed in white vestments after purifying themselves before entering the Temple. Support for this view comes not only from the possible congruence of dates for the lives of Moses and Amenhotep IV, but also from similarities between *The Hymn to Aten*, which is a verse composition of the late Eighteenth Dynasty found carved on a wall of the tomb of Ay but generally ascribed to Amenhotep IV, and the 104th Psalm, which is part of the Old Testament liturgy ascribed to King David (1010-970 BCE). These two beautiful hymns are remarkably alike in both thought and structure, and the similarity has suggested that the Psalmist, who is dated to a much later time than Amenhotep IV, may have been aware of the prior work. Both authors, for example, extolled the Lord for His manifest works on earth: the Bible told how "You clothed the earth with floods of waters covering up the mountains;" while the Egyptian inscription told how "thou has set a Nile-flood in the sky, and it descendeth for them and maketh waves upon the mountains like the Great-Green to drench their fields in the villages."[101] The Bible further described how at night "the young lions roar for their food;" while the inscription said that "every lion is come forth from its lair and all snakes bite."[102] The Bible lamented that when the sun sets, "all is lost," and when "You gather up their breath, they die and turn again to dust;" while the inscription decried that "when thou settest in the western horizon, the earth is in darkness after the manner of death."[103] The Bible praised the Lord for he is "robed with honor and with majesty and light!;" while the inscription proclaimed how "thou art comely, great, sparkling, and high above every land, and thy rays enfold the lands to the limit of all that thou hast made."[104] The Bible further described how "the birds nest beside the streams, and sing among the branches of the trees;" while the inscription extolled that "birds taking flight from their nest, their wings give praise to thy spirit."[105] These similarities could simply be coincidental, but the congruence has suggested to some scholars that one author was aware of the writings of the other.

Dr. Shlomo Izre'el, Professor of Hebrew and Semitic Languages, Tel Aviv University, has gone even further in this similitude, pointing out that there are also similarities between Egyptian Amarna speech-forms and biblical Hebrew verses. Among the many Egyptian idiomatic conventions is the phrase "the strong arm of the king," which was also used by the scribes of Jerusalem and Tyre.[106] The Egyptian word for "strong hand" is denoted by the Sumerian logogram for "right hand," and is recalled in the Old Testament by the notation: "Your right hand,

---

101 Ps 104:7, <u>The Living Bible</u>, 485; Gardiner, <u>Egypt of the Pharaohs</u>, 226.

102 Ps 104:21, <u>The Living Bible</u>, 485; Gardiner, <u>Egypt of the Pharaohs</u>, 225.

103 Ps 104:29, <u>The Living Bible</u>, 485; Gardiner, <u>Egypt of the Pharaohs</u>, 225.

104 Ps 104:1-2, <u>The Living Bible</u>, 485; Gardiner, <u>Egypt of the Pharaohs</u>, 225.

105 Ps 104:12, <u>The Living Bible</u>, 485; Gardiner, <u>Egypt of the Pharaohs</u>, 225.

106 Izre'el, "The Amarna Letters From Canaan," 2415.

O Lord, is majestic in strength; Your right hand, O Lord, shatters the enemy."(107) Furthermore, in an Egyptian letter from Aziru, the son of Abdu-Ashirta and ruler of the Amorites in Amurru, there is the verse "what else should I seek: I seek the beautiful face of the king, my lord;" while in the Bible this appears as "'come,' my heart has said, 'seek my face.' I will seek Your face, O Lord."(108) Other passages also show similar rhythmical natures and metaphoric idioms which support the possibility of either a direct familiarity, or a common origin from indigenous colloquial sources.

What is more important than congruences in literary forms, however, which could simply indicate that the biblical compilers were aware of the Egyptian hymns, is whether Moses and Amenhotep IV can actually be shown to have awareness of each other's religious beliefs, and whether one may have directly influenced the faith of the other by their living together in the palace at the same time. This could be accepted as likely if Amenhotep III was the Pharaoh "who did not know Joseph," and ordered the killing of the Hebrew male newborns. If Moses was saved by one of the royal princesses in his palace, then Moses would have been raised in the same household as Amenhotep IV, and the two men may have then developed their religious principles together. This could have explained the biblical description of the flight of Moses to Midian, for when Amenhotep IV died, Moses would have been forced to flee Egypt as part of the general cleansing which took place after the death of the heretic king, similar to the actions of Sinuhe following the death of Amenemhet I. A possible interaction would also have been possible if the

Exodus took place during the rule of Amenhotep III, so that Amenhotep IV would have become aware of the power of YHWH during the Ten Plagues which were inflicted on Egypt before the Exodus, including the darkness which fell upon the land of Egypt, leaving only Goshen, where the Hebrews lived, bathed in sunshine. Amenhotep IV would have certainly taken notice of this, and seen the possible relationship between the sun and the power of the One and Only Almighty God, YHWH.

The Egyptian author Ahmed Osman has taken the remarkable similarity of the two monotheistic beliefs, and the likely fact that Moses was raised in the palace of Amenhotep III, one giant step further and claimed that Moses and Akhenaten were actually one and the same person, and that Akhenaten/Moses did not die in office, but rather was forced to leave Egypt by rebellious priests, and fled into the Sinai, taking with him much of the Hebrew population who had accepted Aten as the true God. He believes that the Levites functioned as his priests in the religion of Aten, and followed him into the Sinai, before returning to Egypt eighty years later to take part in the Exodus. The succeeding Pharaohs recorded his disappearance as a death, but his mummy has never been found

---

107 Exod 15:6. Ibid., 2416.
108 Ps 27:8. Ibid.

because it does not exist. Osman points to the Talmud, where it is explained that Moses fled Egypt after killing an Egyptian who was beating a Hebrew slave, and traveled to Ethiopia where he became an ally of the reigning king. When the king and Moses returned from an expedition, they found that Bil'am, son of Be'or, an Egyptian who had become one of the king's advisers, had usurped his throne during his absence, but they recovered the city, and when the king died, the Ethiopians claimed Moses as their own king.[109] Bil'am returned to Egypt and became a magician and adviser to the Pharaoh. Moses eventually abdicated his throne when the Queen wished her own son to take over as King, and returned to Sinai, where the biblical story continues. Like Akhenaten, who was both Pharaoh and High Priest in his new religion, Moses saw himself as both the High Priest and the king of the Hebrews during the Exodus.[110]

I do not believe that this claim of Osman that Moses and Akhenaten are one and the same person is true, since such a belief forces us to cast off much of recorded Egyptian history without any factual basis for an alternate explanation. I do think, however, that the two men may have influenced each other if they did indeed live at the same time. This requires an Exodus in the fourteenth or thirteenth century BCE, and I will discuss this further in Chapter 6.

Following the death of Amenhotep IV, according to standard Egyptian chronology, the royal court of Egypt became enmeshed in a series of intrigues to regain control of the throne, and undo the religious changes imposed by Atenism. Some scholars claim that Nefertiti, the wife of Amenhotep IV, immediately sought marriage outside Egypt, and wrote to the Hittite King Suppiluliuma I, requesting one of his sons in matrimony, promising to make the young man king of Egypt. Her ambitions were thwarted, however, when her prospective husband was murdered on the way to Egypt, most likely at the order of Smenkhare, who was in line to inherit the throne. Whether the story is true or not, Smenkhare ascended the throne and ruled from 1337-1336 BCE according to the conventional chronology,[111] although others place his rule as early as 1366-1363 BCE.[112] The parentage of Smenkhkare remains unclear, but some scholars believe he was a son of Amenhotep III and his daughter, Sitamun, and was therefore both a half-brother and a nephew of Amenhotep IV. Others, however, argue that he was either a brother of Tutankhamun, or a son of Amenhotep IV and Kiya, and that Nefertiti preferred Tutankhamun, and married him to her third daughter, Ankhesenpaaten, in order to regain control of the throne. The close physical resemblance between Tutankhamun and Smenkhkare, and recent evidence that

---

109 Osman, Moses and Akhenaten : The Secret History of Egypt at the Time of the Exodus, 22-23.

110 Ibid., 23.

111 Rohl, Pharaohs and Kings, A Biblical Quest, 20.

112 Tadmor, "Chronology of the Ancient Near East in the Second Millennium BCE," 89.

their blood groups are identical, supports the contention that they were indeed blood-brothers, although their exact lineage is still unclear.[113] Smenkhkare only reigned for two years and he died within a few months of his predecessor, so it is not likely that he played much of a role in the biblical tale of the Exodus, and was not responsible for any of the reactionary changes directed at Amenhotep IV's regime.

Tutankhamun, who is well-known today because of the discovery of his remarkably complete tomb by Howard Carter in 1922 CE, ascended the throne after the death of Smenkhkare, and ruled from 1336-1327 BCE, according to the conventional chronology,[114] with some scholars placing his reign as early as 1362-1349 BCE.[115] Soon after becoming king, he married Ankhesenpaaten, the daughter of Amenhotep IV and Nefertiti, and during his reign the revolutionary alterations of his father-in-law were finally put to rest, and the country returned to the religious hierarchy it had worshiped for centuries. Aten was relegated back to the position of a minor divinity under Amun, and the authority of the Amun priesthood was fully reinstated, an act thought by many scholars to have been guided by his wife and her grandfather Ay, the man who would follow Tutankhamun on the throne. In addition to reinstating the religious base of the country, Tutankhamun made social changes which were in conformity with prior Egyptian policy, such as resuming trade with Byblos, which had been interrupted during the reign of Amenhotep IV. His military successes stabilized the political situation in central Palestine, and returned Egypt to a position of authority throughout the Levant. On the Syrian border, however, Amurru had passed into Hittite vassalage, and although the Egyptians attained a victory at Kadesh-on-Orontes, their triumph in Syria was short-lived.

Tutankhamun ruled for three years at el-Amarna, and then transferred his residence to Thebes, changing his name from Tutankhaten, which had been given to him by his father, to Tutankhamun, and his Queen's name from Ankhesenpaaten to Ankhesenamun, reflecting the return in loyalty to Amun. As stated earlier, this type of activity would have supported the decision of Moses to flee Egypt, if he had been raised in the royal household with Amenhotep IV. Tutankhamun died before reaching his twentieth birthday, and was the last male descendant of the Thutmoside Pharaohs, for he failed to produce a male heir. With his death, the Eighteenth Dynasty began to draw to a close. Ay succeeded Tutankhamun on the throne, and according to the conventional chronology ruled from 1327-1323 BCE,[116] although other estimates place his reign as early as 1355-1349 BCE.[117]

---

113 Aldred, Akhenaten, King of Egypt, 293.
114 Rohl, Pharaohs and Kings, A Biblical Quest, 20.
115 Tadmor, "Chronology of the Ancient Near East in the Second Millennium BCE," 89.
116 Rohl, Pharaohs and Kings, A Biblical Quest, 20.
117 Tadmor, "Chronology of the Ancient Near East in the Second Millennium BCE,"

He was the grandfather of Tutankhamun's wife, and had been appointed vizier to the young Pharaoh, so it was natural for the throne to pass to him since he was able to carry out the complex tasks of Pharaoh on short notice. At such an advanced age, however, he was an unlikely choice to guide the country for very long, and many scholars believe that Nefertiti was the controlling force in Egypt during this period of time, directing the kingship along with Ay's Commander-in-Chief, General Horemheb, who would sit on the throne as co-regent. The partnership worked quite well, and the royal court carried on a semblance of ordered rule for the next two years. Upon the death of Ay, the royal line became extinct, as there were no male or female living descendants from any Pharaoh.

Manetho did not end the Eighteenth Dynasty here, however, but kept Horemheb as the last Pharaoh in line. Very little is known of Horemheb's family background, but he had a long history of prominence in the royal court, becoming the Great Commander of the army under Amenhotep IV, the King's Deputy under Tutankhamun, and the vizier under Ay. This regal standing across the reign of three Pharaohs made him the perfect choice to ascend the throne when the genetic thread of inheritance ended upon the death of Ay. According to the conventional chronology, he ruled from 1323-1295 BCE,[118] with others placing his reign as early as 1349-1319 BCE.[119] He continued the restorations begun by Tutankhamun, but took sole credit for all the changes by replacing the name of Tutankhamun on all the monuments with his own, and then demolishing many of the buildings and using the material to construct his own memorials. Since he had no male heir, he designated a long-standing military colleague of his, Pramesse, as senior vizier, thereby assuring that there would be an official heir to the kingdom. This young man would ascend the throne as Ramesses I, the founder of the famous Ramesside Dynasty, an era when most scholars believe the Exodus took place.

B. *The Nineteenth Dynasty, 1295-1186 BCE*

Because so many of the Pharaohs during the Nineteenth and Twentieth Dynasties came from the lineage of Ramesses I, Egyptologists refer to this era as the Ramesside period. The Nineteenth Dynasty is very important to any discussion of the Exodus of the Hebrews, since many scholars place the departure from Egypt during this era, specifically during the rule of Ramesses II, and for this reason, I will discuss the pharaonic succession of this era in greater detail.

Ramesses I belonged to a family from Avaris, in the north-eastern Delta, where for generations all the prominent men had been called Seti or Ramesses.

89.

118 Rohl, Pharaohs and Kings, A Biblical Quest, 20.

119 Tadmor, "Chronology of the Ancient Near East in the Second Millennium BCE,"
89.

Like Horemheb, he was not of royal blood, but ascended to the throne since he was the Pharaoh's vizier and close friend, and Horemheb had died without producing an heir. According to the conventional chronology, Ramesses I ruled from 1295-1294 BCE,[120] although some place his reign as early as 1314-1312 BCE.[121] The differences in the dates ascribed by various scholars for the reign of Ramesses I have become less significant by this time, and it is therefore possible to place contemporaneous events within the rule of a specific Pharaoh with greater accuracy. Ramesses I began the Nineteenth Dynasty by making immediate social and religious changes, including alterations in the hierarchy of the gods. He replaced the southern gods, Thoth and Amun, with the northern gods, Re, Seth and Ptah, and changed the working capital from the city of Thebes, which lay along the southern section of the Nile River, to Tanis, in the Delta, placing the Pharaoh's residence closer to the international concerns of Asia and the Mediterranean Sea. While these changes were similar to the alterations of Amenhotep IV in the sense that they modified the status quo, they were not radical enough to create dissension among those in power, and there was no major opposition to his decisions, either among the populace or the priesthood. Because of his advanced age, when he ascended the throne he almost immediately began to share the kingship with his middle aged son, Seti (Sethos) I. After ruling for only two or three years he died, leaving his son to carry out the alterations which would characterize Egyptian rule during this period of time. Since his reign was so short, few historians have characterized him as playing a major role in the Exodus.

Seti I, according to the conventional chronology, ruled from 1294-1279 BCE,[122] with some scholars placing his reign as early as 1315-1304 BCE.[123] By the time he ascended the throne, the effects of Egyptian isolation during the Amarna Age were still present throughout the Levant, and the whole of Palestine was hostile to Egypt, leaving only the fortresses of Beth-Shean, Megiddo, and Rehob in Egyptian hands. Seti I immediately set out in Year 1 of his reign to destroy an alliance of local princes in northern Palestine from the towns of Beth-Shean, Rehob, Hamath, Pella and Yanoam. His campaign extended from the Suez frontier to the hills of Galilee, and he proved to be an able commander, defeating the Habiru of Mount Jarmuth, near Beth-Shean, and then suppressing a rebellion by the governor of Hamath, in the Jordan Valley, who tried to conquer Beth-Shean. Prisoners from these wars were returned to Egypt as slaves, and if the Exodus took place under Ramesses II, it is possible that some of these captives joined the Hebrew congregation, providing vital information on where to find food, water and shelter during the forty years of wandering in the wilderness of

---

120 Rohl, Pharaohs and Kings, A Biblical Quest, 20.
121 Montet, Everyday Life in Egypt, xv.
122 Rohl, Pharaohs and Kings, A Biblical Quest, 20.
123 Mazar, "The Historical Development," 13.

Sinai and Canaan. To celebrate his victories over the Habiru resurgents, Seti I erected stelae at Beth-Shean, Karnak, and Tyre. Once Palestine was firmly under Egyptian control, he began to consolidate Egypt's position against the Hittites in the northern section of the region. As he extended the distance of his army from the motherland, he built more fortresses along the caravan route in Canaan, in order to protect against attacks behind his flank. This extension of the Prince's Wall would have made avoidance of the northern pathway to Canaan during the Exodus even more imperative during the Nineteenth Dynasty, than during the Eighteenth Dynasty, although this fact alone does not seem important enough to favor one date over the other on the Exodus timeline.

Although Seti I put Egypt back into a position of power and authority in the ancient Near East, it was his son, Ramesses II, who was to propel Egypt forward in more dramatic terms. Ramesses II ruled Egypt for over sixty-five years, an incredibly long period of time, even in our modern era. Referred to as King Sesostris by Herodotus (c. 490-420 BCE), and Sesoosis by Diodorus of Sicily (first century BCE), Ramesses II ruled from 1279-1213 BCE according to the conventional chronology and the Lower Chronology,[124] although others have reckoned the date of accession as 1304 BCE or 1290 BCE.[125] For my purposes, the debate over the accession dates is somewhat academic, for the variance is not great enough to significantly affect the possible relationship of Ramesses II to the Exodus.

During his long life, Ramesses II married eight principal wives, the most important of which was Nefertari. In his later years, he would boast of having sired over one hundred children, and his progeny were so numerous that they became a new privileged class in the country, bearing the seed of a god which made them distinct from other Egyptians. He is often named as the Pharaoh during the Exodus because he finished building the storage cities of Pithom and Ramesses, both of which are mentioned in the Bible as the cities from which the Exodus began, although the actual start of production is not recorded. He expanded his royal residence and administrative center in the northeast Delta into a vast domain, known as Ramesses, Pi-Ramesses the "House of Ramesses Beloved of Amun, Great of Victories," and used so much forced labor in the erection of these two cities that the construction would nicely fit the description of forced Hebrew labor in the Bible.

In the early part of his reign, Ramesses II enjoyed military success throughout the Levant, as did the majority of his predecessors. In Year 2, he defeated the Sherden pirates in a sea battle, initiating the beginnings of social unrest which would be created by the People of the Sea. In Year 4, there was a revolt in Canaan which forced him to mobilize his army and quell the disturbance, and

---

124 Rohl, Pharaohs and Kings, A Biblical Quest, 18, 20, 132.

125 Redford, History and Chronology of the Eighteenth Dynasty of Egypt, 185, 207-208.

this was followed up in Year 5 with a campaign where he marched into Syria and captured Amurru, putting Egypt once again into direct contact with the Hittites who controlled most of western Mesopotamia and northern Syria. That same year, he set out from his new capital in the eastern Delta (Piramesse), and traveled through Canaan and Galilee, up to the springs of the River Jordan beyond Lake Hulah, and then on to Kadesh-on-Orontes (now Tell Neby Mend), and the Beqa' Valley, between the Lebanon and the Anti-Lebanon mountain chains. Kadesh-on-Orontes was a strategically important city, for any northbound army from Egypt had to pass near the city in order to reach the Beqa' Valley. His decision to wrest control of the city from the Hittites was an understandable undertaking, but the campaign was to prove a fateful passage in Egyptian history for, as Nicolas Grimal, Professor of Egyptology at the Sorbonne University in Paris, stated, "it was there that one of the most famous battles in the history of the ancient Near East took place."[(126)] This engagement is probably the most well-known military encounter in ancient times, and detailed accounts from both Egyptian and Hittite texts have provided historians with a fascinating account of wartime maneuvers from the Late Bronze Age.

Kadesh-on-Orontes had initially been brought under Egyptian sovereignty during the reign of Seti I, but in recent years Hittite expansion from Mesopotamia had taken over control of the city. The Hittite King Muwatallis (c. 1320-1294 BCE) had gathered allies from Carchemish, Aleppo, Ugarit, Arzawa, Kizzuwadna, and some of the new People of the Sea, such as the Dardanians and Mysians, in order to gain control of the vital crossroads which ran through Kadesh, carrying commercial traffic throughout the ancient Near East. To meet this serious challenge to Egyptian authority, Ramesses II had reinforced his army with Canaanite units and mercenary troops from the People of the Sea, primarily the Lukka (Lycians), Denyen (Danuna), and the Sherden. The Hittite force was numerically superior, numbering about 37,000 foot soldiers, while Ramesses II had arrived with over 20,000 men, divided into four divisions of 5,000, each named for one of the gods Amun, Re, Ptah and Seth. When Ramesses II reached Kadesh-on-Orontes, two Bedouin Shasu who were employed as guides tricked him into believing that the Hittites were afraid of the Egyptian military prowess, and were hiding in the Aleppo region, north of Tunip. Ramesses II listened to their advice and marched his army directly toward the Hittite camp and into a trap, where he was encircled by 2,500 Hittite chariots which threatened destruction of his entire force. The Hittite army inflicted heavy casualties during their first attack, but when the Egyptians began to retreat, the Hittites paused to collect the valuable booty left behind, rather than following up their initial success with a continued onslaught. This allowed the Egyptians to regroup, and in the ensuing engagement, Ramesses II was able to turn the tide and ultimately win the

---

126 Grimal, A History of Ancient Egypt, 253.

battle. Although Ramesses II celebrated the outcome as a great victory on the walls of his temples, historians have viewed the battle as a draw, since Egyptian authority over Kadesh-on-Orontes was never reinstated and the Amurru switched their allegiance back to the Hittites.[127] Hostilities were not formally ended until Year 21, when a formal treaty was concluded between Ramesses II and King Hattusilis (Khattushili) III (c. 1275-1250 BCE), the brother of Muwattalis. Copies of this pact, known as the "Silver Treaty" because the inscriptions were made on a silver mold, are found both on the walls of Karnak, and in Boghazkoy (modern Boghazkale), cities which lay 1000 miles apart, on opposite sides of the Mediterranean Sea. Both sides were temporarily stunned by the casualties of the battle, and although peace between the two countries continued until the end of the Hittite empire, the power of Egypt and the Hittites had peaked, and both countries would see their dominance dwindle in face of the rising threat from the People of the Sea. The extent of the conflict, and the toll paid by the Egyptians, would have likely favored the success of an Exodus of Hebrew slaves during this era, since Ramesses II was forced to direct his attention more to the Palestine coastland than to the hinterland of Egypt, leaving only a small force of soldiers to man the Prince's Wall and control homeland security.

Consistent with the Exodus occurring at this time is the fact that the first time the word "Israel" was used in extant historical records is the famous Israel Stele, ascribed to the time of his successor Merneptah, as will be discussed in more detail shortly. If Israel was able to be defeated by Merneptah in Canaan, it stands to reason that the Exodus had already occurred, and that the Hebrews were settled in the Promised Land. Since Ramesses II sat on the throne for such a long period of time, an Exodus early in his reign would also leave enough time for forty years of wandering in the wilderness before the Conquest of the Promised Land under Joshua, and the subsequent defeat of Israel by Merneptah.

When Ramesses II died, he had outlived thirteen of his sons, and when his fourteenth son, Merneptah, followed him on the throne, it was clearly "an old man succeeding another old man."[128] According to the conventional chronology, Merneptah ruled from 1213-1203 BCE,[129] although scholars who favor the "Intermediate chronology" place his rule from 1237-1225 BCE, and those who favor the "Low chronology," from 1224-1204 BCE.[130] Although Ramesses II

---

127 The Egyptians claimed in their inscriptions that the cowardly Hittite King sent a letter pleading for peace, while the Hittite records indicate that the battle ended when Ramesses II was forced to retreat in an ignominious defeat. Tyldesley, Ramesses, Egypt's Greatest Pharaoh, 73. The unreliability of national historical records is one reason why scholars believe the Exodus of Hebrew slaves from Egypt would not have been noted on temple or palace monuments.

128 Montet, Lives of the Pharaohs, 197.

129 Rohl, Pharaohs and Kings, A Biblical Quest, 20.

130 Soggin, A History of Ancient Israel, 39.

was the first Pharaoh to encounter and defeat some units of the People of the Sea during his reign, Merneptah was forced to face these same marauders in a full-scale war, rather than minor skirmishes. The first major engagement took place in Year 5 of his reign, when the Libyans, led by prince Maraye (Meryry), made a massive attack against the border of Egypt. The People of the Sea made up a large part of this force, including the Akawasha (Greek Achaeans), Tursha, Luka, Sheklesh (who may have given their name to Sicily), and the Sherden, who had previously been enrolled in the royal guard of Ramesses II. Since most scholars have dated the Trojan War to c. 1180 BCE, a few decades later, as will be discussed in chapter 8, these Greek mercenaries could have included descendants of the dissident Hebrews if the Exodus took place in either the fifteenth or fourteenth century BCE. Even if they had become fully integrated into Greek society by this time, they could have retained memories of the enslavement of their ancestors at the hands of the Egyptians.

This impressive military force, which included the kings of important Canaanite centers such as Ashkelon and Yanoam, presented Egypt with a combined enemy might that was more serious than any foreign threat since the time of the Hyksos. Although he was already a sexagenarian king, Merneptah reacted with vigor, assembling his troops and repelling the initial attack of the Libyans within the boundaries of the Egyptian Delta, thereby preventing their incursion into the populated areas of the country. Merneptah celebrated this great victory in various texts, one of which became known as the "Israel Stele," because it was the first reference to the people of Israel in an extra-biblical text. Discovered in his mortuary temple at Thebes in 1895 CE, this black granite engraving, weighing almost five tons, noted how "Israel is laid waste, his seed is not."[131] The inscription explained that thanks to his own courage, and the murderous effectiveness of his archers, the attackers were checked in a six-hour battle near the border settlement of Per-yeru. Along with Israel were seven other foreign elements with whom Egypt was said to have been at war: Tjehenu (Libya); Hatti (Hittites); Pa-Canaan (Palestine); Askelon (?Ashkelon); Gezer; Yanoam; and Hurru (Syria).[132] The fact that Israel was named as a specific entity has been used by many biblical scholars to argue that the state of Israel was actually in existence at that time, and that the Egyptians regarded them as a distinct people, separate from the Canaanites, Hurrians,

---

131 de Vaux, The Early History of Israel, 490. The stele had originally belonged to Amenhotep III, who had inscribed its *recto* with an account of his building activities. Merneptah then inscribed the *verso* with a poetic account of his victory over the Libyans. Lichtheim, Ancient Egyptian Literature, Volume II: The New Kingdom, 73.

132 The Merneptah Stele, also known as the Israel Stele and the Victory Stele of Merneptah, was discovered by Flinders Petrie in 1896 CE at Thebes, and is an account of Merneptah's victory over the Libyans and their allies. It is the first time the name "Israel" appears in any extant document, and has been taken to mean that the Hebrew people were settled by at least that date following the Exodus.

Shasu-bedouin, or other migratory groups in Canaan.[133] Whether they were seen as existing alongside other Canaanite cities, or a truly non-Canaanite entity, cannot be determined precisely, but the fact that they were specifically named is a clear date-certain that their existence was noted by the Egyptian scribes. One cautionary note, however, is that the designation of the name "Israel" as a political entity did not occur until the time of the United Monarchy, and so the exact meaning of the term in the Israel Stele is therefore still unclear, although few scholars dispute that the reference is linked to the Hebrews who participated in the Exodus.[134]

One nagging problem associated with the recording of the name "Israel" is that if the designation was important enough to appear in a description of a military engagement by the Egyptians, it would seem that the battle should have been recorded by the biblical compilers as well. No such passage appears in the Bible, however, and this has concerned scholars who argue for the historical reliability of the biblical text. The most common explanation for the discrepancy is that the event was seen as being of trivial significance to the Hebrews, even though the Egyptians boasted of a significant victory. If the engagement was grossly over-exaggerated by the chroniclers of Merneptah, it would not be expected that the biblical compilers would have felt the need to memorialize the event. In addition, even if a significant number of Hebrews were lost in the battle, the confrontation may not have been seen as important to the biblical compilers, since the recording of Hebrew defeats were not intended to be a detailed history of the Hebrew people, but rather lessons which taught how Israel would be punished for transgressions against the edicts of the Lord. If the defeat by Merneptah was not connected to a discipline inflicted because of immorality on the part of the Jews, it was not worthy of inclusion in the biblical text. Such a circumstance is found in the ninth century BCE, when Jehu, the king of Israel who had succeeded in ousting Omri's dynasty, was shown bowing in submission to the Assyrian king Shalmaneser III (859-824 BCE) in the famous "Black Obelisk," a battle that was not mentioned in the Bible.[135] These explanations seem reasonable, and I

---

133 The word "Canaan" is written with a specific linguistic feature that denoted land (a replica of hills), while the word "Israel" was written with the determinative for people (a replica of a person) . Smith, The Early History of God: Yahweh and the Other Deities in Ancient Israel, 26.

134 The next appearance of the name of Israel is not found until 830 BCE, when Mesha, the king of Moab, was said to have fought with King Jehoram (Joram) of Israel and King Jehosaphat of Judah in an inscription on a black basalt monument known as the Mesha Stone (Moabite Stone). The inscription gives a totally different version of the battle as recorded in 2 Kgs 3:5-27. Freund, Digging Through the Bible: Modern Archaeology and the Ancient Bible, 36-37. The Mesha Stone also contained the first reference to YHWH in connection with Israel in non-biblical sources. The Oxford Illustrated History of the Bible, 9-10.

135 Coogan, The Old Testament: A Historical and Literary Introduction to the Hebrew

consider, like most historians, that the Exodus took place at some time before the reign of Merneptah, although the interval between the Exodus and the Israel Stele is still open to question.

Although Merneptah was able to stem the invasion of the Libyans, he could not break their power completely, and attacks were eventually renewed against Ramesses III, as will be discussed shortly. When Merneptah died, his son did not ascend the throne, and a hiatus in Ramesside descendants occurred during the reigns of Amenmesses, Seti II, Siptah, and Queen Twosret (Tausert), which lasted for seventeen years, from 1203-1186 BCE, according to the conventional chronology.[136] In 1186 BCE, Setnakht then ascended the throne, and the Twentieth Dynasty began. After only three years, his son, Ramesses III, became king, and although almost every scholar agrees that the Exodus had already taken place by this time, I will briefly outline the reign of Ramesses III because of his intimate connection with the People of the Sea, whose invasions effectively ended the Late Bronze Age.

C. The Twentieth Dynasty, 1186-1069 BCE

Ramesses III was the last of the great Egyptian Pharaohs, and following his death, the role of Egypt as a major participant in the political structure of the Levant came to an end. He ruled from 1184-1153 BCE according to both the conventional chronology and the majority of scholars, and he is primarily remembered as the great campaigner against the People of the Sea, fighting a number of battles against these invaders, including an attack by the Libyans in the Nile Delta during Year 5 of his reign, and another attack by the Libyans under Prince Mesher during Year 8 of his reign. These engagements were recorded on battle reliefs carved on the walls of the temple at Medinet Habu, the mortuary temple built by Ramesses III in western Thebes, and in the Great Harris Papyrus, which was compiled by Ramesses IV in honor of his father's achievements. In Year 11 of his reign, Ramesses III had to repel another attack by the Libyans, and in this engagement, Mesher was captured and killed, and more than forty thousand cattle were taken as booty to add to the temple coffers. Many of the conquered People of the Sea were conscripted into the army of Ramesses III, or were made to serve as slaves throughout the land, primarily in the service of the palace, or landed and temple estates. Some of the Philistines settled in Palestine, eventually controlling a large part of the land south of Phoenicia. The tide had begun to turn, however, and Ramesses III soon had to face an even greater invasion by the People of the Sea, including the Peleset, Weshwesh, Tjekker, Sheklesh, and a new wave of Sherden. During one of these campaigns, he was killed, and the glorious Egyptian Empire came to an end, but by now, "Troy was a memory,

Scriptures, 293.
   136 Rohl, Pharaohs and Kings, A Biblical Quest, 20.

Mycenae a ruin and Hattusi, the Hittite capital, leveled."[137]

At this period of time, the Exodus had ended, and the Conquest of the Promised Land was well on its way to completion. The Hebrew Monarchy is believed to have begun with the reign of King Saul (1020-1006 BCE), a century away, and so I will end my discussion of Egypt and move on to the history of the Hebrews, beginning with the patriarchal generation.

---

137 Johnson, The Civilization of Ancient Egypt, 98.

Chapter 3

THE HEBREWS – FROM
ABRAHAM TO THE EXODUS

While extreme diversity separates the social and religious practices of modern Jews, Christians and Moslems, all three religions nevertheless share the same monotheistic origin in the worship of the one Almighty God of the Old Testament. Known as YHWH to the Hebrews, the Father in the Christian concept of the Trinity, and Allah to the Muslims, this image of a single all-powerful God, as opposed to the multitude of deities which characterized other Bronze and Iron Age religions, varied significantly between the three faiths, but each faithful adherent held firmly to the unity of belief in the existence of only one God Who ruled the earth alone, without the presence of other, more minor, deities. The traditional lore of all three religions included the stories of the lives of the Hebrew Patriarchs, as well as the Exodus from Egypt, the theophany on Mt. Sinai where God gave Moses the Ten Commandments, and the legal precepts contained within the Mosaic Code.[1] The New Testament and Koran (Qur'an) both acknowledge the sanctity of their Hebrew roots, while emphasizing their development in different directions from the mother faith: Jesus was the Messiah from the house of David that was forecast in the book of Micah;[2] and the Moslems were descendants of Ishmael, the son of Abraham, who was evicted from his father's home after the birth of Isaac.[3]

While this evolution of monotheistic practice helps explain the foundation of the three modern religions, it is important to remember that the defining moment

---

1 The descendants of Jacob were known as "Hebrews" to the biblical compilers, a word which generally is thought to be derived from the name of Eber, the great-great-grandson of Noah. The term "Israelite" was used when the patriarchal families were compared to foreigners, but it is not known what the Patriarchs were called by their contemporaries. For simplicity, I will not attempt to differentiate the appropriate use of these names in this book, and will use the term "Hebrew" to refer to the descendants of Abraham before their passage into the Promised Land, and "Israelite" for after the Conquest had begun.

2 Micah 5:2-4. See e.g., Isa 11:1; Jer 23:5-6; Exek 34:23-24; Matt 2:5-6; John 7:42. The classic formulation of the idea that Jesus was the royal messiah from the line of King David, and would be born from a human but become the adopted son of God, is found in Nathan's oracle in 2 Sam 7:11-17. Collins, The Scepter and the Star: The Messiahs of the Dead Sea Scrolls and Other Ancient Literature," 22-23.

3 The names of Abraham, Isaac, and Jacob never occur in the Bible with reference to other individuals, but the name of Ishmael is used for five other people (2 Kgs 25:25; Jer 40:41; Ezra 10:22; 1 Chron 8:38; 9:44; 2 Chron 19:11; 23:1). Abramaovitch, The First Father Abraham: The Psychology and Culture of a Spiritual Revolutionary, 98.

of Judaic monotheism was the declaration in the Decalogue that YHWH was the one and only God, a concept that was unknown to the Patriarchs, as I will discuss in more detail in Chapter 11. The pre-Mosaic Hebrews held steadfast to the ancestral worship of the Patriarchs, unaware of this monotheistic commandment and closely resembling the other Bronze Age polytheistic Semitic tribes who roamed the ancient Near East during the second millennium BCE, and their resistance to change forced Moses to kill more than 40,000 Hebrews during their wandering in the Sinai desert as part of the parricidal punishments demanded by the tenets of the Mosaic Code.[4] Abraham, Isaac, and Jacob were never warned to refrain from idol worship, and the biblical text contained frequent notations to the construction of pillars and images to commemorate important sites where the Patriarchs were favored by divine assistance. This custom of erecting a stone stela to show appreciation to God was common among Semitic people in ancient times, but such practices were later forbidden in the books of *Leviticus* and *Deuteronomy*.[5] The patriarchal families also were not restricted to the worship of YHWH alone, as evidenced by the fact that Rachel took the household idols of Laban along as security when Jacob left the home of his father-in-law with his extended family.[6] No punishment accrued for this apostasy, as would later descend upon those Hebrews who made a golden calf-idol after Moses ascended Mt. Sinai to receive the Ten Commandments. It is this alteration in the manner of appropriate worship that I believe caused some of the Exodus participants to literally flee for their lives and travel to Mycenae, where they could freely practice their ancestral faith.

In order to understand why I believe a group of dissidents fled the Exodus, I will outline the social history of the Patriarchs in this chapter, the life of Moses before the Exodus in Chapter 4, the Exodus itself in Chapter 5, and the dating of the Exodus in Chapter 6. By intently analyzing the history of the Patriarchs from their earliest beginnings to their era of enslavement in Egypt, and then comparing this lifestyle to the rigid regulations set forth by Moses during the Exodus, I hope to verify my hypothesis that a group of dissidents were forced to flee the Exodus following the parricidal reprisals of Moses, and travel to Mycenae before the Trojan War. I should state at the outset of this chapter, that I staunchly deny the attempts of many modern biblical scholars to totally discard the historicity of the Patriarchs by claiming that they were fictional constructions of the historians of the monarchic era, intended simply to promote the primacy of either the northern kingdom of Israel (c. 975-721 BCE; Iron IIA-B) or the

---

4   Many modern scholars have concluded that the pre-exilic Hebrew faith was "thoroughly polytheistic." Keel & Uehlinger, Gods, Godesses, and Images of God in Ancient Israel, 2.

5   Lev 26:1; Deut 7:5; 12:3; 16:22.

6   Gen 31:21.

southern kingdom of Judah (c. 960-586 BCE; Iron IIA-C). I will discuss this in greater detail throughout this book, but for now I will proceed with the history of the Patriarchs as outlined in the biblical text, with the presumption that the facts contained therein are based on a modicum of truth, attested to by the oral tradition which has survived the centuries from the Late Bronze Age to our modern era. In doing this, I follow the opinion of Arnaldo Momigliano (1908-1987 CE), former Professor of Ancient History at the University of London, who warned that "archaeology and epigraphy cannot take the place of the living tradition of a nation as transmitted by its literary texts," accepting that veracity does not depend upon the survival of textual documentation alone.[7]

A. The Patriarchs in Canaan Before Entry Into Egypt

The majority of biblical scholars who accept the general truth of the biblical tradition, if not all of the details, believe that the Patriarchs lived during the end of the Early Bronze Age (3000-2000 BCE), or at the start of the Middle Bronze Age (2000-1600 BCE). While actually placing the origins of the Patriarchs in this era has been attacked by some pundits, beginning with Thomas Thompson's *The Historicity of the Patriarchal Narratives: The Quest for the Biblical Abraham* (1974), and John Van Seters' *Abraham in History and Tradition* (1975), both of whom argued that the book of *Genesis* cannot provide information of any historical value in this regard, I am going to accept the majority view in this chapter that the patriarchal generation did arise during this period of time, and that the origin of the Jews was reflected by the stories that were handed down from generation to generation. This view is buttressed by numerous Egyptian records which document Semitic movements that are very similar to the patriarchal wanderings reflected in the biblical text. This includes the story of Sinuhe, from the second millennium BCE, which describes the rescue of Sinuhe by pastoralists who had been in Egypt, much like Abraham, and pictorial representations, such as that found at Beni Hasan, which are particularly suggestive of the Patriarchs,[8] as well as descriptions of Habiru tribes, some of whom were designated as Benjaminites.[9] Many historians accept that Asiatic pastoralists from Canaan, many of whom "very readily matched the Biblical account of the 'sons of Jacob'," settled in large numbers on the eastern part of the Nile Delta between the eighteenth and

---

7 Momigliano, Essays on Ancient and Modern Judaism, 4. Momigliano decries the modern attempt "to treat historiography as another genre of fiction." Ibid., 5.

8 The tomb chapel of the local governor Khnumhotep II at Beni Hasan c. 1870 BCE shows thirty-seven "Asiatics" visiting Egypt bringing eye paint. Their leader is named Ab-sharru (Abishai), a West Semitic name. Kitchen, On the Reliability of the Old Testament, 318. Their pictorial representation is classically Semitic, with dark hair, long noses, the men bearded and the women long-haired, and they wear multicolored woolen frocks.

9 Wilson, The Bible Is History, 39-40.

sixteenth centuries BCE.[10]

The social practices of the Patriarchs as described in the Old Testament also resemble in many ways the law and customs of the Amorites who settled in Mesopotamia, as attested to in the cuneiform texts discovered in the city of Mari from c. 1800 BCE, and those from c. 1500 BCE from Nuzi, where the Hurrians gathered. This type of congruence helps support the dating of the Patriarchs to this era, and the towns that figure in the patriarchal stories, like Shechem, Bethel, and Jerusalem, were all in existence in the Middle Bronze Age. While this type of data does not prove that Abraham actually existed during this era, it clearly is consistent with the description of the patriarchal lifestyle in the book of *Genesis*, and supports the concept that Abraham, Isaac, and Jacob may very well have been part of the infiltrative process, either in the rapid process often termed as the "Amorite Hypothesis," or in a more gradual fashion, as is more commonly accepted today.[11] The fact that the Patriarchs' names have been identified with those of places or ethnic groups from historical documents "makes it plausible that they are the mythical residue of ancient traditions about ancestral wanderings."[12]

It is important to realize that proving the existence of the Hebrew Patriarchs by factual evidence is almost impossible, since the Hebrew language and lifestyle were very similar to other Semitic groups of the Middle Bronze Age.

Over time, the individual Semitic tongues were modified into discrete languages that made communication between adjacent cultures difficult, and allowed for verification of the presence of the Hebrew tongue in surviving texts, but during the years following the Amorite Invasion, communion between the various Semitic tribes was still possible, as evidenced by the fact that the Patriarchs conversed with other indigenous Canaanites in the Bible who spoke a similar form of the Northwest Semitic dialect.[13] Although the Bible claims that a written alphabet was available to the Hebrews during the Exodus,[14] the earliest

---

10 Wilson, The Bible Is History, 40.

11 Finkelstein, "Patriarchs, Exodus, Conquest: Fact or Fiction?" 43. Not all scholars accept the Amorite Hypothesis, as evident in the statement of Gosta W. Ahlstrom (1918-1992 CE), former Professor at the University of Chicago Divinity School and Department of Near Eastern Languages and Civilizations, who considered the theory "nothing more than a mistake." Ahlstrom, The History of Ancient Palestine, 133.

12 Graves & Patai, Hebrew Myths, the Book of Genesis, 132.

13 The language spoken by the Israelites was not called Hebrew until the use of that term in the prologue to *Ecclesiasticus*, c. 130 BCE. Before that time, it was generally called the "language of Canaan" (Isa 19:18), or "Judean" (Isa 36:12-13). Isserlin, The Israelites, 204. The Canaanite alphabet appeared at the very start of the second millennium BCE, and contained only consonants, like the Hebrew writing, allowing anyone with a knowledge of biblical Hebrew to communicate with those who spoke the Canaanite tongue. Tubb, Peoples of the Past: Canaanites, 14.

14 Reference to writings during the Exodus include the Decalogue, book of the Covenant, inscriptions on the frontlet of the High Priest, recording of the victory over the

example of Hebrew writing in any extant inscription is from 1200 BCE, at an early Hebrew settlement at Izbet Sartah, which contains five lines resembling either Phoenician or ancient Hebrew letters.[15]

In addition to sharing a similar Semitic language and lacking any specific racial trait, the ancient Hebrews also led an analogous way-of-life as a wandering, semi-nomadic people, who lived in tents, raised sheep, cattle, and goats, and moved from one place to another, rather than settling in one particular area. Evidence of caravaneer activity can be found across the Sinai and Negev during the Twelfth Dynasty (1937-1759 BCE) in Egypt, an era contemporaneous with most estimates for the age of Abraham, and before the appearance of permanent caravan stations. In addition, merchants crossed the wide steppes and plains of Mesopotamia with donkey caravans numbering up to hundreds of pack animals. Although the Bible did not specifically mention seasonal wanderings, most scholars have assumed that the Patriarchs spent the rainy spring season in the southern, drier Negev region, and then moved to the cooler highlands in the summer, in order to adequately maintain their grazing flocks. It is believed that they did not follow a typical bedouin existence, however, which extended travel into the desert and along routes where an adequate supply of water was not available, but rather chose to camp in the immediate neighborhood of towns, and with time to try their hand at agriculture, in order to assure a more stable food supply. There is no evidence that they practiced strict dietary restrictions until the regulations instituted by the Mosaic Code, and their requirement of circumcision was not unique, despite the fact that the Bible claimed it was a sign of their covenant with God.[16] Although the Patriarchs were sometimes forced to move from one area to another in Canaan because of envy over their successful economic status, there is no documentation that they engendered cultural and racial animosity until they migrated into Egypt and came under the protection of Joseph. Martin Noth (1902-1968 CE), Professor of the Old Testament at the University of Bonn, has attempted to sub-categorize these Early West Semitic groups which resembled

---

Amalekites, Aaron's blossoming rod, and the station catalogue. Exod 17:14; 24:4, 7, 12; 32:15-16, 32; 34:1, 27-28; 39:30; Num 5:23; 11:26; 17:17; 21:14; 33:2.

15 Hoffman, In the Beginning: A Short History of the Hebrew Language, 29.

16 Although the Bible portrayed circumcision as becoming the unique sign of faith in YHWH, it was not a Hebrew invention, and had been practiced by the Egyptian priesthood for centuries, as depicted on a relief from the tomb of Ankhmahor at Sakkara, from the Sixth Dynasty (second half of the third millennium BCE). The Illustrated Family Encyclopedia of the Living Bible, I.57. Herodotus claims that in addition to the Egyptians, circumcision was practiced "from the first" by the Colchians and the Ethiopians, and that the Phoenicians and Palestinian Syrians (which included the Jews) "agree that they learned this from the Egyptians." Herodotus, The History, II.104, 173. Following the Conquest of the Promised Land, of all the nations which bordered ancient Israel, only the Philistines did not practice circumcision. Plaut, Genesis, The Torah: A Modern Commentary, 162.

the patriarchs as Proto-Aramaeans, although this label has not been uniformly accepted.

1. Abraham

With the birth of Abraham, the Old Testament took a turn from the description of the Creation of the world and mankind in general, to the story of the evolution of the Hebrew descendants as God's Chosen People. Abraham, we are told, was born in the region of Ur of the Chaldeans, in Lower Mesopotamia. The Bible does not specifically mention that Abraham was born in that region, but because his brother Haran, the father of Lot, was said to have been born there, it has been assumed that it was the birthplace of Abraham as well.[17] The Septuagint, which is the name given to the Greek translation of the Jewish Scriptures c. 300-200 BCE, and sometimes abbreviated LXX for its translation by seventy interpreters, speaks only of "the land of the Chaldeans," rather than the region of Ur, and other biblical passages place his home in Haran in northwest Mesopotamia.[18] Since the Chaldeans did not infiltrate Babylon until around 1100-1000 BCE, and did not appear on the historical stage until the ninth century BCE, the information provided in the biblical text is anachronistic, and we therefore cannot reliably know where the progenitor of the Hebrews was actually born.[19]

Although Abraham's father, Terah (Terach), and two brothers, Nahor (Nakhur, Nachor) and Haran, were prominently mentioned in the book of *Genesis*, his mother was never identified. This absence is strange, for although the ancient Hebrews were clearly a patriarchal society, like most other Semitic cultures of that era, the Bible prominently described the lives of other Hebrew women as integral to the structure of the family and nation, especially the Matriarchs Sarah, Rebekah, Rachel and Leah. Why the compilers of the Old Testament chose to ignore the name of Abraham's mother is not clear, but rabbinic legend explained that her name was Amathlai (Amitlai, Emtelai), daughter of Karnebo, and that she had forfeited her right to be identified because she had abandoned Abraham at birth.[20] The legend of this little-known event held that sages had forecast to King Nimrod that a man would be born who would rise up against him. The king therefore commanded that all the pregnant women be gathered, and at their birth, the male offspring were to be killed, and the females be allowed to live, an edict clearly reflective of the Pharaoh's decree to kill the newborn male Hebrew children at the time of Moses' birth. Abraham's mother was able to hide her

---

17 Gen 11:26-28.

18 Anderson, Understanding the Old Testament, 27.

19 Ahlstrom, The History of Ancient Palestine, 182. It is this type of anachronism that helps buttress the claims of skeptics who argue that the biblical stories are pure fiction.

20 Scherman, The Chudash, 51.

pregnancy, and then gave birth to Abraham in a cave, where she abandoned him because of the king's proclamation. God then sent the Angel Gabriel to nourish Abraham, and when he was eight days old, Abraham walked out of the cave on his own, a sign that he was to have the support of the Lord for the rest of his life.[21] While this myth clearly seems to be tied to the abandonment of Moses, it is nevertheless reflective of how the rabbinic oral tradition attempted to expand the limitations of the written Torah in order to provide a cohesive tale of consistent religious tradition, and I will refer to their explanations frequently throughout this book.

As I noted, the exact location of Ur of the Chaldeans at the time of Abraham's birth cannot be known with certainty, but most scholars favor that it was either the Sumerian city of Ur that flourished in southern Mesopotamia in the third millennium BCE, or the city of Ura (modern Urfa), in northern Mesopotamia, near the city of Haran.[22] The ruins of the Sumerian city of Ur are at Tell el-Muqayyar, 220 miles from Baghdad in southern Iraq, a location that fits the biblical details of the migration quite well. The city flourished and reached its zenith under the kings of the Third Dynasty, about 2060 BCE, and was destroyed by the Elamites a little before 2000 BCE, eventually being rebuilt into a prospering trading center shortly thereafter.

While still living in Ur, Abraham married his half-sister Sarah, a union which was legal at the time, although it would later be prohibited by the Mosaic Code.[23] At some later date, Terah decided to move his family from Ur to Canaan, and although the Torah is silent as to the reason for his decision, if the Patriarchs did live around the start of the Middle Bronze Age it is likely that Terah was concerned for their safety, since Ur was destroyed around 2000 BCE. Haran, one

21 Ginzberg, The Legends of the Jews, I.186-189. A child who walks and talks soon after birth is also apparent in the Greek myths of Hermes and Achilles. Graves & Patai, Hebrew Myths, the Book of Genesis, 139.

22 Mariottini, "Ur and Haran, Abraham's Background," 51-52. Cyrus Gordon favored Ura as Abraham's birthplace, because of his belief that Abraham was a merchant with Hittite sponsorship, rather than a wandering shepherd. It is also the city which Muslims regard as Abraham's birthplace. Gordon, Before the Bible: The Common Background of Greek and Hebrew Civilizations, 25-36. Some ancient traditions, including that of Maimonides (Rabbi Moses ben Maimon, Rambam)(1135-1204 CE), have placed Abraham's birth at Cuthah, twenty miles northeast of Baghdad. Maimonides, The Guide for the Perplexed, III.XXIX, 315.

23 Gen 11:31. This close family background of Abraham and Sarah was later revealed by Abraham when he told King Abimelech that he and Sarah had the same father. Gen 20:12. In reality, she was his brother's daughter, and not his father's, but Rashi (Rabbi Shelomo Yitzchaki 1040-1105 CE), the highly-respected medieval sage who is widely considered the greatest of all the biblical commentators, claimed that his statement was justified since grandchildren were considered as children, and Sarah could have therefore been called his sister in the figurative sense of the word. Scherman, The Chumash, 93.

of Abraham's brothers, had died sometime before this move, leaving his orphaned son Lot to travel along with the rest of the nuclear family, but Milcah, Haran's daughter, had married Abraham's surviving brother, Nahor, and they decided to remain in Ur and not accompany the rest of the family on their emigration to a distant destination.[24] No reason was given in the biblical text for the division of the family at this early stage of Hebrew generation, but it seems reasonable to assume that the separation was intended to provide a link with the land of Abraham's birth, since Isaac and Jacob would both return to the land of their relatives when it came time to marry within the genetic confines of the evolving Hebrew culture. Nahor and Milcah had a son, Kemuel, whose son Aram has been linked with the ancestry of the Arameans in some traditions, although these people are usually seen as evolving from another Aram, who was one of Shem's sons.[25] When Isaac married Rebekah, an Aramean, and Jacob married Leah and Rachel, the link between the Canaanite and Mesopotamian roots of the developing Hebrew tribal society was fulfilled. Moses reminded the Hebrews before they crossed over into the Promised Land that their ancestors were migrant Arameans who went to Egypt for refuge and became a mighty nation there, referring to the contribution of Abraham's brother.[26] This strong identity of the roots of patriarchal evolution from both Canaan and Mesopotamia will prove valuable, in my opinion, to the ability of the dissident Hebrews who later left the Exodus to find support during their travels though Canaan to Ugarit, and eventually over to Mycenae, as will be explained in the chapters which follow.

Terah never actually reached Canaan after leaving Ur, settling instead in Haran, a caravan center 600 miles northwest, on the Balikh River in the middle of the Euphrates Valley in Upper Mesopotamia (southern modern-day Turkey). Haran is often referred to as Paddan-Aram (Aram-Naharaim) in the Bible, and along with the city of Ur was one of the three great centers of trade in Mesopotamia. The confusion created by the similar spelling of the names of Abraham's brother Haran, and the city of Haran in English, does not occur in Hebrew where the

---

24 The lineage of Sarah is not given in the biblical text, but Rashi identified her as Iscah (Yiska), the sister of Milcah. Abramaovitch, The First Father Abraham: The Psychology and Culture of a Spiritual Revolutionary, 55. This identity is also accepted by many Muslim traditions, and the fact that Sarah was thereby Abraham's cousin is not a problem of incest, since such a marriage was an acceptable kinship at the time. Firestone, Journeys in Holy Lands: The Evolution of the Abraham-Ishmael Legends in Islamic Exegesis, 29.

25 Gen 10:22; 22:21-22. The Arameans were an Amorite, Semitic-speaking people who emerged from the Syrian desert in the latter half of the second millennium BCE, eventually settling in Syria and along the Euphrates River, making their capital at Damascus in the fourteenth century BCE. Livingston, The Pentateuch in Its Cultural Environment, 31.

26 Deut 26:5.

initial letter of Haran, the man, is "h," while that of Haran, the place, is "kh."[27] Other towns in the region of Haran during the first millennium BCE also had names of Abraham's relatives, including his father Terah, grandfather Nahor, and great-grandfather Serug, but there is no evidence that any of these cities were linked with the naming of Abraham's family.[28] It does suggest, however, a consistency of the biblical story with local contemporary social conditions, and lends some credence to the positioning of Abraham's birth in Mesopotamia.

While Terah was still alive, God commanded Abraham to leave Mesopotamia, the land of his birth, and travel to Canaan, where his descendants would become a great nation.[29] The encounter is not further described, and we do not know how Abraham knew this was God speaking, or whether this was the first occasion he had contact with the Lord. Abraham was seventy-five years old at the time, and this divine covenant with God, known as the Abrahamic covenant, formed the basis for defining the Jews as the Chosen People of the Lord.[30] By telling Abraham to migrate out of Mesopotamia into Canaan, God was ordering him not only to break with the secular past, but with the religious one as well, since the authority of the pagan gods ended at the frontiers of the kingdom at that time. Because the wives of Isaac and Jacob were said to come from the region of Haran, rather than from Ur, it is believed that Nahor and Milcah moved to Haran after the departure of Abraham in order to be with Terah in his declining years.

Abraham obeyed the commandment of the Lord to leave Mesopotamia, and traveled to Canaan, following the well-known caravan route that existed for thousands of years. It followed the river Balikh as far as the Euphrates River, and then continued on to Damascus, Hazor, Shechem, Jerusalem, Mamre, and the Lake of Galilee. He set up his first stationary camp beside the oak tree at Moreh, near Shechem, where the Lord now "appeared" to Abraham and told him that "I will assign this land to your offspring."[31] The manner in which

---

27 Alleman, "The Book of Genesis," 184.

28 McCarter, Jr., "The Patriarchal Age, Abraham, Isaac and Jacob," revised by Ronald S. Hendel, 23.

29 Gen 12:1-2. God's commandment to "go forth" (*lek-leka*) from Mesopotamia would be repeated in the Akeda when he was told to "go forth" to an unspecified height in the land of Moriah to sacrifice Isaac (Gen 22:2). Levenson, The Death and Resurrection of the Beloved Son: The Transformation of Child Sacrifice in Judaism and Christianity, 138. According to tradition, this took place three years after their arrival in Haran. Rappoport, Ancient Israel, Myths and Legends, 254-255. Other scholars believe that the call for Abraham to leave his homeland actually came while he was living in his homeland of Ur of the Chaldeans, and that the Bible only states that he "set out from Haran." Sailhamer, "Genesis," 109. See e.g., Neh 9:7 and Acts 7:2-4.

30 Terah would live for sixty more years after Abraham's departure, since he was seventy years old when Abraham was born, and would die when he was 205 years old. Gen 11:26, 32; 12:4.

31 Gen 12:6-7. Levenson, "Genesis," 31. The oak tree was a representative of the

this conversation took place is not described, but Abraham built an altar beside the tree, commemorating the location as evidence of his covenant with God, an act which again would later be forbidden as a form of paganism by Moses.[32] Jacob would also erect an altar beside this same oak tree when he later traveled to Paddan-Aram to find a wife, naming it *El-Elohe-Israel,* or the "Altar to the God of Israel," an indication that the pre-Mosaic Hebrews put great faith in a visual show of respect to the Lord, a practice which was common among the other Semitic tribes.[33] In my opinion, these actions of the Patriarchs were likely passed down by oral tradition to the Hebrews during their years of enslavement in Egypt, and may help explain why some of the participants of the Exodus so fervently resisted Moses' directive to alter the religious practices of their ancestors. Old habits do not die easily, and even a series of parricidal retributions were not enough to convince the dissident Hebrews to give up their ancient polytheistic religious beliefs.

Abraham continued his travels toward the hills east of Bethel and Ai, where he built another altar to the Lord, this time without an apparent epiphany, and he then continued to the Negev, a path which Jacob would repeat when he returned to Canaan from Haran.[34] He built three more campsites following the one at

---

"tree of life," and was the site where Jacob would later bury the idolatrous appurtances of his family (Gen 35:4), where Joshua set up a great stone (Josh 24:26), and where Abimelech was proclaimed King of Israel (Judg 9:6). In Greek religion, sanctuaries were also marked by special trees, with an old and sacred oak tree aiding the oracle at Dodona with the rustling of its branches. Burkert, Greek Religion, 85-86. The oak tree at Dodona is first mentioned by Homer in the *Odyssey,* but it does not appear in the *Iliad.* Homer, Odyssey, 14:327, 257; 19:296, 362. This worship of trees (Gen 12:6; 13:18; 18:1; 21:33), stones (Gen 28:18, 22), and wells (Num21:17) convinced some early scholars to see the patriarchal religion as a form of primitive animism. Saggs, "Pre-Exilic Jewry," 40.

32 Deut 16:21. Moses reminded the Hebrews that they were not to worship other gods after their entry into the Promised Land, ordering them to tear down the altars they found in Canaan, as well as "smash their pillars, cut down their sacred posts, and consign their images to the fire," or face obliteration by the Lord for their impiety. Deut 7:4-5. Tigay, Deuteronomy, 86.

33 Gen 33:20. Sarna, Genesis, 232. There are hundreds of sites containing standing stones (*massebot*) in Canaanite cult places in the Negev and Sinai from the fifth to the third millennia BCE. Zevit, The Religions of Ancient Israel: A Synthesis of Parallactic Approaches, 256. Biblical notations of these stones are noted at Gen 28:10-22; 31:13, 43-54; 35:16-20; Exod 24:4; Josh 24:26; 2 Sam 18:18; 2 Kgs 3:2; 10:27; 17:10; 23:13-14; and 2 Chron 34:4. Ibid. 260. Archaeologists have discovered these stones at Gezer, Dan, Hazor and Arad. Their association with Asherah, Baal and other Canaanite deities is the basis for their being condemned as a rival to YHWH worship. Walton, Matthews, & Chavalas, The IVP Bible Background Commentary: Old Testament, 403, 435.

34 Gen 12:8-9, 13:3.

Moreh, erecting altars at Beth-el,[35] Mamre,[36] and Beer-sheba.[37] This sequence indicates that once Abraham left Moreh, he traveled southward through the hill region of Canaan, along the watershed route from Shechem to Hebron, and then into the Negev. This path was reflective of the seasonal wanderings which was necessary to provide adequate grazing land for the flocks of sheep that sustained the nutritional needs of semi-nomadic people at the time. At Beth-el, Abraham invoked the name of YHWH for the first time, raising the appellation again on his return from Egypt.[38] This placed a special sanctification on the city, and the biblical compilers highlighted its importance by having Jacob's name changed to "Israel" at the same location.[39] Mamre also became a hallowed site in the Bible, for it was there that the three strangers later appeared to Abraham to tell him that the Lord was going to give he and Sarah a son.[40] Beer-sheba, the final city to be honored by Abraham, lay in a strategic location at the narrowest point of the Negev valley, and guarded the main southern gateway into the highlands of Israel.[41]

It is not possible to know if these passages by the Patriarchs were recognized by other inhabitants of the land connecting Egypt and Mesopotamia, given the lack of any corroborating extant records, but the fact that the details were later recollected by the biblical compilers indicates that some oral tradition was maintained throughout the centuries by succeeding generations of Hebrews, providing the members of the Exodus congregation some familiarity with the land they were entering. I believe that the dissident Hebrews who refused to change their traditional ways of worshiping the patriarchal gods, traveled north to Ugarit, and eventually to Mycenae, utilizing this same information to aid their passage, even encountering distant relatives along the way who were familiar with the very same tales. When they arrived in Greece, they transmitted this very same account to the Greeks, explaining the close resemblance in the legendary traditions of both cultures. I will discuss this further in the Conclusion to this book.

The Negev, where Beer-sheba was located, lay at the southern end of Canaan,

---

35 Gen 12:8; 13:3.

36 Gen 13:18.

37 Gen 21:33.

38 This use of YHWH's name contradicts the passage in the book of *Exodus* when YHWH appeared to Moses at the burning bush and said that He did not reveal His name as YHWH to the patriarchs, indicating that it is a likely addition from a later Redactor. Exod 6:2-3.

39 Gen 35:10-15. Beth-el was mentioned more often than any other city in the Bible except Jerusalem. Plaut, Genesis, The Torah: A Modern Commentary, 280.

40 Gen 18:1, 10.

41 The Bible made a special note of the city with respect to paternal piety by having God appear to Isaac when he first arrived at the site, saying "I am the God of your father Abraham," and by having Jacob offer sacrifices to the "God of his father Isaac." Gen 26:23-24; 46:1. Sarna, Genesis, 187, 312.

a relatively short distance across the Sinai desert from the Egyptian border, and when famine swept across Canaan and prevented Abraham's ability to live off the land, he traveled to Egypt where he hoped to find assistance in feeding his family.[42]   As was customary at the time, when Abraham arrived at one of the Egyptian border stations, he requested permission from the Pharaoh to remain in the region long enough to feed his flock.[43]   Fearing that the Egyptians would kill him in order to take his beautiful wife Sarah into the king's harem, Abraham withheld the fact that they were married and told the king that Sarah was his sister, thereby hoping to secure his own safety.[44]   This deception was not necessarily an outright lie, as some rabbinic traditions claim that Sarah was his half-sister from a different mother,[45] and Nuzi (Nuzu) records from the fifteenth and fourteenth centuries BCE have confirmed that wifehood and sistership were sometimes equated under Hurrian law, making Abraham's ruse not as egregious as might appear on the surface.[46]   Nevertheless, the subterfuge put Sarah's life into a position of grave danger, and this lack of concern for the safety of his wife has caused some commentators to chastize Abraham for his action, although the Bible makes it clear that no harm actually accrued to Sarah.[47]   The length of time that Sarah spent in the Pharaoh's harem is not mentioned in the biblical text, but

---

42   Egypt was not reliant on rainfall to supply irrigation for agriculture, since the annual inundation of the Nile River protected their land from the effects of drought which were devastating to other areas of the Near East. Many contemporary records indicate that Asiatics frequently entered the Delta during the end of the Old Kingdom and throughout the Second Intermediate Period, a time sequence which is compatible with the postulated era of the Patriarchs. Finegan, Handbook of Biblical Chronology, 210.

43   The Pharaoh is not named in the Bible, but *Genesis Apocryphon,* which is one of the seven major Dead Sea Scrolls that were found in Cave 1 at Qumran in 1947 CE, identifies him as "Pharaoh Zoan, the king of Egypt."

44   Gen 12:13, 19. This claim of sister-wife is repeated by Abraham to King Abimelech of Gerar (Gen 20:2, 5, 12), and by Isaac to King Abimelech of Gerar (Gen 26:7, 9).

45   As discussed above, it has also been claimed that Sarah was the daughter of Haran, and therefore Abraham's first cousin.

46   Speiser, "The Patriarchs and Their Social Background," 164. These records also contained a parallel of the Sarah-Hagar episode, where a childless wife was allowed to select a concubine (a woman without dowry) for her husband in order to assure that his bloodline would be continued. Ibid., 166. According to Cyrus Gordon and Gary Rendsburg, no set of texts "offers as many parallels to the patriarchal narratives" as the Nuzi material, and the society at Nuzi was "the single society closest to the lives of the patriarchs." Gordon & Rendsburg, The Bible and the Ancient Near East, 111.

47 The medieval sage Ramban (Rabbi Moses ben Nachman, 1194-1270 CE) commented that the ruse perpetrated by Abraham was a "great sin." Scherman, The Chudash, 57. The *Genesis Apocryphon* from the Dead Sea Scrolls (first to second centuries BCE), however, explained that it was Sarah who told Abraham to utilize this subterfuge so that his life would be spared, thereby absolving Abraham of guilt. "The Genesis Apocryphon," The Other Bible, 204.

in the Dead Sea Scrolls' *Tales of the Patriarchs*, it is suggested that she was there for two years, and to obviate the possibly that she was violated, the Pharaoh was said to be impotent.[48] When the Pharaoh discovered that the pestilence which arose in his country was due to his keeping another man's wife, he questioned Abraham as to why such a dishonest deed was necessary. Abraham's answer was not recorded in the biblical text, but it must have been a satisfactory excuse for when Abraham left Egypt, he was given gifts of animals and slaves, including an Egyptian slave girl, Hagar, who was eventually to bear his first son, Ishmael.

Since it is not known if the Torah was simply a verbatim recording of a Mosaic treatise, or a compilation of accurate oral traditions, we will likely never know why the biblical compilers decided to complicate the story of Abraham's early married life by interposing this apparent entrance of Sarah into the harem of the Pharaoh. While it seems reasonable to assume that the tale of his migration into Egypt was necessary to provide a non-Hebrew mother for Ishmael from a country other than Canaan, it is surprising that Sarah was included in the manner she was, given the general assumption that the Pharaoh frequently had sexual relationships with all of his concubines. I believe, however, that the pre-Mosaic Hebrews identified more easily with these types of possibly flawed behaviors than with the rigid pronouncement that would be put forth in the Mosaic Code, and were therefore more likely to remain loyal to the traditions of the Patriarchs than obey the holier-than-thou requirements of the Mosaic Law. When parricide became the punishment for disobedience, they fled the Exodus and traveled to Mycenae, where they could follow the faith of their fathers.

When Abraham returned to Canaan after this brief sojourn in Egypt, he was not only wealthier than when he first arrived, he also carried with him clear evidence of the favor of the Pharaoh, something which would place him in good stead with Palestinian princes he would encounter in the years to come. The importance of this manifest sign of Egyptian respect is seen in the Egyptian *Story of Sinuhe*, as discussed in chapter 2, which dates, according to most biblical scholars, to the same era of Abraham's migration. Few Semitic tribes had Egyptian slaves as part of their extended family, and the presence of such servants in Abraham's entourage was indicative of Egyptian beneficence. This economic and political advantage placed the Hebrews on a level of prominence above that of other wandering tribes in Canaan, and was likely one reason why the Patriarchs were allowed to travel so freely throughout the Canaanite region.

After leaving Egypt, Abraham set up camp at Beth-el, the site where he had first invoked the name of YHWH. Lot had not been mentioned as being part of Abraham's entourage in Egypt, but he now suddenly reappeared in the biblical text, and quarreled with Abraham over joint possession of the land. The text explains that the land could not support them both for their possessions were

---

48 Wise, Abegg, & Cook, The Dead Sea Scrolls: A New Translation, 89.

too great, language that mimics the situation that would occur between Jacob and Esau, once Jacob reunited with his brother, as will be discussed later in this chapter. Abraham offered to split the property equally, attempting to prevent strife within the family, and Lot chose the acreage along the Jordan plain near the town of Sodom, the richest, but most corrupt, part of the country. This act likely was intended to show Lot's decadent nature, and eventually this seamy side of his character found disfavor with the Lord, resulting in his descendants being forced to become servants to the Hebrews. Most commentators have concluded that the purpose of this story was to underscore the fact that the nations of Moab and Ammon, which descended from Lot's children, had no right to inherit part of the land which God had promised to Abraham, even though Lot was ceded this section of land by Abraham.[49] God alone determined the rightful ownership of property, and human contracts or gifts were subject to the divine will: what the Lord giveth, the Lord could taketh away. As if to emphasize this hierarchy of divine control, after Lot packed up his family and departed, God repeated His promise to Abraham that his descendants would inherit all the land he saw in Canaan, and not simply what he was left with after dividing the property with Lot. Abraham then moved his tents to the plains of Mamre in Hebron, where he built another altar to the Lord for the reassurance of His blessing.

I think it is important to pause for a moment and contemplate why the biblical compilers chose to include the story of Lot's fall from grace at this juncture in the biblical text. Lot is Abraham's only relative who follows him from Mesopotamia into Canaan, except for his wife Sarah, and Lot's descendants, although stricken from the Chosen line of preference through the progeny of Isaac and Jacob, will remain in Canaan, eventually evolving into the population which become the enemies of the tribes of Israel following the Exodus. Not only are the progeny of Lot excluded from the benefits afforded to Abraham's descendants, there are set up as the enemies of the future Israelite population, as dangerous and hated as any of the non-Semitic population of the Promised Land. The dissident Hebrews who refused to follow the edict of Moses to worship only one god, similarly create a schism as great as that which took place between Lot and Abraham, and as meaningful as that which developed between Isaac and Esau. In my opinion, these conflicts were highlighted by the biblical compilers to teach that those who

---

49 Plaut, Genesis, The Torah: A Modern Commentary, 127. After the destruction of Sodom and Gomorrah, Lot fled to a cave, where his daughters lay with him, fearing that all humanity had died in the conflagration. The older girl gave birth to Moab, the ancestor of the Moabites, and the younger girl gave birth to Ben-ammi, the ancestor of the Ammonites. Gen 19:37-38. Lot's incestuous action, although not of his own doing, would doom his descendants for all time. This myth is similar to the Greek myth of Adonis, or Tammuz, whose mother Smyrna made her father, King Theias of Assyria, drunk and laid with him for twelve nights. Graves & Patai, Hebrew Myths, the Book of Genesis, 171.

do not follow the directives of the Lord should expect that not only their own future, but also the future welfare of their entire family line, will become as an anathema to the Almighty God. While such a lesson will form the primary basis for the punishments inflicted during the impiety perpetrated by the inhabitants of the Divided Kingdom, resulting in the fall of Israel and the Babylonian Exile, it helps to support my thesis that some of the Hebrews during the Exodus felt the need to break off their alignment with the congregation now headed by Moses, a man they viewed as impious to the teaching of their ancestors, and migrate to a distant land where they could practice their religions without the threat of parricidal punishment.

Once Abraham and Lot were separated, war broke out in the region between Amraphel, king of Shinar, who is identified by the Sages as Nimrod of Babylon,[50] and his northern allies Arioch (Ariokh), king of Ellasar, Chedorlaomer, king of Elam, and Tidal, king of Golim (Goiim), against the southern kings Bera, king of Sodom, Birsha, king of Gomorrah, Shinab, king of Admah, Shemeber, king of Zebolim (Tzevoyim), and the king of Bela (Zoar).[51] This was the so-called battle of the four kings against the five kings, and the crucial engagement between the two forces was fought at the Valley of Siddim. The northern forces were victorious, and during the retreat of the southern kings, Amraphel took Lot captive. When Abraham was told of Lot's fate, he gathered 318 men who had been born in his house, and pursued the captors as far as the city of Laish (*Lasham*), eventually rescuing Lot and all his possessions.[52] Abraham was referred to as a Hebrew (*Ivri*) for the first time in this passage, and when the king of Sodom offered him a reward for his assistance, Abraham refused the bequest so as not to appear to be beholden to the gratitude of a king for his wealth, rather than the blessing of the Lord.[53] This episode showed that Abraham was not

---

50 Nimrod was the king of Goiim (nations) who told Abraham to plunge into the fiery furnace, according to rabbinic legend. Rashi, Pentateuch With Targum Onkelos, Haphtaroth and Rashi's Commentary, Genesis, 54.

51 Gen 14:1-2. Although the names of the kings are authentic, none of them have been identified with kings who are known to have reigned in their respective regions at the time the engagement was said to have taken place. Walton, Matthews, & Chavalas, The IVP Bible Background Commentary: Old Testament, 45.

52 Gen 14:13-14. The meaning of the number 318 is not known, although it is equal to the number of men killed in the *Iliad*. Plaut, Genesis, the Torah: A Modern Commentary 138. Abraham continued his pursuit of Lot's captors all the way to Hobah, eighty miles northeast of Damascus, which may be the basis for the opinion of some ancient authors, including Nicolaus of Damascus (first century CE) and Trogus Pompeius (first century CE), that Abraham ruled as king in Damascus for a time. Bartlett, Jews in the Hellenistic World, 148-149.

53 The word *ivri*, or "Hebrew," was a title for Jews, in contrast to gentiles, and was used by Joseph (Gen 40:15) and Jonah (Jon 1:9) to describe their heritage, as well as by God, Who referred to Himself as the God of the Ivrim when He commanded Moses to

only devoted to the welfare of all his family members, but that he also possessed the traits of military strength and bravery that was to carry on through the years of enslavement of his descendants in Egypt, and into the resiliency of those who participated in the Exodus.[54] The Hebrews were a fearsome force throughout the Late Bronze (1600-1200 BCE) and Iron Age (1200-587 BCE), and were often victorious in military engagements, even when they were out-numbered by their opposition. It is this reputation of valorous tenacity that I believe impressed the Mycenaeans enough to welcome the dissident Hebrews into their country after they left the Exodus, and incorporate them into military service before the Trojan War, thereby meshing Hebraic traditions into early Greek mythology.

One interesting sidelight in this story of Abraham's rescue of Lot is his meeting King Melchizedek of Salem, the forerunner of the city of Jerusalem, who was referred to in the text as a priest of "God Most High," or Elyon, a deity mentioned in ancient Phoenician records.[55] The reference to Elyon in this fashion has been taken by some scholars to indicate that Melchizedek was a monotheist like Abraham. By uniting Abraham and Melchizedek in this passage, the biblical compilers were likely not only honoring the holy city of Jerusalem, but also accentuating the similarity between the Patriarchs and certain religious traditions which were present in Canaan at that time. This concordance will be discussed in more detail in chapter 11, when the origins of Yahwism are analyzed in greater detail.

Following his rescue of Lot, God appeared to Abraham in a vision and said, "fear not, Abram, I am a shield for you; your reward is very great."[56] Abraham was not entirely pleased with his favored status, however, for he had not yet been blessed with a son to carry on the family name. The survival of a family in ancient times depended upon the birth of children to carry on the family name, and all potentates strove to assure their legacy through the production of male descendants. Since Sarah was still barren at such an advanced age, Abraham's fears were warranted, but God assured him that he would one day have a son to inherit everything he owned, emphasizing the extent of his future bounty by pointing to the stars in the sky, telling him that "so shall your offspring be!"[57]

---

visit Pharaoh (Exod 3:18).

54 The Jewish philosopher, Martin Buber (1878-1965 CE), points to this episode as evidence of Abraham resembling the activities of the Habiru. Buber, Moses: The Revelation and the Covenant, 30.

55 Gen 14:17-19. Melchizedek was the first king of Salem, as well as a priest of Elyon who founded a sanctuary in Jerusalem. Kugel, The Bible As It Was, 153.

56 Gen 15:1. Sarna, Genesis, 112. This assurance became the *Amidah/Shemoneh Esrei* prayer, which blessed God as the "Shield of Abraham," securing the image of YHWH as a powerful warrior for generations to come. Scherman, The Chudash, 66.

57 Gen 15:2-5. Levenson, The Death and the Resurrection of the Beloved Son: The Transformation of Child Sacrifice in Judaism and Christianity, 88. This passage has been

Abraham's future destiny would not be without trial and tribulation, however, for God added that although his descendants would be numerous, they would also be aliens in a land not their own, and would be oppressed and enslaved for 400 years before being allowed to enter the Promised Land.[58] The future was not entirely bleak, for after this passage of time, his descendants would overcome the nations of the Kenites, Kenizzites, Kadmonites, Hittites, Perizzites, Rephaim, Amorites, Canaanites, Girgashites, and Jebusites, and repossess the land which Abraham had been given. In gratitude for God's beneficence, Abraham sacrificed a three-year old heifer, a three-year old she-goat, a three-year old ram, a turtle-dove and a pigeon. This use of animal sacrifice would become an integral part of the ancient Jewish religion, although the practice would be abandoned by the levitical Judaic religion that evolved following the destruction of the Second Temple. The covenant was then ratified by the vision of a smoking furnace and a burning lamp which then passed between the carcasses of the sacrifice.

This description of God's covenant with Abraham is the initial explanation for how the future Israelites were to become the Chosen People in the Promised Land, but the very next biblical passage reported the birth of Ishmael, implying to the reader, and likely to Abraham as well, that the promise of the Lord for future progeny might be provided through the genesis of an illegitimate, albeit firstborn, son, and not through the child of Sarah. Because Sarah assumed that she could not become pregnant at her advanced age, she had agreed to let her Egyptian maidservant, Hagar, lay with Abraham in order to generate a son to carry on the family name.[59] God had not declared that Sarah would necessarily be the

---

pointed to as an explanation of why many ancient authors, including Josephus, Aristobulus, and Eupolemus, claimed that Abraham was learned in astronomy and astrology. Bartlett, Jews in the Hellenistic World, 147-148. The comparison of the number of Abraham's descendants to that of the stars will be repeated as a promise to Isaac (Gen 26:4) and Moses (Exod 32:13). It also will be repeated following Abraham's willingness to sacrifice Isaac in the Akeda (Gen 22:17).

58 Gen 15:13. The Bible does not specifically say they would be in the land of Egypt for 400 years, but in a foreign land that was not theirs. This choice of words will become important in trying to date the Exodus, as will be discussed in Chapter 6.

59 Gen 16:1-3. Translations of the Bible variously refer to Hagar as Abraham's wife or concubine, since the Hebrew word for wife and concubine is the same. The social status of the concubine, however, did not equal that of the wife, and when Hagar became Abraham's concubine, she still remained the servant of Sarah. Plaut, Genesis, The Torah: A Modern Commentary., 148. The custom of an infertile wife providing her husband with a concubine in order to have children through a substitute source was well documented in other ancient Near East cultures. An Old Assyrian marriage contract from the nineteenth century BCE stipulated that an infertile wife must purchase a slave woman for her husband if she did not provide him with offspring within two years. Sarna, Genesis, 119. A Nuzi contract provided for such a circumstance and ordered that if the slave girl had a child, the wife would have authority over the offspring. Plaut, Genesis, The Torah: A Modern

mother of his descendants, even though the promise likely implied a connection to Sarah, so it is possible, in my opinion, that Abraham would identify his future guarantee of children with the birth of Ishmael. This conclusion would explain many of the future actions of Abraham which have created intense controversy over the ages. The Bible pointed out that Hagar quickly conceived, proving that Sarah's barrenness was not the fault of Abraham, and Hagar took this to be a sign of Sarah's inability to function as a wife, and immediately began to consider herself on an equal par with Sarah, rather than as simply her maid-servant. This attitude added insult to Sarah's already injured self-esteem, and she reacted by treating Hagar very harshly, eventually forcing the expectant mother to become so despondent that she attempted to run away into the wilderness and return to Egypt, putting her life, and the life of her future son Ishmael, in danger. During this traumatic episode, Hagar encountered the Angel of the Lord at an oasis who assured her that there was a glorious future for her offspring, despite the travail she had to now undergo, and she agreed to return to Abraham's house and accept her position as a menial servant.[60]

Hagar eventually delivered a son to Abraham when he was eighty-six years old, eleven years after he left Haran, and Abraham named the boy Ishmael, which means "God heeds," a clear indication to me that Abraham believed this was indeed the child which God had promised him.[61] The future direction of Abraham's legacy, as earlier promised by the Lord, now appeared secure, but thirteen years later, when Abraham was ninety-nine years old, and apparently happy with the extent of his immediate family, the Lord unexpectedly appeared to him again and reaffirmed His covenant to make his progeny "exceedingly numerous."[62] God did not identify Ishmael as the heir on this occasion, but instead promised Abraham that he would now have a son with Sarah, despite their advanced age, in order to carry on the divine promise for numerous descendants. To sanctify the sacred nature of this event, and to show how truly different this new generation would be, the Lord directed that every male child was to be circumcised at the age of eight days, and that all adult male Hebrews, including household slaves, and apparently Ishmael, were to be circumcised as well.[63] This rite of circumcision, which had

---

Commentary, 149.

60 Gen 16:6-9. This was the first appearance of an Angel in the biblical text. It has been pointed out that on this occasion, as opposed to what would take place during the Exodus, the oppressor (Abraham) was Israelite, while the slave (Hagar) was Egyptian. Levenson, "Genesis," 37.

61 Gen 16:15. Sarna, Genesis, 122.

62 Gen 17:1-2. Ibid., 123.

63 Gen 17:9-13. The eighth day was particularly significant for it indicated that the newborn had to live for seven days, a unit of time corresponding to the process of Creation, before it would be accepted into the covenant with God. Sarna, Genesis, 125. Abraham was ninety-nine years old when he was circumcised, and Ishmael was thirteen,

apparently been unknown to Abraham before this date, now became the indelible sign by which all future generations of Jews would identify themselves as members of the Chosen People of God.[64] By aligning the necessity of circumcision with the future birth of Isaac, and requiring that all present members of Abraham's clan undergo the rite, a clear delineation was being made between the status of the descendants of Abraham's children. As we will see shortly, although Abraham only had one child at this point in his life, he would not only have Isaac in the near future, but would remarry and have many more progeny after the death of Sarah, and these descendants would also fall outside the newly favored Chosen line of Isaac. The Lord further charged that the child to be born was to be named Isaac, which means "He laughs," and that even though Ishmael was not to be part of the divine covenant, he would nevertheless be blessed by being made fertile. This latter promise was likely made to assure Abraham that the son he thought would carry on the family name for the past thirteen years would not be utterly forgotten and cast aside, but rather would become the ancestor of a great nation, albeit one less prominent than the Hebrew nation.

I believe it is difficult for many readers of the Bible today to appreciate how severe this announcement that Ishmael was not to be the scion of his future descendants must have affected Abraham, since the delegation of Isaac as the second Patriarch is so indelibly written into the history of the Jews. Abraham had been raising his family with Ishmael as his only child for thirteen years, and he would have not only developed a close relationship with Ishmael, but also would have likely broadcast the news to his neighbors and friends that his firstborn son was to inherit all of his standing and wealth. Everyone in that era understood the elevated role which a firstborn son held in the family hierarchy, and the birth of a newborn son thirteen years later would not have been take as a sign that the firstborn child was no longer favored. Now, not only would the status of Ishmael as the heir of Abraham be utterly destroyed, but all of the men in his family would become marked by a strange rite of assembly, which must have seemed to be a sign of emasculation to those who did not practice the bizarre observance. Whether Abraham had second thoughts about not following the directive of God will never be known for sure, but the Bible recorded that he obediently accepted all that he was told, immediately circumcising all of his household on that very day, including his son Ishmael. This incredible faith of Abraham in the word of God would be tested again after YHWH later directed him to sacrifice Isaac, but for now, Abraham was unwavering in his allegiance to God's commandment. The circumcision of Ishmael kept him integrally related to the covenant between

---

the age when he legally became an adult. Gen 17:24.

64 According to Paul, circumcision was not a requirement for Jews under Christianity, since God approved of Abraham before he was given the command to practice circumcision. Rom 4:10-12.

Abraham and God, despite the fact that he would stand outside the Chosen line, but he was not only to lose his right of primogeniture, but the nations he would eventually father would become the enemies of the Jewish people.

In order to sanctify the importance of the future birth of Isaac, God then changed the name of Abram (Avram), or "Exalted Father," to Abraham (Avraham), the "Father of Nations," and Sarai to Sarah, the "Princess," the names by which they would be known to the generations which followed.[65] The Lord went on to tell Abraham that both he and Sarah would be the father and mother of nations, and that kings would come from their progeny. Not only would their descendants be as numerous as the stars in the sky, which reiterated God's previous forecast to Abraham, but they also would be of royal lineage, a pledge that must have astonished Abraham, for even though he had become quite rich in the caravan trade by this time, amassing a wealth in flocks, silver and gold, he had not considered the possibility that his children would become kings, since such an elevation was generally the result of genetic inheritance, a trait which was not present in Abraham's own family heritage. The forecast of royal pedigree may very well have been given to ease the loss which Abraham felt about the demotion of Ishmael to the rank of a second-class child.

Sarah had not yet heard the incredible news of her future insemination, and the sudden vision of all the male members of her family undergoing circumcision must have been a shocking experience, convincing her that something important had happened to assure that Ishmael was to carry on Abraham's legacy. Ishmael was thirteen years old at the time, and even though the practice of honoring the passage of a Jewish son into adulthood at this age would not become a ritual until centuries later, it was still a time of puberty that was recognized throughout the ancient Near East as an age associated with the ability to procreate. As will later be seen later in the story of Dinah, circumcision was a very traumatic procedure, and the men were incapacitated for days before their wounds were healed. Although we now know that other people had practiced circumcision before this event, according to biblical tradition no one else had yet performed this procedure, and the willingness of the men to undergo such a painful procedure must have indicated a strong faith in Abraham's authority and countenance with God.

This assumption by Sarah that the rite was intended to celebrate the ability of Ishmael to now have children of his own may very well explain her unusual behavior in the very next biblical passage, when three strangers appeared at Abraham's home by the terebinths of Mamre, informing him that the Lord's

---

65 Gen 17:1-5, 15-16. The Living Bible, 12. The changing of a name in ancient cultures was a critical element in the development of an important person, for a name was not only a means of identification in the ancient Near East, but also was intimately bound up with the very essence of a person. Joshua would also go through a name change when his importance was elevated, as will be discussed in chapter 5. Sarna, Genesis, 124.

promise was about to be fulfilled, and that he would be given a son in the following year.[66] When Sarah overheard the news, she laughed at the guarantee of a future pregnancy, disbelieving the forecast of her becoming pregnant at such an advanced age. This response was taken as an affront by the strangers who asked Abraham why she would laugh at their forecast, forcing Sarah to lie in an attempt to deny her rude reply.[67] These early descriptions of Sarah treating Hagar harshly, and then acting with little decorum in front of strangers, is not the kind of conduct which one would normally expect to see from the first Jewish Matriarch, but the ancient Hebrews, like other Semitic tribes, were a patriarchal society, and Sarah's demeanor in the Bible was presented with a litany of faults that reflected the general attitude placed upon women in the Late Bronze Age.[68]

The appearance of three strangers who turn out to be deities forecasting the future birth of a son resembles a theme found in the ancient Greek legend concerning the birth of Orion. In that tale, three passing strangers appeared before an old farmer named Hyrieus in Boetia, a man who had worked so hard for most of his life that he and his wife were never able to have children.[69] The visitors were actually the gods Zeus, Poseidon and Hermes, and after they had eaten a carefully prepared meal, they asked Hyrieus if he had any wishes that they could repay for his kindness. Hyrieus confessed that he and his wife Tamagra would have liked to have had a son, and the gods then promised to fulfill his wish,

---

66 Gen 18:1, 10. That these three men were meant to represent the presence of the Lord is suggested by the careful use of the singular and plural verbal forms, indicating that God was indeed appearing to Abraham, but not face-to-face in his own physical form. In addition, Abraham addressed the men as "Lord." Sailhamer, "Genesis," 144-145. According to Rashi, the three men were the Angels Michael, who informed Abraham that Sarah would have a son; Gabriel, who eventually would overturn Sodom; and Raphael, who later healed Abraham and saved Lot. Scherman, The Chumash, 79. When Abraham later attempts to sacrifice Isaac, it again will be an Angel, rather than the Lord Himself, who will intervene.

67 When Abraham first heard the news from God of Sarah's future pregnancy, he also fell face down and laughed at the thought of such an event at their advanced ages, but there is no indication that his behavior was questioned as being improper. Gen 17:17.

68 Women were frequently portrayed in negative terms in the Torah, beginning with the enticement of Adam by Eve to eat the forbidden fruit. According to rabbinic legend, there was also a woman named Lilith who God had formed out of the dust before forming Eve from Adam's rib. Lilith only remained on earth for a short period of time because she was insistent upon enjoying full equality with her husband. When refused, she took her revenge by trying to kill all newborn babies. This sexist conflict continued into patriarchal times, where the "daughters of Zion were haughty and walked with stretched forth necks and wanton eyes; Sarah was an eavesdropper in her own tent, when the Angel spoke with Abraham; Miriam was a tale-bearer, accusing Moses; Rachel was envious of her sister Leah; and Dinah was a gadabout." Ginzberg, The Legends of the Jews, I.65-66.

69 Ridpath, "Orion the Hunter," 2-3.

telling him to bury the ox hide they had just consumed, and in due time a boy would be born, despite their advanced age. The gods urinated on the hide first, and when nine months later a newborn baby appeared at the site where the hide was buried, Hyrieus named the boy Urion, which later was changed to Orion because the neighbors thought that the first name sounded horrible.[70] Whether the Orion fable was a variant of the biblical legend is not known, but the similarity is reflective of many other close parallels in Greek and Hebrew mythology, as will be discussed throughout this book, and I believe my theory of dissident Hebrew migration to Mycenae, bringing oral legends which later would be compiled into the biblical text, is the best explanation for why these concurrences are so common.

The strangers then told Abraham that the outrageous, sinful behavior of the nearby towns of Sodom and Gomorrah was so great that the Lord was coming to witness for Himself the extent of their transgression. After the three men left, God then appeared to discuss the fate of the cities directly with Abraham, the first time that an actual debate between man and God took place in the Bible, as opposed to a simple theophany or revelation of future events, as occurred earlier with both Noah and Abraham.[71] After YHWH revealed His plan to destroy the two cities in order to discipline the inhabitants for their impious activity, Abraham interceded and asked the Lord for compassion, arguing that if the cities were destroyed, innocent men, women, and children would perish along with those who acted immorally.[72] This concern of Abraham for the welfare of those who led a righteous life has been used by many commentators to illustrate the magnanimous nature of Abraham, a man who not only piously obeyed the commandments of God, but cared enough for humanity to argue that all men deserved to be protected by the Almighty God if they remained free of sin. While such a conclusion is supported by the facts of this particular passage, the silence of Abraham, and his failure to try and change God's mind when he was ordered to sacrifice his beloved son Isaac for no apparent reason at all, seems strangely inconsistent with such a description of munificence. Why Abraham had so much concern for the innocent inhabitants of Sodom and Gomorrah, and on the surface so little concern for the life of his own child, has created a controversy that still leaves many readers today without a satisfactory answer. For the moment, it remains one of those biblical inconsistencies that requires a show of faith, rather

70 Kuhl, "Orion, The Tale of Orion, Canis Major, Canis Minor, Lepus and Scorpio," 1-3.

71 A theophany refers to the manifestation of a deity to a person or community, whereby the god communicates his authority and power to be the sovereign of that person or community. It generally does not entail a two-way discussion, as was about to take place with Abraham and YHWH. Moses would also later have a similar discussion with YHWH at the burning bush.

72 Gen 18:23.

than a use of common sense, to explain the vagaries of biblical theology.

Abraham's method of attempting to change God's mind utilized arguments of reason and compassion, which shows how the biblical compilers portrayed the Almighty God with human characteristics. Abraham argued that there was iniquity in calling for an entire annihilation of the city, and asked the Lord if He would destroy the city if there were fifty innocent persons there. God agreed to withdraw the punishment if He was shown evidence that fifty of the inhabitants were pious. Abraham then proceeded to ask for similar mercy if there were forty-five, then forty, then thirty, then twenty, and finally, even if there were only ten innocent people living in the city. When God agreed to spare Sodom and Gomorrah if there were ten innocent people present, Abraham did not pursue the argument further.[73] This ten-person figure would later become the basis for the quorum necessary to have a minyan in Jewish worship. Abraham would not be able to find ten worthy people in order to save the cities from destruction, and the wrath of God then swept over the land, destroying the two cities and reminding all those who questioned His power that disobedience would ultimately lead to devastation and death. This use of capital punishment to discipline those who did not follow God's commandments set the stage for the parricide which Moses brought to bear on large numbers of Hebrew dissidents who refused to alter their age-old ancestral practices of idol-worship following the theophany on Mt. Sinai, and would become the hallmark warning of the Prophets who forecast a prolonged Exile to the residents of Israel and Judah during the era of the Divided Monarchy. The biblical compilers followed the lead of the characterization of pagan gods as being capable of violent wrath if their commandments were not obeyed.

If any reader had sympathy for the fate of the "innocent" residents of Sodom and Gomorrah who would succumb in the conflagration, their view was likely softened in the next section of the Bible, when two of the Angels in the guise of travelers entered the city of Sodom and were invited by Lot into his house. The Sodomites gathered outside and called to Lot, asking to see the men so "that we may know them," a vernacular phrase which meant that they wanted to have intercourse with the strangers (sodomy).[74] Lot asked them to please leave his guests alone, and offered two of his daughters in exchange for the Sodomites to

---

73 The theologic principle that an entire city of sinners would be saved if certain righteous men could be found in their midst is prominent in rabbinic literature, where it underlies the notion of the thirty-six righteous individuals for whose sake the world endures. Levenson, "Genesis," 40. The Lord would later tell Jeremiah that if he could find one fair and honest man in Jerusalem, the city would be spared of destruction. Jer 5:1. This concept was not followed in the book of *Ezekiel*, however, where God angrily vowed that "if Noah, Daniel and Job were here today, they alone would be saved by their righteousness, and I would destroy the remainder of Israel." Ezek 14:14. The Living Bible, 641.

74 Gen 19:5. Scherman, The Chumash, 85, 87.

do with as they pleased.[75] Like Abraham's failure to try and change God's mind when asked to sacrifice Isaac, this passage has received extensive attention over the years, given the willingness of Lot to spare a grievous insult to two strangers by failing to protect his own children from harm. Even though hospitality in ancient days involved an implied promise of safe passage, as is seen throughout the *Iliad* and the *Odyssey*, Lot's concern for the security of his visitors in face of his blatant disregard for the safety of his daughters seems grossly misplaced.

Despite our modern distaste for Lot's action, the Angels appreciated his assistance, and warned him that they were sent by God to destroy the city, and that he must leave at once with his entire family, if he hoped to survive.[76] His two sons-in-law refused to abandon their home, so Lot took his wife and two remaining daughters, and ran from the upcoming devastation. The Angels had commanded them not to turn back and look at the destruction, but Lot's wife could not contain her curiosity, and when she looked back she was immediately turned to a pillar of salt. It was at this point that Lot went to Zoar, and then to a cave in the mountains where he cohabited with his two daughters, giving rise to Moab and Ben-Ammi, the ancestors of Moab and Ammon, who were to become the vitriolic enemies of the Hebrews after their entry into the Promised Land.[77]

The turning of Lot's wife into a pillar of salt provides another parallel with Greek mythology in the story of Orpheus and Eurydice. In that legend, Orpheus, the mythical musician and poet who is considered as the "father of poetry," was renowned for the beauty of his verse and music, which was so powerful that he

---

75 Lot's offering of his daughters may have been the basis for a similar story in the book of *Judges*, where an old man in Gibeah, a village of the tribe of Benjamin, volunteered a young couple from Judah the safety of his house for the night. A gang of sex perverts soon gathered outside and demanded that the husband be turned over to them so they could rape him. The old man begged them not to injure his guests, and offered his virgin daughter and the man's wife instead. The husband pushed his wife out the door, and she was repetitively raped to death, eventually leading to a war between the tribe of Benjamin and the other Hebrew tribes for the offence of the old man's offer. Judg 19:16-30.

76 Although the book of *Genesis* only mentioned the cities of Sodom and Gomorrah as being destroyed, the book of *Deuteronomy* stated that the cities of Admah and Zeboiim were also decimated. Gen 19:24-25; Deut 29:23. Josephus, the Midrash, and early Christian writings added a fifth city to the toll of devastation, the city of Bela, also called Zoar (Tzoar), which made up the Pentapolis, or the 5 Cities of the Plain, with the other four. The Illustrated Family Encyclopedia of the Living Bible, I.60.

77 Some commentators have suggested that this sinful act was possibly a measure-for-measure justice meted out to Lot for his willingness to have his daughters be raped by the men of Sodom in order to protect the strangers who had earlier appeared at his door. Alter, The Five Books of Moses, 92. As if to provide Lot a moral excuse for his actions, the Bible relates that his daughters first got him drunk with wine. Gen 19:32.

could cast a spell over wild beasts with the sound of his lyre.[78] He fell in love
with the nymph Eurydice, and after they were married, she went strolling through
the grass with a group of Naiads, and was suddenly attacked by Aristaeus, the son
of Apollo and Cyrene. As she ran from his advancements, she was bitten in the
ankle by a poisonous snake and died on the spot. Orpheus was so grief-stricken
that he descended into Hades to try and retrieve his beloved wife, despite the fact
no living person was allowed to cross the River Styx into the underworld. His life
was spared only because his lyre-playing assuaged the ferryman Charon, the guard
dog Cerberus, and the gods of the underworld, Persephone and Hades. Hades
was so taken with Orpheus' grief that he promised Orpheus that he could lead
his wife back into the upper world if he did not turn back to look at her. At first,
Orpheus was able to obey this command, but before long he was unable to contain
his desires, and when he turned back to see her beautiful face, she slipped away
into the oblivion of the darkness for all eternity. The two stories are very similar,
and while the story of Orpheus reflected his own disobedience, and Lot's grief
was due to an error by his wife, the loss of a beloved mate because of an inability
to keep one's gaze directed forward when warned to do so by a divine agent is an
unusual theme, and again raises the possibility that the ancient Greek culture was
introduced to the story by dissident Hebrews who traveled to Mycenae before the
Trojan War.

Following the devastation of Sodom and Gomorrah, Abraham moved further
south and settled between Kadesh and Shur, in Gerar, on the southern border
of Palestine. He again feared he would be slain by the inhabitants of the region
because of the beauty of his wife, and claimed to King Abimelech that Sarah
was his sister, rather than his wife. Like the Pharaoh in Egypt a few years
earlier, Abimelech believed the ruse and took Sarah into his harem, once more
threatening the sanctity of her marriage bed. God appeared to Abimelech in a
dream, however, and warned him that he would die if he violated Sarah because
she was a married woman.[79] Abimelech responded that Sarah had also told him
that she was the sister of Abraham, thereby dissolving him of any foreknowledge of

---

78 Orpheus' power was widely known, and he was invited to accompany Jason and
the Argonauts, helping them to overcome many difficulties with the tranquility of his
music. Graves, The Greek Myths: 1, 28.b, 112. His mother was the Muse Calliope,
and his father was said to either be Apollo or the Thracian Oeagrus. He is also seen as
a founder of religious mysteries, known as "Orphism," which teaches the transmigration
of souls in some versions. Schmidt, The First Poets: Lives of the Ancient Greek Poets,
5, 16.

79 Gen 20:3. This was the first dream recorded in the Bible, although God had
appeared to Abraham in a vision earlier, which some scholars interpret as being a dream.
Gen 15:1. God would appear to Jacob twice in a dream. Gen 28:12; 46:2. The appearance
of YHWH before pagans also occurred with the prophet Baalam and Hagar, indicating that
one need not be a pious Hebrew to have contact with the most Holy God of the Jews.

this subterfuge. God reassured Abimelech that He knew his heart was innocent, but that he should return Sarah to Abraham at once, and ask Abraham to pray for his survival, since he was a prophet of God.[80] When Abimelech confronted Abraham with his deception, Abraham claimed that she was indeed his sister, since she was the daughter of his father. Satisfied with this excuse, Abimelech rewarded Abraham with a gift of servants and livestock, in addition to all the land upon which he resided. Abraham also received a thousand shekels of silver, a sizable sum which provided him the means by which he later would be able to purchase burial plots for his family.[81] Since Abraham was successful both times he used this ruse with foreign kings, it is no wonder that his son Isaac would resort to a similar ploy in the future.

Abraham's good fortune was immediately followed by the birth of Isaac, initiating a new phase of Hebrew religious evolution. While there have been some raised eyebrows over Isaac's birth following the taking of Sarah into Abimelech's harem, the birth of Ishmael is a sign that Abraham was not impotent, and Isaac was his biologic son. Isaac was circumcised when he reached the age of eight days, the first Hebrew male specifically mentioned in the biblical text to undergo this procedure at the prescribed date, and Abraham's status in the community increased greatly because of his respected combination of wealth and male progeny. He was able to negotiate the buying of a well at Beer-shema ("Well of the Oath") from Abimelech, thereby acknowledging and guaranteeing his rights of ownership of land as a Hebrew for the first time. When the pact was concluded, Abraham planted a tamarisk tree at the well, invoking the name of the Lord in appreciation of his good fortune. To all appearances, the divine contract between God and Abraham was proceeding on a steady course, but the warning of the Lord that the path would not be smooth was soon to surface in a strange and uncharacteristically fierce manner.

The peace of Abraham's extended family took a turn for the worse when Sarah began to fear that Ishmael would endanger Isaac's inheritance, even though Hagar was not a true wife.[82] She told Abraham to get rid of "that slave-woman

---

80 Gen 20:7. This passage is used to derive the premise that one who injures his neighbor is not absolved from his sin until he seeks forgiveness from the wronged party. Scherman, The Chumash, 93. This is the only reference to Abraham as a prophet in the Bible.

81 Gen 20:16. Walton, Matthews, & Chavalas, The IVP Bible Background Commentary: Old Testament, 52. The sum of one thousand shekels of silver was also the bride price paid among the gods in Ugaritic literature. Ibid. When Delilah agreed to find out and divulge the secret of Samson's strength to the Philistines, she was paid eleven hundred shekels of silver by each of the five Philistine kings, a sum that was 550 times the average annual wage of a laborer at that time. Judg 16:5.

82 According to the laws of Hammurabi (1848-1806 BCE), the son of a slave-wife would share equally in the inheritance of the father if he had been sanctioned as his son, something which Abraham did when he accepted Ishmael into his family. Sarna,

and her son," and Abraham was caught in a dilemma, not wanting to offend his wife who had recently given birth to his first legitimate son, but not wanting to lose Ishmael, whom he had loved for the past seventeen years, and whom he had believed was to carry on the family name. God reassured Abraham that Sarah's advice was correct, since Isaac would be the one to bear His chosen descendants, and so Abraham evicted Hagar and Ishmael from his house, leaving Isaac as the only heir to his entire estate.

During Hagar's emotional and distraught flight, the Angel of the Lord appeared once again and reassured her that Ishmael would not only survive, but that he would become the founder of a great nation, thereby sparing Abraham the shame of causing the death of one of his own children by abandonment and neglect. The nation, of course, was the future Arab religion of Islam, and while the Jews would lord over the descendants of Ishmael for many centuries to come, great conflicts would once again divide the legacy of the children of Abraham in periods of violence and bloodshed, as seen with the events of our modern day.[83]

The tribulations of Abraham were just beginning, however, for this expulsion was eventually followed by the ultimate trial of Abraham's faith in God, when the Almighty Lord "put Abraham to the test," and asked him to sacrifice his only son Isaac, to show that he was devoted to all that God commanded.[84] Known as the "Akeda," this passage is believed to have taken place when Isaac was thirty-seven years old, although he is often represented in descriptions of the event as

---

Understanding Genesis, 156.

83 The Arabs, according to the Bible, were derived from the twelve sons of Ishmael (Gen 21:9-21; 25:12-18), Abraham's six sons with his second wife Keturah after the death of Sarah (Gen 25:1-6), and from Esau, who took two Arab wives (Gen 26:34). According to Islamic genealogists, all Arab tribes were derived from either Qahtan, who gave rise to the southern Arabs, or 'Adnan, who gave rise to the northern Arabs. When Ishmael was evicted from Abraham's house, he grew up with the Jurhum, a tribe derived from Qahtan. Firestone, Journeys in Holy Lands: The Evolution of the Abraham-Ishmael Legends in Islamic Exegesis, 72-73.

84 Gen 22:1. Ibid. The fact that God "tested" Abraham by requiring him to possibly sacrifice his son to show his allegiance clearly delineates, in my opinion, the difference between ancient and modern attitudes towards the importance of children in the grand scheme of things. The ancients did not give much value to the importance of young children, as evidenced by the attitude of Aristippus, the student of Socrates, who replied, after being accused of exposing his son, that "phlegm too, and vermin we know of our own begetting, but for all that, because they are useless, we cast them as far from us as possible." Diogenes, "Aristippus," Lives of Eminent Philosophers, vol. I, II.81, 209. Christian canon law also considered a person before the age of seven years as an incompetent, and without the use of reason. Bouscaren & Ellis, Canon Law: A Text & Commentary, 88.2, 77.

a young child.[85] Such a divine demand is not matched by any other secular or religious mythology except for the Greek story of the sacrifice of Iphigenia by Agamemnon, as the Greek armada prepared to leave for the Trojan War. In that tale, Agamemnon was told by the seer Calchas that the reasons the winds had died down, stalling the Armada in still waters, was because a proper sacrifice had not been given to Artemis, as required under the Greek religious code. Agamemnon would have to choose between offering his daughter to the gods so that the expedition to Troy could continue, or forsaking his loyalty to the Greek state, which he held as commander-in-chief. It is this singular use of infanticide by both the ancient Hebrew and Greek legends to provide a basis for accepted obedience to the divine will which forms the core of my belief that there was a common heritage between the two cultures, and I will discuss both the abandonment of Ishmael and the attempted sacrifice of Isaac in greater detail in chapter 9. For now, I will only mention that Abraham agreed to follow the Lord's directive, and placed his son Isaac on the altar, but that Isaac's life was spared at the very last moment by the intervention of an Angel of the Lord, likely the same one who had twice saved the life of Ishmael.

When Abraham returned to his camp after the Akeda, he packed up the family and departed for Beer-sheba, where he had previously erected altars to God, and then to Hebron, where Sarah died at the age of one hundred and twenty-seven years.[86] In order to properly bury his beloved wife, he purchased the cave of Machpelah, in southern Canaan near Mamre, from Ephron the Hittite. This transaction was reflective of the importance of family loyalty to the Hebrews, for rather than buying acreage for a permanent residence, Abraham's first landed property was a graveyard, which became the burial plot for all three Patriarchs and three of the four Matriarchs.[87] Abraham paid 400 shekels of silver for the property, a price which was similar to other real estate transactions recorded in

---

85 Since Sarah was ninety years old at the birth of Isaac (Gen 17:17), and 127 years old at her death, Isaac is calculated to have been 37 years old at the time of the Akeda. Rabbinic tradition held that Sarah died when she heard that her son had been taken to be slaughtered. Scherman, The Chumash, 100. An alternate midrashic calculation makes Isaac twenty-six years old (*Gen Rab* 56:8), and a pre-rabbinic Jewish tradition, fifteen years old (*Jub* 17:15-16). Levenson, The Death and Resurrection of the Beloved Son: The Transformation of Child Sacrifice in Judaism and Christianity, 133. These estimations would place the age of Isaac close to the age of Iphigenia, who was sacrificed by Agamemnon, as will be discussed in Chapter 9.

86 Gen 23:1. According to the midrash *Pirkei d'Rabbi Eliezer*, Samael (Satan) told Sarah before Abraham returned from the Akeda that Isaac had been sacrificed and she immediately gave up the ghost and died. Zornberg, Genesis: The Beginning of Desire, 124.

87 Gen 23:2, 9. Rachel would be buried elsewhere, near the site of her death, as will be discussed later in this chapter.

texts from Ugarit during the fourteenth and thirteenth centuries BCE, although some biblical scholars have considered the cost to have been inflated, suggesting that Abraham was taken advantage of in his attempt to own land in the vicinity of the Hittite domain.[88] Abraham could well-afford the cost, however, for he was rich in his own right by this time, and the additional one thousand shekels of silver that he had earlier received from King Abimelech would have made his negotiations secure.

Abraham then took another wife named Keturah, and more sons were born to complicate the future family relationships of the Hebrews with their neighbors-to-be, including Zimran (Zambran), Jokshan (Jazar), Medan (Madan), Midian (Madian), Ishbak (Josabak) and Shuah (Sous).[89] The children of Abraham and Keturah became the tribes known for the incense and spice trade, and were not in the linear passage of inheritance which YHWH promised the children of Israel.

2. Isaac

The tale of Isaac is the briefest biography of any Patriarch in the biblical text, and is primarily concerned with his marriage to Rebekah which, as a literary device, united the life of Abraham in Canaan with that of his relatives who remained in Mesopotamia.[90] Because of the sparse treatment of his role as an adult in the patriarchal evolution, a number of scholars have postulated that Isaac was primarily a literary creation whose only function was to link the traditions of Abraham, who was seen by later rabbinic commentaries as the ancestor of the Jewish state of Judah, with those of Jacob, who was identified as the ancestor of the state of Israel. While this may be true from a teleologic standpoint, Isaac's life nevertheless contains important facts which help define the chronologic era of patriarchal existence, and I will therefore discuss his role in the evolution of the Hebrew faith in some detail.

To find a worthy wife for his only legitimate son, Abraham turned to

88 Gen 23:15. Sarna, Genesis, 160; Whybray, "Genesis," 54. To put the price in perspective, many generations later Jeremiah would buy a field in Anathoth from his cousin Hanamel for seventeen silver shekels, a sum greatly below that paid by Abraham. Jer 32:9.

89 Keturah was called a wife in the book of *Genesis* (Gen 25:1), but she was referred to as a concubine by the Chronicler (1 Chron 1:32). Friedman, Commentary on the Torah, 85.

90 Abraham's family had remained in Mesopotamia had grown quite large. His brother Nahor was blessed with twelve sons, eight from his wife Milcah, including Uz, Buz, Kemuel, Chesed, Hazo, Pildash, Jidlaph, and Bethuel, and four from a concubine, Reumah, including Tebah, Gaham, Tahash, and Maacah. Gen 22:20-24. There also was a grandson Aram from Kemuel, and a grandson Laban and grand-niece Rebekah from Bethuel and his wife Milcah. Gen 24:16; 25:20.

Mesopotamia, and the members of his ancestral home in Paddan-Aram, 700 miles away. He sent his oldest servant Eliezar to the city of Nahor, and made him swear not to pick a wife for Isaac from the daughters of the Canaanites, but only to choose a woman from his own tribe.[91] This is the only instance in the Bible where the parents arranged a marriage for their son. Upon being appointed to carry out this important mission, Eliezer prayed to God for assistance, becoming the first person in the Bible to specifically utilize this manner of divine communication. As if to emphasize the value of prayer for future Jews, his request was quickly granted, for immediately upon arriving at a well near the city, he met Rebekah, the daughter of Bethuel, who was the son of Milcah and Abraham's brother Nahor. Once Bethuel and Rebekah's brother, Laban, were told of Abraham's desire to have a wife for Isaac, they quickly agreed to the proposal, likely aware of Abraham's prominence and wealth.[92] Rebekah returned home with the servant to marry Isaac, and thirty-five years later, when Abraham died at the age of 175 years, Isaac inherited all of Abraham's possessions, and then settled near Beer-lahai-roi.[93]

When famine hit the land once again, Isaac prepared to travel to Egypt, as did Abraham a generation earlier, but the Lord told him to stay in Canaan, assuring him that he would survive the crisis. Isaac obeyed, and went instead to the court of King Abimelech for assistance, where he perpetrated the same ploy which Abraham had used with Sarah, claiming that his wife Rebekah was his sister in order to protect his life from the nearby residents. The king was not misled by the claim, however, having noticed that Isaac and Rebekah acted more like husband and wife than siblings. Although the names of the kings that Abraham and Isaac each attempted to deceive are the same, it is not likely that they were the identical person, given the passage of a generation of time, but it must be remembered that Ramesses II sat on the throne of Egypt for sixty-six years, so the possibility does exist that Abimelech's intuition was due to a prior experience. Abimelech warned all the citizens to not molest the young couple, realizing the potential danger which could be inflicted upon those who violated the sacred marriage bond. Rebekah thereby never passed into the king's harem, and Isaac was not

91 Gen 24:10. Intermarriage with the Canaanite tribal populations was not yet prohibited, although it later would be banned in Deut 7:3, and be considered as an apostasy in Ezra 9:2, 12, 14; 10:2.

92 Before they agreed, however, they asked Rebekah whether she would marry Isaac, and she said yes, indicating Hebrew women would have to give their consent to any betrothal. Gen 24:57-58.

93 Abraham lived to see his twin grandsons achieve the age of fifteen years. At his death, it is said that "he was gathered to his kin," (Gen 25:7), but this could not refer to his father and brothers since they died in Mesopotamia. Abramaovitch, The First Father Abraham: The Psychology and Culture of a Spiritual Revolutionary, 140. His sons buried him in the cave of Machpelah, alongside his wife Sarah. Gen 25:9-10.

rewarded with gifts as was his father, but he nevertheless became very successful in his farming endeavors through the blessing of the Lord, and soon emerged from the crisis as an extremely wealthy man. His prosperity engendered envy and hostility among his neighbors, however, and he was forced to move from place to place, eventually settling in Beer-sheba, where he had earlier lived with his father following the Akeda. The Lord appeared to him at that site, and Isaac constructed an altar, showing the same manner of respect which Abraham had initiated during his travels in Canaan.

As with Sarah, Rebekah had difficulty in becoming pregnant, and Isaac pleaded with the Lord to lift the cause of her barren condition. Sterility was often seen as reflective of a problem with the woman in ancient days, and generally blamed on some form of divine punishment. The Lord immediately responded to his pleas, and Rebekah became pregnant at still a relatively young age. Her happiness was short-lived, however, for she soon felt pain in her abdomen which left her in a constant state of anguish. When she asked God why she was in so much misery, the Lord answered that she was bearing two children in her womb, and that they were competing with each other, for they were destined to become separate peoples.[94] He added that the older child would eventually serve the younger, instead of the usual pattern of dominance by the firstborn son. This forecast of sibling rivalry eventually came true, and ultimately split the two descendants of Isaac into two separate nations, just as Abraham's own descendants were split into two nations from Isaac and Ishmael. As predicted, Esau, the eponymous ancestor of Edom, emerged first, a strong infant with reddened skin covered with hair, while his brother Jacob, the ancestor of the Israelites, held on to his heel, an indication of his intent to surpass the priority offered to the firstborn son. Although the name "Jacob" is often said to be a play on the word *ekev* (*akev*), which means heel, evidence now favors that the name came from the word *Yakub-el*, "May El protect," an appellation found in numerous Syrian and Mesopotamian documents from the early second millennium BCE. Whatever the actual derivation of the name, the imagery clearly portended the sibling rivalry that would characterize not only the relationship between Esau and Jacob, but also the children of Jacob, as we will see in the story of Joseph. At the time of their birth, Isaac was sixty years old, indicating that Rebekah had been barren for twenty years, since they were married when Isaac was forty years old.

Despite the fact that God had revealed to Rebekah that the older child would eventually serve the younger after his birth, Isaac still viewed Esau as his firstborn

---

94 This questioning by Rebekah was the first instance of a divine response to a woman's request in the Bible. Although the Angel of the Lord had earlier appeared before Hagar to assure her of what the future held in store for Ishmael, there had been no actual request by Hagar for assistance from God. The quarrel between twin brothers in the womb was also seen in Greek mythology with the story of Proetus and Acrisius, the twin sons of King Abas of Argolis. Graves, The Greek Myths: 1, 73.a, 237.

son, and Jacob therefore had to find a way to achieve the privileged status of the firstborn child in order to become recognized as the third Patriarch of the Jews.[95] God was not bound by the natural order of birth, which generally delegated divine approval to the firstborn son, and many of Israel's renowned leaders came to prominence because God took them out of their natural inferior position as younger sibling and placed them at the front of the line. Other examples of Jewish men who achieved an exalted status despite not being the primogeniture were Joseph, Ephraim, Moses and David. This possibility was not to be taken for granted, however, and Jacob eventually sought to obtain the status of firstborn son by forcing Esau to transfer his birthright in order to eat bread and lentil stew which had been prepared for the evening meal after he came home famished from hunting in the field. One might wonder at the devious manner in which Jacob forced Esau to relinquish his inheritance, but the biblical compilers did not seek to deny the cunning aspect of Jacob's personality, much as the Greeks did not hide a similar trait in Odysseus (Ulysses), the hero of Homer's great poem the *Odyssey*, as will be discussed later in this chapter. Although Esau sold his birthright for food at this time, he could have retained the privilege if he was anointed by Isaac on his deathbed, and so the final outcome was still uncertain, and Jacob would have to resort to trickery once again in order to permanently step to the front of the inheritance line.

The life of Isaac passed quickly in the biblical text, and despite the fact that he was disappointed by Esau's earlier choice of two Hittite women as wives, he still planned to bless him as his firstborn son, not aware of the forfeiture which had earlier taken place to Jacob. As his final days approached, Isaac sent Esau out to hunt some game, in order to prepare a savory dish before receiving his final blessing.[96] Rebekah overheard the conversation and plotted with Jacob to fool Isaac into placing the blessing upon him instead of Esau. To assist Jacob in his endeavor, Rebekah helped him prepare two choice kids as a tasty meal for Isaac,

---

95 The hegemony of the firstborn son was widely attested to in the ancient world, with the firstborn son afforded a double share of the inheritance in the Middle Assyrian laws (fifteenth to twelfth century BCE), as well as those from Mari and Nuzi a few centuries earlier. The Bible also accepted this concept (Deut 21:15:17), and emphasized the favored position by having YHWH tell Moses to say to the Pharaoh that "Israel is my firstborn son," when he asked to let the Hebrews be freed, and that in retribution for the refusal, the firstborn sons of the Egyptians would be killed. Exod 4:21-23. Levenson, The Death and Resurrection of the Beloved Son: The Transformation of Child Sacrifice in Judaism and Christianity, 37. Primogeniture was not universal in the ancient Near East, however, and a number of Mesopotamian law codes explicitly mandated equal division of property among heirs. Greenspahn, "Primogeniture in Ancient Israel," 72.

96 Although the Bible presents this scene as taking place on Isaac's deathbed, Isaac did not die until he was 180 years old, well after the disappearance of Joseph from Jacob's household. Gen 35:28.

and then placed the skin of the kids on Jacob's hands and neck, in order to mimic the appearance of Esau.[97] Jacob followed all of her instructions and brought the food to Isaac, ready to receive the blessing which would assure his primogeniture rights. At first, Isaac was confused by how quickly the game was caught, and hesitated to pronounce the desired blessing. Jacob explained that it was due to God granting him good fortune, but Isaac was still unsettled, since the voice seemed to be that of Jacob, rather than his eldest son. When he felt the furry hands offered to him, however, he decided that it must be Esau, so he kissed Jacob and gave him his final blessing.

Esau then arrived home from the hunt, and when he realized that Jacob had conned him for a second time, taking both his birthright and his blessing, he pleaded with Isaac to give him the honor he deserved by being the firstborn son. Isaac explained that once the blessing was given, it could not be returned, and as a result he would have to serve his brother, despite his innate right of primogeniture. He reassured him, however, that "when you grow restive, you shall break his yoke from your neck."[98] Esau was so angered by the turn of events, that he vowed to kill Jacob when the period of mourning for his father had passed. Rebekah overheard his threat and sent Jacob to her brother, Laban, to remain until Esau's anger dissipated. Jacob's exile would last for twenty-two years, and Rebekah would never see her beloved son again, but her mission was accomplished, and it was through the seed of Jacob, rather than that of Esau, that the Hebrew people would descend. Before Jacob left his father's house, Isaac let bygones be bygones and blessed Jacob, instructing him to not take a wife from the Canaanite women as Esau did, but to go to Paddan-Aram and take a wife from the daughters of Laban, the same region where Abraham had sent his servant to find Rebekah.

The story of the machinations used by Jacob to win the birthright afforded a firstborn son was something that the Mycenaeans would have seen as heroic, since it resembled in many ways the character of their great legendary hero Odysseus, who was famous for his wily and crafty exploits. Best known for his idea of building a wooden model of a horse filled with Greek warriors to fool the residents of Troy into believing the Greek force had surrendered and sailed away from the siege of their city, Odysseus, like Jacob, stood for the concept of victory at all costs. He was adept at fooling not only men, but also the immortals, as witnessed by his victory over Circe and Polyphemus in Homer's the *Odyssey*.[99] Jacob, as well, was able to stand up to the immortals, as evidenced by his wrestling with an angel of God during his return from Mesopotamia, as will be discussed

---

97 Gen 27:12. The use of deception will be turned back upon Jacob when his sons bring Joseph's coat soaked in kid's blood to convince him that his favored son had died.

98 Gen 27:40. Sarna, Genesis, 194.

99 Athena was particularly impressed with this trait of Odysseus, telling him how they were "two of a kind, we are, contrivers, both. Of all men now alive you are the best in plots and story telling." Homer The Odyssey, 13:294-296, 239.

shortly, and his ability to obtain Esau's birthright for a bowl of soup, and the blessing of Isaac by the wearing of the skin of a kid, would have been admired by the Mycenaeans as representative of the type of victory-at-all-costs ethic that was eventually embodied into the saga of the Trojan War. His ruse of saving the best sheep from Laban's herd for his own, as will be discussed shortly, also was equivalent to Odysseus telling the Cyclops Polyphemus that his name was "Nobody," so that after he blinded him, and Polyphemus exhorted his neighbors to help, no one would come since the answer to the question who is doing this to you was "Nobody."[100] Harold Bloom, Professor of the Humanities at Yale University, believed that "Jacob is no Heracles," but I believe he erred in his choice of comparison.[101] The similarity in the personality traits of Odysseus and Jacob are very extensive, and while they are not unusual enough to prove that their relationship was necessarily built on contact between the two ancient societies, the many similarities between the two heroic figures provide another reason to lay the Eastern influence in Greece on Hebraic contributions, rather than from Egypt, Babylon, or Phoenicia.

3. Jacob

The travels of Jacob from Beer-sheba in southern Canaan to Paddan-Aram in northern Mesopotamia, a distance of about 850 miles, once again reconnected the life of the Patriarchs in the region of the Promised Land to their land of origin in Mesopotamia. That the integrity of the Semitic heritage between the two sides of the family was still intact after over 150 years of separation shows that the attachment between generations was not affected by time or place, and reflects the kind of loyalty to one's ancestors that I believe reflected the decision of the dissident Hebrews to leave the Exodus when Moses attempted to modify their religion from polytheism to monotheism. The Hebrews were a close-knit pedigree that maintained an oral tradition of allegiance which carried them through difficult periods of time in their evolution, and the compilers of the Bible were careful to integrate this cohesiveness in their tale of pre-Mosaic patriarchal life. While Moses was able to initiate the reformation of patriarchal religious beliefs into a monotheistic faith, it would take centuries before the Hebrew faithful agreed to the modifications, as evidenced by their years of impiety following the crossing of the Jordan River into the Promised Land, leading up to their eventual Exile into the land of Babylon. Judaism would not become the model of a monotheistic faith until the time of the prophet Ezra, as will be discussed later in this book.

Shortly after his hastened departure following the death of his father, Jacob encamped at an unnamed place, near the village of Luz, and that evening lay

---

100 Homer, The Odyssey, 9.407, 157.
101 Bloom, "Introduction," 3.

down on the ground to sleep. During the night, he dreamed of a ladder reaching up to the sky, on which the Angels of God were going up and down. The Lord stood next to him in the dream, and reconfirmed the covenant He had made to Abraham and Isaac that his descendants would be blessed and spread over the earth.[102] Jacob may have been told of the covenant with God before this event, but this personal contact with YHWH nevertheless astonished him, and he declared that the place was "the abode of God, and that is the gateway to heaven."[103] In homage to the Lord for providing him with this new blessing, Jacob took the stone he was sleeping on, and set it up as a pillar, renaming the place Beth-el, or "house of God." He then poured oil on the stone as a means of anointing his contractual bond with God, a practice which was common in the ancient Near East in effectuating business contracts and international treaty relationships. This sanctuary at Beth-el would attain paramount importance in the later religious history of Israel, and the theophany to Jacob was an integral part of its sanctity. Although Moses and Joshua carried on the tradition of showing gratitude to the Lord for His assistance in a similar fashion during the Exodus, such homage was later declared illegal as idolatrous in the book of *Deuteronomy*, and the dissident Hebrews were faced with another alteration in the manner of showing appropriate appreciation to God, which they had learned from their ancestors.

Jacob continued his journey to Haran and upon his arrival he met Rachel, the daughter of Bethuel, at a well attempting to water her father's flock.[104] As Rachel drew near the well's opening, Jacob moved a heavy stone cover by himself, displaying what Robert Alter, Professor of Hebrew and Comparative Literature at the University of California, Berkeley, called an "Homeric" feat of strength.[105] Not only would Jacob mimic the ingenuity of Odysseus in the stealing of his brother's primogeniture birthright, he would also win his wife by an heroic show of strength, a trait which was characteristic of heroes in Greek mythology. Overjoyed at finding his cousin so quickly, Jacob kissed Rachel and was brought to her house, where he was greeted by her brother Laban. This act of kissing is the only time in the Bible where a man kissed a woman who was not his mother or his wife, and it revealed that the future marriage of Rachel and Jacob was to be more than a match arranged by parents for the sake of family connections, but evidence of true love. Jacob's preference for Rachel from the time of their first meeting is likely the reason why his favorite sons were Joseph and Benjamin, the offspring of Rachel, rather than those who were born earlier to Leah.

---

102   God promised that his "seed shall be as the dust of the earth" (Gen 28:14), although He later would say "as the sand of the sea" (Gen 32:12). Rashi, Pentateuch With Targum Onkelos, Haphtaroth and Rashi's Commentary, Genesis, 157.

103   Gen 28:17. Sarna, Genesis, 199.

104   Gen 29:6. This meeting was similar to the manner in which the servant of Abraham found Rebekah for Isaac, and how Moses met his future wife Zipporah.

105   Alter, Genesis, 152.

Jacob stayed with Rachel's family, assisting with the labors of the land, and after one month Laban inquired of what wages Jacob would expect to receive if he remained for a longer period of time. Since Jacob had fallen in love with Rachel at first-sight, he answered that he would serve Laban for free for seven years, if he then could be given her hand in marriage.[106] Laban agreed to the proposal, likely seeing the offer as a way of bypassing the cost of an expensive bridal dowry, but when the time came for Jacob and Rachel to marry, Laban exchanged her older and more homely sister, Leah, in their premarital bed the night before the wedding. Since Leah could no longer satisfy the pre-marital requirement of being a virgin, she was unable to marry another man, and Jacob was therefore required to marry Leah before being allowed to wed Rachel. Jacob was infuriated by this ruse, but Laban explained that where they lived it was customary for the older sister to marry before the younger one.[107] He told Jacob that if he still wanted to marry Rachel, he would have to work for another seven years, a task which Jacob grudgingly undertook. Whether the biblical compilers intended the subterfuge of Laban to counterbalance the devious actions Jacob used to obtain Esau's birthright is not clear, but it seems evident that they were not going to let dishonesty go totally free, and the long indenture of Jacob may very well have been the price he had to pay for the manner in which he achieved his exalted position in the Hebrew hierarchy. This prolonged period of servitude resembles the twenty years which Odysseus had to spend away from his beloved Penelope: ten years fighting the Trojan War, as chronicled in the *Iliad*; and ten years returning home, only to find his wife besieged by suitors, as detailed in the *Odyssey*.

Jacob worked as promised for Laban another seven years, and then was finally allowed to marry Rachel, and begin his family in earnest. From these two wives, and their two handmaids Zilpah and Bilhah, would come twelve sons who were the progenitures of the twelve tribes of Israel. This tribal organization is discussed more completely in chapter 10, but the summary of his future progeny is as follows: his first wife, Leah, bore Reuben, Simeon, Levi, Judah, Issachar, and Zebulun, as well as a daughter, Dinah; Bilhah, Rachel's handmaid, bore Dan and Naphtali; Zilpah, Leah's handmaid, bore Gad, and Asher; and Rachel,

---

106 Gen 29:18. An Assyrian tablet recorded the case of a man who voluntarily undertook to work for ten years in return for a wife, food, and clothing. Sarna, Genesis, 204. In the Nuzi texts, a typical bride price was thirty or forty shekels of silver, and since a shepherd would be expected to be paid ten ordinary shekels a year, Jacob was paying a higher price than usual for his bride. Walton, Matthews, & Chavalas, The IVP Bible Background Commentary: Old Testament, 62. The Nuzi tablets also allowed a man to work to pay off the bride price, suggesting that the story reflected a well-known practice at the time. Gordon & Rendsburg, The Bible and the Ancient Near East, 124.

107 This tradition was also a generally recognized practice among the peoples of the ancient Near East, and is still a custom that is followed today. Walton, Matthews, & Chavalas, The IVP Bible Background Commentary: Old Testament, 62.

who was barren for many years, finally gave birth to Joseph, and then Benjamin. Biblical commentators have noted that throughout the text reference to the order of Jacob's sons varies, suggesting that any significance that may have initially been apparent was blurred by the time the traditions were fixed. The difficulties which Sarah, Rebekah, and Rachel all faced with becoming pregnant was not a feature of Greek mythology, although it was not uncommon in the Greek and Roman era for infertility to interfere with the ability to procreate. According to John Boswell (1947-1994 CE), former Professor of History at Yale University, this problem resulted in the widespread practice of exposure, whereby mothers who gave birth to an unwanted child were allowed to leave it exposed in a specific location, where couples who desired to raise a child of their own could take the infant home, and keep it as a means of assuring offspring.[108] Exposure was also a prominent component of Greek mythology, as will be discussed in later chapters. Although fertility problems impeded the birth of children in the Bible, it did not eliminate it altogether, and despite the difficulties which the Hebrew Matriarchs faced, the twelve tribes of Israel were clearly marked by fecundity which carried over into the Egyptian era of enslavement, when the rise in population of the Hebrews so worried the Pharaoh "who did not know Joseph" that he ordered the casting of all newborn males into the river to control their rapid growth.

As time passed, and his family grew larger in number, Jacob yearned to see his parents again, and finally asked Laban to allow him to return home with his wives and children. The language he used was reminiscent of how an indentured servant would ask leave of his master in the ancient Near East, for it was the master who owned the offspring of his slaves, and not the biologic parent.[109] Jacob's tactic of asking permission, rather than demanding his freedom, was also consistent with ancient Hebrew filial loyalty, and the respect he showed apparently worked, for Laban agreed to let Jacob leave, answering that he had learned by divination that the Lord had blessed him on Jacob's account. This use of foretelling the future by divination would later be prohibited in the Mosaic Code, but it did not prevent other Hebrew tribes from utilizing the practice during the period of the Judges, especially the tribe of Dan, as will be discussed in chapter 7. In addition, the Hebrew prophets clearly expressed their ability to foresee the future, as will be discussed in Chapter 14, something which all nations believed that certain people had the ability to perform.

Laban also offered to pay Jacob the wages he was due for his fourteen years of

---

108 For an excellent discussion of this process, see John Boswell's The Kindness of Strangers.

109 Gen 30:26. In the Mosaic Code, if a master gave a slave a wife, when the man was allowed to go free, the wife and any children she bore still belonged to the owner. Exod 21:4. When Moses later asked the Pharaoh to let the Hebrews leave Egypt, he spoke the same words that Jacob did when asking Laban to let him return home. The New Interpreter's Bible, 560.

labor, and Jacob responded by saying that he would forgo any money payment, and instead take with him the dark and spotted animals from Laban's flock, leaving all the white sheep so Laban would know if any were stolen. Laban agreed, clearly not aware of Jacob's devious nature, and Jacob then used both guile and intelligence to trick Laban into paying him a greater reward than he would have received by accepting a monetary payment. Jacob accomplished this by placing fresh shoots of poplar, almond and plane trees with peeled white streaks in front of the sturdier animals in Laban's flocks as the ewes drank, causing them to bear lambs with dark patches.[110] In this manner, he assured that his spotted progeny would be strong, while Laban's would be feeble. Once again, the oral tradition of Jacob would clearly comport with the personality makeup of Odysseus.

When Jacob finally packed up his family and left for Canaan, he was a prosperous man, but not devoid of the type of practices which would label the patriarchal faith as polytheistic. While Abraham may have been called by God and changed his faith to YHWH alone, his family back home had continued to worship other gods, as Joshua reminded the congregation at Shechem. This is clearly revealed in Rachel's theft of her father's household idols (*teraphim*) when the family caravan departed Mesopotamia. These objects were small hominiform images of gods, corresponding to the *ilani*, or family gods of the Nuzi household, and to the *penates*, which were the Roman household gods who assured the general well-being of the family and the right of inheritance. Although the *teraphim* were later included in the list of idolatrous abominations outlawed by King Josiah of Judah (639-609 BCE), it is clear that Rachel believed that they were a valuable addition, an indication that the family line of Abraham which remained in Mesopotamia had maintained the tradition of his ancestors by worshiping family gods through the use of iconic images. It is this same ancestral faith which I believed caused many of the Hebrew participants in the Exodus to disobey the demands of Moses that such idols be discarded, under the threat of parricidal reprisal. If Rachel felt the need to carry these idols when she left her father's home, the departing Hebrews surely did the same when they left Egypt. This is evidenced by the biblical notation that Micah, who lived in the hill country of Ephraim following the Conquest of the Promised Land, also owned some teraphim and idols which were stolen by the tribe of Dan when they were trying to find a place to settle.[111]

The importance of these objects is attested to by the fact that when Laban found out that his treasured idols were missing, he pursued Jacob to recover them and finally overtook him ten days later, as the family encamped in the hill country

---

110 Gen 30:35-43. Folklore at the time held that what animals saw while mating determined the appearance of their young. Levenson, "Genesis," 62-63. The Greek legend of Autolycus, son of Chione, included his ability to metamorphose whatever beasts he stole, such as turning them from black to white. Graves, The Greek Myths: 1, 67.c, 216.

111 Judg 17:3-5; 18:14, 17, 20, 27, 30-31.

of Gilead, east of the Jordan River between the Yarmuk and Dead Sea, a distance of 400 miles. Laban's concern was reflective of the Hurrian custom that a man's possession of the household idols insured his leadership of the family and his claim on the family inheritance. Jacob was unaware of Rachel's theft, and was offended when Laban charged that his idols were stolen by someone in Jacob's entourage. He let Laban search all the tents, and Rachel was forced to hide the images under a cushion on which she sat in order to prevent their discovery. When Laban motioned for her to move so he could look under the cushion, she claimed that she was unable to rise, for her menstrual period was upon her.[112] This was a double deception, for not only was she hiding the idols under the pillow where she sat, but she could not have been menstruating, for she was pregnant with Benjamin at the time. Her outright lies, coupled with the theft of her father's idols, continues to reflect the devious nature of the patriarchal generations, and it is not entirely clear why the biblical compilers saw fit to highlight this dishonest, and at times heretical, behavior. It may be that they simply wanted to accentuate the unsaintly nature of mortal beings in general, even those considered heroic in the Hebrews sense of the word, but the fact that many members of the hallowed Hebrew ancestry were guilty of acts that would later be severely punished by the Mosaic Code indicates that the tradition of the pre-Mosaic Hebrews were more akin to the lifestyles of the adventurous Greek heroes than to the rigid ethics of the Mosaic Code. Modern Jews, who willingly accept the tenets of monotheism, have also maintained an honored position for the Patriarchs and Matriarchs, and this devotion, in my opinion, is reflective of why the dissident Hebrews during the Exodus refused to give up the polytheistic practices of their ancestors, and chose instead to flee the parricidal reprisals of Moses.

The search of Jacob's camp turned up nothing, and Jacob then indignantly told Laban that he was incensed by the implication of theft thrust upon his family. He reminded Laban that he had spent many years in service to pay for his wives, all of which were unblemished by any misdeed, and the present accusation was an affront to his stellar performance. It is not known for sure if Laban was satisfied that Jacob's family was innocent of the charge he leveled, but he nevertheless put the loss of his idols aside, and the two men made a pact of mutual nonaggression. To seal the contract, they erected two pillars, and Laban swore to uphold the terms by the "god of Abraham and the god of Nahor," referring to the god of Terah, who was the father of both Abraham and Nahor, while Jacob swore by the "Fear of his father Isaac."[113] Whether Laban's listing indicates that there are two separate gods cannot be known with certainty, but his use of idols, combined with this declaration, strongly supports a polytheistic theism belief. The next

112 Gen 31:35. This excuse would have been expected to ward off Laban, for in ancient days menstruation was considered a danger of evil contamination. Walton, Matthews, & Chavalas, The IVP Bible Background Commentary: Old Testament, 64.
113 Gen 31:45-54. Sarna, Genesis, 222.

morning, Jacob and his family left Laban, never to meet again, and the patriarchal connection with Mesopotamia in the Torah was permanently severed.

It has been noted by many scholars that this pact between Jacob and Laban followed the pattern of many ancient Near Eastern treaty formulae, supporting the conclusion that the biblical compilers utilized historical facts when detailing the historicity of the Jews.[114]

These treaties included:

(1) a proposition, "Come let us make a covenant," (Gen 31:44);
(2) a pillar and boundary markers (Gen 31:44-46);
(3) a covenant meal: "They ate there by the heap," (Gen 31:46);
(4) the naming of the heap as witness of the treaty (Gen 31:47-48);
(5) a divine invocation (Gen 31:49-50);
(6) a stipulation: "I will not pass beyond this heap to you," (Gen 31:51-52);
(7) an oath of allegiance (Gen 31:53);
(8) a sacrifice to seal the promise before God (Gen 31:54).[115]

This same process was used in the covenant associated with the giving of the Ten Commandments, as will be discussed in chapter 5. While not a definite proof that the event actually occurred around this period of time, the resemblance strongly supports the oral tradition, in my opinion, and again suggests that the biblical account may be a recollection of a factual account.

Rather than accept an historical basis for this pact between Jacob and Laban, some scholars argue that the legend was rather created to represent the needs of the Israelite state in the late-monarchic and post-exilic times, and not reflect an actual event. Under this analysis, the biblical compilers were not interested in preserving a reliable historical account, but were rather attempting to promote their own concerns at the time. The tension between Jacob and Laban, and the eventual commemoration of a boundary stone, reflected "the territorial partition between Aram and Israel in the ninth to eighth centuries BCE," providing "a clear case of seventh century perceptions presented in more ancient costume."[116]

---

114 The British Egyptologist and ancient Near Eastern scholar, Kenneth Kitchen, has pointed out that work at Mari and Tell Leilan has produced almost a dozen treaties that took place between 2000 and 1500 BCE, and that their format is "wholly distinct" from those which occurred in the third millennium and the middle and late second millennium BCE. The four treaties which are described in the book of *Genesis*, including the one between Jacob and Laban, "correspond quite closely" with the Mari documents. Kitchen, <u>On the Reliability of the Old Testament</u>, 323. Kitchen used this evidence in his argument that the Patriarchs likely lived during the Middle Bronze Age. Many scholars have suggested that the Decalogue was modeled after the Hittite state-treaties from the archives at Boghazkoy. Beyerlin, <u>Origins and History of the Oldest Sinaitic Traditions</u>, 50-51.

115 Matthews, A Brief History of Ancient Israel, 8.

116 Finkelstein, "Patriarchs, Exodus, Conquest: Fact or Fiction?" 47.

The story was not an attempt to document historical accuracy, but was created to help politically unify an heterogeneous Israelite population.[117] I am not going to try and analyze the ultimate purpose of the biblical compilers in this book, but the fact that so many sections of the Torah are consistent with known customs of the Middle Bronze Age is very suggestive, in my opinion, that knowledge of the Patriarchs, as reflected by the many references to their actions by the biblical compilers, was gained, at least in part, by oral traditions which were carried on for centuries prior to the compilation of the Bible, as will be discussed in the next chapter. The details speak more of a reflection of real ancestral ties, than of imaginary people who never actually existed, and I will accept this view throughout this book.

Once Jacob neared the land of Seir in Edom, where Esau lived, he remembered the dangerous threats made by his brother when they last met, and decided to send gifts ahead in an attempt to assuage his brother's anger. Esau sent back word that he planned to meet Jacob with 400 men, and in response, fearing the worst, Jacob divided his family and goods into two camps in order to make a direct attack more difficult, concluding that the size of the party indicated that his brother planned an assault of retribution. In the interlude before the meeting, Jacob lay down to sleep, but was soon awoken by a man who wrestled with him throughout the night.[118] The reason for the contest was never made clear in the biblical text, but the encounter was so traumatic that Jacob dislocated his hip, leaving him with a permanent injury for the rest of his life.[119] In exchange for his valorous strength, the man told Jacob that he would now be known as "Israel, for you have strived with beings divine and human, and have prevailed."[120] Jacob was

117 As first suggested by Martin Noth. Ibid., 49.

118 Gen 32:24-5. Tradition holds that the name of the stranger was Samael, guardian angel of Esau and the incarnation of Evil. Kaplan, The Living Torah: The Five Books of Moses and the Haftarot, 157. This passage is referred to by the prophet Hosea. Hos 12:4-5.

119 Gen 32:26. This injury reflected that the event was real, and not a dream like the episode of the ladder reaching to heaven. The biblical text related that the damage was not caused by the violence of the struggle, but rather that the man "touched his hip-socket," implying that it was either magical or divine. Gen 32:26. Alter, The Five Books of Moses, 179-180. In the *Iliad*, Homer told how Diomedes threw a large stone at Aeneas' hip, smashing the socket and tearing the tendons. Homer, The Iliad, 5.305-308, 136. The type of abnormal gait, or lameness, which results from the heel being permanently raised is also similar to that attributed by Homer to the God Hephaestus. Graves & Patai, Hebrew Myths, the Book of Genesis, 229. While the use of such an injury in both the Bible and Homeric poems does not mean one necessarily was suggested by the other, it is another similarity which, in my opinion, supports a knowledge of the one to the other, again favoring the Bible as the originating source, based upon accepted timelines.

120 Gen 32:29. Sarna, Genesis, 228. The name Israel, or Isra-El, means "power with El." Benson, The Origins of Christianity and the Bible, A Critical Scholarly Investigation

so taken with the news that he named the place Peniel, later known as Penuel, which means "Face of God," saying: "I have seen a divine being face to face, yet my life has been preserved."[121] Jacob may have been the weaker, younger brother when he fled his home years before, but upon his return he was now to be known by a name which would come to signify a mighty nation that would become one of the primary forces in the ancient Near East. Once again, the strength of Jacob would match that of his heroic Greek counterpart, Odysseus.

When Jacob and Esau finally met, the two men reconciled warmly, without any threats of reprisal, as the passage of time had healed old wounds, despite Jacob's initial concerns. Jacob then traveled to Succoth, where he stayed for a brief time before moving to the city of Shechem. He bought land to live on from the sons of Hamor the Hittite for one hundred pieces of silver, and set up an altar, calling it *El-Elohe-Israel*, "El, God of Israel," acknowledging his own name change, and his acceptance of his role of covenantal heir that had been promised to him by God at Beth-el. Jacob's stay in Shechem would soon prove to be anything but peaceful, however, for an episode was about to take place that was very reminiscent of the Greek "Helen of Troy" motif, where vengeance against the distant Trojans was carried out by the Greeks after Paris abducted Helen, the wife of King Menelaus.

In the biblical version of this legend, Dinah, the only daughter of Jacob, was visiting the neighboring women of Shechem, when she was assaulted by Prince Shechem, the son of Hamor (Chamor) the Hivite, who had sold Jacob the land on which they presently lived. This violation was apparently precipitated by the young man's love for Dinah, and after the attack Shechem asked his father to obtain Dinah as his wife.[122] Despite the honorable intentions of the suitor, Simeon and Levi, two of Dinah's brothers, were outraged by the atrocity, and planned to avenge the defilement of their sister. When Hamor arrived to formally present the marriage proposal, Jacob's sons answered that it was not possible for Dinah to marry someone who was not circumcised. Hamor accepted this explanation, perhaps as a sign of displeasure with how his son had defiled Dinah, and ordered all the men in town to immediately undergo the operation. When all the Hivite

---

of the Sources of Christianity and the Bible, 66. The name Jacob was used forty-five times in the book of *Genesis*, and Israel thirty-four times, the latter when the spiritual side of Jacob was emphasized. Plaut, Genesis, The Torah: A Modern Commentary, 343.

121 Gen 32:31. Sarna, <u>Genesis</u>, 228.

122 Gen 33:19; 34:1-2. This sequence of rape followed by a marriage contract was not uncommon in the ancient Near East, and according to Jewish law, if a man raped a virgin, he not only had to marry her and pay compensation to her father, but he was prohibited from ever divorcing her if the marriage was not a success. Exod 22:16-17; Deut 22:29-29. This regulation followed Middle Assyrian and Hittite laws (fifteenth to twelfth century BCE). Walton, Matthews, & Chavalas, <u>The IVP Bible Background Commentary: Old Testament</u>, 66.

men were disabled by pain on the third day following the procedure, Simeon and Levi entered the town and killed every male inhabitant.[123] The other brothers then ravaged the town and took all their children, wives, and goods as booty. The subterfuge, like that of the Greek Trojan Horse, had taken the Shechemites totally by surprise, but when Jacob found out about the attack, he berated Simeon and Levi for recklessly endangering the entire family by inviting retribution from the Canaanites and Perizzites. The two brothers stood their ground and answered that they could not sit back and let their sister be treated like a whore, but the episode played heavily upon Jacob's will and testament, and in his final speech, Jacob called Simeon and Levi a pair whose weapons were tools of lawlessness, forbidding them from being included in the tribal assemblies. This punishment did not carry over into the generation of Moses, however, as the Levites became a priestly caste who carried out Moses' instructions to kill the dissident Hebrews who failed to follow the monotheistic regulations, as will be discussed in chapter 5. While I do not contend that this story was important enough, or so unique, to influence the Greek legend of the Trojan War, this motif of blood-vengeance is once again another similarity in the legendary material of the ancient Hebrews and Greeks to support a feeling of kinship which I believe led to the Mycenaean acceptance of the dissident Hebrew integration into their society. I will discuss this in greater detail in the Conclusion to this book.

Immediately following this violent event, God told Jacob to go to Beth-el and remain there, instructing him to build an altar at the place He appeared when Jacob was first fleeing Esau. Jacob obeyed, but first instructed the members of his household that they had to rid themselves of all the alien gods they had picked up during their travels. He collected all their jewelry and buried it under the terebinth trees near Shechem, an act of purification that would contrast sharply with the impious actions of the Hebrews who melted their golden earrings at Mt. Sinai to provide material for the construction of a golden calf-idol.[124] This was the only time during pre-Mosaic times that one of the Patriarchs mandated

---

123 In tribal societies which lacked a strong central authority, it was the responsibility of the kinship group to be the primary defender of its members. This led to the practice of "blood-vengeance," whereby a person who killed one of the clan members would himself be killed in order to "redeem" the blood of the slain member. 2 Sam 3:27-30. Tigay, "Exodus," 153. Such retaliation, however, would not excuse the amount of bloodshed against the town of Shechem, since Dinah was not slain, and the townfolk were not responsible for the outrage. When Tamar, the daughter of King David was raped by her half-brother Amnon, her brother Absalom killed him, and all of his allies, to avenge Tamar's outrage, but did not extend the carnage to innocent people. 2 Sam 13:1-29. According to Maimonides, the citizens were considered accomplices in the crime because they did not penalize Shechem. Kaplan, The Living Torah: The Five Books of Moses and the Haftarot, 165.

124 Gen 35:1-4.

the behavior of his family members, except for the time Abraham ordered the rite of circumcision for all male members of his tribe, and it is likely that the biblical compilers were using this occasion to set the standard of behavior that was expected of the Hebrews before the episode of the golden calf-idol in order to legitimize the actions of Moses to institute the punishment of parricide. God then appeared before Jacob to bless him once again, reminding him that his name was now "Israel," and that the land He gave to Abraham and Isaac would forever be assigned to him and his offspring. Jacob anointed the pillar at Beth-el with oil, establishing the authority of the sanctuary there for generations to come.

Jacob then moved south toward Ephrath (Bethlehem), and during the trip, Rachel gave birth to Benjamin, Jacob's twelfth, and final, son. This blessed event was marred by tragedy, however, for Rachel did not survive the difficult delivery. The death of Rachel fulfilled the curse of Jacob who had told Laban when he came looking for his stolen idols "let the one with whom you'll find your gods not live," not realizing that it was his own beloved wife who was at fault.[125] Despite the fact that they were only a short distance from the Cave of Machpelah in Beer-sheba, Jacob did not return there to bury Rachel, but rather had her interred by the roadside. The Bible did not comment on the reason for his action, which caused Rachel to be the only Matriarch missing from the family tomb, but rabbinic tradition held that it was to provide a place of prayer where Jews could come and "ease their grieving hearts in times of personal and national need."[126] The Midrash, on the other hand, explained that she was buried secretly so as not to let Esau know of the funeral.[127]

The death of Rachel not only caused Jacob grief because she was his favored wife, but it was followed by a serious fracture in the unity of his family, for shortly after Rachel died, Reuben, the firstborn son of Jacob and Leah, lay with Bilhah, the handmaid of Rachel, who had given birth to Dan and Naphtali. While this act may have been Reuben's way to publicize his firstborn's right during his father's lifetime – a typical maneuver among rulers during the Bronze Age – such sexual contact was culturally forbidden by the Hebrews at the time, and Jacob responded in his final testament by disenfranchising Reuben from his priority position as firstborn son, and transferring his birthright to Joseph, his favorite son

---

125 Gen 31:32. Friedman, Commentary on the Torah, 119. This oath is reminiscent of the one made by the biblical Judge Jephthah when he swore to sacrifice the first thing he saw upon returning home if God would assure him a victory against the Ammonites. Thinking it would only be his pet dog, it turned out to be his daughter. Judg 11:31.

126 Scherman, The Chumash, 271.

127 Gen 35:8. Ibid., 187. This difference of opinion occurs frequently in biblical exegesis, which involves drawing out the meaning implicit in Scripture, and eisegesis, which reads meaning into Scripture. It is due to debate over what is the "plain meaning" (Peshat) of the words, versus what rabbis over the centuries have expanded the meaning to be (Midrash), often dependent on historical situations which have modified what the canonized text intended.

and firstborn of Rachel.[128] In the *Iliad*, a similar punishment was inflicted upon Phoinix, who lay with the mistress of his father Amyntor after his mother asked him to avenge the dishonor which had befallen her. When Amyntor heard of Phoinx's action, he cursed him and invoked the Fates to prevent his ever bearing a son.[129] Once again, while stories of this nature were not uncommon during that era, the use of multiple motifs in Greek mythology that were highlighted in the Torah by the biblical compilers suggest the possibility that the Greeks learned of these tales by the oral tradition of the dissident Hebrews who fled the Exodus.

These two tragedies culminated the story of Jacob's life as a primary Patriarch, and the biblical history of the Jews then shifted to the tale of Joseph's sale into slavery, and his eventual rise to the position of vizier in Egypt. Before leaving the story of Jacob, however, I want to emphasize once again how much his actions compared favorably with those of Odysseus, the Greek hero who stood for the concept that the end justified the means. Christian commentators have at times derided Jacob's resolution to advance his own interests, promoting an interpretation which has led to anti-Semitic conclusions about the nature of the Jews. This is evidenced by the commentary of the Scottish biblical scholar Marcus Dods (1834-1909 CE), who noted that "in this respect Jacob is the typical Jew – ruthlessly taking advantage of his brother, watching and waiting till he was sure of his victim; deceiving his blind father, and robbing him of what he had intended for his favorite son; outwitting the grasping Laban, and making at least his own out of all attempts to rob him unable to meet his brother without stratagem; not forgetting prudence even when the honor of his family is stained; and not thrown off his guard even by his true and deep affection for Joseph."[130] I am not going to analyze whether such a view is anything more than an anti-Semitic appraisal of Jacob's personality, but it seems clear that during the Late Bronze Age, the actions of Jacob would not have been judged as demonstrative of weakness, or ruthless behavior, but rather of strength by the Mycenaean populace, who were primed to view the actions of their heroes more by the ends achieved, than by the means chosen. The Classical Greeks emphasized traits which were valorous and brave, and the Patriarchs would have been seen as heroic fighters, who took no quarter and bowed to no one who stood in their way. The inclusion of Hebraic tradition into the developing Greek mythology would have been an easy assimilation, and not an impervious barrier, as might appear by the comments of later religious preachers.

One other aspect of Jacob's life which adds possible extrabiblical evidence of the existence of the Patriarchs is the fact that a number of scarabs have been found in Egypt, Sudan, and Palestine from the middle to late seventeenth century BCE, which contain the name of an early Hyksos king named *Y'qb-HR*, that is

128 Gen 49:3-4.
129 Homer, <u>The Iliad</u>, IX.447-457, 210.
130 Dods, "The Book of Genesis," 69.

transliterated as *Y'aqub-Hadda*, or Jacob (Yaakov) in Semitic form. A similar scarab was found in a Middle Bronze Age II tomb at Shiqmona, a suburb of Haifa, Israel, which was dated a hundred years earlier than that of the Hyksos king. Professor Aharon Kempinski (1939-1994 CE), from the Department of Archaeology and Ancient Near Eastern Cultures of Tel Aviv University, believed that this scarab represented a Canaanite ruler named Jacob-Hr, who may have been an ancestor of the Hyksos pharaoh.[131] While it is not clear exactly what relationship there is between these individuals and the Hebrew patriarch, it certainly is possible that aspects of the movements of Jacob in the *Genesis* text were derived, in part, from legends of these people.

B. The Hebrews in Egypt

The story of Joseph's rise to the position of vizier in Egypt is the longest tale in the Bible, and contains elements of sibling rivalry and intra-family jealousy that paint a picture of ambition and resentment, more consistent with the Darwinian concept of survival-of-the-fittest, than with the notion of brotherly love. The compilers of the Bible nevertheless saw fit to use this fascinating saga as reflective of the final evolution of the Jewish culture at the end of the patriarchal line, and it is therefore important to study the lessons which were taught, and analyze their possible reference to contemporary Bronze Age events, so that the most likely date-certain for a chronology of Hebrew history can be determined. The narrative of Joseph's life is thought by most biblical scholars to have been written independently from the other patriarchal accounts, and was probably passed down as an oral tradition in the territory of the tribes of Ephraim and Manasseh (Menashe), around the towns of Shechem and Dothan, where the compilers of the Bible searched for stories that accentuated the plight of the Jews.

According to the biblical account, Joseph was favored by Jacob above all his other siblings, and this privileged status caused enmity among his brothers, who hated him because of his cocky attitude, his ability to explain the nature of dreams, and mostly because he reported their misdeeds to his father. Joseph was well aware of his special station in life, and particularly provoked his brothers by relating two dreams which reflected how he was going to reign over them, despite their elder ranking. One dream had the boys binding sheaves in the field when Joseph's sheaf suddenly stood high above all the others; and the second involved the sun, moon and eleven stars bowing down to him, each reflective of the superior nature of his position in life, when compared to his older siblings.[132] Jacob accentuated this jealousy by giving Joseph a very special gift – a brightly-colored coat which was a sign of wealth and honor, thereby showing his own

---

131 Kempinski, "Jacob in History," 45-46.
132 Gen 37:5-11.

favoritism in an undeniable manner.[133] The brothers' resentment grew with each passing year, and their hostility finally reached a point where they decided to kill Joseph once they had him alone.

Their time for retribution finally came when Joseph was seventeen years old. The brothers were grazing the family sheep in Dothan, near Shechem, when Jacob sent Joseph to bring back news of the welfare of the flock. When Joseph arrived on the scene alone, the brothers realized that this was a perfect opportunity to kill their detested sibling and blame it on an unfortunate accident. As they prepared to carry out their plan, guilt over performing an act of fratricide set in, and at the last moment they refrained from actually shedding their brother's blood, and instead left him stranded in a deep well, where he would die of "natural causes," rather than by their own hand, thereby excusing them from the guilt of outright murder.[134] The brothers were spared even this veiled fratricide, however, for a group of Ishmaelite traders suddenly appeared, taking gum, spices and herbs from Gilead to Egypt, allowing them a more expedient method of disposing of Joseph by selling him into slavery for twenty pieces of silver.[135] This sale price has been used to help place the estimated date of Joseph's life, for the correct average cost in the Middle East for a slave around 1700 BCE was twenty pieces of silver, while by the fifteenth century BCE it had risen to thirty to forty pieces of silver.[136]

If the biblical sale was accurate, Joseph would have lived during the Hyksos regime, a date which is also favored for other reasons, as will be discussed shortly. It should be noted, however, that the Bible states the traders were carrying their goods on camels, which were not domesticated until the first millennium BCE, suggesting that any attempt to date the event by the biblical details is flawed by anachronistic means. In an attempt to support the biblical recording, however, the British Egyptologist Professor Kenneth Kitchen has pointed out that there

---

133 Gen 37:3. An Egyptian tomb-painting at Beni-Hasan, from about 1890 BCE, showed a Semitic clan with the men and women wearing multicolored tunics draped over one shoulder and reaching below the knees, a fashion similar to Joseph's coat. Sarna, Genesis, 255.

134 In the "E" source, it was Reuben who made this suggestion (Gen 37:21-22), and in the "J" source, it was Judah (Gen 37:26-27). Friedman, The Bible With Sources Revealed, 94. Many cisterns hewn out of the rock in order to store water in the rainy season have been found in excavations all over Israel, ranging in depth from six to as much as twenty-four feet. Sarna, Genesis, 259. Some traditions hold that it was Simeon who threw Joseph into the pit, while others claim it was Reuben. Kaplan, The Living Torah: The Five Books of Moses and the Haftarot, 187.

135 Gen 37:26-28. In addition to the Ishmaelites, Midianite traders are also mentioned, possibly a reflection of the different "J" and "E" sources, although it is possible that Joseph was sold more than once. Gen 37:28. Levenson, "Genesis," 76. Rashi held that the Ishmaelites sold him to the Midianites, who then sold him to Potiphar. Scherman, The Chumash, 205.

136 Finegan, Handbook of Biblical Chronology, 220.

are references to camels in external sources between 2000-1200 BCE, and that the use of camels "was *not* wholly unknown or anachronistic before or during 2000-1100."[137] The brothers returned home and told Jacob that Joseph had been killed by an animal, showing him the multicolored coat which they had been dipped in the blood of a goat.[138] Jacob examined the garment and believed their tale, renting his own clothes in response and mourning the loss of his son for many days.[139]

Joseph's indenture to the Ishmaelites was short-lived, as the traders decided to make a quick profit on their purchase by selling him to Potiphar, the captain of the Pharaoh's palace guard in Egypt. The traits which had earlier infuriated his brothers did not irritate Potiphar, who was greatly impressed by the young man's intelligence and management capability. Joseph rose quickly in his master's estimation, and was soon put in charge of all his business affairs, as well as his entire household. Such a reward was not uncommon in the first half of the second millennium BCE, as evidenced by the Papyrus Brooklyn (c. 1833-1742 BCE), which listed the names of forty Semitic servants in one Egyptian estate of the late Middle Kingdom. In that particular document, the Asiatic slaves enjoyed a superior status, working skilled jobs of household management, while the Egyptian slaves were given the more onerous labors of working in the fields.[140] Although the average Egyptian reacted to the Asiatics with contempt, once settled inside the country, they were able to rise in society, and even marry Egyptians and acquire important jobs. This internal consistency of facts associated with the story of Joseph and standard Egyptian practice has been used to support the likelihood that the biblical compilers were relying on historical material when they completed the final draft of the book of *Genesis*.

Despite his initial successful rise in authority over Potiphar's domain, Joseph's tenure did not last very long, as his good looks and impressive demeanor attracted the attention of Potiphar's wife, who attempted to seduce him, thereby putting his position of confidence in jeopardy.[141] Joseph repeatedly refused her advances,

---

137 Kitchen, On the Reliability of the Old Testament, 339. Some date the domestication of the camel to between the fifteenth and thirteenth centuries BCE. Bright, A History of Israel, 81.

138 The irony of the use of goat blood is noted by Jon Levenson, who relates that just as Isaac's life was spared by the sacrifice of a ram, "the goat dies, but the son lives and will yet be restored to his father." Levenson, The Death and the Resurrection of the Beloved Son: The Transformation of Child Sacrifice in Judaism and Christianity, 149. This is just one of a series of pay-backs for deception that form a chain in the "J" narrative. Friedman, The Bible With Sources Revealed, 94.

139 Some rabbinic commentaries claim that Isaac also wept for the death of Joseph, as he was still alive at the time of the event. Kaplan, The Living Torah: The Five Books of Moses and the Haftarot, 189.

140 Brooklyn 35.1446. Sarna, Genesis, 271.

141 Although she was never named in the biblical text, later tradition called her

remaining loyal to the confidence of his master, but she persisted and one day grabbed his coat, demanding that he follow her into the bedroom. Joseph managed to slip away, leaving his coat in her hands, and the wife was so incensed at his rebuff that she screamed that he tried to rape her, showing his coat as evidence of his repulsive intent.[142] When Potiphar heard the news of the attack, he sent Joseph to prison for his outrageous conduct.

This seduction scene has received prominent attention in many biblical commentaries, with the Koran devoting most of sura 39 to the story. Hebrew Midrash differed on the details of the seducement, but all agreed that the extreme beauty of Joseph was the reason for Potiphar's wife's attraction. Some stories have suggested that he was so beautiful that women cast precious jewels at his feet, and even cut their hands with knives while contemplating his face. It has been proposed by some critics that Joseph's comeliness was not necessarily natural, but rather due to his primping himself so that he became a handsome man through artificial means, rather than by his genetic constitution. In the *Genesis Rabba*, for example, Joseph was compared to a marketplace dandy, displaying deeds of youthful foolishness whereby "he bedaubed his eyes and smoothed back his hair and raised his heel."[143] But the Bible does not suggest that Joseph's imprisonment was due to any sin of vanity, and rather portrays him as a man of principles unfairly punished by a woman scorned for love.

This episode of enticement has had numerous parallels in the literature of the ancient world, where the plot line of a Chaste Youth and a Lustful Stepmother was a theme that attracted worldwide attention. Many cultures developed fables of temptation as part of their religious and literary heritage, the earliest of which was the Egyptian *The Tale of Two Brothers*, from the Nineteenth Dynasty (c. 1225 BCE). In that popular narrative, a wife tried to seduce her brother-in-law when her husband was out of town, and when the ruse was discovered, she was slain for bearing false witness.[144] Because earlier portions of the story have been dated to the Eighteenth Dynasty, near the time when Joseph is believed to have lived, some scholars have suggested that the biblical compilers may have been influenced by the storyline,[145] but the plot is quite different, and there is little evidence that other Egyptian legends played much of a role in the development of biblical folklore.

Zuleika (Zulaykha). Plaut, <u>Genesis, The Torah: A Modern Commentary</u>, 382.

142 It is ironic that Joseph's ill-fated problems with Potiphar was related to the false representation of a coat, the very garment that got him in trouble with his brothers in the first place.

143 Gen Rabba 84:7. Kugel, In Potiphar's House, The Interpretive Life of Biblical Texts, 30-35, 45.

144 Lichtheim, Ancient Egyptian Literature, Volume II: The New Kingdom, 203.

145 Joseph and Potiphar's Wife in World Literature: An Anthology of the Story of the Chaste Youth and the Lustful Stepmother, 8.

Greek mythology, on the other hand, contains a quite similar seduction scene in the legend of Hippolytus, which suggests a possible generative influence. In that tale, Phaedra, the sister of Ariadne, blamed the bastard son of Theseus, Hippolytus, for attempting to rape her, when in fact she herself had desired the boy but was angered when he scorned her advances. The Roman playwright Seneca (4 BCE - 65 CE) told how Theseus responded angrily by wishing for the death of his son, praying that he not be allowed to "live to behold another sun's bright rays."[146] The gods acquiesced, and Hippolytus was killed when the horses of his chariot bolted and dragged him to a bloody end. The Hellenized Jews of Alexandria were very taken with this Greek story, and *The Testament of Joseph*, a Hebrew work belonging to the class called *Pseudepigrapha*, clearly seems to have incorporated the Hippolytus theme into a retelling of the Joseph encounter with Potiphar's wife.[147] A similar Greek legend is found in the tale of Bellerophon, the son of Glaucus, who was so handsome that Anteia, the wife of king Proteus (Proitos), fell in love with him and then falsely blamed him with attempted rape when he spurned her advances.[148] It is quite fitting, in my opinion, that the Hellenistic Jews (323-100 BCE) should have developed a fascination with Greek legends, since I believe it was their own ancestral stories that were incorporated by the Greeks from dissident Hebrews, rather than from Egyptian or ancient Near Eastern sources, making the underlying lessons congruous, and easier to understand.[149] The question remains unanswered as to which tale preceded the other, but, in my opinion, the oral legends brought by the dissident Hebrews to Mycenae were the primary source of the Greek mythologic tales.

Unlike the other ancient stories which told of a Lustful Stepmother who caused harm when her advances were spurned, the Old Testament utilized the imprisonment of Joseph as a springboard for explaining how Joseph came to rise to the position of vizier in the Egyptian political hierarchy. After incarceration, Joseph lingered in jail for thirteen years, until he was thirty years old, when he was finally called upon to interpret the nature of a dream to the Pharaoh, who had been left unsatisfied by the explanations of all the magicians and sages in Egypt. The king's wine-taster, who had also been wrongly imprisoned, had earlier asked

146 Seneca, Phaedra, III.946-947, 134-135.
147 Joseph and Potiphar's Wife in World Literature: An Anthology of the Story of the Chaste Youth and the Lustful Stepmother, 16. The *Pseudepigrapha* is a collection of apocryphal works from 200 BCE-200 CE which were rejected by the orthodox Jewish hierarchy, but mothered by the Roman Catholic Church. They contained Greek writings of Hellenistic Jews, as well as Latin, Syrian, Ethiopic, Aramean, Arabic, Persian, and Old Slavic products. Ginzberg, The Legends of the Jews, I.xxvi.
148 Homer, The Iliad, VI.155-165, 157.
149 Entire communities of Hellenistic Jews who considered themselves Jews, "spoke Greek, thought in Greek, and knew hardly any Hebrew or Aramaic," for seven or eight centuries. Momigliano, The Classical Foundations of Modern Historiography, 25.

Joseph about a dream he had while in prison, and was impressed by the veracity of Joseph's interpretation. When he was reinstated to his former position, he suggested to the Pharaoh that he ask for Joseph's advice about the dream which had left him disturbed. Joseph was then given a quick shave and change of clothes to appear more like the aristocracy and middle-class in Egypt, rather than a Semitic Canaanite, and was brought to the Pharaoh to explain a strange dream sequence of seven fat cows coming out of the river to graze on the grass, followed by seven skinny cows, who stood by the fat cows and proceeded to devour them. This was followed by a second dream where seven plump heads of grain were swallowed up by seven shriveled heads of grain. The interpretation was easy for Joseph, since the images were very similar to his own dreams which had so infuriated his brothers that they attempted to kill him. Joseph told the Pharaoh that the dreams meant that there would be seven years of plenty in Egypt, followed by seven years of famine, and that preparations should be made to prepare for the privations.[150] A stela from the Ptolemaic period (2nd century BCE), stated to be describing conditions during the reign of King Djoser of the Third Dynasty (28th century BCE), tells of a time when there was a famine that lasted for seven years, which then was followed by years of plenty, the exact number of which were not given.[151] It is not known if the biblical compilers were aware of this remarkably similar occurrence, or if the Ptolemaic text was an accurate reflection of Egyptian lore, but since the compilation of the Bible appears to have been completed near the time of the Ptolemaic period, it is intriguing to wonder if one legend was suggested by an awareness of the other, and which one may have been the inspirational source.

The Pharaoh took Joseph's exposition seriously, knowing full-well that although the Nile river generally provided adequate irrigation through the annual flooding of the adjacent Nile Valley, there were years when the rainfall in the southern Sudan did not provide a sufficient volume of water to cause the river to rise during the summer months, and this led to cycles of famine. Joseph suggested that the Pharaoh take three measures to deal with the crisis: the selection of a national commissioner who should be a "man of discernment and wisdom;" the appointment of regional overseers; and the storage of large amounts of grain during the years of plenty, in order to assure that there would be provisions during the years of famine.[152] The Pharaoh agreed to Joseph's proposal, and appointed him

---

150 Gen 41:1-7, 25-32.

151 Inscriptions of such occurrences exist from the time of King Djoser (c. twenty-eighth century BCE), the First Intermediate Period (c. 2250-2000 BCE), and the reign of Sesostris I (c. 1971-1928 BCE). Sarna, Genesis, 290. In the famine from the time of Djoser, the Nile failed to overflow its banks for seven successive years. The Illustrated Family Encyclopedia of the Living Bible, I.108.

152 Gen 41:33-35. Sarna, Genesis, 285.

vizier, second-in-command in charge of all Egyptian property.[(153)] When famine later spread over the land, the government was able to sell food to the starving populace, eventually collecting all of their livestock and farmland in payment for the sustenance which normally would have been grown at home, creating even greater wealth for the royal court. Joseph became very rich and prosperous during these seven years of famine, but it is likely that the Egyptian populace viewed him with anger, for although they were able to survive the famine, it was Joseph who was seen as responsible for their loss of independence and property.[(154)] This enmity may very well have been the cause for the enslavement of the Hebrews, to be followed by even greater retribution by the ascension of the Pharaoh "who did not know Joseph."

As evidence of his exalted position, Joseph was given robes of fine linen, a gold chain to wear around his neck, and the chariot of the second-in-command of the Pharaoh. In addition, the people were commanded to shout "Abrek" as he passed by, kneeling down as they would for the Pharaoh himself.[(155)] As further evidence of Joseph's authority to dispense his personal brand of authoritarian justice, he was allowed to wear the Pharaoh's signet ring around his neck, providing him with an immediate sign of royal agreement to any proclamation he made. He was given Asenath, the daughter of Potiphera (Petephres), priest of On, for his wife, and his name was changed to Zaphenath-paneah (Psothom Phanech, Tzaphnath Paaneach), which meant "Revealer of hidden things," because of his power to interpret dreams.[(156)] That Joseph would be rewarded with such high office, despite the fact that he was a non-Egyptian Semite, has been used to argue that he rose to power during the Hyksos Dynasty, a time when Semites were often favored

---

153 Gen 41:44. His appointment put him in a position of great power, since there was no codified law in Egypt at the time, allowing the vizier to dispense justice as he saw fit, with no right of appeal if a defendant felt ill-used. Wilson, The Culture of Ancient Egypt, 172.

154 Although the Egyptian theory of government gave the Pharaoh the supreme right of ownership of the land by virtue of his divine status before the famine, private landed property did exist in all periods of Egyptian history. Sarna, Genesis, 322. As the famine spread throughout Egypt, Joseph eventually collected all the money in Egypt and Canaan for the king, and when the money ran out, he accepted their cattle, horses, flocks, herd and donkeys in exchange for food. Finally, when the Pharaoh controlled most of the land and goods, the people were forced to sell themselves into slavery, thereby becoming serfs on their own land. Gen 47:14, 16-21. The only people who did not have to sell their land for food were the priests, who had been given a food allotment by the Pharaoh. Gen 47:22.

155 Abrek (Abrech) is not an Egyptian word, but recalls the Assyrio-Babylonian *aberaku*, a title given to the highest dignities, meaning "Divinely Blessed." Graves & Patai, Hebrew Myths, the Book of Genesis, 263.

156 Gen 41:45, 51-52. Like Moses, Joseph married the daughter of a pagan priest, and from this marriage would come his two sons, Manasseh and Ephraim. Sarna, Genesis, 287-288.

over natural-born Egyptians.[157] The legend of his rise from the position of slave to vizier has even been summarized by Baruch Halpern, Professor of Ancient History at Pennsylvania State University, as "a reinterpretation of the Hyksos period from an Israelite perspective."[158] If true, this would provide a reasonably narrow date of a contemporary event that would help date the Exodus, as will be discussed in chapter 6.

Arguing against placing Joseph in the era of the Hyksos, however, is the fact that the Bible noted that Joseph's beard was shaven before he was brought to the Pharaoh, and making him look less Semitic would not be something that would seem necessary if it took place during the Hyksos regime. In addition, rewarding a Semite with such honors, although unusual, was not unheard of, as it also occurred during the reign of Akhenaten, who promoted a Semite named Tutu to a high position that entitled him to act as the representative of the crown in certain areas. Tutu's tomb in el-Amarna shows him being given a gold chain by Pharaoh, riding in Pharaoh's chariot, and being acclaimed by the people, who prostate themselves before him.[159]

While Egypt was undergoing the privations of an extended famine, a similar condition was affecting the land of Canaan, and Jacob was so concerned that his provisions would soon run low, that he sent ten of his sons to Egypt in order to obtain food, keeping only his youngest son Benjamin at home. When the brothers approached Joseph to request the purchase of grain, they did not recognize him, given the Egyptian nature of his dress and countenance, and showed their veneration by bowing low, with their faces to the ground.[160] Joseph immediately recognized his brothers, however, and set up a plan to both frighten his siblings for their prior act of revenge, and also to spare them any harm in order to assure the return of his beloved father. He put on a display of harsh authority, claiming that they were spies and ordering them to be taken into custody. When they responded through an interpreter that they were only in Egypt to obtain food for their family, Joseph ordered one of them to return for the supposedly missing youngest brother, who was said to have remained with their father, in order to verify their story. The brothers resisted this demand, and spoke among themselves,

---

157 Under standard Egyptian law, a slave could not be appointed to a high administrative position. Scherman, The Chumash, 227. Although there is not precedent for a Hebrew rising to an administrative position, a Semitic general named Yanhamu is mentioned in the Tell-Amarna letters as governing the Egyptian domains in Palestine, and there has been speculation that his high-ranking colleague, Dudu, may have actually been a Hebrew. Graves & Patai, Hebrew Myths, the Book of Genesis, 262.

158 Halpern, "The Exodus From Egypt: Myth or Reality?," 98.

159 Anderson, Understanding the Old Testament, 42.

160 Gen 42:6. This act was actually a reflection of Joseph's first dream, when the sheaves of his brothers bowed down before his own, although it is not known whether the compilers of the Bible intended to highlight the irony of the action. Gen 37:6.

concluding that their troubles were due to what they had done to Joseph long ago. They did not know, of course, that Joseph could understand their Hebrew discourse, and when they argued that Jacob would never let Benjamin leave, since he then would fear that all twelve of his sons would perish, Joseph agreed to let all of them return, except for Simeon, who was retained as a hostage until the request was fulfilled. The nine brothers arrived home, and told their father how the vizier had demanded that they return with Benjamin if they wanted the release of Simeon. Jacob was distraught with the potential of all remaining eleven sons being killed, and did not agree until the food supplies they brought back were exhausted. When the brothers returned to Egypt, Joseph was overcome by the sight of Benjamin, his only blood-brother, and invited them all into his house to dine, still maintaining his visage as vizier.[161]

Although it must have been difficult to hide his emotions, Joseph was not yet finished with his ruse, for he still had to find a way to convince his father to come to Egypt without revealing his true identity. The methods he used would have made his grandfather proud, and also would have impressed the early Greek myth-makers, as the next day he allowed his brothers to leave for home with provisions, but this time he hid a silver goblet which was used for divination in Benjamin's saddlebag. After the men departed, he sent his steward after them, claiming that they repaid his goodness with thievery. The brothers were brought back to Joseph's house, and Joseph threatened to keep Benjamin as his permanent slave because of their egregious act. Judah pleaded with Joseph not to keep Benjamin in Egypt, for their father Jacob would surely die of grief if they returned home without the young man. At the mention of his father's name, Joseph could no longer hide his emotions, and admitted his real identity to the astonished men. He told them to return to Canaan and bring Jacob and the rest of the family back to Egypt, for there would still be five more years of famine. He forgave their prior sin of selling him into slavery, explaining that it was Divine Providence that caused their actions.

Despite the fact that Joseph's gracious pardon was portrayed in the Bible as having stemmed from true familial love and devotion, it is likely that he also foresaw the need to have the support of his brethren in Egypt, as there were probably signs of resentment already brewing in the land against his economic policies. When Jacob heard of the proposal, he quickly agreed, overjoyed at finding that his favorite son was not dead, and the whole family, numbering seventy persons

---

161 It is evident that Joseph was not integrated into Egyptian society at this time, despite his exalted position, as he was forced to dine alone, since the Egyptians abhorred the prospect of sitting down to eat with a Hebrew. Gen 43:32. This supposedly was due to the fact that the Hebrews ate sheep, thereby contaminating their mouths and utensils, since sheep were sacred to the Egyptians. Kaplan, The Living Torah: The Five Books of Moses and the Haftarot, 219.

in all, moved to Goshen and began the long sojourn of the Hebrews in Egypt.[162] Before starting his journey to Egypt, Jacob made sacrifices at Beer-sheba, where Abraham and Isaac had both built altars, and that night had his last revelation with the Lord who assured him, once again, that He would make a great nation of his descendants. Jacob lived with Joseph in Egypt for another seventeen years, the same period of time Joseph had lived in his house before being spirited away to the land of Egypt, and upon his death, Joseph ordered that Jacob be embalmed, and then received permission to return his body for burial in the cave of Machpelah.[163] After the death of their father, Joseph's brothers were afraid that they might now be subject to retribution for the evil they did their sibling, and they told Joseph that Jacob had instructed them to remind Joseph to not punish them, for he had forgiven them for their misdeed. Joseph reassured them that they would receive his blessings, and at the age of one hundred and ten years, Joseph died and was embalmed and placed in a sarcophagus in Egypt.[164] At this point, the book of *Genesis* ends, and the Bible shifts its focus to the birth of Moses.

One important point to discuss before leaving my analysis of the Hebrew Patriarchs, is the fact that when Joseph assigned land to his brethren to live in Egypt, he assigned them "the best of the land, in the land of Ramesses, as Pharaoh had commanded."[165] This passage has importance to the dating of the Exodus, for many scholars have argued that Ramesses II was the Pharaoh of the Oppression, pointing to the fact that he had built the store-city of Ramesses, from which the Hebrews left the Exodus, and therefore must have been the Pharaoh at that time, since no other Pharaoh was named Ramesses before his father, Ramesses I. This particular *Genesis* reference, however, supports the proposal that the city was in existence during the time Joseph lived, and was not restricted to the thirteenth century BCE. I will discuss this aspect in more detail in Chapter 6.

C. Habiru

As discussed at the start of this chapter, there is contention over the dating of

---

162 Gen 46:26-27. The Septuagint lists the total number of family members as 75, adding the names of Joseph's three grandsons and two great-grandsons. Kaiser, "Exodus," 303. This same total of 75 members is present in one of the Dead Sea Scroll fragments, an indication that the Greek translation was followed by at least some of the Jewish faithful.

163 Gen 50:2, 4-6, 13. It is against Jewish law to embalm a body, which must be interred in such a way that it will "return to the ground from which [it was] taken." Gen 3:19. Levenson, "Genesis," 99. It is possible that the process was necessitated by the length of time it would take to return Jacob's body to the land of Canaan, and this would also explain why Joseph had himself embalmed, as well. Gen 50:26.

164 Gen 50:26.

165 Gen 47:11. Friedman, Commentary on the Torah, 154.

the Patriarchal generation, and even their factual existence, because of the lack of any reference to them in extra-biblical contemporary sources. The Exodus, as well as the Conquest of the Promised Land, are also not specifically mentioned in surviving texts for the Middle and Late Bronze Age, leading to speculation by some scholars that the entire event was only a fictional tale, meant to legitimize the kingdoms of Israel and Judah with an imaginary tale of land-ownership. I will discuss this latter position in greater detail in chapter 5, but with respect to the existence of the Patriarchs, scholars have found possible concurrent references to the Hebrews in the description of a band of social outcasts who operated in Canaan under the term *'abiru* (*'apiru*), generally translated as Habiru. These records are contemporary with the most favored estimates of the Patriarchs and the Exodus, and because of their importance in helping to both prove and date the existence of the Patriarchs, I will discuss the history of the Habiru at this time, and highlight their resemblance to biblical events.

The Habiru were first mentioned in records from the Sumerian Ur III Dynasty, c. 2150 BCE, an era when Semites migrated from the Arabian desert into regions throughout the ancient Near East, eventually resulting in the Amorite Invasion, when Abraham is thought to have left his homeland in Mesopotamia and emigrated to Canaan. Egyptian references to Habiru did not appear until the beginning of the fifteenth century BCE, when the miscreants were termed *'pr.w*, and listed as workers in a winepress in the eastern Delta. From that point forward the Habiru were generally seen as menial laborers, such as quarry workers and stone haulers, or as a disturbing element in Palestine up to the time of Ramesses IV (1164-1157 BCE).[166] These descriptions could be applied to the biblical descriptions of the Hebrews, both in their role as slaves in Egypt, and as a migrant force during the Exodus, encountering hostile kings who forbade their passage toward the Promised Land.

Scholars initially suspected a relationship between the Hebrews and Habiru because of the similarity of the term *'pr.w* with the word *'ibri* (*'ivri, 'ibrim*), which was used thirty-three times in the Old Testament as a designation for the Hebrews.[167] The designation of *'ibri*, which means "the other side," originated with Abraham, who was called an *ibri* because he came to Canaan from Mesopotamia, on the other side of the Euphrates River. The term was usually used in the Old Testament either by foreigners to refer to the Israelites, by Israelites when speaking of themselves to foreigners, or by the narrator when attempting to set off Israelites from their foreign surroundings. The term was not restricted to Israelites, however, as it was a long-accepted adage that "all Israelites were Hebrews, but not all Hebrews were Israelites," referring to the term *ibri*,

---

166 Greenberg, "HAB/PIRU and Hebrews," 195-196.
167 Weippert, The Settlement of the Israelite Tribes in Palestine, 84.

even though biblical writers did not share this usage.[168]

The Egyptian *'pr.w* was also very similar to the Ugaritic *'prm (*'pr*)* of the Ras Shamra texts, and both of these references were equated with a group of people in Mesopotamia represented by the cuneiform ideogram SA.GAZ, a group of raiders who were associated with towns, rather than with a nomadic existence.[169] This naturally led to the conclusion that the use of SA.GAZ in the Hittite treaties, Amarna tablets and Ugaritic texts, all referred to the same people who were labelled as Habiru in Canaan.[170] These citations consistently reflected that the Habiru were engaged in illegal, or unauthorized, actions, and that they were in essence a "stateless, landless folk who lacked permanent status."[171] Not only were robbers and foreigners who were disturbing the social order part of this group, but also escaped slaves who often found asylum with the Habiru, even though the practice of providing refuge to slaves was forbidden by contemporary treaties. Once again, this description is consistent with the actions of the Hebrews in the biblical text, and provide a possible contemporary acknowledgment of their existence in the historical record.

In the Amarna correspondence, the Habiru were often associated with rebels such as Aziru of Amurru and Labayu of Shechem, and the towns of Gezer, Ashkelon, and Lachish all were accused by the Egyptians of supporting the Habiru, and providing provisions for their survival. While I am not attempting to claim that the leaders themselves were actually Hebrews, because the Habiru were seen as undesirable trouble-makers by all of these ancient Near East potentates, if the Hebrews who fled Egypt in the Exodus left around the same period of time, it is distinctly possible that they were simply identified as joining the ranks of the Habiru, since they clearly fit the description of "landless folk who lacked permanent status," and would have trouble finding work in any other type of occupation. If they were recorded in contemporary chronicles at all, the Hebrews would have been catalogued under the rubric of Habiru, rather than differentiated as a distinct entity, separate from the general class of miscreants, since there was nothing to distinguish them as unique followers of YHWH in

---

168 Greenberg, The Hab/piru, 92-93.

169 The term SA.GAZ first appears in Sumerian tablets c. 2500 BCE, and then in the Accad period (twenty-fourth to twenty-second centuries BCE), and in Ur III (2060-1955 BCE). Later texts include referring to them as agricultural workers, or as robbers. Albright, Yahweh and the Gods of Canaan, 75-76.

170 In the final invocation of the Hittite treaties of the fourteenth and thirteenth centuries BCE, the phrase "the gods of the SA.GAZ" alternates with the phrase "the gods of the Habiru," indicating that the two groups were the same. de Vaux, The Early History of Israel, 105.

171 Greenberg, "HAB/PIRU and Hebrews," 188-189. The term eventually became a pejorative to be understood as "rebel," "traitor," or "reprobate." Newgrosh, Rohl, & van der Veen, "The el-Amarna Letters and Israelite History (I)," 8.

the years immediately following the Exodus. It is therefore important to see if complementary descriptions between the biblical text and the Habiru can be identified.

Some support for this deduction is found in contemporary Egyptian inscriptions which show large numbers of Habiru slaves transporting stones from the quarries for use in the construction of monuments throughout Egypt,[172] and in Leiden Papyrus 348, a decree of an official of Ramesses II concerning work on building his new capital, where grain was said to have been distributed to the Habiru who were working on the great pylon of Ramesses.[173] Although there is no proof that any of these Habiru slaves were actually Hebrews, their representation in a manner similar to that described for the bondage of the Hebrews in Egypt in the Old Testament suggests that some of these workers could have been Hebrews, who then departed in a great Exodus under the leadership of Moses, or were slaves who had fled in the Exodus and were then recaptured and returned to Egypt.

Richard Gabriel, former Professor of Politics and History at the U. S. Army War College in Carlisle, Pennsylvania, has taken the similarity between the Hebrews and Habiru a step further and concluded that Abraham's descendants were actually never enslaved in Egypt, but were rather corvee laborers paid to aid in the large construction projects that were common at that time.[174] This would not only explain why they were strong and healthy enough to survive during their forty years of wandering in the wilderness, but also why they were such effective soldiers, able to defeat the Pharaoh's army at the Reed Sea, and various Canaanite kings before their passage into the Promised Land. He supports this view by pointing out that the description of some scholars that the term "resolute" and *hamushim* to describe the manner by which the Hebrews left Egypt can also be translated as "well girted, armed, equipped," indicating that they were prepared for battle from the very day they began their Exodus from Egypt.[175]

According to Gabriel, when Jacob moved his family to Egypt to join his son Joseph, they were settled in Goshen because that region was the most vulnerable to military attack, and the Egyptians housed them at the border of Egypt, to provide security, an appointment equal to that which would have been given to Habiru mercenaries.[176]

The possibility that the Hebrews were part of the Habiru population has led to the proposal by some scholars that although the Hebrews during their forty years of wandering in the wilderness were portrayed in the Bible as a unified force under Moses, they were actually a split movement from the very start, with the twelve

172 Albright, Yahweh and the Gods of Canaan, 89.
173 Malamat, "Let My People go and Go and Go and Go," 64.
174 Gabriel, The Military History of Ancient Israel, 62.
175 Exod 13:17-18. Ibid., 71-72.
176 Ibid., 68.

tribes migrating separately throughout the Sinai and Canaan, and not uniting until sometime after passage into the Promised Land. Under this supposition, there were two waves of Hebrew migration that followed closely on one another: the first involved a group of Rachel tribes, which was testified to in *Numbers* 33; and the second was a group of Leah tribes, as described in the book of *Judges*.[(177)] The Rachel tribes included the members of the House of Joseph, which consisted of tribes appearing in the genealogical lists as children of Rachel and Bilhah, while the original group of Leah tribes were Reuben, Simeon, Levi, Issachar and Zebulun, with Zilpah replacing Levi later in the Exodus tradition. Most of the tribes traveled to the Lower Galilee, and then spread to the seacoast, while others turned south and settled in the Ephraim hills, on the border of the inheritance of the Joseph tribes. Some support for this deduction can be found in the Papyrus Anastasi I, from the end of Ramesses II's reign, which contains a description of danger from Aser, a chief of an ethnic group who was plundering travelers on the road from Megiddo to the Sharon.[(178)] It is possible that this was a reference to the tribe of Asher, thereby placing some of the Hebrews in the western Palestine in the middle of the thirteenth century BCE, while others remained in Egypt. If the Exodus was not a unified effort until after the Conquest began, the size of the congregation would have been much smaller, and less likely to be distinguished as a separate group of rebel slaves.

Further similarity between the Habiru and the Hebrews, as described in the Bible, is even more evident during the era of the Hebrew Monarchy, leading to the suggestion by some scholars that the accepted chronology of the Bible should be revised in order to place these two events together in time. David Rohl, Chairman of the Institute for the Study of Interdisciplinary Sciences (ISIS), has claimed that Labayu of Shechem, one of the rebels named in the Amarna letters, and King Saul were one and the same person in his New Chronology, thereby placing the Amarna Age in the late eleventh century BCE, rather than in the fourteenth century BCE, which is the accepted date in the conventional chronology of the ancient Near East.[(179)] This identification is supported by the correspondence in the names of the children of each man, with the son of Labayu called Mutbaal,

---

177 Mazar, "The Exodus and the Conquest," 84, 88. Manfred Weippert, Professor Emeritus at the University of Heidelberg, concluded that the Leah tribes left Egypt first, while the Rachel tribes followed closely thereafter. Weippert, The Settlement of the Israelite Tribes in Palestine, 41.

178 Mazar, "The Exodus and the Conquest," 81. Papyrus Anastasi I is an Egyptian literary controversy between two scribes about Syria-Palestine geography, generally agreed to reflect a description of Canaan and Syria under Ramesses II. Yurco, "Merenptah's Canaanite Campaign and Israel's Origins," 29.

179 Newgrosh, Rohl, & van der Veen, "The el-Amarna Letters and Israelite History (I)," 7. The New Chronology goes on to synchronize the Eighteenth Dynasty of Egypt with the early Israelite Monarchy, as will be discussed in chapter 6.

and the son of Saul called Ishbaal, both names meaning "man of Baal."[180] In addition, in Amarna letter EA 256, Mutbaal sent a missive to Amenhotep IV mentioning men called Dadua and Yishuya, suggesting the names of David, and his father Jesse, thereby adding further support to the comparison.[181] Finally, both Labayu and Saul were seen as rebellious rulers who sought to reconquer territory which had been taken by their Philistine neighbors. Since Labayu had a fairly extensive kingdom in the central hill-country and Transjordan according to the Amarna letters, the same region which the Hebrews controlled after the Conquest, the geographical location of the Habiru and the Hebrews were the same.

The activities of David and his mercenaries also closely paralleled the Habiru of the Amarna period, an indication to Rohl and his supporters that David may have become an Habiru chief, and taken part in the Habiru uprising.[182] These battles continued during his tenure as king, leading to the designation of the strongholds of the Habiru mentioned in the Amarna letters EA 298, 284, and 306 as being one and the same as the fortress of Zion captured by David in his eighth regnal year.[183] The son of Saul has also been implicated as a threat in some of the letters, and although David was Saul's son-in-law, rather than his son, there are a number of instances where Saul referred to David as his son in the Bible, lending credibility to the possibility that contemporary chroniclers would have seen the relationship in this manner.[184] These postulates, if proven true, would legitimatize the historical existence of King Saul and King David by referring to individuals who are extant in extra-biblical sources, but there still remains a lack of references to the Exodus itself by any contemporary chronicler, leaving open the debate on whether the biblical story is true or simply a fictional event.

Even if the Hebrews did not actually comprise a majority of the Habiru leadership, it is easy to see why their activities may have been ascribed to the Habiru by chroniclers at that time. The identification of the Hebrews with the Habiru is not uniformly followed by all present-day biblical scholars, however, with many pointing out that while the two terms are related philologically, ant their activities are indeed somewhat aligned, their usage cannot be harmonized, since the term

---

180 de Meester, "Saul, David and Solomon and the Amarna Period," 2.

181 Ibid., 3. It has also been pointed out that when Labayu wrote to the Pharaoh claiming that he did not know his son was consorting with the Habiru, this was very similar to the biblical story of Saul's son Jonathan having a friendship with David after he was banished from Saul's court. EA 254. Newgrosh, Rohl, & van der Veen, "The el-Amarna Letters and Israelite History," 14.

182 The use of mercenaries and conscripts were described at 1 Sam 8:11-14; 14:52; 22:7; 2 Chron 12:22; and 2 Chron 13:6-7.

183 2 Sam 5:7. Rohl, Pharaohs and Kings, A Biblical Quest, 227.

184 1 Sam 24:16; 26:17, 21, 25. Newgrosh, Rohl, & van der Veen, "The el-Amarna Letters and Israelite History, (I)" 15.

"Habiru" refers to a social classification, without ethnic or geographical distinctions, while the word "Hebrew" specifically designates the Israelites as descendants of Eber.[185] This distinction, while valid from an entomologic standpoint, does not negate the fact that contemporary historians may have simply seen the Hebrews as members of this generalized social class, irrespective of the name applied, and not attempted to identify them with greater specificity. Unlike the situation with the People of the Sea, as will be discussed in chapter 8, the Habiru may not have been divided into distinct categories of warriors since they did not appear to have migrated from distant countries, or segregated into discrete city-states following the Amarna Age. If the migration of the Hebrews was noted by chroniclers during the Exodus, there is no reason to believe that they would have isolated this one group alone, and highlighted the fact that they were the slaves who escaped Egypt under the leadership of Moses.

Another group of Bedouins who have sometimes been identified as possibly being mistaken for the Hebrews are the "Shasu" (*Shosu*), a term which the Egyptians applied to tent-dwellers in the region of Midian during the New Kingdom.[186] Donald Redford, Professor of Near Eastern Studies at the University of Toronto, has included the early Israelites under the rubric of Shasu/Israel during the thirteenth century BCE, basing his conclusion on the similarity in their lifestyles, and the fact that the verb *sasa(h)* was used in both the Canaanite and Hebrew languages to mean "to plunder."[187] During the Year 9 campaign of Amenhotep II (1427-1392 BCE), the Shasu played a disruptive role as political insurgents along with the *'Apiru*, *Kharu* and the *Ngs*-people, and one of the areas in southern Palestine during this era was designated by the name *yhw*, the consonants of which are the same as the Old Testament divine name YHWH, suggesting the possibility that the Israelites were involved in the process.[188] This is supported by the fact that there are two territories southeast of Canaan that are mentioned in the lists of Amenhotep III (1382-1344 BCE): one is designated the "land of the Shasu: *S'rr*," which is believed to be identified with Seir; and the other is known as the "land of the Shasu: *Yhw3*," which is the Egyptian designation of YHWH.[189] If the Hebrews were part of the Shasu contingency, it would be likely that they would have been referred to, in part, by the name of their deity. In addition, the Shasu were described in the hill country of Canaan in the

---

185 Greenberg, "HAB/PIRU and Hebrews," 197.

186 Rogerson, Chronicle of the Old Testament Kings, 34. This term generally was used to refer to a federation of tribes, but also was used as the name of the region where they dwelled during the Eighteenth Dynasty in Egypt. Nibbi, The Sea Peoples and Egypt, 18.

187 Redford, Egypt, Canaan, and Israel in Ancient Times, 272, 275.

188 Knapp, Society and Polity at Bronze Age Pella: An *Annales* Perspective, 41; Herrmann, A History of Israel in Old Testament Times, 76.

189 Stager, "Forging an Identity: The Emergence of Ancient Israel," 145.

Papyrus Anastasi I, from the reign of Ramesses II (1184-1153 BCE), shortly before the name of Israel appears in the Merneptah Stele.[190] Since contemporary Egyptian sources specifically named the god of these people *Yhw*, a name clearly identifiable with *YHWH*, the God of the Hebrews,[191] and the Shasu lived in the land of the Midianites, where Moses fled after killing an Egyptian, and where he married the daughter of a Midianite priest, many find the coincidence suggestive of identification. If the Hebrews were actually referred to as a group of Shasu by the Egyptians, then extra-biblical evidence for an Exodus of Hebrews from Egypt would exist in the extant archaeologic record, as is the case with the Habiru.

The importance of these conjectures about the alignment of the Hebrews with either the Habiru or Shasu is not that an agreed-upon exact identification will ever be made, but rather that a reasonable explanation for the absence of specific reference to the Exodus in the extant record from the Late Bronze Age is not proof of a fictional nature to the event. In our modern era of debate over competing claims of Palestinians and Jews about priority-rights to the land of Israel, many scholars have attempted to attack the historicity of the Bible by emphasizing the absence of references to the Exodus in the historical record, and thereby negating the factual existence of an Iron Age Jewish state. Accepting that the Hebrews who took part in the Exodus existed as a portion of the Habiru or Shasu insurgency would go far in supporting the reliability of the biblical text.

---

190 Matthews, A Brief History of Ancient Israel, 28.
191 Wilson, The Bible Is History, 58.

Chapter 4
EXODUS: THE PREPARATION

The mass departure of the entire Hebrew population of slaves out of Egypt in a grand Exodus under the leadership of Moses may very well be the most discussed event in the religious history of the Western World, even if there are many modern scholars who doubt that the occurrence ever took place. Most of the religions of the world have been centered around the teachings of a single individual who was either the incarnation of God, or inspired by divine inspirations, and the religion of Israel followed this format by basing the Torah on the recollections of Moses about what God told him during the great Exodus from Egypt where YHWH, the one and only true God of the Universe, directed Moses to take His people out of bondage in Egypt and into the Promised Land in Canaan. Despite the fact that there is no corroboration of an Exodus of Hebrews actually taking place in extant records from contemporary Late Bronze Age (1600-1200 BCE) societies, the Bible's story of the emigration has generally been viewed in the past as an actual historical happening by the allied religions of Judaism, Christianity and Islam.

Those who accept that the Exodus actually took place point not only to the story represented in the Torah, but also in the later books of the Bible, such as the Psalms, where God is said to have delivered His people out of Egypt[1] as well as the words of the some of the prophets.[2] Ancient historians such as Josephus (first century CE), Eusebius (c. 260-340 CE), and Cosmas Indiopleustes (sixth century CE) even paid their respects to Moses by referring to him as "the first historian in the world."[3] Gerhard von Rad (1901-1971 CE), the respected Professor of Old Testament at the University of Heidelberg, went so far as to claim that "the Old Testament is a history book,"[4] and for much of the nineteenth and early twentieth century CE, this premise was accepted as a reasonable and accurate assessment by most biblical scholars.

Over the past century, however, many scholars have begun to argue that the account of the Exodus is a purely fictional story, invented by rabbis to promote a Jewish history that fit their particular religious needs at the time of the return from the Babylonian Exile (587-538 BCE). Rather than qualify as "sacred history," the Bible is instead seen by these skeptics as "*historicized* prose fiction."[5] Such

---

1 Pss 77:21; 78:12-16; 103:7; 105:26-43; 114:1-2; 136:10-21.
2 Amos 9:7; Hos 2:16-17; Jer 2:1, 6-7; 23:7.
3 Cosmas, Christian Topography, III.227, 93.
4 Smend, "Tradition and History: A Complex Relation," 49.
5 Alter, "Sacred History and the Beginnings of Prose Fiction," 22.

historians, often referred to as "revisionists," or "historical minimalists," claim that the biblical story is simply a myth developed by a group of people, socially similar to adjacent Western Semite tribes, who settled in the Palestine region and set themselves apart by writing a self-serving history.[6] In the words of Bustenay Oded, from the University of Haifa, "the Jews during the Hellenistic period invented a series of myths, a myth of Origins, a myth of the Patriarchs, a myth of the Promised Land, a myth of the Pollution of the Land by the Canaanites, a myth of the Conquest and Judges, a myth of the United Monarchy, a myth of Exile and Return, a myth of Ezra, a Myth of the Empty Land – myth, myth, myth."[7] In other words, the Exodus, as recorded in the Bible, never actually happened, it should be read literally, and not literarily.[8] Even Norman K. Gottwald, Professor of Old Testament Emeritus at New York Theological Seminary, who is considered the leading figure in the social scientific criticism of the Old Testament, labels the Mosaic age as "a synthetic creation of canonical Israelite tradition."[9]

Some of the criticism clearly appears to step outside of an academic argument, and seems to be directed against the supporters of Israel, rather than those promoting the Jewish faith, such as the claim of Keith W. Whitelam, Professor of Religious studies and Head of Department at the University of Stirling, who charged that the theology of Western scholarship has promoted the Bible only to silence Palestinian history, and not to advance an understanding of history or religion.[10] Others, however, include well-respected mainline biblical scholars as

---

6 As the debate over the reliability of the Hebrew Bible, and the biblical version of land of "Israel" heats up, the epithets have rapidly expanded, so that we now have traditionalist vs. revisionist, maximalist vs. minimalist, positivist vs. nihilist, credulist/theist vs. skeptic, and neo-conservative vs. scientific. Dever, What Did the Biblical Writers Know & When Did They Know It?: What Archaeology Can Tell Us About the Reality of Ancient Israel, 47.

7 Oded, "Where is the 'Myth of the Empty Land' to be Found: History Versus Myth," 55-56.

8 Thomas L. Thompson, who teaches at the Biblical Studies program of the University of Copenhagen, has concluded that "we can now say with considerable confidence that the Bible is not a history of anyone's past." Thompson, The Mythic Past, Biblical Archaeology and the Myth of Israel, xv. He added that the story is "a theological and literary creation." Ibid., 78. His view is supported by such notables as R. B. Coote, teacher of Old Testament at San Francisco Theological Seminary, and Niels Peter Lemche, who also teaches at the University of Copenhagen, among others.

9 Gottwald, The Tribes of Yahweh: A Sociology of the Religion of Liberated Israel, 1250-1050 BCE, 40. Gottwald claims that Israel was formed by disparate groups of people in Canaan, only a few of which may have actually taken part in an exodus from Egypt. The historical awareness of a few groups were cast in the form of symbolic descriptions which eventually became part of the "lived-through experience" of the entire Israel population. Ibid., 84.

10 Whitelam, The Invention of Ancient Israel: The Silencing of Palestinian History, 3.

seen in a symposium on the "Rise of Ancient Israel" sponsored by the Biblical Archaeology Society and the Smithsonian Institute in 1991 CE, where the principal speakers, including Baruch Halpern, Chaiken Family Chair in Jewish Studies at Pennsylvania State University, William G. Dever, Professor of Near Eastern Archaeology and Anthropology at the University of Arizona in Tucson, and P. Kyle McCarter, Jr., William Foxwell Albright Chair in Biblical and Ancient Near Eastern Studies at Johns Hopkins University, all agreed that the Exodus from Egypt and the Conquest of Canaan are "myths rather than true history."[11] Professor Robert S. Bianchi, former curator in the Department of Egyptian, Classical, and Ancient Middle Eastern Art at the Brooklyn Museum, has summarized the debate by concluding that the subject has become polarized into "an issue of 'blind faith' versus 'scientific scepticism.'"[12] Either you believe that the story is true, and is part of the canon provided by the Almighty God, archaeologic proof aside, i.e., you are accepting the story out of blind faith; or you restrict your beliefs to attributes which can be verified by references in the extant historical record, i.e., you are from the state of Missouri and adhere to the adage "show me."[13] Israel Finkelstein, Professor of Archaeology at Tel Aviv University, claims to hold a centrist position, whereby he believes that much of the *Pentateuch* and Deuteronomistic History (DtrH) actually reflects real events, but that they promote only the view of the surviving political program in Judah in monarchic times, and that "we can only imagine how different a history of Israel written by scribes from the Northern Kingdom or by other factions of Judahite society would be had it survived."[14]

This uncomfortable divisiveness is not only found in academic corners, but has surfaced in synagogues around the world, where many Reformed and Conservative rabbis also accept that the story of the Exodus is not a factual event, while at the same time maintaining a reverence for the Torah as scriptural proof of the existence of an Almighty God. This view, which sidesteps the need to equate the words of the Bible with modern scientific studies, makes it easier to correlate the concepts of evolution and the age of the earth with seemingly diverse biblical views, but it nevertheless continues to provide a roadblock to those scholars who

---

11 Stewart, Solving the Exodus Mystery, Volume I: Discovery of the True Pharaohs of Joseph, Moses and the Exodus, 1.

12 Bianchi, "Foreword," in Rohl, Pharaohs and Kings, A Biblical Quest, ii.

13 The debate has even affected funding of archaeologic projects which have been carried out at biblical sites in order to prove the historicity of the Bible. In an attempt to downplay the religious nature of any important fieldwork, the American Schools of Oriental Research in 1999 CE changed the name of their popular journal from *Biblical Archaeologist* to *Near Eastern Archaeology*, eliminating any suggestion that they were biased in favor of biblical historiography.

14 Finkelstein, "Digging for the Truth: Archaeology and the Bible," The Quest for the Historical Israel: Debating Archaeology and the History of Early Israel, 15.

have argued that the Exodus was a real event, and that the lack of proof is simply reflective of the dearth of material available after a span of over 3,000 years. James K. Hoffmeier, Professor of Near Eastern History and Archaeology at Trinity International University, has spent his entire career investigating the reality of the wilderness tradition and agrees with the historian David Hackett Fischer that those who attempt to deny the event with this type of "negative evidence" have "no evidence at all."[15]

Supporting the view that the lack of mention of the Exodus in extra-biblical records is no evidence at all is the clear circumstantial support that the Hebrews did exist in Canaan, as evidenced by the mention of Omri, the king of Israel from 886-875 BCE, in the stela of Mesha, the king of Moab in the late ninth century BCE, and the annals of the Assyrian kings Shalamenser III (859-824 BCE) and Tiglath-pileser III (745-727 BCE).[16] In fact, of the fourteen Israelite kings named in the Bible, nine appear in external sources, and of the five missing, three were ephemeral (Zechariah, Shallum, Pekahiah), and two reigned (Jehoahaz, Jeroboam II) when Assyria was not active in the southwest Levant.[17] In addition, Josephus, the first century CE Jewish historian, noted in *Against Apion* that the public records of the Tyrians stated that king Solomon built his temple in Jerusalem one hundred and forty-three years before the Tyrians built Carthage, and that Dius, an Hellenistic historian, in his *Histories of the Phoenicians*, recorded that Solomon, "when he was king of Jerusalem, sent problems to Hirom to be solved."[18] There still remains, however, a dearth of archaeologic evidence for the existence of kings David and Solomon, who are depicted as being wealthy and illustrious in the Bible, suggesting that other countries should have left some record of their existence.

In this book, I do not intend to intensely analyze these contentious positions about the validity of the Exodus, and will put the entire academic discussion on the sideline. While I do not necessarily believe that the Torah is a reliable portrayal with regard to all individual specific facts, I will accept the reality that

15 Hoffmeier, Ancient Israel in Sinai, The Evidence for the Authenticity of the Wilderness Tradition, 19-20.

16 Kitchen, On the Reliability of the Old Testament,16-17. Other kings of Israel and Judah are also found in surviving records. Ibid., 17-21. The following kings of Assyria and Babylon appear in the Bible in correct order: Tiglath-pileser III (745-727 BCE) (referred to as King Pul at 2Kgs 15:19), Shalmaneser V (727-722 BCE), Sargon II (722-705 BCE), Sennacherib (705-681 BCE), Merodach-Baladan II (722-710, 703 BCE), Esarhaddon (681-669 BCE), Nebuchadrezzar II (605-562 BCE,) and Evil-Merodach (562-560 BCE). Ibid., 23.

17 Ibid., 62. In the case of Judah, eight out of fifteen kings are mentioned. Ibid.

18 Josephus, "Against Apion," The Complete Works of Josephus, I.17, 612. He added that Menander of Ephesus (early second century BCE), an historian of Tyre whose work has been lost, confirmed the existence of Solomon. Ibid., I.18, 612. Josephus mentions the *Annals of Tyre* as one of his sources, but this treatise is not extant.

an Exodus from Egypt actually took place in a fashion akin to the biblical tale, and then concentrate my attention on outlining what is likely to have occurred if the basic storyline presented in the Torah is true. This approach is similar to that of H. H. Rowley, retired Professor of Old Testament at the University of Manchester, England, who concluded in the Edward Cadbury lectures, that "while, then, we cannot regard the stories as scientific history, we may accept the probability that they preserve accurate historical memories."[19] While it would be nice to have archaeologic proof that an Exodus of Hebrews from Egypt *actually* took place, there is no question that the story of the Exodus is an *actual* recollection of an oral account that then was transmitted into a written document. As the renowned Jewish philosopher Martin Buber (1878-1965 CE) contended, the entire story of Israel's traditions remains an historical process, because "it derives from historical connections and sets off fresh historical connections," – rather than calling it a "historization of myth," Buber preferred to label it as "a mythisation of history."[20] It is not necessary to totally disregard the possibility that oral traditions were passed on for generations, and eventually collated into a reasonably cohesive remembrance of the original event. I will follow a similar assessment of the Trojan War, as will be discussed in Chapter 8, for although archaeology has uncovered proof that a walled city existed at the supposed site of the Trojan War, there is no evidence a Greek force undertook the siege and sacked the city, as portrayed in the *Iliad* by Homer. Just as there are sceptics about the reliability of the historicity of the biblical text, there are those who claim that the aim of the *Iliad* "is to provide the far-flung members of the Greek people with an epic that would help weld them into a great nation."[21] The Exodus and the Trojan War may be the two most famous events in the history of Western civilization, but the lack of archaeologic proof that either event actually took place has left modern believers with an array of academic naysayers, of which I am not one.

Once the validity of the oral traditions about both events is accepted, I can then put forth my theory of dissident Hebrew migration from the Exodus to Mycenae on a framework that will rely not only on imaginary similarities in the legends of the two societies, but also on factual chronologic events which support the likelihood that the ancient Hebrew teachings were transmitted to the early Greeks during the same era when the mythologic basis of the Hebrew and Greek civilizations were first being formulated. New data is continually appearing in the archaeologic literature on findings which support the biblical text,[22] and the lack

19 Rowley, Worship in Ancient Israel, Its Forms and Meaning, 6.

20 Buber, Moses: The Revelation and the Covenant, 17.

21 Gordon, Homer and the Bible: The Origin and Character of East Mediterranean Literature, 20.

22 In 1994, a fragment of a victory monument erected by King Hazael of Aram-Damascus was found from the ninth century BCE which mentions a king of the "House of

of support for an Exodus in the manner described in the Bible is not enough, in my opinion, to negate entirely the fact that such an event did take place. Modern archaeologists have attempted to overstate the importance of their field of endeavor by claiming that "archaeology is the only real-time witness to many of the events described in the biblical text, mainly for the pre-ninth century B.C.E. formative periods."[23] They denigrate the biblical text as being a self-serving account written only to "convey theological, cultural, and political messages," and believe that "only archaeology can assist scholars in identifying such earlier traditions."[24] I would point out that, much like the ruins of the famed city of Troy, archaeology may indeed be able to advance knowledge by examination of ruins that are almost 3,000 years old, but the inaccuracies in the interpretation of their recordings limit our ability to find the "truth" in an equivalent manner to the vagaries of the intentions of authors of written material. I will analyze what the biblical text recorded about the Exodus, and explain why I believe it led to a schism of the participants, such that many elected to leave the Exodus and flee to Mycenae. I do this in a manner somewhat akin to the Egyptologist Jan Assmann's advocation of an approach he terms "mnemohistory," where the past "as it is remembered" becomes the primary focus of interpretation.[25]

Once it is accepted that the Hebrews actually left Egypt en masse under the direction of Moses, the next critical task is to analyze how the Bible explains the process by which the patriarchal polytheistic Semitic faith was modified into a monotheistic religion, as manifested by the Mosaic Code. This alteration did not come about easily, and Moses was forced to resort to a series of parricidal reprisals against those Hebrews who refused to follow his commandments, in order to cull out those idolaters who remained obedient to their ancestral teachings. While the end might very well have justified the means to those who were willing to follow the regulations of Moses, this adage of do-it-my-way-or-die surely created, in my opinion, a crisis of immense proportions to those Hebrews who were unwilling to forgo the faith of their parents who had taught them to practice and obey the teachings of their ancestors for many generations. Like most other tribal societies, the ancient Hebrews were organized by their household, clan, and tribe, and this kinship entailed a common religious devotion. The Ten Commandments clearly

---

David." This writing is known as the House of David inscription ("Tel Dan inscription"), and it appears to be the oldest reference to Israelite kings outside the biblical text, providing more evidence that events described in the Bible indeed took place, even if they are at times exaggerated. Although their full names have not survived intact, the two kings are believed to have been king Jehoram of Israel, and king Ahaziah of Judah. Kitchen, On the Reliability of the Old Testament, 36-37.

23 Finkelstein, "Digging for the Truth: Archaeology and the Bible," 19.

24 Ibid., 17.

25 Assmann, Moses the Egyptian: the Memory of Egypt in Western Monotheism, 8-9.

followed this practice by mandating the honoring of your mother and father in the Fifth Commandment.[26] Some of the participants must have surely believed that they were not following the practices they were taught as children if they obeyed the dictates of Moses, and as they watched their brethren die in opposition to the Mosaic edicts, I believe that some of the congregation felt forced to leave the Exodus and migrate to Mycenae in order to adhere to their age-old belief in the polytheistic faith of their ancestors. To analyze how this eventual rupture occurred, I will discuss the Exodus in detail in the next three chapters, beginning with the life of Moses up to the time he led the Hebrews out of Egypt in this chapter, the details of the Exodus which forced certain of the Hebrews to either leave or face annihilation in Chapter 5, and the arguments favoring particular dates for the Exodus in Chapter 6.

A. Documentary Hypothesis

All we know about the Exodus is what is found in the Jewish Torah, often referred to as the *Pentateuch*, from the Greek *pente* and *teukos*, which means "the work comprising five scrolls," referring to the books of *Genesis, Exodus, Leviticus, Numbers,* and *Deuteronomy*.[27] To Orthodox Jews, the Torah was written by Moses after he was directed by God to record the history of the world.[28] This commandment to write the history of the Hebrews from the time of the Exodus carried with it the force of divine authority, so that no Hebrew could dispute what Moses said about YHWH's directives. According to Maimonides (Rabbi Moses ben Maimon, Rambam) (1135-1204 CE), every letter and word of the Torah was given to Moses by God, and therefore could never be modified by man.[29] Each

---

26 Exod 20:12; Deut 5:16.

27 Some scholars, beginning with the Swiss biblical scholar Wilhelm M. L. de Wette (1780-1849 CE), consider the first four books, known as the *Tetrateuch*, as the true literary unity of the Torah, and do not include the book of *Deuteronomy*, which originally was an introduction to the Former Prophets (Joshua through 2 Kings). Mann, The Book of the Torah: The Narrative Integrity of the Pentateuch, 2. Because the book of *Joshua* describes the actions of Moses' successor, the first six books of the Old Testament (the Pentateuch plus the book of *Joshua*) is sometimes referred to as the *Hexateuch*, but this is a product of critical theorizing, and not an historical entity. Greenberg, Understanding Exodus, 13.

28 The Torah records five instances when Moses was commanded by God to write the history of the Exodus: Exod 17:14; 24:4, 7; 34:27; Num 33:1-2; Deut 31:9, 24.

29 Maimonides cautioned that whoever did not believe that the Torah was composed by Moses under inspiration "denies that the Torah is of Divine origin." "Maimonides to Joseph Ibn Gabir," Letters of Maimonides, 89. The basis of this opinion was Moses' directive to the people before they crossed over to the Promised Land that they must follow the rules and laws of the Lord which he now gave them, and "you shall not add anything to what I command you or take anything away from it." Deut 4:2. Levinson, "Deuteronomy," 370.

Israelite was obliged to believe that everything found in the Torah was absolutely true, and that Moses did not record anything on his own, without input from Almighty God. Biblical scholars, however believe that the written Hebrew script did not develop until about 1200 BCE, which would therefore require that any description of the events must have been carried on by an oral tradition, and then later recorded by someone other than Moses.[30] This does not mean, if true, that what Moses said or did was not directed by the Spirit of YHWH, but rather that his teaching was not made available by any scroll that as yet been uncovered.

The fact that oral transmission was clearly an important part of the evolution of the Hebrew faith created a bitter conflict during Hellenistic times, when a written version of the *Torah* was finally made available to a multitude of people, between the Pharisees, who believed that both the Written Law (*Torah shebikhtav*) of the Torah, and the Oral Law (*Torah shebe'al peh*) of the rabbinic interpretations, which would later be collected in the Talmud, the so-called "dual torah," were sacrosanct, and the Sadducees, who argued for the primacy of the Written Law alone.[31] The Talmud, or Oral Torah, according to the "Sayings of the Fathers" in the Mishnah, held that "Moses received the Torah from Sinai and transmitted it to Joshua, and Joshua to the elders, and the elders to the prophets, and the prophets transmitted it to the men of the Great Synagogue."[32] Because these men were all part of the evolutionary process which faithfully transmitted the teaching of Moses to later generations, they were felt to be worthy of divine guidance in their own actions, just as Moses was in his initial recordings. The Sadducees, on the other hand, refused to allow for any reinterpretation of the written text of Moses, and demanded that only what was actually recorded in the Torah was worthy of being imbued with divine guidance. Pharisaic Judaism eventually won out, but differences of opinion remained as divergent rabbinic schools evolved around sages like R. Akiba (Ben Joseph Akiba, 50-132 CE) and R. Ishmael (Ishmael

---

30 The Swedish scholar H. S. Nyberg (1889-1974 CE), from the Scandinavian school of scholarship which emphasized the importance of oral traditions, explained that writing in pre-exilic Palestine was principally used for practical matters and official registers, "but the actual tradition of history, the epic tales, the cult-legends, doubtless generally the laws too, must in the main have been handed down orally." Nielsen, Oral Tradition, 24. The written Old Testament, which we read today, is believed to have been created between the destruction of Jerusalem in 587 BCE and the time of the Maccabees (167-160 BCE). Ibid., 39.

31 The Talmud, is the compendium of Jewish rabbinical literature, or "Oral Law," composed of the *Mishnah* (*Mishna*), collected by Rabbi Judah Ha-Nasi (the Patriarch) (c. 135-c. 200 CE) in the second century CE, and the commentaries on the *Mishnah*, which are known as the *Gemara*. The Palestinian, or Jerusalem, Talmud was compiled around the fifth century CE, and the Babylonian Talmud, which is the larger of the two, a century or two later. Goldenberg, "Talmud," 131, 135.

32 Kedourie, "Introduction," 9.

b. Elisha, died c. 135 CE), who disagreed on exactly how Scripture was to be interpreted.[33]

In addition to differences of opinion on how a text was to be interpreted, The Pharisees believed that in the written text of the Torah possible changes were introduced by scribes who failed to reproduce texts without adding their own editorial comment.[34] This problem was evident in the complaint of the prophet Jeremiah (625-587 BCE), who found that the scribes "reject the word of the Lord, so their wisdom amounts to nothing."[35] By failing to reproduce faithfully what prior manuscripts had copied, their training was wasted, and so the collected views of respected rabbis about how the Torah should be interpreted were important enough to carry the designation of God-inspired.

In time, the view that Moses was the author of the Torah eventually fell by the wayside as closer analysis of the text clearly indicated to most scholars that the writing must have been compiled by more than one person. This realization began in the seventeenth century CE, when Thomas Hobbes (1588-1679 CE) in England, the philosopher who helped develop the fundamentals of European liberal thought, and the Dutch pantheistic-rationalist Baruch Spinoza (1632-1677 CE) in the Netherlands, both pointed out that various passages in the Torah indicated that the writer had lived at some time after Moses had died.[36] In the 1700s, Henning Bemhard Witter (c. 1711 CE), a German pastor of Hildesheim, and Jean Astruc (1684-1766 CE), the French physician to King Louis XV and son of a Protestant minister who converted to Catholicism, provided additional support for this conclusion by recognizing that the text of the book of *Genesis* used two names for God: *Elohim* and *Jahweh* (*Jehovah*, *Yahweh*), another indication that more than one author was responsible, since Moses would not have varied the name of the deity. Other discrepancies were found over the years which indicated to non-orthodox biblical scholars that the Torah was compiled from a number of independent literary documents, each promoting a tradition which stemmed from different periods in Israel's history. These traditions were transmitted orally over many centuries, and were then eventually compiled into written texts which

33 The school of R. Akiba was characterized by the closest possible text study, while that of R. Ishmael was centered around a more liberal use of logic and hermeneutical rules, such as inferences and analogy. The Classic Midrash: Tannaitic Commentaries on the Bible, 20.

34 Scribes not only copied the texts they were given, but also responded in diverse ways dependent upon the formulations they found in earlier manuscripts, thereby not only transmitting, but reinterpreting the texts and traditions. Fishbane, Biblical Interpretation in Ancient Israel, 23-24.

35 Jer 8:9. Sweeney, "Jeremiah," 941.

36 Coogan, The Old Testament: A Historical and Literary Introduction to the Hebrew Scriptures, 22. One of the first indications of this fact was that the Edomite king list (Gen 36:31-43) was made up of names of person who would have reigned long after Moses had died. Friedman, The Bible With Sources Revealed, 92.

contained conflicting details by successive generations of scribes. By the 1800s, most scholars supported the Supplementary Hypothesis which held that the original core of the *Pentateuch* was a document known as the Book of Origins, and that additions were made by a variety of sources.

Julius Wellhausen (1844-1918 CE), a German biblical scholar from the University of Greifswald, finally developed a satisfactory answer to these concerns when he proposed in 1878 CE, in his famous treatise *History of Israel*, that the final edition of the Torah was written in four stages: a history by the Jahwist (J), or Yahwist, who used *Jahweh* for the name of God throughout the book of *Genesis*, written in the tenth century BCE, during the rule of King Solomon (970-930 BCE), or shortly thereafter in the ninth century BCE;[37] a history by the Elohist (E), using *Elohim* as the name of God, written in the ninth and eighth centuries BCE;[38] a history by the Deuteronomist (D), found primarily in the book of *Deuteronomy*, written in the seventh and sixth centuries BCE, during the Josianic reforms;[39] and a history by the Priestly (P) source, which added material related to worship and genealogical lists, written in the fifth century BCE.[40] This theory

37 The "J" source is often ascribed to an attempt by the surviving southern kingdom of Judah, based in the Jerusalem court, to declare its primacy over the northern kingdom of Israel, which was earlier dispersed by the Assyrians, c. 721 BCE. Finkelstein, & Silberman, The Bible Unearthed: Archaeology's New Vision of Ancient Israel and the Origin of its Sacred Texts, 46. It can be identified in the books of *Genesis, Exodus,* and *Numbers*, and some elements, much revised, in the books of *Joshua* and *Judges.* Gottwald, The Hebrew Bible–A Socio-Literary Introduction, 137. The "J" source has been called "Israel's earliest great theologian," having given to his nation a national epic, and to the world its first major theological opus. Ellis, The Yahwist: The Bible's First Theologian, 21.

38 It is believed that the "E" document originated in the northern kingdom of Israel, and was then brought south to Judah, where a Redactor combined their stories into one "JE" document. Exodus 1-18, 49. It covered most of the same ground as the "J" source, but differed in vocabulary, style, mood, and emphasis. Gottwald, The Hebrew Bible–A Socio-Literary Introduction, 137-138.

39 When Josiah (639-609 BCE) began to repair the Temple in Jerusalem, he found a "book of the law" which caused him to initiate reforms that corresponded to the details of the specific language and injunctions in the text. It is believed that he uncovered a copy of the book of *Deuteronomy.* Cook, The Social Roots of Biblical Yahwism, 57-58. The books of *Joshua, Judges, 1-2 Samuel,* and *1-2 Kings* (Former Prophets) are also attributed to the Deuteronomist, while the books of *1-2 Chronicles*, and possibly *Ezra* and *Nehemiah*, are ascribed to the Chronicler. Chronicles and Its Synoptic Parallels in Samuel, Kings, and Related Biblical Texts, xii.

40 Campbell & O'Brien, Sources of the Pentateuch: Texts, Introductions, Annotations, 5-6. Most of the latter half of *Exodus*, and the whole of *Leviticus*, come from the "P" source. Gottwald, The Hebrew Bible–A Socio-Literary Introduction, 140. Recently, many scholars have revised the traditional view of "P" as an independent narrative strand, and consider the activity more redactional. Davies, A Royal Priesthood: Literary and

became known as the "Documentary Hypothesis," and it surmised that the various sources were then combined into larger units by theologians, whose efforts labeled them as Redactors (R).[41] One Redactor combined "J," "E," and "D," c. 550 BCE, and then "J," "E," "D," and "P" were redacted c. 200 BCE.[42] Most scholars do not ascribe an active role to the Redactors in the formation of the biblical text, but primarily see them as "passive tradents, whose primary aim was to preserve tradition, rather than creative theologians who critically transformed tradition."[43] It is not known whether these various sources were individual authors, or were schools of narrators.[44] The final formation of the Old Testament as the Hebrew canon is believed to have been completed between 100 BCE and 100 CE, with some contribution made by the Synod held at Jamnia (Yavne) in the late first century CE, also known as the Council of Javnia.

While this cursory summary of an extremely complex issue is clearly inadequate to convince skeptics who deny the underlying concept, the favored belief among biblical scholars today is that the general proposition of some type of "Documentary Hypothesis" to explain the generation of the Bible remains viable, although there continues to be active debate over who the sources were, and when the manuscripts were written and collated.[45] In this book, I will not attempt to support any particular aspect of this topic, but will rather accept the conclusion that the Torah was indeed collated by various sources who compiled the material into

---

Intertextual Perspectives on an Image of Israel in Exodus 19.6, 22.

41 Some have included an earlier Grundlage (G) source, which linked the patriarchal tradition with that of Moses and Joshua to form a continuous narrative. Fohrer, Introduction to the Old Testament, 128. "G" was likely an oral, poetic composition of the twelfth to the eleventh centuries BCE, relating an account of the Sons of Israel and their forefathers. Mandell & Freedman, The Relationship Between Herodotus' *History* and Primary History, 98.

42 Hoffmeier, "Exodus," 39. The Chronicler is believed to have been a Redactor who composed his works based on earlier traditions. Chronicles and Its Synoptic Parallels in Samuel, Kings, and Related Biblical Texts, xv.

43 Dozeman, God on the Mountain, 2.

44 Richard Elliott Friedman, Professor of Jewish Studies at the University of Georgia, believes that the Redactor was the priest Ezra, who was described as "the scribe of the law of the God of heaven." Ezra 7:12. Finkelstein, "Patriarchs, Exodus, Conquest: Fact or Fiction?" 50. Other scholars also consider Ezra the Priest as one of the Redactors. Freund, Digging Through the Bible: Modern Archaeology and the Ancient Bible, 13.

45 Richard Elliott Friedman summarized the evidence supporting a Documentary Hypothesis as including seven main arguments: Linguistic, which examines the stage of Biblical Hebrew used in each source; Terminology, where phrases are unique to one source; Consistent Content; Continuity of Texts; Relationships of the source to each other and to history; and Convergence of evidence. Friedman, The Bible With Sources Revealed, 7-31. Some scholars would disagree with this assessment, claiming instead that the theory is in "a state of advanced *rigor mortis*." Nicholson, The Pentateuch in the Twentieth Century: The Legacy of Julius Wellhausen, 96.

our modern version by some method akin to that first proposed by Wellhausen. I will also take this assumption one step further, and argue that the manuscripts which were collected by the learned priests, prophets, and scribes, were circulated in the ancient Near East during the post-exilic period, c. 450 BCE, and were available to early Greek authors and philosophers, as I will discuss in greater detail in Chapter 14.

B. The Life of Moses

The man who represents the true lifeblood of modern Jewish religion and thought is Moses, the charismatic leader who led the Hebrew people out of bondage and into the Promised Land, which God had given to the descendants of Abraham as a reward for his loyal obedience. Although Abraham was the veritable genetic progenitor of the Hebrews, since it was from his children that all future Jews descended, it was Moses who introduced the monotheistic tenets to the Semitic Hebrew tribes, and thereby set the Jews apart from all other religious faiths at that time. His hallowed position as the father of monotheism is accepted by both the Christian and Islamic faiths, who continued to pay homage to the Mosaic Code as the basic moral base from which their respective messiahs set forth the ethical principles of the Divine Law, even after they broke ranks with the practice of Rabbinic Judaism. When we talk about the origins of monotheism, we talk about the teachings of Moses, and so an understanding of how he came to fulfill the position of commander-in-chief of the Hebrews is vital to explaining why I believe many of the dissident Hebrews refused to follow his lead.

The story of the life of Moses begins at the very start of the book of *Exodus*, when we are told that a new contentious situation between the Egyptians and their Hebrew slaves had arisen in Egypt because of the ascension of a Pharaoh "who did not know Joseph."[46] Although some scholars have claimed that the Hebrews were not actually slaves in the modern sense of the word, and lived in their own homes in Goshen, the general interpretation of their position, according to the biblical text, is that by the time of the Exodus, their position had deteriorated into that of slavery. None of the Pharaohs in the Torah are actually named, and this is the only king who carries an explanatory title, with the appellation generally interpreted to mean that the Hebrews had fallen from their favored position in Egyptian society, which Joseph had maintained while holding

---

46 Exod 1:8. Sarna, "Exodus," 4. Rabbinic tradition holds that the pharaoh's name was Malol, the son of Magron, who had waged war against Zepho, the grandson of Esau, and despite the aid of the Israelites in that engagement, he feared that the strength of the Hebrews might turn against him. Ginzberg, The Legends of the Jews, II. 246. It should be noted that the Bible does not say that the prior Pharaoh died, leaving the possibility that the Pharaoh was not another ruler, but rather had changed in his opinion of Joseph, a view that is followed by the Kabbalists. The Kabbalistic Bible: Exodus: Technology for the Soul, 20.

the position of vizier.[47] While part of the disfavor may have been due to anger generated by Joseph during the seven years of famine, as discussed in chapter 3, the Pharaoh "who did not know Joseph" was also concerned that the large numbers of Hebrews in the kingdom provided a serious danger to the safety of the country.[48] He therefore attempted to contain the procreative strength of the Hebrews by making them work even harder building the store-cities of Pithom and Ramesses. These cities were already in existence at the time, but had to be fortified in order to function as a depot for food supplies. When the extra work failed to reduce the population growth of the Hebrews, the Pharaoh decided to kill all future newborn Hebrew male children in an attempt to suppress their ever-enlarging numbers.[49] He directed the Hebrew midwives, Shiphrah and Puah, to ensure that every Hebrew male newborn was immediately suffocated, allowing the female newborns to live, since they were not seen as dangerous to homeland security.[50] This command reflected the events of the paschal night before the Exodus, when all newborn Egyptian male children perished as punishment for the refusal of the Pharaoh to all the Hebrews to leave Egypt, and also anticipated the Slaughter of the Innocents prior to the birth of Jesus, when King Herod ordered all male children, two years of age or under, to be killed.[51] While the Pharaoh "who did not know Joseph" was acting in a bestial manner by ordering

---

47 Ronald Hendel, Professor of Hebrew Bible and Jewish Studies at the University of California, Berkeley, has suggested that the pharaohs may not have been named in order to enable the Exodus story to take root in early Israel by allowing the memory of Egyptian oppression to extend to all who had felt that oppression in their remembered past, even if they had not immigrated from Egypt. Hendel, Remembering Abraham: Culture, Memory, and History in the Hebrew Bible, 60.

48 The Bible notes that although only seventy family members accompanied Jacob to Egypt, their descendants were very fertile, increasing rapidly in numbers. Exod 1:5, 7. The Midrash claims that each woman gave birth to sextuplets, and some claim up to sixty at each birth. Greenberg, Understanding Exodus, 19. Fear that the Hebrews were too numerous (Exod 1:9) was also voiced by Abimelech to Isaac (Gen 26:16), and King Balak to Balaam (Num 22:6). Ibid., 20.

49 The choice to spare newborn female infants is believed to have originated from the ancient belief, as expressed by Philo of Alexandria (20 BCE-50 CE), the first century CE Jewish philosopher and theologian, that "a woman, by reason of the weakness of her nature, is disinclined to and unfitted for war." Philo, "On the Life of Moses, I," The Works of Philo, III.8, 459.

50 Exod 1:15-16. Most scholars accept that the midwives were Hebrew, since their names were Semitic in origin, but some traditions claim that they were Egyptian. Kaiser, "Exodus," 307. Rashi claimed that Shiphrah was Jochebed, and Puah was Miriam. Rashi, Pentateuch With Targum Onkelos, Haphtaroth and Rashi's Commentary, Exodus, 3. Abarbanel (1437-1508 CE) argued that they must have been Egyptian, as the Pharaoh would never hire Hebrew midwives to kill Hebrew newborns. Greenberg, Understanding Exodus, 26.

51 Exod 12:29; Matt 2:16.

the death of all newborn male Hebrews, he was not behaving in an unusual way for the historical times.

The plan failed, according to the biblical text, because the women feared God even more than they did the Pharaoh, and therefore allowed the newborn boys to live, explaining to the king that the Hebrew women were quicker than Egyptians at giving birth, and the babies were already born by the time they arrived.[52] The Pharaoh may have initially accepted their excuse, but remained convinced that infanticide was still the proper technique to control Hebrew population growth, and therefore commanded that the people themselves be required to throw their newborn males into the Nile River, without the presence of a midwife at the birth. This would eliminate any excuse for a male child to survive.

This demand that parents dispose of their own male children at birth seems to many modern readers an unparalleled brutality, even for the violent times of the Late Bronze Age. We pride ourselves today in being more humane in our legislative actions toward destructive behavior against other human beings and animals, even though the front page headlines of newspapers across the globe belie this admirable concern. What is even worse about the Pharaoh's demand, is that it is one thing to order infanticide for punishment or protection, it is ghastly to require that the parent perform the act of execution. The fact remains, however that the use of infanticide as a means of population control was a well-accepted technique in the ancient world, although the most widely used method was female infanticide, rather than the killing of males.[53] Such population-control methodology was sometimes necessary because of a depletion of the food supply, due either to climactic conditions which created widespread famine, or wars which prevented the gathering of agricultural products. Parents at times would resort to infanticide in order to spare their children the slow agonizing death of starvation, or the bondage into slavery following a defeat by an invading army. But forcing the parents to actually drown their own children was a unique act, not recorded in any other historical record or legend. When Moses punished the Midianites for leading the Exodus into idolatry by decimating the adult male population, the women and children were taken into captivity, rather than be killed.[54]

---

52 Exod 1:17-19.

53 Milner, Hardness of Heart/Hardness of Life: The Stain of Human Infanticide, 156-157.

54 Num 31:7, 9. The program of adult male-murder was reinforced by Moses in his address to the people in the book of *Deuteronomy*, when he instructed them that once they began their Conquest of the Promised Land, they were first to offer a city the option of surrender, and then, if the city refused to cede, the males were to be killed, and the women and children were to be taken as booty. Deut 20:13-14. Rabbi Ishmael, one of the greatest Tannaim of the third generation, taught that the primary intention of the Torah was to "remove idolatry and expunge its memory," even if such an action resulted in the loss of life. Heschel, Heavenly Torah: As Refracted Through the Generations, 75. Singling out

The Bible provides some support for the Pharaoh's fear of rebellion, given the rapid growth in the size of the Hebrew slave population. According to the standard translation, the number of Hebrew men who took part in the Exodus was over 600,000, and even though the exact tally is still in dispute, as will be discussed later in this chapter, it is clear that there were enough soldiers involved to survive numerous battles with the indigenous Canaanites, both before and after entry into the Promised Land. Under the threat of such an obvious population explosion, it was not unreasonable for the new Pharaoh to believe that such a large force of tenant slaves could provide a security risk to the country-at-large if they ever rose in rebellion, especially if a large contingent of the Egyptian militia was away on campaigns in Canaan or Syria. It must be remembered that throughout much of the Middle and Late Bronze Ages, Egyptian sovereignty over Canaan was aggressively pursued, and this meant that large numbers of military personnel were not available to protect homeland security.

Moral judgements on the Pharaoh's edict to destroy all Hebrew male newborns aside, when the directive was in effect, Moses was born to Amram, the son of Kohath, and Jochebed, the daughter of Levi.[55] This meant that Moses was the great-grandson of Levi, who was Jacob's third son. Jochebed was Amram's aunt, and although marriage between a nephew and aunt would later be prohibited by the Mosaic Code, during patriarchal times a marriage between close relatives was permitted, as was evident in the fact that Abraham married Sarah, his half-sister; Isaac married Rebekah, the daughter of his cousin; and Jacob married the two daughters of his second cousin. At the time of his birth, Moses had a three-year old brother, Aaron, and a sister, Miriam, who in various biblical sections was said to be both older and younger than Moses, evidence of the occasional confusion which appears in the Torah because of compilation from varied sources. The standard tradition is that Miriam was the eldest child, since she was old enough to witness the abandonment of Moses, as will be discussed shortly.

Despite the presence of the order to kill all newborn males, Moses' parents were able to initially hide his birth from the authorities for a period of three months. Their subterfuge must have been very dangerous, for the Midrash explained that the Egyptians used to visit the homes of the Hebrews with a baby that they would

children, however, was unusual.

55 Exod 2:1. Amram is only identified as a man of the house of Levi in this passage, but is named by the Chronicler as the father of Moses. 1 Chron 5:29; 6:3; 23:13. See e.g., Exod 6:20. He is also named as the father, with Jochebed as the mother, in Num 26:59. The Septuagint and Syriac versions render Jochebed to be his cousin rather than his aunt. Jamieson, Fausset & Brown, <u>Commentary Critical and Explanatory on the Whole Bible</u>, 52. The Hebrew name of Jochebed was *Yokheved*, the first name in the Bible to be constructed from the divine elements of the name YHWH, supporting the notion that God directly interceded in the history of the Hebrews through Moses in order to designate them as the Chosen People. Sarna, <u>Genesis</u>, 40.

make cry in order to evoke a similar response from an infant possibly hidden away.[56] How Moses was kept hidden under the circumstances will never be known for sure, but the time soon came that his presence could no longer be kept secret, and other measures would have to be taken to assure his survival. The parents decided to cast Moses into the Nile River in a little boat made of papyrus reeds, close to where the Pharaoh's daughter was bathing. This choice of setting him adrift in a papyrus boat was particularly appropriate, for in performing this deed, Jochebed was in fact obeying the Pharaoh's command to cast her newborn into the river. It also closely resembled the legend of Sargon I of Akkad (Sargon the Great, c. 2334-2279 BCE), whose mother set him adrift on the Euphrates River in a watertight wicker basket soon after his birth, where he was eventually rescued by Akki, the drawer of water. The Greek myth of Oedipus also has the future king being abandoned by his parents, who were warned that their child might grow up and kill his father, but the tale of Oedipus fits the genre of exposure, more than being set adrift in a basket by a parent.[57] Many biblical scholars believe that the saga of Moses' abandonment was likely drawn from the Mesopotamian legend of King Sargon, but the Greek myth, in my opinion, was more likely to have been a product of Hebraic origin, given the large number of similarities between the two ancient cultures, as described in this book, and the sparse resemblances with ancient Mesopotamian culture.

Moses did not have to float very far before he was discovered by an Egyptian Princess and her entourage. Although Egyptologists generally are skeptical about the likelihood that women of rank went to the Nile river to wash, ancient authors, such as Strabo (63 BCE-21 CE), Pliny the Second (62-115 CE), and Aelian (c. 175-235 CE), held that the waters of the Nile were regarded as sacred, and so immersing would have an effect of ablution, even for the daughter of a king.[58] The Princess apparently recognized that the infant was a Hebrew, either by his clothing, because of her father's decree, or because the child was circumcised, and despite the order for all the newborn male Hebrews to be killed, she decided to rescue Moses and raise him as her own. The name of the Princess, like that of her father, was never mentioned in the biblical text, but various traditions have held that she was either called Tharmuth,[59] Thermuthis,[60] Bithiah,[61] or Merris.[62]

---

56 Greenberg, Understanding Exodus, 39.

57 The most popular versions of the myth have the parents maim the ankles of Oedipus, and then expose him, where he is found and rescued.

58 Kaiser, "Exodus," 309.

59 Jub, xlvii:5.

60 Josephus, "Antiquities of the Jews," The Complete Works of Josephus, II.IX.5, 56.

61 This was her name in Jewish folklore. Luban, The Exodus Chronicles: Beliefs, Legends & Rumors from Antiquity Regarding the Exodus of the Jews from Egypt, 66. She appears in 1 Chron 4:18 as the wife of Mered.

62 Eusebius, Pr. Ev., ix:27, cited in Alleman & Flack, "The Book of Exodus," 210.

The entire rescue was witnessed by Miriam, who was sentried nearby to watch the action, and when she spied the Princess lift her brother from the water, she approached and asked whether she should go and find a wet-nurse to suckle the baby. The Princess agreed to this advice, and the mother of Moses was chosen to nourish her own son. It is likely that this aspect of the story was retained by the biblical compilers to provide evidence of Judaic nourishment to the young child, since there certainly would have been an ample supply of Egyptian wet-nurses at the Pharaoh's court, given the fact that Princesses seldom breast-fed their own children. While the truth of the rescue may never be known, the legend nevertheless fits in with other ancient tales that help to possibly identify source materials utilized by the biblical compilers.

Eventually, Moses was weaned and returned to the Princess' care to be raised in the royal household as one of the Pharaoh's adopted children. There is no record of what Jochebed called her young son,[63] but the Princess named him "Moses," which means to have "drawn forth from the water," because she rescued the infant from the Nile River.[64] Many scholars have denied this explanation, claiming that the real meaning of the name, which is *Mosche (Mosheh)* in Hebrew, was more likely taken from the Egyptian verb, *msi*, which means "to give birth," or *msw*, which means "child of."[65] This latter derivation is supported by the fact that the term was also used as a half-name in Egypt, and was sometimes combined with the name of a god in the Pharaoh's numen, as seen with the nomens of Ahmose and Thutmose. There were also two papyri from the time of Ramesses II (1279-1213 BCE), which listed officials named "Mose."[66]

Although most scholars have accepted that Moses was born of Hebrew parents, a number of commentators have suggested that the man who led the Hebrew Exodus out of Egypt was actually a natural-born Egyptian. This allegation was initially made by Manetho, the Egyptian priest of Heliopolis who first outlined the history of the Egyptian Dynasties in the third century BCE which are still in use today. Manetho, according to Josephus, claimed that Moses was not a natural-born Hebrew, but rather an Egyptian native of Heliopolis, called Osarseph (Osarsiph) after the god Osiris, and that he changed his name when he later joined the Jews in order to claim an Hebrew heritage.[67] He led a large group of

---

63 Jewish legend held that Moses' father called him Heber, his mother called him Jekuthiel, his sister referred to him as Jered (Jared), and his brother as Abi Zanoah. Ginzberg, The Legends of the Jews, II.269.

64 Josephus explained that his name was *Mouses*, from the Egyptian *Mo*, which means "water," and *Uses*, which means "saved from." Josephus, "Antiquities of the Jews," The Complete Works of Josephus, II.IX.6, 57.

65 Hoffmeier, Israel in Egypt, The Evidence for the Authenticity of the Exodus Tradition, 140.

66 Sarna, Exodus, 10.

67 Greek and Latin Authors on Jews and Judaism, 83.

lepers from Egypt to join with the Hyksos against the Egyptians who had evicted them from their land, and framed the laws which later were followed by the Jews.[68] Since for centuries Manetho was held to be the most reliable Egyptian historian when it came to details about the Egyptian monarchy, his opinion that Moses was not of Hebrew origin was given serious credence among his contemporaries.[69]

Most ancient authors, however, viewed this aspect of Manetho's history as anti-Semitic nonsense, and the characterization of Moses as an Egyptian was generally discarded by the majority of scholars until the modern age, when this view was resurrected by the prominent founder of Psychiatry, Sigmund Freud (1856-1939 CE). Freud argued that Moses was not born to a Hebrew family, but was rather an Egyptian whose story was put forth as an invention by the compilers of the Bible who needed to make Moses a Hebrew for dynastic purposes.[70] Since Freud was a respected physician, and also a Jew, his opinion was given a more credible position by some scholars for a brief period of time. Once again, however, the attempt to disprove the Hebrew ancestry of the man who was responsible for the very initiation of Jewish monotheism has generally fallen by the wayside, and while suggestions that Moses was an Egyptian rather than a Hebrew are intriguing, few scholars accept their authenticity, myself included.

Even though Moses would have physically resembled a Semite rather than a natural-born Egyptian as he grew up in the royal court, he would not have necessarily stood out as unique. Thutmose III (1479-1425 BCE) had initiated a policy of having the sons of subject kings of western Asia be sent to the palace as hostages to guarantee their fathers' obedience, and since most of them were Semitic it was common for boys of non-Egyptian habitus to be seen in the Royal court. The children were raised in Egyptian ways, and indoctrinated in the policies of the Pharaoh, to prepare them to eventually replace their fathers once they returned home in a fashion conducive to Egyptian interests. All the male children raised in the palace were known as "Child of the Royal Harem," and this position provided them with honors which were respected throughout the country.[71] Non-royal subjects were also sometimes allowed to live in the royal court, either through marriage, or, as in the case of Joseph, through evidence of unusual talents which particularly impressed the Pharaoh. Given the size of the

---

68 Manetho, 129-31.

69 The view of Manetho was followed by the Greek historians Tacitus (55-117 CE) and Strabo (63 BCE - 21 CE). Assmann, Moses the Egyptian: The Memory of Egypt in Western Monotheism, 21.

70 Freud, Moses and Monotheism, 16. Freud's proposal was that Moses became intrigued with Atenism under the tutelage of Amenhotep IV (1352-1336 BCE), and when the heretic king died, he brought the practice of circumcision, and the worship of Aten alone, to the Hebrew slaves, eventually replacing Aten with the image of YHWH during the Exodus wandering. Ibid., 31.

71 Tyldesley, Hatchepsut: The Female Pharaoh, 54-55.

Pharaoh's harem, with foreign wives frequently present as part of alliances with distant rulers, and the likelihood that the Exodus took place during or after the reign of Thutmose III, it is not likely that the sudden appearance of a new infant of foreign origin would create suspicion as to his racial origin.

The training Moses received in the Egyptian royal court provided him with all of the necessary tools he would later need to successfully lead the Hebrews out of bondage. This included instruction in all aspects of Egyptian wisdom, as well as training in both the Egyptian hieroglyphic and Akkadian cuneiform systems of writing and language. Akkadian was the international language of the Amarna Age throughout the Levant. Just as the city-states in Syria and Palestine were able to communicate directly with the Egyptian Pharaoh utilizing the Akkadian language, Moses would have been able to interact with most of the people he encountered during the Exodus. In addition, Hebrew was a dialect of the Canaanite tongue, and although Moses may not have been familiar with the ancestral language of his people, God had agreed to let his brother Aaron function as his spokesman during the Exodus, providing him with the means to converse with Semitic Bedouins and local Palestinian kings, as well as the Hebrews he led.[72] Other Hebrew elders would likely have also learned these methods of communication, and enabled the Hebrews who fled the Exodus to obtain assistance during their travels, although their conversations with Canaanites would not have been as easily conveyed as by Moses himself.

Moses also would also have received instruction in discipline and military techniques, skills that would prove to be very necessary during the forty years spent wandering through the Sinai Wilderness. Children in the royal educational programs were taught to maintain attention by their tutors in a manner that was summarized by one proverb which stated that "a boy's ear is on his back; he hears when he is beaten."[73] Such a disciplinary approach obviously took root in Moses' nature, and surfaced when he ordered parricidal reprisals against those Hebrews who resisted the changes he demanded. Along with training in reading, writing, and mathematics, the royal students were taught military maneuvers to prepare them to defend their country's colonial possessions. Moses may not have been born to a family of military leaders, but he was certainly trained to become the type of powerful commander that was essential to successfully manage such a large contingency of slaves, and convert their religious faith from the polytheistic creed of the Patriarchs to the monotheistic worship of YHWH. While the dissident

---

72 The ancient Hebrew language was a distinct dialect of Canaanite, and fully comprehensible to their neighbors. Brown, <u>Ancient Israel and Ancient Greece: Religion, Politics, and Culture</u>, 8. Canaanite and Hebrew so closely overlapped that the ability to distinguish them today is usually based on historical information, rather than on linguistic criteria. Smith, <u>The Early History of God: Yahweh and the Other Deities in Ancient Israel</u>, 20.

73 Fletcher, Chronicle of a Pharaoh, The Intimate Life of Amenhotep III, 26.

Hebrews would have been well-trained to function as warriors on the frontline, their value was greater as mercenaries in Mycenae, rather than an independent armed force remaining in Canaan under their own leadership without Moses, since they did not have experience in the skills necessary to become a high-ranking officer.

In addition to the diversity of language available to him, and the wide array of leadership skills, Moses also had first-hand knowledge of the territory into which he led the Hebrew Exodus. When he was forty years old, the Bible told how he killed an Egyptian taskmaster who was beating a Hebrew slave, and the text made a point of noting that it was not an accidental killing, but rather Moses looked around to be sure no one was watching, and then killed the Egyptian and hid his body in the sand.[74] This violent action by the man who was to become the true progenitor of the Jewish faith was not ignored by the Sages, with one Midrash claiming that God said to Moses before he died: "Did I ever tell you to kill the Egyptian?" and Moses responded "You killed all the Egyptian firstborn, and I should now stand to die for one single Egyptian!"[75] That his action did not go unnoticed is evident in the very next passage, when Moses was visiting the Hebrews again and broke up a fight between two men, one of which asked him if he was planning to kill him like he did the Egyptian.[76] We do not know if Moses was bothered by realizing that he had killed an Egyptian for beating a Hebrew slave, and now was interrupting a physical confrontation between two possibly related Hebrews, but his witnessing of the deed frightened Moses, forcing him to flee Egypt in order to escape prosecution by the Pharaoh.[77] The Pharaoh in question was not named in this passage, but since he was not designated as the Pharaoh "who did not know Joseph," most scholars have assumed that it was one of his successors. This was the first reference to a violent act by Moses in the Bible, although it was certainly not the last, given the parricidal acts which would follow during the years of wandering in the Sinai desert. We may never know why the biblical compilers decided to highlight this violent episode, but I believe

---

74 Exod 2:12.

75 Heschel, Heavenly Torah: As Refracted Through the Generations, 445.

76 Exod 2:13-14. Rashi claims the two men were Dathan and Abiram, who would later join the rebellion of Korah. Rashi, Pentateuch With Targum Onkelos, Haphtaroth and Rashi's Commentary, Exodus, 8.

77 Exod 2:15. The Torah does not actually explain how old Moses was when he fled to Midian, but in the New Testament, Stephen stated that Moses was forty years old. Acts 7:23. Jub 48:1 held him to be forty-two years old. According to various rabbinic traditions, he was aged 12 years (*Sh'moth Rabbah* 5:1), 18 years (*Sh'moth Rabbah* 1), 21 years (*Yov'loth* 47:10), 29 years (*Shalsheleth HaKabbalah*) 32 years (*BeMidbar Rabbah* 14:40), 40 years (*Sh'moth Rabbah* 1), 50 years (Artapanus) or 60 years old (Rabbi Moshe HaDarshan, *Bereshith Rabathai*, pg 13) at the time. Kaplan, The Living Torah: The Five Books of Moses and the Haftarot, 262.

it was necessary to point out that the eventual role of Moses as judge, jury, and executioner of those who did not follow the guidelines of the monotheistic Mosaic Code at the very start of the Exodus story, to show that the killing of Jews by Jews was performed by a man who had already shown a homicidal trait that cannot be blamed on God's wrath alone. As I will argue later in this book, I believe, as well, that while this nature served the purpose of YHWH well during the years of the Exodus, it was not the type of leadership that would be necessary following the entry into the Promised Land, and was a primary reason why Moses would have to die before the Jordan River was crossed because the capitol punishment he inflicted on the Hebrews who failed to follow the monotheistic demands of the Ten Commandments bloodied his hands in the same manner which King David's hands were bloodied, causing YHWH to disallow his building of the First Temple.[78]

After fleeing over the border of Egypt, Moses took refuge in Midian, a land in the southern stretches of Transjordan, along the eastern bank of the Jordan River and the Gulf of Aqaba.[79] The Midianites were traders in gold, spices, and slaves, and also shepherded flocks throughout the deserts of Canaan and Sinai. They were the same caravanners who bought Joseph when he was about to be killed by his brothers, and were relatives of Abraham's second wife, Keturah, whom he married after the death of Sarah. When Moses rescued the daughters of Jethro from shepherds at a well, the girls told their father that they were saved by an Egyptian, likely because Moses was dressed in his typical Egyptian garb. He later was allowed to marry one of the women, Zipporah (Tziporah), an indication that the Midianites saw him either as one of their own, because of his facial characteristics, or as a prominent Egyptian who could assist them in times of need. His time spent in Midian gave him extensive knowledge of the land the Hebrews would have been led into during the Exodus from Egypt.

Now that he was isolated from the land of his birth, distant from both the Hebrews and Egyptians alike, Moses took on the psychological demeanor of a man without a country. He had grown up in the Egyptian royal court, but it was clear that he was not a legitimate son of the Princess, given the fact that his Semitic appearance would have borne little resemblance to other Egyptian citizens. While he may have thought at first that his father was a Semitic dignitary married to the Princess, there is no evidence in the biblical text that such a subterfuge was undertaken, especially once Moses was old enough to ask questions about

---

78 1 Chron 22:8.

79 Midian derived its name from the fourth son of Abraham and Keturah. Gen 25:2. The exact location is not known, and some scholars have even placed it in the Sinai peninsula, rather than in Canaan. Exodus, The Torah, A Modern Commentary II, 18. The Midianites were considered kinfolk by the Israelites, which may explain why Moses went there. Gen 25:2. Ibid.

his parentage. He must have felt some identity with the Hebrews, since he saved a Hebrew slave from being beaten by an Egyptian, but the reasoning behind this compassion has never been elucidated, and it is generally accepted that the attachment was due to some type of blood-bond that led to his protecting the slave from harm, rather than from his belief that he was the son of a Hebrew slave. This inference is likely related to his being breast-fed by his own mother, and thereby ingesting the essence of a Hebrew identity. Perhaps as a result of this separation from his homeland, Moses named his first child Gershom, or "foreigner," a reflection that he had become a "stranger in a foreign land."[80] Over the next forty years, he prepared himself for whatever destiny awaited him by developing a steadfast belief in the validity of his own decisions, unaffected by any cultural restrictions which would have been part of the formal education of most other men. He grew to manhood with the attitude of a loner, owing no man, or country, a payment for the benefits he received. When YHWH appeared and offered him His unique bond of friendship, Moses accepted the task and became acclimated to the lonely life at the top of the Hebrew political pyramid. During the forty years of wandering in the Sinai Wilderness following the Exodus from Egypt, this quality put Moses in direct conflict with the devotion of the Hebrews to their ancestral beliefs, the result of which was a campaign of parricidal punishment that would put more than 40,000 Hebrews to death.

The lack of an Hebrew identity during the first eighty years of Moses' life is highlighted by the fact that Moses apparently did not circumcise his sons, as required by Jewish Law. As discussed in the previous chapter, circumcision was mandated by God to Abraham as a positive sign of acquiescence to His commandments. When God first appeared to Abraham and guaranteed to make a mighty nation of him, He told Abraham that he had to obey the terms of the contract, and "that every male among you shall be circumcised" as proof of the acceptance on the eighth day after birth.[81] Abraham obediently circumcised every member of his family at that time, and from that time forward, all Hebrew children were circumcised at the appropriate time, beginning with the birth of Isaac. A strange passage in the book of *Exodus*, however, seems to indicate that Moses had not adhered to the requirement, for as he was traveling back to Egypt with Zipporah and his two children, preparing to meet the Hebrews for the first time, the family encamped at night, and YHWH suddenly appeared, threatening

---

80 Exod 2:22. Sarna, <u>Exodus,</u> 12. In the "J" source, Moses has only one son Gershom, while in "E" there is a second son, Eliezer. Friedman, <u>The Bible With Sources Revealed,</u> 125.

81 Gen 17:9-12. <u>The Living Bible,</u> 12. This mandate was so sacrosanct that a Second Temple source reported that when the Seleucid King Antiochus IV Epiphanes (reigned 175-163 BCE) prohibited circumcision, Jewish mothers chose martyrdom and death over neglect of the commandment. 1 Macc 1:60-61. Levenson, "Genesis," 39.

to kill Moses with a knife.[82] No reason was given for God's anger, but Zipporah apparently realized that the cause was the uncircumcised condition of her son, and she immediately picked up a flint-knife and performed the rite, throwing the foreskin at Moses, saying "you are a bridegroom of blood to me!"[83] It is not known if Moses knowingly refused to submit his son to this rite or did not know of the requirement because of his ignorance of Hebrew lore, but this act of Zipporah appears to have pacified God, for He let Moses continue the rest of the journey unharmed, while Zipporah and the children returned home.

Since the Bible does not directly state whether Moses was circumcised or not, the meaning of this passage has never been satisfactorily clarified, and debate continues as to why the Lord was angry enough to try and kill Moses so soon after appointing him to lead the Hebrews to the Promised Land. If Moses had not circumcised his son, as required by the covenant with Abraham, how could God choose such a man to save His Chosen People from their ill-fated life in the first place? If he had not been circumcised himself because of the danger of being discovered because of crying from pain, how could he be worthy of the task ahead? It is possible that Moses may have bypassed the rite because he did not realize he was a Hebrew by birth, but the actions of Zipporah would seem to indicate that she was aware of the oversight. Perhaps her understanding came about by knowledge of Moses' own circumcised state through their moments of intimacy, although, as discussed in the previous chapter, this did not necessarily mean that Moses was Jewish by birth. Commentators have pointed out that the incident may have had a literary foundation, for it resembles many other ancient tales that told about heroes having to master some challenge while on their way home, overcoming an onslaught by mysterious powers that blocked their way.[84] Whatever the explanation, the bond between Moses and God was now firmly attached until the days just before the crossing of the Jordan River, when Moses was forced to die because of an incident where he struck a rock to produce water, rather than speak to it as commanded by God, as I will discuss at the end of the next chapter.

A final factor in the "foreignness" of Moses' nature to the Hebrews was the important role played by his father-in-law, a mysterious figure who was called Reuel, Jethro (Jether, *Yitro*), and Hobab at various times in the biblical text. The variety in names appears to come from differences in the documentary sources who did not agree on his appellation: the Elohist (E) referred to him as Jethro;[85]

---

82 Exod 4:24. Although Moses was actually never mentioned by name in the text, it is generally assumed that the reference was to him. Sarna, Exodus, 24.

83 Exod 4:25. Sarna, Exodus, 25.

84 Exodus, The Torah, A Modern Commentary II, 53. The most famous of these myths was the *Odyssey* by Homer, where Odysseus faced a series of challenges arranged by the god Poseidon.

85 Exod 3:1.

the Jahwist (J) as Reuel;[86] and other biblical sources called him Hobab.[87] Since Hobab was said to be the son of Reuel, and brother-in-law of Moses, in the book of *Numbers*,[88] some scholars have ascribed the multiplicity of names to transposition of the terms for father and grandfather, but the reason for the discrepancy is not pertinent to my thesis, and I will simply refer to him as Jethro in this book. Jethro was a priest of the Midianites, and this prominent position in a pagan religion has suggested to many scholars that the changes which Moses was to later incorporate in the Law Code of the Torah were reflective of the religious and social beliefs of the Midianites.[89] This view is suggested by the fact that the first sacrifice mentioned in the book of *Exodus* was performed by Jethro when he came to visit Moses with Zipporah, Gershom and Eliezer.[90] The close relationship between Moses and Jethro would indeed explain how Moses became familiar with the gods which formed the kernel of Semitic worship, particularly the god El who is believed to have been the forerunner of YHWH, as will be discussed in chapter 11. Although rabbinic tradition has downplayed the pagan nature of Moses' religious background, it is difficult to deny a possible Midianite contribution to the alterations which were introduced in the Mosaic Code, even though the *Haggadah* skirts the polytheistic nature of the pre-Mosaic practices by claiming that by the time Moses arrived in Midian, Jethro had realized that idol worship had no substance, and rejected it, turning to God for penitence.[91] The fact that Jethro appeared to the participants of the Exodus, and was known to be a pagan priest, lends credence to my thesis that many of the Hebrews refused to follow the monotheistic mandates of Moses, choosing instead to follow the lessons they were taught by their ancestors.

The manner in which Moses was called to return to Egypt after tending the flocks of Jethro for forty years, is important in understanding why I believe the Hebrews eventually rebelled against his rigid regulations. He had been forced to

---

86 Exod 2:18. Other Reuels in the Bible included a Benjamite, a Gadite, and a son of Esau. Gen 36:4; Num 2:4; 1 Chron 9:8. Exodus 1-18, 172.

87 Judg 4:11.

88 Num 10:29.

89 In the books of *Exodus* and *Numbers*, he was referred to as a Midianite, while in the book of *Judges* he was a Kenite. Houston, "Exodus," 70. Some scholars go as far as to claim that Jethro and the Midianites were the first worshipers of YHWH, ascribing the monotheistic changes brought about by Moses to have been a part of his pagan training, rather than a natural evolution from his Hebraic origins. Greenberg, Understanding Exodus, 48.

90 Exod 18:12. There is debate among biblical scholars whether this took place before or after the theophany on Mt. Sinai, but Jethro confessed at the time that YHWH was greater than any other deity because of the miracles He provided. Exod 18:10-11. Wellhausen, Prolegomena to the History of Ancient Israel, 53.

91 The Book of Legends/Sefer Ha-Aggadah, 4.25, 62.

flee Egypt because of his unprovoked murder of another Egyptian, but he was able to legally reenter the land of his birth because the Pharaoh "who did not know Joseph," from whom Moses was forced to flee after killing the Egyptian taskmaster, had died, initiating the established custom of a new Pharaoh celebrating his accession by granting amnesty to those who had been found to be guilty of a crime in the past. The narrative of his calling was not a brief encounter with God, followed by an immediate acceptance, however, as Moses repeatedly sought to excuse himself from the task, believing that he was simply unworthy of such an important undertaking. This humble response was understandable, given the fact that Moses had not yet witnessed any of the miracles God could perform, or have been privy to how powerful a warrior YHWH could be when circumstances demanded His assistance. All of YHWH's majesty would become apparent later, both in the manner with which He convinced the Pharaoh to allow the Hebrews to leave Egypt, and the magical methods He used to assuage the concerns of the Hebrews during the forty years of wandering in the Sinai Wilderness. He also, however, must have realized that he had no identity with the people he was being directed to return to, and little reason to believe that they would follow his directives.

While the biblical compilers may have desired to accentuate Moses' initial reluctance to become a savior as indicative of a humble nature, rather than a desire to become a powerful leader, by emphasizing that it was the directives of God, and not the personal opinions of Moses, which altered the Hebrew religion from a polytheistic to a monotheistic belief, there can be no denying the fact that Moses took on an extremely despotic attitude once he realized the extent of his powers. As we will see in the years during the wandering in the Sinai Wilderness following the Exodus, his initial reluctance to become the savior of the Hebrews quickly dissipated, and he took on the role of religious leader with a particular vengeance. Many of the Hebrews were killed for not following his monotheistic directives, and I believe that it is possible that some of these parricidal punishments may have even exceeded the directives of YHWH, and instead been the desire of Moses to fully apply the extent of his awesome powers. We will never know the true nature of the account, since the Bible only recounts Moses' side of the story, but we do know that despite the remarkable task which Moses was given to bring the Hebrews out of slavery and into the Promised Land, he was not allowed to cross the Jordan River and step foot onto the holy land he so desperately desired to reach.

The calling of Moses by God to become the savior of the Hebrews in Egypt began as he was tending a flock of sheep in the fields of Midian around Mt. Horeb (Mt. Sinai). All at once, the Angel of the Lord appeared before him in the guise of a burning thorn-bush, and spoke his name twice: "Moses! Moses!"[92]

---

92 Exod 3:2-4. The reason the Lord chose to appear in a thorn-bush has fascinated

This double recitation of his name allied Moses with other seminal leaders in Hebrew history, including Abraham, Jacob and Samuel, each of whose name was repeated when the Lord first appeared in their midst.[93] The identity of Moses with these eminent predecessors was accentuated by his response of "Here I am," which was the same answer that the other three replied when their names were called by God.[94] Although Moses may have been an Egyptian by adoption, and a Midianite by marriage, he was now being realigned with the great men of the Hebrew faith through his birth, and it was this Hebrew parentage that identified him as one of the Chosen People whom God elected to take over control of the Promised Land. The Elohist highlighted the importance of this seminal event by identifying God for the first time in the Bible as YHWH, thereby linking Him with the God of Abraham, Isaac, and Jacob, but clarifying that He was truly the one and only God, and not a deity who appeared in other forms.[95]

YHWH initiated the discussion with Moses by first directing him to remove his sandals, since the place on which he stood was now holy ground in the presence of the Lord. He then told Moses that He had seen the deep sorrows of His Chosen People in Egypt, and for this reason He was now asking Moses to free Abraham's descendants from their prolonged bondage, and deliver them into a land "flowing with milk and honey."[96] To fulfill this destiny, Moses was to return

---

commentators for centuries, and most answers seem to revolve around the fact that of all the bushes in the world, the thornbush is the most apt to inflict harm. The Book of Legends/Sefer Ha-Aggadah, 4.29, 62. Rabbinic commentary has suggested that God chose to dwell in the stunted thorn-bush to convey the knowledge to Moses that He suffered along with all of Israel. Ginzberg, The Legends of the Jews, II.303. Philo of Alexandria (20 BCE-50 CE), the first century CE Jewish philosopher and theologian, believed that the burning bush was a symbol of the oppressed people, and it not being consumed was an emblem of the fact that those oppressed would not be destroyed. Philo, "On the Life of Moses, I," The Works of Philo, XII.65, 465. Jon Levenson, Associate Professor of Hebrew Bible in the Divinity School of the University of Chicago, believes that the similarity in the sounds of *sene* (bush) and *Sinay* (Sinai) cannot be coincidental, and suggests that the emblem of YHWH was a tree. Levenson, Sinai and Zion: An Entry into the Jewish Bible, 20. The burning bush has also been identified as the black raspberry (*rubus sanctus*), sana plant (*Casia obovata*), the shurbu (*Colutea istria*) or the wild juju (*Xizyphus spina*). Kaplan, The Living Torah: The Five Books of Moses and the Haftarot, 268. A number of commentators have compared the burning bush which Moses encountered with the burning lamp which Abraham saw when he was promised an heir by God, after he rescued Lot and was blessed by Melchizedek. It was then that God told Abraham that his descendants would be kept captive for four hundred years, and then go free with great wealth. Gen 15:17.

93 Gen 22:11; 46:2; 1 Sam 3:4-5.
94 Gen 22:11; 46:2; Exod 3:4; 1Sam 3:4. Sarna, Exodus, 14.
95 Exod 3:6. Alt, Essays on Old Testament History and Religion, 13-15.
96 Exod 3:5, 8. Sarna, Exodus, 15. Milk and honey were nutrients which could

to Egypt and demand from the Pharaoh that he be allowed to lead the Hebrews out of their bondage. Moses reacted to this pronouncement by claiming that he was not capable of performing such a dangerous undertaking. He argued that he had no experience in leadership, aside from his education in the royal court, and that he had been a simple shepherd for forty years, tending his flocks in Midian, far from his Egyptian homeland and Hebrew brethren.[97] The Bible does not mention how Moses was aware that he was born a Hebrew, but his reaction lends support to his likely having some inkling of this relationship when he killed the Egyptian taskmaster who was beating a Hebrew slave. He also was concerned that if he returned to Egypt with such a demand, he would not be welcomed by his own people, let alone the Pharaoh, because of his prolonged absence. "Who am I that I should go to Pharaoh and free the Israelites from Egypt?" he asked, a worry that was sensible for an eighty year old man who had never even lived among the Hebrews, except in infancy. It would take some time for the Lord to allay Moses' apprehension in a debate which the great Jewish philosopher Martin Buber (1878-1965 CE) labeled as "the great duologue in which the God commands and the man resists."[98] Although Nelson Mandela easily returned to South Africa to become President of his country after an exile of twenty-six years, Moses did not have the reputation, or the identity, of that great man among his own people.

Many biblical commentators have applauded Moses for his humility in this regard, but I believe that his initial reaction was more representative of how foreign he felt among the Hebrews, than any lack of desire for imperial power. Although Moses may have understood the religious practices of the Hebrew slaves through his years in the land of Midian, he had never lived in a Hebrew community, or become educated in their specific theologic practices. How was he going to convince the tribal elders to bind their allegiance to him, and risk personal injury, or even annihilation, by demanding that the Pharaoh free them from their bondage, when he was not known to them as a scholar or leader of the Hebrew faith? This deficiency would prove to be well-founded during the

---

sustain life for many months by themselves, and therefore were considered the epitome of beneficence. Sarna, Exodus, 16. In the Egyptian *The Story of Sinuhe* (nineteenth century BCE), which some scholars believe resembled the story of Abraham, the presence of cattle and honey, instead of milk and honey, was used to describe the wealth of the land of Yaa. Exodus, The Torah, A Modern Commentary II, 30. The phrase "flowing with milk and honey" is used fourteen times in the Pentateuch and five times in the rest of the Old Testament. Harris, "Leviticus," 614.

97 Joseph, Moses, and David were all shepherds who became rulers in the Bible, reflecting the ancient image of the king as a shepherd, or servant, of his people. Levenson, The Death and the Resurrection of the Beloved Son: The Transformation of Child Sacrifice in Judaism and Christianity, 144-145.

98 Buber, Moses: The Revelation and the Covenant, 46.

Exodus, when the Hebrews frequently questioned the authority of Moses during their forty years of wandering the wilderness before crossing into the Promised Land. God reassured Moses by telling him that "I will be with you; that shall be your sign that it was I who sent you," a clear indication that Moses would somehow be imbued with the identity, or at least the support, of a God.[99]

Moses accepted that this emblem of divine support was a critically important element, but still questioned God on how he could convince the Hebrews that he had the support of their preferred Divine Being, and not some other regional deity. He boldly asked what name he should use to convince the Hebrews that it was indeed the God of their Fathers, and God answered that He was the "God of Abraham, Isaac, and Jacob," indicating that a new name was not needed, since the elders would thereby know who He was by that appellation.[100] Moses persisted, asking for more specificity, and God said tell them that I am *Ehyeh-Asher-Ehyeh*, or "I Am That I Am," a phrase which denoted the Tetragrammaton YHWH (*Yud, Hei, Vav, Hei*), which would become the primary recording of the divine name from that point forward.[101] This passage has been pointed to as evidence of the polytheistic nature of the Hebrews before Moses appeared on the scene, as there would be little reason for Moses to be concerned about the name of God if there were not other deities who were worshiped by the Hebrew people. While modern Jews clearly understand that the God of Abraham, Isaac, and Jacob is one and the same with YHWH, the pre-Mosaic Hebrews were apparently not so uniform in their awareness. The complex terminology of the patriarchal gods will be discussed in greater detail in chapter 12, but Moses' concern for accuracy makes sense, given the fact that he was totally unknown to the generation of Hebrews who presently were enslaved on Egyptian soil, and he would need to be assured that the God who he was identified with was the One Who carried the greatest influence and power.

While we cannot know the mind set of Moses when he was suddenly faced with this vision of God telling him to return to Egypt to become the deliverer of the Hebrew people out of bondage, we can make a very educated guess on what he must have known, or at least believed, about his origins on the basis of what this passage says about his response to YHWH's request. Moses did not react with any astonishment that he was to become the leader of the Hebrews, but

---

99 Exod 3:12. Sarna, Exodus, 17.

100 Exod 3:6. Alt, Essays on Old Testament History and Religion, 16.

101 Exod 3:13-14. Ibid., 19. Other translations include "I-Will-Be-Who-I-Will-Be," and "I Am He Who Endures." Alter, The Five Books of Moses, 321. In Kabbalah, the name YHWH is often translated as "Is-Was-Will-Be," which in reverse means "existence." Green, EHYEH: A Kabbalah for Tomorrow, 2. This was not the first time the name YHWH appeared in the Torah, as it was used when Enosh was born to Seth (Gen 4:26), but this passage was the first time God revealed His name to a human being. Mondriaan, "Yahweh and the Origin of Yahwism: A Critical Evaluation," 580-581.

only with concern about how he would be received. This indicates to me, that he somehow either knew, or thought he might be, a Hebrew by birth, and then raised as an adopted child of the Egyptian princess, likely based on his learning the history of Egypt while being schooled in the Pharaoh's palace. He clearly was not Egyptian in appearance, and as soon as he was aware of his age, and what had happened the year he was born to the Hebrew slaves, he would have wondered if it was possible that he was born a Hebrew and then exposed by his mother, in order to spare his life. He also would have considered this possibility after his murder of the Egyptian taskmaster who was beating a Hebrew slave. Although his initial reluctance to return to Egypt is natural, given the manner in which he was forced to leave, and the stability of his life in Midian for forty years, there is no indication in the biblical text that this trepidation prevented him from finally accepting YHWH's offer.

YHWH then directed Moses to assemble the Hebrew elders once he entered Egypt, and inform them that the time had come for their Exodus out of the bondage which had tortured them for so many years. After the Hebrews had agreed to follow his leadership role, he was then to go to the Egyptian Pharaoh and request permission to take all of the Hebrews on a three-day trip into the wilderness in order to sacrifice to God. The wording of this solicitation implied that the trip was only temporary, a clear deception since the Exodus was planned as a permanent affair from the very start. The Lord added that the Pharaoh would not agree to this proposal, and that Moses would have to change his mind by causing various plagues to paralyze the economy of the country through widespread devastation. After the Egyptians were exhausted by their losses, and made fully aware of the power of the Lord, the Hebrews would then finally be able to leave, taking with them a cache of valuable objects they would strip from the grieving Egyptians.[102] This latter guarantee of riches to be taken from the Egyptians when the Exodus began has created much controversy over the years, but rabbinic tradition has generally accepted that the treasure was payment for the years of service the Hebrews had given as indentured slaves.

It is no surprise that Moses listened to this frightful forecast of the events leading up to the Exodus with some degree of astonishment and fear, and that he

---

102 YHWH told Moses at the time that each "woman shall borrow from her neighbor and the lodger in her house objects of silver and gold, and clothing, ... thus stripping the Egyptians," an indication that it was only the women who would receive the booty. Exod 3:21-22. Sarna, Exodus, 19. Just before the final Plague, however, the Lord told Moses that he was to "tell the people to borrow, each man from his neighbor and each woman from hers, objects of silver and gold," evidence that the rewards were not restricted to only women. Exod 11:2. Ibid., 52. Finally, once the Hebrews were packing up to leave, the Bible recorded that "the Israelites had done Moses' bidding and borrowed from the Egyptians objects of silver and gold, and clothing," and that all the Egyptians let their holdings be stripped. Exod 12:35. Ibid., 61.

answered that he simply did not have the ability to perform such a complicated task. He might have accepted the fact that he was born to Hebrew parents, and looked forward to returning to Egypt as the future leader of his people, but undertaking a direct attack on the Pharaoh was another thing altogether. The people would never believe him, he argued, and the power of the Pharaoh was greater than anything he could bring to force compliance. God replied that He would give him a magic rod that would turn into a snake, and that this miracle would be strong enough to convince the Egyptians that the God of Abraham, Isaac, and Jacob was on his side.[103] In addition, He would provide Moses with the magical ability to turn his hand white with leprosy, and to take water from the Nile River and have it turn into blood when poured upon the dry land.[104] These promises were intended to impress Moses, for he was aware that the Egyptian religion was permeated with superstition and magic, and that the people, as well as the Pharaoh, would have been awed by the performance of such miracles. The Bible does not record if the Patriarchs were also swayed by such magical powers, but it is clear that these same superhuman acts were going to be vitally important in maintaining the loyalty of the Hebrew congregation. It seems clear that the primary reason the elders agreed to commit to his sole leadership was his use of magic, and not his intellectual or religious mystique, for the biblical text told how the Hebrew people believed that Moses was sent by God after Aaron told them what the Lord had said, and Moses "did the signs."[105] It was the use of wizardry that initially impressed the Hebrews, but as the Exodus wore on, and Moses forbid their maintaining the faith of their ancestors, more and more dissidents became tired of his sleight-of-hand mastery, and less impressed with his claim of being the only one to be conversant with God.

Despite this impressive promise of divine assistance with magical powers, Moses was not entirely assuaged, and replied that he was not a good speaker, and had a speech impediment, making it difficult for him to sway the awesome power of the Pharaoh. The precise nature of this defect remains unclear, although it is often translated as "uncircumcised lips," which suggests that he was not only unable to effectively present his demands to the Pharaoh, but that he would be impotent before the Hebrews as well.[106] Moses was so concerned about his

---

103 Exod 4:1, 3, 5. The rod in ancient Egypt was a symbol of royal authority, and the snake represented the patron cobra-goddess of Lower Egypt. This combination would therefore be doubly impressive, and serve as a menacing symbol of death. Sarna, Exodus, 20.

104 Exod 4:6-8. Leprosy was generally seen as a sign of divine punishment for human behavior, uncleanliness rather than a disease, and the alteration of water from the Nile River, which was deified in Egypt, indicated that YHWH's rule was sovereign over subordinate gods. Ibid., 21.

105 Exod 4:30-31. Noth, Exodus, A Commentary, 48.

106 Exod 4:10. The phrase was repeated at Exod 6:12, 30. Sarna, Exodus, 21.

inability to communicate that he asked the Lord to send someone else. God grew impatient with these repetitive excuses and "became angry with Moses," but agreed to send his brother Aaron, a capable orator, to serve as his spokesman to the people.[107] This was the first time in the Torah that the emotion of anger was ascribed to God, although His ire would frequently flare against the obstinate Hebrews during the years which followed. Moses realized that he could no longer refuse God's offer at this point, and assented to undertake the task of leading the Hebrews out of Egypt. Although he seemed to be insecure and unsure of his ability to fulfill the requirements necessary for a successful outcome during his monologue with God, over the next forty years his confidence would grow, and he would develop such a severe dictatorial style of rule that thousands of his brethren would be killed because of their failure to follow the new monotheistic principles of the Mosaic Code.

C. Number of Participants in the Exodus

Before proceeding with an analysis of the actual Exodus in the following chapter, I want to discuss the size of the Hebrew force that left Egypt, in order to estimate how many dissidents may have eventually withdrawn and emigrated to Mycenae. The standard translation of the "E" source in the book of *Exodus* indicates that over 600,000 men of military age, in addition to older men, women and children, made up the congregation which took part in the migration.[108] A similar total of 603,550 is listed in the book of *Numbers*, also attributed to the E source, where it is clarified that the men were of military age, which began at the age of twenty years old.[109] The "P" source gave a closely aligned total of 603,550 men in the book of *Exodus*, following the episode of the golden calf-idol, and 601,730 in the book of *Numbers*, seven months later when the Tabernacle was completed.[110] After the plague at Acacia, near the end of the Exodus, when a census of the men of Israel except for the Levites who were twenty years old or older was taken, the total was said to be 601,730, which is incredibly close to the number which began the Exodus.[111] To buttress the validity of these figures,

---

107 Exod 4:14. Ibid., 22.

108 Exod 12:37. A "mixed multitude," or *erev rav*, was part of the total. Exod 12:38. The Chumash, 359.

109 Num 1:2, 46. Exodus 1-18, 122. The definition that a male achieved physical maturation at age twenty years is similar to other nations of the classical world. In Sparta, a man could enter military service at twenty years of age; in Athens, it was eighteen years; and in Rome, it was seventeen years. Milgrom, Numbers, 5. The Talmud added that men over the age of sixty years were no longer able to enter the military, and therefore were not included in the census. Scherman, The Chumash, 727.

110 Exod 38:26; Num 26:51. Halpern, "The Exodus From Egypt: Myth or Reality?," 90.

111 Num 26:51.

when a census was taken by King David near the end of his reign, it was reported that 800,000 men of conscription age were present in Israel, and 500,000 in Judah, numbers which would support a total of 600,000 men during the Exodus, a few centuries before.[112] Finally, during the building of the Tabernacle on Mt. Sinai, each man was valued at a half-shekel, and the silver obtained from the community was listed as 100 talents and 1,775 shekels.[113] Since there are 3,000 shekels to a talent, this would equal 301,775 shekels, making the total number of men 603,550, a figure very close to the census compilation.[114]

Despite the consistency of the census totals in these various passages, many commentators have insisted that the figures listed are simply too large to be believed. If one adds to this total the number of Hebrew women and children, in addition to the "people of various sorts" that went with them, the sum would be almost 2 million, a figure that would seem to be unmanageable for any era, but especially impossible during the Late Bronze Age.[115] J. Maxwell Miller and John H. Hayes, from the Candler School of Theology at Emory University, have pointed out that if the Hebrew contingent was this large, they would have stretched for 150 miles standing ten abreast, and it would have taken eight or nine days to march by any fixed point.[116] According to Richard Friedman, Professor of

112 2 Sam 24:9. The Chronicler gave the totals as 1,100,00 men in Israel, and 470,000 in Judah, adding that the tribes of Levi and Benjamin were not included in the numbering. 1 Chron 21:5. The American historian Salo Baron (1895-1989 CE) has estimated that there were 1.1-1.35 million Jews in the ancient world at the end of the eighth century BCE, and 1.8 million in 100 BCE, although he gave no basis for these estimations. McGing, "Population and Proselytism: How Many Jews Were There in the Ancient World?" 89-91. Gregory Bar-Hebraeus (b. 1226 CE), the thirteenth century Syriac Christian writer claimed that Claudius Caesar took a census of the Jews that numbered 6,944,000 and Tacitus reported a total of 5,984,072 Jews, to put these numbers in greater perspective. Ibid., 92-94.

113 Exod 30:13; 38:25-26. In the system of weights and measures used in the ancient Near East, the talent was the highest unit of weight, equivalent to sixty minas or three thousand shekels. One hundred twenty talents of gold would weigh about four tons. Walton, Matthews, & Chavalas, The IVP Bible Background Commentary: Old Testament, 364.

114 Kaiser, "Exodus," 495.

115 Exod 12:38. The Living Bible, 58. The description of the "people of various sorts," known as *erev rab*, was used in the book of *Nehemiah* to refer to the Ammonite and Moabite foreigners, who were later expelled from the assembly at the Temple for their belief in Balaam. Neh 13:3. Manetho claimed that this designation referred to 80,000 Egyptian lepers and other diseased persons who allied themselves to the Hebrews and eventually settled in Jerusalem. Exodus 1-18, 414.

116 Miller & Hayes, A History of Ancient Israel and Judah, 60. According to another estimate, the back of the line would have taken a couple of weeks to reach the starting point of the front of the line. Walton, Matthews, & Chavalas, The IVP Bible Background

Hebrew and Comparative Literature at the University of California, San Diego, if they had marched eight abreast, by the time the first Hebrew reached Mt. Sinai, half of them would still be in Egypt.[117] In addition, there seems to be no way such an assembly could be fed with the resources available in the Sinai wilderness during the Late Bronze Age. While semi-nomadic Semitic tribes were able to survive in this region for centuries, most were forced to enter Egypt periodically when resources became limited from climactic and social reasons from the time of the Old Kingdom (2700-2190 BCE) forward. In the more arable areas of the Levant, the population density was limited, and it is generally believed that only about 250 persons per hectare resided in urban areas of the Canaanite Middle Bronze IIb, giving a total population in both the urban and rural regions of about 200,000 people.[118] Even if agricultural advances were made by the Late Bronze Age to significantly increase the food and water supply, there would still seem to be little chance that an infusion of 2,000,000 people could be supported by the available natural resources.

Not only is the number of participants unwieldy, but it is hard to believe that the slave population in Egypt was that large, given the fact that estimates place the total number of people in Egypt at about 2,000,000 during the Old Kingdom, and 3-4,000,000 during the New Kingdom (1550-1069 BCE).[119] Even if one accepts Donovan Courville's estimation that the population of Egypt at the time of the Exodus was almost 8,000,000, the loss of this many citizens at one time, even if they were slaves, would have likely decimated the Egyptian economy, and left them open to invasion by outside forces.[120] In addition, many estimates of the total population of Canaan at that time are only 1,000,000 people, and recent calculations place the number even lower, below 150,000.[121] These totals clearly argue against the infusion of two million Hebrew slaves, given the fact that no contemporary chronicler recorded their presence.

A smaller total is also supported by Moses' summary of the history of the Hebrew people as they were camped in the wilderness of Moab, forty years after they left Mount Sinai. He reminded the gathering that the Lord had chosen them to inherit the Promised Land because He loved them, and not because they were a large nation, since they were actually "the smallest of all."[122] If the total population of Hebrews was actually two million, it certainly would be greater than most of the other principalities in the Levant during that era, and would

---

Commentary: Old Testament, 88.

    117 Friedman, Commentary on the Torah, 428.

    118 Kempinski, "The Middle Bronze Age," 194.

    119 Hassan, "The Wealth of the Land," 67; Manley, The Penguin Historical Atlas of Ancient Egypt, 94.

    120 Courville, The Exodus Problem and Its Ramifications, I.31.

    121 Isserlin, The Israelites, 95.

    122 Deut 7:7. The Living Bible, 156.

not, by any stretch of the imagination, be construed as the smallest of all the principalities.

Support for lowering the actual total is also found in other biblical passages, such as the statement that there were only 22,273 firstborn sons over the age of one month when a census was taken on Mt. Sinai, a few years after the Exodus began.[123] If the true number of men over age twenty years was 603,550, this would mean that only 3.7% of the men had firstborn sons, a ratio of males above the age of twenty years to firstborn male children of approximately 27:1. This figure, according to Rabbi W. Gunther Plaut, the leading historian, scholar, and representative of the Reform Judaism movement, "exceeds the bounds of likelihood," given the fact that the Hebrews in later texts were said to only fulfill their destiny by having children, and is more consistent with a population of about 250,000 adult males.[124]

Since many modern biblical scholars consider the Bible to be a fictional treatise, the most common explanation for this exaggerated total is to simply ignore the claims as inflated and false. Norman K. Gottwald, for example, simply disregarded the biblical text and considered the number of Levitical worshipers of Yahweh under Moses to number only in the few hundreds, or thousands at the most.[125] Rather than conclude that the original Hebrew text is inaccurate, however, and thereby contaminate the reliability of biblical historicity, other scholars have theorized that the problem lies in the translation of the original text, which wrongly interpreted the Hebrew words which explained the tabulations. The one which has gained the greatest modern support is the explanation put forth by George Mendenhall, retired professor of Near Eastern Languages and Literature at the University of Michigan, that the primary problem was not an allegorical use of the total number of participants intended to demonstrate the miraculous power of YHWH to sustain such a large throng in such a small space, but rather an erroneous interpretation of the meaning of the Hebrew word *elef*, which was used to make the census determination in most biblical sections. Mendenhall first proposed in 1958 CE that *elef* could mean both the number 1,000, which was how most translations interpreted the word in order to come to the 600,000 figure, but also a subsection of a tribe, which was originally a military term and indicated units of men which in pre-monarchical times may have only averaged six to nine men, rather than one thousand.[126] In the Amarna letters,

123 Num 3:43.

124 Plaut, Numbers, The Torah, A Modern Commentary IV, 18. Attempts to explain the discrepancy have often centered on claiming that the total only represented the firstborn sons born after the Exodus began, although there is no direct indication of this in the biblical text. Allen, "Numbers," 729.

125 Gottwald, The Tribes of Yahweh: A Sociology of the Religion of Liberated Israel, 1250-1050 BCE, 40.

126 Pixley, On Exodus, A Liberation Perspective, 67.

for example, when King Rib-addi of Byblos asked the Egyptian Pharaoh for an emergency contingent of men to help defend his city, the number of troops in each contingent totaled 10-20 men.[127] If the interpretation that *elef* refers to a unit of six to nine men is applied to the biblical tradition, then the tribe of Reuben, which was listed as having "46 elef 500" in the biblical text, for a total of 46,500 under the standard translation, would become 46 contingents of men, equaling about 500 troops.[128] This would make the number of people fleeing with Moses as somewhere between 18-72,000, and the fighting force of adult males 6-18,000, rather than the 600,000 figure which resulted if the word *elef* was taken to mean 1,000 men.[129] The total force of fighting men in the Exodus under this interpretation would then compare to other armies mentioned in non-biblical texts, and would better explain how Moses was able to single-handedly maintain control during the forty years of wandering in the Sinai wilderness. A military force of 10,000 men was still a significant force during the time of Hammurabi (1848-1806 BCE), and raiding parties during the Amarna Age (1353-1336 BCE) often were composed of about 300 men.[130] During the Middle and Late Bronze Ages, Egyptian armies occasionally totaled as many as 10,000 men, reaching 20,000 during the battle of Kadesh, again validating that the Hebrew congregation would likely have totaled this approximate range.[131]

This smaller total fighting force would also still be large enough to account for the military success of the Hebrews during the Exodus, since the kings of individual towns in Canaan had small armies, which generally did not include more than fifty chariots.[132] With respect to the Canaanite cities, the inhabitants of the towns varied as to size and likely included a few thousand people for cities like Beth-shean, Dothan, Megiddo, Shechem, Gezer, Lachish, and Beth-shemesh. Hazor, which was much larger in area, probably accommodated several tens of thousands inhabitants, but the defense of the town was mostly provided by fortifications and superior defense arrangements, such as an adequate water supply, and it is likely that not more than 25% of the population would represent men who could act as defensive warriors.[133] The smaller Hebrew force also would comport with campaigns elsewhere in the Mediterranean, where Robert Drews, Professor of Classics and History at Vanderbilt University, has estimated that

127 Noth, Numbers, A Commentary, 22-23.
128 Plaut, Numbers, The Torah, A Modern Commentary IV, 18-19; Humphreys, "The Numbers in the Exodus From Egypt: A Further Appraisal," 323.
129 Choi, "Exodus: How Big was the Population?" 115-116.
130 Harrison, Numbers, An Exegetical Commentary, 1992.
131 Yadin, "Warfare in the Second Millennium BCE," 138-139. When Alexander the Great defeated the Persian army, he was estimated to have had between 30-43,000 infantry and 4,000 calvary. Plutarch, "Alexander," 15, 267.
132 Yadin, "Warfare in the Second Millennium BCE," 139.
133 Ibid., 151.

the early PIE speaking warriors who invaded Greece c. 1600 BCE and formed the Shaft Grave Dynasty in Mycenae were composed of thousands or tens of thousands of people, and not hundreds of thousands.[134] An Hebrew force of 10,000 would have been large enough to contend with the armies they came up against, but small enough to not affect the delicate balance of power or be recognized by contemporaneous sources.

This modification would necessitate, however, a reassessment of the number of Hebrews killed by Moses. The biblical text indicates that over 40,000 people were slain, as I have detailed in the preceding chapters. This is approximately 7% of the total number of Hebrew males, and under the revised calculation the number would be equivalent to about 1400, assuming the majority of the people killed were men. Similarly, the number of dissident Hebrews who left the Exodus would have to be small enough to not drain the resources of the remaining force which took part in the Conquest of the Promised Land. I estimate that this would have been in the range of 1000-1500 men, not counting their wives and children, which would be a size both relevant to the needs of the Mycenaean war effort, and capable of being important enough to transmit traditions that would be retained by the survivors of the Trojan War. Movement of this many people would have been relatively easy, and their effect on the Mycenaean economy would have still been significant enough to result in transmission of traditions, as discussed throughout this book.

While I accept that the theory put forth by Mendenhall and others is probably accurate, one problem with the theory is that the word *'lp*, which later was vocalized as *'elef*, was translated as "thousand" rather than "troop" in the Siloam tunnel inscription (c. 700 BCE), and the Moabite Stone (c. 840 BCE), as well as other ancient Hebrew, Aramaic, and Ugarit inscriptions.[135] In addition, *elef* was also used when indicating that the number of firstborn Hebrew males was 22,273, and the use of the word to refer to a clan would be inappropriate since firstborn sons do not constitute clans.[136] I nevertheless agree with those scholars who claim that a force of two million Hebrews taking part in the Exodus is simply too large to be believed, and that the proper interpretation of the word *elef* should be as a group of men, rather than as a thousand individuals.

---

134 Drews, The Coming of the Greeks, 195.

135 Humphreys, "The Number of People in the Exodus From Egypt: Decoding Mathematically the Very Large Numbers in Numbers I and XXVI," 200.

136 Friedman, Commentary on the Torah, 432.

Chapter 5

EXODUS: THE EVENT

y premise that much of the Classical Greek culture originated from ancient Hebraic traditions that were introduced by dissident Hebrews who fled the Exodus in fear for their lives and traveled to Mycenae before the Trojan War relies on details of the Exodus account which indicate that Moses imposed parricidal retributions against those Hebrews who followed the religious practices of their ancestors, rather than obeying the new monotheistic regulations imposed by the Mosaic Code. These actions infuriated the Hebrews, who "felt that the bond of blood was stronger than any tie of citizenship," and that loyalty to the family overrode loyalty to the laws promulgated by Moses.(1) As they watched their brethren die for the sake of their ancient beliefs, I believe that they realized that they had no choice but to depart for the distant Mycenaean shore, if they expected to survive the unforeseen mandates of the Mosaic Code.

As I have already discussed, many historians do not believe that the Exodus ever took place, but I will follow the lead of others who accept that the biblical description is based in some degree on recollections of factual traditions, and in this chapter I will analyze the biblical account of the Exodus, examining both the sites in question, and the confrontations which took place between Moses and the Hebrews who were regarded as "stiff-necked" and disobedient, in order to show why my theory of a rebellion in the wilderness is the most likely explanation for an Hebraic contribution to ancient Greek culture.

This task is difficult because the stories of the fabled passage are scattered throughout the Torah, and many of the sites are either unidentifiable today, or are not agreed upon by modern historians. In addition, the route taken varies in different biblical sections, primarily because the placement of names in the Bible was not meant to be an exact compilation, but rather was intended to educate the people about the miracles God wrought, so that they could follow the regulations set forth in the Mosaic Code with appropriate compliance. The generally accepted axiom among biblical scholars, stemming from the school of Ishmael, is that "there is no chronological order in the Torah."(2) This inexactitude has resulted in heated debates over where such important sites as Mt. Sinai and the Reed Sea are located, and exactly what order of travel actually took place.

The term "itinerary" has been applied to the determination of the pathway taken through the wilderness, and the controversy is so extensive that most scholars accept it as a distinct literary genre. One prominent example of this uncertainty is exactly when Jethro, Moses' father-in-law, arrived at the foot of Mt. Sinai to

---

1 Bowra, The Greek Experience, 41.
2 Heschel, Heavenly Torah: As Refracted Through the Generations, 240.

help Moses formulate the management of the Exodus from an administration standpoint. The biblical text states that Jethro came with Zipporah and her two sons, Gershom and Eliezer, before the revelation and delivery of the Ten Commandments.[3] Most scholars, however, believe that Jethro actually appeared after the theophany, leaving many to conclude, as summarized by the Orthodox Jewish Rabbi Jacob Milgrom, that "the wilderness traditions survived, in the main, without fixed dates, and they were clustered at the beginning and at the end of the wilderness sojourn."[4] While the details of the pathway taken are not critical to my theory of why a group of dissidents left the Exodus, the events which took place are crucial to my interpretation of what happened, and I will therefore discuss the generally accepted placement of the various sites, in order to provide a consistent base to parallel the explanations provided by other biblical scholars.

While I envy the ability of scholars like Arnaldo Momigliano (1908-1987 CE), former Professor of Ancient History at the University of London, to read the Bible in Hebrew, Livy in Latin, and Herodotus in Greek,[5] I am not fluent in any of these languages, and will not be providing my own translation of the original Hebrew text in this book. Because no one translation is accepted as authoritative by biblical scholars, and because I want my quotations to be open to academic scrutiny and debate, but still appropriate to the point I want to emphasize in that passage, I have utilized widely-accepted sources, choosing one over another dependent upon the clarity of the specific quotation in question. While this technique may subject my work to criticism based upon my favoring renderings which buttress my theory, I believe in the advice of Maimonides who taught his students that it made no difference whether you studied the Torah or Talmud in the holy tongue or in Arabic or Aramaic, for "what really matters is whether it is done with an intellectual perception."[6] I have kept this adage in mind, and believe my choice of textual material will satisfy the requisites of Maimonides throughout the citations in this book.

---

3 Exod 18:1-5.

4 Milgrom, <u>Numbers</u>, xi. The debate dates back to the earliest rabbinic commentaries as evidenced by the opinion of Ramban (Rabbi Moses Ben Nachman, 1195-1270 CE), who maintained that the events in the Torah should always be assumed to have occurred chronologically, while Rabbi Abraham Ibn Ezra (1090-1164 CE) argued that Jethro arrived after the theophany, despite being placed before in the biblical text. Scherman, <u>The Chumash</u>, 394.

5 Momigliano, Essays on Ancient and Modern Judaism, 3.

6 "Maimonides to Joseph Ibn Gabir," <u>Letters of Maimonides</u>, 87.

A. The Path of the Exodus

1. Ramesses to the Reed Sea

According to the biblical text, the Exodus from Egypt began on the fifteenth day of the first month, following the night of the demise of the firstborn Egyptian children, when the Pharaoh, grief-stricken over the loss of his eldest son, finally relented to Moses' request to "let my people go."[7] Whatever the true size of the group that left Egypt under the direction of Moses, as discussed in the previous chapter, the Bible relates that they began their emigration from Ramesses, the major city in Goshen, where Jacob and his family lived after migrating to Egypt at the bequest of Joseph, in the northeast section of the Delta.[8] The name Ramesses refers to the city that was initially begun by Seti I (1294-1279 BCE) as a rebuilding of the Hyksos capital city of Avaris, and later completed by Ramesses II (1279-1213 BCE) to function as one of the Egyptian "store cities," along with the city of Pithom.[9] Although the exact location of the city is still disputed today, most scholars place it in the region of the Wadi Tumilat, a narrow stretch of land that runs from the eastern arm of the Nile River to the Great Bitter Lake.[10]

Once the congregation left Ramesses, they traveled to Succoth along the Wadi Tumilat, a journey that would normally be expected to take one day to complete. The strip functioned as one of the primary highways leading into and out of Egypt during the Late Bronze Age (1600-1200 BCE), and movement along its path was recorded in a number of ancient Egyptian sources, such as the Papyrus Anastasi 5, where a communication from a troop commander in Tjeku during the Eighteenth Dynasty noted that two runaway servants traveled this same route from Ramesses to Succoth in an attempt to escape from Egypt. Succoth is a Hebrew word meaning "tents," and was an area of bivouac for mobile peoples, rather than a

---

7 Exod 7:5; 8:1, 20; 9:13, 17; 10:3. The Living Bible, 53-56. The Jews were spared the death of their own firstborn children by placing a spot of blood from the sacrificial lamb on their doorposts, similar to the mark God placed on the forehead of Cain as a sign of divine protection. Gen 4:15; Exod 12:23. Jews have celebrated this event ever since the Exodus at the start of spring with a special meal known as the Passover (*Pesach*) seder, in appreciation of their being spared when the Angel of Death passed over their homes. Not only were the firstborn children killed, but also the firstborn of the cattle (Exod 12:29), leading the school of Ismael to ponder on what sin the cattle were guilty of. Heschel, Heavenly Torah: As Refracted Through the Generations, 229. It took place on the fifteenth day of the first month. Exod 12:18; Num 33:3.

8 Gen 45:10; 47:11; Exod 12:37; Num 33:3.

9 Stiebing, Out of the Desert? Archaeology and the Exodus/Conquest Narratives, 58-59.

10 Sarna, Genesis, 309-310.

specific city. It corresponds to the Egyptian toponym Tjeku, and may refer to either the region, or a specific location, although its most favored site is near the border fortress of Tell el-Maskhuta, west of modern Ismailiya, between Goshen and the Great Wall.[11]

As the Hebrews collected themselves at Succoth and prepared to undertake their first taste of extended freedom in centuries, Moses searched to find the bones of Joseph, who had made his brethren vow that they would take his bones with them if they ever left Egypt.[12] While this promise was made generations earlier, Moses nevertheless believed that they could not depart without Joseph's remains, since it would betray the wish of a revered ancestor. Such devotion is admirable, and, in my opinion, validates the inherent ancestral worship which the Hebrews had practiced for centuries in Egypt. Even Moses, who would soon begin to order a modification of this allegiance, showed how important it was to obey ancestral directives. The *Haggadah* claimed that Moses knew where Joseph was buried because Serah (Serach), the daughter of Asher who was of Joseph's generation, was still alive and directed him to the bank of the Nile River where Moses was able to call out Joseph's name and locate his coffin by bubbles which appeared upward in the waters.[13] The message that piety to forefathers was sacrosanct, even if it placed the lives of the Hebrews in danger by delaying the Exodus, is also consistent with the Fifth Commandment, which requires that the Hebrews honor their mother and father.[14] The Hebrews were taught for centuries to practice the polytheistic faith of their ancestors, and Moses, at the very start of the Exodus, validated the sanctity of this practice by honoring Joseph's bequest. When Moses later insisted that they no longer set up pillars or idols to give thanks to God for His beneficence in the manner of the Patriarchs, the dissident Hebrews rebelled, earning them the designation as being "stiff-necked" and stubborn throughout the Old Testament gleanings. Even when Moses attempted to force them to alter their ways with parricidal punishments, some of the Hebrews held steadfast to their filial traditions and eventually bolted, in my opinion, from his tyrannical rule, fleeing to Mycenae, where they could practice ancestral devotion in the same manner which Moses had initially done with Joseph's remains.

---

11 Hoffmeier, Israel in Egypt, The Evidence for the Authenticity of the Exodus Tradition, 179, 181.

12 Exod 13:19. The Bible states that the bones of Joseph, which Moses had brought with from Egypt, were buried in Shechem, in the parcel of ground which Jacob had bought from the sons of Hamor. Josh 24:32. Joseph was embalmed and placed in a coffin after he died, however, so it would not only be his bones which were transported, but his entire body. Gen 50:26.

13 The Book of Legends/Sefer Ha-Aggadah, 4.71, 71-72. Serah is mentioned as one of the seventy family members to accompany Jacob to Egypt, and was the daughter of Asher. Gen 46:17.

14 Exod 20:12; Deut 5:16.

With their task completed, the Exodus moved on, and a few days later the Hebrews encamped at Etham, "on the edge of the wilderness," a reference which explains their next forty years being the "wilderness tradition."[15] The Hebrews had now reached the southern border of the Sinai peninsula, and although the exact location is not certain, many scholars believe that it lay at the eastern end of the Wadi Tumilat, in the Lake Timsah region. Since the word Etham is similar to the Egyptian term *ḫtm* (fort), or *Khetem*, it may also refer to one of the military installations in the area, although the Hebrew pronunciation does not match the strong Egyptian guttural sound.[16] Another possibility is that Etham referred to the "mouth of the canal," an ancient structure called the Frontier Canal, which has recently been excavated along the eastern border of Egypt, adjacent to the Sinai Peninsula.[17] This edifice was seventy meters wide at water level, and ran from Pelusium down to Lake Timsah, just to the east of the Wadi Tumilat. The purpose of the canal has not yet been determined, but it is thought to have been part of the defensive structure set up by the Egyptians against the Semitic tribes, in addition to being used as a waterway for irrigation.

Since the Hebrews likely believed that their gateway to freedom was soon to be opened, given the location of Etham at the eastern edge of Egypt, it must have come as a surprise when God ordered Moses to take a sudden change of direction, north toward Pi-hahiroth (Mouth of Water), which lay between Migdol (Mt. Migdol) and the Sea, opposite Baal-zephon (Beelsephon), rather than continue directly into the desert, as the location of Etham would have suggested.[18] Scholars have theorized that this was necessitated by the defensive line of fortifications known as the "Prince's Wall" ("Wall of Horus," "Wall of the Ruler"), which barred roads leading into and out of Egypt toward the desert.[19] It was begun by Amenemhet I (1937-1908 BCE), the first king of the Twelfth Dynasty, and was intended to

15 Exod 13:20; Num 33.6. Sarna, Exodus, 69.

16 Kaiser, "Exodus," 385.

17 Hoffmeier, Israel in Egypt, The Evidence for the Authenticity of the Exodus Tradition, 164, 166, 170.

18 Exod 14:1-2; Num 33:5-7. God did not lead them by the more direct route, known as the "Way of the land of the Philistines," or the Philistine Highway, and most biblical scholars believe that this choice was mandated because the Hebrews would encounter armed resistance by the direct passage, and lose heart and return to Egypt. He instead made them take a roundabout path by way of the desert to the Reed Sea. Exod 13:17-18. Kaplan, The Living Torah: the Five Books of Moses and the Haftarot, 321. Baal-zephon, which literally means "lord of the north," was a deity in the Ugaritic pantheon associated with Mount Casius, just north of Ugarit. Sarna, Exploring Exodus, The Origins of Biblical Israel, 108-109. Migdol appears in Egyptian as *mktr*, which means "fortification" in both the Semitic and Egyptian language of the time, and therefore may have been one of the fortresses built by Seti I to protect the eastern frontier against the Asiatics. Hoffmeier, Israel in Egypt, The Evidence for the Authenticity of the Exodus Tradition, 189.

19 Sarna, Exploring Exodus, The Origins of Biblical Israel, 105.

protect the Delta region against invasion by Bedouin nomads. Seti I (1294-1279 BCE) extended the fortifications to protect the path which the Egyptian forces took when they campaigned in Asia, and by the time of Ramesses II (1279-1213 BCE), fortresses were present along the entire southern end of the *Via Maris,* ending with Migdol of Men-maat-re at the Egyptian border and Sile.[20] Staying clear of the Prince's Wall not only would hide the movements of the Hebrews from Egyptian sentries, but also would keep them away from cities where treaties may have required that they be returned to Egypt if they were discovered to have left the country without permission.[21] Whether the Exodus took place in the fifteenth, fourteenth or thirteenth centuries BCE, Moses would have been aware of these treaties, and likely led the Exodus away from the Prince's Wall, even if not directed to by YHWH.

The Bible credits the decision to change direction to God's directive, rather than Moses, but the order would only seem to make sense if the total number of participants was less than that given in the standard translation of the biblical text, as described in the previous chapter. Even though the Hebrews did not have military training during their years of slavery in Egypt, they were still a formidable force, as was proven in the years to come, and it is likely that anonymity was not the only reason for God's order. If safety was the primary goal, it may have actually been better to move directly into the desert, rather than toward the *Via Maris,* for the Hebrews would then have been offered some degree of freedom from the Egyptians who "regarded the desert with a mixture of awe and fear."[22] The wilderness was infested with dangerous animals, like the wolf, panther and leopard, and snakes hid everywhere in the sand, making travel by foot hazardous. There were also few maps available, except for the regions of the gold mines, and this made expeditions so dangerous that when Ramesses III (1184-1153 BCE) sent caravans into the desert, he commissioned a special corps of police and archers to protect the participants.[23] Such concerns would not have likely

---

20 The *Via Maris* ran for a distance of 184 miles, from Pelusium to Heliopolis, and by the time of the New Kingdom, according to Diodorus of Sicily (first century BCE Greek historian), a regular military road was constructed with fortifications along the way, especially at watering places. In the Amarna letters there are numerous references to various tribes being allowed to pass these fortresses for a fee. Herrmann, A History of Israel in Old Testament Times, 58.

21 In the first decades of the fifteenth century BCE, a number of treaties were signed among the regional powers in order to control "the extradition of political fugitives and the cross-border movements of transhumant populations." In these treaties, kings agreed to return fugitives who had revolted from their respective country and fled to the neighboring land, in addition to returning populations "including its women, its goods, and its large and small cattle." Beckman, Hittite Diplomatic Texts, 12.

22 Montet, Everyday Life in Egypt, 175.

23 Ibid., 177-178.

bothered the Hebrews, since they had the protection of God who set a light in the sky to guide Moses on where to lead and where to encamp at night, a system which lasted throughout the forty-year span of time.[24] Although the Bedouin tribes presented an armed danger to most intruders into their territorial space, the size of the Hebrew caravan would have frightened off most brigands looking for booty. It therefore seems more likely that the reason for the change of direction is that God had told Moses that He would harden the Pharaoh's heart in order to show how powerful was the might of the Lord, and by first traveling to Pi-hahiroth, away from the desert, the Hebrews were brought to the vicinity of the Reed Sea, where the congregation would soon be attacked by the Pharaoh's army. In essence, the change in direction did the exact opposite of keeping the Hebrews hidden from view, and allowed God to publicize His power to the world by the parting of the Reed Sea. Once again, the conclusion that the story of the Exodus was primarily a way of validating the right of the Hebrews to claim authority in the Promised Land is not an altogether rash opinion, but it still does not prove that the Exodus did not take place in a fashion similar to what is recorded in the books of *Exodus* and *Numbers*.

It is while the Hebrews were encamped at this site that the Pharaoh reconsidered his earlier decision to free the slaves, and ordered his men to attack the Hebrews, and punish them for the havoc they had wrought in Egypt during the period of the Ten Plagues. Some scholars have suggested that the Pharaoh was only reacting to their failure to return after a brief absence, arguing that he had believed that their request to leave was only to take part in a short religious festival, which would have typically taken three days, rather than a permanent grant of emancipation. This view is based on the fact that when Moses first asked for permission to leave, he only requested a three-day trip in the wilderness in order to sacrifice to YHWH.[25] While such a misunderstanding was possible, most commentators have blamed the Pharaoh's action on his intense hatred of the Hebrews, which resulted from the Lord's decision to harden his heart against the repeated requests of Moses to have God's Chosen People be set free.

The Egyptian militia reached the Hebrews at the Reed Sea, and when the people saw the troops approaching, they immediately turned their anger upon Moses, blaming him for encouraging them to leave their homeland.[26] They

---

24 The biblical text noted that "the Lord went before them in a pillar of cloud by day, to guide them along the way, and in a pillar of fire by night, to give them light, that they might travel day and night." Exod 13:21; 40:38; Num 9:15-17; 10:11; Pss 78:14, 105:39. Sarna, Exodus, 70. The Roman historian Quintus Curtius (fl. mid-first century CE), in his *History of Alexander*, noted that Alexander the Great used a similar method, placing a fire on top of a pole to signal where his troops were to move. The fire was visible at night, and the smoke by day. Gabriel, The Military History of Ancient Israel, 75.

25 Exod 5:3.

26 Exod 14:9. Although the body of water where the battle took place is often referred

reasoned that it would be "better for us to serve the Egyptians than to die in the wilderness," and many had a change of heart about the reliability of their new-found leader.[27] This was an understandable reaction, for the Egyptians presented an imposing fighting force, led by a calvary of 600 chariots and charioteers.[28] Moses may have performed miracles to sway the resistance of the Pharaoh, but he now faced an attack from the most experienced army in the Levant, without the support of his fellow congregants.

It should not have been unexpected that most of the Hebrews questioned Moses' authority at such an early date in the Exodus, given the fact that Moses was still a relatively unknown mentor to the Hebrews. He had first appeared to them for forty years as a member of the Egyptian royal house, and then was absent for another forty years before his sudden return and elevation to the position of commander-in-chief. Even if there had been an oral tradition about his hidden birth and rescue which promoted his Hebrew origins, his ability to guide such a large group into the wilderness was certainly untested, and because the Hebrews had never set foot outside Egypt, the sudden appearance of the dreaded Egyptian army returning to punish them for the havoc they caused, would have surely sent a wave of fear that shook the very foundation of their faith. Moses later referred to this episode in his speech to the Hebrews before they crossed over the Jordan River to the Promised Land, and reminded the Hebrews that they always defied his attempted reformations, "from the day that you left the land of Egypt until you reached this place."[29]

Despite the paramount danger which the Pharaoh's soldiers presented, Moses was up to the task and performed the most well-known miracle in the biblical text by stretching out his hands and causing the waters of the Reed Sea to miraculously part, allowing the Hebrews to walk safely to the other side. Once the congregation had crossed over, the Egyptians began to follow from the opposite bank, and Moses stretched out his hands once again, causing the waters to sweep over the Egyptians, drowning the entire force in an awesome display of divine power.[30] To accentuate the extent of their conquest, the dead

to as the "Red Sea," referencing the term used in the Septuagint translation for reasons unknown, the correct translation is generally believed to be the "Reed Sea." Currid, Ancient Egypt and the Old Testament, 135.

27 Exod 14:12. Sarna, Exodus, 72.

28 Exod 14:9. The first Pharaoh to employ chariotry as a separate section of the army was Amenhotep III (1382-1344 BCE), suggesting that the Exodus took place either during or after his reign. Fletcher, Chronicle of a Pharaoh, The Intimate Life of Amenhotep III, 106. Although the Bible contains many anachronisms, the mention of chariots is an important argument for placing the Exodus in the thirteenth century BCE.

29 Deut 9:7. Tigay, Deuteronomy, 98. See e.g., Ps 106:7-9.

30 Exod 14:27. This parting of the waters to allow a miraculous passage was repeated in the biblical text when Joshua crossed the Jordan River to attack the city of Jericho. In that event, the priests carried the Ark to the water's edge, and when they entered the

soldiers washed up on the seashore, providing the Hebrews with a large supply of weapons that would enable them to succeed in later military battles. This cache of arms, coupled with the amount of jewelry and goods they were given before they departed Egypt, made the rag-tag armada a formidable force to reckon with. It was a spectacular victory, and as the waters of the Reed Sea once again settled into the comfort of a defensive barrier, Moses led the satisfied Hebrews deeper into the Sinai wilderness, far away from the dangers of Egyptian retribution. It is not known if the man who had ordered the killing of Hebrew male newborns by throwing them into the water of the Nile River was himself killed by drowning in the Reed Sea, since the biblical text says that not one of his army who followed the Hebrews into the sea survived, but it was, in any case, a fitting punishment for the tyrant who had caused the shedding of so many Hebrew tears.

The story of the parting of the Reed Sea, and the resultant defeat of the Egyptians, was celebrated in the book of *Exodus* by a hymn, variously called the "Song of (at) the Sea," or the "Song of Moses," extolling the attributes of YHWH as a warrior God Who led the victory, and thereby frightened the enemies of Israel in Canaan.[31] It told how God controlled the sea and then built His sanctuary for all to acclaim, a declaration that God was the "Warrior responsible for the present victory; it is His right hand that crushed the enemy."[32] It was followed by the "Song of Miriam," which was sung while the Hebrew women joyously danced to the music of timbrels in celebration of the victory over the Egyptians.[33] This

---

river stopped flowing as if held back by a dam, allowing the army to pass. Josh 3:13-14. Josephus related how Alexander the Great was also said to have parted the Pamphylian Sea in order to allow his army to pass through, a story which was attested to by Callisthenes (c. 360-328 BCE), Strabo (63 BCE - 21 CE), Arrian (86-160 CE), and Appian (95-165 CE). Josephus, "Antiquities of the Jews," The Complete Works of Josephus, II.XVI.5, 64. The region of the Reed Sea was known to be subject to large tidal flows, and Diodorus of Sicily (first century BCE) recorded that during the invasion of Egypt by Xerxes in 340 BCE, a troop unit of his army drowned when they were caught in the surging waters. Gabriel, The Military History of Ancient Israel, 78.

31 Exod 15:1-19. The poem at the end of the book of *Deuteronomy* has also been called the "Song of Moses," and some scholars have restricted this terminology to that passage. Deut 32:1-52. Levinson, "Deuteronomy," 440.

32 Goldin, The Song at the Sea, 31.

33 Exod 15:19-21. Some commentators have also referred to the "Song of Miriam" as the "Song of the Sea." Friedman, Commentary on the Torah, 221. Miriam was referred to as a prophetess in this section (Exod 15:20), the first person in the Bible to be so-called, a trait which she shared with Deborah (Judg 4:4), Huldah (2 Kgs 22:14), Noadiah (Neh 6:14), and Hannah (1 Sam 2:1). The Song of Miriam is the oldest Israelite poetry of any length, and belongs to the category of triumphal songs or hymns, which include celebrations of the Egyptian Pharaohs Ramesses II (1279-1213 BCE) at Kadesh, and the triumph of Marniptah (Merneptah, 1224-1211 BCE) over the Libyans, and the victory of the Assyrian king Tukulti-Ninurta I (1243-1207 BCE) over the Cossaeans of Babylonia,

jubilant reaction quickly evaporated the fear which paralyzed the Hebrews when they first saw the Egyptians approaching , but the congregants would remain frightened of their precarious survival in the years ahead, continuing to claim with each crisis that they never should have left their homeland only to die in an arid wasteland. For now, their fate appeared secure, and the blessings of the Promised Land close at hand.

2. *From the Reed Sea to the Wilderness of Shur*

Following the celebration, the congregation then traveled for three days before arriving at Marah in the Wilderness of Shur.[34] Scholars have basically outlined three separate pathways that Moses could have taken during this next phase of migration: the Northern, or "Yahwistic," route, which followed the coastal road, or *Via Maris*, to the land of the Philistines; the Southern, or "Elohistic," route, which took a southeasternly direction into the Wilderness; and the Central pathway, which lay intermediate between the two. I will briefly outline the arguments for each of these proposals before continuing with the story of the Exodus itself, for the direction of the Exodus helps determine the site of Mt. Sinai, where the theophany setting forth the principles of monotheism took place.

The northern "Yahwistic" route followed a north-easterly direction from Goshen, taking the *Via Maris*, which left Egypt at the fortress of Tjeku, north of Lake Serbonis. It continued up the Palestinian coastal plain to Gaza, and then to the Carmel chain where it crossed to the Plain of Jezreel through a narrow pass at Megiddo. First uncovered in 1888 CE by the German archaeologist, Gottlieb Schumacher (1857-1925 CE), the *Via Maris* was also known over the years as the "Way of the Sea," "Great Trunk Route," "Sea Route," and the "Coastal Highway," although what it was actually called in ancient days is not certain. Because the Hebrews would have had to pass the fortress at Tjeku in order to reach the coastal highway, and then travel through marshy lagoons before finally reaching the Eastern Frontier Canal, most scholars believe that the chance of success in this direction was very limited, given the fact that the direction was heavily used by military forces and trading caravans that connected Egypt with the mercantile centers in Syria during the Late Bronze Age. It was heavily guarded, even during times of peace, and this was likely the reason that God told Moses not to lead the Hebrews in this direction in the first place, even though it was the most direct route to Canaan from their point of departure. Because of these circumstances, the British Egyptologist Kenneth Kitchen has concluded that it is necessary to

all from the thirteenth century BCE. Albright, Yahweh and the Gods of Canaan, 12.

34 Also known as the "Desert of Shur" (Gen 16:7; 20:1; 25:18), and the "Desert of Etham" (Num 33:8), this region represents the whole district ranging from Egypt's northeastern frontier into the northwestern and southern quarters of the Sinai peninsula. Kaiser, "Exodus," 398.

"compel rejection of this option once and for all."[35] Despite the limitations which such a passage would have imposed, some scholars believe that the Hebrews still followed the northern route, making the shrine of Zeus Casius, located on the Mediterranean coast at Ras Qasrun, the biblical Baal-zephon; Lake Sirbonis the Reed Sea; and Jebel Halal, west of Kadesh, the site of Mt. Sinai.[36]

The route which most scholars favor is the southern "Elohistic" one, which moved up Sinai's west coastlands, then east through the mountains and wadis to a southern Mt. Sinai, near the modern Gulf of Suez, then back up northeastward along Sinai's east coast and desert to Kadesh-barnea. This path connected the Wadi Tumilat with central Sinai, along a road which had been used for centuries by mineworkers from Egypt during the Middle and New Kingdoms.[37] Known as "the Way of Shur," or *Yam Sooph* (*Yam Suph*), in ancient times, it was the direction taken by travelers who left Egypt and then crossed the Sinai peninsula to Canaan, south of the *Via Maris,* in the direction of Beer-sheba in the Negev.[38] This was the same path that Hagar likely took when she became pregnant and tried to flee to her homeland from Sarah's beatings.[39] Mt. Sinai in this southern direction would then be identified with Jebel Musa, Jebel Katherina, or Jebel Sirbal.[40]

Since many Semites, including the Hebrews, had likely worked in the mines during their years of slavery in Egypt, this route would have been well-known both to Moses, and the Exodus participants. It was also the direction taken by escaping slaves in a letter written by a frontier official at the end of the thirteenth century BCE. Although the southern route was the most safe, with respect to hostile Egyptian forces, the land was less productive and settled, making it difficult to find enough food and water to support a large contingent of men, women and children, no matter what the actual number. This would have resulted in a frequent lack of supplies, and may explain why there were so many confrontations between Moses and the Hebrews over a lack of water and food in the early part of the Exodus.

Some scholars believe the Hebrews kept clear of the *Via Maris,* which was the direction of the northern pathway, but did not travel deep into the Sinai wilderness, as suggested by the southern pathway, and instead took a more moderate central direction into the broad limestone shield of Et-Tih. There are two basic theories concerning this view. The first holds that the Exodus traveled

---

35 Kitchen, On the Reliability of the Old Testament, 266.

36 Robertson, On the Track of the Exodus, 59; Exodus, The Torah, A Modern Commentary II, 150.

37 Hoffmeier, Israel in Egypt, The Evidence for the Authenticity of the Exodus Tradition, 188.

38 It is today the great Hajj route from Egypt toward Mekkeh. Trumbull, <u>Kadesh-barnea, Its Importance and Probable Site</u>, 352.

39 Gen 16:6-9.

40 Exodus, The Torah, A Modern Commentary II, 150.

from Goshen eastward toward the Bitter Lakes, at the southern end of today's Suez Canal, where they crossed the Reed Sea and then traveled to Mt. Sinai, which would then be located at Jebel Sinn Bishr, about thirty miles southeast. The other passage took the Hebrews across the Sinai peninsula all the way to Eilat, at the northern tip of the Gulf of Eilat, and then to Mt. Sinai in the land of Midian, today's southern Jordan or northern Saudi Arabia. Both of these paths had few wells to allow for the passage of a large body of people, thereby providing a basis for the deficiencies of water noted in the biblical text, but did not proceed into the deep southern reaches of the Sinai wilderness, where the most favored site for Mt. Sinai is located. For this reason, the central pathway is not followed by the majority of biblical scholars.

3. From the Wilderness of Shur to Mt. Sinai

Whichever route they chose to follow after leaving the Reed Sea, the Hebrews eventually reached the Wilderness of Shur, which was part of the great desert beyond the border of Egypt, covering all of the Sinai peninsula except for some coastal strips and inland oasis. Their first stop in this locale was at Marah, where they found the water to be bitter, indicating that it was a desert spring, rather than the sweet water they were used to in the Nile Valley.[41] Despite being exhausted and parched, the Hebrews found the taste of the water so unpleasant that they could not drink, complaining to Moses that they were going to die of thirst because of his inept leadership.[42] This was the second time that they questioned his competence, and their accusations became so heated that Moses actually feared for his life. He turned to the Lord, pleading for help in order to assuage the anger of the Hebrews, and YHWH showed him a tree which had magical properties to cure the unstable situation. When Moses threw branches from the tree into the tainted well, the water miraculously became drinkable, allaying the immediate threat of death from dehydration.

Although the crisis had passed, Moses realized that his command was in jeopardy from this ungrateful throng, and he sternly reminded the Hebrews that they had to heed his advice, for he was not making decisions by himself, but was only transmitting the directions of the Lord. He warned them that God would bring down the same diseases He caused the Egyptians to suffer during the ten plagues if they did not follow His commandments and keep all of His Laws.[43]

---

41 Exod 15:23. The word *Marah* means bitterness in Hebrew, and the waters in that location are still quite bitter today.

42 It was at this point that the people were said to have "murmured" against Moses, in Hebrew "*wayilonu*," a phrase which would be repetitively used throughout the Exodus narrative to indicate that they complained, expressed resentment, or grumbled. Alter, The Five Books of Moses, 405.

43 Exod 15:26. There was no threat of capital punishment at this juncture, but only

He also reminded them that he was the only one to know God's intentions, for he alone was in touch with the Lord. This argument was not consistent with the patriarchal pattern of worship, where many Elders, and not just one man, were in touch with family gods, as will be discussed in more detail in chapter 12. The attack of Pharaoh's army was still fresh in their minds, however, and the Hebrews were convinced enough by Moses' power over the bitterness of the water to agree to follow his command. Moses' threat had allowed him to survive the confrontation without disruption of his autocratic rule, but he once again had to resort to magical demonstrations of the Lord's power in order to maintain control, a tactic that he would be forced to use over and over during the forty-year passage to the Promised Land. He was isolating himself from the standard method of tribal decision-making, and the time would soon come when discipline would require more than a show of power over nature to keep the unruly Hebrews in check.

The group next proceeded to Elim, where there were twelve springs of water and seventy date palms, providing the congregation with abundant sustenance to refresh themselves. Fertile oases such as these were formed by subterranean waters which collected in sufficient quantities for palm-groves to thrive in the middle of the wilderness of the Sinai peninsula, allowing Bedouins a chance to water their flocks as they constantly moved throughout the region. Elim, which means "terebinths" or "oaks," still retains a plentiful supply of good water today, and is used as a stopping place by modern Bedouins who make the region their home. The nearby plain of el-Marhah made this position a convenient camp site for the Hebrew enclave, enabling them to reconnoiter the land before moving forward.

After Elim, the Hebrews moved into the wilderness of Sihn (Desert of Sin), not to be confused with the Wilderness of Zin. The name Sihn is sometimes interpreted to be a short form of the word Sinai, but some scholars have instead attributed the derivation either to the word *Senneh*, from the name of the burning bramble bush where Moses had his theophany, or to the moon-god Sin, who was worshiped in the Sinai peninsula by the Bedouins.[44] Once again, the exact location is not certain, but since the book of *Numbers* lists Dophkah, which means "smeltry," as the next stop after Sihn, it is often thought to refer to the Egyptian turquoise and copper mining center at Serabit el-Khadim (Debben er-Ramleh), a sandy tract north of the Gebel Musa.

It was now six weeks since the departure of the Hebrews from Egypt, and soon after arriving in Sihn their food supply ran out and hunger once again left the entire community uncertain as to whether they should have ever listened to

---

the threat of sickness and disease.

44 Exod 16:1; Num 33:10. Exodus 1-18, 592; Alleman & Flack, "The Book of Exodus," 223.

Moses and left the safety of their homeland. For the third time, a rebellion spread among the people as they complained that he was risking their lives unnecessarily. They demanded to return to Egypt, where they would at least be spared of starvation, and where the complaints at Marah were made only by "the people," it was now "the whole Israelite community" that was upset with Moses' command.[45] Commentators have puzzled over the sudden disappearance of the food supply at this relatively early stage of the Exodus, since the Hebrews were said to have taken "large droves of livestock, both flocks and herds," when they departed Egypt.[46] Even with the large numbers of participants, it would seem reasonable that the animals could have provided adequate sustenance, although it is possible that Moses had only prepared for a shorter voyage, not knowing that the Lord was going to direct him away from the *Via Maris* and into the southern reaches of the Sinai. I believe it is more likely that the biblical compilers were simply amplifying the storyline by showing how Moses was faced with the triad of necessities which all migratory peoples must meet in order to survive a wilderness trek: safety from hostile forces (Pharaoh's army), and relief from the privations of water and food. To survive each of these crises, Moses was forced to rely on the assistance of the Lord, rather than on his own foresight and ingenuity. When the people now complained that they had nothing to eat in the Sihn Wilderness, Moses argued that their complaints were not really against him, but rather were directed against the Lord, a sin that was more dangerous than the perils they faced. He identified himself as the only one able to contact the Lord for assistance, and in so doing was continuing to detach himself from the authority of the Hebrew Elders, many of whom may have been inciting anger among the Hebrews in order to regain their former positions of power. The biblical compilers were likely utilizing these natural dangers to set the stage for the more important necessity for survival – faith and obedience in the words of the Almighty God. Not only would failure to comply with this requirement cost thousands of Hebrews their lives, it would also prevent Moses from being allowed to cross over the Jordan River into the Promised Land, as will be discussed later in this chapter.

Moses called the people together and admonished them for their constant moaning and complaints. He told them that the Lord would make provisions for their need, and in the morning, the miracle of quails and manna appeared, covering the land with ample supplies of food.[47] For the third time in only six

45 Exod 15:24; 16:2. Sarna, Exodus, 84, 86.

46 Exod 12:38. The New Interpreter's Bible, 780.

47 Exod 16:13-15, 31, 35; Pss 78:21-28, 105:40. Manna would continue to appear throughout the Exodus, until the Passover offering when they were encamped at Gilgal, in the steppes of Jericho, and an overabundance of quail would recur following the departure of the Hebrews from Mt. Sinai at Kibbroth-hattaavah. Num 11:6, 31-32; Josh 5:10-12. In the book of *Exodus*, manna was described as being like coriander seed, white in color, and tasting like wafers in honey. Exod 16:31. In the book of *Numbers*, the color was like

weeks, Moses utilized his awesome power to miraculously turn the tide of events and prove that YHWH was truly the one and only God, and that he was God's one and only chosen prophet (*nabi*). While his actions may have converted some of the Hebrews to have faith in his directives, others were growing intolerant of being excluded from the process of communicating with God, and their discontentment would simmer until it eventually boiled over into a full-fledged rebellion following the theophany on Mt. Sinai.

Scholars have long tried to account for the appearance of manna with scientific, rather than religious, explanations. One widely accepted view is that manna was actually the lichen *Lecanora esculenta*, which grows on rocks in the region, and produces pea-sized globules that are light enough to be blown by the wind. This sweet, edible substance has been collected for years by the natives of central Asia, and is still found in the inland regions of the Sinai peninsula, where it is referred to as *mann* by the nomadic inhabitants, and preserved in leather gourds, like honey, for future use. Another possibility for its origin is the tamarisk thicket, on which a droplike formation appears during the month of June from the secretions of insects. The sweet liquid of the hammada plant, common in southern Sinai, and the seed of the coriander, have also been put forth as possible candidates for the sudden availability of food. In a similar scientific vein, the sudden appearance of quail has been explained by the known migration of vast flocks of common quail (*Coturnix coturnix*), which return to the Levantine region in the Spring, during their flight from Africa to Central Europe, the very season in which the Exodus took place. They generally fly low and land frequently because of exhaustion during this lengthy process, and are thereby easily captured with nets or by hand.

Whether the miracle of manna and quail was provided by natural means, or through the intervention of the Lord, Moses was initially able to quell the hunger of the Hebrews without resorting to bloodshed. He had directed his followers not to collect manna on the Sabbath, however, for that was a day that was holy to the Lord, and no one was allowed to participate in any food-gathering activity. How the Hebrews should have known this rule is not entirely clear, since the Ten Commandments had not yet been given on Mt. Sinai, and there is no evidence in the biblical text that Moses had yet explained the regulations of the Mosaic Code.[48] Whether out of ignorance, or simply because they feared running out of food, some of the people disobeyed the restriction and proceeded to gather both manna and quail on the Sabbath. At this point, the Lord showed frustration over the ungrateful behavior of the Hebrews, and asked Moses: "How long will you people refuse to obey My commandments and My teachings?"[49] This is the first

bdellium, and the taste like rich cream. Num 11:7, 9. Classical Jewish thought reconciled this difference by suggesting that manna could take on various flavors and colors. Fox, "Numbers," 306-307.

48 The law of the Sabbath relates back to Gen 2:1-3.

49 Exod 16:28. Sarna, Exodus, 91.

time in the biblical text that God was revealed as being directly annoyed with the descendants of Abraham as His Chosen People, although His frustration would be repeated many time in the future. The battle line between Moses and God on one side, and the dissident Hebrews on the other, was now clearly drawn, and the final determination of who would control the passage into the Promised Land would eventually result in a program of parricidal punishments that was directed at weeding out all Hebrews who refused to follow the Mosaic Code.

Moses then led the congregation to Dophkah, Alush, and finally to Rephidim, where the people discovered that they were once again without water. Forgetting the admonitions they had recently received over their complaints of the lack of food, they protested so bitterly that Moses told YHWH that they were "almost ready to stone me."[50] The rhetoric of dissatisfaction in this section is more threatening than earlier confrontations, indicating growing impatience with the futility of their flight into the wilderness. It conjured up a picture of an angry and hostile confrontation between Moses and a large collection of Hebrews who were clearly disappointed with their newly found freedom in a strange land. The biblical text did not suggest at this point that there were philosophical reasons for this embattlement, but rather that the disgruntlement stemmed from concern over their ability to survive in the wilderness without the aid of the Egyptian royal house. Disunity had fractured the Hebrews into factions who were not ready to risk their lives for this foreigner from Midian.

In order to quell the disturbance, the Lord told Moses to strike the rock with his rod in front of the people, and Moses obeyed, causing water to miraculously flow from the solid stone.[51] This directive, although quite effective, would prove to be very fateful at a later date, when a lack of water once again threatened to disrupt the Exodus and the Lord directed Moses to *speak* to the rock, rather than *strike* it. On that occasion, Moses hit the rock with his rod, as he had been instructed to do on the first occasion, and was punished severely by being forbidden to pass into the Promised Land before he died. When the crisis passed, Moses named the place Meribah (Massah), meaning "place of faultfinding," because it was there that Israel had "found fault" with him and with the directives of God.[52] Although

---

50 Exod 17:1, 4; Num 33:12-14. The Living Bible, 63, 146.

51 Exod 17:5-6. This miracle is reminiscent of what happens with porous rocks in the mountainous country of southern Sinai, where water is seen at times to drip from internal collections through openings on the surface. Pearlman, In the Footsteps of Moses, 95. An ancient Egyptian inscription told of a similar occurrence when Egyptian soldiers had been sent to quarry stone in the Wadi Hammamat for the tomb of King Mentuhotep (c. 2060 BCE), and found water sprouting from the porous limestone rocks of the area. Great Events of Bible Times, 38.

52 Exod 17:7; Deut 6:16; 9:22; 33:8. Noth, Exodus, A Commentary, 140. The event is recollected in Pss 81:7 and 95:8. The names, Massah (Testing) and Meribah (Quarrel), are derogatory symbols which indicate the seriousness of the people's questioning God's

Moses was able to once again save the Hebrews from death through dehydration, it was apparent that his popular appeal was at an all-time low.

Following the confrontation at Rephidim, the Hebrews were attacked by a group of people known as the Amalekites, and the congregation resisted and fought back, rather than retreat, as when they were faced with the threat of the Pharaoh's army at the Reed Sea. The Amalekites were distant cousins of the Hebrews, descended from Amalek, the son of Esau's firstborn son Eliphaz, who roamed the deserts of northern Sinai and the southern Negev during the second half of the second millennium BCE, a territory similar to the Ishmaelites. There are no literary sources outside of the Bible which have proven their existence, but they are believed to have been a late adherent to the twelve-tribe Edomite confederation, and likely interpreted the sudden appearance of the Hebrews in this region as a threat to their control of the regional trading routes. It is not known whether their animosity toward the Hebrews was in any way related to the stealing of their ancestor's primogeniture birth-right by Jacob, but hereditary enmity is certainly possible.[53] Moses named Joshua to command the Hebrew forces against the Amalekites, and this appointment would be the first of many positions Joshua filled to assist Moses before he was later designated to lead the crossing of the Jordan River into the Promised Land.[54] Joshua was eventually victorious, but once again they had to rely on the assistance of Moses, who was able to magically keep his hands raised until sunset, with the help of Aaron and Hur, in order to assure that Israel would win the war.[55] A similar scene was depicted by Homer in the *Iliad* after the Trojans were driven back from the Greek ships during an attack on the retreating Greeks. Zeus watched the slaughter and pitied the plight of Hector in that passage, so he ordered a stay in the fighting and sent Apollo to assist the Trojan cause. Apollo led them back into battle, and as

providence. Friedman, Commentary on the Torah, 227.

53 Balaam would later declare that because the Amalekites were the first of the nations to attack the Israelites, their destiny would be one of destruction, rather than victory. Num 24:20. They were the most warlike nation that lived in the region, and their struggle with Israel has often been seen as "the eternal struggle of good versus evil." Scherman, The Chumash, 391.

54 Exod 17:9. Joshua was forty-five years old at the time, and his name was originally Hoshea, but Moses changed it to Joshua, even though it would not be recorded as such in the biblical text until a year later. Num 13:16. Scherman, The Chumash, 391. He was the grandson of Elishama son of Amihud, a prince of the tribe of Ephraim, and the son of Nun. Num 1:10; 1 Chron 7:27. Joshua is named eleven times in the "E" source, but never in "J." This is reflective of his being a northern hero, from the tribe of Ephraim. Friedman, The Bible With Sources Revealed, 149.

55 Hur (Chur) would later be put in charge of the camp with Aaron when Moses ascended Mt. Sinai with Joshua (Exod 24:14), but it is not known whether he is the same Hur who was the son of Caleb and Ephrath (1 Chron 2:18-20). There is a Jewish tradition that he was the husband of Moses' sister, Miriam. Kaiser, "Exodus," 408.

long as he held up the aegis which Hephaistos had made for Zeus, Hector and his comrades were victorious.[56]

This victory over the first military force they encountered must have encouraged the Hebrews to see the triumph as part of their destiny as the Chosen People, but the fruits of their labor would come back to haunt them, for they collected a great deal of gold and silver as a result of their conquest, and it is likely that much of this material was used to construct the golden calf-idol at the foot of Mt. Sinai. As a result of that apostasy, the killing of dissidents who disobeyed the Mosaic Code began, and the bloodshed would not end until over 40,000 Hebrews lost their lives. In commemoration of the victory over the Amalekites, Moses built an altar which he called "Adonai-nissi," meaning "the Lord is my standard flag."[57] The Amalekites would later reap some revenge over this defeat when they joined with the Canaanites at Kadesh-barnea to defeat the Hebrews.

It was at this juncture that the Lord instructed Moses to write the events of the battle into a permanent record in order to assure that the story, and the lessons it told, would be remembered forever.[58] This was the first mention of any type of writing in the Bible, and although it meant that a written script must have been available to the Hebrews at the time, there is no extant archaeologic evidence of Hebrew writing until an inscription from 1200 BCE, at an early Israelite settlement at Izbet Sartah, which contains five lines resembling either Phoenician or ancient Hebrew letters.[59] Later biblical passages indicated that Moses followed the Lord's directive, thereby becoming the author of the Torah, as discussed in the preceding chapter.

Following the victory over the Amalekites, Jethro, the father-in-law of Moses and priest of the Midianites, heard of the Hebrew triumph, and came to visit Moses at the "mountain of God," bringing with him Zipporah and her two sons, Gershom and Eliezer.[60] Many commentators have concluded that this passage is not in proper chronological sequence, and have instead placed the visit after the revelation at Mt. Sinai, rather than before.[61] The arrival of Jethro, whenever it took place, marked a turning point in the administration of control over the Hebrew enclave, as Jethro told Moses that the task of governing the Hebrews

56 Homer, The Iliad, 15:318-319, 317.

57 Exod 17:15-16. Sarna, Exodus, 96.

58 Exod 17:14.

59 Hoffman, In the Beginning: A Short History of the Hebrew Language, 29.

60 This passage is the only section in the Torah which mentioned Moses' second son. Exodus, The Torah, A Modern Commentary II, 184.

61 Sarna, Exodus, 97. Ramban maintained that the events in the Torah should always be assumed to have occurred chronologically, while Ibn Ezra believed Jethro arrived after the theophany on Mt. Sinai, and that the Torah placed the arrival at this juncture in order to contrast between Jethro, an outsider whose counsel was of benefit to Israel, and Amalek, an outsider who launched an unprovoked attack against Israel. Scherman, The Chumash, 394.

by himself was too great for only one man. He encouraged Moses to set up a new secular judiciary which bypassed the Elders, and instead elected "God-fearing men, truthful men, haters of bribes."[62] These men, of course, would be chosen by Moses, thereby allowing him to extend his authority over decision-making without having to always be the one in charge at the time. He would therefore be able to pick and choose the issues he deemed most important, and pass the minor cases off to judges he trusted to arbitrate. This policy set forth the future direction of Judaism as a formulation of the Mosaic Law, and helped give Moses the power and time he would need to carry out his demands, as well as his parricidal punishments. If such a stratified system of control had not been in place, it is unlikely that Moses would have been able to control the dissidents after the reprisals for the golden calf-idol incident.

4. Mt. Sinai and the Golden Calf-Idol

By the third month after leaving Egypt, the Exodus had reached deep into the wilderness of Sinai, and the Hebrews now encamped at the foot of Mt. Sinai, in preparation for the theophany which was to set forth the sacred tenets of their new monotheistic faith. Although the mountain is uniformly referred to as Mt. Sinai today, in the Bible this designation was only used by the "J" and "P" sources, while the "E" and "D" sources designated it as Mt. Horeb.[63] Some scholars have suggested that the name Horeb alluded to the whole region, while Sinai referred to a specific peak, but all agree that the biblical compilers did not intend to suggest that there were separate mountains referenced by the different names, since the events recorded in the books of *Deuteronomy* and *Exodus* by the various sources are the same.

The location of Mt. Sinai has never been identified with certainty, but Christian tradition, and the majority of scholars, have placed it at the southern end of the Sinai peninsula, where food and water are plentiful, and the travel distance best fits the wilderness itinerary. The highest peak in south Sinai is Jebel (Gebel) Musa, the mountain which in Arabic means "Mount of Moses." It stands 7,345 feet high, and St. Catherine's Monastery (Santa Katerina) was founded on the site in 527 CE to mark the location which Christianity held that Moses received the Ten Commandments. Another candidate is Ras es-Safsafeh (Willow Peak), which is adjacent to this site and stands 7,046 feet high. The two peaks sit at

---

62 Exod 18:21. Alter, <u>The Five Books of Moses</u>, 419-420. This language was very similar to language for the recruitment of judges in both Hittite and Egyptian documents from the late second millennium BCE. Ibid., 419.

63 <u>Exodus 1-18</u>, 198. The term "Sinai" is applied sixteen times in the Old Testament, and the term "Horeb" is used seventeen times. Hoffmeier, <u>Israel in Egypt, The Evidence for the Authenticity of the Exodus Tradition</u>, 114.

opposite ends of a three mile long granite ridge, with Jebel Musa at the southern end, and Ras es-Safsafeh at the northern end. The valley in between the peaks is large enough to accommodate the large Exodus population, and this geographical configuration is one reason why it is generally favored among biblical scholars as the correct site of the holy theophany. Other possible locations, if either the northern or central pathway was taken following the crossing of the Reed Sea, include Gebel Helal, thirty miles west of Kadesh-barnea in the northeastern Sinai, Har Karkom, Gebel Sin Bishr, and a volcanic site in the region of Midian, east of the Sinai Peninsula near the Gulf of Aqabah.[64]

The arrival at Mt. Sinai opened a new chapter in the history of the covenant between God and Israel, for the only requirement for the descendants of Abraham to maintain their status as the Chosen People up to this point was to undergo the rite of circumcision, a painful but relatively simple rule to follow. Now, Moses would expand the requisites by soon presenting a list of Ten Commandments, in addition to a litany of regulations, which were ordained by God as compulsory behavior to maintain one's status as a Jew.[65] For hundreds of years, the Hebrews had practiced their religion with circumcision as the only required social restriction; they were allowed a variation in their choice of family gods, and did not have a long list of forbidden activities. That the generations of Hebrews who grew up as slaves in Egypt were not aware of the importance of YHWH, the God of Moses, is evident from the book of *Ezekiel*, where the Lord explained that He first let Himself be known to the Hebrews during the time the Exodus began.[66] As will be discussed in later chapters, the early Hebrew tribes, like their Semitic neighbors, had each worshiped their own tribal and family gods. The father was the head of the nuclear family clan (*paterfamilias*) in the early Hebrew tribes, which was then part of the extended family or clan (*mishpahah*), and then part of the larger tribal lineage (*shevet, matteh*), and finally part of the whole people of Israel (*bene-yisrael*).[67] Although many of the Hebrews likely worshiped YHWH in some manner before the theophany at Mt. Sinai, they did not restrict their devotion to one God alone, and their fathers were the ones to tell them what was required to remain pious. Never again, however, following the presentation of the Ten Commandments, would Hebrews be allowed to show adherence to their ancient faith in the manner taught to them by their ancestors without subjecting themselves to capital punishment. This alteration, in my opinion, splintered the

64 Tullock, the Old Testament Story, 74; Hoffmeier, Israel in Egypt, The Evidence for the Authenticity of the Exodus Tradition, 124.

65 The Ten Commandments are listed at Exod 20:1-17 and Deut 5:6-21, and are believed to have been assembled for the Elohistic source of the Pentateuch. Fohrer, Introduction to the Old Testament, 68.

66 Ezek 20:5.

67 Dever, Did God Have a Wife? Archaeology and Folk Religion in Ancient Israel, 19-20.

Hebrews into two philosophic categories: one favoring the polytheism of their ancestors; and the other adhering to the regulations as interpreted by Moses. Brother would turn against brother in this religious civil war, and the nature of Jewish faith would forever be changed into a creed of monotheism.

Moses would have been familiar with the standard location of Mt. Sinai, for this was the same region that the Lord appeared to him in the guise of a burning bush, and directed him to return to Egypt to lead the Exodus of the Hebrew slaves. Moses must have thought that his task of leading the Hebrews out of Egypt was almost over when he arrived at the mountain base, for he had come full circle from that fateful day, and the region seemed a logical location as a staging area for passage into the Promised Land. They had been on the move for three months, and when Moses finally ascended the peak to receive instructions on what to do next, he probably did not realize that it would eventually take four more ascensions before the theophany was completed, and forty more years until the entry into the Promised Land was achieved.[68]

At the first meeting, God directed Moses to tell the people that if they would obey Him faithfully, and keep His covenant, they would be "My treasured possession among all the peoples."[69] He added that He would come and speak to Moses from a thick cloud in front of the congregation so the people would hear his words and "trust you ever after."[70] That YHWH knew he was having a problem with some of the dissident Hebrews certainly must have been a reassurance to Moses, and likely set the stage for the type of parricidal cleansing that would cull the unbelievers from the ranks of the Chosen People. It was not all the Hebrews who were destined to become part of the future elite, but only those who obeyed the tenets of the Mosaic Code. When Moses returned to the camp, he summoned the people to tell them of God's plan, and the congregation agreed to do all that the Lord requested.

Despite all of the disagreements leading up to this stage, the Hebrews were apparently mollified enough by the magical powers of God they had seen, and the sanctity of the scene at Mt. Sinai, to once again accept the leadership of Moses, giving credence to the impressive nature of the mountain, which was something that few of the slaves, if any, had ever seen before. Even without the added effects of lightning and thunder, which would later accompany the appearance

---

68 This initial ascension took place almost immediately according to the "E" source, and about seven days later in the "P" source. von Rad, From Genesis to Chronicles, 12. Moses went up at Exod 19:3, 8, 20; 24:9; 34:4, and came down at 19:7, 14, 25; 32:15; 34:29. There is some confusion on the first ascension as to whether Moses went up once or twice, as the text contained two directives by God to ascend before the theophany, although only one ascension is actually mentioned.

69 Exod 19:5. Sarna, Exodus, 103. The phrase "treasured possession," was also used by a Hittite king to describe one of his vassals. Tigay, "Exodus," 146.

70 Exod 19:9. Ibid.

of the Lord, the visual imagery of the moment obviously evoked sincere piety, and the Hebrews eagerly awaited the confirmation of their favored status. Moses then returned to the mountain top a second time to tell the Lord that the entire congregation agreed to follow His command. YHWH instructed Moses to have the people prepare themselves to receive the Torah after a three-day waiting period, during which time they were to sanctify themselves and wash their clothing, in preparation for hearing what God had to say. Moses was also cautioned to set boundaries around the mountain to prevent the people from getting too near, lest they die by being too close to the Lord's presence. These requirements were clearly setting the stage for a seminal religious event, and the Hebrews were not to be disappointed by the display which was soon to follow.

On the morning of the third day after this pronouncement, as the throng gathered in their designated space, a huge cloud appeared over the top of Mt. Sinai, and a terrific storm rumbled with paroxysms of thunder and lightening, causing the entire mountain to tremble violently as the top filled with smoke.[71] Moses brought the people to the bottom of the mountain as instructed by God, and the entire congregation watched in awe as the Presence of the Lord descended and spoke to them in a thunderous Voice. God was only heard, and not seen, but if there ever was any doubt about the close relationship between Moses and God, this open spectacle, for all to see, should have forever silenced any criticism or incertitude. God then called for Moses to return to the mountain top a third time, and told him to warn the people not to break through the barriers in order to gaze upon the Lord or they would perish. He added that Moses was to bring Aaron with him on the next trip to the summit.

This description of the preparation for the giving of the Ten Commandments on Mt. Sinai closely resembles the scene in the *Iliad*, when Hector strove to recover the body of Patroklos. To assist Hector in this brave act, Zeus shrouded Ida in a deep mist, and "let go a lightning flash and a loud thunderstroke, shaking the mountain," and terrifying the Achaians.[72] Later, Athena intervened to assist Achilles in frightening the Trojans by encircling his head with a golden cloud from which a fire rose like a flare into the bright air.[73] Although the use of meteorologic similes does not prove a contribution of one to the other, since the imagery was not unique to Hebrew and Greek mythology alone, it does provide another example of a congruous writing style, which supports the possibility that one author was aware of the writings of the other. The fact that Moses met with

71 Exod 19:16-18. Scholars believe that the description of the storm theophany came from the "E" account, while that of the seething volcano came from the "J" account. Dozeman, God on the Mountain, 25. Both the names of Elohim (v. 17, 19) and YHWH (v. 18, 20) appear in the passage, an indication that the scene was compiled by someone who utilized separate sources. Schmidt, The Faith of the Old Testament, 40.

72 Homer, The Iliad, 17:591-595, 370.

73 Ibid., 18:196-236, 380-381.

God on top of Mt. Sinai, and God descended to speak the Ten Commandments, is similar to the habitat of the Greek gods on top of Mt. Olympus, but it is not unique enough to suggest a cause-and-effect relationship. Each resemblance nevertheless adds a further mark of veracity to my proposed relationship between the ancient Hebrews and Greeks.

God's theophany was "direct, public, and communal," so that all the Hebrews experienced the phenomenon of God speaking from heaven, and as the people witnessed the awesome display, they fell back and told Moses "we will obey; but let not God speak to us, lest we die."[74] They were truly awestruck by this event, and willingly relegated to Moses the authority to communicate with God alone, thereby ceding their rights which existed under the polytheistic format of the Patriarchs. At the time, it probably seemed like a good idea, given the obvious danger which the spectacle of the Lord presented in the awesome display of power, but as we will see with the passage of time, this transference of authority to Moses alone was the start of a schism that would end in violent parricidal actions. I will not discuss the various implications of these Commandments at this time, except to note that the only ones which would have likely created controversy were the declaration of the first, which stated that "you shall have no other gods beside Me;" the second, which stated that you shall not make any image or idol of Me; and the fifth, which commanded the people to honor their mother and father, thereby creating a major problem for those Hebrews who felt that the edicts of Moses went against the teachings of their parents.[75] How could they honor their mother and father if they could not worship the gods they obeyed?

Moses underscored his sole authority over judging how to punish those Hebrews who disobeyed the Lord's directives by reminding the people that the Lord was an impassioned God, and there would be a "vigorous, intensive, and punitive nature of the divine response to apostasy and to modes of worship unacceptable to Himself."[76] This statement set the legal groundwork for Moses' authority to inflict capital punishment on those Hebrews who did not follow his pronouncements. Moses read these instructions aloud to the gathered throng, and the people solemnly promised to obey. In the presence of the Almighty God, it was easy to forget the teaching of your ancestors, but we will see that as time passed, and the memory of this awesome event vanished, the Hebrews returned to their polytheistic roots in order to maintain a faith that had been hundreds of years in the making.

In order to ratify the covenant which He had just presented, the Lord told Moses to come bach to the top of the mountain with Aaron, Nadab and Abihu, and seventy elders, but to leave the others at a distance and approach God alone

74 Exod 20:16; Deut 5:20-22. Sarna, Exodus, 115-116.
75 Exod 20:1-4, 12; Deut 5:6-9, 16. Sarna, Exodus, 109-110.
76 Exod 20:5. Ibid., 110.

when he neared the summit.[77] The purpose of this fourth trip was for God to give Moses the stone tablets upon which He had written the Ten Commandments heretofore transmitted orally, thereby making a permanent record of the requirements of the covenant. Before ascending the peak, Moses repeated all of the commandments and ordinances the Lord had given, and the people agreed with one voice to solemnly obey. He then set up an altar at the base of the mountain with twelve pillars for each of the Hebrew tribes, and sacrificed burnt-offerings (*olah*), spreading the blood on the altar and the people, as later described in the book of *Leviticus*.[78] As the group climbed to the top, "they saw the God of Israel: under His feet there was the likeness of a pavement of sapphire, like the very sky for purity."[79] Moses then ordered the others to remain where they were, and climbed to the apex alone to receive the tablets which God had inscribed, allowing Joshua to follow a short distance further to serve as his attendant. He would remain on the mountain peak for forty days, telling the people later that he neither ate nor drank during that entire period of time.[80]

Once Moses and the tribal elders left the camp, the people found themselves without the security of their trusted leaders, and their despondency rapidly

---

77 Exod 24:1. Nadab and Abihu, two of Aaron's four sons, received this honor on this occasion, but would later be burned to death as punishment for burning incense without permission. Exod 6:23; Lev 10:1-2.

78 Exod 24:4-8. The twelve pillars symbolized that all twelve tribes accepted the covenant. Scherman, The Chumash, 441. When Joshua crossed the Jordan River into the Promised Land, he similarly set up twelve stones to commemorate the parting of the waters to allow the Ark of the Covenant to pass. Josh 4:5-6. These are the same structures which God had just told the Hebrews to smash when they later enter the Promised Land. Exod 23:24. The spreading of the blood upon the people is unique to this episode alone, although it somewhat is reminiscent of the Bridegroom of Blood episode where Zipporah threw the foreskin of her son at Moses after circumcising him when God threatened Moses' life on their way to Egypt. Alter, The Five Books of Moses, 456.

79 Exod 24:9-10; Deut 9:9-10. Sarna, Exodus, 152-153. This vision is generally not seen as a perception by the senses, which would result in the death of the observer, but rather as a "perception by the intellect," or a prophetic vision. Ibid., 153. God had warned Moses that "a man cannot have a vision of Me and still exist." Kaplan, The Living Torah: The Five Books of Mose and the Haftarot, 457.

80 Exod 24:18; 34:28. The length of time that Moses spent on the mountain top alone has fascinated scholars for centuries. According to Cosmas Indicopleustes (sixth century CE), a Greek sailor from Alexandria who traveled to Ethiopia, India and Sri Lanka before becoming a monk of Nestorian tendencies, during the forty days Moses remained on the mountain top, God taught him all the wonders of His creation of the world, and gave him a new form and soul. Cosmas, Christian Topography, III.96, 81. The prophet Elijah the Tishbite also fasted for forty days on Mt. Horeb (1 Kgs 19:8), and Jesus Christ for forty days in the Wilderness (Matt 4:2). Fasting for extended periods of time, drinking water but eating no food for up to one year, has successfully been used as a means of weight control.

increased as their isolation grew from days into weeks. They soon forgot the promise they had made during the theophany a few days before, and pined for the faith of their ancestors which had carried them through their years of slavery in Egypt. Although this may have been the moment that Moses planned for Judaism to drastically change from its polytheistic beginnings to a unified faith in YHWH alone, much of the congregation was not willing to bypass their time-tested traditions, especially since Moses was nowhere to be found. They therefore turned to Aaron, the second-in-command, and demanded that he construct an idol to worship god in the manner of their forefathers. "Make us a god who shall go before us," they said, "for that man Moses who brought us from the land of Egypt we do not know what happened to him."[81]

The choice of Aaron to head their idol-worship was logical, for although Moses was a stranger to the Hebrew community, Aaron had been a member of their suffering in Egypt his entire life, and understood the ways of their forefathers. The fact that Aaron agreed to their demands supports the proposition that his faith in the Mosaic Code may have been shaken as well, given the fact that his brother was absent for such an extended period of time. Aaron asked the people to bring him all of their golden earrings in order to provide appropriate material to make an idol in the form of a golden calf, making it clear that he was not simply an unwilling participant in this apostasy, as he would later claim when confronted by Moses.[82] The die of religious schism was now cast, and although Aaron escaped the punishment which was inflicted on those who were responsible for the building of the idol, he would nevertheless be forced to die with the entire generation of Hebrews who left Egypt before the entry into the Promised Land, as will be discussed shortly. In a strange way, the Pharaoh would have some degree of revenge for the havoc which Moses brought upon his land, for the gold used to construct the apostatic idol was a good part of the wealth which the Hebrews were given from the populace before they left on the Exodus.[83]

The jewelry was collected and melted down in order to prepare a proper offering, and when the golden calf-idol was completed, the people showed their pent-up

---

81 Exod 32:1. Sarna, <u>Exodus</u>, 202-203.

82 Calves were the reflection of syncretism, the reverting to the religious and cultural characteristics of the Canaanites and Egyptians. The bull was associated with the god Baal and the fertility cult in Ugaritic texts. Walton, Matthews, & Chavalas, <u>The IVP Bible Background Commentary: Old Testament</u>, 368.

83 Exod 3:22; 12:35. The Egyptians were literally stripped of their possessions when the Hebrews departed following the Paschal night. The Talmud tells how the Egyptians filed suit against the Hebrews before Alexander of Macedon, claiming that gold and silver was taken from them during the Exodus, and they demanded that it be returned, but the Jews responded by requiring payment for the 600,000 men who were enslaved for 430 years. van der Horst, "The Interpretation of the Bible by the Minor Hellenistic Jewish Authors," 522.

relief and exclaimed "this is your god, O Israel, who brought you out of the land of Egypt."[84] Quickly thereafter, burnt-offerings were brought to the altar, and a wild party and feast ensued. It should be noted that while the Hebrews were disobeying the edicts of Moses in making an idol to represent God, they were not necessarily violating the First Commandment, which directed that there should be no other god but YHWH. By declaring that "this is your god, O Israel," the Hebrews were giving homage to one god alone, perhaps even to YHWH, an indication that the idol was a remonstration against Moses' authority, rather than an apostasy against the power which was demonstrated up to this time by YHWH. Although the Bible makes it clear that YHWH was angered by the decision to build the idol, we must remember that we are hearing only one side of the story – that of Moses, the victor in the battle to convert Judaism into a monotheistic faith. If my theory of Hebraic influence on Classical Greek culture is true, the other side of the story is told in the tales of Greek mythology, and the dissident Hebrews may have believed that the God they witnessed during the theophany before Moses left, was pleased to have been worshiped in the manner they did.

While the decision to build the idol was a violation of the Ten commandments, which had been spoken by God but not yet been written down, it was not a denial of the authority, or the power, of the Almighty God. The Bible did not find fault with Aaron's decision to accede to the Hebrew's demands, but his response contrasted sharply with the actions of Jacob, who, after his arrival at Bethel, had asked all his family members to bring him the idols and golden earrings they had accumulated in their travels.[85] Rather than use these substances as the source of gold for a new idol, Jacob demanded that the material be buried in the ground, for earrings were generally coupled with alien gods and had to be ritually interred to cleanse the community of heretical contamination. The willingness of Aaron to go along with the apostasy demanded by the Hebrews cannot be excused as easily as the Bible wants us to believe, however, and it is amazing that the very priesthood which was charged with the responsibility of managing the ritualistic adoration of the Lord was nevertheless entrusted to Aaron and his descendants, as will be discussed in chapter 12. It is true that Aaron himself would die before the

---

84 Exod 32:8. Sarna, Exodus, 204. When Jeroboam I was made king of Israel in 931 BCE, he worried that the people would return to Jerusalem, and the rule of King Rehoboam of Judah, so he constructed two golden calves, one at Bethel and one at Dan, and told the people that "this is your god, O Israel, who brought you up from the land of Egypt!" the same phrase used by the people at Mt. Sinai. 1 Kgs 12:28. Zevit, "First Kings," 702. The Old Testament scholar Walter Beyerlin finds that the parallels between the two Golden Calf accounts "are so numerous and obvious that one cannot refrain from suspecting a connection between the two texts." Beyerlin, Origins and History of the Oldest Sinaitic Traditions, 126.

85 Gen 35:1-4.

entry into the Promised Land, but his lineage would still become the progenitors of the sacred High Priesthood.

The choice of a golden calf figurine to idolize makes sense, since the Hebrews are believed to have worshiped some of their early deities in the form of a storm-god standing on a young bull ever since entering the land of Egypt. The worship of animals was characteristic of groups in almost every part of Egypt and Canaan during the Middle Bronze Age, and the Hebrews, like most Semitic tribes, would have delineated the figure of their god by depicting a powerful animal, rather than a human image. According to William Foxwell Albright (1891-1971 CE), the former Professor of Semitic Languages at Johns Hopkins University, "this practice had doubtless been shared by pre-Mosaic Hebrews with the pagans among whom they lived."[86] Rather than attempt to delineate the figure of a god in human terms, which would bring in images of human beings whose frailties would belie the potency of the deity, the use of an animal allowed the people to concentrate on an image of power.

The capital punishment which would be meted out for the building of the golden calf-idol was the pivotal turning point in the process of monotheistic change in the ancient Hebrew religious practice, for it utilized a culling out of the dissident Hebrews, rather than any further attempts at education and change. While Moses was occupied with God on the summit, preparing the tablets which contained the Ten Commandments, God told Moses to return to the camp because "your people, whom you brought up out of Egypt, have become corrupt."[87] He threatened to destroy all of the Hebrew "stiff-necked people," and make a great nation out of Moses instead, eliminating the Hebrews as His Chosen People. Moses did not accept this honor, and instead interceded on behalf of the Hebrews, and attempted to persuade the Lord to have a change of heart. He pointed out that the Egyptians would say that it was with evil intent that He brought them out of Egypt, only to be destroyed in the mountains, and that this would demolish the image of a powerful but just God, which YHWH had worked so hard to create during the trials and tribulations of the plagues in Egypt before the Exodus. According to rabbinic tradition, Moses put the fate of the Hebrew people before his own aggrandizement, and his modest actions showed that his true goal was not one of self-centered greed, but rather of a true liberator whose only concern was that of the Hebrew people. One wonders, however, if the part about his being offered the chance to stand in the stead of Abraham was an accurate remembrance, or a chance to fluff his feathers of virtuousness, given the fact that the Torah was clearly written with this intent in mind. Whatever interpretation is true, Moses was now to care only for those Hebrews who agreed to follow his Mosaic Code, and when he returned from the mountain top, his course of action turned from verbal castigation, which had characterized his

---

86 Albright, Yahweh and the Gods of Canaan, 197.
87 Exod 32:7. <u>The New Interpreter's Bible</u>, 928. See e.g., Deut 9;11-14.

previous encounters with the Hebrew dissidents, to a sentence of death against all those who did not follow his religious directives.

After convincing God to have compassion on at least some of the Hebrews, Moses began to descend the mountain with the two tablets on which God had inscribed the Ten Commandments on both sides with His own finger. Joshua was still waiting near the summit, and told him that there were sounds of song coming from the camp, an indication that people might be preparing for war. Moses answered that the sounds were not a cry for military action, but of revelry and joy, and when they entered the camp, they found people dancing around the golden calf-idol, celebrating in pagan, impious ways. Moses became enraged at the sight, and angrily threw the tablets to the ground, shattering the hallowed words of God into little pieces.[88] This action not only expressed Moses' wrath, but it actually annulled the covenant God just made with the Hebrew people, just as a modern pact would be void if the contract was torn up before it was signed. Moses' patience with the actions of the ungrateful Hebrews had vanished, and the extent of his anger now erupted into a violent rage. He ordered the idol to be melted down and then ground into a powder for the people to drink as punishment for their sins.[89] He then turned to Aaron and berated him for his role in the apostasy, asking how he could perform such a terrible transgression. Aaron replied with an excuse that Moses could surely understand: "You know what a wicked bunch these people are," he said, adding that all he did was throw the gold into the fire, "and out came this calf!" as if the idol fabricated itself.[90] Moses apparently accepted Aaron's response, and despite the gravity of his brother's offense, he did not order any punishment for his complicity. This exoneration was likely due to his remembering the tribulations he himself had been put through by the stiff-necked Hebrews, and Moses would later tell the people when he addressed them before the crossing of the Jordan River into the Promised Land, that the Lord was angry enough with Aaron to destroy him, but Moses interceded on his behalf.[91]

Although Moses was willing to forgive Aaron for his transgression, he was not so lenient toward those who were the instigators of the impious act. After forcing the revelers to drink the powdered remains of the idol, he called the Levites to his side and ordered them to kill the culpable evil doers: "even your brothers, friends and neighbors," he warned, emphasizing that family bonds were to offer

---

88 Exod 32:19; Deut 9:17. The Koran claimed that Moses "put down the Tablets," rather than break them on the ground. Sur 7.18.150. Ali, The Meaning of the Holy Qur'an, 387.

89 Exod 32:20; Deut 9:21. This action was similar to a story in the Ugaritic texts where the goddess Anath destroyed the god Mot by burning him and then grounding the remains as grain in the handmill before casting the residue into the field for the birds to eat. Davis, Moses and the Gods of Egypt, 288.

90 Exod 32:22, 24. Sarna, Exodus, 208.

91 Deut 9:20.

no protection from harm.[92] It seems natural that Moses would have turned to the Levites for this task, since they were not only his tribal brethren, but along with the Simeonites, were the ones who initiated the savage slaying of the Shechemites in retribution for the rape of their sister Dinah, as discussed in chapter 3. The Levites would later become the assistants to the priests after the building of the ark, perhaps as a reward for their loyal service, a task which in the future could not be performed by those who had blood on their hands, an odd requirement given the history of the Levites up to the founding of the priestly sect. Moses was dedicated to cleansing the congregation of their illegal ancestral practices, but he would find that the dissidents did not give up easily, for, as Maimonides later explained in *The Guide for the Perplexed*, "it is contrary to man's nature that he should suddenly abandon all the different kinds of Divine service and the different customs in which he had been brought up."[93]

This was the first instance where one Jew actually killed another in the biblical text, although Abraham had attempted to sacrifice Isaac, and the brothers of Joseph had hoped to eliminate their sibling through an act of abandonment that would have been equivalent to murder. Moses may have previously been reluctant to have Hebrew blood on his hands, but after the meeting with God on Mt. Sinai, his attitude had radically changed. Moses knew that he need not worry if he destroyed those who seemed to be the most resistant to change, since God Himself had threatened to exterminate all the Hebrews for their rebellious behavior. Rashi (Rabbi Shelomo Yitzchaki 1040-1105 CE), considered by many to be the greatest of all biblical commentators, justified Moses' action by noting that one of the crimes for which capital punishment was authorized was sacrificing to a god other than the YHWH.[94] While this rationalization carries a significant element of truth, the extent of the parricide which was to follow in the ensuing years was more akin to a commission of genocide, than it was to corporeal harm. Any Hebrew who did not agree to follow the regulations of the Mosaic Law was at risk for losing his life, and this lesson was surely not lost upon those who disagreed with Moses' radical alteration of the faith of their fathers.

Three thousand Jews were executed on that day, and Moses then returned to the mountain top to receive another set of the Ten Commandments, and to ask the Lord to forgive the sin of the Hebrew people. On this occasion, Moses carved the terms of the covenant on the tablets by himself.[95] This has led some scholars

---

92 Exod 32:27. <u>The Living Bible</u>, 78.

93 Maimonides, The Guide for the Perplexed, 32, 324.

94 Exodus, The Torah, A Modern Commentary II, 373.

95 Exod 34:1-4; Deut 10:1-4. The book of *Deuteronomy* says that God wrote on the second set of tablets, just as He did on the first. Deut 10:2, 4. The translations of the book of *Exodus*, however, vary as to whether it was God or Moses who wrote on the second set. While all state that God told Moses to write the Commandments at Exod 34:27, some revert to having God write the commandments at Exod 34:28. See, e.g., <u>The Living Bible</u>,

to infer that God did not totally forgive the Hebrews for their impious actions, for if He had, He would have inscribed the tablets Himself.[96] God reinforced the appropriate nature of Moses' punitive action by sending a plague upon the people as further punishment for worshiping a false idol, raising the death total above 3,000, although the nature of the scourge, and the exact number of Hebrews killed, was never fully disclosed in the biblical text. He ordered the people to stop wearing jewelry, a task they obeyed, and told Moses that He would no longer travel in their midst as He drove out their enemies from the Promised Land, for they were such a stiff-necked people that He might decide to suddenly destroy them along the way if He remained nearby.[97] These actions transformed Moses from simply a military leader in charge of the migration of a group of enslaved Hebrews to freedom, into a High Priest and King with the authority to inflict capital punishment upon all who disobeyed his commands. The Mosaic Code was the ultimate Law of the land, and Judaism was now the first religion on earth to worship the One and Only Almighty God.

When Moses descended with the second set of stone tablets after spending another forty days and nights on the mountain top, his face glowed with a strange aura, forcing him to always wear a veil over his face, which he only removed when he went into the Tabernacle to speak to God.[98] It was as if he had become fearful for other humans to behold, and the Latin Bible of Jerome (347-420 CE) translated this event into a description which suggested that Moses had grown horns on top of his head, which was the basis for the way Michelangelo depicted Moses in his famous statute. The ancient Greek translation of the Septuagint, however, interpreted the phrase as sending forth beams of light, rather than horns.[99] In whatever manner Moses' face was altered, it was becoming clear to the rest of the Hebrew congregation that the word of Moses was now Law, and that philosophical debate over the sanctity of ancestral worship was a topic that could never again be broached.

80; Scherman, The Chumash, 515.

96 Tigay, Deuteronomy, 104.

97 Exod 33:3-6. As a sign of this loss of favor, Moses pitched his Tent of Meeting, where he communed with God, outside the camp. Exod 33:7. In the Tent itself, hidden from view of the rest of the congregation, the Lord continued to appear to Moses "face to face, as a man speaks to his friend." Exod 33:11. The Living Bible, 78. Joshua never left the tent. Exod 33:11.

98 Exod 34:29, 34-35. The day Moses returned with the Second Tablets of the Law was ordained as Yom Kippur, the eternal day of forgiveness. Few Jews remember that their pious behavior on the holiest day of the year celebrates the killing of thousands of their brethren for the construction of the golden calf-idol. Scherman, The Chumash, 637.

99 Kirsch, Moses, 5, 275.

5. From Sinai to Kadesh-barnea

Once the Sinaitic revelation was completed, and a Tabernacle to house the Ten Commandments was constructed, Moses took a census of the Hebrews as they prepared to march through the wilderness of Sinai, away from the site of the mountain itself.[100] Over the next twenty days the camp was organized into a secure military structure which protected both the Tabernacle and the tribal members as they prepared to march through the adjacent hostile environment on their way to the Promised Land. It was now the twentieth day of the second month of the second year since they left Egypt, and eleven months after they arrived at Mt. Sinai, and the Hebrews were anxious to complete their journey and settle into a more secure environment.

As with the passage from the Reed Sea to Mt. Sinai, there is disparity over the route next taken, for according to the book of *Deuteronomy*, which in essence is a long speech by Moses to the Hebrews at the Jordan River summarizing their history up until that point, the Hebrews next traveled to Kadesh-barnea, on the border of the Promised Land, where the episode of the spies took place; while in the book of *Numbers*, the first stop listed was the Wilderness of Paran, before traveling on to Kadesh-barnea.[101] There are a variety of names for this site in the Bible, including Kadesh-barnea, Meribah-kadesh, Enmishpat, and Kadesh, but in order to not confuse this locale with the city of Kadesh, which was a stronghold of the Hittites in the north of Syria, and the site of many battles between the Hittites and the Egyptian Pharaohs during the Eighteenth and Nineteenth Dynasties, I will use the name Kadesh-barnea throughout this text. The different terminology in the two books is not necessarily inconsistent, for the Wilderness of Paran is generally thought to be a collective term for all the wilderness areas on the eastern edge of the central plateau of the Sinai peninsula, with Kadesh-barnea laying on the border of the Wilderness of Paran and the Wilderness of Zin, close to the territory of Edom. Biblical scholars have pointed out that it was reasonable for the Hebrews to move into this area, since the locality contained the largest oasis in the northern Sinai, with a perennial spring and nearby pasturage land, allowing enough productivity to sustain a large congregation of people for an extended period of time.

The distance from Mt. Sinai to Kadesh-barnea was said to have taken eleven

100 The desert Tabernacle tent which the Lord instructed Moses to make was very similar to the one used by Ramesses II in the battle of Kadesh in both shape and dimensions, including the placement of the entrance on the eastern wall. Gabriel, The Military History of Ancient Israel, 95. Both structures included a central Holy of Holies, where God spoke to the leader in order to direct the military campaign. Ibid., 96-97.

101 Num 10:12; Deut 1:19-20. It is generally believed that the book of *Deuteronomy* followed the "JE" source, while the book of *Numbers* combined that information with variant data coming from the "P" source. Tigay, Deuteronomy, 427.

days to travel by foot, and since the average distance traveled in a day's journey by caravan in the Late Bronze Age ranged from fifteen to eighteen miles a day, the location is believed to have been nearly two hundred miles away. The congregants had evidently not learned much of a lesson from the recent killings following the incident of the golden calf-idol, however, for upon their first stop at Taberah, three days later, they immediately voiced their dissatisfaction with Moses, complaining bitterly of all the misfortunes which had befallen them throughout their year-long journey. Although the specifics for their misery were not stated in the biblical text, Rashbam, a twelfth century CE French biblical commentator and grandson of the respected Rashi, claimed that their objections were due to the harsh living conditions they had to endure in the wilderness.[102]

When God heard them once again berate the leadership of Moses, He did not wait for Moses to request assistance, but instead sent a fire which ravaged the outskirts of the camp. The people screamed for Moses to help, aware that the destruction must have been sent by God, and when Moses prayed for the fire to stop, the conflagration miraculously ceased, and the place thereby became known as *Taberah*, or "The Place of Burning," as a warning to all those who disobeyed the directives of Moses that they faced a continued threat of annihilation for their violations.[103] How many Hebrews died in this conflagration is not recorded, but it should have been crystal-clear to all the dissidents that Moses was not going to abide any disagreement about how the Exodus was to be conducted.

Despite the fact that the Hebrews understood the seriousness of Moses' intent to alter their religious beliefs by now, family traditions were not easily forgotten, and it would take many years, and many more killings, before the Hebrews who remained with the Exodus finally modified their ways. When they next arrived at Kibroth-hattaavah, in the Wilderness of Paran, they complained about the absence of meat, grumbling that they were tired of eating only manna, and wanted some variance in the quality of their diet. This dissatisfaction was blamed on the "rabble," who simply craved other food, and caused the Hebrews to wail for fish, cucumbers, melons, leeks, onions, and garlic, which had been provided for them in Egypt.[104] Moses lost all patience with their demands, and vented his frustration to the Lord: "Where am I supposed to get meat for all these people? ... I cannot carry this nation by myself!"[105] He was so distressed by the continuous grumbling that he told the Lord he could no longer bear the burden of leading the Exodus: "If You would deal thus with me, kill me rather, I beg You, and let

---

102 Num 10:33, 11:1. Milgrom, Numbers, 82.

103 Num 11:3. The place name "Taberah" came from a Hebrew noun meaning "burning," and was mentioned only here and in Deut 9:22. Allen, "Numbers," 787.

104 Num 11:4-5. This is the only time that the term "rabble" appears in the Masoretic Text (MT). Allen, "Numbers," 795.

105 Num 11:13-14. Milgrom, Numbers, 86.

me see no more of my wretchedness!"[106]

The Lord understood Moses' dilemma, having been ready to utterly destroy the Hebrews following the incident of the golden calf-idol, and directed him to gather seventy of Israel's elders, the same number which were taken with to Mt. Sinai at the time of the theophany, and He would imbue them with some of Moses' spirit so that they could assist him in the governance of the people.[107] According to the Mishnah, which is the core legal document of the Talmudic oral tradition, this was the institution of the Great Sanhedrin, which would become the highest judicial authority in Jerusalem during the centuries following the Conquest of the Promised Land.[108] The Lord then told Moses to tell the people that since they whined so much for meat, He would give them meat to eat for a whole month, "until it comes out of your nostrils and becomes loathsome to you."[109] Moses questioned the Lord on how it was possible to have enough meat to feed 600,000 men for that long of a period of time, an indication that his faith in miracles might be beginning to wane. Rashi considered this vacillation of faith an error as grave as that which Moses later committed at Meribah, but the majority of traditional Jewish commentators have exculpated Moses for this action.[110] The Lord then sent a wind which swept quail from the sea and strew them over the camp to a depth of two cubits for a distance of one day's journey. The appearance of the quail was similar to the provisions which had been provided at the Sihn wilderness, only this time a severe plague followed, which killed many of those who complained, leading to the name Kibroth-hattaavah (Chatzeroth), meaning "Graves of Craving," for those who had the gluttonous craving were buried there.[111]

The congregation then moved on to Hazeroth, where Miriam and Aaron grumbled to Moses about the Cushite woman he married, providing further evidence that the disunity among the Hebrews was not restricted to the general assembly alone, but also involved his own siblings.[112] They complained that they

---

106 Num 11:14-15. Ibid. This tirade has been referred to as "Moses' Lament." Allen, "Numbers," 791.

107 Rabbinic tradition holds that these were not the same seventy men who accompanied Moses on his fifth ascent to the summit of Mt. Sinai. Milgrom, Numbers, 86-87.

108 Scherman, The Chumash, 791. The Mishnah is anonymous, but by tradition was compiled c. 210 BCE in Palestine by Rabbi Judah Ha-Nasi (Judah the Patriarch, 135-220 CE). The Mishnah then was carefully studied by the great sages, and their commentaries were collected into the Babylonian and Palestinian Talmuds. The sayings are divided into six principal sections, which are then subdivided into sixty-three tractates.

109 Num 11:20. Numbers, The Torah, A Modern Commentary IV, 107.

110 Ibid.

111 Num 11:33-34. Ibid., 110.

112 It is possible that the reference to her being "Cushite" was a slanderous term stemming from racism. Allen, "Numbers," 797. Cush was generally used to represent

were being delegated a minor role in the religious hierarchy by his belief that he was the only one who was in touch with the Lord. "Has He not spoken through us as well?" they asked, raising a question that had no other basis-in-fact in the extant biblical text.[113] As if on cue, YHWH descended in a Cloud at the entrance of the Tabernacle, and told Miriam and Aaron that while He may choose to speak through prophets in visions and dreams, He only would communicate face-to-face with Moses, and that they should never dare to criticize their brother for his hallowed position.[114] This declaration would seem to clarify that no one but Moses could expect to have a one-on-one conversation with the Lord, but the issue would soon be raised again with the rebellion of Korah.

As punishment for her questioning the role of Moses, YHWH struck Miriam with leprosy, a normally fatal disease. Moses pleaded with the Lord to spare the life of his sister, and God cured her after a seven-day confinement.[115] Aaron was also spared retribution for his role in the castigation of Moses, but since he died before entry into the Promised Land, some scholars have suggested that his impious behavior at this time, in conjunction with his role in the building of the golden calf-idol, may have been the underlying cause for his early demise. We no longer hear of any strife between Moses and his siblings, although at the end of the Exodus, Moses warned the Hebrews to remember what the Lord did to Miriam as punishment for her improper accusations, and that they had better follow His instructions during their Conquest of the Promised Land if they did not want to suffer a similar fate.[116]

With their arrival at Kadesh-barnea, the Hebrews reached the southern

---

the Ethiopians, south of Egypt, and the Kossaeans, east of the Tigris, who the Greeks called Libyans. Asimov, Asimov's Guide to the Bible, Volume One: The Old Testament, 47-48.

113 Num 12:2. Milgrom, Numbers, 94.

114 In making this statement about only speaking face-to-face with Moses, the Lord was speaking directly to Aaron and Miriam, but it was in the form of a spiritual Cloud, rather than in His Divine Essence. Many biblical passages suggest that seeing God was too awesome for humans to survive if they actually were in face-to-face contact. Gen 32:30; Exod 19:21; 33:20; Judg 13:22; Isa 6:5. Exceptions include Exod 24:10-11; Num 12:8; Deut 34:10; Ezek 1:27-28. Tigay, "Exodus," 111. In ancient Mesopotamia, the gods displayed their power through their divine brilliance, which struck terror in the heart of the observer, but was not fatal. Walton, Matthews, & Chavalas, The IVP Bible Background Commentary: Old Testament, 266. In Greek mythology, however, seeing the god Zeus in all of his glory was similarly fatal, as occurred with Semele, the mother of Dionysus (Bacchus, Iankos). The gods in Greece usually had contact with humans by taking on the guise of another human being.

115 Num 12:10-15. Leprosy was considered a punishment for offenses against the Deity in both Israel and other countries of the ancient Near East. Milgrom, Numbers, 97.

116 Deut 24:9.

boundary of Canaan, leaving only the greater part of the Negev to separate them from the hill-country of the Amorites in Palestine. They likely expected to remain at that location for a short period of time before moving on to the Promised Land, as the region resembled a staging area, but as it turned out, they stayed for the next thirty-eight years. At the time they first arrived, they knew very little about the land of Canaan, and in order to prepare for their next move, Moses sent out scouts to reconnoiter the lay of the land. The account of this mission varies in the books of *Numbers* and *Deuteronomy*, once again suggesting that the story was compiled from separate sources. According to the book of *Numbers*, Moses decided on his own to send out twelve spies, one distinguished chieftain from each tribe, including Caleb, from the tribe of Judah, and Joshua, from the tribe of Ephraim.[117] Their task was to survey the region and determine if the soil was rich or poor, if the residents were strong or weak, and if the towns were open or fortified. Since it was the season of the first ripe grapes, the journey must have taken place in the summer months of July or August, and the men were said to have scouted the entire length of the land of Canaan, from the wilderness of Zin, which lay above the wilderness of Paran, north to Rehob and Lebo-hamath, an important city on the southern border of the kingdom of Hamath, which would later coincide with the northern boundary of Israel under Kings David and Solomon. They followed the watershed along the mountain range, and did not enter the closely settled lands of the Shepelah and Coastal Plain, which would have exposed them to detection by the forces they hoped to eventually encounter by surprise. They traveled about two hundred and fifty miles in each direction, and their journey lasted a total of forty days.

In the book of *Deuteronomy*, on the other hand, the people were said to have come to Moses after being told to immediately possess the Promised Land, and asked for men to first be sent ahead to reconnoiter the land, in order to determine which was the best route to follow. Moses agreed, but the scouts only traveled as far north as Hebron, by the Wadi Eshcol, about seventeen miles south of Jerusalem, a much shorter journey, but enough to convince them that "it was indeed a good land."[118] In both books, the men returned with a report that the land was bountiful, but filled with fortified cities and strong people, including the Anakites.[119] They advised against entering the Promised Land at this time,

---

117 Num 13:2-3, 6, 8, 16; 32:8. Moses changed the name of Hoshea, son of Nun, to Joshua in this section. Num 13:16.

118 Deut 1:22-25. The Living Bible, 149.

119 The Anakites (Anakim) belonged to a race of giants known as Rephaim, or Nephilim giants, from the word *nafal*, or "fall," because they were believed to be "the fallen ones" mentioned in the book of *Genesis*. Plaut, Genesis, The Torah, A Modern Commentary, 55. They were descended from Anak, who lived in the hill country. Josh 11:21. The Nephilim are first mentioned in Gen 6:4, before the great Flood, suggesting that it was not only Noah's family who survived the deluge. Og, the Anakite King of

despite the suggestion of Caleb and Joshua that the Hebrew force could overcome the obstacles which appeared to be present.

The fear expressed by most of the scouts is consistent with illustrations from Egyptian reliefs of Seti I (1294-1279 BCE), which showed a town of Canaan standing on a mound with steep, smooth sides topped by turrets and parapets, protected by two towers and surrounded by a deep moat, a seemingly impregnable object for the poorly-equipped Hebrews.[120] Such defenses protected the inhabitants from all manner of attack, and could only be breached by a prolonged siege, which required resources not available to the Hebrews at that time. While the reluctance to attempt such a battle may have been a reasonable tactical choice, the congregation failed to take into account the fact that Moses had divine powers which went beyond man-made defenses, and that the Lord had ordered them to proceed at once. Instead of obeying the divine command, the Hebrews refused to advance, opting instead to elect a new leader to take them back to Egypt. Moses, Aaron, Caleb, and Joshua all tried to dissuade the people from their lack of faith, but the Hebrews would not listen, and even talked of stoning their leaders to death. The Lord became so angered by this reaction that He once again threatened to disinherit and destroy the Hebrews, telling Moses that He would make a new nation from his descendants that would be far more numerous and successful than the present band of ingrates. Moses pleaded with the Lord not to proceed in this manner, just as he had done when the Lord was angered by the golden calf-idol on Mt. Sinai, but where Moses earlier had argued that the Egyptians would claim God was merciless, he now told the Lord that His reputation in the world would suffer, for the other nations would say that He was not strong enough to bring them into the land He swore to give the Hebrews. He reminded God that His nature was to be merciful, "slow to anger and abounding in kindness; forgiving iniquity and transgression."[121] Although the Lord had primarily been portrayed up to this point as a warrior and avenger, Moses now expounded a trait that would become of greater importance in later Judaic theology. God agreed to follow Moses' advice, but vowed that not one person in the entire generation would live

---

Bashan, was said to have an iron bed that was thirteen and a half feet long, and six feet wide. Deut 2:11, 3:11. Tigay, Deuteronomy, 17. The Moabites referred to these gigantic aborigines as Emim, and the Ammonites called them Zamzummim (Zumzumim). Deut 2:11, 20. The concept that sons of God could have relations with women became very popular in Greek mythology, and some scholars have proposed that both the Hebrews and the Greeks learned this legend from Hittite mythology. Alter, The Five Books of Moses, 38. I believe, however, that the origin of the Greek legend was more likely transmitted by the dissident Hebrews who traveled to Mycenae before the Trojan War.

120 Illustrated Family Encyclopedia of the Living Bible, II.94. The walls of ancient Canaanite cities were often 30-50 ft. high, and sometimes 15 ft. thick. Milgrom, Numbers, 105.

121 Num 14:18. Sarna, Exodus, 216. This is how the Lord described Himself before Moses on Mt. Sinai. Exod 34:6.

to see the land they were promised, except for Caleb and Joshua.[122] In the book of *Deuteronomy*, Moses told the people that you had "no faith in the Lord your God," and for this sin you were all condemned to die in the wilderness.[123]

This forecast of banishment was intended to separate the generation of Hebrew children who were being taught to worship YHWH alone, from their parents, who had grown up with the traditions of their ancestors. At the time, Moses and Aaron probably did not realize that they also would be included within this category of exclusion, although in the final days before his death, Moses connected his punishment with that of the people's negative reaction to the spies' report, rather than with the episode which had taken place at Meribah, where he struck the rock to give water rather than speak to it as God had commanded.[124] This connection has led some scholars to surmise that Moses may have had more complicity than was suggested by the biblical account, and that he may have sinned by altering the terms of the scouts' assignment, thereby causing the negative response to their report.[125] Abarbanel (1437-1508 CE), the Portugese Jewish philosopher and leader of Spanish Jewry at the time of the Expulsion in 1492 CE, held Moses partly culpable for the failure of the spies because he asked them to report on the strength of the Canaanites and their cities, which gave the spies the opening to deliver their frightening report in the first place, rather than simply proceeding to march into Canaan when directed to do so by God.[126] Most biblical scholarship, however, has accepted that Moses' action at Meribah was the primary reason for his being barred from entering the Promised Land, and that the punishment directed against the adult generation of Hebrews who began the Exodus was because of their failure to properly accept the tenets of monotheism and the edicts of the Almighty Lord.

The result of this entire episode was that the Hebrew congregation would be forced to bear their punishment for another thirty-eight years, and during that period of time, all of the adult generation would die off in the wilderness, leaving only their children under the age of twenty years to inherit the Promised Land. God had pardoned the sins of those who participated in the Exodus too many

---

122 Num 14:30, 38; 32:12. Only Caleb was mentioned at Num 14:24 and Deut 2:36. YHWH explained that the Hebrews had "disobeyed me and tested me ten times," and no one who had so treated Me with contempt would be allowed to see the Promised Land. Num 14:22-23. Allen, "Numbers," 819, The ten episodes included actions at the Reed Sea (Exod 14:10-12); Marah (Exod 15:22-24); the Desert of Sin (Exod 16:1-3, 19-20, and 27-30); Rephidim (Exod 17:1-4); Mt. Sinai (Exod 32:1-35); Taberah (Num 11:1-3); Kibroth Hattaavah (Num 11:4-34); and the Desert of Paran (Num 14:1-3). Ibid., 822. God would prove true to His word, for not even Moses or Aaron would enter the Promised Land.
123 Deut 1:32. Levinson, "Deuteronomy," 365.
124 Deut 1:37.
125 Tigay, Deuteronomy, 19.
126 Scherman, The Chumash, 947.

times, and He now decided to renew the covenant with the next generation, a sign that those who had grown up in Egypt were too set in their ways to ever change into a people willing to follow the precepts of YHWH alone.[127] This resistance to change was something which should have been expected by both Moses and YHWH, however, for the Fifth Commandment demanded that the Hebrews "honor thy mother and father," and if their parents had worshiped idols all of their life, it would have been impossible for the children to both follow the new Mosaic Code, and honor the beliefs which their ancestors retained through generations of enslavement in Egypt. In order to prevent those Hebrews who were attached to the polytheism of their forefathers from being part of the new Jewish monotheism, God demanded that the entire pre-Mosaic generation die off in order to begin anew with children trained in the Mosaic Law. A new chapter in Hebrew theology was being written, and the conquest of Canaan was to involve a clean slate of apostles. For the next thirty-eight years, the Hebrews would wander through the Sinai Wilderness until the Lord decreed that they could successfully cross the Zered Brook. As for the ten spies whose evil report instigated the Hebrew's fear, they were not granted such an extended stay of execution, and were immediately struck dead for their role in the crime of disobeying the edict of God.

The enormity of this divine decision to withhold the ultimate goal of the participants of the Exodus from entering the Promised Land is critical to understanding why I believe it is likely that some of the Hebrews who were already at odds with Moses felt it necessary to leave the Exodus, and strike out for a distant land, rather than risk further confrontation. Not only were they required to forgo the religion of their ancestors under the tenets of the new Mosaic Law, and thereby subject themselves to parricidal punishment if they were discovered to have disobeyed the Ten Commandments, but they were now being told they would never be allowed to cross over into the Promised Land during their lifetime, even if they remained and followed the regulations which were so abhorrent to their tradition. Certainly the promise of a free life in Canaan, as opposed to forced slavery in Egypt, was something which encouraged many of the Hebrew slaves to undertake this incredibly dangerous journey into an unknown region in the first place. They had been willing to follow the direction of a foreign leader, who was not even part of their community, only because they were promised a future

---

127 That this covenant would later be annulled is evident in the book of the prophet Jeremiah, where it is told that YHWH decided that a new covenant would be made with Israel and Judah after the Babylonian Exile that "will not be like the covenant I made with their fathers," since they broke the prior covenant by failing to follow the requirements set forth in the Ten Commandments. Jer 31:31-32. Sweeney, "Jeremiah," 991. Ezekiel, on the other hand, says the Lord said "I will remember the covenant I made with you in the days of your youth, and I will establish it with you as an everlasting covenant." Ezek 16:60. Sweeney, "Ezekiel," 1071.

life that was secure in the advantages of becoming the Lord's Chosen People. Once they were settled in a new location, they could practice their religion in the manner they had become accustomed. As earlier discussed, the wilderness of Sinai was a dangerous and violable region, and no one seriously thought of the wilderness as a destination in which to permanently settle down. But now, if they remained with Moses, they would have to wander through the desert for the rest of their lives, relying only on the guarantee that their children would have a better life because of the sacrifices they made. Such unselfish goals may very well have characterized a certain number of Hebrews at the time, but for many others, once the killings reached a point where their very existence was at stake, their only choice was to leave the Exodus and search for a better life elsewhere.

Before the people had much time to ponder their fate, God told them to march back into the wilderness by way of the Sea of Reeds, in order to amplify His refusal to let them enter the Promised Land. He warned them not to fight the descendants of Esau who resided in the land, for He had given those inhabitants the hill country of Seir as a possession. This communication must have come as a shock to the men who had prepared themselves for a chance to finally taste the fruits of freedom, despite the initial fears raised by the spies' report. The very next morning, the Hebrews regained their courage and decided not to follow God's second directive, but instead reverted back to the original order to march directly into the hill country. Moses cautioned them not to disobey God's words, and warned that they would be defeated by the Amalekites and Canaanites since the Lord would not be with them, but their collective mind was made up, and they would not be turned back. The Hebrews marched forward, likely encouraged by their previous success against the Amelekites, when Moses had assured their victory by keeping his arms raised with the assistance of Aaron and Hur. Moses was not with them now, however, and they were dealt a shattering defeat at Hormah shortly after entering enemy land. The survivors regrouped after the catastrophe, and Moses then led the Exodus away from Elath and Ezion-Geber, southward into the Sinai wilderness, as directed by YHWH. The Amelekites would centuries later be defeated in a holy war by king Saul, and after king David avenged their raid on a Philistine outpost, they disappeared from the historical scene.

Rather than have a direct access to the Promised Land which was available at Kadesh-barnea, the Exodus now had to travel eastward and then northward, through the five regions which ran the length of the Transjordan: Edom, Moab, Ammon, and the Amorite kingdoms of Sihon and Og. This forced them to encounter resistance from kings who refused their request for safe passage at each step of the way. The Bible only presented what took place during a few isolated events of this thirty-eight year tenure, but each one is pertinent to understanding why the dissident Hebrews could not remain part of the original congregation which took part in the Exodus from Egypt, so I will continue my analysis of the biblical historicity in the sections which follow.

6. *The Rebellion of Korah*

Despite the extreme nature of the punishment inflicted upon the dissident Hebrews by Moses after the incident of the golden calf-idol, severe confrontations between many of the participants and their beleaguered leader continued to arise as the Exodus moved into the prolonged wilderness stage. The next serious fracture in the tenuous relationship came with the insurrection mounted by the prominent Kohathite leader Korah,[128] along with his Reubenite allies Dathan, Abiram, and On.[129] This was not a rebellion of rogues or ruffians, as was seen in earlier confrontations over the lack of water, food, or safety, but was rather a dispute that involved credible leaders and esteemed men of rank. Korah was a distinguished Levite, the son of Izhar (Yitz'har), who was the son of Kohath, and he was renowned not only because of his family and wealth, but because of his ability to speak well and persuade the people to follow his pronouncements by the brilliance of his oratory. Dathan and Abiram were members of the senior tribe of the Hebrews, and they carried the support of 250 princes who were eminent leaders in the other eleven tribes. The tents of the Kohathites and Reubenites were close to one another on the south side of the camp, and this gave the disaffected ones the opportunity to confer together. That such a respected coalition would raise complaints about the leadership of Moses was evidence of a significant disagreement at the highest level of tribal command, and the very future of Moses' monotheistic revolution was at stake if the revolt succeeded.

Some scholars have suggested that Korah, who was a cousin of Moses, was discontented because his Kohathite division of the family had been passed up in the appointment of Elizaphan, the son of Uzziel, as leader of the tribe of Levi

---

128 According to tradition, Korah was extremely wealthy, and was one of Pharaoh's officials in Egypt. Kaplan, <u>The Living Torah: The Five Books of Moses and the Haftarot</u>, 74.

129 This story is believed to have been compiled from two separate sources, with the account of Korah coming from the "P" source, while the tale of Dathan, Abiram and On came from the "J" source. Coats, <u>Rebellion in the Wilderness: The Murmuring Motif in the Wilderness Traditions of the Old Testament</u>, 156. The intent of the conspiracy by Korah and his followers was directed against the levitical order instituted by Moses, and the conspiracy of Dathan and Abiram against the civil authority of Moses. The Redactors blended the stories together to convey the anger directed against Moses by those who disputed his right to have the only prerogative to proscribe the manner by which Judaism became a monotheistic faith. <u>Numbers, The Torah, A Modern Commentary IV</u>, 155, 164.

when the Levites were appointed as the assistants of Aaron.[130] Whether it was for this reason, or simply because these men, like Miriam and Aaron, felt excluded from the tyrannical rule which Moses set up during this prolonged period of wandering in the wilderness, may never be known, but the outcome of this dispute was to make an exclamation point in what would happen to those Hebrews who questioned the authority of the leader who had taken it upon himself to alter the course of Jewish development.

Where and when this final event of rebellion occurred is not specified in the biblical text, although tradition has held that it took place at or near the encampment at Hazeroth, shortly after the episode of the spies.[131] The primary complaint against Moses was that he had only brought them out of Egypt to make himself king, a charge which was reminiscent of the accusation made by one of the Hebrews who Moses had angered shortly after smiting the Egyptian who was beating a Hebrew slave. The man at that time was assaulting another Hebrew, and when Moses intervened to save the victim, the aggressor responded by asking Moses, "who made you chief and ruler over us?"[132] The Semitic mode of government involved a Council of Elders who were responsible for determining the policy of the tribal conclave. While a single person may have been elected by the Elders at times to negotiate with foreign kings, no one person ever held the kind of power which was now wielded by Moses. Korah was upset that Moses alone controlled the leadership of the Hebrews, and that he extended his authority by placing his brother Aaron in control of the priesthood. Despite his magical powers, Korah argued that Moses was no better than anyone else in the congregation, and he had no right to say that he was the only one who could interpret what the Lord commanded.

Such a claim does not seem out of line under the circumstances, since the combination of both political leader and seer under one man alone was unique among all the great powers during the Late Bronze Age. Even in Egypt, where the Pharaoh was imbued with divine qualities, there was a strong priestly caste who was called forth to advise on matters of the gods. In the story of Joseph, for

---

130 Anderson, "The Book of Numbers," 283. Korah was the eldest son of the second son of Kohath, while Elizaphan was the son of Uzziel, the youngest son of Hohath, and Korah believed that his elder status should have placed him in the position of being head of the family. Milgrom, Numbers, 129.

131 Scherman, The Chumash, 939. The book of *Numbers* is frequently cited to support the occurrence of the rebellion in the fortieth year of the Exodus, and the book of *Deuteronomy* in the third year. Milgrom, Numbers, 164. A fragment of the Dead Sea Scrolls states that the rebellion took place five years after the Exodus began. Wise, Abegg, & Cook, The Dead Sea Scrolls: A New Translation, 565.

132 Exod 2:14; Acts 7:27. Sarna, Exodus, 11. According to rabbinical tradition, it was Dathan and Abiram who betrayed Moses to the authorities for striking down the Egyptian taskmaster. Kirsch, Moses, 298.

example, the Pharaoh consulted seers to determine what the gods meant by the nature of his dream, despite the fact that he was considered to be a replica of god on earth. When Joseph provided an interpretation that turned out to be true, the Pharaoh told him that he was a man "in whom is the spirit of God."[133] This separation-of-powers would also become apparent during the United Monarchy, when King Saul proceeded with a sacrifice, rather than wait for Samuel to arrive, and was cursed by Samuel and denied the blessing of God for his impudence.[134] Moses was vehement about not allowing any other man to claim divine inspiration, and his rigid denial infuriated the Hebrew elders, who had always participated in the religious hierarchy before the leadership of Moses.

Korah's charge directly threatened the autocratic control of Moses, however, and the entire stability of the movement toward monotheism was in danger of disruption if Moses was forced to cede his despotic rule. Rather than offer the malcontents some modicum of authority, Moses faced the challenge in his typically belligerent manner, denying any possibility of change, since God had decided that he alone was to direct the enactment of the Mosaic Code. He told Korah that YHWH would make known in the morning which of them was truly in charge, and directed him to take the incense burners and light them in front of YHWH at that time. Moses knew, of course, that only the priests were permitted to burn incense, and that Nadab and Abihu, the sons of Aaron, were previously burnt to death for their earlier attempt to burn incense without proper authorization. He therefore prayed to the Lord to not accept the grievances of Korah and his allies, and to punish them for their accusations. He reminded the Lord that he had never even hurt one of them, conveniently forgetting the golden calf-idol incident, where he had directed the Levites to kill thousands of Hebrew idolaters.

The next day, when the dissenters gathered and Korah burned incense in the fire pan in direct violation of the Mosaic Code, Moses told the rest of the community to withdraw to a distance away from the abodes of Korah, Dathan and Abiram. Dathan and Abiram then came out from their tents, along with their wives and children, and the ground suddenly split open and swallowed them up, along with Korah's family, throwing them into the depths of Sheol, the abode of the dead.[135] This was followed by a great fire which burnt up the other two

---

133 Gen 41:38. Sarna, Genesis, 285.

134 During the battle with the Philistines at Gilgal, Samuel arrived late to offer the burnt (*olah*) and peace-offerings (*shelamim*), so Saul proceeded with the sacrifice, which was not allowable under the Mosaic Code. When Samuel returned, and found out what Saul had done, he told him that he had disobeyed the commandment of the Lord and that his dynasty must now end. Samuel cursed him and denied him the blessing of God, even though God had first favored the choice of Saul as King of the Jews. 1 Sam 13:9-14.

135 Num 16:30-32. In this passage, and in Deut 11:6 and Ps 106:17, only Dothan and Abiram were said to have been swallowed up. Korah was not specifically named, but later sections testify that he was included with the others. Num 26:10. The Samaritan

hundred and fifty men who were allied with the rebels, and had volunteered their services in the offering of incense to God. The fire pans which were used to burn the incense were then removed from the ashes and hammered into sheets of plating for the altar, as a sacred reminder of the dangers of encroaching upon the sanctuary without the permission of the Lord.

Although God enabled Moses to thoroughly dispose of the leaders of the revolt in a clear and decisive manner, many of the Hebrews remained sympathetic to the rebels' cause, and did not believe that parricidal retaliation of the most respected men in the community was an appropriate punishment. An angry mob formed to show their displeasure with Moses' actions, telling him that he had killed the Lord's people! Their anger fomented in a manner which was greater than that which accompanied the golden calf-idol incident, and the Lord was so incensed by their actions that He sent a plague which killed another 14,700 people before the dissidents finally agreed to obey His commands.[136] Moses sent Aaron forth among the people to burn incense in order to make atonement for their sins, and then took a staff from each tribe and deposited them in the Tent of Meeting. The next day, only the staff with the name of Aaron had sprouted and brought forth almond blossoms, indicating that Aaron alone held the authority of the priesthood, and no one else could claim to challenge the edicts of the Lord. Any Hebrew who hoped to retain allegiance to their ancestors must now have been convinced that there was no way to practice their age-old faith and still remain part of the Exodus assembly.

The story of Korah is often given little attention in Bible-class study, but it is an extremely important part of the conversion of the Jewish faith from ancestral-worship, which characterized the Patriarchal and pre-Mosaic religious life, to monotheism, as demanded by the Mosaic Code. It is likely that the biblical compilers placed the tale at the critical point following the episode of the spies to accentuate the fact that the Lord had let it be known with absolute certainty that not only the congregation-at-large, and Miriam and Aaron in particular, were required to obey Moses' interpretation of the Word of God, but also the elite elders of the Hebrew enclave. Anyone who questioned the authority of Moses would be subject to the penalty of death. It was similar to the proscription of the death penalty to those who cursed their mother and father (Exod 21:17), a capital punishment that did not require any physical harm to the victim. No one should ever wonder again about the direction of the evolution of monotheism under the tenets of the Mosaic Law, and those who remained loyal to the teachings of their ancestors would now have to decide to either change their ways, or change their

---

Pentateuch says that Korah was burnt up as well, although this does not appear in the Masoretic translation. Carson, "Numbers," 236. All descendants could not have been killed, since the sons of Korah are listed as gatekeepers of the temple in 1 Chron 26:1.

136 Num 16:49.

address to a distant land.

It is at this point that I believe the dissidents finally decided to part ways with the Exodus. It was clear from the defeat at Hormah that those who remained would never reach the Promised Land, and their attempt to oust Moses from their midst had clearly failed with the death of Korah, resulting in the demise of many more of their own leaders. The time had now come to get out on their own, and find a land that would offer them a place to work and raise their families, and freely worship their own gods in the manner of their family traditions.

7. *Kadesh-barnea to the Promised Land*

It is not possible, using the biblical text alone, to know if any of the Hebrew dissidents actually left the Exodus at this point in time, but there were still more parricides to come, indicating that at least some of the disbelievers still remained. Following the disruption of Korah's rebellion, the Hebrews moved to the Wilderness of Zin, and stayed at Meribah, where Miriam died and was buried. Once again, a lack of water resulted in a rebellion against Moses, and the people complained that he had brought them from Egypt only to die in this horrible place. Moses and Aaron went to the Tent of Meeting to query the Lord for help, and YHWH told Moses to take his staff and assemble the people and then *speak* to the rock before their eyes, and it would give out water. As previously discussed, at the earlier incident Moses had been commanded to *strike* the rock rather than *speak* to it, and no reason for the difference in commands was now given. Moses struck the rock twice with his staff, instead of speaking to it as instructed by God, and water miraculously appeared, assuaging the thirst of the unruly mob. YHWH was furious with Moses because of this seemingly minimal oversight, and He punished the man who had spent the last forty years of his life leading the Hebrews through an incredible journey of strife and aggravation, by having him die before he could enter the Promised Land. The reason YHWH gave for this devastating penalty was that "because you did not trust Me enough to affirm My sanctity in the sight of the Israelite people, therefore you shall not lead this congregation into the land that I have given them."[137] The site was then named the Waters of Meribah, meaning that "the Israelites quarreled with the Lord - through which He affirmed His sanctity."[138]

This incredible turn of events has prompted extensive debate among biblical commentators over the years, as most people believe that the man who was so instrumental in formulating the precepts of the monotheistic Jewish religion should have been allowed some leeway in the rigidity of his obedience, given

---

137 Num 20:12. Milgrom, <u>Numbers</u>, 166. This explanation is repeated in Ps 106:32-33.

138 Num 20:13. Ibid. The event is recollected in Pss 81:8 and 95:8.

the enormous stress which he had been placed under as leader of an unruly, polytheistic group of slaves, who continuously refused to follow the edicts of God. As Rabbi W. Gunther Plaut, the leading historian, scholar, and representative of the Reform Judaism movement queried, how could the Lord let such a minor transgression, "committed in frustration and justifiable anger, wipe out a lifetime of merit and service."[139] Moses had devoted the greater part of his adult life to aiding the Hebrews departure out of slavery in Egypt to freedom in the Promised Land, and to have his dream unfulfilled for this one episode of insubordination seemed an extraordinary punishment, out of proportion to the intensity of his crime. Some scholars have attempted to answer this question by pointing out that by hitting the rock, rather than trusting in God's directive, Moses had begun to place more confidence in his own decision-making than in the Lord's command.[140] In addition, when he approached the rock with Aaron at his side, he asked the people "shall we get water for you out of this rock?" implying that it was going to be his action, rather than God's, which was important.[141] In some sense, Moses was assuming the magical powers of God as his own, and thereby acting more like a messiah, than a prophet. If God allowed Moses to cross over the Jordan River with this inflated opinion of his own self-worth, the continued identification of Moses as the savior of the Hebrews would jeopardize the basic tenet that it was YHWH alone Who was responsible for the fate of the Chosen People. If anyone doubted the word of God, the reliability of the Torah was put in jeopardy, and such a legacy would destroy the basic principle which Judaism stood for: the total authority of the one and only Almighty God for Whom Abraham had been willing to place his only son on the sacrificial altar. Since the chronology of the event is not certain, we do not know for how long Moses was forced to live with this knowledge that he was, in essence, a lame-duck leader, but the biblical text does not indicate that he modified the methods of his authoritarian control, and the parricidal punishments did not end, as will be discussed shortly.

Another possible explanation for the decision, in my opinion, was the fact that Moses was put directly in the role of executioner by the parricides that were necessary to force obedience to the monotheistic principles of the Mosaic Code, and this was not a role which would favor the tenets of Judaism which evolved following passage in the Promised Land. Whether all the deaths as recorded in the biblical text were in fact due to the direct or indirect influence of God, or whether some may have been due to an abuse of authority by Moses himself, cannot be known with certainty, since the recording of events was not an independent assessment of the facts. The text is clear, however, that the parricides were mandated by the need to educate future generations that the Mosaic Code

---

139 Numbers, The Torah, A Modern Commentary IV, 197.
140 Friedman, Commentary on the Torah, 495.
141 Fox, "Numbers," 323-324.

carried a death sentence as punishment for those who disobeyed, and letting Moses cross the Jordan River and continue to be in charge of the congregation would have blurred the difference between secular and religious responsibilities. In addition, YHWH told King David that he could not build the First Temple, and must leave that task to his son Solomon, because he had blood on his hands from his years as military commander.[142] This impurity could easily be connected with Moses, who not only was tainted by numerous killings, but responsible for causing the death of Hebrews, rather than enemies of the Israelite people.

Although the period of the Judges and the United and Divided Monarchies were filled with many episodes of apostasy, the biblical text indicates that it was YHWH, using the might of foreign countries against Israel and Judah, and not one of the leaders, who was responsible for the punishments inflicted upon the people-at-large. It would have been very difficult for Moses to maintain the type of governmental control that would be necessary to gain control of the land they wrested from the indigenous population, given his history of violence during the forty years of wandering in the desert. Transferring the secular leadership to a man like Joshua, and leaving the religious community under the direction of the High Priest, was a necessary step in assuring the success of this process. That both YHWH and the people understood the difficulty of the task ahead is evident in the very first chapter of the book of *Joshua* where the Lord tells Joshua three times, and the people once, to "be strong and resolute."[143]

Despite the unsettling news of his limited tenure, Moses set up a plan of action to finally lead the Exodus toward the crossing of the Jordan River into Promised Land. He sent messengers to the king of Edom, whose country was on the border of Kadesh, and asked for permission to pass through his land on the way to the King's Highway.[144] The king refused this request, and Moses was therefore forced to turn south, back toward the Reed Sea, in order to skirt the borders of Esau, remembering the Lord's command not to fight the Edomites directly.[145] It was at this juncture that the Lord directed Moses, Aaron, and Eleazar, the son of Aaron, to climb Mt. Hor, for it was time for Aaron to die.[146] At the summit,

---

142 1 Chron 22:8.

143 Josh 1:6-7, 9, 18. Meyers, "Joshua," 464-466.

144 Num 20:14-17. The King's Highway was the main road that ran through the entire length of Transjordan from north to south. The Exodus would follow this road up to the city of Jericho, where they crossed the Jordan River into the Promised Land. Milgrom, Numbers, 168.

145 In the book of *Deuteronomy*, Moses told the Hebrews before they entered the Promised Land not to despise the Edomite, for "he is your brother," being descendants of Esau. Deut 23:8. Kaplan, The Living Torah, The Five Books of Moses and the Haftarot, 976-977.

146 Num 20:22. This site was also mentioned in Num 33:38 and Deut 32:50, although Deut 10:6 recorded a different tradition, whereby Aaron died at Moseroth. Aaron died at the age of 123 years.

Aaron stripped his vestments and gave them to his son, symbolizing the passage of priestly authority that would characterize the future policy of the Hebrew High Priesthood. As previously discussed, although the biblical text does not expound upon the reasons for Aaron's death at this juncture, his role in the golden calf-idol incident, and his siding with Miriam against Moses, both provide a possible explanation for why his value to the survival of the Exodus was now at an end.

After turning away from Edom, the Hebrews were again refused safe-passage by the Canaanite King Arad, and this time they had no choice but to wage war against the inhabitants in order to continue their travels toward the Promised Land, since alternate routes of travel were not available. Although they suffered a defeat at the start of hostilities, the Hebrews eventually destroyed the major cities of the region, naming the place Hormah, which means "destruction."[147] These battles may have resulted in a significant loss of valuable supplies, however, for following the triumph, the people again complained of the lack of food and water as they continued to skirt the land of Edom, encamping at Zalmonah and Punon. Their complaints were directed against both God and Moses, and God retaliated by sending a plague of serpents which killed many of the Hebrews, although an exact number was not given in the biblical text. Moses interceded on behalf of the Hebrew people once again, and YHWH told him to make a bronze model of the snake and mount it on a standard which would protect all those who were bitten. Although the biblical compilers took great care to not implicate Moses as judge and jury in this episode, it is likely that the people nevertheless allied him with the disaster, since he so carefully identified himself as God's partner in the disasters which followed Korah's rebellion. Misbehavior would be harshly punished during the Exodus, and with each passing year, the message was clear: you either obeyed the Lord's commandment as promulgated by Moses, or you died.

As was seen following the crossing of the Reed Sea, and the departure from Mt. Sinai, the Bible then described the ongoing passage toward the crossing of the Jordan River in disparate ways. According to the book of *Numbers* 21, the Exodus continued through the Transjordan, encamping first at Oboth and then at Iye-abarim, which bordered Moab on the east. The congregation then stopped at the Wadi Zered, and passed beyond the Arnon River, into the wilderness that extended from the territory of the Amorites. From there, they continued to Beer, Midbar, Mattanah, Nahaliel, Bamoth, and then to a valley in Moab, near the peak of Pisgah.[148] This description, along with that of Judges 11:17-

---

147 Num 21:2-3. Ibid., 172.

148 Num 21:10-13, 16-20. This section contains a reference to the *Book of the Wars of the Lord*, which is believed to be an extrabiblical collection of material which has been lost, possibly the *Book of Jashar*. Num 21:14; Josh 10:13; 2 Sam 1:18. Numbers, The Torah, A Modern Commentary IV, 213. Most scholars believe it is an ancient collection of songs of war in praise of God. There are 21 other books mentioned in the Bible that have never been found. These are believed to cover some chapter in ancient Israel's sacred

18, envisioned a southerly route down to Ezion-Geber, and then northward along the eastern edge of Edom and Moab. The itinerary of the book of *Numbers* 33, however, described a northerly route from Kadesh-barnea, along the King's Highway through Edom and Moab.[149] Biblical scholars have not yet been able to resolve these two pathways into a unified passage, and some have suggested that the Exodus may have split into two tribal populations, eventually joining at the Arnon, east of the Jordan River.[150]

When the enclave reached the Amorite territory, Moses once again sent messengers to seek peaceful passage through the kingdom of Sihon. King Sihon is not mentioned in any extra-biblical text, although some scholars believe that his name may have been preserved in the name of Tell Shihan, in Moab, south of the Arnon River. His territory was bordered by the Dead Sea and Jordan River on the west, Wadi Jabbok on the north, Ammon and the desert on the east, and Wadi Arnon on the south. Moses promised that he would only use the King's Highway, as he did with the king of Edom, and assured Sihon that they would not wander into the fields, or use water from the wells. Sihon nevertheless refused his request, and attacked the Hebrews at Jahaz, where he was defeated, allowing the Hebrews to take control of the Transjordan. All of Sihon's subjects were killed, and the cattle and spoil of the cities were taken as booty. This was the first actual conquest of land by the Hebrews, and they took possession of the towns, rather than leaving the region barren. They followed up this victory with a defeat of King Og of Bashan, who ruled the area which is known today as the Golan Heights. Sixty towns were destroyed in that campaign, and once again the Hebrews took no captives, eliminating the pagan infidels who polluted the land with their worship of false gods.

The Hebrews now had a base of operation with agricultural resources that assured them a steady supply of food and water. Once secure in their defenses, they marched northward to the steppes of Moab, across the Jordan River from Jericho. Seeing how the Hebrews so thoroughly defeated the Amorites, Balak, the king of Moab, sent messengers to Balaam in Pethor, asking him to come and curse the Hebrews, since they were too numerous for him to defeat without divine assistance.[151] This account has some possible historical support, as there was a man named Balaam, son of Beor, who lived in Pethor and was mentioned on a fragmentary wall-plaster inscription from a temple at Deir 'Alla in Transjordan, from the ninth or eighth century BCE.[152] The writings of that prophet bear

---

history. Miller, & Huber, The Bible: A History, 42-43.

149 Num 33:37-49.

150 Numbers, The Torah, A Modern Commentary IV, 212.

151 Num 22:2-6; Josh 24:9-10. There was a King Balak who lived about 1300 BCE. The Balaam referred to here is not believed to be the same as the one mentioned in Gen 36:32. Numbers, The Torah, A Modern Commentary IV, 221.

152 Fox, "Numbers," 328.

striking similarities to the story of Balaam in the Bible, indicating that the literary traditions of the two may very well have been the same.[153]

When the elders of Moab and Midian arrived at Balaam's abode, he told them to wait the night, so that he might receive instructions from the Lord in a dream. While prophecy throughout the ancient Near East often relied on portents from sources found in nature, the Bible generally utilized dreams to convey messages from God. That evening YHWH came to him during his sleep, and told him not to curse the Hebrew people, for they were blessed. Balaam complied with God's order, and refused to travel to Moab, but when Balak received word of the refusal, he sent another contingency of dignitaries to ask Balaam to change his mind. This time, God told Balaam to go to Balak, but to do only what He commanded. Balaam then set out for Moab, where Balak took him to Kiriath-huzoth to see the shrine of Baal known as Bamoth-baal.[154] Balaam directed Balak to build seven altars so that he could sacrifice a bull and ram on each one in order to encourage the Lord to grant him a manifestation. The Lord then appeared to Balaam, and told him to give an oracle which blessed the Hebrews instead of cursing them. Balak was angered by this prophecy, and took Balaam to Sedehzophim to offer a second sacrifice on seven altars. The second oracle was no different than the first, and Balaam explained to Balak that God was "not man to be capricious, or mortal to change His mind," indicating that his omens would not change simply because they came from a different location.[155] Balak did not give up, however, and finally took Balaam to a third site on the peak of Peor, where the spirit of God came upon Balaam after sacrificing a bull and a ram on the seven altars, and as he looked upon the Hebrew tribes camped in the wilderness, he compared the might of Israel to cedars planted beside the water, and prophesied that they would defeat and rise above Amalek's Agag. Balaam added that the enemies of the Hebrews would be crushed, and anyone who cursed them would themselves be accursed. The reason why such a long passage involving Balaam was incorporated into the Bible is uncertain, although most scholars believe that the story was composed independently, and inserted into the Pentateucal corpus at a later date to accentuate the power of YHWH over the pagan Canaanites.

---

153 Burnett, A Reassessment of Biblical Elohim, 37.

154 Num 22:39, 41. During this voyage, God sent an Angel to block Balaam's path, and when the donkey he was riding saw the Angel, she refused to pass. Balaam struck the animal three times, trying to force her to move, and God caused the donkey to respond verbally to his abuse. Num 22:22-30. This was the only instance in the Bible of an animal speaking, except for the serpent's address to Eve in the Garden of Eden. Gen 3:1. Numbers, The Torah, A Modern Commentary IV, 225.

155 Num 23:19. Milgrom, Numbers, 199. This contrasted with pagan gods who, when appealed to by man, would change the content of their message. Ibid.

8. *Acacia*

After successfully defeating the Amorite kings on their way to the Promised Land, the Hebrews were optimistic about their prospects, and in sight of their long sought legacy across the Jordan River. Most of the original generation had died out by now, and the Hebrews who survived had never known the shackles of slavery, or the comforts of a secure and stable homeland. Now that they seemed on the verge of successful independence, some of the younger men felt the need to celebrate after they settled in Acacia, and so began to go to wild parties with the local Moabite girls, rather than accept the confinements of orthodox Jewish teaching under the strict Mosaic Law. Before long, all Israel was joining freely in the prohibited worship of Baal-peor, the local deity.[156]

This was the first time the Hebrews were actually said to worship Baal in the biblical text, but their fascination with this particular god would continue to result in apostasy for centuries to come, as will be discussed in chapter 12. The Lord's anger furiously exploded at this vile behavior, and He ordered Moses to execute all the tribal leaders responsible for the outrage. Moses responded by sentencing all those who worshiped Baal to death, and by the time the carnage was over, another 24,000 Hebrews had died.[157] In order to publicize how egregious their behavior was, the Lord decreed that the guilty men be impaled after they were killed to show how despicable was their affront to God.[158] Even more would have been killed, but the anger of the Lord was assuaged when Phinehas, the son of the incumbent High Priest Eleazar, and grandson of Aaron, killed Zimri, the son of a leader of the tribe of Simeon, and a Midianite princess named Cozbi, who were lying together in a tent.[159] According to Josephus, Moses had warned Zimri that

---

156 Num 25:1-3. Baal is the name of the god, and Peor the site of worship. Ibid., 212. In pagan religions, women were often associated with images of sexual worship. Some scholars believe that this may have been one reason why women were not allowed to be priests in the Jewish religion. Allen, "Numbers," 920.

157 Num 25:9. The New Testament put the total number at 23,000. 1 Cor 10:8.

158 Num 25:4-5. Normally, a person who was executed for a crime, and his body hung on a tree, was buried that same day, for leaving the body overnight would defile the land. Deut 21:22-23. The public impalement here was intended not only to be a deterrent to others, but also as expiation for Israel's apostasy. Milgrom, Numbers, 213. The only other incident of impalement in the biblical text occurred with the sons of King Saul in 1 Sam 21:6, 9, 13. Some translators have interpreted the word as hanged, instead of impaled. Numbers, The Torah, A Modern Commentary IV, 251.

159 Phineas was the son of Eleazar, the third son of Aaron. Exod 6:23, 25; 1 Chron 6:4; 9:20. Like Moses, Phinehas is a name of Egyptian origin, meaning "the Nubian," or "the Negro." Numbers, The Torah, A Modern Commentary IV, 252. The Talmud identifies Zimri with Shelumiel, son of Tzuri-Shaddai, and Cozbi is also called Sh'vilani, Shelonai, or Shulani. Kaplan, The Living Torah: The Five Books of Moses and the Haftarot, 798.

his marrying outside of his faith and sacrificing to other gods was against the laws of YHWH, and that he must change his ways and stop acting madly, now that he was living in relative prosperity. Zimri refused, and berated Moses in front of the entire assembly for his tyrannical commands, saying that he was harder upon the Hebrews than were the Egyptians. He defended his right to worship others gods in order to come at truth by inquiring of many people, and it became obvious that his beliefs were detrimental to the sanctity of the entire group.[160] As a reward for his actions, Phinehas was promised that he and his descendants, the Zadokites, would be priests forever. This remained valid for many centuries, but during the rule of the Seleucids and following the Maccabean rebellion (167-160 BCE), this pledge was not followed, and it is believed that the Zadokites then formed the Essene sect, which has been identified with the Dead Sea Scrolls.

The parricidal slaughters ended at this point in the biblical text, but by now, in the words of the popular author Jonathan Kirsh, "Moses the emancipator" had become "Moses the exterminator."[161] Adding up all the Hebrews who were killed, the total reached over 41,700, not including the unnamed number who died when God sent venomous snakes as punishment when they complained about the lack of food and water on their way to Edom (Num 21:6), those who succumbed to the plague at Kibroth-hattaavah (Num 11:33-34), or those who were killed when God sent a fire to destroy the objectors at Taberah (Num 11:1-3). That the tribe of Simeon may have been singled out in this slaughter is suggested by the fact that the exceedingly wicked Zimri was a prince of the house of Simeon, and the census taken just before the passage into the Promised Land showed that their total numbers had decreased by 37,100, when compared to the census taken at Mt. Sinai, a drop of about 63 percent.[162] It is also possible, however, that the decline could also have been due to many of their number joining the Hebrew dissidents who fled from Moses' iron fist, as will be discussed in greater detail throughout this book. Other tribes which suffered a loss of men between the first and second census, and therefore are candidates for having joined the migration, are Reuben, with a loss of 2,770 (6 percent), Gad, with a loss of 5,150 (11 percent), Ephraim, with a loss of 8,000 (20 percent), and Naphtali, with a loss of 8,000 (15 percent). The total loss in the number of participants between the two censuses was 61,020, a figure very similar to the 41,700 parricides mentioned in the biblical text, when the miscellaneous who died are also taken into account. Whether all of these killings were restricted to only these five tribes will never be known for sure, but it seems reasonable that many of the deaths were explained by the biblical compilers

160 Josephus, "Antiquities of the Jews," The Complete Works of Josephus, IV.VI.10-12, 93.

161 Kirsch, Moses, 10.

162 In the first Hebrew census, the tribe of Simeon numbered 59,300. Num 1:23, 2:10-12. By the end of the wilderness wanderings, this number was reduced to 22,200. Num 26:12.

as an act of punishment for their apostasy. It is also possible, however, that many of the names were stricken from the roster of tribes because the families fled the Exodus, were there thereafter considered as dead. Interestingly enough, the other tribes all increased their numbers, including Judah (3 percent), Issachar (18 percent), Zebulun (5 percent), Manasseh (64 percent), Benjamin (29 percent), Dan (3 percent), and Asher (29 percent).[163]

B. The Death of Moses

The time for passage into the Promised Land had finally arrived, and the generation of adult Hebrews who refused to follow the order of God to immediately enter the Promised Land from Kadesh-barnea had now died out. Despite the impiety of some of the younger generation, it was nearing the time for the Chosen People to fulfill their destiny in the land of Canaan, but before ordering the death of Moses, the Lord directed him to carry out one final mission in order to execute retribution upon the Midianites for their role in causing the apostasy of the Hebrews at Baal-peor. Twelve thousand men were picked for the campaign, one thousand from each tribe, and Phinehas served as both commander and priest, equipped with trumpets for sounding the blasts of attack, which would later prove so powerful at the walls of Jericho. Phineas, rather than Joshua, was placed in command of this enterprise because the struggle assumed a religious character as "the Lord's vengeance."[164] The Hebrews were victorious in this battle, slaying every enemy male soldier, in addition to the five kings of Midian, and Balaam, son of Beor. Rather than destroy all the populace, the expedition brought the women and children back as captives, but Moses ordered that all the male children, and all the women who were not virgins, had to be slain because of the role of the women in the orgy at Acacia. Although there is scholarly debate over whether the Conquest of the Promised Land was a military take-over, or an infiltration of pastoralists , as will be discussed shortly, this final chapter in the wanderings of the Exodus clearly supports the theory that the mindset of the Hebrews was that of a conquering force, rather than a peaceful group prepared to take control by a gradual political resurrection.

The forty-year Exodus was now about to end, and Moses gathered the Hebrews on the plain in Moab in order to present his farewell address, since he would be prohibited from crossing the river with them. He reviewed what had transpired over the past forty years, and then summarized the laws and lessons which the Hebrews were to follow in order to maintain their position as the Chosen People.[165]

---

163 Allen, "Numbers," 928-937.

164 Num 31:3. Numbers, The Torah, A Modern Commentary IV, 295-296.

165 When he was finished, Moses wrote down the Torah and gave it to the priests, sons of Levi. Deut 31:9. In the Amoraic period, the view was expressed that Moses wrote thirteen Torah scrolls on that day, twelve for the twelve tribes, and one to place in the Ark.

It has been estimated that this speech would have lasted for about three hours uninterrupted, but since tradition held that it took thirty-six days to deliver, it must have been presented piecemeal, rather than all at once.[166]   During this speech, Moses recapped his view of God in words which have become the mainstay of Judaism to the present day:

Listen, Israel: YHWH is our God. YHWH is one. And you shall love YHWH, your God, with all your heart and with all your soul and with all your might. And these words that I command you today shall be on your heart. And you shall impart them to your children, and you shall speak about them when you sit in your house and when you go in the road and when you lie down and when you get up. And you shall bind them for a sign on your hand, and they shall become bands between your eyes. And you shall write them on the doorposts of your house and in your gates.[167]

Moses had pleaded with the Lord to be allowed to cross over the Jordan River and see the Promised Land before giving up his life, but God refused this request, and Moses was forced to cede the leadership to this trusted second-in-command, Joshua. He then composed a poem, known as the "Shirat Ha'azinu," which warned that the Hebrews would betray God despite the fact that He treated them with justice and kindness, and because of this ingratitude, they deserved the punishment that would be inflicted upon their descendants.[168] The poem related how "Jeshurun," (Israel) grew fat and sacrificed instead to gods they had never known: "You neglected the Rock that begot you, Forgot the God who brought you forth."[169] While the majority of Hebrews had by now been converted from polytheism to monotheism, their obedience to the word of God was not yet secure, and many Hebrews would continue to turn back to the oral traditions of their own fathers and elders, before settling into a rigid code of proper behavior following the return from the Babylonian Exile. He handed the written Teaching he had prepared to the priests, and told them to read it aloud to all the people of Israel every seven years at the Feast of Booths.[170]

Moses then told them that once the Promised Land was settled, they were to erect a large stelae covered with lime, upon which was to be written all the laws which he had outlined in the book of *Deuteronomy*, as a reminder of what was required to follow the tenets of God. To show their acceptance of this directive, the tribes of Simeon, Levi, Judah, Issachar, Joseph, and Benjamin then stood upon Mount Gerizim and proclaimed a blessing, while the tribes of Reuben,

---

Heschel, Heavenly Torah: As Refracted Through the Generations, 549.

166 Tigay, Deuteronomy, 5.

167 Deut 6:4-9. Friedman, Commentary on the Torah, 586-587.

168 Deut 31:19. Tigay, Deuteronomy, 295, 298.

169 Deut 32:15, 17-18. Ibid., 306-307.

170 Deut 31:9-10. Some believe that this was the book of the law which was discovered in the days of Josiah. 2 Chron 34:14.

Gad, Asher, Zebulun, Dan and Naphtali stood on Mount Ebal and proclaimed a curse, setting forth the principle that the Lord's covenant with Abraham provided both benefits and punishment, depending on whether the people were obedient or not.[171] Moses then ascended the heights of Abarim to view the Promised Land before he died in the book of *Numbers*, while in the book of *Deuteronomy*, he was told to go to the summit of Pisgah, which was later identified as the specific peak of Mount Nebo.[172] God explained to Moses that "You shall die on the mountain that you are about to ascend, and shall be gathered to your kin, as your brother Aaron died on Mount Hor and was gathered to his kin; for you both broke faith with Me among the Hebrew people, at the waters of Meribath-kadesh in the wilderness of Zin, by failing to uphold My sanctity among the Hebrew people."[173] In this moving scene, God again reminded Moses that "I have let you see it with your own eyes, but you shall not cross there."[174] With the death of Moses, the political leadership of the twelve tribes now fell back into a more democratic system, headed by a Council of Elders with Joshua, and other Judges who followed, being allowed to manage the security of the nation, while the priests maintained theologic consistency.

C. The Conquest of Canaan

Before concluding the discussion of the Hebrew Exodus, I want to briefly outline what transpired in the land of Canaan when the Hebrews, now under the direction of Joshua, crossed the Jordan River and entered the Promised Land. The historicity of this event has been hotly debated, as has the validity of the Exodus itself, but the nature of the Conquest is important to the dating of the

---

171 Deut 11:29; 27:12-13. Mt. Gerizim lies about one mile to the west of Shechem, and is currently known as Jebel et-Tor. Mt. Ebal is the highest point in Samaria, and lies about two miles north-east of Mt. Gerizim. Kaplan, <u>The Living Torah: The Five Books of Moses and the Haftarot</u>, 925.

172 Num 27:12-13; Deut 32:49. Nebo is also possibly one of the three mountains which Balak, the king of Moab, sent the seer Balaam to ascend in order to curse Israel, specifically the summit of Pisgah. Num21:20; Deut 34:1.

173 Deut 32:50-51. Tigay, <u>Deuteronomy</u>, 317.

174 Deut 34:4. Ibid., 337. According to rabbinic tradition, Moses died four months after the death of Aaron, and one year after the death of Miriam. Ginzberg, <u>the Legends of the Jews</u>, III.317. Jewish tradition holds that he died on the seventh day of the twelfth month. Rashi, <u>Pentateuch With Targum Onkelos, Haphtaroth and Rashi's Commentary, Deuteronomy</u>, 3. Moses died on his 120th year birthday, spanning three generations of forty years each. Deut 31:2; 34:7. This was the age which God determined to be the maximum a human should reach before the Great Flood. Gen 6:3. He was buried in a depression of the land of Moab by God, in a place that remains unknown to this day. Deut 34:5-6. Rabbi Ishmael (90-135 CE) claims that Moses buried himself. Rashi, <u>Pentateuch With Targum Onkelos, Haphtaroth and Rashi's Commentary, Deuteronomy</u>, 178.

Exodus. I believe it is necessary to discuss some of the details before proceeding to an analysis of the chronologic theories.

In his final speech to the Exodus congregation, Moses explained that the Lord was going to dislodge seven large nations in order that the Hebrews could possess the Promised Land: the Hittites, Girgashites, Amorites, Canaanites, Perizzites, Hivites, and Jebusites.[175] The invasion was to be a Holy War, and Moses warned the Hebrews that no matter how many people inhabited the land, "you must doom them to destruction," and not be swayed by pity to allow those who did not follow the Mosaic Code to live.[176] All emblems of idolatry were to be destroyed, for, as Moses indicated, "you are a people consecrated to the Lord your God; of all the peoples on earth the Lord your God chose you to be His treasured people."[177]

Exactly how this cleansing of the land was to occur was not clearly detailed in the book of *Deuteronomy*, but the books of *Joshua* and *Judges* described many military battles, beginning with the destruction of the city of Jericho at the time of the crossing of the Jordan River. Known as the "Conquest Model," this view describes the twelve tribes of Israel joining in a concerted campaign to conquer and destroy the inhabitants of Canaan, and then fill the void with their own distinctive culture and religion. As with many other issues concerning the historicity of the Bible, confirmation that these events took place as represented in those passages is lacking in many of the archaeologic remains of these cities, and this has resulted in great controversy over the manner in which the twelve tribes eventually conquered the territories of the Promised Land, if, in fact, the story is true. Archaeologic evidence at Jericho, for example, indicates that the walls "came tumbling down," not in the time of Joshua, but in the third millennium BCE, and that the city was destroyed again in the middle of the sixteenth century BCE, possibly during the expulsion of the Hyksos from Egypt.[178] There is no evidence of violent destruction of Jericho during the fifteenth to the twelfth century BCE, although there is evidence that some of the Canaanite cities were violently destroyed in the late thirteenth century BCE, including Lachish, Hazor, Bethel, Debit, and Eglon, although there is no clear evidence that it was the Hebrews under Joshua who led the assault.[179] The end of the Late Bronze Age was an era of constant battling between the armies of Egypt and Mesopotamia to control this region, and

---

175 Deut 7:1. Tigay, <u>Deuteronomy</u>, 84-85. In other sections of the Bible, the nations were said to number anywhere from six to twelve. Ibid., 84.

176 Deut 7:2. Ibid., 85. The extermination was to mimic the destruction of Sodom and Gomorrah.

177 Deut 7:6. Ibid., 85-86.

178 Anderson, Understanding the Old Testament, 124-125.

179 Ibid., 126. The city of Hazor suffered a series of destructions, culminating in one major catastrophe c. 1275 BCE, when many of its cult statues were deliberately smashed. This may have been the same destruction ascribed to Deborah and Barak in Judges 4:23. Wilson, <u>The Bible Is History</u>, 83.

it is not possible to detail the combatants of each city by extant records. In their zeal to downplay any validity in the biblical story of the Hebrews, many scholars have taken this dearth of evidence to deny that a conquest of the Promised Land ever took place, so much so in fact that Frank Moore Cross, Professor Emeritus of the Harvard Divinity School, snidely remarked that "widespread evidence of destruction in Canaan at the end of the Late Bronze Age and the beginning of the Iron Age" is attributed to the violence of "almost anyone – except Israel."[180] Others, however, take a more cautious view, and include the possibility that some of the destruction could have reflected biblical descriptions. Robert Coote, Senior Research Professor of Hebrew Exegesis and Old Testament at the San Francisco Theological Seminary, for example, notes that while "biblical literature is virtually entirely state literature, and ancient state literature typically conceals as much as it reveals of the real contours of social organization under state sovereignty," it seems reasonable to state "with some assurance that Israel was organized as a tribal alliance," at the time the cities were destroyed.[181]

Despite the academic debate, many biblical scholars still accept the biblical story that the Hebrews crossed the Jordan River and set up a base camp at Gilgal, on the eastern edge of Jericho's territory, as described in the book of *Joshua*, and then attacked and destroyed the city of Jericho after Joshua directed the priests to blow their horns, causing the walls of the city to come tumbling down. This was followed by a number of successful attacks against other cities, until the Hebrews eventually subdued the Canaanites, and turned the territory into a land that was ruled by the Israelite tribes.[182] Thirty-one kings and their armies occupied the land, and Joshua "vanquished them all."[183] W. F. Albright (1891-1971 CE), the former Professor of Semitic Languages at Johns Hopkins University, and his followers have staunchly defended this "Conquest Hypothesis" as the true account of the triumphant passage.[184] Eugene Merrill, Professor of Old Testament Studies at Dallas Theological Seminary, has explained the paucity of archaeologic data supporting this view by pointing out that there were only three cities placed

---

180 Cross, From Epic to Canon: History and Literature in Ancient Israel, 70.

181 Coote, "Social Organization in the Biblical Israels," 37.

182 The Bible did not say for how long these wars continued, although the book of *Joshua* listed thirty-one towns where the cities were overrun and their kings slain. Josh 12:24. The victory was very extensive, with the whole of the region brought under Hebrew control, including the hill country of Judah, the Negeb, the entire land of Goshen, the Shephelah, the Arabah, and the Coastal Plain. Josh 11:16. Many areas remained under Canaanite control, however, including the districts of the Philistines, Geshurites, Gebalites, Sidonians, and Avvim. Josh 13:2-6.

183 Wiesel, Five Biblical Prophets, 20.

184 Stager, "Forging an Identity: The Emergence of Ancient Israel," 130-131; Hess, "Early Israel in Canaan: A Survey of Recent Evidence and Interpretation," 126; Younger, "Early Israel in Recent Biblical Scholarship," 178.

under the directive of *herem*, which demanded that the inhabitants be killed and the city totally destroyed, and so it is very possible that the scarcity of widespread destruction in the archaeologic record of this era is consistent with the biblical account.[185]

Many scholars, however, have found the lack of archaeologic verification too significant to validate the description in the biblical text, and have therefore offered a number of other explanations. One theory is the "Pastoral Nomad Hypothesis," "Immigration Model," or "Peaceful Infiltration Model," first proposed by the German Old Testament scholar Albrecht Alt (1883-1956 CE) in 1925 CE, which claimed that the ancient Israelites peacefully infiltrated the hill country of Canaan, rather than conquering the area militarily, as was suggested by the *Joshua* text.[186] Alt concluded that the hill country of Canaan was sparsely settled, and therefore offered little resistance to the nomadic or semi-nomadic Israelites, who took their flocks from east of the Jordan into the hills west of the river and created settlements where few Canaanites lived. Gradual sedentarization then took place, and the land eventually became dominated by Israelites as their numbers grew to become a majority of the inhabitants. In this way, control over the region did not require devastation of city walls, and archaeologic sites would not be expected to show any changes.

This type of political evolution was common in Palestine at that time, and city-states often were expanded by agriculturists who concentrated their grazing land around fortified cities in order to provide protection against an invasion by outside forces. As their various habitations were secured, the twelve Hebrew tribes then formed a political league with the worship of YHWH at its core. Alt's pupil, Martin Noth, found support for this view in the lack of evidence for warfare in the archaeologic remains at Jericho and Ai, cities which were said to be destroyed by the *Joshua* text.[187] Military confrontation, and subsequent territorial expansion, did eventually take place under Alt's proposal, but not until late in the period of Judges and United Monarchy, near the end of the eleventh century BCE. This would explain why the archaeologic data is not consistent with an immediate destruction following the crossing of the Jordan River under the leadership of Joshua in the thirteenth century BCE.

There are problems with this assesment, however, the primary one of which is that many scholars believe that the Hebrews were agriculturalists, accustomed to village life, rather than a roving band of nomads, and that they were therefore more concerned with their local existence, than with regional aggrandizement.[188]

---

185 Merrill, Kingdom of Priests: A History of Old Testament Israel, 137.

186 Hess, "Early Israel in Canaan: A Survey of Recent Evidence and Interpretation," 126.

187 Callaway, "The Settlement in Canaan, The Period of the Judges," 70.

188 Anderson, Understanding the Old Testament, 126.

To believe that they had the resources, and the desire, to take over the Promised Land, simply because they had become the majority of inhabitants in the region, does not fit with what is generally known about such people. In addition, recent research has downplayed the presence of nomadic peoples in the steppes at that time, making it unlikely that there would have been enough tribes to infiltrate, and then take over, the land of Canaan.[189]

Another concept which allows for more violent confrontations, but not of the type detailed in the book of *Joshua*, is identifying the Hebrews with the Habiru, as discussed in chapter 3. While the nomadic Habiru frequently were in conflict with the ruling princes of the region who were allied with the Egyptians, they were often favored by the authorities who remained in control of various city-states independent of Egypt, and as Egyptian presence became less entrenched throughout the Levant, these self-reliant sovereigns regained control of the land. The Hebrews who were misidentified as Habiru then occupied a number of cities, and eventually extended their control over much of the land. This explanation is known as the "Symbiosis Hypothesis," and William Dever, Professor of Near Eastern Archeology and Anthropology at the University of Arizona in Tucson, has argued that this would explain the archaeologic surveys and excavations from the twelfth century BCE, which shows 300 small, unfortified hilltop villages that were founded *de novo*, rather than built on the remains of destroyed Late Bronze Age Canaanite cities.[190] This theory views the Hebrews following the Exodus as combining both nomadic and agriculturalist traits.

This hypothesis has the same problem as the Pastoral Nomad Hypothesis, however, in that the pastoral component rarely exceeded 10-15% of the total population, and it is difficult to believe that all of the new Iron Age I (1200-1000 BCE) settlements emanated from this single source alone. It must be remembered, however, that the Hebrews populated the more rural area of Canaan, away from the urban centers of population, and so their numbers may therefore have ranged higher than usually estimated by archaeologic remains, especially if they were allied with the Habiru element. In addition, if there was a friendly relationship between the semi-nomadic Hebrew groups and the city populace, it is possible that a more amicable take-over was possible, allowing for a transfer of power over time without destruction of the city walls.

Another related theory envisions a social revolution from within Palestine, as opposed to either an invasion from without or a peaceful infiltration by pastoralists, and is commonly referred to as the "Peasants' Revolt Hypothesis," or "Sociological Model," most prominently advocated by George E. Mendenhall, former Professor of Near Eastern Languages and Literature at the University of Michigan, and Norman K. Gottwald, Professor of Old Testament Emeritus at

---

189 Finkelstein, "When and How Did the Israelites Emerge?" 75.
190 Dever, "Archaeology and the History of Israel," 123.

New York Theological Seminary.[191] According to this hypothesis, the Habiru were not immigrants from outside Palestine, but rather were part of the autochthonous peasant population, who "cut themselves free from their responsibilities towards the community in which they lived and had set up in opposition to the system of government which was established in the country."[192] They allied themselves with a small but vital group of Hebrew slaves who brought with them the myth of deliverance from bondage by the god YWHW, and revolted against the Canaanite aristocracy of the city-states because of excessive taxation which was ordered to pay tribute to the Egyptian Pharaoh. This concept fits well with the description of the Habiru in the Amarna letters and other texts throughout the ancient Near East, and contemporary evidence for this type of activity can be seen in one of Seti I's stelae at Beth-shean, which recorded how he suppressed the rebellion of the governor of Hammath (Tell el-Hammeh in the south of the Beth-shean valley).[193] Once again, if the Hebrews were indeed allied with the Habiru in any of these battles, it is possible that they would not have been mentioned by name, but only have been included under the general rubric of Shasu or Habiru. Such anonymity, however, would require that the size of the Exodus be much smaller than that listed in most modern translations of the Bible. Gottwald labels this theory as the "Revolt Model," whereby a group of slaves or 'apiru, who were worshipers of the god YHWH, revolted against their overlords and joined forces either with infiltrators from the desert, or indigenous Canaanites who converted to Yahwism.[194]

A variant of this model, recently suggested by Volkmar Fritz, from the German Protestant Institute of Archaeology, is a symbiosis of the other four, and is known as the "Ruralization Hypothesis." Fritz claims that the earliest Israelites lived for a long time alongside the Canaanites, and then emerged out of the Late Bronze Age urban Canaanite society in the late thirteenth century BCE, when the pastoralist sector found it more advantageous to shift toward farming with stock-raising, rather than shepherding.[195] Niels Peter Lemche, Professor at the Institute for Biblical Exegesis at the University of Copenhagen, Denmark, has agreed with this theory, arguing that since there was no archaeologic evidence for the presence of a new people in Canaan in the Late Bronze Age and Iron I Age, the Hebrews did not come from outside Canaan, but instead were derived from

---

191 Callaway, "The Settlement in Canaan, The Period of the Judges," 71. Gottwald differs from Mendenhall by equating the rise of Israel with a political revolution along the lines of Marxist ideology. Younger, "Early Israel in Recent Biblical Scholarship," 181.

192 Weippert, The Settlement of the Israelite Tribes in Palestine, 58-59.

193 Mazar, "The Historical Development," 15.

194 Gottwald, The Tribes of Yahweh: A Sociology of the Religion of Liberated Israel, 1250-1050 BCE, 210-11.

195 Stager, "Forging an Identity: The Emergence of Ancient Israel," 141; Dever, "How to Tell a Canaanite From an Israelite," 30.

the Habiru who were living there at the time. This concept that the Israelites were derived from pastoral Canaanites is known as the "Evolutionary Hypothesis," and its primary appeal is once again to explain how the Israelites could take control of the Promised Land without resorting to a violent incursion.[196]

A final proposal to explain the development of a twelve-tribe confederacy c. 1200 BCE, without postulating an Exodus as described in the Bible, or a Conquest of Canaan by a combined force of Hebrews, is the "Traditio-Historical Model" developed by Martin Noth. This school of thought claims that the twelve tribes did not merge until the end of the Late Bronze Age, brought together by common religious and historical traditions, rather than because they shared a common origin as the children of Jacob. Many of the tribes had settled in Canaan as Amorite immigrants, with only the tribes of Levi and Joseph, and possibly Ephraim and Manasseh, having settled in Egypt.[197] Moses then led at least the tribe of Levi to Sinai, where he had already been introduced to the concept of Yahweh by the Midianite priest Jethro. They later encountered Judah at Kadesh-barnea and converted them to Yahwism, following which the other tribes also eventually converted in their respective Canaanite domains. The different traditions which all of the tribes agreed upon included their inherited rights to rule the land of Canaan, a miraculous deliverance conceived to take place at Sinai, a manifestation of God in covenant, a wilderness wandering, and a conquest or inheritance of the land.[198] I mention this theory for the sake of completeness, but since I have already declared that I believe an Exodus from Egypt by the twelve tribes of Israel did indeed take place, I will not spend further time arguing the pros and cons of this construct.

While it is not yet possible to prove which of these theories is a more accurate representation of how the Hebrews conquered the Promised Land, I believe that the data at the present time does support a relationship between the Hebrews who took part in the Exodus, and the Habiru who are mentioned in surviving texts from multiple contemporary societies. The exact mechanism by which the Conquest took place is not pertinent to my theory, since I am concerned with Hebrews who left the Exodus before passage into the Promised Land, but the method does have some relationship to the chronology, and so I will discuss this aspect again in the next chapter.

D. Discussion

The story of the Exodus from Egypt is an incredible saga, filled with miracles and wonderment of the power of YHWH to guide His Chosen People into

---

196 Hoffmeier, Israel in Egypt, The Evidence for the Authenticity of the Exodus Tradition, 26-27.

197 Merrill, Kingdom of Priests: A History of Old Testament Israel, 139-141.

198 Ibid., 142-143.

their favored status as rulers of the Promised Land. It embodies more than an explanation of how the Hebrew people were saved from enslavement in Egypt by God and then led into the land of milk and honey to receive their destiny as the Chosen People, however, as it also represents an important stage in the evolution of the Jewish faith from a typical Semitic polytheistic way-of-life during the era of the Patriarchs, into a monotheistic religion, which set the Jews apart for centuries to come. The Patriarchs may have been the genetic progenitors of modern-day adherents to the Jewish faith, but they did not live their lives according to the tenets later demanded by the Mosaic Code. Following the passage into the Promised Land, many generations of Hebrew descendants would also stray from the path demanded by the Mosaic Law, and the die was not firmly cast until the return of the Jews to Jerusalem from the Babylonian Exile in 538 BCE.

Monotheism has become the characteristic trait of almost every Western religious faith today, while the worship of multiple gods has been relegated to the historical record of ancient, pagan beliefs. This theologic transformation was not an easy path, however, and the Exodus story graphically described the toll it took on the disparate group of Hebrews that followed Moses out of Egypt and into the Sinai wilderness. If one looks only at the storyline set forth in the biblical text, it appears that most of the danger to Hebrew existence after the Exodus from Egypt came from Canaanite kings who resisted the infusion of Hebrews into their realm. This is not the case, however, for internal dissension created by the changes of the Mosaic Law killed more Hebrews than any foreign enemy. Philosophical differences between the Hebrew participants who wanted to remain loyal to their ancestors and Moses erupted into a full-blown civil war which resulted in the deaths of over 40,000 dissenters. I believe those resisters who survived the parricidal punishments fled the Exodus and traveled to Mycenae, where they could practice their religion freely, in a manner which they believed was faithful to the teachings of their ancestors.

Chapter 6
EXODUS: THE DATE

alculating the precise date of the Exodus of the Hebrews from Egypt has proven to be a very popular subject over the ages, with estimations spanning centuries of time, generally falling between the sixteenth and thirteenth centuries BCE. Ancient scholars were quite dogmatic in their conclusions, despite the fact that their proposals were based entirely on oral traditions, yet many of their claims fell remarkably close to modern estimations, suggesting the possibility that they may have had access to documentary sources which have not survived the ravages of time. The oldest complete extant Jewish chronicle which contained an opinion on when the event occurred is the Seder Olam Rabbah, or "Book of the Order of the World," attributed to Rabbi Yose ben Halafta (c. 150 CE), which announced that the flight from Egypt occurred 2448 years after the birth of Adam (AAd) and 792 years after the Great Flood, a date that would be equivalent to 1312 BCE.[1] Demetrius (350-280 BCE), the Hellenistic Jewish chronographer and pupil of Theophrastus (372-287 BCE), calculated a date of 3839 AAd, or 1468 BCE, placing the birth of Abraham 1948 years later than that found in the Hebrew text,[2] and Josephus, the first century CE Jewish historian, maintained in Against Apion that Phoenician records indicated the Exodus took place 612 years before Solomon built the First Temple, making the date 1582 BCE.[3]

---

1 Finegan, Handbook of Biblical Chronology, 110-111. Many ancient scholars timed the Exodus to the birth of Adam, a chronology designated as *annus Adami*, or AAd. Under this timeline, Adam died in 1 AAd, Noah was born in 1056 AAd, and died in 2006 AAd, and the Great Flood took place from 1656-1657 AAd, which is equivalent to 2319 BCE. Ibid., 109-110. The *Book of Jubilees* claims the Exodus happened 2,410 years after the creation of the world, while Josephus says 4,053 years. Meyers, "Biblical Archaeology: The Date of the Exodus According to Ancient Writers," 5. Other Hebrew authors estimated the time from Adam to the Flood was 2,242 years. Manetho, 7.

2 Finegan, Handbook of Biblical Chronology, 142, 145. The Hebrew Bible calculated the interval from Adam to Abraham as 1,948 years but the Septuagint determined it to be 3,314 years. Sterling, "The Jewish Appropriation of Hellenistic Historiography," 235. Others have determined that Abraham was born 2,008 years after Adam, and that by using the chronologies in the Bible of various events, and knowing that the Kingdom of Judah fell to Babylon in 586 BCE, the date of Creation was then determined to be 4004 BCE. Jones, The Chronology of the Old Testament, xiii.

3 Josephus, "Against Apion," Complete Works of Josephus, II.2, 623. It is generally agreed that King Solomon came to the throne c. 970 BCE, and the foundation of the First Temple was laid around 966 BCE. In *Antiquities of the Jews*, Josephus modified

The Samaritans count the calendar years differently from the Hebrew sources, and date the Exodus to 1682 BCE.[4]

Dating the Exodus was also popular among a wide spectrum of ancient historians. Hecataeus of Abdera (fourth century BCE), a Greek historian and Sceptic philosopher who rose to fame under Alexander the Great (356-323 BCE), and was in the service of Ptolemy I Soter (305-283 BCE), added specific reasoning for his opinion, placing the Exodus during the time of Danaus, in the fifteenth century BCE.

In his panegyrical ethnography of Egypt, *Aegyptiaca* (*On the Egyptians*), Hecataeus described how a pestilence swept the land in ancient Egypt, which the people ascribed to the workings of gods angered by the presence of foreigners in the country.[5] To resolve their troubles, the Egyptians ousted the aliens, including Danaus, Cadmus, and a colony headed by Moses. Danaus and Cadmus migrated to Greece, and the greater number, led by Moses, were driven into the land of Judea, where Moses founded the city of Jerusalem and divided the Jews into twelve tribes.[6] This explanation deserves closer scrutiny because it takes into account legendary sources which tie the Exodus closely to the foundation of Greek civilization. Danaus is generally dated to 1480 BCE, around the time of the great Grecian Flood, and Cadmus to 1400 BCE, along with the foundation of

this figure somewhat, claiming that there was 592 years from the Exodus until the First Temple construction was started, rather than 612 years. Josephus, "Antiquities of the Jews," The Complete Works of Josephus, VIII.III.1, 174. He claims that the accuracy of his account is attested to by Dius in his *History of the Phoenicians*, and by Menander the Ephesian. Josephus, "Against Apion," The Complete Works of Josephus, I.17-18, 612.

4 Luban, The Exodus Chronicles: Beliefs, Legends & Rumors from Antiquity Regarding the Exodus of the Jews from Egypt, 56.

5 Hecataeus, according to Josephus, had also written a treatise called *On the Jews*, which has not survived. Bar-Kochva, Pseudo-Hecataeus, "On the Jews": Legitimizing the Jewish Diaspora, 1. Many scholars have theorized that the work was a forgery, however, and written instead by a man labeled Pseudo-Hecataeus, a Jewish author who lived at the turn of the first century CE. Ibid., 122, 139, 145. Hecataeus was the first Greek to discuss the origin of the Jews, while Theophrastus, the disciple of Aristotle, is generally credited as being the first Greek author to mention the Jews. Stern, Greek and Latin Authors on Jews and Judaism, 20. These authors lived during the Hellenistic Age (323-100 BCE), when the Old Testament was translated into the Greek Septuagint, thereby making the biblical history available to non-Jewish scholars for the first time.

6 Hecataeus of Abdera, 1-3, as cited in Stern, Greek and Latin Authors on Jews and Judaism, 28-28. Hecataeus ascribed the conquest of the territories of the Promised Land to the leadership of Moses after he had founded the city of Jerusalem, rather than to the standard biblical account, which put Joshua in command. Ibid., 32. Josephus believed in a variant of these histories, claiming that the Hyksos built the city of Jerusalem with 240,000 people after their expulsion from Egypt. Josephus, "Against Apion," Complete Works of Josephus, I.14, 611.

Thebes, which preceded the founding of Mycenae by 50-100 years.[7] The Parian Chronicle, and other ancient chronologers, placed both Danaus and Cadmus somewhat later, c. 1516-1519 BCE.[8] This assessment that the Hebrew Exodus was allied with the flight of Danaus was followed by a number of other ancient historians, and I will discuss how this proposal fits in with a possible relationship between Danaus and the Hebrew tribe of Dan in the next chapter, but it should be noted that Afrocentrists have claimed that Danaus, Aegyptus (Mestraim), Cecrops, and Erechtheus were all black Egyptians, and along with Cadmus, a "Negroid" from Canaan, they accounted for the development of Greek culture.[9] I will not attempt to argue for or against a particular racial make-up for these legendary heroes, but will mention the mythological evidence, along with that available from archaeologic sources, in order to account for all arguments that have been put forth by those attempting to analyze the evolution of the Classical Greeks.

Today, debate over when the Exodus took place remains a hotly contested issue because there are no extra-biblical historical records which refer to the event, or even to the presence of an Hebrew enclave in Canaan during any period of time before the Merneptah Stele (c. 1208 BCE). This means that biblical references alone must be relied upon to formulate a chronology, and because there is inconsistency in the intervals of time which the biblical compilers used to describe the sequence of events, scholars must search for ways to explain the discrepancies, and collate the material into a unified whole. In this chapter, I will summarize the arguments which have been presented to place the Exodus in each commonly proposed era, and then discuss why I believe the Exodus most likely took place during the fifteenth century BCE.

A. Sixteenth Century BCE

The earliest date suggested by modern scholars for the Exodus is the sixteenth century BCE, when Ahmose I (1539-1514 BCE) defeated the Hyksos and

---

7 "Mythical Chronology," 3. Greek mythology claimed that Cadmus, the son of the Phoenician King Agenor and brother of Europa, was sent in search of his sister after her abduction by Zeus, and found a grove protected by a fearful dragon. Cadmus killed the beast and sowed its teeth, from which a crop of armed men grew. He built a city on the site and called it Thebes. Schwab, Gods & Heroes: Myths & Epics of Ancient Greece, 57-59.

8 Robertson, The Parian Chronicle: Or the Chronicle of the Arundelian Marbles; With a Dissertation Concerning Its Authenticity, 25. The Parian Chronicle is an engraved marble slab, of unknown origin, found on the island of Paros, and thought to have been written c 264 BCE. It details the chronology of Greece for 1318 years, from the reign of Cecrops 1582 BCE, to the archonship of Diogenus 264 BCE. Ibid., 43-44. Its authenticity is often doubted because it is not mentioned by any writer of antiquity.

9 Diop, Civilization or Barbarism: An Authentic Anthropology, 92.

forcibly evicted them from Egypt, initiating the Eighteenth Dynasty. Ancient authors, such as Africanus (c. 180-250 CE), Diodorus of Sicily (first century BCE), Herodotus (c. 490-420 BCE), Manetho (third century BCE), and all of the early Church Fathers, except Eusebius, agreed with this timeline, identifying the Hebrews as being part of the Hyksos multitude which left Egypt en-masse after being expelled by Ahmose I.[10] Such a conclusion makes sense from a practical standpoint, for when the Hyksos fled Egypt they were a large band of Asiatics whose flight into Palestine closely resembled the path taken by the Hebrew Exodus. If the Hebrews were indeed part of the Hyksos multitude, it would help explain why the Exodus was not specifically mentioned in contemporary chronicles, since the expulsion of the Hyksos would have taken precedence over the loss of Semitic slaves who simply followed the Hyksos out of town.

Although the biblical compilers chose to represent the event as the culmination of YHWH's desire to allow His Chosen People to finally cross over the Jordan River into the Promised Land, Late Bronze Age historians would have logically seen the role of the Hebrews as nothing more an escape from investiture when the borders of Egypt were opened by the fleeing Hyksos militia. Donald Redford, Professor of Classics and Ancient Mediterranean Studies at Pennsylvania State University, has supported this view, pointing out that although the historicity of the Bible is generally unreliable, "no one can deny that the tradition of Israel's coming out of Egypt was one of long standing."[11] The only chain of historical facts that could fit the basis for the longevity of this tradition, according to Redford, is the Hyksos descent and occupation of Egypt.

Archaeologic remains are also consistent with an Exodus in this era, as evidenced by destruction of a number of important cities which are mentioned in the Bible as having been attacked during the Conquest of the Promised Land, including Jericho, Gibeon, Hebron, Hormah/Zephath, Ai, Arad, Debir, Lachish, Hazor, and Bethel.[12] While there is no proof that any of these sites were actually demolished by the Hebrews, if you believe that the Conquest was a violent affair, rather than a peaceful infiltration of Hebrews into a position of power, as discussed in chapter 5, then the sixteenth century BCE is an acceptable time frame for the Exodus to have taken place.

Although this argument is very appealing because of the ability to explain the lack of direct extra-biblical evidence for the Exodus, it places hardship on attempts to correlate other aspects of the timeline of Hebrew evolution which are mentioned in the biblical text. The primary problem with a sixteenth century BCE Exodus date is the declaration in the book of *1 Kings* that there were 480 years

---

10 Meyers, "Biblical Archaeology: The Date of the Exodus According to Ancient Writers," 14.

11 Redford, Egypt, Canaan, and Israel in Ancient Times, 412.

12 Setterfield, "Creation and Catastrophe Chronology," 4-5.

between the Exodus and the founding of Solomon's Temple, a fact which would date the event to c. 1446 BCE, in the fifteenth century BCE, rather than in the sixteenth century BCE, since the First Temple is generally dated to c. 966 BCE.[13] A number of attempts have been made to alleviate this dilemma by claiming that the biblical compilers did not intend the 480 year figure to be a rigidly defined interval, but rather a total which could be modified by alternate interpretation of other biblical sections. While most of these reassessments have been directed at arguing for a thirteenth century BCE Exodus date, as will be discussed later in this chapter, some non-academic commentators have used a similar analysis to extend the 480 year interval even further. Kenneth Doig, a retired purchasing agent with an interest in biblical chronology, has argued that the 480 year total was not meant to include the 105 years when God departed from the Tabernacle during the time of the servitude, thereby making the true sum 585 years, allowing the Exodus to have taken place c. 1552 BCE, in the sixteenth century BCE.[14] Doig based his conclusion on Psalm 78, which told how God was so angered by the impiety of the Hebrews when they reverted to idol worship, that He abandoned the dwelling place at Shiloh, and did not support the Hebrews in their quest for permanent control of the Promised Land.[15] Other amateur biblicists, like the Australian astronomer Barry Setterfield, have used a similar reasoning to modify the *1 Kings* reference, although there is slight variation in the number of years missing from the biblical account in each of their propositions.[16]

Another way to bypass the 480 year limitation, without assuming hidden biblical intentions, is to individually add up the length of time each Judge ruled in the biblical text, coming up with a sum of 553-596 years, rather than 480 years, depending upon how each biblical passage is interpreted.[17] This method directly argues that the 480 year total was not intended to be a factual period of time, but rather a generalization for approximation purposes only. The New Testament supports this modification, for Paul told the people of Antioch that after Israel defeated the land of Canaan, the Judges ruled for about 450 years. When the forty year reign of King Saul, and the forty year reign of King David, is added to this figure, the total is 530 years, rather than 480 years, and the Exodus would

---

13 1 Kgs 6:1. The 480 year figure mentioned in *I Kings* is validated by adding the first four years of Solomon's rule, the forty-two regnal years of King Saul and King David, the 136 years from Tola to Eli, the 200 years of peace under the savior judges, the fifty-three years of oppression after the death of Joshua, and the forty-five years implied in *Joshua* 14:1, where the conquered lands of Canaan were allotted to the remaining tribes of Israel. Judges, The Anchor Bible, 23.

14 The total of 105 years came from references in the book of *Judges*, including Judg 3:8, 14; 4:2-3; 6:1; 10:8; and 13:1. Doig, "The 1552 Exodus," 4.

15 Ps 78:58-61.

16 Setterfield, "Creation and Catastrophe Chronology," 3.

17 de la Torre, "Dating the Exodus, The Hyksos Expulsion of 1540-1530 BCE?" 3-5.

once again fall in the sixteenth century BCE.[18] Josephus also may have followed this interpretation when he said that the Exodus occurred 592 years before the Temple of Solomon was built, placing the event about 1552 BCE.[19]

Even if one accepts that the 480 year reference is not reliable, and concludes that an extra century of time should be added to the total, however, there are other reasons for not accepting an Exodus during the sixteenth century BCE. The first of these problems is that there is strong support for placing Joseph in Egypt during the rule of the Hyksos, as discussed in chapter 3. Joseph's brothers sold him to Ishmaelite traders for twenty pieces of silver, a price which was the correct average cost in the Middle East for a slave around 1700 BCE, while by the fifteenth century BCE, it had risen to thirty to forty pieces of silver.[20] In addition, it is more likely that his elevation to the position of vizier would have taken place with an Hyksos Semite on the throne of Egypt, rather than a natural-born Egyptian. Since the conventional chronology dates this period to 1648-1550 BCE, there would only be about one hundred years between the era of Joseph and Moses, not enough time to allow for the growth of the Hebrew population from the seventy people who entered Egypt with Jacob to the numbers associated with the Exodus.[21]

The second problem is that according to the Priestly Chronology, there were four generations from the time of Levi, who was a son of Jacob, to the life of Moses.[22] If Moses returned to Egypt to lead the Exodus when he was eighty years old, then five generations of time would have passed, as Moses had sired one or two sons by that time, adding one more generation to the four previously mentioned. Even if Joseph entered Egypt at the beginning of the Hyksos invasion, this would leave only a twenty-year generation interval, and the most common interval for a generation in the Bible is forty years, as reflected in the fact that it took forty

---

18 Acts 13:20-21. There is some dispute among scholars as to whether Paul said that the 450 years elapsed from the Egyptian oppression to the deliverance of the Promised Land to Israel, or whether it ran from the time of the Conquest to the days of Samuel. Ibid., 13.

19 Josephus, "Antiquities of the Jews," The Complete Works of Josephus, 8.3.1, 174.

20 Gen 37:26-28. Finegan, Handbook of Biblical Chronology, 220.

21 The Book of Sothis, purported to have been written by Manetho but uniformly believed to have been written by someone else referred to as pseudo-Manetho, claimed that Joseph arrived in Egypt and became vizier under Apophis, the last king of the fifteenth Dynasty. Luban, The Exodus Chronicles: Beliefs, Legends & Rumors from Antiquity Regarding the Exodus of the Jews from Egypt, 124. Ahmed Osman has identified Joseph with Yuya, the father of Queen Tiye, and explains the fact that although the number of Jacob's family to travel to Egypt is listed as seventy, only sixty-nine are named, with the unnamed person being Tiye, who was Joseph's daughter. Osman, Moses and Akhenaten: The Secret History of Egypt at the Time of the Exodus, 54.

22 Exod 6:16-20.

years for a generation to die off during the Exodus.[23] To now apply a twenty-year generation interval would be a departure from standard biblical exegesis, although we will see that proponents of a thirteenth century BCE Exodus date often reduce the 480 year figure of *1 Kings* by arguing for a more reasonable generation interval of twenty-five years.[24]

A final problem with an Exodus in the sixteenth century BCE is that there is good reason to identify Ahmose I, who ruled either from 1539-1514 BCE in the conventional chronology, or 1570-1546 BCE according to many Egyptologists, as the Pharaoh "who did not know Joseph," or at least one of the Pharaohs who followed shortly thereafter. If Joseph was vizier during the rule of the Hyksos, as many scholars believe, the Egyptians would have had good reason to include his Hebraic ancestors as being responsible for the earlier overthrow of their country, and therefore sought retribution to avenge the magnitude of their dishonor. The order of the Pharaoh "who did not know Joseph" to kill all newborn Hebrew males would then have been part of this vengeful process, and since Ahmose I sat on the throne during the eviction of the Hyksos, he seems to be the most likely candidate for this biblical description. If the Exodus took place in the sixteenth century BCE, however, Ahmose I would have been the Pharaoh of the Exodus, rather then the Pharaoh "who did not know Joseph," leaving one of the Hyksos kings as the man who attempted to prevent the birth of Moses eighty years earlier. It is difficult to explain why a Semitic Hyksos ruler would have wanted to so decimate the reproduction of male Semitic slaves. I agree with the arguments of the nay-sayers in this regard, and therefore do not accept that the Exodus took place in the sixteenth century BCE.

B. Fifteenth Century BCE

The two most favored dates for the Exodus are 1446 BCE, the so-called Early Date of the fifteenth century BCE, and 1290 BCE, the Late Date of the thirteenth century BCE. Those who favor the Exodus taking place during the Early Date generally rely on the reference in the book of *I Kings* which states that the Exodus took place 480 years before King Solomon began to build his temple

---

23 Num 32:13; Ps 95:10. In addition, the life of Moses was divided into forty year increments, and when God was angered by the wickedness of Man before deciding to send a Flood to destroy all of those remaining except for the righteous Noah, he shortened the life of men to one hundred and twenty years, a figure which clearly represents three conventional generations of forty years each. Gen 6:3.

24 Biblical historicity aside, many modern scholars believe that a twenty, or twenty-five, year generation interval is more reasonable than a forty year interval. Kaiser, "Exodus," 290. The fact that it took forty years of wandering in the desert for the adult generation of Hebrews to die out is more reflective of the time from manhood to death, than it is from birth to birth. Rohl, Pharaohs and Kings, A Biblical Quest, 117.

in the fourth year of his reign, which is generally taken to be 966 BCE.[25] If that date is accurate, then simple addition would place the date of the Exodus in 1446 BCE, during the reign of Thutmose III (1479-1425 BCE), according to the conventional chronology, or Amenhotep II, under other popular chronologies. This timing is very attractive, for it would identify Ahmose I as the Pharaoh "who did not know Joseph," as just discussed, thereby providing an adequate explanation for why the newborn Hebrew male children were to be killed as part of the retaliation against the hated Hyksos regime, and it would leave enough time for four or five generations to pass before the Hebrews left Egypt, approximating the forty-year generation interval found elsewhere in the Bible. It would seem to not leave enough time for the number of Hebrews to reach the census totals listed in the Torah, however, although, as discussed in Chapter 4, this large number is subject to modification by the interpretation of the word *elef.* The interval would be adequate to approximate the more moderate estimations of the total number of participants in the Exodus, in my opinion, especially when the amount includes the non-Hebrews who were said to join the migration following the death of first-born Egyptians in the last Plague.

An Exodus in the fifteenth century BCE is also appealing because it would provide an explanation as to why the event was ignored by contemporary chroniclers, since the Conquest of the Promised Land would have taken place in the Amarna Age, when conditions in Egypt were in disarray because of the isolationism imposed by Amenhotep IV (1352-1336 BCE). The movements of the Hebrews throughout Canaan would have been much easier during this era, for Amenhotep IV ignored the region during the time he sat on the throne of Egypt, resulting in a reduction of the number of Egyptian military maneuvers. The Hebrews could have been seen as another group of Habiru, who local Palestinian kings said were creating problems in the area, as discussed in chapter 3. This would answer why there was no extra-biblical reference to the presence of the Hebrews, since there is little reason to believe they would have been identified as a separate group within the Habiru category. It also would account for the lack of letters from Jericho, Gibeon, Bethel, and Hebron to the Egyptian Pharaoh, for these cities would have been captured by the Hebrews, while letters from Jerusalem, Megiddo, Ashkelon, Gezer, and Acco continued to appear, due to the fact that these cities remained in Canaanite hands.[26] Finally, archaeologic evidence of widespread demolition of cities including Jericho, Debir, Lachish, Hebron, Bethel, Gibeon, Arad and Hazor are found during this period of time, consistent with a violent Conquest as outlined in the books of *Joshua* and *Judges.* Some commentators have even conjectured that the name "Israel" in the Merneptah Stele could refer to the six tribes of Israel who fought against Sisera in the Song of Deborah, one of the

---

25 1 Kgs 6:1.

26 Stiebing, Out of the Desert? Archaeology and the Exodus/Conquest Narratives, 42.

oldest pieces of Hebrew poetry.[27]

Proponents for the Early Date have searched for consistency in other sections of the Bible to buttress the claim that the biblical compilers intended the 480 year period of time figure to be taken literally, and not just a rough estimate. The section which is most often cited in this respect is in the book of *Judges,* where Jephthah, one of the last biblical Judges before the coronation of king Saul, was said to have told the king of Ammon that the Israelites controlled the area east of the Jordan near the Arnon River for 300 years.[28] Since Jephthah is generally dated to around 1100 BCE, the 300 year span would place the Hebrews in Canaan c. 1400 BCE, and by then adding thirty-eight years to cover the amount of time the Exodus took for the Hebrews to reach Heshbon, where the 300 year period began, the Exodus would have taken place c. 1438 BCE, very close to the 1446 BCE date calculated from the book of *1 Kings.*[29] Those who oppose the fifteenth century BCE Exodus date have denigrated the importance of this passage by arguing that Jephthah was not portrayed in the Bible as having access to historical records which would detail how long the Hebrews had controlled the region, and his 300 year statement was simply intended as a rough estimate of time, rather than an exact determination, even more unreliable than the 480 year period itself.[30]

Ancillary support for the Early Date has been put forth by a group of scholars who argue that the Ten Plagues which Moses wrought upon the Egyptians when they refused to free the Hebrews from bondage are best explained by natural disasters which are known to have taken place in the fifteenth century BCE. The devastations which appeared throughout Egypt were destructive enough to convince the Pharaoh that the God of Moses was too Almighty to refuse Moses' request to "let my people go," and he eventually broke down and allowed the Hebrews to leave. One of the more popular theories is that the volcanic eruption at Thera (Santorini), one of the biggest volcanic eruptions on earth in the last few thousand years, led to atmospheric changes which caused a tidal wave that devastated the Minoan civilization on Crete, and also eventually led to the ruination of the ten plagues.[31] The event was dated by Hans Goedicke, the former Chairman of the Department of Near Eastern Studies at Johns Hopkins

---

27 Lipinski, <u>On the Skirts of Canaan in the Iron Age: Historical and Topographical Research,</u> 62. Deborah and Barak were said to have led a force of soldiers who had been living as peasants from Ephraim, Benjamin, Machir, Issachar, Zebulun, and Naphtali. Judg 5:11-18.

28 Judg 11:26.

29 In addition, if you add the one hundred and forty-four years the Judges and Kings ruled, from Jephthah to the fourth year of Solomon, the total comes to 484 years, a figure which is remarkably close to the 480 years mentioned in *1 Kings.* Davis, <u>Moses and the Gods of Egypt,</u> 30.

30 Bratcher, "The Date of the Exodus: The Historical Study of Scripture," 6.

31 Finegan, Handbook of Biblical Chronology, 230.

University, to 1475 BCE, and a number of biblical scholars used this identity to then date the Exodus to the years following this event, placing the migration in the fifteenth century BCE.[32] Recent research, however, has questioned the reliability of this date as sea cores from Crete and the eastern Mediterranean have shown that it is extremely unlikely that Thera's eruption could have effected Egypt the way the proponents of this theory believe.[33] In addition, radiocarbon dating indicates that the eruption more likely occurred between 1650-1600 BCE, probably c. 1628 BCE, adding more uncertainty to the conclusion, but there is continued debate on how accurate these measurements are, and whether they are reliable enough to discount the archaeologic evidence which favored the fifteenth century timeline.[34]

Under currently accepted ancient Near-East chronologies, if the Exodus did indeed take place in the fifteenth century BCE, then Ahmose I (1539-1514 BCE) was likely the Pharaoh "who did not know Joseph," and the Pharaoh who sat on the throne of Egypt when Moses returned from his self-induced exile was either Hatshepsut (1473-1458 BCE), Thutmose III (1479-1425 BCE), or Amenhotep II (1427-1392 BCE), since their reigns most closely approximate the eighty years which would have passed before Moses returned to lead the Exodus from Egypt. Hans Goedicke, head of the Department of Near Eastern Studies at Johns Hopkins University, has argued that Hatshepsut was likely the Pharaoh of the Exodus, because inscriptions from the Speos Artemidos, a temple built by Hatshepsut during the time of her reign, indicates that she was angry over a group of Asiatics who lived in the Delta, and that these residents were probably the Hebrew slaves.[35] Most scholars, however, find this evidence meager, given the fact that she utilized Semitic workers and sailors on her ships, and would not have therefore likely singled out the Hebrews in this manner, and favor either Thutmose III or Amenhotep II as the Pharaoh of the Exodus, both of whom had tomb paintings showing major building projects which utilized Semitic slaves, providing pictorial evidence of the type of labor which the Bible mentioned as becoming intolerable to the Hebrews.[36] Thutmose III is particularly favored in this regard because he had a palace at Memphis, placing him closer to Goshen than the palace at Thebes where most of the other Eighteenth Dynasty Pharaohs were located. Since Moses had to make multiple trips to plead with the Pharaoh

---

32 Stiebing, Out of the Desert? Archaeology and the Exodus/Conquest Narratives, 44, 102.

33 Ibid., 44.

34 "Santorini," 1.

35 Stiebing, Out of the Desert? Archaeology and the Exodus/Conquest Narratives, 43-44. The Semites in the text are called "Aamu," and their leader is "Abisha." Luban, The Exodus Chronicles: Beliefs, Legends & Rumors from Antiquity Regarding the Exodus of the Jews from Egypt, 30.

36 Bimson, Redating the Exodus and Conquest, 249.

"to let my people go" during the time of the Ten Plagues, it would have been much easier to travel from Goshen to Memphis, than it would have been to Thebes.

Timing the Exodus to the reign of Thutmose III would also be consistent with the writings of Manetho, who named Misphragmuthosis as the Pharaoh of the Exodus, an Egyptian whose Greek name was Menkheperre-Thutmose III.[37] Although Manetho said that the Exodus occurred under Pharaoh Amenhotep in another section of his *Aegyptiaca*, Thutmose III's son, Amenhotep II, sat in co-regency at the end of his reign, providing an explanation for the variation in terminology in the two sections of Manetho's work.[38] Placing the Exodus during the reign of Thutmose III would nicely fit the birth of Moses eighty years earlier, during the reign of Ahmose I, and would mean that the Pharaoh from whom Moses fled at age forty years would likely have been Amenhotep I (1514-1493 BCE) or Thutmose II (1493-1479 BCE), a course which could then identify Hatshepsut as the daughter of the Pharaoh who rescued Moses from the Nile River, even though she was actually the Pharaoh's wife. Although Hatshepsut is known to have had two daughters, Neferura and Merira-Hatshepset, she never gave birth to a son, and since the Egyptian crown was generally passed to a male, this could very well explain why she was anxious to adopt a newborn boy as her own, and why Moses received preferential treatment at the royal court, despite the fact that he was of Semitic origin.

Not only does this chronology conveniently match biblical and accepted Egyptian historical data, it would also explain why the dissident Hebrews decided to migrate to Mycenae, for through his successful international programs, Thutmose III was able to make many contacts with the Aegean world, receiving a plethora of gifts, including gold and silver vessels in the Mycenaean style.

Mycenaean settlements were established in Rhodes and Cyprus during this time, and the Hebrews would have been able to easily make contact with their representatives in Ugarit. While the Mycenaeans would not have likely risked Egyptian anger at receiving Hebrews who were sympathetic to Moses, a man who would have been high on the Egyptian hit-list, a contingent of Hebrews so opposed to the Exodus that they fled the parricidal reprisals would have been welcomed, and even remunerated for the information they could provide about the one man who was ultimately responsible for the devastation in Egypt. This would place the Hebrews in Mycenae at the beginning of the palace-oriented period, an era which has revealed evidence of significant Egyptian influence, including the use of gold masks for burial, monuments of carved stone on the graves, metal-inlay techniques, and the placement of extremely large stones in the palace walls. Who else but the laborers responsible for the construction of these

---

37 "The True Date of the Exodus," 14-15. Africanus called him King Amosis. Ibid., 15.

38 Ibid., 14-15.

edifices could helped the Mycenaeans complete the construction of their city with such precision?

Some scholars have argued that Thutmose III could not be the Pharaoh of the Exodus because he was so powerful and active throughout the ancient Near East that the Exodus could not have succeeded while he sat on the throne. This premise is flawed, however, for in many ways his exploits makes success more likely, since the bulk of the Egyptian army would have been busy on maneuvers along the *Via Maris*, where most of the prosperous cities were located. This left the central and southern regions of Palestine, where the Hebrews fled and wandered for the ensuing forty years, relatively free from strict Egyptian control. In addition, if the Exodus from Egypt occurred while Thutmose III was on a military maneuver deep in the Levant, the defensive force left at home may not have been large enough to offer much resistance to the Exodus. His topographical list of victories mentions 119 towns in Palestine and southern Syria which were conquered, and this meant that a large percentage of the Egyptian fighting force would have been away from home for prolonged periods of time.

Despite all of these supporting arguments for an Early Date Exodus, the majority of scholars today have concluded that "there could not have been a mass exodus from Egypt followed by a dramatic conquest of Canaan in the fifteenth and fourteenth centuries B.C."[39] Part of the reasoning for this conclusion is that archaeologic remains do not show occupation at Ramesses, the store-city which the Bible tells the Hebrews built before the Exodus, during part of the sixteenth century and all of the fifteenth century BCE. There are also very few sites mentioned in the Conquest narratives which indicate occupation at that time as well, including the cities of Kadesh-barnea, Heshbon, Jericho, Ai, Gibeon, Hazor and Dan.[40] As discussed in chapter 3, however, there is active debate about the nature of the Conquest, and how much damage might have been expected, since it is quite possible that the Hebrews gained control by a gradual infiltration, rather than by a military invasion. The cities which were occupied may have sustained little damage by this process, although some sites may have been destroyed by forces other than the Israelites. In addition, if the Hebrews were involved in the construction of the store cities of Ramesses and Pithom, it is not necessary that the cities would have been completed by the time the Exodus began, but only that the work had begun at some earlier date, under Pharaohs who ruled before Ramesses II. The Bible makes it clear that the city, or at least an area associated

---

39 Propp, "Jewish Origins," 8.

40 Stiebing, <u>Out of the Desert? Archaeology and the Exodus/Conquest Narratives</u>, 94. If Heshbon is identified with Tell Hesban, there are no remains prior to Iron Age I, but if the site is rather Tell Jalul, or Tell el-Umeiri, there is evidence of Middle and Late Bronze Age occupation. Chavalas & Adamthwaite, "Archaeologic Light on the Old Testament," 83. This emphasizes the uncertainty in relying on archaeologic evidence when attempting to prove the chronology of ancient events.

with the site where the city was eventually built, existed much earlier, for when Joseph assigned land to his brethren to live in Egypt, he assigned them "the best of the land, in the land of Ramesses, as Pharaoh had commanded."[41] This clearly means that the city was in existence during the time Joseph lived, and was not restricted to the thirteenth century BCE, unless it was an anachronistic usage of the name.

More problematic for proponents of this era is the fact that settlements in the highland areas of Canaan were relatively sparse at this time, and did not increase until the Iron Age period (1200-587 BCE), which would favor a thirteenth century BCE Exodus date. Based on this type of data, William Dever concluded that "only a handful of diehard fundamentalists" would favor a fifteenth century BCE date.[42] The territories which were ultimately associated with the tribes of Judah, Benjamin, Ephraim, and Manasseh showed a nearly ninefold increase in the number of settlements, from 36 to 319, during the twelfth century BCE, a population density which had never before been the seen, making the Late Date a much more likely scenario.[43] It is very difficult to identify the remains of nomadic and semi-nomadic tribes, however, and although the Bible tells how the Conquest under Joshua was very successful, it would have been many years before they necessarily built settlements which survived the ravages of time. This negates some of the contrary evidence, although the lack of a significant population density remains a point of contention.

To actively disprove that the Exodus took place in the fifteenth century BCE, critics point to more than a lack of archaeologic confirmation, but extend their criticism to argue that a literal reading of the *I Kings* text is unreliable and not determinative of the Exodus date. This exegesis is generally accomplished by arguing that the total of 480 years is an artificial figure, created during the compilation of the Bible in order to satisfy a schematic, rather than a literal, outline. Many numbers in the Old Testament were used symbolically, rather than for purposes of simple counting, as earlier shown for the span of forty years, which was the time frequently allotted for a generation in biblical times. Under this reasoning, the 480 year figure was simply the addition of the twelve generations of priests that would have existed from the time of Aaron to Azariah of the House of Zado, the first priest to officiate in King Solomon's Temple, and not a literal calculation of the time interval.[44]

This argument is supported by the fact that two other biblical sections, if literally interpreted, are not consistent with the 480 year total. The first section,

41 Gen 47:11. Friedman, <u>Commentary on the Torah</u>, 154.

42 Dever, Who Were the Early Israelites and Where Did They Come From?, 8.

43 Meyers, "Early Israel and the Rise of the Israelite Monarchy," 72.

44 Stiebing, Out of the Desert? Archaeology and the Exodus/Conquest Narratives, 47; Mazar, "The Exodus and the Conquest," 72.

written by the "E" or "J" source in the book of *Genesis*, claimed that Abraham's descendants would be slaves in a foreign land for 400 years, and then return to Canaan after four generations.[45] The location of the enslavement is not detailed, and the start of the 400 year period is not defined in the biblical text, but most scholars take it to begin when Jacob entered Egypt with his family, since it was then that the Hebrew sojourn in Egypt truly began, even though they were not slaves while Joseph was still alive.[46]

Some Rabbinic exegesis has claimed that the 400 years began instead with the birth of Isaac, pointing to the claim of Sarah that Isaac was abused by Ishmael, Abraham's illegitimate Egyptian son, thereby initiating a period of affliction.[47] This interpretation is generally not favored today, however, since nothing in the biblical text supports the oppression of the Hebrews during their stay in Canaan.

If the Hebrews were in Egypt for 400 years, and there were 480 years between the Exodus and the building of the First Temple, then Joseph would have been born c. 1915 BCE and risen to the position of vizier in Egypt before the Hyksos invasion, while Jacob would have entered Egypt c. 1876 BCE. Abraham, under this timeline, would have been born c. 2166 BCE, and arrived in Palestine c. 2091 BCE, before the Amorite Invasion, which is commonly dated to the years following 2000 BCE. All of these dates are unacceptably early to most biblical scholars, who generally synchronize the movements of Abraham to the Amorite Invasion, and the elevation of Joseph to vizier during the rule of the Hyksos, making the Early Date timeline impossible.

Proponents of the Early Date downplay the reliability of this section, pointing out that since there were four generations from Levi to Moses during this period of time, there would have to be a one hundred year generation interval to explain a 400 year separation, and this is not only inconsistent with most biblical sections, which allot a forty year generation interval, but is clearly too long to be taken seriously, even with the long lifespans allotted the Patriarchs in the Bible.[48] They instead conclude that since the starting date for the 400 year period of time is never actually defined, it is too inexact to be seriously used as a reliable chronologic gauge.

Another inconsistency with the *1 Kings* passage is found in the book of *Exodus*, where the "P" source stated that the descendants of Jacob spent 430 years in Egypt, not referencing whether they were slaves or not, and not defining exactly when the 430 year period began.[49] This passage coincides reasonably well with the 400 year

---

45 Gen 15:13, 16. Since it was Levi who came to Egypt, the four generations would be Levi, Kohath, Amram, and Moses. Kaplan, The Living Torah: The Five Books of Moses and the Haftarot, 71.

46 de Vaux, The Early History of Israel, 291.

47 Sarna, Genesis, 116.

48 Exod 6:16-20.

49 Exod 12:40-41. Gal 3:17 also describes the period of time the Hebrews spent in

interval of the book of *Genesis*, but once again is lacking a definite starting date. Even though the passage refers to the descendants of Jacob, rabbinic tradition has understood the 430 year period to actually begin on the day of the covenant with Abraham, despite the fact that Abraham did not reside in Egypt with his family in the biblical text.[50] This interpretation would place the Patriarchs in a more appropriate era, but would still be inconsistent with the interpretation of the *1 Kings* passage, making the Early Date determination wrong.

The Septuagint (LXX), Samaritan, and Syro-Palestinian (SP) translations of the book of *Exodus* passage obviate this confusion by interpreting the sentence to read that the Hebrews dwelt in Egypt *and in the land of Canaan* for 430 years, leaving 215 years for the time dwelt in Egypt, and 215 years in Canaan.[51] This conclusion was reached by combining the begetting ages of Abraham and Isaac, and adding Jacob's age on entering Egypt to give a total of 290 years, and then subtracting Abraham's age of seventy-five years when he left Mesopotamia for Canaan to give an aggregate of 215 years.[52] The result nicely divides the 430 year total into two equal divisions, following a standard biblical practice of using symmetrical patterns to determine time spans during the lives of the Patriarchs.[53] It also allows for the reference of four generations to more closely approximate the 40 year generation interval found elsewhere in the Bible, creating consistency in the interpretation of the various biblical texts.

If the Septuagint interpretation is taken as an appropriate reading, and applied to the literal 480 year interval of *1 Kings*, the Patriarchal chronology fits quite nicely with acceptable timelines, placing Abraham's birth c. 1951 BCE, during the Amorite Invasion; Isaac's birth c. 1852 BCE; Jacob's birth c. 1792 BCE; and Joseph's birth c. 1701 BCE.[54] Joseph would have been sold to Potiphar c. 1684 BCE, and risen to the position of vizier c. 1686 BCE, during the early period

---

Egypt as 430 years.

50 Kaiser, "Exodus," 379.

51 This 215 year period was also followed by the Samaritan Tolidah Chronicle, the Hellenistic Jewish chronographer Demetrius, Ibn Ezra, the renowned twelfth century CE Spanish biblical commentator, and Josephus. Hughes, <u>Secrets of the Times, Myth and History in Biblical Chronology</u>, 35; Sarna, <u>Exodus</u>, 62; Josephus, "Antiquities of the Jews," <u>The Complete Works of Josephus</u>, II.XV.2, 62.

52 Hughes, Secrets of the Times, Myth and History in Biblical Chronology, 33.

53 Symmetry is observed in the fact that Abraham lived seventy-five years in the home of his father, as well as during the life time of his son Isaac; he lived one hundred years in Canaan, and was one hundred years old when Isaac was born; Jacob lived seventeen years with Joseph both in Canaan and in Egypt; and there were ten generations from Adam to Noah, and a similar ten generations from Noah to Abraham. Sarna, <u>Exodus</u>, 62.

54 This would be consistent with the New Testament statement of Paul that God gave the Ten Commandments 430 years after the time of Abraham. Gal 3:17.

of Hyksos rule according to the conventional chronology.[55] The 215 years of sojourn in Canaan would have then taken place from 1877-1662 BCE, and in Egypt from 1662-1447 BCE, placing the birth of Moses c. 1527 BCE, during the rule of Ahmose I, and his flight from Egypt to Midian c. 1487 BCE, during the rule of Thutmose II.[56] Moses would return to lead the Exodus forty years later c. 1437 BCE, in the fifteenth century BCE during the rule of Thutmose III, dates which are all very consistent with the majority opinion of patriarchal historicity, and are the ones which I believe best explain the migration of Hebrew dissidents to Mycenae in an early enough era before the Trojan War for Hebrew tradition to be incorporated into the developing Greek cultural base. While it is clear that biblical exegesis and archaeologic data cannot date the Exodus to any specific period of time, it seems appropriate to consider the Early Date for the Exodus as a reasonable likelihood, if the conventional chronology of Egyptian pharaonic history is accepted.

C. *Fourteenth Century BCE*

A fourteenth century BCE date for the Exodus is supported by only a few biblical scholars, with the calculation usually based on data from the Talmud, which held that the First Temple stood for 410 years, followed by a 70 year Exile, and then the building of the Second Temple, which stood for 420 years.[57] Since the Second Temple was destroyed in 70 CE by the Romans, this means that the First Temple would have been constructed in 830 BCE, about 140 years later than the date that is generally fixed for the rule of King Solomon. If the 480 year period from the book of *1 Kings* is then added to this date, the Exodus would have taken place in 1310 BCE, in the fourteenth century BCE, rather than 1446 BCE, in the fifteenth century BCE.

Most scholars do not accept the reliability of this Talmudic statement, however, and continue to date the construction of the First Temple to 966 BCE, but some support for claiming a fourteenth century BCE Exodus date still exists from the fact that Amenhotep III (1382-1344 BCE) or Amenhotep IV (1352-1336 BCE) would then have been the Pharaoh of the Exodus, thereby allowing for a simultaneous development of Hebrew and Egyptian monotheism. Sigmund

---

55 Klassen, The Chronology of the Bible, 11-14, 17-18.

56 Ibid., 19.

57 Yoma 9a. Adler, "Dating the Exodus: A New Perspective," 51. The Second Temple was built by the Jews who returned from the Babylonian Exile in 538 BCE following a decree from Cyrus the Great of Persia (c. 600-529 BCE), and was completed in 515 BCE. Rabbinic sources date the building to 350 BCE. While a close replica of the First Temple, it lacked the Ark of the Covenant, the Urim and Thummim, the holy oil, the sacred fire, the Ten Commandments, the pot of manna, and Aaron's rod. "Second Temple of Jerusalem," Wikipedia, http://en.wikipedia.org/wiki/Second_Temple_of_Jerusalem, 1-2.

Freud (1856-1939 CE), the founder of the practice of psychoanalysis, was so intrigued with the similarities of Moses and Amenhotep IV that he suggested in his monograph *Moses and Monotheism*, that Moses was actually an Egyptian high official in the regime of Amenhotep IV, rather than a Hebrew, who became enamored with the Aten religion espoused by Amenhotep IV. When Amenhotep IV died, Moses brought the worship of the sun-god to the Hebrew slaves, along with the Egyptian practice of circumcision, and during the forty years of wandering in the wilderness, the worship of Aten was replaced by homage to YHWH, which Moses was introduced to by his father-in-law Jethro.[58] Manetho, the third century BCE Egyptian priest and historian, was the first to suggest that Moses was an Egyptian, and, like Freud, also considered that he lived during the reign of Amenhotep III.[59]

While few biblical scholars support this heretical view of Moses' heritage, the reign of Amenhotep III could easily be seen as consistent with the biblical tale of heightened labor placed upon the Hebrew slaves during the rule of the Pharaoh "who did not know Joseph," since he undertook a program of self-glorification that was second to none in the history of Egypt. Many magnificent temples were constructed throughout Egypt during his reign, with one of the monuments including the largest statute of a Pharaoh ever built, a massive structure rising seventy feet above the south side of the tenth pylon at Karnak. He was particularly known for building large limestone shrines, and the full extent of his work is often obscured by the fact that many of the buildings were completed by later Pharaohs, such as Ramesses II, and therefore not ascribed to his hand.[60] Although many of his most stupendous structures were built around Thebes, he also constructed magnificent temples at Athribis, Bubastic and Letopolis in the Delta, placing the work near Goshen, where the Hebrew slaves were domiciled.[61] If the Hebrew slaves working on these projects were subjected to extremely harsh conditions in order to complete their allotted tasks on time, it is conceivable that the oral recollections could have become embellished enough to explain their working conditions at the time of the Exodus. In addition, Amenhotep II, his father, was the first Pharaoh to employ chariotry as a separate section of the army, suggesting that the Exodus took place either during or after his reign, given the biblical description of Pharaoh's attack on the Hebrews at the Sea of Reeds.[62]

---

58 Freud, Moses and Monotheism, 31-32.

59 Osman, The Lost City of the Exodus: The Archaeological Evidence Behind the Journey Out of Egypt, 39. Josephus rejected these claims of Manetho. Ibid., 40

60 Aldred, Akhenaten, King of Egypt, 147.

61 Ibid., 150. In addition, he had many connections to the Delta region, since three of his top advisers, all named Amenhotep, were from that area, including his Scribe of the Elite Troops who also served as Superintendent of All the works, his High Steward in Memphis, and his northern Vizier. Ibid., 164-165.

62 Fletcher, Chronicle of a Pharaoh, The Intimate Life of Amenhotep III, 106.

This sequence is also quite intriguing, for if Moses was present in the palace of Amenhotep III, he then would have had contact with Amenhotep IV, and the two men would have had ample time to talk about their unique monotheistic religious beliefs. Amenhotep IV was the most controversial of all Egyptian Pharaohs, due to his attempt to modify the long-standing religious practices of the nation by instituting a monotheistic worship of the sun disc Aten, and this revolution in many ways did indeed mimic the changes which Moses put forth in his theophany on Mt. Sinai. A number of scholars, aside from Sigmund Freud, have attempted to connect the lives of the two men, since their attempt to convert their respective cultures from polytheism to monotheism is so unique that the likelihood they acted totally independent, one completely unaware of the teachings of the other, is relatively remote.

If indeed the Exodus took place at this time, then Moses would have had to been born eighty years earlier, during the reign of Thutmose III. This would then mean that the edict to kill all the newborn male children would then have been a reaction against the reign of Hatchseput, who was friendly with many Semitic workers and sailors who supported her naval expeditions and buildings. Thutmose III did show anger against her reign by eliminating her name from any of the monuments after he became Pharaoh, and he could have imposed his order against the Hebrew slaves as part of this same vindictive retribution.

There are also good connections to Greek legendary material if the Exodus took place in the fourteenth century BCE, as many historians believe that Mycenae and Troy were founded c. 1350-1300 BCE, during the time of Perseus and Pelops.[63] Argive kings at this time would have included Atreus, Thyestes, Euresxtheus, Agamemnon, Aegisthus, and possibly Perseus, and the Hebrew dissidents who fled the Exodus could then be identified with the coming of Pelops from Phrygia, the coming of Ion and Cecrops II to Athens in 1320 BCE, and the exploits of Heracles, who is believed to have lived c. 1350 BCE, two generations before the Trojan War.[64]

While appealing because of the alignment of Moses and Amenhotep IV, and the possible legendary alignment of the founding of Greece by Hebrew dissidents fleeing the Exodus, there is so far no evidence to support that there was actual contact between the two men, or that the knowledge of one was personally transmitted to the other, despite the fact that both revolutions were ignited at the end of the Late Bronze Age. This scenario therefore has very few supporters, but the fourteenth century BCE date does allow more time for the incorporation of biblical motifs into the developing Greek mythologic base before the Trojan War than the thirteenth century BCE date, and therefore should still be considered

---

63 "Mythical Chronology," 3.

64 Duncker, History of Greece: From the Earliest Times to the End of the Persian War, I.134.

seriously.

It should be noted that if the Exodus took place in the thirteenth century BCE, as will be discussed next, then Amenhotep IV may very well have been the one to first suggest a monotheistic God, rather than Moses, and Moses would have been influenced by philosophic discussions of the event during his years of growth in the Egyptian royal court, later incorporating the concept into his Mosaic Code.

D. Thirteenth Century BCE

The most-favored date among biblical scholars for the Exodus today is in the thirteenth century BCE, during the reign of Ramesses II (1279-1213 BCE), or a little later under his successor Merneptah (1213-1203 BCE).[65] This conclusion is primarily based on the description in the book of *Exodus*, where the Hebrews are said to have built the store-cities of Ramesses and Pithom.[66] Since the city of Ramesses is believed to have been constructed by Ramesses II, if the Hebrews were still enslaved it seems reasonable to conclude that the Exodus took place during that period of time, or shortly thereafter. Support for this deduction is found in contemporary Egyptian inscriptions which show large numbers of Habiru slaves transporting stones from the quarries for use in the construction of monuments,[67] and in Leiden Papyrus 348, a decree of an official of Ramesses II concerning work on building his new capital, where grain was said to have been distributed to the Habiru who were working on the great pylon of Ramesses.[68]

Although there is no proof that the Habiru slaves were actually Hebrews, the fact that many scholars have often identified the Habiru with the Hebrews makes it likely that the workers were part of the congregation which eventually left Egypt under the command of Moses.

In addition to the biblical reference of Ramesses and Pithom, a thirteenth century BCE date is also favored by the fact that Moses had to make multiple trips to the Pharaoh's home in order to continually request that the Hebrews be freed during the time of the Ten Plagues. Since Moses would have been living in Goshen at the time, such a repetition could only take place if the capital city of Egypt was close to the region of Goshen. Most of the Pharaohs of the Eighteenth Dynasty had their capital city in Thebes, which was a three-day trip from Goshen,

---

65 Bimson, <u>Redating the Exodus and Conquest</u>, 22; de Vaux, <u>The Early History of Israel</u>, 392. According to William Dever, former Professor of Near Eastern Archaeology and Anthropology at the University of Arizona, "the specific time frame for the Exodus is now confirmed as the middle to late 13th century B.C., not the 15th century B.C. as formerly thought." Dever, <u>Who Were the Early Israelites and Where Did They Come From?</u>, 8.

66 Exod 1:11.

67 Albright, Yahweh and the Gods of Canaan, 89.

68 Malamat, "Let My People go and Go and Go and Go," 64.

making travel up and back very unlikely. Ramesses II, however, spent much of his time in the city of Ramesses, which was only one day away from Goshen, and so the biblical description of events would have been able to be completed in a reasonable manner.

As I discussed in chapter 2, the literary compositions Of the *Psalms* and the *Hymn to Aten* by Amenhotep IV show congruences which could indicate that the biblical compilers, or even Moses, were aware of the Egyptian hymns, making it possible that Moses and Amenhotep IV were actually aware of each other's teaching by their living together in the palace at the same time. This would be particularly likely if Amenhotep III was the Pharaoh "who did not know Joseph" and ordered the killing of the Hebrew male newborns. If Moses was saved by one of the royal princesses in his palace, then Moses would have been raised in the same household as Amenhotep IV, and the two men may have then developed their religious principles together. This could have explained the biblical description of the flight of Moses to Midian, for when Amenhotep IV died, Moses would have been forced to flee Egypt as part of the general cleansing which took place after the death of the heretic king, similar to the actions of Sinuhe following the death of Amenemhet I. When Moses returned to Egypt from Midian forty years later, the Pharaoh of the Exodus would then have been Ramesses II.

There is also support for a thirteenth century BCE Exodus in the fact that the list of people which the Bible claimed the Hebrews encountered as they traveled to Canaan through Midian, Amalek, Edom, Moab and Ammon is most reflective of social conditions during that era. The kingdoms of Edom, Moab and Ammon did not exist before the thirteenth century BCE, making it impossible for the Hebrews to be warring with these rulers as they sought passage to the Promised Land.[69] If the recollection of the travels is literal, the Exodus could not have taken place in the fourteenth or fifteenth century BCE, but such an argument is not completely determinative, since it is clear that the biblical compilers were interested in theologic, rather than purely historical, issues in most sections of

---

69 Sarna, "Israel in Egypt, The Egyptian Sojourn and the Exodus," 40. Archaeologic evidence supports the view that Edom was devastated earlier in the nineteenth century BCE, and did not have permanent villages and fortresses until the early Iron Age, making resistance of this type not possible before the thirteenth century BCE. Davis, Moses and the Gods of Egypt, 21. The fact that walled cities were not yet developed in the region does not negate the fact that there were nomadic occupants in the Transjordan at the time, however, for the word for "city" in the Hebrew text does not necessitate the presence of a fortified town, but also could refer to a nomadic settlement. Bimson, Redating the Exodus and Conquest, 69. This could explain why there is scarcely any evidence of settlement in Edom and Moab in the fifteenth century BCE. Bratcher, "The Date of the Exodus: The Historical Study of Scripture," 11. Moses would have been expected to face resistance from whatever local population ruled the land as he skirted the direct route to the Promised Land, and traveled up the King's Highway to his crossing of the Jordan River near Jericho.

the Bible. Their audience was familiar with the descendants of those countries as present-day foes, and the authors of the Bible may have simply identified their ancestors as having fought against Moses, just as their contemporary progenies were resisting the political existence of Judah and Israel. The biblical compilers simply took advantage of present-day awareness to make events of the past more understandable and informative to the Jews who had returned from the Exile to live once again in the Promised Land. The fact that contemporary designations during the time of the Exodus may have been changed to reflect prominent names during the writing of the Torah does not negate the fact that the Exodus was, in actuality, a real event, nor demand that it be placed in the thirteenth century BCE.

Archaeologic data has been used to both support and denigrate a thirteenth century BCE Exodus date. A number of important sites, such as Jericho, Hazor, Lachish, Bethel, Debir, and Hazor all show evidence of destruction around 1220 BCE,[70] and although the devastation at Hazor and Jericho had earlier been dated by the British archaeologist John Garstang (1876-1956 CE) to c. 1400 BCE, later excavations at Jericho by Dame Kathleen Kenyon (1906-1978 CE), and at Hazor by the Israeli archaeologist Yigael Yadin (1917-1984 CE), have correlated the dates with those of Bethel, Lachish and Debir, all of which provide evidence of violent destruction toward the end of the thirteenth century BCE.[71]

A number of cities do not show evidence of ruination, however, including Gibeon, Hebron, Arad and Hormah, which would be expected if the Conquest took place in a manner as outlined in the books of *Joshua* and *Judges*.[72] In addition, there is no way to prove that the devastation was caused by the Hebrews, as opposed to other groups, such as the Egyptians or People of the Sea, or even from natural disasters, such as earthquakes or accidental fires.[73] The archaeologic remains are therefore consistent with, but not proof of, a thirteenth century BCE Exodus date.

The most important piece of extra-biblical evidence for the Exodus actually have taken place during this period of time, or just before, is the famous "Israel Stele" of Merneptah, which commemorated the battle between Egypt and a coalition of tribes from Libya and the People of the Sea, who invaded Egypt under the Rebu prince Mereya, so-named because it is the first appearance of the name Israel in a non-biblical text. This 7.5 foot high, hieroglyphic-covered black granite slab was commissioned by Merneptah in his fifth regnal year to commemorate his military

---

70 Davis, Moses and the Gods of Egypt, 24.

71 Bimson, Redating the Exodus and Conquest, 51.

72 Ibid., 52.

73 There is no sure way to distinguish Israelite culture from other types during the period in question. Ibid., 61.

successes against the Libyans, and has been used to claim the existence of Israel in Palestine at the end of the thirteenth century BCE.

The message described the political situation as follows:

- Canaan is plundered with every hardship.
- Ashkelon is taken, Gezer captured, [and] Yano'am reduced to nothing.
- Israel is laid waste, his seed is no more.[74]

The importance of this Stele is that an entity called Israel clearly existed in Canaan in 1212 BCE, and its presence was vital enough to cause the Pharaoh to recognize the Israelites as a substantial force, which acted against the interests of Egypt. Proponents of a thirteenth century BCE Exodus claim that if Israel was already settled in Palestine during the middle of Merneptah's reign, and their presence had not yet been seen as worthy of mention by other contemporary chroniclers, the Hebrews must have been a relatively new addition to the Canaanite political environment. This suggests that Ramesses II was likely on the throne at the time of the Exodus, and the Hebrew tribes then gathered strength to make their presence known, prior to the time they invaded the Promised Land. Some support for this deduction is found in the Papyrus Anastasi I, from the end of Ramesses II's reign, which contains a description of danger from Aser, a chief of an ethnic group who was plundering travelers on the road from Megiddo to the Sharon. It has been suggested by some scholars that this might be identified with the tribe of Asher, thereby placing some of the Hebrews in the western Palestine in the middle of the thirteenth century BCE, although the entire tribal amphictyony of Israel which developed during the Conquest was not yet complete.[75]

While the presence of the name Israel does strongly support an Exodus in the thirteenth century BCE, it does not prove that the Exodus had just taken place, however, for the language used in the text only indicates that Israel was a people living in that area, and not a free-standing political unit. This is consistent with the fact that Israel was not seen as a distinct entity until the time of the Monarchy, and so the mention of the name may only be a reference to certain Semitic tribes living in a nomadic, or semi-nomadic, state, either as Hebrews or indigenous Canaanites. It is also quite possible that there was an earlier Exodus, followed by a prolonged period of settlement, during which time at least some of the Hebrew tribes became involved in an encounter with the forces of Merneptah, and were cited as having been soundly defeated, along with some of their neighbors. This possibility is buttressed by the possible identity of the Hebrews with the Habiru, as discussed earlier.

If the Exodus did take place while Ramesses II was on the throne of Egypt,

---

74 "The Merneptah Stela: Israel Enters History," 30.
75 Mazar, "The Exodus and the Conquest," 81-82.

as many scholars suggest, the Pharaoh "who did not know Joseph" would then have been either Tutankhamun (1336-1327 BCE) or Horemheb (1323-1295 BCE), given the fact that Moses was eighty years old when he returned to lead the Hebrews out of Egypt. While either of these men would have obviously hated anyone identified with the rule of Amenhotep IV, it is hard to imagine why they would have initiated a policy of newborn male infanticide against the Hebrew slaves. There is no evidence to believe that Semites were seen as an integral part of the reign of Amenhotep IV, as possibly could have occurred with Hatshepsut, and this means that the biblical compilers would have simply invented the story to falsely amplify the vile nature of the Egyptian Pharaoh, a supposition I find too fanciful to be accepted as credible.

There are also problems with biblical exegesis concerning the 480 year interval of *I Kings* if the Exodus is placed in the thirteenth century BCE. In order to place the Exodus at this time, and not find serious fault with the reliability of the Bible, proponents have argued that the original translation was simply following a forty-year generation interval that lasted for twelve generations, and was not intended to be taken as a literal historical fact. If one instead uses a more likely generation interval of twenty-five years, which modern scholars generally find more reasonable, then the twelve generation total is 300 years, rather than 480 years, and the Exodus would have taken place in 1266 BCE, rather than 1446 BCE, given a date of 966 BCE for the construction of the First Temple. This interpretation may indeed be more logical to those who seek to analyze the intent of the biblical compilers with modern, rather than contemporary, standards, but I believe that this type of reassessment is flawed by its presumption that our present level of understanding is superior to those of our ancestors.

We cannot ignore the 480 year total in *1 Kings* by a recalculation that does not take into account the fact that the Bible saw the generation interval to be forty years, and replacing that figure arbitrarily in order to reinterpret the Exodus date is exegesis based on emotional bias, rather than rational cogitation.

Even if one was to accept an alteration in the 480 year interval, a thirteenth century BCE Exodus would also place the Patriarchs in an inappropriate era, depending upon how the *Exodus* 12:40 passage is translated. If the Masoretic rendering of a 430 year total in Egypt is applied to an Exodus in the thirteenth century BCE, Jacob would have joined Joseph in the eighteenth century BCE, a placement that is acceptable to most biblical historians. If the Septuagint 215 year interval is applied to a thirteenth century BCE Exodus date, however, Joseph would have arrived in Egypt c. 1500 BCE, more than fifty years after the expulsion of the Hyksos, making the patriarchal timeline inconsistent with most scholarly evaluations. As I discussed earlier, the Septuagint interpretation makes more sense, in my opinion, for it correlates the period of time with other biblical generation intervals, whether the Hebrews lived in Egypt for four or five generations.

Finally, the Late Date leaves only about 300 years to accommodate the era of the Judges, and the reigns of King Saul, King David, and the first four years of King Solomon's reign.[76] Even if one accepts some overlapping of the periods, the span of time is very short, and negates the words of Paul the apostle to the synagogue at Pisidian Antioch, where he claimed that the era of the Judges, up to the time of Samuel, was 450 years.[77] While this aspect of the chronology is open to a more liberal interpretation, its discrepancy still adds further uncertainty to the thirteenth century BCE date.

In addition to these arguments, a thirteenth century BCE Exodus date is particularly inappropriate from my perspective, because the Trojan War would have take place only a half-century later, leaving little time for the Hebrews to become enmeshed in Mycenaean society so that their traditions could be transferred to the early legends of Classical Greece. It also would not correlate with the legends of Danaus, which are presumed to have take place in the fifteenth century BCE. As described earlier, Danaus is often identified with the Hebrew tribe of Dan, providing extra-biblical identities which I believe support a biblical historicity, at least with legendary and linguistic, if not archaeologic, data. Such correlations do not fit well with a thirteenth century BCE Exodus date.

E. Twelfth Century BCE

Cyrus Gordon, Professor Emeritus of Mediterranean Studies at Brandeis University, and Gary Rendsburg, Professor of Near Eastern Studies at Cornell University, have recently dated the Exodus to 1175 BCE, much later than most scholars, by not interpreting the biblical numbers literally, but rather as "idealized figures very typical of the epic tradition."[78] Their recalculation of the patriarchal lifespans put the Patriarchs into the Amarna Age, with Abraham living in Canaan c. 1385 BCE, Isaac c. 1355 BCE, and Jacob c. 1325 BCE, placing Joseph's arrival in Egypt c. 1295 BCE.[79] This placement of Abraham in the Amarna Age was felt to be necessary because of the Nuzi texts, which offered many parallels to the patriarchal narratives.

The society at Nuzi, according to Gordon and Rendsburg, was "the single society closest to the lives of the patriarchs."[80] Under this timeline, Ramesses II is dated to 1291-1224 BCE, and identified as the Pharaoh "who did not know Joseph," rather than the Pharaoh of the Exodus, with the flight from Egypt taking place during the reign of Ramesses III (1184-1153 BCE), at the time the People

---

76 Merrill, Kingdom of Priests: A History of Old Testament Israel, 169.
77 Acts 13:20.
78 Gordon and Rendsburg, The Bible and the Ancient Near East, 112.
79 Ibid. This would place Joseph during the reign of Seti I. Ibid., 139.
80 Ibid., 112.

of the Sea began invading the Levant, c. 1175 BCE.[81] The reason God directed the Hebrews to avoid traveling through the land of Philistines in this scenario was not because the Egyptian military force presented a danger to the escaping slaves, as is surmised by most biblical scholars, but because the Philistines were attacking along the coast at that time, and were too strong for the Hebrews to face.[82]

While this view of the biblical story is based on a rational attempt to validate the existence of the Patriarchs by aligning them with extra-biblical conditions that support their lifestyle as described in the biblical text, I believe this assessment is erroneous because it ignores standard biblical traditions, without attempting to provide an acceptable adequate reason to totally set aside the interpretations discussed above. It also places the Patriarchs in what most scholars consider to be an unacceptable era, and ignores the importance of references to Israel as a force to be reckoned with in the Merneptah Stele, thereby failing to take into account one of the most important factual pieces of data which exists in extra-biblical records from that era.

It may not be possible to know exactly how long before the Merneptah Stele the Exodus took place, but the fact that the Israelites were set apart from other Canaanites in this record, and were not referenced as part of the People of the Sea movement, speaks strongly against an Exodus in the twelfth century BCE. In addition, this timing would be inconsistent with my postulated migration of the Hebrew dissidents to Mycenae before the Trojan War, and the resultant incorporation of Hebrew traditions into the developing Greek mythology.

Manfred Bietak, Director of the Austrian Archaeologic Institute, has also argued for an Exodus during the twelfth century BCE, basing his opinion on the findings of reed huts at Medinet Habu in the second half of the twelfth century BCE, which have the same floor plan as the "Israelite houses" found in Israel.[83] He believes that the occupants were either Israelites or Proto-Israelites employed to demolish the Temple of Ay and Horemheb during the reign of Ramesses III, and that their presence indicated that the Exodus had not yet taken place.[84] Baruch Halpern, Professor of Ancient History at Pennsylvania State University, noted that if this estimate is correct, it would provide an explanation for the composition of the Song of the Sea, which is generally placed between 1125-1000 BCE.[85] Once again, attempting to date the Exodus by aligning the event with a single piece of archaeologic evidence fails to satisfactorily answer all components of the Late Bronze Age timeline, and is therefore, in my opinion, a false assumption.

---

81 Ibid., 142, 152.

82 Ibid., 151. This removed the claim that the use of the word "Philistine" was anachronistic.

83 Bietak, "Israelites Found in Egypt," 41, 82.

84 Ibid., 46-47.

85 Halepern, "Eyewitness Testimony," 57.

F. Discussion

As stated in the very beginning of this chapter, most scholars favor either a fifteenth century BCE or a thirteenth century BCE date for the Exodus, modifying various biblical references to fit a timeline primarily determined by emphasizing one section over another. While arguments for both are reasonably strong, I believe that biblical data, coupled with archaeologic and legendary evidence, best supports an Exodus during the fifteenth or fourteenth century BCE, for the description of the anger of the Pharaoh "who did not know Joseph" against the Hebrews is best correlated with the expulsion of the Hyksos by Ahmose I. The rise of Joseph to the position of vizier in Egypt also fits the Hyksos regime nicely, since it would have been unlikely that a Semitic slave could have been held such a position of power during any other era, given the fact that Egyptian animosity against Semitic people was very profound since the time of the First Intermediate Period (2190-2106 BCE). Joseph's family would have been offered preferential treatment by the Hyksos, and the Egyptian populace would have therefore identified the Hebrews as being part of the ruling regime. When the Hyksos were evicted from the country, any Hebrew slaves who remained would have been both hated because of their identity with the Hyksos, and feared because of the danger they posed to the security of the homeland defense. During the time Ahmose I was away from home, pursuing the Hyksos into Palestine and extending the sovereignty of Egyptian rule, a revolt by the remaining Hebrew population would have been devastating, so he had ample reason to try and reduce the number of male slaves. A final advantage of affixing Joseph to the era of the Hyksos would be the placing of the Patriarchal chronology near the end of the Amorite Invasion, a timeline preferred by most biblical scholars.

Coupling the birth of Moses, and the Exodus eighty years later, with the expulsion of the Hyksos also explains why so many ancient authors referred to Moses as being part of the emigration of people out of Egypt and into Greece under the leadership of Danaus and Cadmus. It not only fits appropriate chronologic timelines, but, if my thesis is correct, provides the best explanation for why there is so much Eastern and Egyptian influence in the early Greek civilization.

If the anger of the Pharaoh "who did not know Joseph" was not associated with the Hyksos expulsion, the other two possible instances when Egyptian retribution could have reasonably been directed against Hebrew slaves living in the country to such a degree that an order to destroy all newborn males would have been promulgated, was when Thutmose III ascended the throne in the fifteenth century BCE, and destroyed the name of his stepmother Hatshepsut from all the monuments throughout Egypt, and when the revolutionary changes of Atenism were overturned following the death of Amenhotep IV in 1336 BCE. The actions of Thutmose III against the memory of Hatshepsut were certainly violent, and filled with the desire to reap revenge upon her delaying his reign by aspiring to the rule of Pharaoh herself, but there is little reason for him to have included the Hebrews in his desire for vengeance against his stepmother, unless they were somehow allied with her regime, which appears unlikely from all that is known about her reign. While she did utilize Semitic workmen to construct her ships which opened the trade route to Punt, there is no evidence that the Semitic slave population in Egypt was diverted to benefit her name alone. Even if there was a reason to suspect his being the Pharaoh "who did not know Joseph" because of these actions, the Exodus would have taken place eighty years later, in the fourteenth century BCE, rather than during the Late Date, which is favored by most biblical scholars, leaving Horemheb to be the Pharaoh of the Exodus, as discussed earlier in this chapter. This scenario has little biblical support and would require a difficult exegesis to explain the 480 interval of *1 Kings*.

With respect to the royal reaction against Amenhotep IV, there is similarly no reason to believe that the Hebrews would have been singled out as being responsible for this revolution, and although most Pharaohs likely felt antipathy for the Hebrews, as they did for Semites in general, it seems unlikely that they would have feared the slave population to such an extent that they thought the safety of the country was at stake. Even if Tutankhamun or Horemheb detested the Hebrews, the natural succession of pharaonic power eliminated all of the monotheistic changes of Atenism, and the population, including the Hebrew slaves, posed little threat to the autonomy of the new administration.

A fifteenth or fourteenth century BCE Exodus date therefore best fulfills the criteria for naming the Pharaoh "who did not know Joseph," and, in my opinion, is also consistent with conditions that favored success of the endeavor, since Moses would have led the Exodus during the reign of Pharaohs who were often away from Egypt on military maneuvers, leaving the border defenses of the country in a weakened position. This not only would have encouraged the infiltration of the country by outside forces, it also would have allowed those inhabitants who wanted to leave the country a relatively easy avenue of exit, since the border stations would have had a reduced contingency of troops. Once the congregation had passed the last line of defense, communication to military commanders in the Levant could have alerted the forces of the Pharaoh to return to Egypt, and stage an attack against the Hebrews at the Reed Sea, once again providing an explanation for the biblical description of events. Thutmose III particularly fits this criteria, and God's warning to Moses to not follow the path of the *Via Maris* into the coastal region of Palestine, was very understandable because the armies of Thutmose III were most concentrated in that region. It was natural for the Hebrews to instead travel into the wilderness of Sinai, and later into the hill country following the passage into the Promised Land, for these were the regions which were not infiltrated by Thutmose III's forces.

The fifteenth and fourteenth century BCE dates are also preferred, because it places the Hebrews in Canaan during the period when the Habiru were described as a "stateless, landless folk who lacked permanent status."[86] This would have included not only those miscreants who were robbers and foreigners disturbing the social order, but also escaped slaves who often found asylum with the Habiru, even though the practice of providing refuge to slaves was forbidden by contemporary treaties.[87] In the Amarna correspondence, the Habiru were often associated with rebels such as Aziru of Amurru and Labayu of Shechem, and the towns of Gezer, Ashkelon, and Lachish all were accused by the Egyptians of supporting the Habiru and providing provisions for their survival.[88] Because the Habiru were seen as undesirable trouble-makers by all of these ancient Near East potentates, the Hebrews who fled Egypt around the same period of time were likely to join their ranks, since they clearly fit the description of "landless folk who lacked permanent status," and would have trouble finding work in any other type of occupation. If they were recorded in contemporary chronicles at all, the Hebrews were likely to have been catalogued under the rubric of Habiru, rather than differentiated as a distinct entity, separate from the general class of miscreants, since there was nothing to distinguish them as unique followers of YHWH in the years immediately following the Exodus.

The final reason to favor a fifteenth or fourteenth century BCE date is that the Hebrews following the Conquest would have had adequate time to become entrenched as a people in Palestine to be recognized by Merneptah, and also to become an integral part of the Mycenaean culture which became embodied in the mythology of the Trojan War.

For the Greeks to have included the legends of the Torah in their evolving mythology, as well as utilizing the amphictyony system of government as discussed in chapter 10, the dissident Hebrews would have had to arrive at an early date before the Trojan War, and this is best explained by an Exodus in the fifteenth or fourteenth century BCE, as opposed to the thirteenth century BCE. They would have brought engineering skills which enabled the Mycenaeans to construct their palaces with Cyclopean stones, and would have provided enough military assistance to allow for the expansion of the Mycenaean empire, while still providing man-power at home. This close assimilation would also explain the inclusion of Semitic words into the developing Greek language, rather than presuming a Phoenician source from mercantile contacts alone.

In addition to the Hebrews providing the Semitic language source, my thesis also explains the variety of other Egyptian and Phoenician attributes which Marin Bernal, as summarized by Walter Slack, claimed the Greeks borrowed, including "about twenty-two gods, goddesses, and mythic heroes (BA 2:79-111), place

---

86 Greenberg, "HAB/PIRU and Hebrews," 188-189.

87 Ahlstrom, The History of Ancient Palestine, 235.

88 de Vaux, <u>The Early History of Israel</u>, 108; Greenberg, "HAB/PIRU and Hebrews," 193.

names, trade terms, loan-words, floating islands, water plants, date palms, linen (BA 1:79), the Phoenician alphabet (BA 1:34), aspects of West Semitic mythology (BA 2:438), stone bowls, a button seal, a marble cup (BA 2:147), Mycenaean Shaft Grave goods such as gold-leaf death masks, bronze weapons, a crystal bowl, a sycamore box, lapus lazuli scarabs, flint arrowheads, jewels and carved ivories from Hyksos Egypt (BA 2:394-97), an alabaster amphora, gold 'Vaphio cups,' beads, fragments of Egyptian pottery (BA 2:450), and trade goods such as copper, bronze, ivory, gold, spices, papyrus, possibly cotton, ostrich feathers and eggs, ointments and spices (BA 2:466-67, 484-85)."[89] Many historians have claimed that the monuments and religious notions in Greece came primarily from contact with the Phoenicians,[90] but in my opinion the Phoenicians were simply the men who manned the ships bring the Hebrews to the Mycenaean shore.

In answer to those who argue for a thirteenth century BCE Exodus date, the fact that the Bible describes the Hebrews as being involved with the building of the store-cities of Ramesses and Pithom does not necessarily mean that the construction had to take place under Ramesses II. The cities dated back to the time of the Hyksos, where it was their capital city of Avaris, and the modifications completed by Ramesses II were actually begun much earlier, under Seti I. Ramesses II constructed a monument to celebrate the 400-year anniversary of the city, known as the Stele of the year 400, an indication that the city was first founded c 1730 BCE.[91] There is no reason to assume that the Hebrew slaves could not have been working on repairs in the original city, as opposed to the later revisions made under Ramesses II.

The necessity for Moses to make frequent trips to the Pharaoh's home is also not of decisive importance, as no time limit is given in the Bible for the period of the Ten Plagues, nor is there any reason to presume that Moses had to be stationed in Goshen, as opposed to some other work camp closer to the cities occupied by Thutmose III. The presence of Edom, Moab, and Ammon as the countries opposed to the migration of Moses toward the Jordan River does not require that the countries be at the height of their power for the biblical compilers to use them as reflective of the people who fought with Moses during the Exodus.

For all of these reasons, the fifteenth or fourteenth century BCE is the most likely time when the Exodus of the Hebrews from Egypt took place. This

---

89 Slack, White Athena: The Afrocentrist Theft of Greek Civilization, 133.

90 In the words of the German historian Max Duncker (1811-1886 CE), "Special cults which are foreign to the religious notions of all the Arian races, but are evidently in harmony with those of the Phoenicians, and which we find regarded as old and traditional customs in more than one canton of Greece in historical times, lead us to the conclusion that they were brought by the Phoenicians to the coasts of Hellas, and adopted by the Greeks." Duncker, History of Greece: From the Earliest Times to the End of the Persian War, I.59.

91 Finegan, Handbook of Biblical Chronology, 219.

determination has the added benefit of allowing the patriarchal timeline to be placed in the Middle Bronze Age, during the era of the Amorite Invasion. It also allows the Conquest to take place during the era of the Habiru infiltration in Canaan, providing an explanation as to why the Hebrew Exodus was not mentioned in extant extra-biblical texts.

Chapter 7
MYCENAE AND CLASSICAL GREECE

I have spent the first six chapters of this book outlining the history of the ancient Near East and Egypt, along with the biblical story of the Patriarchs and the Exodus, and I now will cross the Mediterranean Sea, as I believe the dissident Hebrews who fled the Exodus did, and outline what is known about the development of the early Greek civilization. The Classical Greek culture (500-323 BCE) is widely regarded as the intellectual foundation for all of Western civilization, but very little is known about the origin of that society, primarily because it developed during a poorly understood era known as the Greek Dark Age (1000-850 BCE).[1] Contributing to the mystery is the fact that the early Greeks left no written record of their history, a happenstance which Josephus, the first century CE Jewish historian, remarked as being the primary deficiency of the Greeks, when compared to the Egyptians, Babylonians, and Hebrews, and the one which led to subsequent misinformation and lies.[2] The conspicuous lack of hard facts about the origin of the Greeks led Jonathan M. Hall, Professor and Chair of Classics at the University of Chicago, in his history of the Greek Archaic world, to admit that "the fundamental question which I wish to ask is not so much 'what happened?' in the Archaic period of Greek history, but rather 'how do we know what (we think) happened?'"[3]

The generally accepted beginning of culture on the Greek mainland which can be labeled as truly Greek is Mycenae, the homeland of King Agamemnon, who was appointed commander-in-chief of the Greek force that sailed to Troy and avenged the dishonor of their county, as memorialized in Homer's the *Iliad*, thought to be composed in the eighth century BCE.[4] Mycenae was a strong

---

1 The first Olympic games began in 776 BCE, providing an acceptable end to the Greek Dark Age for those who follow the standard chronology of the ancient Near East.

2 Josephus, "Against Apion," The Complete Works of Josephus, I.4-6, 608. Josephus also castigated the veracity of the Greek historians, including the works of Hellanicus, Acusilaus, Ephorus, Timeus, Herodotus, Antiochus, Philistius, Callias, and even Thucydides, pointing out that there were great differences of opinion on the details of their various genealogies. This was due to their neglect of preserving records of their history. Ibid., I.3-4, 608. The Jews, on the other hand, had kept meticulous records of the genealogy of their priests for two thousand years. Ibid., I.7, 609.

3 Hall, A History of the Archaic Greek World, ca. 1200-479 BCE, 15. Although it is "extremely probable that the Greeks came to their country from somewhere else," the ancient Greeks nevertheless thought of itself as an original authochthonous population. Burckhardt, The Greeks and Greek Civilization, 15-16.

4 Spyridon Marinatos (1901-1974 CE), Professor of Archaeology at the University of Athens, has defined the Mycenaeans as "the people who were the first to organize military and political power throughout a large part of Greece during the second millennium BC;

maritime power in the Late Bronze Age (1600-1200 BCE), occupying the region on the lower slopes of the Euboea Mountain. It dominated the northern Mediterranean Basin following the decline of the Minoan civilization in Crete in the fifteenth century BCE, and became the primary source of Aegean influence in the ancient Near East until the widespread destructions by the People of the Sea during the thirteenth and twelfth centuries BCE. From the fourteenth century BCE onwards, these early Greeks constructed fortified palaces at Mycenae, Tiryns, and Midea in the Argolid, Pylos in Messenia, Thebes in Boeotia, and Volos in Thessaly, and although they were smaller than their Minoan counterparts, these citadels functioned effectively as economic centers.[5] During this period of time, the Mycenaeans not only took part in the extensive trade which developed among the countries surrounding the Mediterranean Sea, but also sent colonists to distant lands in order to manage the extensive commercial endeavors of their mother country. What exactly happened to this magnificent civilization in the intervening Dark Age is not well understood, but there is no question that much of Mycenaean tradition, language, and culture was instrumental in formulating the details of the Greek mystique. In this chapter, I will discuss the many vagaries of ancient Mycenaean and Classical Greek culture and mythology, pointing out which aspects appear I believe were derived from the dissident Hebrews, who arrived during the Late Bronze Age, before the Trojan War.

A. Background

The Mycenaean civilization, which lasted from c. 1580-1200 BCE, was the first society on the Greek mainland to gain international prominence, although signs of human life in the region dates back to the Upper Paleolithic (Old Stone Age) period (45,000-13,000 BCE), typified by remains found in Epirus, Thessaly, and Argolis.[6] As the mainland society changed from an hunter-gatherer to an agrarian and livestock-raising culture, complex communities arose as early as 9000 BCE, leaving evidence of their existence in multiple stone wall enclosures. These early complexes were in contact with the nearby Cycladic islands, as evidenced by obsidian (volcanic glass) remains from the island of Melos in the Franchthi Cave in southeast Greece.[7] As a result of this initial enterprise, larger villages

---

who first built urban capitals or developed existing settlements into strong centers; whose rulers became the first petty kings and eventually great monarchs of Greece; who created the first royal dynasties and thus gave birth to the Greek heroic legends." Marinatos, "The First 'Mycenaeans' in Greece," 107. The Mycenaeans are generally seen as including the kingdoms of Mycenae, Thebes, Tiryns, and Pylos. Strauss, The Trojan War: A New History, xviii.

5 Hall, A History of the Archaic Greek World, ca. 1200-479 BCE, 42.
6 Durando, Ancient Greece: The Dawn of The Western World, 20.
7 Fragments suggesting actual organized human habitation can be found in the

developed, the oldest of which is Nea Nikomedia, in Macedonia, dated to around 6,218 BCE. Although these settlements were quite complex, they still lagged behind those found on the southern and eastern Mediterranean shore, where the remains of a walled-city at Jericho, and at Catal Huyuk in southern Anatolia (Asia Minor), have been dated to as early as 7000 BCE. Despite the fact that there was sporadic seafaring activity during this early era, a true maritime trading culture did not develop until the Early Bronze Age (3000-2000 BCE), when the necessity to import large amounts of the elements that were needed for the metallurgy of bronze forced the inhabitants to increase their import capabilities. This initiated a more rapid growth of sophisticated habitation as immigrants from distant areas began to invade the territory and construct a number of permanent settlements.

The aboriginal inhabitants on the mainland have been known by various names over the years, including *Cranaan*, *Lelegian* (*Lleges*), and *Carian* (*Kares*), but the commonest name used by the Classical Greek writers for their ancient ancestors was *Pelasgian*.[8] Heinrich Schliemann (1822-1890 CE), the man who first uncovered the remains of the capital of Mycenae in 1876 CE, as well as the city of Troy in 1870 CE, labeled these earlier settlers as *Minyans*, since he discovered their presence at Orchomenos in Boeotia, the home of the legendary King Minyas. Modern scholars have followed this designation by identifying the characteristic pottery style of these early Bronze Age inhabitants as "Minyan."[9]

At the start of the Middle Bronze Age (2000-1600 BCE), the same time Abraham is believed to have begun his migration from Mesopotamia to the Levant, a great assault of peoples from the north hit the Greek mainland,

---

Franchthi cave from as early as 20,000 BCE, but evidence of complete villages did not appear until the Neolithic Age (c. 8800-4700 BCE), when farming began to allow for the development of larger, more stable settlements. Martin, Ancient Greece, From Prehistoric to Hellenistic Times, 5. Obsidian first appeared in the Upper Paleolithic period, but in the second phase of the Mesolithic period (c. 8300-6000 BCE), obsidian from Melos, as well as large quantities of fish bones, were found in the cave, indicating that the inhabitants of Franchthi not only sailed to Melos, which was 93 miles away, but also fished in deep water for the first time. "Prehistoric Archaeology of the Aegean: Lesson 1: The Southern Greek Palaeolithic, Mesolitic, and Neolithic Sequence at Franchthi," 2-3.

8 Myres, Who Were the Greeks?, xxii, 95. Herodotus (*The History*, II.56) and Thucydides (*The History of the Peloponnesian War*, I.iii.1) both accepted that the *Pelasgoi* were the primitive population of Greece. Georgiev, "The Arrival of the Greeks in Greece: the Linguistic Evidence," 243. According to Aeschylus, King Pelasgus was the first king in Arcadia, and was on the throne when Danaus arrived with his fifty daughters from Egypt. Aeschylus, "Prometheus Bound," 240, 61. The Pelasgians were eventually driven out by the Hellenes. Duruy, History of Greece, and of the Greek People, From the Earliest Times to the Roman Conquest, vol. 1, 162.

9 Marinatos, "The First `Mycenaeans' in Greece," 108. Minyan clay occurs in Gray, Black (Argive), Red, and Yellow varieties, and was used to construct goblets and kantharoi. "Prehistoric Archaeology of the Aegean: Lesson 9: Middle Helladic Greece," 3.

destroying the settlements of the Early Bronze Age inhabitants at Asea, Malthi, Tiryns, Korakou, Zyouries, Aghios, Kosmas, Orchomenos, and Eutresis, leading Robert Drews, Professor of Classics and History at Vanderbilt University, to label this interface of the Early and Middle Bronze Age periods as "the coming of the Greeks."[10] Recent debate has suggested that Drew's timeline may be in error, and that the destruction took place either somewhat earlier, c. 2100 BCE, or later, c. 1600 BCE, but the fact remains that the origin of the Mycenaean civilization was contemporary with the Amorite Invasion, as discussed in chapter 1, and that the true initiation of the cultures of our modern world can be found in the efforts of these MBA migrants. Ancient historians referred to these early invaders of the Greek mainland as Achaeans, Aeolians, Danaans, and Ionians, consistent with the names applied by Homer to the Grecian force in the Trojan War,[11] but modern scholars have not agreed upon who these primal people were, and where they came from.[12] For convenience, they are generally labeled as Indo-Europeans, or "Hellenes," because they spoke an early form of Indo-European languages, known as PIE language, uniting them with the people who eventually populated Europe, Persia, and India.[13]

This conception that the origin of Greece is from Aryan Indo-European stock has been criticized by some modern scholars as being racist and not consistent with legendary evidence. It has been referred to by Martin Bernal, Professor of Government and Near Eastern Studies at Cornell University, as the "Aryan model," because rather than being based on historical accuracy, it reflects the slaveholding mentality of the eighteenth and early nineteenth century academic communities in

---

10 Drews, The Coming of the Greeks, 16, 19, 45.

11 The Achaeans are thought to have originally come from Thessaly, and then settled in Argos and Lacedaemon (southern Peloponnesus), mingling with the Danaans, who dwelled in Argos and were the descendants of Danaus, while the Argives were simply named for their residence in Argolis. Parada, "The Trojan War," 6-7. Ionians were the Greek inhabitants of Ionia, a region in western Asia Minor (today's Turkey), and were referred to as such in the Bible. Joel 4:6. Zvi, "Joel," 1166.

12 Starr, The Origins of Greek Civilization, 1100-650 B.C., 30. Recent data suggests that either north-west Anatolia, or Bactria, in modern Afghanistan, may have been their site of origin. Guthrie, "The Religion and Mythology of the Greeks," 855; Drews, The Coming of the Greeks, 25-26.

13 Starr, The Origins of Greek Civilization, 1100-650 B.C., 8. *Hellenes* is the name which was eventually applied to all Greek speaking Indo-Europeans. The name is derived from the mythical Hellen, the son of Deucalion. His sons included Aeolus, who succeeded Hellen in Thessaly; Dorus, who emigrated to Mount Parnassus; and Xuthus, who fled to Athens where he married Creusa, daughter of the Athenian King Erechtheus, who bore him Ion and Achaeus. Thus, the four most famous Hellenic nations – Ionians, Aeolians, Achaeans, and Dorians – were descended from Hellen. Graves, The Greek Myths: 1, 43.b, 158.

Europe and the United States.[14] According to Bernal, the history of Greece was written by Indo-European victors, who were interested in identifying themselves as the generators of the Classical Greek culture, ignoring the true reality that Greece was founded by people of color: Egyptians and Phoenicians, who followed Danaus and Cadmus during their expulsion from Egyptian soil, and arrived on the mainland during the Heroic age, around 1500 BCE. Because scholars from the Classical Greek (500-323 BCE) and Hellenistic (323-30 BCE) Ages accepted this latter view, Bernal labeled it the "Ancient model" of Greek origin, rather than the "Aryan model."[15] Bernal sanctioned, in essence, the Ancient model, but modified it to accept that Indo-Europeans did initially invade Greece in the Early Bronze Age, but were replaced by the Egyptians and Phoenicians during the invasion of the Hyksos c. 1600 BCE.[16] In so doing, Bernal believed that his explanation would answer how both elements played a part in the development of the Classical Greek culture.

Bernal's claim that racial categorization affected the view of many historians in the nineteenth century CE has offended many of his colleagues, but the charge seems clearly evident in the conclusion of the German historian Max Duncker (1811-1886 CE), who asserted that the Greeks could not have built the walls of Mycenae without outside assistance because "the Arian races are differently constituted from the Egyptians and the Semites of Babylon and Assyria; their general character and the greater prominence among them of the individual in the conduct of life unfitted them for undertaking laborious architectural works."[17] People of color and Jews were seen by Duncker as making for a good slave population, but they never could be expected to engender the type of intellectual

---

14 Bernal, Black Athena, I.1.; Yurco, "Black Athena: An Egyptological Review," 62. Bernal separates this theory into the Broad Aryan Model, which accepts possible Phoenician, but not Egyptian, colonization of Greece, and the Extreme Aryan Model, which does not even accept Phoenician colonization of Greece. Berlinerblau, Heresy in the University: The *Black Athena* Controversy and the Responsibilities of American Intellectuals, 23-25. Bernal's position followed that first propounded by Marcus Garvey (1887-1940 CE), the founder of the Universal Negro Improvement Association, who wrote that "the white world has always tried to rob and discredit us of our history." Lefkowitz, "Ancient History, Modern Myths," 7. Bernal also pointed out that academicians were prejudiced against Jews, and that "anti-Semitism provided an explanation for the denial of the role of the Phoenicians in the formation of Greece." Bernal, Black Athena, I.xiv. His claim of prejudicial intent did not apply to modern classicists after 1945 CE. Ibid., I.28.

15 Ibid., I.1.

16 Bernal referred to this as the "Revised Ancient Model." In this modification, he also maintained that the Pelasgians who were living in Greece at the time spoke an Indo-Hittite language. Berlinerblau, Heresy in the University: The *Black Athena* Controversy and the Responsibilities of American Intellectuals, 24-26, 45.

17 Duncker, History of Greece: From the Earliest Times to the End of the Persian War, I.48.

and artistic achievements of the Classical Greek era. Obviously, this narrow racist view is today viewed by most scholars as both morally and factually wrong, but the fact remains that Aryan involvement was a major factor in the development of the early Greek culture, and that an Eastern influence was an important part of the evolutionary process, although not likely of primary importance. My thesis that dissident Hebrews left the Exodus and traveled to Mycenae before the Trojan War is somewhat similar to Bernal's modified Ancient model, since it proposes that the Hebrews arrived from Egypt around 1500 BCE, but where Bernal proposed that the immigrants were the initial founders of the Greek race, I accept that the Mycenaeans were of both Indo-European and Eastern stock, and that their Greek descendants eventually developed their cultural traits from a variety of adjacent sources, including the Hebrew dissidents.

The Indo-European invaders, from wherever they came, settled mostly in central Greece, and continued to establish contact with the inhabitants of the Cyclades, as well as nearby Crete. The mixture of Indo-Europeans, Pelasgians, and, eventually, colonists from Egypt and Phoenicia, led to the formation of a number of cities, which, according to the English historian William Mitford (1744-1827 CE), included Sicyon, on the northern coast of Peloponnesus, founded by Aegialeus; Corinth, in the neighborhood of Sicyon, founded by Sisyphus, Glaucus, and Bellerophon; and Argos, which was the first to acquire political eminence, founded by Inachus or Phoroneus.[18] The administration they set up remained in power until the end of the seventeenth century BCE, when the Mycenaean civilization took over control of much of the Greek mainland.[19] The city of Mycenae lay at a particularly powerful position, controlling the land route to central Greece through the Isthmus of Corinth, and the Mycenaeans took advantage of their strategic location to expand their authority to distant lands. Archaeologic remains indicate that their culture was characterized by great dominance and wealth, with chieftains whose power and prosperity grew through the development of new weaponry, including the sword and body-shield, as well as improved chariots, which allowed them to overpower defenses that relied on stationary manpower alone.[20] Debate continues among historians as to whether this take-over was sudden, over one to two generations, or whether it developed more slowly, as a result of infiltration rather than invasion, but in either case the resultant Mycenaean society strengthened their hold on the region and became identifiable as a distinct cultural entity by the start of the Late Bronze Age.

18 Mitford, The History of Greece, Volume I, 23-28.

19 According to legend, Mycenae was founded by Perseus, son of Danae and Zeus, and great-great-great-grandson of Danaus. He was also a contemporary of Pelops. Ibid. 31-32.

20 Emily Vermeule (1929-2001 CE), Professor *emerita* at Harvard University, has attributed this success to their being "mobile, highly trained soldiers everywhere seeking new stations of power." Vermeule, Greece in the Bronze Age, 108.

In order to identify who these Mycenaean immigrants were in more detail, scholars have generally turned to archaeologic and linguistic evidence, which is based on scientific, rather than mythical grounds. This type of data is clearly essential to making a reasoned analysis of the origin of the Greek people, but it is still vital to remember Bernal's argument that the views of the ancient Greeks are nevertheless important, for "given the unreliability and patchiness of other sources of information on the Bronze Age Aegean ... one should use those elements of myths and legends with plausible historicity as aids in setting up working hypotheses to be tested in other ways."[21] I will therefore first outline the mythical traditions surrounding the founding of Greece, in order to provide a template of oral history on which to then add a support of scientific proof. Although the legends are quite contrived, and not based on any known historical individuals, much like the stories of the Hebrew Bible, I will spend some time on explaining the details in order to try and point out where I believe the oral tradition of the Bible may have influenced the developing Greek beliefs, or perhaps been influenced by the Greek history itself, since the Greek and Hebrew stories were being formulated in contiguous periods of time.

B. Tradition

The ancient Greeks generally accepted that Homer's description of the Trojan War was factual, and that their ancestors came from the region of Mycenae, a city they believed was initially founded by Perseus, the son of Zeus and the mortal Danae, the daughter of King Acrisius of Argos, who was supposed to have lived in the fourteenth century BCE. This would place the rise of Mycenae in an era congruous with estimates for the Exodus of the Hebrews from Egypt, and I believe the legendary material which evolved about the foundation of the Greeks was greatly affected by stories of the patriarchal generations brought by the dissident Hebrews who fled the Exodus and traveled to Mycenae. I therefore will discuss the Greek tradition in more detail in order to point out the many similarities.

According to the standard version of the story, Perseus had fortified the city of Mycenae with a wall composed of stones so large that the construction had to be carried out by the Cyclopes, superhuman beings strong enough to lift even the heaviest boulder without the aid of mechanical assistance.[22] The archaeologic remains of the city, which I will discuss shortly, show this composition quite clearly, and it is easy to see why the Greeks infused their recollection with the assistance of the gods as evidence of their favored position in the hierarchy of civilized life. Upon the death of Perseus, legend holds that the kingdom passed to his son, Sthenelus (Sthenelos), who was eventually succeeded by his son Eurystheus, the man who captured Argos and assigned Heracles to perform the

---

21 Bernal, Black Athena Writes Back, 28.
22 Graves, The Greek Myths: 1, 241-243.

twelve labors. This period of rule, at the very start of Greek history, was known as the dynasty of the Perseidae, referring to the name of its founder, Perseus. The Perseidae dynasty ended abruptly when Eurytheus died without leaving a male heir. He had provided for an orderly succession of hereditary control in case of this event, however, by directing that upon his death the kingdom be ruled by his uncle, Atreus of Elis, the son of Pelops and Hippodameia. Pelops had come from Lydia in Anatolia, and married into the royal family of Elis, near Olympia, eventually siring two sons, Atreus and Thyestes. When the boys had grown into manhood, a dispute with their father caused them to be driven out of their home, and they took refuge with Eurytheus in Mycenae. At first, the brothers appear to have gotten along very well, but soon after Atreus was appointed king of Mycenae, his position of power made him fear a rebellion by his brother, and he therefore sent his own two sons, Agamemnon and Menelaus, to seize Thyestes in Delphi and bring him to Mycenae, so that he could be imprisoned and kept under close guard. As often happens during the intrigues associated with dynamic succession, Atreus was eventually assassinated, and Thyestes then ascended the throne as king. Agamemnon and Menelaus were forced into exile, and fearing that they in turn would be eliminated by Thyestes, the young men sought refuge with King Polyphides of Sicyon, and then with King Oeneus of Calydon. In time, they eventually returned to Mycenae and dethroned Thyestes with the help of King Tyndareus of Sparta. Agamemnon married Clytemnestra (Clytaemestra, Klytaimnestra), one of the daughters of Tyndareus, and became king of Mycenae, while Menelaus married Helen, another daughter of Tyndareus, and became king of Sparta. These two rulers would later form the core of leadership for the Greeks during the Trojan War, and the details of their marriages are discussed in the next chapter, when I analyze the history of that fabled conflict.

It is important to note at this juncture that if the Exodus took place in the fifteenth century BCE, then the dissident Hebrew migration to Mycenae would have taken place during this early phase of Mycenaean development, while if it was in the thirteenth century BCE, it would have been closer to the time of the Trojan War itself. In either case, the mingling of Hebrew and Greek mythology would have still been taking place at the very start of what later could be incorporated into the Classical Greek ethos. The rivalry between Atreus and Thyestes for control of the Mycenaean kingdom in many ways resembles the biblical tales of rivalry between Esau and Jacob for the blessing of Jacob, and in my opinion may have been introduced by the stories transmitted by the dissident Hebrews, but the Greek rendition was much more grotesque, and included a ghastly version of the feud, which provides the basis in Greek tragedy for children inheriting the sins of their fathers and mothers. The plot began when Thyestes seduced Aerope (Europe), the wife of Atreus, and to revenge his dishonor, Atreus killed the sons of Thyestes, and served their remains to him as a meal on one of his visits. While infanticide itself was not uncommon throughout the ancient world, cannibalism was never resorted to except in rare and tragic instances, and the vial nature of this offense led to a tragic fate that befell generations to come.[23] To initiate the retaliation, Thyestes impregnated his own daughter, and then married her to Atreus, so that the child she bore, although appearing to be the son of Atreus, was actually the offspring of Thyestes. When the newborn son, Aegisthus, was grown, Atreus told the young man to kill Thyestes, but Aegisthus knew that Thyestes was his true father, and together they planned to complete their vengeance by killing Atreus and taking over the throne. Once this revenge was accomplished, the intricate plot did not end, for Agamemnon, the son of Atreus, eventually succeeded Thyestes as king, and when he returned from the Trojan War, his wife, Clytemnestra, along with her lover, the very Aegisthus who had earlier helped to kill Agamemnon's father, assassinated Agamemnon in reprisal for his sacrificing his daughter Iphigenia as the Greek armada lay dormant in the bay of Aulis. The events continued to unfold in the next generation, when Orestes, the son of Agamemnon, killed both Aegisthus and Clytemnestra.

This inherent fate that doomed generations of the House of Atreus was a tragic concept that may very well have been introduced by the traditions of the dissident Hebrews, for in the Torah, God warned the Hebrews not to worship other gods or idols or guilt would fall upon the children, up to the third and fourth generation.[24] In addition, in the Bible, cannibalism is not described as having taken place, but among the many curses that Moses warned the Hebrews would befall them if they did not follow all of God's commandments and decrees after they crossed the Jordan River into the Promised Land was to be so famished by a siege that they would "actually eat the flesh of your sons and daughters."[25] Later Israelite civil and criminal law did not incorporate the legal principle of guilt passing down to subsequent generations, and instead restricted punishment to the agent alone, but the Hebrews who participated in the Exodus were not subject to the modifications of the post-Exilic rabbis, and their view of Justice was very similar to that espoused on the Greek stage. This influence may explain why Agamemnon followed the example of Abraham in obeying the divine command to sacrifice his child, although God interrupted the immolation of Isaac, while Artemis allowed Iphigenia to die. The Greek details are much more violent and repellant, but the underlying lessons they taught are quite synonymous with Jewish tradition.

Another popular legend about the foundation of Mycenae, which is even more

---

23 According to Aeschylus, after Thyestes became aware of what he had eaten, he spat the meat out and cursed the house of Atreus to bring doom upon all of his descendants. Aeschylus, "Agamemnon," 1602, 87.

24 Deut 5:9.

25 Deut 28:53. Kaplan, The Living Torah: The Five Books of Moses and the Haftarot, 1005.

suggestive of an arrival of a group of Hebrew dissidents following the Exodus, is the myth which claimed that the Mycenaeans descended from Danaus, who fled Egypt with his fifty daughters and traveled to the Greek mainland, reaching Lerna in Argos via the island of Rhodes. Danaus had quarreled with his brother Aegyptus over their inheritance, and when Aegyptus proposed that the fifty daughters of Danaus marry his own fifty sons, Danaus fled to Mycenae, fearing a plot against his own life if he either refused or agreed to this request. His concerns were not unwarranted, for fathers and husbands often feared for their lives once the women of their family were noticed by other rulers in ancient times, as evidenced in the Bible by the subterfuge which Abraham and Isaac presented to the Pharaoh and King Abimelech about the relationship of their wives as sisters. Danaus and his family first landed in Rhodes, but failing in an attempt to establish his colony there, he preceded to Argos, where Gelanor reigned over the Pelasgians. When Aegyptus discovered the escape, he sent his sons in pursuit and the men overtook Danaus' family at Argos, where Danaus finally agreed to arrange a mass marriage. The acceptance was feigned, however, for Danaus had convinced his daughters to kill each husband on their wedding night with a sharp pin he had hidden in their bedclothes. All but one, Hypermnestra, agreed to the deception, and she fled with her husband Lynceus to the city which later bore his name. Danaus then became the king of Argos, and his descendants became known as the Danaoi, or Danaans, one of the terms which Homer used to refer to the Greeks in the *Iliad*.

Like the story of the Trojan War, the legend of Danaus was accepted by most ancient historians as being based on factual historical events, and Manetho included the tale in his *Aegyptiaca Upomnemata*. According to Manetho, Danaus was known as Aramis, and after five years of ruling in Egypt, he was exiled during the Eighteenth Dynasty, and fled for refuge to the land of the Greeks, where he then ruled as the king of Argos.[26] His brother Aigyptos (Aegyptus) then ascended the Egyptian throne as Ramesses. Hecataeus of Abdera, the Greek historian and Sceptic philosopher who rose to fame under Alexander the Great (356-323 BCE), and was later associated with Ptolemy I Soter (323-283 BCE) in Egypt, was the first ancient author to claim that the Exodus led by Moses took place during the time of Danaus, thereby correlating the mythology of the Greeks with the story in the Bible. In his panegyrical ethnography of Egypt, *Aegyptiaca*, Hecataeus related that there was a pestilence in ancient Egypt, which the people ascribed to the anger of the gods over the presence of a variety of foreigners in the country. To resolve their troubles, the Egyptians ousted the aliens, which included Danaus, Cadmus, and a colony headed by Moses.[27] Danaus and Cadmus migrated to

---

26 Verbrugghe & Wickersham, Berossos and Manetho, Introduced and Translated, 142.

27 Hecataeus of Abdera, 1-3, as cited in Stern, <u>Greek and Latin Authors on Jews and Judaism</u>, 27-28. Hecataeus was the first Greek to discuss the account of Jewish origin,

Greece, while the greater number of Hebrews, led by Moses, were driven into the land of Judea, where Moses founded the city of Jerusalem and divided the Jews into twelve tribes.[28] Hecataeus did not supply a chronological framework for these events, but subsequent authors, such as the Egyptian historian Charemon (first century CE), the Egyptian priest Ptolemy of Mendes (first century CE), and the Roman historian Tacitus (55-117 CE), provided estimates which would place the event in the fifteenth century BCE.[29]

As discussed earlier, Martin Bernal cited this legend as one basis for his Ancient model of Greek origin, where he claimed that people of color from Egypt and Phoenicia were the true founders of Greek culture. From my perspective, this theory is more supportive of a possible migration of Hebrews to Mycenae during the Exodus, for it allies the migration of Moses and the Hebrews with the eviction of Danaus and Cadmus, who then traveled to Greece. Not only does the migration match the Exodus timeline, but the similarity of the name Danaus with the Hebrew tribe of Dan could mean that the founding of Mycenae was due, in great part, to a man who retained Hebraic traditions that were characteristic of the patriarchal traditions before the modifications imposed by Moses.

This theory of origin helps explain why some ancient Hebrew writers declared that there was a consanguinity between the Greek and Hebrew people. Josephus, in *Antiquities of the Jews*, maintained that Areus, the king of the Lacedaemonians, sent a letter to the High Priest Onias claiming that the Lacedaemonians and the Jews were brethren, and that both were descended from the kindred of Abraham.[30] Josephus pointed out that a seal on the letter in the shape of a four-square portraying an eagle with a dragon in its claws was the emblem of the tribe of Dan, supporting the view of Areus.[31] Other evidence of this linkage is found in the book of *I Maccabees*, where the High Priest Jonathan wrote to the Spartans reminding them that Areus once sent a letter to Onias saying that they were kin, and that Onias accepted the emissary with honor.[32] Although many scholars pay little attention to the historical claims in the book of *I Maccabees*, since it was written in Greek and often struggled to find a social relationship between the Hebrews and Greeks, the legend of Danaus nevertheless supports the possibility

---

and may have been the first one to even mention the Jews, although this distinction is usually applied to Theophrastus (372-287 BCE), the disciple of Aristotle. Ibid., 20. The version of the Exodus as related by Hecataeus, where Egypt purged their country of alien people because of a plague, was also followed by Strabo (c. 63 BCE-21 CE). Assmann, Moses the Egyptian: The Memory of Egypt in Western Monotheism, 37.

28 Stern, Greek and Latin Authors on Jews and Judaism, 28.

29 Ibid., 29.

30 Josephus, "Antiquities of the Jews," The Complete Works of Josephus, XIII.IV.10, 256.

31 Ibid., XIII.IV.10, 256; Capt, Missing Links Discovered in Assyrian Tablets, 63.

32 I Macc, XXVIII.xii.7-8, 444.

that a group of dissident Hebrews migrated to Mycenae at the same time Moses led the Hebrews out of Egypt, thereby providing Danaus with a Hebrew, rather than an Egyptian, heritage.

It is interesting that the tribe of Dan is singled out in these connections between the ancient Hebrews and Greeks for not only is there a similarity between the names of Danaus and Dan, but more importantly of all the Hebrew tribes, the attributes of the Danites best fit the role of rebels, lending support to their playing a role in the decision to leave the Exodus. The Danites were generally regarded by rabbinical sources as the black sheep of the house of David, and were frequently cited in the biblical text for their disobedience to the regulations of the Mosaic Code.[33] They were placed at the rear of the Exodus when the order of movement was determined following the theophany on Mt. Sinai, and their behavior following the Conquest of the Promised Land suggests that they may have taken umbrage at their distant position.[34] The tribe of Dan was the only one of the twelve tribes to fail to secure the land allotted to them in the western hills of the Benjamin-Judean territory, forcing them to migrate far to the north to find a suitable location to raise their families.[35] During the process of reconnoitering the region, they asked the Ephramite Micah to have one of his priests inquire of God whether their trip would be successful, evidence of a faith in divination that was prohibited by the Mosaic Law.[36] They also took idols from Micah's home to assist their endeavors, a practice which would have been punished by death if the precepts of the Ten Commandments were enforced.[37] These actions were remindful of the behavior of Rachel, who took idols from her father's house when she left with Jacob to return to Canaan, and of the stories of how the Lord reminded Aaron and Miriam that He spoke to prophets in visions and dreams, thereby encouraging the ability to tell the future. Although Moses gave strict orders to forgo this behavior during his lifetime, this belief in the practices of their ancestors was something which the Danites never forgot, and, in my opinion, is very suggestive of their being part of the group of dissident Hebrews who felt forced to leave the Exodus. When the Danites arrived in Mycenae, their

---

33 New Testament theology followed this tradition, fostering the legend that the Antichrist came from the tribe of Dan. The Jewish Encyclopedia, IV.423.

34 Num 10:25.

35 Josh 19:47; Judg 18:1. The Danites were forced to move to an area not already occupied by other Hebrew tribes, since Moses had earlier told Joshua that once the land was divided, the property would be the permanent possession of each allotted tribe, and no one was allowed to steal a man's land by moving the boundary marker. Deut 19:14; 27:17; Josh 14:9; Hos 5:10.

36 Judg 18:5.

37 Micah had set up a small "house of God" in the mountain of Ephraim and placed in it a graven image, and a molten image to the Lord. Judg 17:4. The Danites stole the idols from the home of Micah, along with an ephod, and some teraphim. Judg 18:17, 30-31.

superstitious recidivism would have been well-received, since Classical Greek mythology strongly accepted the value of oracles, even elevating the priestess at Delphi to the level of a deity.

Further evidence of the disenfranchisement of the tribe of Dan from their post-Mosaic brethren is found in the Song of Deborah, during the early Conquest era, where it was said that the tribe of Dan remained with the ships, rather than fighting with their fellow tribes against King Jabin of Canaan.[38] No reason was given for their isolation in the biblical text, but the battle took place during the period of time that they were beginning to reconnoiter the land to the north, and so the Danites may have already decided to break the relationship with the rest of the congregation.

This identification of the Danites with the dissident Hebrews would also help clear up why there are no explanations of the genealogy of the tribe of Dan in the book of *Chronicles*. If many of the Danites left the Exodus before the Conquest took place, or shortly thereafter, then their failure to conquer their allotted portions in the Promised Land could be due to a reduction in their population census. The book of *Judges* explains how they were forced to migrate north to Laish, thirty miles southeast of Sidon, leaving only a small number of residual members as part of the Hebrew tribal amphictyony.[39] Their history thereby became neglected by the biblical compilers who concentrated their attention on traditions passed down by the dominant tribes of the first millennium BCE. When a census of the tribes was taken in the second year after the Exodus began, the tribe of Dan had the second largest tabulation of men over the age of twenty years, numbering 62,700 men.[40] After the plague which was sent to kill the Hebrews who were worshiping Baal at Acacia, the tribe of Dan still numbered 64,400, the second largest number next to the tribe of Judah.[41] There is no recorded census of the tribes after the Conquest began, but a tribe of this strength should have had little trouble controlling the territory they were given, and I believe it was because a majority of the Danites fled the Exodus with the dissidents before the Conquest, and migrated north to Ugarit, before crossing the Mediterranean Sea to the Mycenaean shore.

Another tribe which may have traveled with the Danites to Mycenae were the

---

38 Judg 5:17. The Song of Deborah (Judg 5:1-31) is one of the earliest surviving texts in the Hebrew language, dating to about 1150 BCE, somewhat later than the Song of Miriam. Albright, Yahweh and the Gods of Canaan, 13. It is generally believed that six tribes went to war (Ephraim, Benjamin, Machir, Zebulun, Issachar and Naphtali), while four tribes (Gad, half of Manasseh, Dan and Asher) refused to join, while Reuben chose not to go. Amit, "Judges," 520.

39 Judg 18:1, 28-29.

40 Num 1:20-46; 2:3-31.

41 Num 26:43. This amount is very impressive, given the fact that Dan had only one son, Shuham. Num 26:42.

Simeonites, as their tribe showed the most dramatic decrease in the numbers of men between the first and last census taken of the Hebrews. After the theophany at Mt. Sinai, the tribe of Simeon numbered 59,300, while just before passage into the Promised Land, the total had plummeted to 22,200.[42] This latter number made the Simeonites the smallest of the Hebrew tribes, even including the tribe of Levi, who numbered 22,000 in the first census, and 23,000 at the end of the Exodus.[43] It is perhaps for this reason that when land was allotted to the various tribes in the Promised Land, Simeon only received a portion within the area given to the tribe of Judah.[44] Since none of the other tribes showed a similar fall in numbers, it is reasonable to conclude that many of the dissidents who were killed for their refusal to follow the edicts of the Mosaic Code may have been comprised of the tribe of Simeon.[45] This is particularly true of the numbers killed for worshiping Baal-Peor at Shittim, where the ringleader of the iniquity was Zimri, a prince of that tribe.[46] That many of them were killed outright during the Exodus is suggested by the fact that the loss of 37,100 is close to the total of over 40,000 Hebrews that were subjected to capitol punishment as enumerated in the biblical text.

A final legendary description of the founding of Greece which has connections to the Exodus is the allied story of Cadmus, who was said to have arrived in Greece with Danaus via Rhodes and Crete. According to the Parian Chronicle (Parian Marble), Danaus and his daughters sailed from Egypt to Greece in the year 1511 BCE, after first stopping at Rhodes.[47] This was just after Cadmus arrived in Greece, c. 1519 BCE, and founded the city of Thebes. Other sources dated the arrival of Danaus somewhat later, to c. 1430 BCE, with that of Cadmus c. 1400 BCE, making a reliable estimate uncertain.[48] The difference in years between these various assessments is not great, and the range would fit many of the Exodus dates as favored by modern scholars, especially my belief that the Exodus occurred in the fifteenth or fourteenth century BCE, as discussed in chapter 6. As will be discussed shortly, the Eastern influence on both the architecture of Mycenae, and the language of Greece, is generally ascribed to the

42 Num 1:23; 26:14.
43 Num 3:39; 26:62.
44 Num 18:1-9.
45 The only other tribes to decrease in numbers between the two censuses were Reuben, which lost 2,770; Gad, which lost 5,150; Ephraim, which lost 8,000; and Naphtali, which lost 8,000. The Chronicler placed the number of men in the tribe of Asher at 26,000, a total much smaller than the 41,500 mentioned in the book of *Numbers*, but this disparity does not necessarily mean a loss equivalent to the other tribes. Num 1:40; 26:47; 1 Chron 7:40.
46 Num 25:14.
47 Jones, Bronze Age Civilization, The Philistines and the Danites, 29-30.
48 Myres, Who Were the Greeks?, 139.

Phoenicians, who plied the trade routes of the Mediterranean Sea during the Late Bronze and Iron Ages (1200-587 BCE).[49] I believe it was the Hebrews, however, rather than the Phoenicians who were responsible for this contribution, and this would make it easy to understand why the legend developed in the manner it did, for the followers of Cadmus were said by the ancients to be Phoenicians, even though the Phoenician migration from the island of Crete did not take place until the invasion of the People of the Sea centuries later, as will be discussed in the next chapter. As I have pointed out throughout this book, much of the Hebrew contribution has been falsely attributed to the Phoenicians rather than the Hebrews, leading Martin Bernal to conclude that it is "overwhelmingly likely" that Homer's reference to "Kadmeans" at Thebes, and Hesiod's describing Europa as "daughter of noble Phoinix" carried by Zeus over salt water, both represent the following of earlier traditions, which indicated that Cadmus was a Phoenician who traveled over the Mediterranean Sea to Greece.[50] Under my analysis, Cadmus, like Danaus, was one of the dissident Hebrews who fled the Exodus after Moses instituted his policy of parricidal punishments for all those who refused to follow the regulations of the Mosaic Code, and not a Phoenician.

C. Historical Evidence

As already mentioned, most scholars today do not place much value on legendary material, and look instead to the scientific historical record, including language characteristics and archaeologic data, for information on who influenced the developing Classical Greek civilization. Although no one has yet named the Hebrews as an important component of this evolutionary process, I believe that the data from these two primary, non-legendary sources also strongly supports the proposition that the changes were due to a group of dissident Hebrews who left the Exodus and became enmeshed within the Mycenae civilization before the Trojan War, rather than Phoenicians who brought their information via the mercantile pipeline.

1. Language

The Classical Greek alphabet, which forms the foundation of the modern

---

49 The first century CE Jewish historian Josephus claimed that the Greeks learned their language from the Phoenicians and Cadmus, and since that time the Phoenicians have been credited by the majority of academicians as the most likely source for this influence. Josephus, "Against Apion," The Complete Works of Josephus, I.2, 607. In the words of Max Duncker, when talking of the presence of foreign cults in Greece, "it could have been Phoenicians who brought them to the Greeks." Duncker, History of Greece: From the Earliest Times to the End of the Persian War, I.60.

50 Bernal, Black Athena Writes Back, 93.

Greek language, is thought to have developed sometime around 850 BCE, just prior to the writings of Homer and Hesiod.[51] The characteristics of this language have been used by scholars to define the heritage of the Greeks, since it is generally accepted that the writing is Indo-European in origin, bearing many resemblances to both Latin and Sanskrit.[52] The Indo-European superfamily includes the Celtic, Slavic, Anatolian and Indo-Iranian groups of languages, and is clearly distinct from the Semitic tongue, which belongs to the Afro-Asiatic superfamily.[53] Because the Greek language appears to have primarily developed from the Indo-European tongue, most scholars have concluded that the ancestors of the Greeks were Indo-European settlers who arrived sometime after 2000 BCE, and that an actual migration of people, rather than a borrowing process, occurred.[54] As discussed earlier, this reasoning was charged with racist overtones by Martin Bernal.

The Greek language is not entirely Indo-European, however, with a high ratio of words identifiable as coming from Semitic and Egyptian sources.[55] Since ancient times, the Phoenicians have been credited with providing this input, and this concept carried over into the modern era, as reflected in the conclusion of the Italian archaeologist and linguist Sabatino Moscati (1922-1997 CE) that "there is no doubt that the Phoenicians taught the alphabet to the Greeks."[56] Herodotus, in the ninth century BCE, also recorded a tradition that the Greeks learned to write from the Phoenicians, and this was supported by the fact that the Greeks called letters *phoinikeia*, or "Phoenician things."[57] Although most linguists have placed this merger in the eighth century BCE, recent evidence has convinced some authorities that the Phoenician contribution may have taken place as early as 1100 BCE, a time when the Greek mainland was entering the Dark Age following the Trojan War.[58] The transmission is believed to have taken place in the Eastern Mediterranean, either in Crete, Cyprus, Euboea, or Al Mina.[59] This hypothesis

---

51 The earliest extant Greek inscriptions date to 775 BCE. Powell, Homer, 25.

52 Myres, Who Were the Greeks?, 101.

53 Jasanoff, & Nussbaum, "Word Games: The Linguistic Evidence in *Black Athena*," 179. The Afro-Asiatic (or Hamito-Semitic) family includes Egyptian, Semitic (Akkadian, Hebrew and Arabic), Berber, Chadic, Cushitic, and Omotic. Davies, "Egyptian Hieroglyphs," 78.

54 Fine, The Ancient Greeks, A Critical History, 4.

55 Myres, Who Were the Greeks?, 90-91.

56 Moscati, The World of the Phoenicians, 88. John Healey, Lecturer in Semitic Studies at the University of Manchester, bluntly states that there is "almost universal agreement that Phoenicia was the starting point." Healey, "The Early Alphabet," 232.

57 Cook, "Greek Inscriptions," 264.

58 Feldman, "Homer and the Near East: The Rise of the Greek Genius," 15; Cross, "Newly Found Inscriptions in Old Canaanite and Early Phoenician Scripts," 17.

59 Hall, A History of the Archaic Greek World, ca. 1200-479 BCE, 57.

places the influence of Phoenicia on the Greek language from external contacts, rather than assimilation by immigrants who lived on the Greek mainland, but this dating would also be consistent with an Hebraic, rather than a Phoenician, input, for an inscription from 1200 BCE found in Izbet Sartah, an early Hebrew settlement, contains five lines which resemble either Phoenician or ancient Hebrew letters, thereby supporting the theory that both Semitic tongues were in use at that time.[60] Because the Phoenician, Hebrew, Canaanite, and Ugaritic languages are all very similar, there is no way to argue for one source over another by the nature of their alphabets alone, but if the dissenting Hebrews did travel to Mycenae after leaving the Exodus, and became integrated into the Mycenaean culture, they would provide a much more plausible source for the infusion of their dialect than by simple trade contacts with merchants from adjacent lands.[61] Since Moses was said in the Bible to have written the record of the Exodus at the time it took place, there is no reason to doubt that many of the Hebrews were able to communicate by writing at that time, and when they left the Exodus and migrated to Mycenae, they could have been responsible for the additions from their advantageous position as citizens of the country. Despite this fact, most scholars believe the Phoenician alphabet "spread south to the Hebrews and was adopted by the Aramaeans to the east," rather than give the Hebrews credit for originating their own script.[62] This is primarily based upon the fact that the sign forms in the earliest inscriptions appear to have been Phoenician, which were then modified by the Aramaic scribes.[63] But it is not always possible to distinguish between the Phoenician and Hebrew recordings, for, with respect to the Gezer Calendar, a small tenth-century BCE stone tablet believed to be an early Hebrew inscription, "it cannot be easily decided linguistically whether this text is actually Hebrew or Phoenician."[64] The modification which the Phoenicians and Hebrews made to the more ancient Canaanite language, however, was not significant enough to prevent their communicating with each other, and the Greeks would have not seen their syntax as being significantly different. It should be noted, however,

---

60 Hoffman, In the Beginning: A Short History of the Hebrew Language, 29. The next extant example of Hebrew writing is the Gezer Calendar from the tenth century BCE. Ibid., 31.

61 The Biblical Hebrew, Canaanite, and Ugaritic dialects are similar phonetically, morphologically, and syntactically. Newgrosh, Rohl & van der Veen, "The el-Amarna Letters and Israelite History," 6-7. Hebrew was even called the "language of Canaan" (Isa 19:18), or "Judean" (Isa 36:12-13) in the book of *Isaiah*. Isserlin, The Israelites, 204. Despite the similarities, it is generally believed that the Hebrews accepted the Phoenician script "along with a whole cluster of other cultural traditions from the peoples they met when they settled in Palestine." Healey, The Early Alphabet, 30.

62 Healey, "The Early Alphabet," 222.

63 The Oxford Encyclopedia of Archaeology in the Near East, vol. I, 77.

64 Healey, "The Early Alphabet," 224.

that both Greek and Ugaritic texts are read from left to right, while Phoenician and Hebrew are read from right to left.[65]

It is not easy to understand why an Hebraic contribution to the developing Greek language has been totally ignored in modern times. The Hellenistic Jewish historian Eupolemus (second century BCE) had concluded that the Phoenicians received their language from the Jews, and then transmitted their script to the Greeks.[66] The basis for his deduction is not detailed in surviving texts, but recent scholarship has upheld his view by showing that the Hebrew modification of doubling up three of the letters to be used as vowels (*h, w, y*) may have been used as a basis for both the Greek and Latin alphabets.[67] This is an important distinction for considering the Hebrew origin, for the Greeks are generally credited with adding a new dimension to alphabetic writing by using some of the letters to represent vowels.[68] Eusebius (c. 260-340 BCE) also mentioned the similarity in the Hebrew and Greek letters to support the notion that the Greeks took their language from Hebrews in ancient Syria, rather than from Phoenicia, but subsequent analysts failed to support his claim.[69]

In more modern times, Francois Rene de Chateaubriand (1768-1848 CE), the French writer and historian, also believed that the Greek language was probably formed from the Hebrew, based upon its roots and ancient alphabet.[70] A variant of this view, which does not differentiate in time the Phoenician and Hebrew alphabets, has recently been championed by Cyrus Gordon, professor emeritus of Mediterranean studies at Brandeis University, who claimed that "the Ugaritic ABC gave rise to the Phoenician-Hebrew ABC which in turn was borrowed by the Greeks."[71] Ugarit was the major center for international commerce in the Late Bronze Age, as discussed in chapter 1, and the nature of its alphabet has

---

65 Ibid., 218. It is generally believed, however, that Greek writing was originally right to left, and changed because it was more convenient. Vase painters would occasionally write in both directions, or in the style of *boustrophedon*, or "ox-turning," where each line begins under the last letter of the previous line. Cook, "Greek Inscriptions," 267.

66 Eusebius, P.E., ix.26.1, as cited by Collins, <u>Between Athens and Jerusalem, Jewish Identity in the Hellenistic Diaspora</u>, 46. The same passage was quoted by Clement of Alexandria (Titus Flavius Clemens, c. 150-215 CE) in the second century CE. Bartlett, <u>Jews in the Hellenistic World</u>, 59-60. Most scholars accept that Eupolemus was a Jew, although Josephus conveyed the impression that he was a Greek. Bartlett, <u>Jews in the Hellenistic World</u>, 56.

67 Hoffman, In the Beginning: A Short History of the Hebrew Language, 3, 23.

68 Healey, "The Early Alphabet," 232.

69 Eusebius, <u>Preparation for the Gospel</u>, V.V.d, 2.507-508.

70 The Hebrew Bible in Literary Criticism, 14.

71 Gordon, <u>Before the Bible</u>, 130. Gordon also has argued that the Minoan Linear A script was Semitic, which supported his view that the Greek and Hebrew civilizations had a common background with both sharing a Northwest Semitic substratum. Gordon, "Recovering Canaan and Ancient Israel," 2787.

suggested that it pre-dated both the Hebrew and Phoenician tongues. It was the earliest West Semitic language represented in an alphabetic script with an important body of decipherable inscriptions from the fourteenth and thirteenth centuries BCE, and was a cuneiform writing with a signification number of abecedaries, the conventional name for the writing out of an alphabet according to an established order.[72] It is believed that it modified a Proto-Canaanite (Proto-Sinaitic) alphabet which was invented c. 1700 BCE.[73] The basic consonantal inventory of Ugaritic was represented by twenty-seven signs, while the southern Canaanite (Phoenician, Byblian) and Hebrew alphabets contained twenty-two signs, and the posited Proto-Canaanite one had twenty-nine phonemes.[74] This back-dating of the origins of the Semitic tongues clearly places the Hebrew language origin as being contemporary with the Hebrew Exodus.

Linguistic analysis alone cannot prove which source was more important, but it seems unlikely to me that the Greeks would have incorporated Semitic elements into their own language simply because they were exposed to Phoenicia or Ugarit through economic intercourse. My theory that dissident Hebrews became totally absorbed into the Mycenaean way-of-life, providing needed manpower to aid in both construction projects at home and military excursions abroad, as well as likely integrating into a practice of their patriarchal faith, which was not yet monotheistic and mimicked in many respects the early Mycenaean religion, provides a much better explanation for why the Greeks incorporated Semitic words, for the exposure of the Mycenaeans to the Hebrew tongue would have been continuous and close, and not derived from economic transactions alone. As Hebrew traditions were assimilated into the developing Greek culture, it would be natural that components of their language would have been included as well. Whether Ugarit played a role in the development of the Hebrew tongue, or whether the influence came from Canaanite sources, is not pertinent to this proposal, for it was the final product that was introduced into the Greek tongue by Hebrew migrants that matter, and not the earlier sources which helped the

---

72 The Oxford Encyclopedia of Archaeology in the Near East, vol. I, 76.

73 Hallo, "Again the Abecedaries," 286, 288-289. The Proto-Canaanite alphabet was composed of letter forms that were originally pictographic, for the most part, and influenced by Egyptian writing. Demsky, "Writing in Ancient Israel and Early Judaism, Part One: The Biblical Period," 8. It is the first step toward actual alphabetic writing, as opposed to the syllabic Egyptian, and cuneiform Akkadian systems, and was discovered in inscriptions c. 1700 BCE carved by miners at the turquoise mines at Serabit al-Khadim in Sinai. Healey, "The Early Alphabet," 210. Although there is Egyptian influence, the script is clearly Canaanite West Semitic. Ibid., 211. The clay tablets discovered at Ebla are also written in the Proto-Canaanite script. Merrill, Kingdom of Priests: A History of Old Testament Israel, 48. Eblaite is the earliest attested Semitic language. Gordon & Rendsburg, The Bible and the Ancient Near East, 71.

74 The Oxford Encyclopedia of Archaeology in the Near East, vol. I, 76; vol. III, 6.

Hebrews formulate their own brand of communication.

While the Hebrews may have been responsible for the introduction of Semitic elements in the Greek language, the island of Crete also clearly was instrumental in helping develop the earliest Greek script. Three types of writing have been uncovered from the island of Crete during the Middle and Late Bronze Ages: a hieroglyphic script; an early linear script, labeled as Linear A and believed to be reflective of the Cretan language; and a later linear script, designated as Linear B and ascribed as the Mycenaean tongue. Today the hieroglyphic script is referred to as Cretan Pictographic, and very little is known of its history because it has not been deciphered. It is generally believed, however, that the Cretan Pictographic script formed on the island independently from Egyptian hieroglyphics, which it resembles, and was not due to migrants from Egypt who brought with them the fundamentals of a written form of communication.[75]

Linear A tablets are few in number, but have been found throughout Crete in archaeologic levels stretching from 1750-1400 BCE, many years before the appearance of Linear B, which were initially found only in Knossos, and nowhere else in Crete, from a stratification of around 1450-1400 BCE.[76] Because Linear A is found in the same time frame as the Hieroglyphic script, and because one-third of the signs in Linear A closely resemble the Hieroglyphic forms, it was initially believed that Linear A developed directly out of the Hieroglyphic Script. It is now generally accepted, however, that the two were virtually contemporary in terms of their appearance, and evolved separately, although no clear explanation of how they were utilized, or why both versions were necessary, has been presented.[77] Linear B is distinguished from Linear A by its more cursive style, and has since been found on the Greek mainland at Pylos and Mycenae from around 1400-1200 BCE.[78] More recently, tablets have also been uncovered at Orchomenos, Tiryns and Eleusis on mainland Greece, and at Chania in Crete, an indication that its use was widespread at the time.

When the famous English archaeologist Sir Arthur Evans (1851-1941 CE) first unearthed evidence of the three scripts, he considered that all three were Minoan in origin. As other Linear B tablets were found on the Greek mainland, however, it soon became apparent that Linear B was of a separate origin from

---

75 Saggs, <u>Civilization Before Greece and Rome</u>, 92-93. Cyrus Gordon claims that the Cretan pictographic had strong affinities with both Egyptian writing, and the Northwest Semitic dialect, and that this indicated the Minoan palace builders were Semitic sealords ejected by the early Pharaohs of the twelfth Dynasty who then immigrated to Crete around 1800 BCE. Gordon, <u>The Common Background of Greek and Hebrew Civilizations</u>, 6-7.

76 Fine, The Ancient Greeks, A Critical History, 3; Hutchinson, Prehistoric Greece, 74.

77 "Prehistoric Archaeology of the Aegean: Lesson 10: Middle Minoan Crete," 10.

78 Chadwick, "The Linear Scripts and the Tablets as Historical Documents: (b) The Linear B Tablets as Historical Documents," 617.

the other two. Since the Linear A script predated Linear B, and the earliest Linear B tablets were found in Knossos, some scholars deemed that Linear A was the actual precursor of the Linear B script, and that the Linear B tablets were developed during the Greek occupation of Knossos, and then brought over to the mainland.[79] Although an appearance of the writing would seem to validate this conjecture, this view is no longer followed, for although Linear B resembles Linear A by using 54 of the Linear A signs, it is deemed to be a different writing, and the actual derivation has so far escaped certain identification, although it is generally accepted that Linear B was at least partially derived from Linear A for the purpose of writing a different, non-Minoan language.[80] The reason for the delay in the appearance of Linear B is now thought to be due to the fact that the Mycenaeans did not become a prominent political force in the region until the fall of Crete, as will be discussed shortly. The appearance of the Linear B tablets in the fifteenth century BCE matches the Early Date estimation of the Exodus, and if my conclusion that this dating is accurate, then the Hebrew dissidents would have arrived in Greece at the very inception of the early Greek alphabet, and would have been instrumental in infusing a Semitic element into the developing Greek alphabet.

Most scholars agree that the language of Linear B was an actual precursor of the Greek tongue, although how the conversion of this early Mycenaean script to the Classical Greek language took place is still uncertain, as there are no extant examples of intermediary writings. The great palaces on the Greek mainland which fostered the art of writing during the Mycenaean era were destroyed during the Dorian invasion, and no surviving tablets have been found from the ensuing era of the Greek Dark Ages. The tablets of Linear B have also failed to add much information about Mycenaean culture, since they appear to be solely administrative documents, lists and inventories, and do not detail any historical events, as do the Egyptian hieroglyphics. In addition, the limited number of documents makes interpretation very difficult, as evidenced by the word *te-re-ta*, which appears often in Linear B texts, and has variously been interpreted as priest; man in feudal service; man of the community subject to taxation; and servant.[81] This leaves historians with little information to reconstruct how the Mycenaean language may have actually originated. For now, we can only hope that some discovery of extant documents on the Greek mainland will provide further evidence of the evolutionary process, akin to the finding of the Dead Sea Scrolls, which provided biblical scholars with evidence of manuscripts that were hundreds of years earlier than those previously known.[82] As I discussed earlier,

---

79 Taylour, <u>The Mycenaeans</u>, 32.
80 Hutchinson, <u>Prehistoric Greece</u>, 73.
81 Vernant, The Origins of Greek Thought, 23.
82 , 8. The modern view is that some of the scrolls date from the second century BCE,

however, I believe the inclusion of Semitic elements into the Greek tongue is much more likely to have come from Hebrew dissidents who were incorporated into the Mycenaean society, than from Phoenician traders who were not part of the indigenous population on the mainland.

2. Archaeologic Evidence

Most of what we know about the Mycenaean physical world comes from the remarkable excavations first begun by Heinrich Schliemann, the German businessman who uncovered the remains of Troy in 1870 CE, Mycenae in 1874 CE, Orchomenos in 1880 CE, and Tiryns in 1885 CE. His expansive research crossed the breadth of the ancient Greek world, eventually proving that the vivid descriptions of Homer were more than the fanciful imaginations of a blind poet, and instead were based on civilizations that truly represented the origins of the Classical Greek Age. While archaeologists have long denigrated Schliemann for his poor excavating techniques and rash conclusions, the sites he uncovered were truly remarkable, and have provided historians a firm model of factual data on which to base their theories of Mycenaean origin.

The earliest signs of the Mycenaean civilization in Schliemann's excavations are the remains of the "Shaft Grave Dynasty," uncovered at the very bottom of the ancient city. Thirty deep shafts which served as graves were unearthed, and the valuable nature of the artifacts contained within the burial sites indicated that the inhabitants lived in a wealthy society. When Schliemann found a gold death mask in one of the graves, he immediately declared in his grandiose fashion that he had uncovered the image of King Agamemnon himself, although we now know that the graves were dated to an earlier era, c. 1600 BCE, suggesting that they came from the era of the Perseids, rather than from the time of the Trojan War.[83] Many Minoan artifacts were also found among the remains, a sign that the Shaft Grave Dynasty, while not actually Minoan in origin, was clearly influenced by a Minoan presence at some time during their early development.

Little is known about where these first Mycenaeans came from, but the chariots and charioteer gear found in the Shaft Graves resemble those which were first used by the Hittites under Hattusilis I (c. 1660-1620 BCE), as well as by the Hyksos in Egypt (1648-1555 BCE), raising the possibility that the warriors came

the vast majority from the first century BCE, and a few others from the first century CE. Wise, Abegg, & Cook, The Dead Sea Scrolls: A New Translation, 14. Before they were discovered, the earliest extant biblical texts were from over one thousand years later. Every book of the Hebrew Bible, except for Esther and Nehemiah, are represented in the Dead Sea Scrolls, in addition to the deuterocanonical books of Tobit, Sirach, and the Letter of Jeremiah. Sanderson, "Ancient Texts and Versions of the Old Testament," 294.

83 Bury & Meiggs, A History of Greece to the Death of Alexander the Great, 21.

from one of those locations. This corollary was pointed out by Robert Drews, Professor of Classics and History at Vanderbilt University, in his analysis of the generation of the early Greek culture:

The kind of event that occurred in the Argolid ca. 1600 B.C. fits squarely within the category of takeovers described in the preceding chapter. Just as charioteers appropriated thrones and states through the East, so PIE-speaking charioteers invaded Greece and took over for exploitation the population they found there. Although circumstances must have varied considerably from one land to another, the rudiments of the pattern were apparently similar in the takeover of northwestern India by the Aryans, of southern Mesopotamia by the Kassites, of Egypt by the *Hyksos*, of Mitanni by Aryans, and of many small Levantine states by Aryan and Hurrian maryannu. All of the takeovers occurred within a few generations after the perfection, around the middle of the seventeenth century B.C., of chariot warfare and the demonstration of its possibilities by Hattusili I and by the *Hyksos* who set themselves up in Egypt.[84]

The concept that PIE-speaking Achaeans entered the Greek mainland and utilized techniques from both the ancient Near East, as well as from the nearby island of Crete, to rise in dominance during the Late Bronze Age is a very attractive theory, although it is not followed by all Greek scholars. The possibility that the Mycenaeans developed from emigres of Hyksos warriors fits extremely well with my theory of an influx of dissident Hebrews who left the Exodus in the fifteenth century BCE, following the overthrow of the Hyksos regime.

Around 1500 BCE, the Shaft Grave Dynasty changed its method for royal burials, and began to utilize beehive-shaped tombs, or *tholoi*, the largest of which was euphemistically labeled by Schliemann as the "Treasury of Atreus."[85] Similar structures have been uncovered elsewhere on the Greek mainland, indicating that the Mycenaeans controlled a large part of the region by this time, but this particular characteristic did not last very long, and shortly thereafter, c. 1450 BCE, near the time when the Early Date for the Exodus is fixed, a palace-oriented society arose, further reflecting the influence of the Minoans. The jewel of this latter period was a truly impressive castle enclosing an area of 2,925 feet in circumference, and fortified by gigantic walls entered on the west by a solid Lion Gate, and on the north by a concealed postern. As with the *tholoi*, the basic plan of the palace was repeated at Tiryns and Pylos, and all three structures differed slightly from the Minoan palaces by being much more heavily fortified, less open to the air, and by having a central fixed hearth instead of a mobile brazier. The similarity of the plans

---

84 Drews, The Coming of the Greeks, 172.

85 This impressive structure measures forty-eight feet in diameter, and forty-three feet in height. Kishlansky, Geary & O'Brien, <u>Civilization in the West</u>, 40. It was the largest domed building in the world for over a thousand years, until the Pantheon was built in Rome. Robbins, <u>Collapse of the Bronze Age, The Story of Greece, Troy, Israel, Egypt, and the Peoples of the Sea</u>, 113.

have suggested to scholars that there must have been a Cretan presence during its construction, although the differences make it evident that the Mycenaeans built their fortresses to withstand invasion by land, while the Minoans relied on their protection by the expanse of sea which under their control.[86] The timing of the construction of these palaces with the large Cyclopean stones to the same era as the Early Date of the Exodus is, in my opinion, due to the immigration of experienced Hebrew dissidents who gained knowledge of the techniques of stone construction during their years of servitude in Egypt.

This would also explain how ideas and techniques from Egypt and the Levant also appear in Mycenae during this period of time. It has already been noted that the first immigrants used chariots which were developed and improved in the region of Anatolia, as well as being used by the Hyksos, but Egyptian influence during the palace-oriented period now included other significant changes, such as the use of gold masks for burial, monuments of carved stone on graves, and metal-inlay techniques.[87] Martin Bernal has suggested that these trivets indicate that the Hyksos actually invaded Greece, and took control of the mainland, but most scholars do not accept that there was an actual Egyptian presence in Mycenae, and rather ascribe the Egyptian influence as being promulgated through other societies, such as the Minoans in Crete.[88] This conclusion is based on the fact that the most typical Hyksos artifacts, such as scarabs and button-based juglets, which would be expected if personnel from that regime settle in Mycenae for any length of time, have not been found on the Greek mainland.[89] My postulate of the Hebrews being responsible for the transference, however, would readily explain these findings, without resorting to a belief in an Hyksos invasion.

The Hebrews would have brought the objects with them after they left Egypt, as described in the book of *Exodus*, which recorded that the Hebrews took many valuable objects of silver and gold when they left Egypt.[90] These products could easily have been part of the cache uncovered in the palace-oriented period, and

---

86 Smith, The Ancient Greeks, 4. The absence of fortifications in Crete led Sir Arthur Evans to conclude that the Minoan empire had a powerful naval fleet which protected the site, consistent with the writings of Thucydides (460-400 BCE). Wood, In Search of the Trojan War, 106.

87 Stubbings, "The Rise of Mycenaean Civilization," 633.

88 Like Schliemann's claim that the gold mask in one of the shaft-graves was that of Agamemnon, Bernal believed that a gold mask found in one of the graves could have been the image of an Hyksos warlord. Tritle, "*Black Athena*, Vision or Dream of Greek Origins?" 319.

89 Vermeule, Greece in the Bronze Age, 109.

90 According to the biblical text: "The Egyptians were practically stripped of everything they owned!" Exod 12:36. The Living Bible, 58. Some of this jewelry was likely used in the construction of the golden calf-idol, but other pieces were retained and brought to Mycenae, influencing artisans to reproduce their design.

their presence would resolve the nature of stone construction methodology found in Mycenae, since the Hebrews would have retained a knowledge of Egyptian engineering and manufacturing technology, enabling the Mycenaeans to quickly learn the workmanship which appears in their remains.

The style of buildings in Mycenae is an important clue to the determination of where the early Greeks received their cultural influence. Three techniques of building have been excavated in Mycenae, one of which has been termed Cyclopean, because the walls were constructed of huge blocks of roughly shaped limestone, packed together with small stones and yellow clay in the interstices, and so large that it would take two horses to move them.[91] Since the ancients believed that super-human strength was necessary to move these stones, they claimed that the walls were built by the Cyclopes, legendary giants imported from Lykia.[92] The other two methods were also conglomerates of large blocks, including one that was well-dressed with a hammer and regularly coursed, and another that was fitted together with great art. The construction of these protective walls showed "familiarity and skill in handling and dressing large masses of stone," as many of the stones weighed as much as five tons, and averaged five to eight meters in thickness.[93]

A number of theories have been proposed to explain how the early Greeks were able to carry out this process, without resorting to the aid of mythical creatures sent by sympathetic gods. Heinrich Schliemann postulated that "as the Phoenicians managed their import, it is possible that this whole decorative style came through that nation to Greece."[94] He pointed out that the Phoenicians were credited with supplying the many words of Semitic origin to the earliest forms of the Greek

---

91   This technique is also known as "Ashlar" masonry. Wace, Mycenae: An Archaeological History and Guide, 49. It can be found in many Hellenic cities, including Mykonos, Mycenae, Tiryns, Athens, Orchomenos, and Lykosoura. Duruy, History of Greece, and of the Greek People, From the Earliest Times to the Roman Conquest, vol. 1, 187.

92   Euripides, "Iphigenia in Aulis," 266, 226. Legend claimed that seven gigantic Cyclopes, called Gasterocheires, earned their living as masons, and accompanied Proetus when he came from Lycia, fortifying Tiryns with massive walls using blocks of stone so large that a mule team could not have moved them. Graves, The Greek Myths: 1, 73.b, 238.

93   Wace, Mycenae: An Archaeological History and Guide, 49, 110.

94 Schliemann, Tiryns, The Prehistoric Palace of the Kings of Tiryns, xlix. Schliemann may have been simply reiterating the view of Josephus, who claimed that the Egyptian influence in early Greece came about through the Phoenicians, who carried wares from the southern Mediterranean shore to the Greek mainland. Josephus, "Against Apion," Complete Works of Josephus, I.12, 610. Duruy believed the workmen were Pelasgians, a people who venerated Inachus as their founder and preceded the Hellenes on the Greek mainland. Duruy, History of Greece, and of the Greek People, From the Earliest Times to the Roman Conquest, vol. 1, 190.

language, and that this evidence of the close intercourse that took place between the two countries could indicate that the gigantic walls of Tiryns, as well as other prehistoric walls throughout Greece, were built by Phoenician colonists.[95] Once again, the Phoenicians are being credited with providing expertise in areas outside their nautical skills. The Phoenicians were never known for being proficient in the areas of masonry and construction, outside of ship-building, and I find it highly unlikely that they were responsible for either the transference of knowledge, or the supply of large amounts of skilled labor. The Hebrews, on the other hand, were very experienced in these manufacturing techniques from their years of working in Egypt as slaves. Although the Torah primarily referred to construction with bricks at the time of the Exodus, there was also much utilization of stone up to that period of time. The construction of the Cyclopean walls in Mycenae and Tiryns took place around 1340 BCE, with the Lion Gate following around 1250 BCE.[96] If the Exodus took place anywhere from the fifteenth to fourteenth century BCE, as I believe it did, the Hebrews could have easily provided the Mycenaeans with a means by which the walls could have been constructed. The Phoenicians may have been the ones to transport Hebrew artisans to Mycenae, but they were not an integral part of the engineering process itself. Once the palaces were built, and the dissident Hebrews were integrated into the expanding Mycenaean culture, the legends and traditions of the Patriarchs became part of the evolving Greek mythology, eventually culminating in the Classical Greek society centuries later.

Although the Hebrews provide a better explanation for the building of the palaces than do the Phoenicians, it is also possible that Cretan artisans played a role in this palace-oriented period, for the palaces on Crete were destroyed in the fifteenth century BCE, a century before the construction in Mycenae began in earnest. The widespread destruction in their own country would have likely forced surviving Cretans to migrate elsewhere, and the most likely place for them to travel was Mycenae, where they then could have taken part in the proliferation of activity that characterized the palace-oriented period. While there is no way to differentiate the contribution of Hebrews and Cretans in this regard, the addition of Semitic and Eastern cultural influences into Mycenae during this same era favors, in my opinion, that it was the Hebrews, rather than the Cretans, who were of primary importance.

D. The Role of Crete

As discussed above, the Mycenaean palace-oriented society was clearly influenced by Cretan culture, but the advancement of Mycenaean power in the Late Bronze Age was affected more by their take-over of Cretan property across the Mediterranean Basin, than by its ideologic assistance. When the palaces on

95 Schliemann, Tiryns, The Prehistoric Palace of the Kings of Tiryns, 27-28.
96 Mylonas, Mycenae & The Mycenaean Age, 33.

Crete were suddenly destroyed in the fifteenth century BCE, the Mycenaeans took over the Cretan worldwide centers of trade and immediately became the sole focus of authority in the Aegean sphere. This conversion from a growing political force into a dominant regional power forced the Mycenaeans to find an infusion of man-power to feed their imperial cravings, and I believe this deficiency was provided by thousands of dissident Hebrews, who not only were able to supply the men needed for this transformation, but also the means by which to accomplish these goals through their experience as slaves in advanced Egyptian construction technology. To better understand what role Crete played in the generation of Mycenaean society, and how they provided Mycenae the ready means to become a dominant world power, it is necessary to analyze their history during the Early and Middle Bronze Ages.

Lying equidistant between the important Bronze Age centers of Mycenae, Cyrene, Troy and the Nile Delta, Crete played an important role in the ancient world by functioning as "a stepping stone between all eastern Mediterranean lands."[97] Next to Cyprus, it was the largest island in the Aegean, and lay only sixty miles from the Greek mainland, and one hundred and twenty miles from Anatolia. Because it was the first Aegean island to maintain a large armada of trading vessels, it had a head start over other countries surrounding the Mediterranean Basin in the development of maritime trade.[98] Archaeologic evidence indicates that the first inhabitants of Crete were Neolithic settlers in the seventh millennium BCE, thought to be migrants who arrived in boats from Anatolia. Although settlements have been found at Knossos as early as 6000 BCE, major expansion did not take place until the Early Bronze Age, referred to as the Early Minoan period (3000-2000 BCE), when new immigrants came in from either the Nile Delta, or from Palestine, particularly in the eastern part of the island. Settlements rapidly began to expand across the island near the end of this period, with palaces beginning to appear as early as 2000 BCE.

Utilizing the ample forests of oak, fir, cypress and cedar which were present in ancient times to provide a wealth of ship timber, Crete became the first maritime expedition force in the Mediterranean region, and rose to international prominence in rapid succession. The success of the Minoans in world trade during the Middle Minoan period (2000-1580 BCE) was aided by the regular winds and currents which made passage from Crete and Rhodes to North Africa possible, even in the second millennium BCE. The direct sea route from Crete to Egypt was only three hundred miles long, and a steady north-west wind in the summer assisted navigation to Egypt, while the return voyage was helped by a sea current

---

97 Grant, The Ancient Mediterranean, 87.

98 Minoan seals show large sea-going vessels consistent with this burgeoning economy as early as 2000 BCE. Hutchinson, <u>Prehistoric Greece</u>, 93.

which flowed northwards from the Nile Delta.[99] The weather was unpredictable, however, and this made the trip more dangerous than the nine hundred mile route that hugged the coastline and led to the ports of Rhodes and Cyprus, and then down the coast of the Levant, a route which would be favored by the Mycenaeans whose maritime expertise did not yet match that of the Minoans.[100] The structure of the Minoan ships, with their higher prow and lower stern than the Egyptians, suggests that they took the direct route from Crete to Egypt, and then returned in a circular fashion, traveling up the coast of Palestine to Cyprus, and back by the way of the Dodecanese.[101]

Chief exports of the island were wine, oil, timber and textiles, but the Cretans functioned more in the importation and exportation of goods, than as exporters of locally-made products, much the way Phoenicians would centuries later during the Late Bronze Age. Their ships were "a common sight in Near Eastern ports," and foreign relations were maintained with Egypt, Asia, Libya and the Aegean world.[102] The Minoan culture blossomed from contact with the ancient Near East, and Cretan merchants were among the most active on the Syrian coast and Egypt. Colonies were founded in many parts of the Aegean world and the Levant during the first half of the second millennium BCE, and their pottery found its way to many of the Cycladic islands including Delos, Ceos, Melos, Thera, Rhodes, Samos, Iasos, and at Miletus on the Asiatic mainland.[103] Evidence of contact with Egypt is present from as early as the fourth millennium BCE, during the predynastic era.

The origin of the name of the island is not agreed upon, although there is no

---

99 Saggs, Civilization Before Greece and Rome, 137. Ships during this era could only sail ahead of the wind, as the technique of sailing into the wind was not discovered until much later with the advent of the Latin sail. The importance of the wind was manifest in the fact that the north wind was named Boreas, the west wind was Zephyr, the east wind was Eurus, and the south wind was Notus. Pillot, The Secret Code of the Odyssey, 21. For navigation, as indicated by the advice of the goddess to Odysseus in the *Odyssey*, the position of the star constellations was critical. Homer, The Odyssey, 5.271-276, 89.

100 That this longer route was also dangerous is evident from the curse that the chorus of suppliants set upon the herald sent to Argos to return them to Egypt: "May the sea swallow you as you round the wooded point of Cyprus!" Aeschylus, "The Suppliants," 872-73, 80.

101 Samuel, The Mycenaeans in History, 33.

102 Willetts, Everyday Life in Ancient Crete, 35, 37.

103 Huxley, The Early Ionians, 15. Minoan influence was strong in the Cyclades from the beginning of the Protopalatial (Old Palace) period (1900-1700 BCE) in MM IB. It became even more marked in the Neopalatial period (1700-1400 BCE), in sites such as Phylakopi (Melos), Paroikia (Paros), Ayia Irini (Keos), and Akrotiri (Thera). This is primarily seen in pottery shapes and decorative patterns, as well as fragments of Linear A tablets. "Prehistoric Archaeology of the Aegean: Lesson 18: The Nature and Extent of Neopalatial Minoan Influence in the Aegean and Eastern Mediterranean Worlds," 2.

lack of traditional explanations. According to Pliny the Second (c. 62-115 CE), Dosiades, a third century BCE writer of inscriptions from Sicily, claimed that the island took its name from the nymph Crete, the daughter of Hesperis.[104] The Bible, however, generally referred to Crete as *Caphtor*, and their people as the *Caphtorim*, from whom the Philistines were said to have originated.[105] Variations on this label included *Kaptara*, which is how the Assyrian texts of the Mari period referred to Crete; *Kpt*, *Kptr*, or *Kaptara*, from the Ugaritic texts; and *Kftiw*, *Kefti*, *Keftar*, or *Keftiu/Kaptaru* in Egyptian.[106] Closely identified with the biblical label of Caphtorites is the term *Cherethites*, which appeared in poetic parallel with the Philistines in the books of *Ezekiel* and *Zephaniah*.[107]

Whatever the true derivation of the name for the island, most ancient historians identified the early Cretan civilization with King Minos of Knossos, the legendary ruler of Crete who was credited with developing the first powerful maritime nation on earth.[108] When Sir Arthur Evans uncovered Knossos in his archaeologic excavation in 1900 CE, he coined the term Minoan for the Cretan civilization in honor of this famous ruler, although there is no factual data on whether the stories are genuine. When the Cretan civilization entered the Middle Minoan era, they "skyrocketed into one of the most extraordinary achievements of mankind."[109] A major expansion of Aegean trade occurred throughout the Levant during the MM II period (c. 1900-1700 BCE), and objects of Aegean origin have been found at most of the centers of trade, including Ras Shamra, Hazor, Megiddo, Tod, Harageh, Lahun, and Abydos.[110] The Egyptian royal graves at Byblos, from the time of the twelfth Egyptian Dynasty (1937-1759 BCE), show pottery fragments that imitated the Aegean models,[111] and depictions in the Thera paintings show ships with Middle Kingdom Egyptian-style construction

---

104 Pliny, <u>Natural History</u>, IV.xii.58, II.161.

105 In the biblical Table of Nations, the *Caphtorim* are one of the peoples descended from Mizraim, the son of Ham. Gen 10:13-14. Sarna, <u>Genesis</u>, 75. See, e.g., Deut 2:23; Jer 47:4; Amos 9:7.

106 Simons, The Geographical and Topographical Texts of the Old Testament, 17; Astour, "Place Names," 294.

107   Ezek 25:15-16; Zeph 2:5. See e.g., 1 Sam 30:14. Howard, Jr., "Philistines," 232.

108 Thucydides recorded that King Minos was the first person to establish a navy, and that he dominated the Aegean world through his command of the sea. Thucydides, <u>The Peloponnesian War</u>," I.4, 37.

109 Starr, The Origins of Greek Civilization, 1100-650 B.C., 37.

110 Hindson, <u>The Philistines and the Old Testament</u>, 17. Architectural palace designs exactly like those found in the palace of Minos on Crete are also evident during the reign of Yarim-Lim (1780-1765 BCE), in the city of Alalakh, in northwest Syria, an indication that Cretan influence extended deep into the Levant. Jones, <u>Bronze Age Civilization, The Philistines and the Danites</u>, 14-15.

111 Lods, Israel, From Its Beginnings to the Middle of the Eighth Century, 70-71.

and sail rigging following the volcanic eruption in 1640-1650 BCE, indicating a Cretan influence.[112]

The island enjoyed great economic advantage from these endeavors, allowing the Cretans to construct grand palaces during the Middle Minoan period, making the region one of the most populated centers on earth. None of the cities were protected by defensive walls, however, an indication that the Minoans downplayed any threat of invasion by either outside forces, or by rebellious inhabitants who sought to overthrow the ruling monarchy. This did not protect them from natural disasters, however, and a general catastrophe destroyed many palaces around 1750-1700 BCE, forcing a period of reconstruction which eventually resulted in the New Palace era (1700-1450 BCE), the true zenith of Minoan civilization.[113] The new palace at Knossos was equal in size to a small Oxford college or a medieval monastery, and since Linear B tablets were found only at Knossos, and nowhere else on the island, most scholars believe that the palace at Knossos was the political center of the Cretan world, and that the Mycenaeans infiltrated that particular area because it functioned as the nerve center of the Minoan civilization.

A final phase of destruction began to spread across the island from 1450-1375 BCE, accompanied by the appearance of a greater Mycenaean influence on Crete, including military themes in the palace frescoes at Knossos, pottery remains reminiscent of Mycenaean styles, and the use of Linear B Script.[114] These changes have been interpreted to mean that the country came under the control of the Mycenaeans, and was followed by a Mycenaean displacement of Minoan colonies on the islands of Rhodes and Cyprus.[115] If the Exodus took place in the fifteenth or fourteenth century BCE, it is obvious that the dissident Hebrews would have dealt with the Mycenaeans, rather than the Minoans, if they chose to travel to the island of Crete, instead of the shore of mainland Greece. They would have then likely been transported to Mycenae to function as construction workers once Mycenae began to take over control of the island.

E. *Mycenaean Presence in the Levant*

Like the Minoans, the early Mycenaean culture paid close attention to the sea as a means of expanding commercial contact with distant lands, thereby

---

112 Yurco, "*Black Athena,* an Egyptological Review," 81.

113 Most historians believe that this devastation was caused by earthquakes. Knapp, "Island Cultures: Crete, Thera, Cyprus, Rhodes, and Sardinia," 1441. The island is set in an area that is geologically unstable, and has been subjected to many earthquakes over the centuries. Willetts, <u>The Civilization of Ancient Crete</u>, 23.

114 "Prehistoric Archaeology of the Aegean: Lesson 10: Middle Minoan Crete," 3.

115 The colony on Rhodes has been identified by some scholars as the country of Ahhiyawa. Knapp, "Island Cultures: Crete, Thera, Cyprus, Rhodes, and Sardinia," 1443.

developing a maritime framework that one day enabled them to effectively control the former Minoan trade routes. Although much smaller in size than both Italy and the Iberian peninsula, the Greek coastline of 2600 miles was longer than that of its neighbors on the northern and eastern coast of the Mediterranean Sea, and the valleys and harbors which faced to the southeast afforded many opportunities for maritime trade throughout the region. In addition, the chain of islands which crossed the sea toward Anatolia and the Levant enabled the Mycenaean captains to guide small ships "in perfect security" to Asia and Egypt, even without the aide of a compass.[116] The Mycenaean take-over of the Minoan colony at Ialysos on Rhodes in the fifteenth century BCE allowed their ships to travel south and then reach a sea-current with a southeasterly direction which brought them directly to the Delta, or to Cyprus, without losing sight of land. Their next settlement was at Enkomi on Cyprus, and during the Late Bronze Age these two islands were used by the Mycenaeans as stepping stones for Levantine trade, with the city of Ugarit functioning as the nerve center for operations throughout the entire Mediterranean Basin.[117] No ship was ever more than forty miles from shore during this voyage, allowing Mycenae to trade with Egypt through ports along the Syrian and Palestinian coasts, rather than relying solely on the direct route usually taken by the Minoans. The Mycenaean vessels had large storage areas, indicating that they were primarily used as cargo ships and not warships, and although they were not among the foreign ships depicted in Egyptian tomb paintings, pottery remains found on Cyprus, and along the entire length of the Syria-Palestine coast, have convinced scholars that Mycenaean merchants "held a virtual monopoly on maritime commerce in the eastern Mediterranean" during the Late Bronze Age.[118] In this capacity, they would have shared the waters with Phoenician entrepreneurs.

The most common type of early Mycenean ship used for these purposes had five pairs of oars, but larger ships had fifteen pairs of oars, and even carried masts for sailing to more distant destinations. By the time of the Trojan War, the average Mycenaean vessel had fifty oars, with the largest up to one hundred oars.[119] Most of the ancient ships were square sailed, and the prevailing winds in the Mediterranean blew from north to south, so while a trip from Athens to Rhodes might take three days, with another four days to reach Egypt, the journey back

---

116 Kitto, The Greeks, 31.

117 In the *Iliad*, Agamemnon's breastplate was a gift of his Cypriote friend, Kinyras (Cinyras), who had heard of the Achaian preparation of war and gave the king the corselet which had ten circles of cobalt, twelve of gold, and twenty of tin. Homer, The Iliad, 11:20-25, 234-235.

118 Vermeule, Greece in the Bronze Age, 258.

119 Jason's ship, like the Mycenaean vessels during the time of the Trojan War, was also a fifty-oared galley (*pentekoter*). Casson, The Ancient Mariners, 55.

would take twice as long.[120] If the Exodus took place at any time between the fifteenth and thirteenth centuries BCE, the dissident Hebrews would have surely sought passage from either Mycenaean or Phoenician seamen, since these two countries monopolized the maritime activity across the Mediterranean Sea.

Despite the relative safety of using the circular trade route, which never lost sight of land, travel was still unpredictable, and subject to uncontrollable direction changes because of sudden weather changes and the uncertainty of the sea currents. Such precipitous alterations were noted by Homer in his description of how Menelaus was forced to land in Egypt during his return home from the Trojan War,[121] and how Odysseus was drawn out to sea past Kythera, and finally on to the strange land of the Lotus Eaters.[122] These disasters were blamed on the gods, who created atmospheric changes which would "shake the Aegean Sea," washing up the bodies of drowned men on the shores of Mykonos, Delos, the Capherean promontories, Scyros, and Lemnos.[123] While these dangers may have ended the career of many a sailor, they were not frequent enough to discourage the use of sea travel for emigration, since the only alternative was to trek on foot through Anatolia, requiring not only an extended period of time to complete the journey, but also the ability to survive an ever-present threat from hostile kings. When the dissident Hebrews realized they had to travel to a distant shore in order to escape the dangers which faced them in the Levant, they would have surely taken the sea route, rather than risk an arduous and dangerous journey overland. Not only would that route take longer, but they would have likely realized in Ugarit, once they attempted to converse with traders from that region, that there was no way to communicate with the indigenous inhabitants, a problem they did not face with the Semitic languages prevalent in the Levant.

The wealth of Mycenae grew steadily once the Minoan culture collapsed, and by the fourteenth century BCE, Mycenaean pottery was found throughout the Levant, from Carchemish in the north to El Arish in the south, a distance of 500 miles. As summarized by Dr. H. W. Catling, from the British School at Athens, "what had been a trickle of Mycenaean trade in the late fifteenth century BCE became a flood during the fourteenth."[124] Commerce carried well into

---

120 Freeman, Egypt, Greece and Rome: Civilizations of the Ancient Mediterranean, 115.

121 Homer, The Odyssey, 3.300-303, 44.

122 Ibid., 9.80-81, 147. Odysseus was again thwarted in his attempt to land at Ithaca when his ship "caught a fresh norther," and ran southward with the wind until it was hit by lightning and sank. Ibid., 14.292, 256. A similar northerly gale swept the ships of Dion (408-354 BCE) from the coast of Sicily to Libya. Plutarch, "Dion," 25, 123-124.

123 Euripides, "The Trojan Women," 88-90, 130.

124 Catling, "Cyprus in the Late Bronze Age," 199. The largest import to Greece was ingots of tin and copper for the armament industry, while the largest export was pottery, much of which was produced in the Argolid. Sandars, The Sea Peoples: Warriors of the

the interior, and followed the valley of the Orontes as far as Hamah, Qatna and Kadesh, and then onto to Alalakh and Jericho. Although the Hittites did not allow Mycenaean traders to enter the hinterland of Anatolia, centers were developed on the coast at Miletus and Colophon, as well as at the city of Troy.

It is at this pivotal period of time, when the palaces on Crete were destroyed, and the Mycenaeans were beginning to expand their commercial enterprise throughout the ancient Near East, that the arrival of a group of Hebrew dissidents in Mycenae would have been warmly welcomed, providing a much needed supply of men to assist both in the construction of palaces on the mainland, and the expansion of military capabilities. No word for "mercenary" has been found in Greek texts, but it is generally accepted that Mycenae, like most of the countries in the ancient Near East, utilized warriors from adjacent lands. Nancy K. Sandars, from the School of Archaeology at Oxford University, even attributed the type of sword known as "northern bronzes," which were found in ruins associated with the Mycenaean military, as coming from individuals who traveled to Greece from Transylvania and Hungary to participate in wartime activities.[125] The military and economic needs of the country were growing daily, and the populations of kingdoms on the Greek mainland were not substantial enough to compete with the larger Hittite and Egyptian populations.[126] An infusion of combat-weathered soldiers numbering in the thousands would have made a significant contribution to the Mycenaean armada, and allowed the Mycenaeans the ability to fortify their increasing need for expansion at home and overseas, while maintaining an adequate militia to protect and expand their growing empire. As the Trojan War drew to a close, and Greece entered the Dark Age, oral traditions about the war were passed from generation to generation, allowing the patriarchal legends time to be modified into the tales of Greek heroism, so famously portrayed in the *Iliad* and the *Odyssey* by Homer. It is clear that much of the populace in that era thoroughly enjoyed listening to these epic tales, as it is estimated that the *Iliad*

Ancient Mediterranean 1250-1150 BC, 74-75. The Uluburun shipwreck off the coast of southern Turkey, dated to about 1300 BCE, contained 10 tons of copper, and one ton of tin ingots, along with an array of other products totaling 20 tons. Pulak, "The Uluburun shipwreck and Late Bronze Age Trade," 290. The pottery which was exported was not only decorative, but was used to store valuable commodities like resins, animal fats, and, most importantly, olive oil. The Mycenaeans also exported weapons, jewelry, hides, timber, wine, olive oil, and purple dye. Casson, The Ancient Mariners, 55.

125 Sandars, The Sea Peoples: Warriors of the Ancient Mediterranean 1250-1150 BC, 94.

126 It is estimated that the population on the mainland totaled 180,000 people in Mycenae, 70,000 in Midea, 90,000 in Tiryns and 60,000 in Argos. Wood, In Search of the Trojan War, 158. These numbers were not large compared to the populations of Egypt and Anatolia, where the forces at the battle of Kadesh in 1275 BCE were over 25-37,000 men on each side.

took about twenty hours to perform, likely over a three day period of time, and the *Odyssey* took two days.[127] In my opinion, the story eventually reduced to writing by Homer, contained elements of Hebrew legends that were supplied by the Hebrew dissidents to embellish the developing evolution of Greek mythologic tradition.

F. Ahhiyawa

The belief that Mycenae had trading contacts in Anatolia was intensified when a small number of references were found to a land called Ahhiyawa among the many Hittite cuneiform tablets found at the capital city of Boghazkoy from the fourteenth century BCE. Ahhiyawa was a prominent political force in the Late Bronze Age, but little factual knowledge existed about the country, and its capital city has never been identified with certainty, although suggestions had included placement in western coastal Anatolia near Miletus, in the Troad, on mainland Greece, and on the island of Rhodes or Crete. One of its well-known rulers was Tawagalawas, the son of Antarawas, who at one time was of sufficient standing for the Hittite king to consider marrying into his family. A missive from the king, called the "Tawagalawas letter," referred to the king of Ahhiyawa as "my brother,"[128] and the fact that King Suppiluliuma I sent an exile there, has suggested that there were friendly relations between the two countries.[129]

That Ahhiyawa may have been part of the Mycenaean empire was first proposed by the Swiss Assyriologist and Hittitologist Emil Forrer (1894-1986 CE), who made the pronouncement in 1924 CE that Ahhiyawa referred to the Achaeans of Homer's the *Iliad* and the *Odyssey*.[130] Forrer went so far as to claim that Attarissyas, a king of Ahhiyawa and contemporary of the Hittite King Tudhalias IV (1250-1220 BCE), was actually Atreus, the father of Agamemnon, although this supposition has not been supported by the majority of scholars.[131] Despite the fact that Alan E. Samuel, Professor of Greek and Roman History at the University of Toronto, has proposed that "there can be no real doubt that *Ahhiyawa* refers to one of the Mycenaean kingdoms,"[132] most scholars still consider the identification tenuous. The possible connection of Ahhiyawa with Homer's Greeks, however,

---

127 Schmidt, The First Poets: Lives of the Ancient Greek Poets, 81.

128 Hutchinson, "The Decadence of Minoan Crete: The Mycenaean Empire," 420.

129 Samuel, The Mycenaeans in History, 124.

130 Robbins, <u>Collapse of the Bronze Age, The Story of Greece, Troy, Israel, Egypt and the People of the Sea</u>, 58. The Achaeans are the name by which the Greek invaders of Troy are generally called, although at times Homer also referred to them as Argives or Danaans. Stapleton, <u>The Illustrated Dictionary of Greek and Roman Mythology</u>, 8.

131 Knapp, "Bronze Age Mediterranean Island Cultures and the Ancient Near East, Part 2," 126.

132 Samuel, The Mycenaeans in History, 126.

is supported by an Hittite text which told how cult idols from Greece were sent from Ahhiyawa to the bedside of the plague-stricken Hittite king, believed to be Mursilis II (1339-1306 BCE), in hopes of resulting in a cure.[133] The fact that the Ahhiyawans were noted seafarers, regularly trading along the Eastern Mediterranean, and were friendly with the Hittites, often sending gifts to the Hittite king, has buttressed the possible connection of the two countries, but more data is needed before a true identity can be made.

If Ahhiyawa was indeed part of the Mycenaean realm, the close relationship between Ahhiyawa and the Hittites would fit nicely with my theory of Hebrew migration to Mycenae, for if the Exodus occurred in the fifteenth century BCE, when there were still friendly relations between the two countries, a group of Hebrew runaway slaves from Egypt would have likely been seen as friendly by the Hittites, who were competing with Egypt for control of the Levant. If the Hebrews wanted to escape the region, Mycenae was an opportune destination, and contact with Ahhiyawa would have been easy to make, given the fact that there was clear communication between the two countries in the era of the Early Date of the Exodus. A later Exodus date would not fit this pattern, however, for by 1300 BCE the Greeks had begun to have significant disagreements with the Hittites, and many of the Hittite letters made reference to political problems between the two countries.[134] If the dissident Hebrews arrived in Hittite controlled land during this period of time, it would have likely been more difficult for them to obtain passage to the Mycenaean shore. By placing the Exodus in the fifteenth, or even the early fourteenth century BCE, however, the Hebrews would have arrived during a period of cooperation between the two countries.

G. Religion

The Classical Greek religion developed from a variety of sources, with two major elements identifiable: the Homeric Olympian religion, which was particularly suited to the warring Greek class and consisted of a society of anthropomorphic gods with whom human relations were maintained by sacrifice and prayer in a spirit of bargaining or seeking for favors; and the chthonian cults, which contained gods who were connected to nature, providing security for a more settled and humble people who wrested their livelihood from the land.[135] Because homage was directed to a large number of gods, the Greeks were willing to incorporate the deities of foreign nations into their own divine panoply whenever circumstances indicated that the god in question was powerful enough to assist in their future endeavors. This receptivity also characterized the religion of the Mycenaeans, who almost always "took over and absorbed into their own system other religious

---

133 Wood, In Search of the Trojan War, 180.
134 Ibid., 180-181.
135 Guthrie, "The Religion and Mythology of the Greeks," 853.

systems with which they came into contact."[136] If the Hebrews conveyed the biblical tales of the incredible might of YHWH, it would seem reasonable to assume that the Mycenaeans would assimilate their beliefs. Along with ascribing attributes of YHWH to Zeus, an incorporation of other biblical tales would also be expected to follow. I will make notice of all these instances throughout this book, and it is my belief that the assimilation took place because of the emigration of Hebrew dissidents from the Exodus.

The characteristics of the polytheistic Hebrew faith before the alterations imposed by the Mosaic Code would have been very compatible with the Mycenaean creed, especially their devotion to the teaching and faith of their forefathers. The pre-Mosaic Hebrews who took part in the Exodus had left bondage in Egypt and walked into the wilderness in order to have the freedom to live as they wished, free from persecution and enslavement. A primary focus of their faith, however, was the honor that was paid to ancestors, something which the Greeks also highlighted in their heroic tales. The regulations of Moses interfered with this devotion by placing limitations on not only what God the Hebrews could honor, but how that homage was to be expressed. Unlike the Mosaic Code, which restricted the worship of YHWH to the sanctuary under the direction of the priestly caste, the God of the fathers (*theos patroos*) was "a nomadic deity, leading, accompanying and guarding the group that was faithful to him."[137] The Patriarchs had diligently taught their children to show their adoration of the gods in ways that Moses now forbade, and the participants who remained with the Exodus were forced to either put such principals aside, or face parricidal retribution. In Mycenae, the Hebrews would encounter a religion which not only allowed them to practice the faith of their ancestors, but also provided the concept that success was achievable through honorable deeds, rather than pious obedience. Moral teachings were not extensive, and the virtues of the Greeks "were preeminently military - above all, physical strength and bravery."[138] These traits would have appealed to the Hebrews who were tired of the prolonged wandering in the Sinai wilderness, and

---

136 Chadwick, The Mycenaean World, 85. Unlike the Greek pantheon, details of Mycenaean worship are sparse, and the Linear B tablets have so far failed to enlarge our understanding, since they do not yet show any evidence of religious practice. It appears, however, that they eventually produced "an amalgam of the forms of worship indigenous to the Aegean basin with the cults and beliefs which they brought with them," unlike the Jews who utterly rejected all other religious beliefs outright. Guthrie, "The Religion and Mythology of the Greeks," 852. The Mycenaeans took deities from all the surrounding countries, including Egypt, Crete, and Indo-European sources, and often made only minor modifications in the attributes of each one. Even Zeus, the most powerful of the Greek gods on Mt. Olympus, originally came from ancestors that were not originally Greek. Chadwick, The Mycenaean World, 86.

137 de Vaux, The Early History of Israel, 272.

138 Botsford & Robinson, Hellenic History, 41.

the realization that they would never be able to enter the Promised Land. For a period of time, the mysteries of the Exodus and the magical tricks of Moses kept their interest and funneled their efforts into survival at whatever cost was required. As tension between their long-held beliefs and the tyranny of Moses increased, however, they found it necessary to leave the unity of their former neighbors and friends, and strike out for a land where they could be free to live the faith of their own ancestors.

In return for the valuable assistance provided by the Hebrews in the construction of the palaces at home and in military maneuvers abroad, the Mycenaeans would have seen the power of YHWH as worthy of respect, since the Hebrews had just fled from Egypt, the strongest nation on earth, and survived in the wilderness with the help of YHWH alone. The Hebrews were a sturdy group of men whose success must have meant that they were favored by the gods, and so absorbing YHWH into their panoply of deities would have been a natural reaction. I will discuss how the attributes of YHWH resembled other Greek gods in more detail in chapter 11, but for now I will only note that the similarities support the proposal that the Greeks learned of YHWH's feats by direct assimilation, rather than by hearsay evidence alone.

H. The End of Mycenae

Shortly after the Trojan war ended, the Mycenaean empire rapidly disappeared from the geopolitical scene as a series of catastrophes materialized throughout the Greek mainland, leading to total or partial destruction of almost every major urban center on the Greek mainland, including Mycenae, Tiryns, Pylos, Thebes, Orchomenos, Araxos, Krisa and Menelaion.[139] Pylos and Mycenae showed signs of destruction c. 1230 BCE, followed by the disappearance of habitation in other cities.[140] There are indications that the danger of invasion was anticipated, as the fortifications at Mycenae and Tiryns were strengthened, and concealed passages were constructed to safeguard the water supply, in the second half of the thirteenth century BCE.[141] As will be discussed in the next chapter, the Trojan War in ancient times was believed to have taken place c. 1180 BCE, but modern

---

139 Desborough, "The End of the Mycenaean Civilization and the Dark Age: (a) The Archaeological Background," 659. Destruction also occurred at Kydonia in Crete; Troy, Mersin, Tarsus and Hattusas in Anatolia; Paleokastra, Kition, and Enkomi on Cyprus; and Ugarit, Kadesh, Qatra, Hamath, and Alalakh in Syria. Zevit, The Religions of Ancient Israel: A Synthesis of Parallactic Approaches, 94.

140 Robbins, Collapse of the Bronze Age, The Story of Greece, Troy, Israel, Egypt, and the Peoples of the Sea, 121. About one-half of the 500 settlement sites identified in mainland Greece during the Late Helladic III B period do not continue into IIIC. Ibid., 126.

141 Hall, A History of the Archaic Greek World, ca. 1200-479 BCE, 43.

scholars have often favored an earlier date, placing the time of the battle closer to the destruction of the cities on the Greek mainland. In either case, there is a clear chronologic congruence between the two events, making it possible that the Homeric heroes may have crossed the sea to Troy as they fled for their lives from their homeland, rather than in an attempt to avenge the honor of Greece because of Helen's abduction by Paris (Alexander).

The demolition of cities on the Greek mainland caused the population to fall by one-half during this period of time, as many inhabitants fled to other areas throughout the Mediterranean Basin. Despite the fact that newcomers from the north migrated in to repopulate some of the towns, the majority of Mycenaeans left their homeland and settled in widely separated areas, ranging from the Ionian islands and Achaea in the west, Chios in the east, and an aggressive emigration to the island of Cyprus. Aeolians sailed across to Lesbos and the Asiatic coast south of the Troad; Dorians moved from Laconia and the Argolid to Crete and the southeastern Aegean islands as well as Caria; and Ionians migrated to the Cycladic islands and over to the western coast of Anatolia. By 1120 BCE, the geography of the ancient Near East had been radically revised, and the Mycenaean Empire "had sunk into final decay."[142]

What happened to cause this sudden dissolution is still subject to debate, with explanations ranging from climactic changes causing a disruption in the ability to maintain adequate food supplies throughout the region, to widespread devastation brought about by an invasion of the People of the Sea. Famine was clearly a problem in Anatolia at the time, as indicated by the Hittite king urging the king of Ugarit to send a ship with grain to the town of Ura in Cilicia as a "matter of life and death."[143] William Stiebing Jr., Professor of History at the University of New Orleans, has argued that drier conditions which prevailed in the Levant from 1300-1100 BCE seems to be the best explanation to account for the collapse of many civilizations during the end of the Late Bronze Age,[144] but evidence of widespread destruction in archaeologic sites favors the more popular view that there was some type of invasion from the outside by forces which displaced the weaker sedentary population.[145] Greek lore labeled this intrusion as being due to the Dorian Invasion on the mainland, a migration of people led by the Heracleidae, an Achaean clan descended from Heracles, hence

---

142 Kirk, Homer & the Oral Tradition, 1.

143 Lipinski, <u>On the Skirts of Canaan in the Iron Age: Historical and Topographical Research</u>, 23. Merneptah also shipped a huge gift of corn to Hatti. Ibid., 24.

144 Stiebing, "Climate and Collapse - Did the Weather Make Israel's Emergence Possible?" 54.

145 Desborough, "The End of the Mycenaean Civilization and the Dark Age," 660. Robbins, Collapse of the Bronze Age, The story of Greece, Troy, Israel, Egypt, and the Peoples of the Sea, 144.

the designation as the "Return of the Heracleidae."[146] They settled in the Argolid and Laconia, displacing the Achaean population to the northern Peloponnesian region of Achaea, where the Ionians were then displaced to the Cyclades and the central coastal belt of Asia Minor. Later expeditions settled the other Dorian cities of the Aegean and central Mediterranean. One problem with this theory is that the tradition does not mention any of the cities that were destroyed during the invasion, and archaeologic evidence clearly reveals a violent destruction of the Mycenaean palaces. In addition, rather than show evidence of Dorian habitation, archaeologic sites during this era reveal a steep decline in identifiable sites, indicating widespread abandonment. Once again, legend and hard facts find little ground for agreement.

Whether the Dorian Invasion is in fact an historical explanation for the fall of the Mycenaean Empire, or simply a legend developed to align the Classical Greeks with the descendants of demigods, is not pertinent to my thesis of dissident Hebrew migration, since the Exodus would have taken place well before this event. I therefore will not attempt to argue for or against its validity at this time, and will only point out that many scholars today are beginning to see the destruction on the Greek mainland as being due to a mass migration of people which took place toward the end of the twelfth, or the beginning of the eleventh, century BCE, rather than a full-scale invasion by outside forces. The newcomers were not restricted to Dorians alone under this theory, but rather involved a variety of people from adjacent lands, each of whom maintained characteristics of language and culture which were identifiable in other regions throughout the Mediterranean Basin. The result of all these changes is that the process destroyed the civilization of the Bronze Age and led to what has been referred to as the Greek Dark Age.

While the history of Mycenae ends at this point of time, the Greek Dark Age remains the hidden resource for what immediately preceded the Classical Greek Age. From the sparse information available, it appears that the society returned to a more primitive level of culture. Barry B. Powell, Professor of Classics at the University of Wisconsin-Madison, notes that Homer only referred to a single text of writing in his 28,000 lines of poetry, and concluded that this was "clear testimony to Hellenic provincialism after the collapse of the Mycenaean world ca. 1150 BC and proof of Hellenic remoteness from the centers of ancient civilization."[147] Archaeology has revealed, however, that while the majority of the mainland may have had a general level of poverty, some areas, such as Lefkandi on the island of

---

146 Taylour, The Mycenaeans, 75. It was called the Dorian Invasion because the leaders came from the Greek region of Doris, a small mountainous district between Mts. Oeta and Parnassus. Pausanias (iv.3.3) and Thucydides (i.12.3) both claimed that the invasion took place around 1100 BCE. Graves, The Greek Myths, 2, 146.1, 211.

147 Powell, Homer, 13.

Euboea, showed signs of a hierarchical social system, with richly furnished burial sites.[148] In the Early Archaic Period (850-725 BCE), from the time of Homer to the Persian Wars, many cities in Greece, including Athens, Argos, Thebes and Sparta, grew into thriving centers of trade, founding colonies and trading posts throughout the Mediterranean Basin, competing with the Phoenicians and the Etruscans.[149] It is thought that the Greeks refined the technology of their own language during this period of time through contact with the literate civilizations of the Near East, resulting in the recording of the oral Homeric traditions of the *Iliad* and the *Odyssey*.[150] By the Middle (725-610 BCE) and Late Archaic Period (610-510 BCE) the political format of the Greeks was finally reorganized into the type of democracy by which the Classical Greeks became widely known, setting the agenda for the rest of Western history.[151] I will end my discussion of Greece at this point, and move on to an analysis of the Trojan War, which set the stage for the birth of the written word in the Western World. In the chapters which follow, I will expand on the reasons why the Hebrews should be given credit for the contributions I just mentioned.

In summary, the founding of Mycenae, and its evolution to a position of power at the end of the Late bronze Age, closely follows the timeline which I believe best dates the Exodus of the Hebrews from Egypt. The legendary, linguistic, and archaeologic data that is available also best fits the supposition that it was the Hebrews, rather than the Phoenicians, or the Hyksos, who provided both literary motifs, as well as experienced manpower to both construct the palaces, and assist in the maintenance of both homeland security and imperial expansion.

---

148 Martin, Ancient Greece, From Prehistoric to Hellenistic Times, 39.

149 Durando, <u>Ancient Greece: The Dawn of The Western World</u>, 26. The Archaic Age (850-480 BCE), which means "Old-Fashioned Age," stems from art history and is the era when the Greeks fully developed their new political form of the city-state (*polis*). Martin, <u>Ancient Greece, From Prehistoric to Hellenistic Times</u>, 51.

150 Ibid., 43.

151 Kishlansky, Geary & O'Brien, <u>Civilization in the West</u>, 44. The Mycenaeans were not totally forgotten, however, for their settlements became the centers that evolved into the sanctuaries at Olympia, Delphi, Dodona, Isthmia and Nemea. Durando, <u>Ancient Greece: The Dawn of The Western World</u>, 40.

Chapter 8

THE TROJAN WAR

From the very inception of the written word, every ancient civilization has sought to memorialize their history in some type of permanent record, as amply reflected in the extensive hieroglyphic records in Egypt and Sumeria, and the literary collections of the Bible and numerous Mesopotamian epics. While events of trade and exploration often made up part of this indelible collection, graphic descriptions of war have taken center stage, with stories of military conflict detailing both the exaltation of victory and the agony of defeat for future generations to remember.

A. Fact or Fiction?

The most famous of these tales in the Western World is the account of the sack of Troy by the Greeks, as recorded in the *Iliad* and the *Odyssey* by Homer.[1] For centuries, people listened to oral recitations of how the Greek heroes battled against their Trojan foes in order to avenge the dishonor of their country brought about when the Trojan prince Paris (Alexander) abducted Helen, the wife of King Menelaus of Sparta, and carried her off to his citadel in the Troad.[2] This epic saga became the first book published in the Western World, and the detailed description of the war provided generations of children and adults the ability to marvel over the details of the destruction of the city of Troy, following a ten-year siege by the brave warriors from Greece. The valorous behavior of the combatants on both sides of the war so inspired readers that potentates in the Aegean courts named themselves after some of the participants, including Hector, Agamemnon, and Achilles. When Alexander the Great (356-323 BCE) entered Ilium in 334 BCE, after defeating the mighty Persian force which had controlled the city since the end of the Late Bronze Age, he immediately made sacrifices to Athena and

---

1 Troy was a Phrygian city in northwestern Anatolia (Asia Minor), in the region called the Troad. At the time of the Trojan War, it was heavily walled, with broad streets and beautiful palaces. Its allies included the Ascanians, Amazons, Lycians, and Eastern Ethiopians. Parada, "Troy," 1. Although the *Iliad* and the *Odyssey* immortalized the Trojan War in Greek saga and legend, the events leading up to the arrival of the Greek force were told in another epic, the *Cypria*, which has not survived extant.

2 That the poems were transmitted orally, before the Greek alphabet was invented, has been surmised by all historians, ancient and modern. The fact of a single reference to writing in the *Iliad*, when King Proetus of Corinth sends Bellerophon to Lycia with a folded tablet containing "baneful signs" (*Il.* 6.168), is discounted as not referring to the general use of written language at the time. Powell, Homer, 11.

Priam in appreciation for his victory, exchanging his own armor for some of the ancient sacred weapons which were said to have been preserved since the time of the Trojan War.[3] He then adorned the temple with votive offerings, and anointed the gravestone of Achilles with oil, crowning it with garlands in honor of what that great warrior had accomplished in his battles against the enemies of Greece.[4] The Roman Emperor Julius Caesar (100-44 BCE) also paid homage to the tributes afforded the heroes of the Trojan War by promising to rebuild the city to the level of its former greatness after witnessing the decline which years of neglect had wrought.[5] Even during the Middle Ages, when interest in classical scholarship fell far below the importance of edicts from the Catholic Church, travelers still stopped at Troy to see for themselves the locality of the city which was made famous by the heroic poem of Homer.

The mystique of Troy has not lost any of its attraction in modern times, as scholars and the public alike have continued to be fascinated by the romance and heroism which characterized the Homeric poems. What is remarkable about all of this attention is the fact that most readers do not even question the reality of the war, even though, like the biblical story of the Exodus, there is no proof that the conflict actually took place. Belief in the factual nature of the event dates back to ancient times, when it was generally acknowledged that the legend of the Trojan War was a recitation of reality, accurately depicting the valorous behavior of the Late Bronze Age Greeks.[6] The Greek historian Thucydides (460-400 BCE) accepted that the story was true, calling it the greatest war that had ever taken place.[7] Herodotus, the "Father of History," recorded that when he traveled to Egypt, the priests told him that the tale of Troy was true, and that the facts were verified by Menelaus himself.[8] More recently, however, skepticism over the veracity of the war began to be raised by a number of nineteenth century

---

3 Arrian, The Anabasis of Alexander, 11.3, 416. Alexander the Great regarded the *Iliad* as a handbook of the art of war, and took a copy on his campaigns that had been annotated by Aristotle. Plutarch, "Alexander," 8, 259-260.

4 Plutarch, Lives, xv.4, VII.263; Strabo, The Geography, 13.I.26, VI.51.

5 Wood, In Search of the Trojan War, 30.

6 According to the French archaeologist and historian, Paul Veyne, "Homer's listeners believed in the overall truthfulness of the account and did not disdain the pleasure of the tale of Ares and Aphrodite." Veyne, Did the Greeks Believe in Their Myths? An Essay on the Constitutive Imagination, 21. He explained that "the difference between fiction and reality is not objective and does not pertain to the thing itself: it resides in us." Ibid. This latter opinion does not satisfy most modern skeptics.

7 Thucydides, The Peloponnesian War, I.10, 41.

8 Herodotus, The History, II.118, 179. It should be noted that many scholars have claimed that Herodotus made up, or falsified, many of the Egyptian historical facts he claimed to have learned from Egyptian priests. Nielsen, The Tragedy in History: Herodotus and the Deuteronomistic History, 41.

historians, but their concerns were silenced when the German businessman and archaeologist Heinrich Schliemann (1822-1890 CE) discovered the remains of Troy in 1870 CE, and announced to the world that the site of the famous conflict had finally been found. Schliemann claimed that the walled-city he uncovered at the site was violently destroyed, and that this meant the Trojan War actually took place. His argument proved to be so persuasive that few naysayers could be found to disparage the weight of the seemingly indisputable archaeologic data.

But just as the remains of the city of Jericho do not prove that it was the Hebrews who crossed the Jordan River and caused the walls to tumble down, thereby validating the biblical tale, the archaeologic remains of a violent devastation of the city of Troy at the end of the Late Bronze Age does not prove that it was a Greek force which sieged, and then finally destroyed, the city once the walls were breached. The data only supports the conclusion that Homer's tale *may* be true, and not that the events of the epic poem *are* based on a factual occurrence. There are many other explanations consistent with the nature of the city's remains, particularly the fact that the wreckage could have come about by a natural disaster, or by an invasion of the People of the Sea (Sea People), rather than a Greek corps under the command of Agamemnon. Homer's tale was intended to do more than simply describe an historical event, it set the stage for a Greek mystique that expanded over the centuries into legends which formed the background of Classical Greek theatrical productions. Just as the Ten Commandments set forth the principles of the Mosaic Law, the actions of Greek heroes in the Trojan War taught a formula of morality which would be copied by the Romans, and then passed on to the rest of the Western World as a model of heroic behavior. These ends are an integral part of our modern heritage, but the fact remains that both events remain unproven conjectures requiring a leap of faith to prove that they actually took place.

If we are to accept that the archaeologic data at Troy is evidence of an actual military event which was recorded in some factual manner by Homer centuries later, it is necessary to compare the legendary account of the Trojan War with what is known about the remains uncovered at the site. It is also necessary to analyze sociologic data from that era to see if there are alternate explanations to the course of events than those composed by Homer. In this chapter, I will discuss these various questions in order to argue that the fact of a conflict taking place at Troy at the end of the Late Bronze Age is true, but that the Greeks alone did not siege and capture the city of Troy, as recorded by Homer, but rather that the People of the Sea, in conjunction with the Mycenaeans and dissident Hebrews, took part in the conflict, helping to create the legends which were so prominently ascribed to the Greeks.

B. The Trojan War Legend

Most of what we know about the Trojan War comes from Homer's epic poem, the *Iliad*, which is believed to have been written in the eighth century BCE.[9] The legend of the war told how Helen, the wife of the Spartan King Menelaus, was abducted by the Trojan prince Paris, causing the Greeks to retaliate by attacking the city of Troy, carrying out a ten-year siege before finally entering the gates through the ruse of the Trojan Horse. The city was burned to the ground, and the inhabitants either killed, or taken back to Greece as slaves. At the center of the controversy was Helen, the daughter of King Tyndareus, and the most beautiful woman in the world. Helen owed her perfection to the fact that she was the biologic offspring of Zeus, who had impregnated her mother Leda after descending to earth in the shape of a swan. Although her sister Clytemnestra did not share this divine background, both women were exceedingly desirable because of their beauty and royal background. Tyndareus realized that every worthy warrior in the land would want to marry one of his daughters, but he was concerned that the rivalry over Helen could create a dangerous situation among her admirers. He therefore made every suitor in the land promise to collectively avenge any insult to her, or to her future husband, before allowing her to marry, a tactic that was recommended to him by Odysseus. The technique worked quite well, and Helen eventually wed Menelaus, the king of Sparta, while Clytemnestra married Agamemnon, the king of Mycenae.

The pact which Tyndareus had required of all the eligible suitors was put to the test when Paris, the younger brother of Hector, made a visit to Sparta as a Trojan ambassador, and fell in love with Helen.[10] She, according to most sources, fully returned his affection, and while Menelaus was away attending the funeral of his

---

9 The earliest surviving transcripts of the *Iliad* are from the tenth century CE, although Homer is believed to have recited his poems in the eighth century BCE. The parts of the Trojan War which are not contained in the *Iliad* are believed to have been part of a work known as the "Epic Cycle," including the *Cypria*, on the first nine years of the war; the *Aethiopis*, which focused on Troy's Ethiopian and Amazon allies; the *Little Iliad*, on the Trojan Horse; the *Iliupersis*, on the sack of Troy; the *Nostoi*, on the return of various Greek heroes, especially Agamemnon; and the *Telegony*, a continuation of the *Odyssey*. Strauss, The Trojan War: A New History, xxi-xxii.

10 The illicit affair was destined to take place after Paris was chosen to judge which of the goddesses was the fairest. His choices were Hera, the goddess of marriage and childbirth, and the wife of Zeus; Athena the goddess of wisdom, war, justice and the arts, and a daughter of Zeus; and Aphrodite, the goddess of love, beauty, and sexual rapture, and another daughter of Zeus. Hera offered him immense power if she was chosen, Athena promised him military glory and wisdom, and Aphrodite offered him the love of Helen, the most beautiful woman in the world. Unable to bypass the opportunity to have the most coveted woman in the world as his wife, he chose Aphrodite. Johnston, "Trojan War," 1.

grandfather Catreus, the two lovers ran away to Troy, taking a large amount of treasure with them.[11] Once they were safely ensconced in the city, they married and Helen bore Paris three sons, Bunomus, Aganus, and Idaeues, and a daughter, Helen, all of whom were killed during the war.[12] When Menelaus returned home and discovered their elopement, he immediately sailed to Troy with Odysseus, the king of Ithaca, and demanded the return of his wife. The Trojans refused his request, and Menelaus then appealed to Tyndareus to enforce the oath which all the suitors had taken. Obedient to their word of honor, the Greeks assembled an army under the leadership of Agamemnon, and prepared to sail to Troy to punish the Trojans for their defamation of the Greek name.

All of these facts leading up to the start of the war are not contained in the *Iliad*, but have rather been gathered from multiple versions of the myth contained in the surviving works of many Classical Greek playwrights, historians, and poets. One critical aspect of the story, which is directly pertinent to my theory of dissident Hebrew migration to Mycenae during the Exodus, is the fact that King Agamemnon, who was chosen as commander-in-chief of the Greek army, was forced to sacrifice his daughter Iphigenia before the battle could take place, an act incredibly similar to the tale of Abraham and Isaac. The Greeks had gathered at the Boeotian harbor of Aulis to sail across the sea to Troy, but the winds suddenly died down, and the armada, consisting of over one thousand ships, became stalled in the water. Calchas, the famous seer brought along to help in the planning of battle, advised Agamemnon that the reason for the atmospheric delay was that the goddess Artemis (Diana) had been angered because Agamemnon had promised to sacrifice the loveliest thing each year in her honor, and, in the confusion of preparing for war, he had neglected the offering that season. In order to now appease the virgin goddess' anger, and assure a change in the weather, Calchas warned "that virgin blood must be shed."[13] Agamemnon readily agreed to this demand, but soon was informed that the girl to be sacrificed was his own lovely daughter, Iphigenia. Like Abraham, Agamemnon was faced with the difficult decision of having to sacrifice a child to appease a god, although he had been made aware of this task by a human interpreter, rather than by a direct conversation with the goddess herself. Unlike the biblical myth, no deity intervened in this tale of tragedy, and Iphigenia died so that the Greeks could sail to Troy and lay siege to the city for ten years before the walls were breached and the Trojans were

---

11 Sappho, the seventh century BCE ancient Greek poetess, claimed that Helen had "left her husband – the best of all men – behind and sailed far away to Troy; she did not spare a single thought for her child nor for her dear parents" as the goddess of love led her astray. Sappho, Poems & Fragments, 21.

12 Graves, The Greek Myths, 2, 159.v, 275. The story of the abduction is similar to the Ugaritic tale of *Keret*, where Keret's lawful wife Huray was carried off to Udm. Ibid., 159.2, 277.

13 Ovid, Metamorphoses, XII.29-30, 286.

put to the sword.

I will discuss the sacrifice of Iphigenia in more detail in chapter 9, when I compare the actions of Abraham and Agamemnon, but the importance of this tragedy rests upon the fact that no other culture in human history highlighted a sacrifice, or an attempted sacrifice, of a child by a parent in order to teach a critical element of their social heritage except the Jews and the Greeks. While infanticide itself was a common occurrence among ancient peoples, and frequently not seen as a crime by contemporary law codes, no other culture, either before or after the Late Bronze Age, placed the event at such a level of importance that it became an integral component of what it meant to be a pious adherent of the Divine command. It is my belief that this unique use of the infanticidal motif indicates that one culture transferred the legend to the other, in a manner that was direct and involved an assimilation of people, as well as literary material. Since I believe the Exodus took place before the Trojan War began, it is most likely, in my opinion, that the dissident Hebrews took the story to Mycenae, rather than surmise that the biblical compilers included reports of the Homeric legend when they gathered material for the book of *Genesis*. I will expand upon my reasoning for this conclusion at the end of this chapter.

C. Archaeologic Data

As discussed above, Heinrich Schliemann, a wealthy German businessman who was obsessed with finding the site of the Trojan War since he first read the story as a young child, uncovered the remains of Troy in the nineteenth century CE, and claimed that this proved that the Trojan War was more than a fictional event. The account of his discovery has been called "the world's greatest archaeological detective story," and the saga began in 1865 CE, when interest in archaeologic sites from the ancient world was at an all time high.[14] Frank Calvert (1828-1908 CE), a United States consular agent and part-time archaeologist, had bought a mound of land from a local farmer at Hissarlik, a mound of rock about 95 feet high that was favored by many enthusiasts to be the location of Homer's city since the setting lay at the point where the Black Sea and the Mediterranean Sea meet. Calvert dug deep trenches which exposed the remains of the classical temple of Athena, but he ran out of money before he could complete the task of uncovering the entire city. On August 14, 1868 CE, Schliemann visited the site and immediately surmised that the remains of Troy were there, for the geographic position commanded the opening of the Dardanelles, and controlled the land route that came up along the western coastal region of Anatolia, where ships could cross the straits from Asia to Europe. He quickly acquired the rights to the property, and began to carry out six major campaigns of excavation between 1870 and 1890

---

14 Wood, In Search of the Trojan War, 12.

CE. In his zeal to prove that Homer's tale was true, he blindly dug through the layers of antiquity with such broad strokes that he cut across and disturbed much of the archaeologic record of the multiple civilizations that thrived at the site. By the time he had completed his project, he had written eleven books, eighteen diaries, and compiled 221 volumes of excavation notebooks.[15] In his excitement and haste, however, most scholars believe that he set back the work of future researchers for years, and perhaps even damaged the site to such a degree that a proper detailed analysis would never be possible. While such a conclusion may be true, there is no question that he uncovered the remains of the fabled city of Troy, and proved to many skeptics that the war may not have been entirely a fictional event, without any basis in fact.

Following Schliemann's astounding discovery, more careful excavations of the site began to be carried out in 1893 and 1894 CE by Schliemann's assistant, Wilhelm Dorpfeld (1853-1940 CE), and then by Carl Blegen (1887-1971 CE), from the University of Cincinnati, between 1932 and 1938 CE. The efforts of these highly skilled professionals revealed that the city evolved through nine successive towns, labeled as Troy I-IX, which later archaeologists have broken down into 47 subdivisions, representing progressive phases of habitation.[16] The oldest settlement, labeled Troy I, was built directly on bedrock in the Early Bronze Age (3000-2000 BCE), and was an extremely small setting, protected by well-planned, eight-foot thick fortifications, which indicated a reasonably high level of defensive sophistication. Most scholars now believe that these fortifications were able to protect the city from forced invasion, but that the metropolis was eventually destroyed by fire, although the exact cause of the catastrophe has never been adequately explained. The remains were not extensive enough to determine who was responsible for the construction, but ceramic shapes recovered from the site were characteristic of those found in a wide area of the northern Aegean islands, as well as neighboring coastal regions, suggesting that the immigrants likely came from a regional abode.

After Troy I was destroyed, another city, labeled Troy II, was immediately built on the site with no apparent disruption in the type of culture that inhabited the location. The impressive fortifications, and steep, well-paved ramp, along with evidence that the structure was destroyed by a conflagration, led Schliemann

---

15 Wood, In Search of the Trojan War, 48.

16 Leveque, <u>The Greek Adventure</u>, 50. Troy I-VII contained the remains of forty-two building phases belonging to the Bronze Age, and on the surface were the remains of Troy VIII (Greek) and Troy IX (Roman). Fields, <u>Troy c. 1700-1250 BC</u>, 13. The estimated dates of each city are Troy I (c. 2900-2450 BCE), Troy II (c. 2450-2200 BCE), Troy III-V (c. 2200-1700 BCE), Troy VI (c. 1700-1250 BCE), Troy VII (c. 1250-1050 BCE), Troy VIII (c. 700-85 BCE), and Troy IX (48 BCE-550 CE). Ibid., 10, 17-27. The delay in habitation at the site between the destruction of Troy VII and the building of Troy VIII is not clearly understood.

to believe that Troy II represented the remains of the city where the Trojan War was actually fought. He uncovered a cache of jewelry at this level and, in his typical grandiose nature, immediately labeled the trinkets as the "Jewels of Helen," and the cups of gold, silver, electra and bronze, as the "Treasure of Priam," the aged king of the citadel. How such valuable ornaments would have escaped the general looting that took place before the city was burned to the ground was never explained, but modern scholars have now shown that Troy II existed in the Early Bronze Age, making it much too ancient to be the residence of Priam, and so Schliemann's exorbitant claims were deprived of serious consideration shortly after they were made.

Once Troy II was destroyed, the next three cities (Troy III-V) were relatively impoverished, making it unlikely that any of the layers was the site of the Trojan War. The citadel did expand to cover an area of 4.4 acres over the ensuing period of time, however, and some scholars believe that the destruction of Troy V may have been carried out by Heracles, who had waged a campaign against the city in the generation before the abduction of Helen by Paris.[17] This supposition does not have broad support, however, since Heracles remains a legendary hero with little evidence of his existence in the historical record.

The next city, designated as Troy VI, expanded even further to encompass an area of 4.94 acres, with fortifications that were superior to any previously used. This was a truly impressive structure, with walls that were 13-16 feet thick, and more than 19 feet high, interspersed with massive towers and five gateways. It clearly was built to withstand a prolonged siege, and at the level designated VIh, there were signs of armed conflict, including bronze spearheads and arrowheads scattered in the debris and lodged in the fortification walls. There also were the remains of horses, leading to the conclusion that chariot-warriors may have been involved in an attack on the city. All of these findings convinced Dorpfeld in 1893 CE that this level was the site of the Trojan War, and once again hopes were raised that the fabled city of Troy had finally been unearthed.

Although Dorpfeld's claims were more reasonable that those of Schliemann, later excavations by Carl Blegen eventually showed that the city had not been destroyed by an army, as was first suggested by Dorpfeld, but rather that the walls had collapsed from a powerful earthquake that occurred around 1275 BCE. Internal walls were found to have fallen over in large heaps, and in one place the foundation of the walls had actually shifted to another position, something which could only be caused by natural movements of the earth. Earthquakes had

---

17 Fields, Troy c. 1700-1250 BC, 21; Graves, The Greek Myths, 2, 137.1, 174. Heracles had been angered by King Laomedon's exposure of his daughter Hesione on the seashore to be eaten by a monster, in payment for a debt he owed Poseidon, and therefore captured the city, burned it to the ground, and set Priam on the throne, one generation before the Trojan War. Ibid., 137.a-l, 169-171.

previously been shown to be involved with the destruction of Troys III, IV and V, so it was not unexpected that a similar fate would befall Troy VI. The remains of horses were explained by the fact that the city had been built by newcomers who brought horses with them, and not because the horses were killed during combat when the walls were breached. These findings, combined with the fact that the city existed during the reign of Hattusilis III (1275-1250 BCE), when Hittite relations with the kingdom of Ahhiyawa had become hostile, rather than at the time of Priam, indicated that Dorpfeld's identification of Troy VI as the site of the Trojan War was erroneous.[18]

Once again, the world did not have to wait long for a new declaration of discovery to be made. Following the destruction of Troy VI by a natural disaster, the site was immediately reconstructed as Troy VIIa, and because the remains of the material culture were identical to that of the preceding settlement, it was presumed that the survivors of the earthquake were responsible for the restoration. Troy VIIa showed more clear signs of armed conflict than did Troy VI, with walls that were marked by the ravages of fire, and so much desolation that Blegen felt there was "little doubt that it had come from the hand of man."[19] Traces of bodies were evident everywhere, including one with an imbedded arrowhead which Blegen believed had been discharged by an invading Achaean. This led Blegen to confidently avow that Troy VIIa was the site of the Trojan War, a view which has so far survived the test of time. Although the remains do seem to indicate that an armed conflict took place, it has yet to be determined whether the destroyers of the city were truly the Greeks, however, as claimed by Homer, or whether some other elements could have played a role in the destruction of Troy, most likely an attack by the People of the Sea who were rampaging throughout the ancient Near East at the time.

Whether archaeology will ever add more information about what took place at Troy VIIa is open to question, since there appears to be little else to be uncovered at the site in pristine condition. Little progress has been made in recent years, except for the findings of the German Archaeologist Professor Manfred Korfmann (1942-2005 CE), who showed that large lower settlements existed outside the walls of the city from the seventeenth to the twelfth centuries BCE. These dwellings indicate that the entire city of Troy was large enough to control access from the Mediterranean to the Black Sea, and from Asia Minor to southeast Europe, thereby making it reasonable to believe that an invading force would spend so much time and effort to wrest control of the city from the Trojan ruling class. Despite the fact that Homer claimed it was the Greeks who sieged, and eventually destroyed, the city of Troy, there is still no way to prove that the force was actually an army led by Agamemnon, rather than some other group,

18 Leveque, The Greek Adventure, 50.
19 Wood, In Search of the Trojan War, 115.

such as the People of the Sea.

As to when the war was fought, the range of estimations fall within a relatively narrow range, unlike the situation with the date of the Exodus. Ancient authors, such as Thucydides (460-400 BCE), believed that the war ended on 1184 BCE,[20] although earlier dates included 1334 BCE, as suggested by Douris (Doulis) (c. fifth century BCE) of Samos; 1250 BCE, by Herodotus (c. 490-420 BCE); and 1135 BCE, by the Greek historian Ephorus (405-330 BCE).[21] The Parian Chronicle, which chronicled many ancient notable events between 1580-263 BCE, made the most exacting claim, placing the sack of Troy on June 5, 1209 BCE.[22] More modern estimates, taking advantage of the details uncovered by the excavation of the city, and utilizing modern scientific analysis, have modified these conclusions, but the dates are still remarkably similar, including 1270-1240 BCE by Professor Carl Blegen (1887-1921 CE),[23] 1200-1190 BCE by the renowned archaeologist Carl Nylander,[24] and 1180 BCE by the Yale historian Michael Wood.[25] What seems clear from all of these estimations is that the war likely took place at some time near the thirteenth century BCE, making it contemporary with the Late Date estimation for the Exodus, and also with the arrival of the People of the Sea. All of this data strongly supports, in my opinion, an Exodus in the fifteenth or fourteenth century BCE, leaving enough time for the Hebrew dissidents to

20 Dothan & Dothan, People of the Sea, The Search for the Philistines, 29. Eratosthenes (276-194 BCE), the librarian of Alexandria and the most influential scholar of his time, followed the view of Thucydides. Wood, In Search of the Trojan War, 28. Other ancient authors who dated the Trojan war to 1183 or 1184 BCE were Dionysius of Halicarnassus (60-6 BCE), Diodorus of Sicily (first century BCE), Tatian (110-180 CE), Eusebius (263-339 BCE), Apollodorus (180-120 BCE), and Solinus (third or fourth century CE). Robertson, The Parian Chronicle: Or the Chronicle of the Arundelian Marbles; With a Dissertation Concerning Its Authenticity, 113-114. The date was determined by reckoning that the interval from the Trojan War to the Return of the Heracleidae was eighty years, and from then to the First Olympiad was 326 years, based upon the reigns of the kings of Lacedaemon. Diodorus, The Library of History, I.5.1, 21.

21 Vermeule, Greece in the Bronze Age, 277. Dates accepted by other ancient scholars included Phanias of Eresus (fl. 332 BCE) 1126 BCE, Callimachus (305-240 BCE) 1127 BCE, Timaius (c. 275 CE) 1193 BCE, Dicaiarchus (third century BCE) 1212 BCE, and Cleitarchus (fourth century BCE) 1234 BCE. Robbins, Collapse of the Bronze Age, The Story of Greece, Troy, Israel, Egypt, and the Peoples of the Sea, 85-86. Sosibius (third century BCE) reckoned it was 1171 BCE, Timaeus (345-250 BCE) 1193 BCE, and Dicaerchus (c. 355 BCE) 1212 BCE. Robertson, The Parian Chronicle: Or the Chronicle of the Arundelian Marbles; With a Dissertation Concerning Its Authenticity, 115-116.

22 Ibid.; Wood, In Search of the Trojan War, 28.

23 Vermeule, Greece in the Bronze Age, 277.

24 "Prehistoric Archaeology of the Aegean: Lesson 27: Troy VII and the Historicity of the Trojan War," 1.

25 Wood, In Search of the Trojan War, 225, 230.

become enmeshed in Mycenaean society before the Trojan War.

D. People of the Sea

While the Trojan War provides the primary historical end-point for my discussion of a dissident Hebrew migration to Mycenae, a correlating factor which helps to identify when the events took place is the widespread destruction of much of the Levantine territory by a group of marauding tribes known as the People of the Sea at the end of the Late Bronze Age. This was the era when a great "folk movement" occurred throughout the ancient Near East, characterized by masses of peoples who began to wander "from the central plains of Asia and eastern Europe across Europe to the Mediterranean Basin and the islands of the sea."[26] A vast migration, according to Nancy K. Sandars, from the School of Archaeology at Oxford University, was the "hall-mark of the times," and the entire Near East was caught up in a period of adjustment that would eventually change the shape of the world to come.[27] Within an incredibly short period of time, the political climate of the Mediterranean Basin was drastically altered as the Hittite Empire collapsed, Egyptian power declined, and the Mycenaeans disappeared from the historical stage, initiating the end of the Late Bronze Age, and the onset of the Iron Age (1200-587 BCE).

The People of the Sea play a critical role in the turbulence of this era, although very little is known of their factual nature, since the extant record is void of a written account by their own hand. They seem to have come from a variety of locations, although scholars have generally divided their origins into two sources: the Anatolian hypotheses places their extraction on the western and southern seaboard of Anatolia, either inland in Lycaonia, or on the south-west coast of Caria; while the Aegean hypothesis traces their origin to the Aegean islands and Greece. The Aegean theory is supported by Egyptian chronicles which depicted some of the People of the Sea, especially the Ekwesh (Akwash), in costumes which resembled those of the Mycenaeans, or the people of Ahhiyawa, a political entity first mentioned in Hittite cuneiform texts of the fourteenth century BCE.[28] This congruence has been contested by others, however, who find the similarity only superficial.[29] The invaders, from wherever they came, nevertheless seem to have first begun to make their way to the lands of the eastern Mediterranean in boats during the fourteenth and thirteenth centuries BCE, seizing the island of

---

26 Hindson, The Philistines and the Old Testament, 37-38.

27 Sandars, The Sea Peoples: Warriors of the Ancient Mediterranean 1250-1150 BC, 198.

28 Hutchinson, "The Decadence of Minoan Crete: The Mycenaean Empire," 421; Yurco, "*Black Athena*, an Egyptological Review," 92.

29 Knapp, "Bronze Age Mediterranean Island Cultures and the Ancient Near East, Part 2," 126.

Alashiya (Cyprus), and then penetrating inland into Anatolia and northern Syria. They disrupted the pattern of international trade which had developed during the Late Bronze Age, as attested by the disappearance of Mycenaean and Cypriote pottery from the land of Canaan, and the arrival of locally made Philistine bichrome ware. Although the People of the Sea are often referred to as a coalition of forces, each with their unique site of origin and style of military dress, there is no evidence that they actually ever formed a unified force which fought under one banner. In point of fact, they were soldiers who often fought on both sides of a battle, taking payment from whoever was able to afford their services. They even were willing to change sides if the outcome was not in their favor, as evidenced by Ramesses II (1279-1213 BCE) converting Shardana (Sherdana) prisoners into active members of his own militia, as will be discussed shortly.

Although some of the invaders traveled inland, most of the People of the Sea used the Mediterranean Sea to move their forces up and down the coast, leading to the appellation applied by the Egyptians.[30] They moved quickly from one locale to another, and fought with fierce brutality. Some scholars have claimed that the Bible also contains allusion to the People of the Sea in a forecast given by Balaam during the Exodus, when he predicted that Moab would fall and ships would come from the coast of Cyprus to destroy both Eber and Assyria.[31] Since Cyprus contained a large contingent of Mycenaean and other People of the Sea tribes during the end of the Late Bronze Age, the biblical description could be seen as congruent with the historical reality, although the reference is too nonspecific to be sure it indicated an invasion by the People of the Sea, as opposed to other enemy forces.

Egyptian records relating to the People of the Sea primarily begin with the reign of Ramesses II, where it is recorded that he "destroyed the warriors of the Great Green Sea" in 1278 BCE, a reference to Shardana mercenaries.[32] At the critical battle of Kadesh, the Shardana fought both with and against the Egyptians, and Ramesses II was so impressed with their attributes as fierce warriors, that he inducted them into his own army after they were taken prisoner. Eventually, they formed some of his best mercenary troops, being memorialized with honor

30 Most of what we know about the People of the Sea comes from Egyptian sources, although there are passing references in an obelisk from Byblos, and in Hittite records. Nibbi, The Sea Peoples and Egypt, 110. In various Egyptian texts, they were called "foreigners who came from their lands and the islands in the middle of the Great Green," or "foreigners from the north who were in their islands." de Vaux, The Early History of Israel, 501.
31 Num 24:23-24. Ziony Zevit, Professor of Biblical Literature and Northwest Semitic Languages at the University of Judaism in Los Angeles, also points to Israelite texts which refer to the People of the Sea *en bloc* as "Pelishtim." Zevit, The Religions of Ancient Israel: A Synthesis of Parallactic Approaches, 96.
32 Wood, In Search of the Trojan War, 218.

on the walls of the Temple of Luxor in the early thirteenth century BCE for their bravery against the Hittites at Kadesh. In addition to the Egyptian sources, the Shardana are also mentioned in Ugaritic texts from the thirteenth century BCE as having been mobilized for military service or having received royal land grants, presumably as payment for military activities. This type of recompense appears to be characteristic of other countries during this era, and is how I believe the dissident Hebrews were paid when they emigrated to Mycenae.

The origins of the Shardana are obscure, with some scholars suggesting that they came from Sardinia, based upon the similarity of their names.[33] They wore characteristic horned helmets, with protection for the back of the neck, short kilts, and carried round shields with a sword or spear, a type of dress that was often found in northern Syria, so it is possible that following their settlement in Cyprus, they then migrated to populate the island of Sardinia, rather than originating there in the first place. A bronze statuette with a similar distinctive headdress has been found at Enkomi on Cyprus, suggesting that the Shardana maintained a strong presence on that island. That some of the Shardana may have come from Mycenae is suggested by the fact that warriors wearing similar horned helmets were found on the famous "Warrior Vase" from Mycenaean ruins, so that an involvement of Shardana in the Trojan War is quite likely, given the contemporary nature of the two events. Some scholars have also linked the Shardana with the area that was the original settlement of the tribe of Dan, although there is no evidence to prove this contention, and Dan's presence in the area of the Aijalon and Sereq vales, as described in Josh 40-47, is not matched by other historical sources.[34]

With the reign of Merneptah (1213-1203 BCE), evidence of other People of the Sea tribal elements appear, including the Shekelesh (Sicily), Lukka (Lycians), Ekwesh (Achaeans or Ahhiyawans), and Tursha (Etruscans), all of whom are listed as being closely allied to the Libyans who attacked Egypt at that time, along with the Shardana.[35] The Tursha prince had a very distinct physiognomy in these representations, with a short, thick nose, wide lips, heavy beard, and hair without a cap. Although they are not mentioned by name, this same type of captive was also pictured in an inscription of Ramesses III (1184-1153 BCE) in 1186 BCE, indicating that the Tursha remained an active participant in raids against Egypt

---

33 de Vaux, The Early History of Israel, 502. This conclusion is supported by the fact that their dress was similar to figures found in the Nuraghe cemeteries of Sardinia. Hutchinson, "The Decadence of Minoan Crete: The Mycenaean Empire," 421.

34 Lipinski, On the Skirts of Canaan in the Iron Age: Historical and Topographical Research, 54-55.

35 Nibbi, The Sea Peoples and Egypt, 102. The Libyans during the Late Bronze Age only appear in Egyptian records as invaders from the west, and include the Meshwesh and Libu tribes. Their original homeland is not known, but may have been Cyrenaica, near the location of the present-day city of Benghasi. Robbins, Collapse of the Bronze Age, The Story of Greece, Troy, Israel, Egypt, and the Peoples of the Sea, 165.

for many years. Like the Shardana, their origin is unknown, but suggestions include northern Assuwa near the Troad, central western Anatolia, where Lydia was later to arise, as well as Tyrsenoi, the Asiatic nation which colonized Etruria. These descriptions would be consistent with the Tursha possibly being aligned with the Trojans when the Greek force landed on the Anatolian coast.

Once Ramesses III ascended the throne, more names of People of the Sea appeared at Medinet Habu, including the Denyen, Tjeker (Teucrians), Peleset (Philistines), and Weshesh.[36] Once again, the pictorial representations indicate distinct forms of dress, with the Peleset, Tjeker and Denyen soldiers wearing feathered headdresses, while the Shekelesh and Teresh (Tyrrhenians) had fillet headbands. The Tjeker also are mentioned in Egyptian literary sources, as pursuers of Wen-Amon, an official in the Temple of Amon at Karnak, who was sent to Byblos to procure timber for the Egyptians around 1100 BCE, and ran afoul of the Tjeker during his stay in the town of Dor. When Wen-Amon was robbed, he had to flee to Cyprus, pursued by the Tjeker in their fleet of eleven ships. These events all post-date the generally accepted timing of the Trojan War, but are near enough to consider the People of the Sea as active participants in the fabled event.

The Denyen are an intriguing element of the People of the Sea, for they are also mentioned in the Amarna Age, appearing in Assyrian records as Danuna. This name is similar to that of the Danaans (Danoi), the name Homer often used to refer to the Greek participants, so it is likely that they could have been part of the Greek coalition of forces. As discussed in chapter 7, the Hebrew tribe of Dan has also been linked with the Danaans, so the involvement of Denyen provides a possible link for the inclusion of dissident Hebrew warriors as well. Although the lack of circumcision in the Denyen would favor their being of Greek, rather than of Hebrew, origin, it must be remembered that many Hebrews during the Exodus did not practice circumcision, as evidenced by the fact that before the crossing of the Jordan River, the Lord told Joshua to circumcise the entire male population, only the second time in Israel's history that this directive was necessary.[37] The fact that the Teresh, Shardana, Akawasha, and Teresh were circumcised, as indicated by their hands rather than their genitals appearing in the representation of the enemy count delivered to the Egyptian king, also provides intriguing possibilities of Hebrew involvement.

A final tribal group which is of particular interest to students of the Bible, as well as to my theory of dissident Hebrew migrations, is the Peleset, who are

---

36 Sandars, The Sea Peoples: Warriors of the Ancient Mediterranean 1250-1150 BC, 158.

37 Josh 5:2-6. It is not known if all of the Hebrews that left Egypt were circumcised, but this passage would suggest that few of the children born during the Exodus underwent the rite, suggesting that many of the adults who migrated to Mycenae may not have been circumcised as well.

believed by most scholars to represent the Philistines, not only because of the linguistic similarity in their names, but also because they settled in the areas in which the biblical Philistines were later found. That the Peleset were intent on settlement of the land from the very start of the invasion, rather than just the retrieval of treasure as mercenaries, is evident in their being pictured on the walls at Medinet Habu with ox-carts, suggesting that they were searching for land to cultivate, rather than for cities to ravage. As discussed in chapter 1, the Philistines are believed to have originated in Crete, where the ideogram of the head of a man wearing a feathered headdress on the Phaestos Disc from southern Crete is believed to reflect he image of a Philistine warrior. On Egyptian wall-reliefs, they are shown as clean shaven, wearing paneled kilts decorated with tassels, and a chest protector with a circle of upright reeds or leather strips on their heads. Their arrival in Canaan from Crete provides a path which I believe the dissident Hebrews duplicated in the opposite direction, a generation or more before the Trojan War took place. It is even possible that the Hebrews brought information about the benefits and dangers of Canaan to the Peleset, encouraging them to begin their migration to that destination when conditions in Crete worsened. It would be quite ironic of such a transmission did take place, since the Philistines became the primary enemy of the Hebrews following the Conquest of the Promised Land under Joshua.

E. Discussion

While archaeologic data clearly supports the proposition that some type of military conflict took place in the city of Troy around the time when many historians claim that the Trojan War took place, it is not possible with present-day information to prove that the invading force was the Greeks, as described by Homer in the *Iliad* and the *Odyssey*. Since Mycenae disappeared from the geopolitical scene shortly after the end of the war, they paid a dear price for their drawn-out effort if they indeed were the victors of the battle. While it is possible that the Greek legend was based on reliable oral traditions, I believe it is much more likely that the Greeks inflated both the nature of their victory, and the dominance of their role in the war, similar to the manner in which Ramesses II claimed that he routed the Hittites at the battle of Kadesh-on-Orontes. The Mycenaens may have played a role in the Trojan War, but rather than being the only invading force, they were probably part of a comprehensive invasion of the People of the Sea, which included the city of Troy as part of their rampage across the entire ancient Near East. The similarity in names between a number of the People of the Sea and the combatants in Homer's tale makes it very plausible that the *Iliad* was a recollection of the events from a strictly Greek standpoint, and that the war in reality was a battle of the People of the Sea, allied with the Mycenaeans, against one of the citadels in Anatolia that had been seen as the lynch-pin controlling trade between Europe and the Levant.

Once the Trojan War is identified as part of a global series of events which brought about an end to the Late Bronze Age, rather than the result of a feud caused by the abduction of a king's wife, it is easy to understand how the dissident Hebrews who migrated to Mycenae in the generation before the war would have participated in the event, infusing their history into stories that later became incorporated by Homer, and the Classical Greek tragedists, into the legends of Greek heroic behavior. The willingness of Abraham to proceed with the sacrifice of Isaac when commanded to do so by YHWH was transformed into the sacrifice of Iphigenia by Agamemnon when Artemis caused the winds to die down at the bay of Aulis. The crafty maneuvers of Jacob to gain the right of primogeniture from his brother Esau became part of the personality of Odysseus, while the dream interpretations of Joseph helped to formulate the ability of the seer Calchas to read the omens of the gods in the nature of present-day atmospheric changes. Biblical legends became incorporated into the Greek mythology, just as Hebrew dissidents were incorporated into the Mycenaean way-of-life. I will discuss this theory again in the Conclusion to this book, but it is clear to me that an Hebrew contribution to the Trojan War provides a better answer for how the conflict actually took place than any other postulate to date.

Chapter 9

ABRAHAM AND
AGAMEMNON

As I stated in my introduction to this book, the similarity between the legends of the attempted sacrifice of Isaac by Abraham, and the completed sacrifice of Iphigenia by Agamemnon, led me to postulate that there must have been some connection between the two ancient cultures in order to account for the fact that no other society in the history of the world put emphasis upon an act of infanticide to teach the important lesson of devotion to God or country. In my book *Hardness of Heart, Hardness of Life: The Stain of Human Infanticide*, I showed how infanticide was a common practice among all cultures, ancient and modern, for reasons that ranged from the necessity to control population growth, to a general disregard for the value of infants and young children. I further estimated that as many as 10% of all children ever born may have died at the hands of their parents, a statistic which is not reached today because of the ready availability of abortion to eliminate unwanted pregnancies. More than 50% of unwanted pregnancies are aborted in the modern Western World, and while this circumstance has generated an intense, and sometimes violent, debate among social activists, it clearly has resulted in a lower rate of child-murder. Despite the fact that numerous societies throughout history accepted the right of a parent to resort to infanticide under a variety of circumstances, only the Jews and the Greeks highlighted the act in a positive light in their traditional lore. Abraham's devotion to YHWH's commands superceded his love for his two sons, Ishmael and Isaac, and is pointed to with pride by Jews, Christians and Moslems alike as a sign of pious obedience. Agamemnon's loyalty to his country superceded the life of his daughter Iphigenia, and is a reflection of the importance of the state over the individual in the Greek ethos, as reflected in the writings of Aristotle. In this chapter, I will analyze and compare the details of the two tales, in order to show why I believe the congruence is due to a Mycenaean incorporation of the Hebrew legend as part of the general inclusion of Old Testament myths, which followed the assimilation of dissident Hebrews who left the Exodus following the parricidal punishments imposed by Moses.

A. Abraham and Isaac

Certainly the most widely discussed sacrifice of all time, and the one which still remains a timeless mixture of mystery and awe, was the biblical tale of the attempted killing of Isaac by his father Abraham, the great Patriarch and eponymous ancestor of the Jews.[1] This action, so instrumental in the institution of the concept of monotheism, was reflective of how deeply the committed Jew was in his trust and faith in the Almighty God, YHWH. All pious Jews were taught to follow the commandments of YHWH, no matter how difficult the task might seem, and Abraham's willingness to sacrifice his only legitimate son in order to prove his obedience to the authority of God was proof-positive evidence of this hallowed acquiescence. The story, known as the "Akeda," which means "binding" and refers to the binding of Isaac on the altar, became part of the High Holy Holiday of Rosh Hashonah in synagogues across the world, presented as a model of unlimited faith, a prime example of how trust in the Lord should be maintained.[2] It was proudly, and reverently, put forth as depicting the very essence of what it meant to be a devout Jew, and, in the words of the Romanian-born Jewish-American novelist and Nobel Laureate Elie Wiesel:

This strange tale is about fear and faith, fear and defiance, fear and laughter ... Here is a story that contains Jewish destiny it its totality.[3]

To try and understand why this saga has held such a sacrosanct place in Jewish theology, and why it maintained its sanctity in the kindred faiths of Christianity and Islam, it is necessary to analyze more thoroughly the events which preceded the Akeda itself, as well as the details of the attempted sacrifice.

When Abraham was eighty-six years old, and Sarah was still barren, Sarah gave her Egyptian handmaid Hagar to Abraham in order to provide for a son to carry on the family name. At the time, Sarah felt that she could no longer expect to become pregnant because of her advanced age, and contemporary practice allowed for a barren wife to offer her husband a concubine, as would later occur with Jacob and Rachel. A bastard child could still inherit the father's wealth, and so Abraham's future descendants would have been secured through the lineage of his illegitimate offspring.[4] Hagar quickly conceived, proving that Abraham's fertility was not at fault, and because she now was carrying Abraham's firstborn child, she began to consider herself Sarah's equal, rather than her servant. Sarah

---

1 In the Koran, Abraham is directed to sacrifice Ishmael, rather than Isaac. Sura 37:99-110.

2 The association of the Akeda with Rosh Hashonah comes from Abraham's vision of the ram caught in the thicket by its horns (Gen 5:13) being seen as the origin of the blowing of the shofar. Ibid., 182. During the Middle Ages, when Christians forced Jews to either accept baptism or die, the Jews took strength from the Akeda saying, "If Abraham could face that ... then we can face this." Henderson, "Sermons From the Pulpit: Beyond All Reason," 3.

3 Wiesel, Messengers of God, 69.

4 The custom of an infertile wife providing her husband with a concubine in order to have children through a substitute source was well documented in the ancient Near East. An Old Assyrian marriage contract from the nineteenth century BCE even stipulated that an infertile wife must purchase a slave woman for her husband if she does not provide him with offspring within two years. Sarna, Genesis, 118-119.

did not accept this rebuke lightly, and treated Hagar harshly, reminding her that she still was only a slave, and not part of Abraham's nuclear family. Hagar was so upset by this ill-treatment that she tried to escape by running away into the wilderness. During her first flight from oppression, Hagar was met by the Angel of the Lord at a well, and was commanded to return to Abraham's household and accept her position of subservience. In return, she was guaranteed that she would become a great nation, with offspring that would "be too many to count," for she was pregnant with a son who would be "a wild ass of a man."[5] Hagar passively agreed to this divine demand, and in appreciation of her blessed encounter, she named the well Beer-lahai-roid, or the "Well of the Living One Who Sees Me."[6] Shortly after her return to Abraham's house, she delivered a son who Abraham named "Ishmael," meaning "God hears," an indication that he accepted the child as his own, and, in essence, the boy was God-sent. [7]

Over the ensuing years, Abraham grew prosperous, and the future of his family name appeared secure by the solid development of Ishmael's maturation. When he was ninety-nine years old, YHWH suddenly appeared and reaffirmed His covenant to make Abraham "exceedingly numerous," and the father of a multitude of nations.[8] The details of how his beneficence was to take place were not provided, but his name was changed from "Abram," which meant "Exalted Father," to "Abraham," which meant "Father of Nations," and he would no longer be responsible only to his limited family alone, but also to the future generations which would comprise a mighty nation favored by God. As further evidence of their change in status before the Lord, Sarai would now be called "Sarah," which meant "Princess." This alteration in their names was a portentous event, for a name was not only a means of identification in the ancient Near East, it was also intimately bound up with the very essence of a person, and in this case it was used to inaugurate a new phase of Abraham's life, much as was the change of name of Amenhotep IV (1352-1336 BCE) of Egypt to Akhenaten after his institution of the sole worship of the Sun god.

The next year, when Abraham was one hundred years old, the Lord reappeared and now declared that His contract to make of him a great nation would take place through the birth of a son to his wife Sarah, who was then ninety years old. The continuation of his heritage was not to be through Ishmael, as Abraham had believed for the past thirteen years, but rather by the miraculous birth of another son. As a further sign of God's favor upon Abraham's descendants, and to symbolize the commitment which was expected of all future Hebrews to follow the precepts of the Lord, YHWH told Abraham that every male child was to

---

5 Gen 16:9-12. Ibid., 120-121.
6 Gen 16:13. Alter, Genesis, 71.
7 Gen 16:15-16; 21:11; 25:9. Sarna, Genesis, 122.
8 Gen 17:1-2. Ibid., 123.

be circumcised at the age of eight days old.[9] To begin the process, all living male Hebrews were to be circumcised, as well as household slaves, so that the covenant would immediately sanctify the entire Jewish household. Finally, the Lord directed Abraham to name the child "Isaac," which means "He laughs," to remind them of the bounty which they received as a reward for their faithful observance of the divine covenant   Abraham obediently followed all of these commands, circumcising all of his household on that very day, including his son Ishmael, who was thirteen years old at the time. This act kept Ishmael integrally related to the covenant between Abraham and God, despite the fact that he would stand outside the Chosen line.

While this biblical section serves to clearly designate Isaac as the future Patriarch of the Jewish people, and Abraham must have rejoiced at the prospect of his beloved Sarah finally being granted the gift of being able to give birth to a son, the news must have nevertheless been bittersweet to Abraham, for he had been raising his family with Ishmael as his only child for thirteen years, and had not simply developed a close relationship with his son, but surely must have proudly broadcast to his neighbors that his firstborn son was to inherit all of his standing and wealth. How would he now explain this sudden change to his family and friends? How would he let Ishmael know that he no longer was to bear the title of primogeniture, a position which he must have been expecting for years, now that he was nearing the age which a child became an adult? In addition to the psychological stress, the sudden performance of a painful operation as circumcision on all the male members of his household must have seemed to be a sign of emasculation to those who did not practice the bizarre observance, and the only explanation Abraham could use to justify the action was that it was a commandment from God, an argument that surely would have been questioned by those who feared submitting to the bloody rite. Whether Abraham had second thoughts or not about following the directive of God will never be known for sure, but the Bible recorded that he accepted all that he was told, and immediately circumcised all of his household on that very same day.

---

9 Gen 17:9-12. This operation would serve as an indelible reminder of "the enduring, irrevocable nature of the covenant." Gen 17:7. Sarna, Genesis, 124. The eighth day was particularly significant for it signified that the newborn had completed a seven-day unit of time corresponding to the process of Creation. Ibid., 125. It should be noted, however, that this covenant was not necessarily irrevocable, for according to the prophet Jeremiah, YHWH later decided that a new covenant would be made with Israel and Judah after the Babylonian Exile that "will not be like the covenant I made with their fathers," since they broke the prior covenant by failing to follow the requirements set forth in the Ten Commandments. Jer 31:31-32. Sweeney, "Jeremiah," 991. Ezekiel, on the other hand, denied that this annulment was made, claiming that the Lord said "I will remember the covenant I made with you in the days of your youth, and I will establish it with you as an everlasting covenant." Ezek 16:60. Sweeney, "Ezekiel," 1071.

The activity on that portentous day must have also shocked and dismayed Sarah, for she had not yet heard the incredible news of her future insemination, and the sudden vision of all the male members of her family undergoing circumcision must have made her believe that something divine had happened to assure that Ishmael was to carry on Abraham's legacy. Ishmael was thirteen years old at the time, and even though the practice of honoring the passage of a Jewish son into adulthood at this age would not become a rite until centuries later, it was still a time of puberty that was recognized throughout the ancient Near East as an age associated with the ability to procreate. Although we now know that other people had practiced circumcision before this event, according to biblical tradition no one else had yet performed this procedure, and the willingness of the men to undergo such a painful procedure must have indicated a strong faith in Abraham's authority and countenance with God. Her natural reaction would have been to associate this scene with Ishmael's passage into manhood, and her shock likely is an explanation of what happened next in the biblical text.

Following the period of recovery from the rites of passage, three strangers appeared at Abraham's home by the terebinths of Mamre, informing him that the Lord's promise was about to be fulfilled, and that he would be given a son in the following year.[10] Sarah overheard the news of her future pregnancy for the first time, and laughed at the prospect of having a child at such an advanced age. As mentioned above, this response was probably due, in part, to astonishment since she had believed that Ishmael's puberty was the cause of the mass circumcision, but her reaction was taken as a direct affront by the strangers who asked Abraham why she would laugh at their prediction, forcing Sarah to lie in an attempt to deny her rude reply. These early descriptions of Sarah treating Hagar harshly, and then acting with little decorum in front of strangers, is not the kind of nature which one would expect to see attributed to the first Jewish Matriarch, but the ancient Hebrews, like other Semitic tribes, were a patriarchal society, and although Sarah would become a respected Matriarch to future generations of Jews, her demeanor in the Bible was presented with a litany of faults that reflected the general attitude placed upon women in the Late Bronze Age.[11] I believe the behavior of Sarah in

---

10 Gen 18:1, 10. According to Rashi, the three men were the Angels Michael, who informed Abraham that Sarah would have a son; Gabriel, who overturned Sodom; and Raphael, who healed Abraham and saved Lot. Scherman, The Chumash, 79.

11 Women were frequently portrayed in negative terms in the Torah, beginning with the enticement of Adam by Eve to eat the forbidden fruit. According to rabbinic legend, there was also a woman named Lilith who God had formed out of the dust before forming Eve from Adam's rib. Lilith only remained on earth for a short period of time because she was insistent upon enjoying full equality with her husband. This continued into patriarchal times, where the "daughters of Zion were haughty and walked with stretched forth necks and wanton eyes; Sarah was an eavesdropper in her own tent, when the Angel spoke with Abraham; Miriam was a tale-bearer, accusing Moses; Rachel was envious of her sister

both situations is more reflective of the fears and pressures placed upon women in the male-dominant Late Bronze Age, than it is from any deficiency in her underlying character, but we will see that her conflict with Hagar is about to take a more confrontational turn with the birth of her own child.

Although Sarah was previously willing to encourage Abraham to have a son with Hagar when she was barren, she now became jealous of Abraham's relationship with his other family, and demanded that Abraham get rid of Hagar and her illegitimate child at once. This concern is understandable, for as long as there was an elder son around to tempt the affections of Abraham, her own child was in danger of losing his due inheritance. She therefore told Abraham to immediately evict Hagar and Ishmael from the household, leaving Abraham with a very difficult decision, since Ishmael was still his firstborn child and abandoning the boy and his mother would certainly put their lives at risk. Abraham hesitated when Sarah first made her request, but God once again appeared to reassure him that Sarah's insistence was proper, and that it was to be through Isaac that his hereditary line would be continued. This divine intercession convinced Abraham that he had no choice but to follow Sarah's mandate, and early in the morning he evicted Hagar and Ishmael from his house, leaving them to survive on their own in the wilderness of Beer-sheba.[12] Hagar aimlessly wandered into the desert, and when her supply of water ran out, she left Ishmael under a bush and sat at a distance, too grief-stricken to watch her child die. The fact that Ishmael was thirteen years old at the time belies the intended empathy which this scene was meant to produce. This emotional scene was to have a happy ending, however, for God heard the cries of the boy and once again sent an Angel to assure Hagar that Ishmael would live, and that a great nation would arise from the boy's descendants.[13] Hagar found the strength to continue her journey, and Ishmael indeed survived, eventually becoming the leader of a people who dwelt in the wilderness of Paran, although he no longer would reside in the house of his father.

This aspect of the Akeda has not received as much attention as that of the sacrifice attempt itself, but the actions of Abraham to first wilfully expose his firstborn son Ishmael to the dangers of the desert, and then later prepare to

---

Leah; ... and Dinah was a gadabout." Ginzberg, The Legends of the Jews, I.65-66.

12 Gen 21:14. While this eviction scene resembles the earlier one when Hagar was pregnant, literary criticism attributes this section to E, and the first one to J. Levenson, "Genesis," 44. Some commentators have hypothesized that Abraham harbored a lasting resentment with Sarah over this expulsion demand, and that their marriage eventually resulted in a separation, which preceded Sarah's death. Abramaovitch, The First Father Abraham: The Psychology and Culture of a Spiritual Revolutionary, 141.

13 Gen 21:17-18. The Midrash holds that the Angels pleaded with God not to perform the miracle and save Ishmael, for his future offspring would one day persecute and murder Jews, but God responded that Ishmael would only be judged by his present deeds, and not according to what would happen in the future. Scherman, The Chodash, 97.

sacrifice his second son Isaac, were a clear indication that the commandments of the Lord were to be followed under all circumstances, even if the repercussions included the possible death of a beloved child. Abraham followed God's directive to kill one of his sons not only once, but twice, having no foreknowledge that either child would survive the event, and leaving no question that the intent of this lesson was that nothing on earth was more important then the edicts of God. The true believer would put his entire faith in the Lord's will, and would obey His orders at all times, trusting that God's way was the best. It should be noted that such total devotion to the commandments of God was not an Hebraic invention, as many religions required an all-encompassing fervor for the orders of their particular deities, but the use of infanticide as an example of this loyalty is unique to the Jews and the Greeks, and I believe the idea initiated with the biblical tale of Abraham and Isaac.

To bring the story back to the Akeda itself, some years after the birth of Isaac, God decided to have Abraham verify his faith and obedience in the ultimate test of faith.[14] God called Abraham personally, rather than through the intermediary of an Angel, and once again we do not know where this event took place, but Abraham answered *Hinne-ni*, "Here I am," a term which implies attentiveness and responsiveness to instructions.[15] This time God told him to make an *olah*, or offering:

Take your son, your beloved one, Isaac whom you hold so dear, and go to the land of Moriah, where you shall offer him up as a burnt offering on one of the heights that I will point out to you.[16]

The description of the son to be offered is often translated as "the one whom you love," requiring that Abraham suppress his most intense paternal affections in placing obedience to God above all else. Rabbi Yoshe-Ber of Brest (d. 1892 CE), who became known for his penetrating insights of the Torah, theorized that the Lord had to tell Abraham of this difficult task because "no angel would have

---

14 The exact timing of the event is not given, and the account simply begins with the phrase "*vayehi akharei hadevarim haeleh*," or "some time afterward." Abramaovitch, The First Father Abraham: The Psychology and Culture of a Spiritual Revolutionary, 128. According to accepted chronology, Isaac was thirty-seven years old, since Sarah was ninety years old when he was born, and 127 years old at her death, which supposedly occurred when she learned he had been taken to be sacrificed. Gen 17:17; 21:5; 23:1. Scherman, The Chumash, 100.

15 Gen 22:1. Levenson, "Genesis," 45.

16 Gen 22:2. Genesis, The Anchor Bible, 161. The exact location of Moriah is not known, but is said by the Sages to be in Jerusalem, at the Dome of the Rock, with the derivation from the word *myrrh*, one of the spices in the Temple incense mixture. Scherman, The Chumash, 101.

accepted the assignment."[17] Without any argument – without even any attempt to question the reason for such a violent request as he had earlier done when God told him he was going to destroy Sodom and Gomorrah – Abraham awoke early the very next morning to carry out his appointed chore. His silence in this regard is quite remarkable, especially since the story of Sodom and Gomorrah is juxtaposed in the same parashah as the Akeda, clearly a sign that the reader was to be aware of a connection in the lessons to be learned. In the words of the noted biblical scholar Nahum Sarna: "He who was so daringly eloquent on behalf of the people of Sodom surrenders in total silence to his own bitter personal destiny."[18]

Why did Abraham silently acquiesce to the Lord's command to kill his beloved son without even a hint of understandable reluctance? It has been pointed out that in the episode of Sodom and Gomorrah, Abraham was challenging God's *plan*, while in the Akeda, Abraham was following a *command*, and that "As always, he obeys his God's wishes."[19] Even so, when YHWH first directed Abraham to leave Mesopotamia and his father's house, He was negating Abraham's past heritage, and when He directed Abraham to have all the males in his house circumcised, He was modifying Abraham's present way-of-life, but now, with the directive to kill Isaac, He was apparently negating the whole future which Abraham had hoped for. In addition, He was commanding Abraham to do something that must have seemed to be an impious action, even though the prohibition of murder had not yet been proclaimed by a direct theophany.

Aside from the fact that the story of Sodom and Gomorrah is attributed to the "J" source, while that of Abraham and Isaac is from the "E" source,[20] biblical scholars have often pointed out that when God forecast to Abraham the future birth of Isaac, He cautioned that you must "walk in My ways and be blameless."[21] Abraham took this to mean that if he did not do as he was told, his reward would be voided. This same phrase appeared in contemporary Akkadian writing, where it was used to mandate the absolute loyalty of a subject to a king.[22] By choosing this phraseology, the author of the Akeda was showing that Abraham could not question a directive of God, and expect to remain in the Lord's good graces. When Abraham had attempted to change God's mind about Sodom and Gomorrah, he had not been personally directed to act, but was only responding to what he viewed as an inequitable killing of innocent people. Now, God had

---

17 Weinreich, Yiddish Folktales, 22.

18 Sarna, Genesis, 151.

19 Levenson, The Death and Resurrection of the Beloved Son: The Transformation of Child Sacrifice in Judaism and Christianity, 130.

20 Hendel, Remembering Abraham: Culture, Memory, and History in the Hebrew Bible, 38-39.

21 Gen 17:1. Levenson, The Death and Resurrection of the Beloved Son: The Transformation of Child Sacrifice in Judaism and Christianity, 130.

22 Ibid.

given him a direct order, and the only thing he could do as a pious adherent was to follow God's bidding without a word of regret. In so doing, Ronald Hendel, Professor of Hebrew Bible and Jewish Studies at the University of California, Berkeley, concludes that he would be able to embody both the moral imperative of the "way of Yahweh" (Gen 18:19, "J"), with the ethical ideal of "God-fearing" (Gen 22:12, "E").[23]

While this explanation suffices for most Orthodox Jews, the reasoning seems insufficient for many modern ethicists, as well as many other faithful adherents to the Old Testament, for as Soren Kierkegaard, (1813-1855 CE), the Danish philosopher and theologian, questioned in *Fear and Trembling*, "there were countless generations which knew by rote, word for word, the story of Abraham – how many were made sleepless by it?"[24] His reasoning was simple, for "to money I have no ethical obligation, but to the son the father has the highest and most sacred obligation."[25] In other words, blood is supposed to be thicker than water, and while one may view the sacrifice as a religious obedience to the commandment of God, the ethical and legal conclusion was that he was willing to murder his son, and no pleading would set that intent aside. In the end, Kierkegaard admitted that "though Abraham aroused my admiration, he at the same time appalls me."[26]

Abraham not only immediately set out to do God's bidding, he did not tell Sarah or Isaac the nature of his trip, perhaps fearing that his family's faith would not be equal to his own. He saddled his ass in the morning, and took two of his servants along. After a journey of three days, they reached their final destination.[27] Abraham bid the two men to remain where they were, and proceeded to climb the mountain with Isaac at his side. The wood for the burnt-offering had been placed on Isaac's shoulders, as one would do with a sacrificial animal, and Christian theologians have compared this act to Christ bearing the cross on his way to the

---

23 Hendel, Remembering Abraham: Culture, Memory, and History in the Hebrew Bible, 40.

24 Kierkegaard, Fear and Trembling and The Sickness Unto Death, 39.

25 Ibid.

26 Ibid., 71. Henry Hanock Abramovitch, Associate Professor in the Department of Medical Education at Tel Aviv University, had a similar reaction, concluding that "the akeda is the psychotic culmination of a severely disturbed personality," a man who "changes his name, his place of residence (at least ten times) and displays severe psychopathology in his interpersonal relation with his wife and sons." Abramaovitch, <u>The First Father Abraham: The Psychology and Culture of a Spiritual Revolutionary</u>, 19. He added that the Kantian approach to the dilemma faced by Abraham should have been decided by the fact that "one can be sure, absolutely, that human sacrifice is morally wrong," but one cannot be sure that the voices one hears are truly the word of God, and that he should have then chosen to remain home. Ibid., 131.

27 The Midrash claimed that the two servants were Eliezer and Ishmael. Scherman, <u>The Chumash</u>, 101.

crucifixion.[28] As the father and son slowly ascended the mountain, each with his own heavy load, Isaac asked innocently: "Father, there is the wood, and the firestone, but where is the sheep for the burnt offering?"[29] Abraham answered solemnly: "God will see to the sheep for his burnt offering, my son."[30] By this show of concern, some scholars believe that Isaac had begun to sense his gruesome destiny, but even though he may have realized that his life was in danger, tradition has taught that he remained unmoved by this fear, and that his path was straight and unaltered, for he knew he had the blessing of the Lord. The Midrash explains that they walked together, "the one to bind, the other to be bound; the one to slaughter, the other to be slaughtered."[31]

When the father and son finally arrived at the site designated by God, Abraham bound Isaac's arms and legs, as he would have done with a sacrificial animal, and then laid him on the altar, in preparation for the final act of immolation.[32] He lifted the knife to plunge into the body of his son, and as the moment of killing approached, the Angel of God suddenly shouted to him from heaven above:

Abraham! Abraham! Lay not your hand upon the boy, nor do the least thing to him! Now I know how dedicated you are to God, since you did not withhold from me your own beloved son.[33]

The need for the sacrifice had evaporated in the willingness of Abraham to perform the deed, and Isaac was allowed to live and fulfill God's promise to populate the earth with a multitude of descendants. Abraham, who had so intently concentrated on his task that the Angel had to call out his name twice, had proven beyond all doubt that he was totally devoted to obeying the commandments of the Lord, showing himself to be "the incontestable paradigm of the truly 'God-fearing' man, one who is wholehearted in his self-determined, disinterested, self-surrender to God's will."[34] In a nearby thicket, Abraham saw a ram caught by its's horns, and knowing that this was a sign from the Lord, he took the creature and

---

28 Origen, "Homilies on Genesis," 6, The Fathers of the Church, 140-141. Already in the *Epistle of Barnabas* from the fourth century CE, "Isaac is referred to as the prototype for the sufferings and trials of Jesus." Spiegel, The Last Trial: On the Legends and Lore of the Command to Abraham to Offer Isaac as a Sacrifice: The Akedah, 84.

29 Gen 22:7. Genesis, The Anchor Bible, 161.

30 Gen 22:8. Ibid.

31 Gen Rab 56:4. Levenson, The Death and Resurrection of the Beloved Son: The Transformation of Child Sacrifice in Judaism and Christianity, 134.

32 Gen 22:9. Jon Levenson, Associate Professor of Hebrew Bible in the Divinity School of the University of Chicago, questions why Abraham bound Isaac, since it was not a common practice to bind animals before the sacrifice. Possible explanations could be that it may have been the standard for human sacrifice, or that Abraham feared that Isaac would not "share his father's unshakable resolve to do the will of God at any price." Ibid., 135.

33 Gen 22:11-12. Genesis, The Anchor Bible, 162.

34 Sarna, Genesis, 153.

sacrificed it on the altar where Isaac had just lain.[35] In appreciation of the sparing of his son's life, Abraham named the place *Adonai-yireh*, meaning "the Lord will see to the substitute for His offering."[36] From that time forward, animals would be substituted for human beings in the sacrificial process, and the *shofar*, the ram's horn, would be blown on Rosh Hashonah to signify a new year and a new life.[37]

The Angel's response that "I know how dedicated you are to God" has suggested to some scholars that Abraham's obedience up to this point was not enough to convince God that Abraham had given up his faith in other deities, and lends support to the belief that the patriarchal faith was polytheistic, as will be discussed in more detail in chapter 12. This is an interesting hypothesis, for Abraham did have many connections with pagans, siring Ishmael through the Egyptian slave Hagar, and conducting business transactions with the Amorites. Could it be that God was uncertain about Abraham's faith in Him alone, and wanted to be assured that he was worthy of being the man to build the first monotheistic religion in the world? If this was the case, Abraham surely passed the test by his willingness to offer up Isaac for sacrifice, but the trauma which Abraham went through may have weakened his faith in the wisdom of YHWH, for following the Akeda and the death of Sarah, Abraham married Keturah, a woman who appears to have had no Hebrew connections.[38] Is it possible that Abraham had second thoughts about God's directives to place his children in harm's way near the end of his life, and reverted to methods of homage which resembled the general polytheistic Semitic faith, more than the monotheist creed which would

---

35 Gen 22:13. It was not unusual for a ram to get caught by its horns while nibbling at thickets, and a pair of figurines depicting such a condition has been found in the royal tombs of Ur, from the middle of the third millennium BCE. The Illustrated Family Encyclopedia of the Living Bible, I.67. In the Greek tale of Phrixus, a youth was saved from death at the hands of his father but the sudden appearance of a ram with a fleece of gold who carried him away from the land of Boetia. Plaut, Genesis, The Torah: A Modern Commentary, 210-211.

36 Spiegel, The Last Trial: On the Legends and Lore of the Command to Abraham to Offer Isaac as a Sacrifice: The Akedah, 68. According to R. Hanina ben Dosa, from the first generation of the Tannaim in the first century CE, not a part of the ram went to waste for "its tendons became the ten strings of the harp that David used to play on; its skin became the leather girdle around the loins of Elihah; as to its horns, with the left one the Holy One, blessed be He, sounded the alarum at Mount Sinai; and with the right one, which is larger than the left, He will in the future sound the alarum at the Ingathering of the Exiles in the Age to Come." Ibid., 39.

37 Many have argued that the story of the Akeda served as an etiology of the substitution of animal for human sacrifice. Levenson, The Death and Resurrection of the Beloved Son: The Transformation of Child Sacrifice in Judaism and Christianity, 111.

38 Her name is almost identical with the Hebrew word for "incense," suggesting that she may have been from one of the tribes who traded in frankincense throughout the Levant. Marks, "The Book of Genesis," 20.

be promulgated by Moses during the years following the Exodus? This somewhat heretical supposition is not generally discussed in the rabbinic literature, but I believe that the event does not accurately reflect how difficult it must have been for Abraham to follow the directive of God, given his initial hesitance when Sarah told him to banish Ishmael from his household. The events which followed his return home must be taken into account when assessing the long-term effects on his commitment to monotheism, and Abraham's seemingly rash decision to marry a person not of his own family can reflect, in my opinion, his anger at YHWH for putting him into a position of possibly having to kill his own son. One can only imagine the nightmares which followed, and the biblical text quickly moves on to a discussion of the next generation once the tale of the Akeda was completed, including Abraham's arranging the marriage of Isaac to someone from the land of his birth, but not to a Canaanite.[39]

When Abraham had completed the sacrificial rite using the ram instead of Isaac, the Angel of the Lord spoke to him again, and repeated the covenant which the Lord had made to guarantee the success of his progeny. He told him that because he had performed this deed, the Lord swore that he would be blessed, and that his offspring would "inherit the gate of its enemy."[40] Although He had previously promised Abraham that his offspring would be as numerous as the stars, He now assured him that they would also prevail over their enemies. To show the reliability of this promise, God swore by His own name, an oath which could not be any more certain.[41]

Although the standard biblical translation presents the Akeda as sparing the life of Isaac, biblical scholars have long noticed that despite the fact that both Abraham and Isaac were said to ascend the mountain, the text only stated that "Abraham returned" to the young men waiting at the base.[42] In addition, when Sarah died soon thereafter, only Abraham was mentioned as having gone to mourn for her, and Isaac's name was not included. This has led some Midrash commentaries to conclude that Isaac was not spared during the sacrifice, but was actually killed and then resurrected at a later time, since his story is continued in the passages which followed.[43] This reincarnation theme is suggestive of Christ's rising from the

---

39 Gen 24:2-4.
40 Gen 22:17. Scherman, The Chumash, 105.
41 Gen 22:16; Heb 6:13.
42 Gen 22:6-8, 19. Spiegel, The Last Trial: On the Legends and Lore of the Command to Abraham to Offer Isaac as a Sacrifice: The Akedah, 3. Not only is Isaac not specifically mentioned as returning with Abraham, the Bible does not relate any further conversation between them, and the next reference is when Isaac and Ishmael bury their father. Gen 25:9.
43 Friedman, Commentary on the Torah, 78. Rabbinic tradition held that Isaac was carried to paradise by Angels, and sojourned there for three years before returning home. When Abraham returned home alone, Sarah was so grieved that her soul fled from her

dead in the New Testament, but such a conjecture is not supported in present-day Jewish theology, and the standard approach to interpreting the Akeda is to accept that Abraham's knife was stayed, and the sacrifice never completed. Since the Bible was written long after the Exodus took place, we do not know what the oral legend may have been soon after the Exodus, and whether the dissident Hebrews brought with them a version which included such a resurrection theme.

As I discussed previously, the willingness of Abraham to sacrifice Isaac when ordered to do so by God has been viewed within the Jewish faith as a mark of devotion to which all truly pious Jews must aim. For the sincere adherent, there must be such intense faith in divine communication that no one must question the commandments of God, no matter how painful the request might appear. This attitude was voiced by the second century BCE Jewish wisdom teacher Joshua ben Sira, who claimed that Abraham, when tested, "was found loyal."[44] Soren Kierkegaard agreed with this conclusion and solemnly noted: "no sacrifice was too hard when God required it."[45] Finally, Philo of Alexandria (20 BCE-50 CE), the first century CE Jewish philosopher and theologian, emphasized that the sacrificial attempt was even more meaningful because it involved the loss of an only son: "For a father to surrender one of a numerous family as a tithe to God is nothing extraordinary, since each of the survivors continues to give him pleasure, but when there is only one son, it shows his acceptability of God."[46] This sentiment is reflected in the fact that the story of the Akeda highlights the synagogue service during Rosh Hashonah, the second holiest day of the year next to Yom Kippur on the Jewish religious calendar. Jon Levenson, Professor of Jewish Studies at the Divinity School and the Department of Near Eastern Languages and Civilizations at Harvard University, points out that it also reflects the cultic norm "that the beloved son belongs to God: 'You shall give Me the firstborn among your sons' (Exod 22:28b)."[47]

An acceptance of Abraham's solemn show of faith is also followed by the Christian and Moslem religions, both of whom incorporated the Old Testament

---

body. Ginzberg, The Legends of the Jews, I.286. R. Judah, the Hebrew grammarian of Toledo, Spain, 1070-1090 CE, explained that at the moment Abraham's knife touched Isaac's throat, his soul flew out of him, but God quickly reversed the process and when Isaac arose he praised the Lord, saying "Blessed art Thou, O Lord, who quickens the dead." Spiegel, The Last Trial: On the Legends and Lore of the Command to Abraham to Offer Isaac as a Sacrifice: The Akedah, 30-31. Another commentary explained that the soul flew out of Isaac when "he beheld the light of the Shekinah, ... but the Holy One, blessed be He, revived Him." Ibid., 31-32.

44 Levenson, The Death and Resurrection of the Beloved Son: The Transformation of Child Sacrifice in Judaism and Christianity, 175.

45 Kierkegaard, Fear and Trembling, 36.

46 Philo, On Abraham, XXXV.196, 97.

47 Levenson, The Death and the Resurrection of the Beloved Son: The Transformation of Child Sacrifice in Judaism and Christianity, 142.

into their own sacred texts: the New Testament and the Koran. Saint Paul (5-67 CE) highlighted the attempted sacrifice by noting that God's promise to give the whole earth to Abraham and his descendants "was not because Abraham obeyed God's laws but because he trusted God to keep His promise."[48] This promise, of course, refers to God's forecast that Abraham's offspring would continue through the body of Isaac, so that even if he completed the sacrifice, God would bring his son back to life again. Abraham knew that the Lord would never renege on His vow, and he therefore went along with the process, knowing full-well that Isaac's life would be spared.[49] While such trust in the Word of the Lord may very well reflect Abraham's extraordinary belief in the Unity of God, it still denotes a willingness to subject his son to harm, especially in light of the fact that he turned Ishmael out of his house, not knowing whether he would survive in the wilderness or not. No matter how much Abraham may have relied on God's promise to assure his legacy of descendants, his readiness to place Isaac on the altar and raise his knife in an act that many ethicists, myself included, find difficult to understand. That the ancient Hebrews, as well as the Greeks, felt that the lesson of willingness to sacrifice you own child was a necessary part of their moral code indicates to me the certainty that the two societies were somehow intimately connected at the time the legend began, and, in my opinion, this was in the years following the Exodus when the dissident Hebrews migrated to Mycenae.

B. *Agamemnon and Iphigenia*

The story of Agamemnon and Iphigenia closely follows that of Abraham and Isaac in many respects. In the fable of the Trojan War, as discussed in the previous chapter, Helen, the most beautiful woman in the world, was seduced and abducted by Paris, the prince of Troy and son of King Hector. Paris had been in Sparta visiting Menelaus, the brother of King Agamemnon, and fell in love with his wife, Helen, while Menelaus was out of the country. The two fled Greece for Troy, and when Menelaus returned home and found his wife gone, he vowed revenge upon the entire Trojan nation for the dishonor wrought by their prince. The Greeks gathered a large armada of ships in the Bay of Aulis, with Agamemnon, the brother of Menelaus, in command as general and chief. As preparations to sail were completed, the winds suddenly died down, stalling the entire fleet in the water. Calchas, the renowned seer brought along to help in the planning of battle, advised Agamemnon that the reason for the atmospheric delay was that Artemis (Diana), the virgin goddess, had been angered because in

---

48 Rom 4:13. The Living Bible, 900.

49 This conclusion obviously predated God's decision to renege on the promise that the Davidic monarchy would endure forever. 2 Sam 7:16; 1 Kgs 2:4; 9:5. It turned out, however, that the promise was based upon the monarchs following God's law. 1 Kgs 9:4-7; 11:11.

the confusion of preparing for war, Agamemnon had neglected to sacrifice the loveliest maiden in all of Greece at the start of the season.[50] In order to now appease her ire, and assure a change in the weather, Calchas warned that virgin blood must be shed.[51] Unlike Abraham, who was never given a reason why God required the killing of Isaac, the Greek legend made it clear that the reason for the sacrifice was to assure proper homage to the gods, thereby preventing divine anger which generally resulted in a disaster for the entire community.

Agamemnon, as a recognized dignitary of the ancient Greek community, would have been well aware of the ability of seers to recognize the wishes of the gods, and he therefore accepted the interpretation of Calchas, not yet realizing whose "virgin blood" it was that had to be shed. He soon found out, however, that it was his own lovely daughter, Iphigenia, that had to be sacrificed, and like Abraham, he was faced with the difficult decision of having to kill his own child to appease the demands of a god, or forsake his loyalty to the entire Greek nation. While his choice was agonizing, his decision was clear, for the ancient Greeks, as Aristotle later summarized in *Politics*, saw that "the state is by nature clearly prior to the family and to the individual, since the whole of necessity is prior to the part."[52] No single person, not even one's own child, retained primary importance in such a system of law, and Agamemnon, like Abraham, did not question the veracity or wisdom of the demand. One critical difference between the two tales, however, was that Abraham had heard the request directly from God, while Agamemnon was relying on the opinion of a human interpreter. Greek mythology did allow some heroes, such as Odysseus and Achilles, to have communion with a god, but for the most part the Greeks believed that seers were the only ones to be in direct contact with the gods, and that their interpretations were therefore to be held as sacrosanct.

This portrayal of a ruler having to grieve over personal tragedy in order to protect the interests of his country became a favorite topic of future Greek playwrights and philosophers, and in many versions of the story Agamemnon's decision has been portrayed as labored and intense. According to Euripides (480-406 BCE), when he first realized it was his daughter who had to be sacrificed, he ordered the herald Talthybius to make a loud proclamation and dismiss the whole army, for

---

50 According to Sophocles (490-406 BCE), it was Iphigenia who had to be sacrificed, rather than one of Menelaus' two children, because Agamemnon had shot a stag in the forest which greatly angered Artemis. Sophocles, "Electra," 637-645, 320. Euripides (c. 480-406 BCE) found it quite strange that Artemis would demand human sacrifice, since she forbid any man whose hands were stained with bloodshed, childbirth, or burial, to approach her altar. Euripides, "Iphigenia in Tauris," 381-383, 136.

51 "Virgin blood must satisfy the virgin goddess' anger." Ovid, Metamorphoses, XII.29-30, 286. See e.g., Euripides, "Iphigenia in Tauris," 18-24, 123.

52 Aristotle, Politics, I.3.1253a, 55.

he never could brutally murder Iphigenia in this manner.[53] "If I did commit this act," he told Menelaus, "against law, right, and the child I fathered, each day, each night, while I yet lived would wear me out in grief and tears."[54] When Menelaus heard of this decision, he argued with Agamemnon, attempting to convince him to proceed with the sacrifice, pointing out that Greece was troubled with grief and it was necessary for him to shoulder a part of the hardship. Agamemnon resisted, answering that "Greece, like yourself, some god has driven mad," but he eventually realized that he must proceed for the army would kill all of his family if he failed to fulfill his obligation of sacrificing to Artemis.[55] His obvious love for his daughter made his resolution pitiful and tragic, expanding the degree of emotional stress which was already placed upon his shoulders as head of the Greek force preparing for war.

This initial reluctance to follow the mandates of Calchas is very interesting, and shows, in my opinion, how the early Greek playwrights tussled with the same problems that troubled the commentators of the Akeda, as discussed above. How can one listen to the mandate of a god that you must kill your own child, without at least questioning the reasons for the demand? Since the Greek legend concluded that Iphigenia was killed, interpretations generally included some reluctance on the part of Agamemnon to proceed, but for the most part, except for some variations which I will discuss further in Chapter 14, Agamemnon finally realized that he had to accede to the wishes of the god, and despite his horrified reluctance to place Iphigenia on the sacrificial altar, the honor of Greece depended upon his obedient response. In the words of the Roman poet Ovid (43 BCE-17 CE), eventually "the king subdued the father," and Agamemnon proceeded with the bloody offering.[56] Kierkegaard labeled this action typical of the tragic hero: "The father will turn his face away, but the hero will raise the knife."[57]

This tragic fate of Iphigenia proved to be fertile ground for Greek playwrights, who generally spared no tears in describing the final event. In *Agamemnon*, Aeschylus (525-426 BCE) dramatized the indecision of Agamemnon by having him explain how his sight would forever be agonized by "the beauty of my house with maiden blood shed staining these father's hands beside the altar."[58] He finally accepted, however, that "when necessity's yoke was put upon him he changed," realizing what he had to do as commander-in-chief of the Greek armada.[59] His determination was stolid as "her supplications and her cries of father were nothing,

---

53 Euripides, "Iphigenia in Aulis," 94-96, 220.
54 Ibid., 398-400, 233.
55 Ibid., 411, 234; 414, 239; 1267-1270, 281-282.
56 Ovid, <u>Metamorphoses</u>, XXII.
57 Kierkegaard, <u>Fear and Trembling</u>, 68.
58 Aeschylus, "Agamemnon," 208-210, 41.
59 Ibid., 218-219, 41.

nor the child's lamentation to kings passioned for battle.[60]

Euripides, on the other hand, portrayed the final speech of Iphigenia to her mother Clytemnestra, who was shocked to hear what Agamemnon was planning, as an heroic offering which became the hallmark of all future altruistic martyrs:

O Mother, if Artemis wishes to take the life of my body, Shall I, who am mortal, oppose the divine will? No — that is unthinkable? To Greece I give this body of mine. Slay it in sacrifice and conquer Troy.[61]

Like Isaac, she would not struggle against the demands of her father, but would give up her life in an act of courageous martyrdom. Unlike the offering of Isaac by Abraham, however, there was no divine intervention in this Greek tragedy, and when the sacrifice was completed, the winds arose and the fleet sailed away to defeat the Trojans in a grisly ten-year war, as chronicled in Homer's famous heroic poem, the *Iliad*.

Some authors nevertheless found the concept of infanticide too grotesque for adulation, and attempted to find ways to maintain the loyalty of Agamemnon to the welfare of his country without resulting in the death of his daughter. In *Iphigenia in Tauris*, Euripides took a different approach, and had Iphigenia survive the sacrificial attempt when Artemis "deceived their eyes with a deer to bleed for me and stole me through the azure sky," setting Iphigenia down in the town of Tauris, where she became a priestess of Artemis in charge of human sacrifice.[62] The replacement of an animal for Iphigenia at the very moment of truth indicated that the god did not need to see the sacrifice completed, an action remarkably similar to that of the Akeda in the Old Testament. The origin of the reason for the two divergent plays by Euripides is not clear, although it appears reasonable to me that Euripides may very well have heard of the Abraham and Isaac story, and was connecting the outcome to the Greek myth in a manner that would preserve the life of the child, while at the same time retaining the basis of the ancient legend.

Ovid, as well, claimed that the innocent young girl was not actually killed. In *Metamorphoses*, he told how Artemis yielded to the drama of the moment, and placed a deer in the stead of Iphigenia as a replacement victim, in much the same way that a ram was accepted with Isaac, and a deer in the story by Euripides.[63] Hesiod (eighth century BCE), according to the ancient Greek guidebook writer Pausanias (fl. c. 160 CE), also could not believe that Iphigenia died, but there are no details as to what the circumstances were to change the final outcome.[64]

What has survived to modern times, however, and what was generally accepted

60 Ibid., 228-230, 41.

61 Euripides, "Iphigenia in Aulis," 1394-1396, 291.

62 Euripides, "Iphigenia in Tauris," 19-20, 26-30, 124; 782-784, 155. She loathed human sacrifice, but piously obeyed Artemis. Graves, The Greek Myths: 2, III.d, 74.

63 Ovid, Metamorphoses, XII.32-33, 286.

64 Pausanias, Description of Greece, I.XLIII.1, I, 229.

by the Classical Greek civilization, is the legend that Agamemnon carried out the murderous deed, and killed his daughter for the good of the country, and the honor of his fellow-men. Despite the fact that the Greeks were victorious at the end of the ten- year Trojan War, the saga of tragedy for Agamemnon, and the entire house of Atreus, did not end, for when Agamemnon returned home triumphantly, he soon paid the ultimate price for his sacrifice of Iphigenia. His wife, Clytemnestra, did not share his proud loyalty to the grandeur of Greece, and the sacrifice of their daughter turned her love for Agamemnon into vengeful hatred. Sophocles (497-406 BCE) in *Electra*, told how Clytemnestra explained to her surviving daughter Electra that she killed Agamemnon for Justice, since he "was the only Greek generous enough to please the gods by killing his own daughter."[65] The refusal of Clytemnestra to accept the heroic nature of Agamemnon's decision was repeated by the Roman tragedist Seneca (3 BCE-65CE) in *Agamemnon*, where Iphigenia's nurse argued that the loss of her ward "freed our Grecian fleet from long delay, and waked from their dull calm the sluggish seas."[66] Clytemnestra, however, answered her scornfully:

Oh, shameful thought, that I, the heaven born child of Tyndarus, should give my daughter up to save the Grecian fleet.[67]

Clytemnestra's action was not generally condoned by most Greek tragedists, even though it might today be accepted as a legitimate claim of defensible homicide against a man who would slit his own daughter's throat in order to promote a war in which the sons of many mothers would be slaughtered for pride alone.

Although Clytemnestra's retribution seems to have stemmed solely from her immense grief over the loss of her daughter, her depiction on the Greek stage soon expanded into that of a vengeful schemer who not only was unfaithful during the valorous interlude of her husband's ten year wartime absence, but who committed murder without cause. Her son Orestes continued the tragical fate of the house of Atreus by killing Clytemnestra to avenge the death of his father. In the *Oresteia* trilogy by Aeschylus, he was then pursued by the Furies who were sent by Clytemnestra to "hunt him down once more, and shrivel him in your vitals' heat and flame."[68] Orestes fled to the sanctuary of Apollo, where he was given refuge, and when the Chorus confronted Apollo on how he dared harbor a matricide, Apollo answered that the killing of a spouse was equal to the killing of a blood relative, for the marriage oath was guarded by a right of nature, thereby invoking the pardonable necessity for blood-revenge.[69] Orestes then fled to the temple of Athena in Athens, where the Chorus agreed to let the goddess try his

---

65 Sophocles, "Electra," 592-94, 318.
66 Seneca, <u>Agamemnon</u>, II.I.160-161, II, 720.
67 Ibid., II.I.162-164, 720.
68 Aeschylus, "The Eumenides," 138-139, 139.
69 Ibid., 217-218, 142.

guilt. Apollo spoke for Orestes in his defense, and expanded the reasoning for legal absolution by arguing that a mother was not the parent of her child, but only the nurse of the newly planted seed that grew in her womb. Once again, the role of the male in Classical Greek society was clearly dominant. Athena took this argument to heart, being that she was born of Zeus directly without the need for a mother, and found for Orestes when the jury was deadlocked.[70]

Of interest, while the Greeks chose to highlight the role Iphigenia's mother played in the sacrifice, the Old Testament simply left Sarah out of the story altogether. As previously discussed, the women in the Bible, and Sarah in particular, did not always evoke images worthy of respect, but the biblical compilers did not feel the need to involve the emotions of Isaac's mother in the most important lesson of the Torah, while the Greek playwrights parlayed the supposed response of Clytemnestra into a starring role. Sarah's presence was not entirely neglected, however, for in the very next passage after the Akeda, Sarah's death was announced, and this has prompted interpretations that she possibly died of grief after hearing of Abraham's intent. While the text does not proved any direct evidence to this effect, such an interpretation seems very plausible, and when the Greeks were first introduced to the fable, they may have very well expanded Sarah's role in their typically gruesome fashion.

C. Discussion

The fact that both Abraham and Agamemnon were forced to stand at an altar with knife in hand as executioner of their own flesh and blood, and then were extolled in posterity for their willingness to do so, forms a unique bond in the history of world mythology because of the remarkable similarity in the message each legend taught about the acceptability of the infanticidal act as a mark of faith in the infallibility of God.[71] In the biblical narrative, Abraham was asked to sacrifice Isaac in order to prove his willingness to follow YHWH's directive, no matter how much personal loss might result. As a result of this single-minded devotion, his descendants became the Chosen People of God, inheriting the Promised Land after first suffering an extended period of enslavement in Egypt. In the Greek legend, Agamemnon was required to sacrifice Iphigenia in order to appease the goddess Artemis so that the Greek armada could sail to Troy and avenge the honor of the Greek nation, something which the Heroic Age in Greece put above life itself. Following the immolation of Iphigenia on the altar, the winds arose as promised, and the Greeks began their ten-year conflict, which was to herald the bravery of Greek heroes for centuries to come. Both societies

---

70 Ibid., 735-740, 161.

71 That the initials of the father's name and the child's name are the same is a coincidence that adds to the mystery of the two events, although it is unclear if it was an attempt by the receiving culture to highlight the connection.

taught that the ends of these killings justified the means, although Agamemnon paid the price of being murdered by his wife Clytemnestra for putting the welfare of the state above that of his family. Clytemnestra's understandable anger was not applauded by the Greeks, and she paid her own price for the killing by being slain by her son Orestes. Abraham, as well, is believed to have lost his beloved wife Sarah to grief over the event, and never again is said to have conversed with God. He may have been applauded by his descendants, but there is a question as to how he was viewed by his conscience.

While the willingness to commit murder in order to prove loyalty to a divine being is consistent with the religious tenets of many ancient and modern societies, highlighting the infanticidal act as a paradigm of this lesson is unique to only the Hebrew and Greek cultures. Human sacrifice was not unusual in ancient times: it characterized many societies besides the Hebrews and Greeks, and otherwise rational and successful civilizations frequently practiced the rite in elaborate ceremonies that were intended to pacify the pertinacious nature of their gods.[72] Participants hoped that by relinquishing the life of an individual, gratuitous repayment would be generated in the form of warding off disease, assuring a harvest, preventing calamity, or saving the state from the threats of a foreign power. This was particularly prominent in the case of the firstborn child, who was often regarded as the property of a god. By offering the child up for sacrifice, the youth was simply restored to his or her rightful owner, thereby cleansing both the individual and the community of sin. Philo of Byblos (64-141 CE), an antiquarian writer of historical works in Greek, noted that: "It was customary for the rulers of a city or nation, rather than lose everyone, to provide the dearest of their children as a propitiatory sacrifice to the avenging deities."[73] The well-known Hellenic Jewish philosopher and theologian, Philo of Alexandria, also remarked that these cultures saw "child sacrifice as a holy deed and acceptable to God."[74]

The Bible highlighted the sacrifice of children in other sections than the Akeda. In the book of *Exodus*, God told Moses that "the firstborn of your sons you shall give to Me."[75] This was intended to be redeemed by the paying of a fixed fee to the priests (*Pidyon haBen*), however, and not refer to child sacrifice, as evidenced

---

72 Milner, Hardness of Heart/Hardness of Life: The Stain of Human Infanticide, 319-340.

73 Philo of Byblos, The Phoenician History, 3.44, 63.

74 Philo, On Abraham, XXXIII.181, 91. It should be noted that Ahaz, king of Judah 735-715 BCE, and Manasseh, king of Judah 687-642 BCE, both worshiped at the altars of Baal, and even sacrificed their own sons in a burnt-offering to the god. 2 Kgs 16:3, 21:6; Jer 7:31.

75 Moses then explained to the people, however, that they must buy back their firstborn sons (Exod 13:13, 15; 34:20), for a payment of five shekels at age one month old (Num18:16). According to Num 3:11-13, God clarified that He would take the Levites in place of the firstborn male children.

by other passages of the book. Despite this clear directive, other Hebrew kings did indeed sacrifice their sons, including King Ahaz of Judah, who followed the heathen custom of his neighbors (2 Kgs 16:3), and King Manasseh of Judah (2 Kgs 21:6).[76] And because he had vowed to sacrifice the first thing he saw when he returned home if the Lord granted him victory in his battles, the biblical Judge Jephthah (c. 1100 BCE) was forced to sacrifice his daughter.[77] In addition, the prophets warned of God's retribution because the people burnt their first-born children as offering to other gods.[78]

With the advancement of time, and the development of more complex civilizations, the importance of human sacrifice maintained its hold, as a sign of pious devotion to the gods. The ancient Syrians sacrificed children to Jupiter and Juno, while the kings of Tyre offered their sons in sacrifice to a variety of Canaanite deities.[79] In Greece, one of the heroes from whom the Athenian tribes received their name – the *Eponymoi* – was a man named Leos, the son of Orpheus, who was said to have given up his three daughters, at the command of the Delphic oracle, for the safety of the commonwealth during a famine.[80] He was revered for this generous act, which saved the fatherland, as was Erectheus of Attica, who sacrificed his daughter to Pherephatta for a similar reason.[81] The carnage reached an incredible peak in the ancient society of Carthage, where infant sacrifice was seen as a necessity to maintain stability of the state, and lasted for a period of almost six hundred years.[82] The practice became so prevalent that it offended ancient moral codes which would be seen as overly tolerant today. When Gelon, the tyrant of Gela, vanquished the Carthaginians in the fifth century BCE, he so abhorred evidence of this practice that he ordered them to stop sacrificing their children to Cronus as part of the peace treaty to end hostilities between the

---

76 Their infanticides mimicked those of the Moabite King Mesha, (ninth century BCE) who burned his eldest son to the God Chemosh (2 Kgs 3:26-27), the Ammonites who offered their sons to Molech (Lev 18:21; 20:2-3), and the Aramaeans of Sepharvaim whose gods were Adram-melech and Ana-melech. Graves & Patai, Hebrew Myths, the Book of Genesis, 175.

77 Judg 11:31.

78 Ezek 16:20-21; 20:26, 31. King Josiah of Judah destroyed the altar of Topheth in the Valley of the Sons of Hinnom so no one could again burn his son or daughter to death as a sacrifice to Molech. 2 Kgs 23:10. This heinous act was condemned by the prophet Jeremiah who said that both sons and daughters were burnt as sacrifices to the gods. Jer 7:31; 19:5; 32:35. The prophet Micah warned both Israel and Judah that sacrificing your oldest child would not make the Lord glad. Micah 6:7.

79 Ryan, "Child Murder in Its Sanitary and Social Bearings," 2.

80 Pausanias, Description of Greece, I.V.2, I, 25.

81 Clement of Alexandria, "Exhortation to the Heathen," III, Writings, I, 48-49.

82 Stager & Wolff, "Child Sacrifice at Carthage - Religious Rite or Population Control?" 32.

two countries.[83] While individuals who performed these sacrifices were often applauded by local beneficiaries, their acts were not condoned in general by the community-at-large.

Dissolution of the union between human sacrifice and acceptable religious worship finally began to develop with the rise of Christianity, as governments around the globe began to classify human sacrifice as an homicidal act. Clement of Alexandria (second century CE), the head of the noted Catechetical school of Alexandria, voiced the modern concept when he declared that "a murder does not become a sacrifice by being committed in a particular spot."[84] Tertullian (155-230 CE), one of the early Church Fathers, scorned those who believed that Diana of the Scythians, or Mercury of the Gauls, or Saturn of the Africans, or Jupiter in Latium would demand that a human be sacrificed in order to appease their insatiable appetite for blood.[85] The stand of the Church was clear: human life was sacred to Christ and could not be offered to any god as evidence of moral behavior. Whether this lesson was apparent to the populace, however, is another matter. The very basis of Christianity was the willingness of a Father, albeit a Divine one, to sacrifice His Son for the future of mankind. In the New Testament, we read that: "For God loved the world so much that He gave His only Son so that anyone who believes in Him shall not perish but have eternal life."[86] When early Christians ingested a wafer and wine representing the body and blood of Christ, the Romans claimed that they practiced cannibalism and infanticide. Tertullian argued that such an accusation was ridiculous, given the abhorrence of murder in the teachings of Christ, but the image of sacrificial benefit still remained.[87]

Although the Christian church condemned the sacrifice of children by pagans as an act of murder, they did not see the willingness of Abraham to sacrifice his son Isaac as evidence of unnatural or criminal behavior. Rabanus Maurus (780-856 CE), in his defense of oblation in 819 CE, pointed to the willingness of Abraham to sacrifice Isaac as proper adherence to a divine law that superseded that of mortal man.[88] One could not always look to human legislation to find an answer to the actions of man, it was necessary to accept the commandments of God as reflective of orders which were to be obeyed above and beyond that which was prescribed here on earth. This interpretation of appropriate faith in the directive of God has carried on to the modern day, and both the Christian and Islamic religions have followed the precept set forth in the Old Testament that Abraham's obedience to the demands of the Lord was worthy of respect, and an indication of reverential faith, rather than felonious assault.

---

83 Plutarch, "Gelon," 175.1, <u>Moralia</u>, 27.
84 Clement of Alexandria, "Exhortation to the Heathen," III, <u>Writings</u>, I, 49.
85 Tertullian, "Scorpiace," 7, <u>Apologetic Works</u>, XI, 395.
86 John 3:16. <u>The Living Bible</u>, 981.
87 Tertullian, "Apology," 7.1, Apologetical Works, The Fathers of the Church, 25.
88 Boswell, The Kindness of Strangers, 440.

Agamemnon's reputation also did not suffer, despite the fact that he was murdered by his wife for his infanticidal action. His sacrifice of Iphigenia was accepted by the ancient Greek civilization as indicative of proper behavior, for it was consistent with the tenet that the life of an individual was subservient to the survival of the state. This concept of loyalty to the mother-country was taught by all of the Classical Greek philosophers as being essential to the survival if the Greek community, and if one of the gods saw fit to demand the sacrifice of a child, then it was appropriate for a father to accede to the divine judgement. This willingness of both the ancient Hebrews and Greeks to stand alone on the world stage, and promote an act of infanticide as reflective of their culture's credo of behavior, is remarkable, and, in my opinion, mandates the conclusion that one society developed its stance from the position of the other.

As to which society influenced the other, we have to look at estimated dates for the origin of the oral legends. As I discussed in chapter 6, the Exodus is generally believed to have taken place in either the fifteenth century BCE (Late Date), or the thirteenth century BCE (Early Date). I believe that the former date seems most probable, placing the arrival of Hebrew dissidents in Mycenae during the end of the fifteenth, or start of the fourteenth century BCE. Since the Trojan War is estimated to have taken place c. 1180 BCE, this would give the Hebrew legendary material over two centuries to become incorporated into the Greek lore, an acceptable period of time under any historical perspective. If the Exodus took place in the thirteenth century BCE, the Hebrews would still have arrived before the Trojan War, but they would have likely been seen only as outside mercenaries, aiding in the fighting of a distant war, as opposed to being an accepted member of the Mycenaean community.

Because the first text of the Old Testament is thought to have been compiled as part of the restoration of Judaism under the Pharisees after the fall of Jerusalem in 70 CE, and then modified into the form we know today from learned scribes, known as the Masoretes, around 900 CE, there is an alternate timeline to consider.[89] The Greek alphabet was developed, c. 850 BCE,[90] and Homer's tales were the first books to be published in the Western World shortly thereafter. It is therefore possible that the biblical compilers knew of the story of Agamemnon, and modified it into the trial of the Akeda as the Old Testament was being collated. Under this scenario, the story of Iphigenia would have likely been seen as worthy of inclusion because it showed how the willingness to put the whole above the part was a vital ingredient for the survival of the Israelite state. The lessons of the Babylonian Exile made it clear to the compilers of the Old Testament that it was vital to maintain a unified front against hostile neighbors who threatened their very existence. The best way to do this was to accentuate the power of the Lord,

---

89 Porter, The Illustrated Guide to the Bible, 13.
90 Starr, A History of the Ancient World, 201.

in the same manner that Moses did in his parricidal reprisals against the Hebrews who did not follow the monotheistic commandments of the Mosaic Code. The Lord could demand that any one life be lost in order to save the whole, and because of Abraham's trust in His judgement, the life of Isaac was spared.

While the reasoning of this latter sequence of events seems to present a believable account, a major problem with the theory that it does not seem likely that the compilers of the Old Testament would have emphasized such a drastic account as a feigned sacrifice of one's own child without some history of acceptance by the Hebrew populace in the generations before the Torah was written. The Bible is filled with warnings from God about not practicing child-sacrifice during the era of the Judges and Prophets, and it does not seem plausible that the inclusion of a fable such as that of the Akeda would have been inserted at this later period of time. For this reason. I believe that the most likely sequence is that the tale of the Akeda preceded that of Agamemnon and Iphigenia, and that the dissident Hebrews carried the story to Mycenae and influenced the Greeks, rather than vice versa.

In support of this decision, I also believe that the Greeks were impressed enough by the biblical tale to include in their legend the killing of Agamemnon by Clytemnestra. While every discussion I have read about the Greek legend, including the *Orestia* triad by Aeschylus, promotes the image of Clytemnestra as an avenging woman attempting to usurp male dominance and control, I believe that almost all of the Greek poets and playwrights also were attempting to find some harmony between the necessity of the sacrifice to continue for the benefit of the state, with the clear moral imperative to not perform infanticide. I have previously described how infanticide was common in ancient times, resulting in up to ten percent of all children born being killed by their parents,[91] but it is clear that the Greek philosophers and playwrights found this act something which could not be totally condoned, and, in my opinion, resulted in the eventual killing of Agamemnon by his wife for what she viewed as a heinous, immoral, act, deserving of divine punishment. The Hebrews may have readily accepted the Akeda because the sacrifice never took place, but the Greeks had to find a way to mesh the story of Agamemnon and Iphigenia with the moral precepts that began to find infanticide as an unacceptable behavior on the part of both mortals and gods.

In conclusion, I believe that the details of the two tales, and the moral lessons they taught, are too similar to postulate that they developed separately, without one initially influencing the other. Since the chronologic timeline of the Late Bronze Age makes it reasonable to place a group of dissident Hebrews in Mycenae before the Trojan War, I contend that the most reasonable explanation

---

91   See, Milner, Hardness of Heart/Hardness of Life, The Stain of Human Infanticide.

of the coincidence is that the story was brought to Greece by the Hebrews, along with many other patriarchal legends and practices, and that the concepts were incorporated into classical Greek mythology and culture, when the dissident Hebrews were becoming incorporated into the Mycenaean society. Although the Abraham and Isaac legend was the most obvious Hebraic addition to Greek culture, other similarities also exist, which I will detail in the chapters which follow.

Chapter 10
TRIBAL AMPHICTYONY

The ancient Hebrew and Greek societies are frequently described as consisting of tribal segments which congregated under a system governed by a central authority in a system of government that was the standard organization for nomadic and semi-nomadic pastoralists during the Late Bronze Age (1600-1100 BCE).[1] Unlike our modern urban way-of-life, which has often dispersed families into smaller units that rely on elected governmental bodies to provide social directives and welfare in order to survive, tribes typically depended on an internal hierarchy which consisted of an administrative chief who bore the responsibility for implementing the recommendations of a Council of Elders. Since the members of a tribe were united by similar religious and social beliefs, less effort was needed to assure that the populace would have common goals in mind.

Although the Mycenaean ancestors of the ancient Greeks did not follow a similar pattern of rule, developing instead a monarchical political system, the Classical Greeks (500-323 BCE) chose to abandon the hegemony of kingship, and formed a political union known as an amphictyony, whereby twelve independent city-states, acting much like tribes, coordinated their efforts in a confederacy that was centered around a central shrine devoted to the worship of a select god.[2] This format bore a distinct relationship to the Hebrew tribal system, but it is not known why the Greeks decided on this particular configuration, or where they obtained the model for its structure.[3] In this chapter, I will discuss my

---

1 Today, tribes are primarily described as gatherings of individuals with a similar ethnic and hereditary background, clustered together in a stable or mobile locale, utilizing cooperative methods to ensure public safety and food-gathering capabilities, a definition that was applicable to both the Hebrews and Greeks. Each tribe is often subdivided into "clans," which then are further subdivided into "families" or "fathers' houses." The clans are reckoned either through the mother (matrilineality) or the father (patrilineality), or sometimes by a mixture or bilateral method. Gottwald, The Tribes of Yahweh: A Sociology of the Religion of Liberated Israel, 1250-1050 BCE, 299. While some analysts of ancient Israelite society have argued that the ancient Hebrews are better described as "complex chiefdoms," rather than tribes, I find the designation of academic interest only, and will continue to discuss the Hebrew social system as consisting of tribes throughout this book. Miller, Chieftains of the Highland Clans: A History of Israel in the 12th and 11th Centuries BC, 6-14.

2 A similar league was formed in Italy, composed of twelve small Etrurian states. de Vaux, "Was There an Israelite Amphictyony?" 41.

3 The affinity between the Hebrew and Greek systems was first noted in 1864 CE by the Old Testament scholar and Orientalist Heinrich Ewald (1803-1871 CE), although

proposal that the dissident Hebrews fleeing the parricidal punishments of Moses brought the fundamentals of an amphictyony to Mycenae through their twelve-tribe model of government, and that this method of political rule was resurrected by the surviving Greeks during the Archaic Age (850-480 BCE).

A. The Hebrew Amphictyony

Many scholars have remarked on the strong identity of the Hebrew people with their twelve-tribal heritage, stemming from the twelve sons of Jacob. One Old Testament scholar, Walter Beyerlin, went so far as to claim that all of the varied Sinai traditions have "one Sitz im Leben: the history of the sacral tribal confederacy of Israel."[4] This clearly defined tribal system is very evident in the biblical text following the Conquest of the Promised Land, but we actually know nothing concrete about the Hebrew tribal structure during the years of enslavement in Egypt before the Exodus took place. It seems reasonable to assume that it was still a twelve-tribe system of government at the start of the Exodus, since Moses built an altar at the base of Mt. Sinai after the theophany was delivered with a structure that had twelve pillars, one for each of the tribes of Israel that had descended from Jacob's male progeny.[5] This assessment is buttressed by the fact that when the congregation prepared to leave Mt. Sinai and march toward the Promised Land, they were organized into the same twelve-tribe pattern.[6] In addition, the ephod worn by the Israelite High Priest had twelve onyx stones on the straps, six with the names of the elder sons of Jacob on one side, and six with the imprint of the younger sons on the other side.[7] These facts strongly support that the tribal format was pre-Mosaic in origin, and was utilized by Moses during the Exodus itself.

---

no suggestion was made at that time that the two were interrelated. Lemche, "The Greek 'Amphictyony' - Could it be a Prototype for the Israelite Society in the Period of the Judges?" 48-49.

4 Beyerlin, Origins and History of the Oldest Sinaitic Traditions, 167.

5 Exod 24:4. The progeny of Jacob, or "Israel" as he later was named by God, came from two wives and two concubines. The sequence of his offspring was as follows: Leah bore him four sons, Reuben, Simeon, Levi and Judah (Gen 29:32-35), and then after a long period of infertility, she bore two more sons, Issachar and Zebulun, as well as a daughter, Dinah (Gen 30:17-21). Rachel's maid, Bilhah, then bore him two sons, Dan and Naphtali (Gen 30:4-8), followed by Leah's maid, Zilpah, who bore him two more sons, Gad and Asher (Gen 30:10-13). Finally, God took pity on Rachel and "opened her womb," allowing her to bear a son, Joseph, and then, in the final years of her life, another son, Benjamin (Gen 30:22-24; 35:18). Sarna, <u>Genesis</u>, 206 The descendants of "Israel" thereby became known as the Israelites.

6 Num 2-3.

7 Exod 28:9-12. The outermost garment worn by the High Priest was an ephod made of gold and twisted linen. Exod 28:6. Linen ephods were worn by lesser priests, as well as Samuel and David. 1 Sam 2:18; 22:18; 2 Sam 6:14.

Martin Noth (1902-1968 CE), Professor of the Old Testament at the University of Bonn, disagreed with this presumption of a twelve-tribe political system during the Exodus, promoting instead the theory that the twelve tribes of Israel did not form a political unit until after the settlement in Canaan, thereby placing the biblical version of events on a level of fanciful reconstruction, rather than historical accuracy.[8] Other modern biblical scholars, who have also questioned the reliability of the historicity of the Bible, have suggested that much of the story was simply intended to set the framework for religious teaching, rather than portray a true historical account. Alternatively, since "biblical literature is virtually entirely state literature, and ancient state literature typically conceals as much as it reveals of the real contours of social organization under state sovereignty," scholars like Robert B. Coote, Professor of Old Testament at San Francisco Theological Seminary, find it reasonable to state "with some assurance that Israel was organized as a tribal alliance," and the biblical texts outline what the writers of the Israel courts thought about tribal identity and organization.[9]

While it matters little to scholars of the history of Israel as to when the twelve-tribe system of rule first developed, it is obviously critical to my theory of dissident Hebrew migration to Greece during the Exodus to try and determine if the immigrants brought with them the concept of twelve-tribal rule. The paucity of reliable archaeologic data on the history of the Jews makes it impossible to prove that the biblical record of the tribal system being present during the Exodus is true, but I am going to accept in this book, as I discussed in chapter 4, that the Bible presents a relatively valid account of the Exodus that can be analyzed for consistencies which point to a reasonable explanation of how and why particular events took place. To this end, I am going to accept that a twelve-tribe format was in place at Mt. Sinai, as related by the biblical compilers, and that it guided the Hebrews during the era of the Judges, before the formation of the United Monarchy, "as a twelve-tribe confederacy organized around a covenant with Yahweh in support of a central shrine," which would fit the definition of an amphictyony.[10] This means that when the dissident Hebrews fled the Exodus and traveled to Mycenae before the Trojan War, they would have been accustomed to this system of rule, and likely continued the same pattern when they arrived on the Grecian shore.

Whenever the twelve-tribe format was accepted, it is clear that the biblical compilers were intent on coupling the political design with the number of Jacob's twelve natural sons, since he adopted the two sons of Joseph – Ephraim and Manasseh – on his deathbed, making the actual number of his "sons" fourteen,

---

8 Noth, The History of Israel, 5.

9 Coote, "Social Organization in the Biblical Israels," 37-38.

10 Gottwald, The Tribes of Yahweh: A Sociology of the Religion of Liberated Israel, 1250-1050 BCE, 345.

rather than twelve.[11] Even though Joseph did not marry a Hebrew woman, the heritage of his sons were in the direct genetic line of Jacob, given the patrilineal format of ancient Hebrew inheritance, but how to deal with assessing the make-up of the various clans proved to be a tricky problem which resulted in two different listings of the composition of the twelve-tribe format in the biblical text. One list included the tribe of Levi, and then reckoned Ephraim and Manasseh, the two sons of Joseph, as being part of their father's tribe; while the other gave Manasseh and Ephraim their own tribe, and eliminated Levi and Joseph altogether.[12] Niels Peter Lemche, from the Institute for Biblical Exegesis at the University of Copenhagen, has argued that this discrepancy supports the premise that the entire system was "a highly artificial one, elaborated on and changed, not according to historical circumstances but because of literary motives and religious concerns."[13] I disagree with his conclusion, and believe that the disparity can easily be explained by the fact that once the tribe of Levi became a tribe of priests in the book of *Exodus*, it became necessary to devise a new membership because the Levites could not then participate in the Council of Elders. The biblical compilers obviously felt that the number twelve had magical meanings, given the fact that twelve sons were born to Abraham's firstborn son, Ishmael;[14] twelve tribes evolved from Abraham's brother Nahor;[15] and twelve Edomite tribes evolved from Abraham's grandson Esau.[16] The pre- and post-Mosaic Hebrews would have also been aware of these numerical omens, and would have wanted to maintain their tribal total at that number by eliminating Joseph along with Levi when the priestly category was completed, and replacing them with the tribes of Joseph's two sons. This is a very reasonable solution to the problem, and does not require a conclusion that the machinations indicated that the whole process was a fictional event.

Accepting the fact that the Hebrews were comprised of a twelve-tribe format throughout their history following the Exodus from Egypt, and that the number of tribes were chosen because of the belief that this total had divine favor, it is still not clear how the union functioned before the formation of the Monarchy. This issue has been the subject of great controversy over the years, with all theories suffering from a dearth of substantive support, since the Bible does not describe the process in any great detail. A. H. Sayce (1845-1933 CE), an Anglican priest

11 Gen 48:5.
12 The first list can be found in Gen 29:31-30:24; 35:22-26; 46:8-25; 49:2-27; Exod 1:2-4; and the second in Exod 1:5-15, 20-43; 2:3-31; 7:12-83; 10:14-28; 13:4-15; 26:5-51; 34:16-29; Deut 27:12-13; 33:6-25. Lemche, The Israelites in History and Tradition, fn 49, 204.
13 Ibid., 104.
14 Gen 25:13-16; 1 Chron 1:29-31.
15 Gen 22:20-24.
16 Gen 36:1-10; 1 Chron 1:35.

and Professor of Assyriology at Oxford, was the first to advance the concept in 1888 CE that the tribes were organized as an amphictyony,[17] a proposal that was supported by Max Weber, (1864-1920 CE), a German economist and founder of modern Sociology, who described Israel during the period of Judges as a warlike confederation which may have had "amphictyonic rites."[18] Martin Noth expanded this proposition in 1930 CE, arguing that the confederacy of Hebrew tribes clearly qualified as an amphictyony because they centered their worship of YHWH in a particular city, which changed on a rotating basis.[19] He was supported by the well-known Old Testament scholar from the University of Heidelberg, Gerhard von Rad (1901-1971 CE), who noted that the coalition of Hebrew tribes during the time of Joshua fit all the criteria of being a "Jahweh Amphictyony."[20] This concept was supported by the Song of Deborah, one of the oldest texts in the Hebrew Bible, which has been used to buttress the claims of those who believe that the Hebrew tribes fulfilled the definition of an amphictyony by performing as a united league who covenanted with YHWH and each other in defense of a central cultic shrine.[21] The ark was placed within the central sanctuary, first at Shechem then at Bethel, Gilgal, and finally at Shiloh.[22] This conception received widespread acceptance among biblical scholars for many years, although no suggestion was ever made that the Hebrews were the ones to introduce the design to the Greeks. In fact, Albrecht Alt (1883-1956 CE), the distinguished German Old Testament scholar, compared the Hebrew model to ones which "had already appeared" in the early history of Greece and Italy, thereby suggesting that the Hebrews followed the Greek pattern, rather than preceding it.[23]

Despite widespread support for considering the political arrangement of the Hebrew tribes as an amphictyony in the past, academicians have recently thrown the idea aside, pointing to the paucity of reliable historical support as insufficient to make such a claim. Arguing that the twelve tribes have never been conclusively shown to be a political institution, and that there is not documented evidence of a central cult or shrine, many scholars have concluded that the concept of an Israelite amphictyony "has been soundly dismissed."[24] Norman K. Gottwald,

---

17 Rowley, Worship in Ancient Israel, Its Forms and Meaning, fn. 4, 58.

18 de Vaux, The Early History of Israel, 695.

19 Gottwald, The Tribes of Yahweh: A Sociology of the Religion of Liberated Israel, 1250-1050 BCE, 346.

20 von Rad, Old Testament Theology, I.9.

21 Sparks, Ethnicity and Identity in Ancient Israel: Prolegomena to the Study of Ethnic Sentiments and Their Expression in the Hebrew Bible, 109.

22 de Vaux, "Was There an Israelite Amphictyony?" 40.

23 Gottwald, The Tribes of Yahweh: A Sociology of the Religion of Liberated Israel, 1250-1050 BCE, 234.

24 Sparks, Ethnicity and Identity in Ancient Israel: Prolegomena to the Study of Ethnic Sentiments and Their Expression in the Hebrew Bible, 8. J. Alberto Soggin (1926-

Professor Emeritus of Biblical Studies at the New York Theological Seminary, has added to this negative reassessment by arguing that the twelve-tribe system did not even appear as an administrative unit until the time of King David, making it an executive convenience, rather than a true political system.[25] These are convincing arguments, but I believe that the label they are attacking is not pertinent to the issue at hand, because it does not matter whether the association of twelve Hebrew tribes can be didactically classified as a true amphictyony or not, but whether the system they used was the model upon which the Greeks developed their own configuration. It is true that the actual history of the Hebrew model of government has not survived in the extant historical record, but the biblical account does provide a reasonable outline of what appears to be a tribal society, with the twelve sons of Isaac forming a cooperative conclave from the time of the Exodus forward. There is clearly a resemblance between the Hebrew and ancient Greek systems, and if there was a Hebrew dissident emigration to Greece during the Exodus, the Hebrew format may very well have been utilized by the Greeks when they formulated a new political arrangement at the end of the Greek Dark Age (1000-850 BCE). The Hebrews during the Exodus, according to the biblical account, clearly saw themselves as being part of a twelve-tribe congregation, and if there were representatives from each tribe who left as part of the dissident Hebrew emigration, it is likely that they would have retained this same model during their travels to the distant Mycenaean shore.

Some scholars have promoted the theory that the suggestion for the Israelite form of government, especially King Solomon's monthly district system, could have been derived from the Bala system of collecting goods that was used in the Sumerian League of Ur III (2060-1955 BCE).[26] First put forth in 1960 CE by W. W. Hallo, Laffan Professor of Assyriology and Babylonian Literature at Yale University, the Bala system rotated contributions calendrically among league members to the sanctuary of Enlil at Nippur.[27] Most historians, do not believe that this system functioned as an amphictyonic league, however, claiming instead that it was composed of more than twelve cooperating cities, each with their own tutelary divinity.[28] Even if the Hebrews were influenced by the function of this

---

2010 CE), former Emeritus Professor of Old Testament at the Waldensian Faculty of Theology, did not even like references to it being a tribal league. Soggin, Israel in the Biblical Period: Institutions, Festivals, Ceremonies, Rituals, 27.

25 Gottwald, The Tribes of Yahweh: A Sociology of the Religion of Liberated Israel, 1250-1050 BCE, 345. Gottwald did not believe that the Hebrew tribal league was a true amphictyony, since the central shrine of Israel was not only at one site and all amphictyonies were "intrinsically bound to a particular shrine." Ibid., 349. Rather than postulating an intertribal body of delegates, Gottwald only found evidence that the tribes had individual leaders, and on occasion consulted together. Ibid., 350.

26 Chambers, "Ancient Amphictyonies, Sic Et Non," 51.

27 Ibid., 52-54.

28 Ibid., 54-55.

format, the desire of the Greeks to follow this model would not have come from the ancient Sumerian records, in my opinion.

B. The Greek Amphictyony

To support my thesis that the Hebrews first suggested the model of an amphictyony to the Greeks, it is necessary to analyze what is known about the evolution of the Greek political system following the end of their Dark Age, when the population began to organize into city-states (*polis*) during the ensuing Archaic Age.[29] The philosopher Aristotle attributed the emergence of the *polis* as being the inevitable result of the forces of nature at work,[30] but modern scholars have credited its development more to the geography of the country, than to the natural order of the universe. The Greek mainland was not conducive to agriculture, and a successful union required that the neighboring city-states cooperate towards common goals of defense and economic stability, rather than relying on independent growth. In order to carry out this ambitious plan, the Greeks chose the amphictyony as their preferred method of political organization over the monarchical system, which was present in Mycenae during the Late Bronze Age. The term "amphictyony," which literally means "union of dwellers," comes from the name of the son of Deucalion and Pyrrha, Amphictyon, who reigned as king from his sanctuary at Thermopylae around 1522 BCE, and later, according to the Parian Chronicle, became ruler of Athens.[31] Amphictyon was said to have gathered his subjects into an amphictyony group at that time, just three years prior to the arrival of Cadmus, and eleven years prior to the arrival of Danaus, at some time during the fifteenth century BCE, the era when I believe the Exodus took place.[32] Nothing is known about why he chose this particular format, or whether it was suggested by other cultures, and most scholars believe that the entire legend was mythical in origin, since Athens was not a political force during that period of time, and no historical documents of Amphictyon's life have survived. That the ancient Greeks chose this particular era to date their first amphictyonic system of rule fits very well with a fifteenth century BCE Exodus timeline, and also aligns the arrival of the Hebrews with Danaus and Cadmus.

---

29 The Greek *polis* was a self-governing and independent physical fusion of villages (*komai*), usually interpreted today as a city-state. Hall, <u>A History of the Archaic Greek World, ca. 1200-479 BCE</u>, 68. An alternate form of government was the *ethne*, which was scattered thinly over a territory without urban centers, and was governed by periodical assemblies. Ibid., 88.

30 "Hence it is evident that the state is a creation of nature, and that man is by nature a political animal." Aristotle, <u>Politics</u>, I.3, 1253a2-3, 54.

31 Robertson, The Parian Chronicle: Or the Chronicle of the Arundelian Marbles; With a Dissertation Concerning Its Authenticity, 24.

32 Jones, <u>Bronze Age Civilization, The Philistines and the Danites</u>, 52-53. Others date Cadmus' arrival thirty years after Danaus. Myres, <u>Who Were the Greeks?</u>, 139.

The first successful amphictyony developed by the Greeks was comprised of twelve *ethene*, or people with a common language, blood, and religion. The political structure involved a central shrine, with a body of officers delegated from each of the twelve member tribes.[33] Why the number twelve was chosen is unclear, although the philosopher Plato, writing a few centuries later, adjudged that the ideal state should always have the city, citizens and property divided into twelve parts.[34] Plato did not explain his reasoning for this conclusion, and may have simply been accepting the fact that his hallowed Greek ancestors were basing their original formulation on knowledge of universal perfection which was unique to the Greek mind. The Greeks considered everyone not of Greek heritage as barbarian, and viewed their own history as being favored by divine choice. What is more likely, in my opinion, is that the number twelve came from the Hebrew model, which was based on the twelve sons of Jacob.

The first amphictyony League was originally set up to protect and administer the sanctuary of Demeter at Anthela, near Thermopylae. By the seventh century BCE, following the Crisean war, Anthela was surpassed in importance by the Delphic shrine, which was formed for Apollo at Delphi c. 650 BCE, and the two sides united to form the Great Amphictyonic League.[35] The members of the Delphic amphictyony changed over the years, but there were always twelve tribes, and meetings were held twice a year at Thermopylae in the spring, and Delphi in the autumn.[36] Delphi became the most venerated shrine in ancient Greece, and the oracle there, known as the Pythia, was visited by people from all over the world seeking advice on how to act in matters of both personal and national importance.[37] For a large sum of money, the Pythia would answer

33 This tribal system of government should not be confused with the classic division of Athenians into ten tribes, which was a later development under Kleisthenes. Dillon & Garland, Ancient Greece, Social & Historical Documents from Archaic Times to the Death of Socrates, xv.

34 Saunders, "Laws," V.745B-D, 1425.

35 Chambers, "Ancient Amphictyonies, Sic Et Non," 43. Delphi, which was first settled c. 1400 BCE, was known to the Greeks as the "holiest of holies, and navel of the world!" Euripides, "Orestes," 332, 131.

36 The original founders included the Aenianes, Boeotians (Thebes), Dolopes, Dorians (Sparta), Ionians (Athens), Locrians, Magnetians, Malians, Perrhoebians, Phocians, Pythia (Delphi), and Thessalians. "Amphictyonic League: Encyclopedia Beta," 1. Each member sent two delegates, or *hieromnemons*, to the Amphictyonic Council. de Vaux, "Was There an Israelite Amphictyony?" 40.

37 Stapleton, The Illustrated Dictionary of Greek and Roman Mythology, 63. According to legend, the origin of the Delphic oracle came through the agency of Zeus, who sent two eagles to fly from the opposite extremities of the earth, and they met at Delphi, establishing it as the center of the world. Ibid., 64. Another legend told how Apollo had found the spot ideal for founding a shrine to guide men, but had to first slay a monster Python who resided there. This gave Delphi its other name – Pytho – and the Oracle came to be known as the Pythia. Broad, The Oracle: The Lost Secrets and Hidden

questions posed to her by crying out inarticulate phrases while in a trance, and an interpreter would write out the official response, which was often vague, and subject to multiple interpretations. Her pronouncements were taken with such credence that the playwright Aeschylus (525-426 BCE) decreed "by judgment given, heads are lopped and eyes gouged out, throats cut, and by the spoil of sex the glory of young boys is defeated."[38]

Although the shrine at Delphi became known more for the fame of the Pythia than for the functions of the Delphic amphictyony, the defensive front which the twelve members presented against hostile enemy forces was an important element of Greek military dominance during the Archaic Age. In joining forces against external threats, the members of the league took a solemn oath to not "destroy any town of the amphictyonic league, not to cut off the waters supplying the towns either in times of war or in times of peace and, if anyone violated these prescriptions, to march against him and to overthrow his towns and, if anyone plundered the treasures of the god or was an accomplice in any act of profanation or tried to lay hands on the sacred things, to joining their hands, feet, voices and all their strength to punish him."[39] Remindful of the oath taken by the Greek suitors for the hand of Helen before her marriage to Menelaus, this expansive vow was put to the test at times, for problems did arise between member city-states, forcing the amphictyony to settle internal disputes, as occurred between Delphi and Cirrha, and later during the Amphissaean war, when a member of a Greek amphictyony was punished for refusing to hand over those who had committed sacrilege.[40] This type of police power also took place among the Hebrews, as when the tribes gathered to punish the tribe of Benjamin for having refused to hand over to the tribunal the perpetrators of a particularly savage crime which took place at Gibeah.[41] Just as the Greek leaders consulted the Pythia before making preparations for battle, the Hebrews generals went to Beth-el, where the Ark of God was located, to counsel God about which tribe should lead the attack.[42] Both the Greek and Hebrew unions realized that the authority of the Whole had to rule over the individual decisions of the Parts if the State was to remain a strong and viable force, a condition remindful of the issues leading up to the American Civil War, when the importance of individual state's rights was subjugated to the decisions of the federal government.

Since the primary aim of the Greek amphictyony was to provide for religious festivals and sacrifices, each member group had a particular god associated with

Message of Ancient Delphi, 25, 27. The earliest references to the Oracle is found in Homer's *Iliad* and *Odyssey*. Ibid., 27.

38 Aeschylus, "The Eumenides," 186-190, 141.
39 de Vaux, The Early History of Israel, 698.
40 Grant, The Rise of the Greeks, 123.
41 Judg 19-20.
42 Josh 20:18, 27.

the central shrine. At the Boeotian amphictyony in Onchestus, the union at Calauria, and the one at Cape Mycale (Heliconius), Poseidon was the god of favor; while at Delphi and Delos, the god who held the venerable spot was Apollo.[43] This commitment to the worship of a single god who was associated with the unique characteristics of the amphictyony members did not affect the loyalty of the Greeks to Zeus, who maintained his position at the head of the Olympian pantheon. Since the Hebrews were all monotheistic, devoted to the worship of YHWH, there was no need for more than one League to represent the interests of all the people. But as will be discussed in the next chapter, the Patriarchs and pre-Mosaic Hebrews did give homage to family gods as well, and the demands of Moses to restrict devotion to YHWH alone, and to forgo the construction of any type of idol, is what led to the schism and resultant parricides. In Mycenae, the dissident Hebrews could practice the faith of their fathers openly, and without concern for their safety. Like Zeus, YHWH was seen as the most powerful of the gods, but there was no demand to give up loyalty to one's family deities as well.

C. Discussion

Although there is disagreement among biblical scholars on exactly how the twelve tribes of Israel functioned in the governance of their people following the Exodus from Egypt and the Conquest of the Promised Land, and whether their chosen format fit the description of an amphictyony or not, it is clear that there was much symmetry between the biblical description of how the Hebrews during the Exodus were categorized under the twelve tribes named for the sons of Jacob, and the Greek amphictyony model, which was composed of twelve city-states. Both entities were centered around an allegiance to a specific god (God), and both functioned as a forum where disputes among fellow members were debated, and, if necessary, settled by violent means. Of particular importance to my theory of Hebraic influence on Classical Greece is the fact that both of these unions utilized a twelve-member format, with the Hebrews readjusting the number of Jacob's "sons" in order to maintain this total, and the Greeks deciding on the number twelve for their first, and most important, League.[44] Although Plato later explained that this likely came about because the number twelve identified the ideal political state, it seems to me more likely that the choice of twelve city-states was based upon the ancient Hebrew political scheme of twelve tribes, and the magical nature of the number twelve as the ideal for the number of sons in a family, which the Greeks became familiar with following the assimilation of the

---

43 Ehrenberg, The Greek State, 109.

44 The maritime Kalaurian League had seven to nine members, and the Boeotian League varied between ten to twelve members, but the first, and most important, Delphic League was composed of twelve members. Rahtjen, "Philistine and Hebrew Amphictyonies," 103.

dissident Hebrews into Mycenaean culture during the Late Bronze Age. The Bible provides other important personages with a family of twelve children, including Abraham's firstborn son, Ishmael (Gen 25:13-16; 1 Chron 1:29-31); Abraham's brother Nahor (Gen 22:20-24); and the twelve Edomite tribes which evolved from Abraham's grandson Esau (Gen 36:1-10; 1 Chron 1:35). This indicates that the number was imbued with some magical quality to the biblical compilers, who felt it was important enough to manipulate the names of the twelve Hebrew tribes in order to maintain that total. When the Mycenaeans incorporated the traditions and legends of the Patriarchs, they took note of the primary importance of the strength and power of YHWH, and also the twelve-tribe division of government, which rose to the surface with the dissolution of the Monarchy following the Trojan War. The integration of the might of YHWH became incorporated into the primary importance of Zeus, as will be discussed in the next chapter, and the twelve-tribe model was resurrected into the design of the amphictyony.

It is important to point out that this proposal does not require that the Hebrew tribal format exactly fit the definition of an amphictyony, as determined by the union of Greek city-states, because the Greeks would have been expected to modify the Hebrew model in order to fit their specific needs. The Greeks were extremely iconic, constructing multiple temples, shrines, and sculptures to honor the image of their gods. Unlike the Hebrews, their security on the mainland was strong, and there was little chance that their efforts would be destroyed. If the location of the member city-states was dependent on the sea, Poseidon was worshiped at the central shrine, since he controlled the dangers which threatened survival of the ships. If the needs of the members were contingent upon knowledge and foresight, Apollo would command their attention, as was evident with the Delphic union. The Hebrews may have maintained strong control of parts of Canaan following the Conquest of the Promised Land, and during the heyday of the United Monarchy, but there was always a significant danger of Philistine incursions, and the Holy Ark was therefore contained within a mobile sanctuary, moving from its initial location at Shechem, to Bethel,[45] Shiloh,[46] and finally Gilgal (near Jericho).[47] Once the First Temple was constructed in Jerusalem, all twelve Hebrew tribes had a single location for worshiping YHWH, fulfilling the

45 Judg 20:18, 26ff.

46 1 Sam 1ff; Jer 7:12ff. The shrine at Shiloh operated as a cultic center during the Judges period and in the time of Samuel, but was apparently destroyed by the Philistines after the battle of Ebenezer. 1 Sam 4:1-11. Walton, Matthews, & Chavalas, The IVP Bible Background Commentary: Old Testament, 272-273.

47 Josh 9:6; 10:6-9; 15; 1 Sam 10:8; 11:14-15; 13:4; 15:12, 21, 33. von Rad, Old Testament Theology, I.21. Gilgal continued to serve as Israel's central sanctuary for special celebrations and convocations of the tribal league, as well as a sacred place where cultic were conducted, until at least the eighth century BCE. Joshua, The Anchor Bible, 26. See e.g., Amos 4:4; 5:5; Hos 4:15; 9:15; 12:11.

criteria of a central shrine, but by that time the Hebrews had chosen a monarchy as their preferred method of government.

By itself, this evidence for an Hebraic contribution to the development of the Greek amphictyony format does not prove beyond doubt that the Greeks received their concept from Hebrew dissidents who arrived in Mycenae before the Trojan War. When the total picture of Hebraic material within the Classical Greek culture and mythology is viewed in its entirety, however, the likelihood that the Greeks learned of the political system from an encounter with Hebrew dissidents who fled the Exodus, fearing the parricidal retributions of Moses, is the best explanation we have for the similarities that exist between the two groupings. Other scholars who dispute the likelihood of an Israelite amphictyony have nevertheless commented on the similarity between the Greek and Israelite traditions, to the point of questioning whether they are not coincidental.[48] Once again, a reluctance to claim an Hebraic contribution to the evolution of Greek civilization overshadows all analysis, but I believe that the similitude bespeaks of cultural contact and that union took place when dissident Hebrews fled the Exodus and traveled to Mycenae. As I have discussed for many other aspects of Greek and Mycenaean practices, a Hebrew contribution is much more sensible than postulating an influence by Phoenicians, or other ancient near-Eastern entities, such as Egypt or Ugarit. No other cultural force during the Late Bronze Age had a political system which resembled the amphictyony model, and there is nothing about Greek history to suggest that they would have independently developed this system on their own account.

In regard to the suggestion that the biblical pattern was a fictional invention constructed by the compilers from information gathered about the Delphic amphictyony, rather than an integral component of the pre-Mosaic tribal system, I believe the system of twelve tribes designed from the sons of Jacob is too ingrained in Jewish lore to be considered as nothing more than fanciful imagination. To postulate that all of this heritage came from an oblique awareness of the Greek amphictyony is to stretch the imagination too far. The Delphic amphictyony began functioning in the seventh century BCE, and all the documentary evidence points to the description of the twelve-tribe Hebrew system as coming from the "J" source writing in the ninth to tenth century BCE, the "E" source in the eighth century BCE, and the "D" source in the seventh century BCE. This means that the biblical sources were already compiling their material well before the formation of the Greek amphictyonies, favoring the thesis that it was the Hebrew system which influenced the Greeks, and not vice versa.

---

48 Sparks, Ethnicity and Identity in Ancient Israel: Prolegomena to the Study of Ethnic Sentiments and Their Expression in the Hebrew Bible, 75.

Chapter 11

GODS

In his expansive history of Greece, the Scottish historian and classical scholar John Gillies (1747-1836 CE) noted that "inquisitive men have endeavored to trace the corrupted streams of Pagan worship to the pure fountain of the Jewish dispensation."[1] Like other Western scholars who accepted that their Judeo-Christian beliefs in the single Almighty God was superior to the base representations of those who followed a polytheistic faith, Gillies nevertheless found it unlikely that there could be any assimilation of Hebrew theology into Mycenaean society, given the clear disparity in the nature of ancient Hebrew and Classical Greek belief in the essence of the Divinity. Despite the claim of some Egyptologists that Atenism predated the tenets of the Ten Commandments, Judaism is widely accepted as the first monotheistic faith on earth, teaching that there was only one Almighty God Who commanded that "You shall have no other gods beside Me," a directive which also became the hallmark of the religions of Christianity and Islam.[2] The Classical Greeks (500-323 BCE), on the other hand, were a polytheistic faith, worshiping a pantheon of gods who not only controlled the elements of nature, but also the destiny of each and every human being.[3] Although Zeus was portrayed as the most dominant of the twelve gods who dwelled on Mt. Olympus, each of the other eleven deities was responsible for a particular area of human endeavor, and unless they were pacified by appropriate sacrifice, the wrath of their displeasure would befall not only an individual person, but possibly an entire community as well.[4] The discrepancy between the faiths of the two cultures was so great that Cyrus Gordon, the renowned professor emeritus of Brandeis and New York Universities, despite finding so many similarities between the Greeks and the Hebrews that he claimed both descended from the ancient community in Ugarit, clarified that "it is in the sphere of religion that our

---

1 Gillies, The History of Ancient Greece, Its Colonies and Conquests, From the Earliest Accounts Till the Division of the Macedonian Empire in the East: Including The History of Literature, Philosophy, and the Fine Arts, 25.

2 Exod 20:2, Sarna, Exodus, 109; Deut 5:7, Tigay, Deuteronomy, 64.

3 In Hesiod's *Theogony*, which predated the Classical Greeks, there were more than one hundred and twenty individually named divinities and characters. Coleman, "Did Egypt Shape the Glory that was Greece?" 285.

4 By the time of the Classical Greeks, twelve Olympian gods stood at the forefront of Greek worship, including Zeus (Jupiter, Jove), Hera (Juno), Athena (Minerva), Apollo, Artemis (Diana), Poseidon (Neptune), Aphrodite (Venus), Hermes (Mercury), Hephaestus (Vulcan), Ares (Mars), Hestia (Vesta), and Hades (Pluto). The two earth gods were Demeter (Ceres) and Dionysus (Bacchus). Roman counterparts in parenthesis.

Greek and Hebrew texts are worlds apart."[5]

This picture of Judaism as a monotheistic creed, however, was a result of the changes brought about by the dictates of the Mosaic Code during the Exodus, and did not reflect the beliefs of the Hebrew people before they left Egypt. That the generations of Hebrews who grew up as slaves in Egypt were not aware of the importance of YHWH is evident from the book of *Ezekiel*, where the Lord explained that He first let Himself be known to the Hebrews during the time the Exodus began.[6] It was confirmed by God's statement to Moses at the burning bush that He appeared to the Patriarchs as El Shaddai, but was now to be known as YHWH.[7] It was Moses, and not Abraham, who demanded the worship of YHWH alone, and although Abraham may have been portrayed in history as the first person on earth to worship only one God, the stories of the pre-Mosaic Hebrews in the Bible suggests that these early Hebrews were actually polytheistic, practicing a religion which resembled their Canaanite neighbors more than the faith which was espoused by Moses.[8]

The initial belief in a polytheistic creed is evident, in my opinion, not only in the descriptions of patriarchal life, but also in the resistance which Moses faced in his initial attempts to force the Hebrews to obey the new monotheistic regulations, as discussed in chapter 5. Many of the Hebrews were reluctant to follow the regulations imposed by Moses, and after he died, and they were about to enter the Promised Land, Joshua summoned the people together at Shechem, and told them that their ancestors worshiped other gods, but they *now* must worship only YHWH, emphasizing the need to obey the monotheistic changes imposed by Moses.[9] Even when the Hebrews were settled in the Promised Land, and supposedly united in the worship of YHWH alone, they over and over again returned to polytheistic idol-worship, forcing God to eventually punish their apostasy by sending the kingdoms of Israel (724 BCE) and Judah (587 BCE) into Exile. So many of the Hebrews were unfaithful to this monotheistic proclamation, that the Lord told the prophet Elijah that only seven thousand of the entire population "has not knelt to Baal."[10] As William Stiebing, Professor of History at the University of New Orleans, noted, "many, if not most, of the new Israelites continued to worship Ba`al and other Canaanite deities along with (or,

---

5 Gordon, Homer and the Bible: The Origin and Character of East Mediterranean Literature, 55.

6 Ezek 20:5.

7 Exod 6:2-3.

8 According to Stephen L. Cook, Associate Professor of Old Testament at Virginia Theological Seminary, the concept that the Israelite religion evolved from polytheism to monotheism "has been a keystone of classic liberal criticism of the Bible." Cook, The Social Roots of Biblical Yahwism, 3.

9 Josh 24:2, 15.

10 1 Kgs 19:18. Zevit, "First Kings," 717.

in some cases instead of) Yahweh, since the Bible does describe such 'backsliding' in the period of the 'Judges' and throughout the era of the monarchy."[11]

Not only were the pre-Mosaic Hebrews similar to the Mycenaeans in the nature of their religious beliefs, the evolution of their historical writings also followed an allied path. Sara Mandell, Professor of Interdisciplinary Arts and Sciences at the University of South Florida, and David Noel Freedman (1922-2008), former holder of the chair of Hebrew Biblical Studies at the University of California, San Diego, pointed out that there are remarkable similarities between Herodotus' *History*, and the Primary History (Genesis-2 Kings) of Ezra, who is credited as the editor who divided the Old Testament into the parts which became the *Pentateuch* and the Prophetic, which were "too numerous to be either accidental or merely characteristic of a shared genre."[12] They went on to suggest that there may have been shared knowledge between the two men that led to this similarity, and that this particularly was evident in the fact that both the Jewish Primary History, and the writings of Herodotus and the Greek tragic playwrights "paid attention to the relationship of a man or a state to the divine."[13] I will discuss this in more detail in chapter 14, but I want to point out now that such a view is very credible, given the fact that Herodotus was the contemporary of Ezra and Nehemiah, and visited Ascalon and possibly Gaza about 450 BCE, during his travels which led to the writing of his *The History*.

The question then of when Judaism became a true monotheistic faith is understandably complex, and has led to intense debate, with valid arguments made by proponents of the various dates. In essence, the disagreements center primarily around whether the Hebrews could be considered to be monotheistic after the Ten Commandments were delivered at Mt. Sinai, and Moses began to punish Hebrews for not worshiping YHWH alone, or whether it did not take place until later, around the time of the Babylonian Exile (587-538 BCE), when the Israelites finally accepted worship of YHWH alone as a state-sponsored religion. While it is clear that the rhetoric of monotheism became more rigid, in the seventh and sixth centuries BCE, the question of whether the biblical declarations were truly monotheistic at Sinai, and not monolatrous or henotheistic, remains open to question.[14] From my perspective, it does not matter when the majority of Hebrews began to follow the monotheistic teachings of Moses, but rather that the dissidents who left the Exodus refused to obey this commandment and brought their own brand of henotheism or monolatry to Mycenae, where it meshed quite

---

11 Stiebing, Out of the Desert? Archaeology and the Exodus/Conquest Narratives, 199.

12 Mandell & Freedman, The Relationship Between Herodotus' *History* and Primary History, ix.

13 Ibid., 143.

14 Smith, The Origins of Biblical Monotheism; Israel's Polytheistic Background and the Ugaritic Texts, 151.

nicely with the developing image of Zeus as the head of a pantheon of gods. To better understand the expansive manner of these similarities, I will first analyze the nature of patriarchal and Greek theology in this chapter, and then compare the methods each culture utilized to practice their faith in the next chapter.

A. Judaic Monotheism

When Moses saved the Hebrews from annihilation by miraculously parting the waters of the Reed Sea and drowning the Pharaoh's army who followed them out of Egypt shortly after the Exodus began, the people celebrated by extolling YHWH and asking "who is like You, O Lord, among the celestials?" clearly singling out YHWH from the other deities because of the strength He showed in saving their lives.[15] This same distinction was later made by Jethro, the father-in-law of Moses, who visited the congregation after hearing of their rescue. In his enthusiasm for the Hebrew victory, Jethro declared that "now I know that the LORD is greater than all gods," because He delivered His people from the Egyptians.[16] In the book of *Deuteronomy*, Moses told the people that YHWH "is the God of gods and the Lord of lords,"[17] and in the book of *Psalms*, it is related that those who bow down to idols are foolish, for "all divine beings bow down to Him."[18] These pronouncements clearly show that although the Hebrews were enthralled with the solitary might of YHWH, they were also aware of the existence of other gods, which would have been expected in an era of polytheistic belief.[19] After the theophany on Mt. Sinai, Moses set forth the edict that all of these other deities were to be ignored, and that any idol-worship was strictly forbidden, for YHWH would not abide any show of disrespect by continuation of their ancestral polytheistic practices.[20] This warning was repeated before the crossing of the Jordan River into the Promised Land, when Moses reminded the Hebrews that YHWH was a "consuming fire, an impassioned God," Who would utterly wipe them out if they did not forgo the adoration of idols.[21] The first commandment – you shall have no other gods beside me – clearly set forth the unique principal of monotheism, but by forbidding the Hebrews to worship other gods, it also presupposed their existence, and set up a strict rule to disavow any

15 Exod 15:11. Sarna, Exodus, 79.

16 Exod 18:10. Ibid., 99.

17 Deut 10:17. Friedman, Commentary on the Torah, 600-601. At Deut 4:35, however, Moses says that He is God and "there is no other outside of Him." Ibid., 579.

18 Berlin & Brettler, "Psalms," Pss 97:7. 1390.

19 How the Hebrews interpreted the existence of other gods among the pagans has been a hotly debated issue, since in Hebrew, "God" and "gods" is rendered by the same word, and there is no use of capital letters to distinguish a higher authority God, as in our language. Heschel, Heavenly Torah: As Refracted Through the Generations, fn. 1, 106.

20 Exod 20:3, 5; Lev 26:1; Deut 5:7-9.

21 Deut 2:24-26. Tigay, Deuteronomy, 51-52.

acceptance of the faith of their fathers.[22]

Despite the fact that Moses demanded that YHWH be recognized as the One and Only God, the Bible records that many Hebrews refused to give up their ancient ancestral beliefs, and continued to accept the fact that other gods existed, and that they had to be placated or some disaster would befall the community. The congregants may have lauded YHWH as the most powerful of the gods, and the one which needed the most attention, but they were not ready to stake their lives on YHWH's might alone. This type of faith, sometimes labeled as monolatrous or henotheistic, rather than polytheistic, by a number of scholars, was clearly a better label for the Hebrews then true polytheism, but because Moses set forth the commandment that the acceptance of any other deity was an apostasy punishable by death, there is little reason to segregate these other views. For this reason, I will not attempt to distinguish between monolatry and polytheism in this chapter, and will label any homage outside the parameters of the Mosaic Code as polytheistic.

1. Patriarchal Theology

While it is clear that Moses was preaching a monotheistic belief, it is not as easy to rigidly define exactly how the Patriarchs worshiped their gods. It appears that the relationship between the Patriarchs and YHWH was quite personal, but the designation of their God varied, with Abraham entering into a relationship with the God known as the "Shield' of Abraham (Gen 15:1), Isaac with the "Fear of Isaac" (Gen 31:42, 53), and Jacob with "the Mighty One of Jacob" (Gen 49:24).[23] Most biblicists do not believe that the Bible intended these names to indicate different deities, and contend that in time, the three family cults were combined, with YHWH becoming known as the God of the ancestors, the fathers, or simply of Abraham, Isaac, and Jacob.[24] But some scholars, such as John Bright, the former Cyrus H. McCormick Professor of Hebrew and the Interpretation of the Old Testament at Union Theological Seminary in Virginia, argue that the Patriarchal faith was "a clan religion, in which the clan was quite really the family of the patron God," adding that "it would be wrong to call this type of religion a monotheism."[25] In addition, Albrecht Alt has suggested that the term "gods of the Fathers" means that they were all initially distinct deities that coalesced into the Unity of YHWH when the Hebrew religion evolved from

---

22 Exod 20:2; Deut 5:7.

23 Anderson, Understanding the Old Testament, 41,

24 Exod 3:6, 15; 4:5; 1 Kgs 18:36. According to the Elohist, the God Who revealed Himself to Moses was "the God of Abraham, the God of Isaac and the God of Jacob." de Vaux, The Early History of Israel, 267-268.

25 Bright, A History of Israel, 101-102.

a form of polytheism into the monotheism of Yahwism.[26]

Most biblical scholars, even those who disagree and see Abraham as a true monotheist, conclude that there was little to separate Abraham from his Canaanite contemporaries, both before and after the seminal occasion when God presented him with the divine covenant which promised inheritance of the land of Canaan to his descendants if he followed the precepts of the Lord.[27] The Bible does not discuss the religious practices of Abraham's father Terah, but it is generally accepted that he was an idol-worshiper, and perhaps even a maker of idols.[28] Maimonides claimed that Abraham was brought up in the religion of the Sabeans, who believed in the divine nature of the stars.[29] The Bible did not attempt to portray Abraham, or his son Isaac and grandson Jacob, as rigidly adhering to faith in YHWH alone, for, in the words of the Austrian religious scholar Claus Schedl, Abraham "sacrifices and prays at the Canaanite holy places, worships the supreme god El just as Melchizedek, and is even prepared to undertake the heroic act of child sacrifice, a ritual known to us from the Canaanite religion."[30] Abraham may have been the eponymous founder of the Judaic race, and for all we know as rigidly observant as any modern orthodox Jew, but the story of the Exodus makes it clear that it was Moses, rather than Abraham, who truly engineered the world's first monotheistic faith. The fact that the great prophet Jeremiah related that even the covenant that was modified by Moses was not irrevocable, and would later be annulled, is an indication of how angry YHWH was at the impiety of the Patriarchs and their descendants. According to Jeremiah, YHWH decided that a new covenant would be made with Israel and Judah after the Babylonian Exile that "will not be like the covenant I made with their fathers," since they broke the prior covenant by failing to follow the requirements set forth in the Ten Commandments.[31]

Abraham overtly showed the manifestations of his pagan upbringing when

26 Cross, Canaanite Myth and Hebrew Epic: Essays in the History of the Religion of Israel, 3-5. Stephen L. Cook, Associate Professor of Old Testament at Virginia theological Seminary, refers to the scriptural beliefs as "biblical Yahwism," in order to clearly separate it from Canaanite forms of Yahwism. Cook, The Social Roots of Biblical Yahwism, 1-2.

27 Because the term "Canaanite" is controversial, and difficult to define, it has been proposed that the designation "West Semitic" be substituted in this regard. Niehur, "'Israelite' Religion and 'Canaanite' Religion," 28.

28 Klinghoffer, The Discovery of God: Abraham and the Birth of Monotheism, 20-21.

29 Maimonides, The Guide for the Perplexed, XXIX, 315.

30 Schedl, History of the Old Testament II. God's People of the Covenant, 97.

31 Jer 31:31-32. Sweeney, "Jeremiah," 991. Ezekiel, on the other hand, came to a different interpretation, noting that the Lord said "I will remember the covenant I made with you in the days of your youth, and I will establish it with you as an everlasting covenant." Ezek 16:60. Sweeney, "Ezekiel," 1071.

he first set up a stationary camp beside the oak tree at Moreh, following his emigration from Mesopotamia. He constructed an altar beside the tree, and commemorated the location as evidence of his covenant with God.[32] Details of how the altar was constructed are not revealed in the biblical text, but most scholars believe it contained representations of the Lord, since this form of worship was common in Canaan at the time, and was later prohibited by the Mosaic Code. A number of campsites then followed, with Abraham continuing his devotional practice by erecting altars at Beth-el,[33] Mamre,[34] and Beer-sheba.[35] Isaac and Jacob followed this same practice, as did Moses on Mt. Sinai,[36] but when the Hebrews were ready to cross the Jordan River and enter the Promised Land, Moses ordered them to tear down the altars they found in Canaan, as well as "smash their pillars, cut down their sacred posts, and consign their images to the fire," or face obliteration by the Lord for their impiety.[37] The Patriarchs may have been allowed to show their gratitude by the construction of altars, but the aniconic regulations of the Mosaic Code sternly eliminated all such pagan activities. For the dissident Hebrews who fled the Exodus before the entry into the Promised Land, however, such a show of devotion was the standard practice.

Other evidence of adherence to Canaanite beliefs among the Patriarchs is apparent in the response of Jacob to his dream of a ladder rising to heaven at Beth-el, when he rested on his way to Haran after fleeing Esau's wrath over the loss of his father's deathbed blessing. Jacob made a vow to God at that time that if He would remain with him and protect him then "the Lord shall be my God."[38] This promise clearly indicates that Jacob had not yet decided to give exclusive allegiance to YHWH alone, and had accepted the importance of other family deities. After Jacob was married, and living in Laban's home, his family continued their faith in idols, as evidenced by the fact that Rachel took Laban's teraphim with her when she left with Jacob to return to Canaan.[39] Although

---

32 Gen 12:6-7. Jacob also erected an altar beside this same oak tree when he later traveled to Paddan-Aram to find a wife, naming it *El-Elohe-Israel*, or "The Altar to the God of Israel." Gen 33:20. The Living Bible, 30. The oak tree was a representative of the "tree of life," and this reverence of nature was the reason Moses later forbid the planting of trees within the precincts of an altar. Deut 16:21. Sarna, Genesis, 91. In Greece, the rustling of the branches of an old and sacred oak tree at Dodona similarly provided the oracle with insights into future events. Burkert, Greek Religion, 85-86.

33 Gen 12:8; 13:3.

34 Gen 13:18.

35 Gen 21:33.

36 Exod 24:4.

37 Deut 7:4-5. Tigay, Deuteronomy, 86.

38 Gen 28:21. Sarna, Genesis, 200.

39 Gen 31:21. That the teraphim were used for divination, which was prohibited by the Mosaic Code, is apparent in other biblical sections. Judg 17:5; 18:5, 14-20; 1 Sam 15:23; 2 Kgs 23:24; Ezek 21:21, 26; Zech 10:2. Van Dam, The Urim and Thummim: A

Jacob was unaware that his wife had hidden the holy figures in her luggage, he must have known about his wife's illicit beliefs before the departure took place, since the patriarch of the Semitic family determined the manner in which the family gods were worshiped.

In addition to the actions of Jacob and Rachel, some of their children acted in a fashion which was clearly more in line with pagan Canaanite practices, than with the edicts that were later to be set forth by Moses in the Mosaic Code. Judah, the fourth son of Jacob and Leah, left home as an adult and moved to Adullam, where he married a Canaanite girl, the daughter of Shua, and had three sons, Er, Onan, and Shelah.[40] Since marriage outside the religion was barred by the Mosaic Law, such behavior would have been seen as abhorrent under the monotheistic code. Reuben also violated one of the most basic patriarchal taboos of incest by sleeping with his father's concubine Bilhah while Jacob was still alive,[41] and Joseph, whose actions could probably be excused because of his difficult situation in Egypt, married an Egyptian woman and took on an Egyptian name and life.[42] Through this act, Joseph's two sons, carrying Egyptian blood in their veins, would eventually become the heads of two of the twelve tribes of Israel after being adopted by Jacob on his deathbed.[43]

That these pagan practices were also prevalent among Jacob's relatives is confirmed by his actions following the tragedy at Shechem, when Simeon and Levi massacred the Shechemites for the rape of Dinah. This event took place years later, when all of Jacob's children were grown, and YHWH directed Jacob to go to Beth-el after the slaughter in order to make an altar for forgiveness, adding that he must rid himself of all the alien gods in his midst. Jacob obeyed this command, and ordered his family to bring him "all the alien gods that they had, and the rings that were in their ears, and Jacob buried them under the terebinth that was near Shechem."[44] This action shows that many members of Jacob's family had remained loyal to the polytheistic beliefs that characterized most of the ancient Near East during the Middle Bronze Age, even though Jacob himself may have begun to give allegiance to YHWH alone. Unlike Moses, who demanded that the Hebrews involved in the building of the golden calf-idol be punished by death because they disobeyed the earlier commandments of God, Jacob simply asked

---

Means of Revelation in Ancient Israel, 149-150.

40 Gen 38:1-5. His first son Er married Tamar, but was wicked and died, and so his brother Onan married the widow, but would not have a child by her and so the Lord had him killed as well. Tamar disguised herself as a harlot and lay with Judah, eventually giving birth to twin sons Perez (Pharez) and Zerah. Gen 38. Both King David and Jesus Christ were descendants of Perez.

41 Gen 35:22.

42 Gen 41:41-46.

43 Gen 48:5.

44 Gen 35:4. Sarna, Genesis, 240.

his relations to forgo their practice at that time, and did not mention any form of punishment which would result if they did not follow his demand. This passive order may very well explain why the Hebrews resorted to building a golden calf-idol during Moses' prolonged absence at Mt. Sinai, unaware that their action would provoke parricidal punishments when Moses returned to the camp. Although the message conveyed by Moses after the theophany may have been crystal clear about the need to forgo homage to other gods, there was no way the Hebrews who were reluctant to change their methods of adoration could have realized that failure to obey would result in capital punishment.

The names which the Patriarchs chose to honor God at various sites throughout Canaan also point to similarities between the polytheistic Canaanites and pre-Mosaic Hebrews. The Patriarchs frequently used the words "El" or "Baal " in the naming of their honorary structures, appellations which referred to the two major Canaanite gods. El was the oldest Canaanite deity, and was worshiped as the "father of mankind," although he played only a minor part in the Canaanite cult and legend.[45] Baal was a younger deity, but he eventually became the chief of the Canaanite gods, and was personified as the Storm, a role similar to that of Zeus.[46] His female counterpart was Baalath, often referred to by the personal name Astarte (alternatively known as Ashtoreth, Asherah, Athirat, Ashtar, and Ishtar).[47] As will be discussed shortly, many scholars believe that these designations indicate that the Patriarchs worshiped Canaanite gods before the rise of Yahwism, although others argue that the terms were simply intended to mean "master" or "lord," and not a reference to a specific god.[48] This process of

---

45 The epithets of El were "the King," and "the Father of Gods," an indication that he was the head of the pantheon. With the rise of Baal, however, his position appears to become ceremonial and without power. Coogan, Stories From Ancient Canaan, 12.

46 The name of Baal appears seventy-six times in the Old Testament. Cooper, "Divine Names and Epithets in the Ugaritic Texts," 348. See Num 25:3, 5; 32:38; Deut 3:9; 4:3; Josh 11:17; 12:7; 13:5; Judg 3:3; 20:33; 2 Sam 5:20; 13:23; 2 Kgs 4:42; 19:23; 1 Chron 4:33; 5:8, 23; 14:11; Pss 29:5-6; 106:28; Ezek 25:9; Song of Songs 8:11.

47 Asherah was a popular goddess in the Near East, worshiped at Sidon (1 Kgs 11:5, 33), Tyre, and by the Philistines (1 Sam 31:10). Wooden poles or pillars were erected in her honor (Exod 34:12), and some say that any tree planted at the entrance to a house of worship is called an Asherah. Kaplan, The Living Torah: The Five Books of Mose and the Haftarot, 461, 948. Worship of Asheroth idols is also noted at Judg 2:14; 3:7; 6:25, 30; 10:6; 1 Kgs 18:19; 2 Kgs 21:4, 7; 23:13-15; and 2 Chron 17:6. Jeremiah tells how women offered cakes to "The Queen of Heaven," who was Ishtar (Inanna), the Mesopotamian goddess of love and war. Jer 7:18; 44:17-19.

48 Lods, Israel, From Its Beginnings to the Middle of the Eighth Century, 120. Albrecht Alt (1883-1956 CE), the well-known German Old Testament scholar, believed that the Judaic faith was initially a form of the El religion, which included the God of Abraham, the Fear of Isaac, and the Mighty One of Jacob as "numina which originally had nothing to do with one another," but which came together under the worship of YHWH

adopting the titles of foreign gods and then attributing them to a God of your own choosing is a method known as "assimilation,"[49] and was frequently used by the Greeks and Romans when they incorporated deities from cultures they vanquished.

That the Hebrews continued to practice idolatry during the Exodus is evident in many biblical passages, which explained Moses' intent to alter their impious actions. The very building of the Tabernacle was intended to stop the people from sacrificing to evil spirits in the open fields, and to bring their offerings to the priest at the entrance of the Tabernacle, in order to have it be performed properly.[50] According to Rabbi Ishmael, as understood by Maimonides, "the primary intention of the entire Torah was to remove idolatry and expunge its memory."[51] For the dissident Hebrews who fled to Mycenae, however, such an alteration would have been an impious sacrilege.

2. Post-Conquest Theology

When the forty years of wandering in the Sinai Wilderness was over, and the generation of Hebrews who had refused to follow God's commandments had all died off, Joshua led the remainder of the Exodus congregation into the Promised Land, initiating a Conquest of Canaan that would assure the fulfillment of God's promise that the Hebrews were His Chosen People. After their victory was secured, and the twelve tribes were settled in their allotted domains, Joshua summoned the people together at Shechem and told them that they must now decide whether they were going to "revere the Lord and serve Him with undivided loyalty," or follow the gods which their ancestors worshiped in the land of Canaan, once again proving that the Patriarchs were seen as adhering to a polytheistic faith.[52] The generation of impious Hebrews who had been raised in Egypt were gone, but Joshua still felt the need to question the younger generation on whether they understood that the patriarchal belief was no longer an acceptable practice under the edict of the First Commandment. The people enthusiastically answered that they would serve YHWH as their One and Only God, a covenant which Joshua

---

alone. Alt, "The God of the Fathers," 9, 55. Jon D. Levenson, Professor of Jewish Studies at the Divinity School and Department of Near Eastern Languages and Civilizations at Harvard University, points to the statement of Frank Moore that "El in biblical tradition is often used simply as an alternate name of YHWH," and adds that "El as the kind, compassionate, and wise creator and father of gods and humanity lives on in the God of Israel." Levenson, <u>The Death and Resurrection of the Beloved Son: The Transformation of Child Sacrifice in Judaism and Christianity</u>, 34.

49 "Ugarit and the Bible," 3.

50 Lev 17:5-7.

51 Heschel, Heavenly Torah: As Refracted Through the Generations, 75.

52 Josh 24:14-16. Meyers, "Joshua," 504.

then commemorated with a great stone that was set next to the oak tree beside the Tabernacle.[53]

Although the Hebrews agreed to Joshua's mandate at the time, their actions soon belied the reliability of their intent. Following their victories during the era of the Judges, generations of Israelites began to once again bow down to the idols of Baal,[54] and Asherah,[55] and intermarry with the pagan Canaanites, Hittites, Hivites, Perizzites, Amorites, and Jebusites, something which they were specifically prohibited from doing by Moses.[56] Many Prophets warned the Israelites that their impiety would bring down the wrath of God, but faith in the power of the Canaanite gods was too firmly entrenched to be modified at once, and strict observance of the Mosaic Code would not take place until the return of the Israelites from the Babylonian Exile (587-538 BCE), as will be discussed shortly. Because the Israelites so readily fell back upon the practices of their Canaanite neighbors, some scholars see the two religions as syncretistic, with tenets that attracted adherents from both camps. Professor Hans Magnus Barstad, from the University of Oslo, supports this view by claiming that the idol-worship during this period of time was so great that "all the evidence available today points towards the fact that belief systems in Israel and other Near Eastern cultures in the Iron Age were fairly similar," with several different deities commanding

---

53 Josh 24:25-26. To signify the importance of this pact, the bones of Joseph, which had been retrieved by Moses before the Exodus began and then carefully transported during the forty years of wandering in the wilderness, were buried at Shechem. Josh 24:32. Joshua's address to the Hebrews gathered at Shechem is believed by some scholars to include some who probably had entered Canaan from the south or west, or who had already been living in the land among the Canaanites, as opposed to having taken part in the entire Exodus. Anderson, Understanding the Old Testament, 139.

54 Complaints about Baal worship are seen in Judg 2:11, 13; 6:25, 28, 30-31; 1 Sam 7:4; 12:10; 1 Kgs 16:31-32; 18:19-21, 25-26; 22:54; 2 Kgs 3:2; 10:18-23, 25-28; 11:18; 23:4-5; Jer 9:13; and Hos 2:15, 18-19.

55 Judg 3:7; 1 Kgs 18:19; 2 Kgs 13:6; 23:4, 7. Figurines indicating worship of the goddess Asherah have prominently been found in rural parts of Israel during the Assyrian period (721-586 BCE), away from the central monotheistic cult practiced in the Jerusalem Temple. Keel & Uehlinger, Gods, Goddesses, and Images of God in Ancient Israel, 202. Two ancient Hebrew inscriptions at Kuntillet 'Ajrud and Khirbet el-Qom even contain benedictions in the name of "YHWH and his Asherah," suggesting that some of the Hebrews may have seen Asherah as a consort of YHWH. Geller, "The Religion of the Bible," 2022. William Dever, Professor Emeritus of Near Eastern Archaeology and Anthropology at the University of Arizona in Tucson, has intensively studied this aspect of ancient Hebrew folk-religion and identified the representation of trees at sacred sites throughout ancient Israel with the presence of Asherah. Dever, Did God Have a Wife? Archaeology and Folk Religion in Ancient Israel, 94.

56 Deut 7:3.

attention from the Israelite population.[57] The French biblical scholar Adolphe Lods (1867-1948 CE) likewise explained that during this period of time, "the worship of Jahweh and of the baals was carried on simultaneously," with the people worshiping "Jahweh when they were in trouble, and the baals when they were prosperous."[58]

This bipolar behavior of the Israelite population during the era of the Judges was clearly heretical, and God sent many messages to the Chosen People through the warnings of the Prophets, admonishing them for their behavior and cautioning them that although He had promised to not ever break His covenant with them, He would refuse to help them in their contests against the foreign nations in their midst if they continued to worship heathen altars.[59] These threats did little to change the evil ways of the Israelites, however, and worship of the gods of Aram, Sidon, Moab, the Ammonites, and the Philistines continued unabated through the period of the United and Divided Monarchies. Eventually, God's threats culminated in the destruction and Exile of Israel by Assyria in 724 BCE, and Judah by Babylon in 587 BCE, but before that dreadful event took place, the Israelites modified their government into a monarchical system that characterized most of the ancient Near East during the Iron Age (1200-587 BCE).

The impiety reflected by the Israelites during the era between the Conquest and the end of the Divided Monarchy is important to my thesis because it proves that many of the ancient Hebrews were unwilling to follow the mandates of the Mosaic Code, even once they were entrenched in the Promised Land and were not subject to parricidal punishment. Threats of God's vindictive retribution did not change their beliefs, and it is easy to understand why some of their ancestors who were subject to capital punishment during the forty years of wandering in the Wilderness decided to leave the Exodus altogether, and travel to a distant land.

3. The United and Divided Monarchies

The modification of the political format of the Hebrews from a tribal system of government to a Monarchy was a gradual evolution. During the period of the Judges, many biblical scholars believe that there were pre-monarchial experiments where regional warlords were elected to provide *ad hoc* solutions for immediate

57 Barstad, "Deuteronomists, Persians, Greeks, and the Dating of the Israelite Tradition," 68.

58 Lods, Israel, From Its Beginnings to the Middle of the Eighth Century, 404. This evidence of widespread idol-worship prompted Ephraim Stern, Director of the archaeologic excavations at Dor, to call the religion practiced in those regions "pagan Yahism." Stern, "Pagan Yahwism: The Folk Religion of Ancient Israel," 21, 28.

59 Judg 2:1-3.

problems, with powers that closely resembled that of a king.[60] This was evident when the people asked Gideon to be their monarch, although he refused, saying "the Lord alone shall rule over you."[61] His son Abimelech was more ambitious, however, and overtly desired to become king. He eventually was elected to the job by the citizens of Shechem,[62] but never became ruler of all the Israelite tribes, and so could not realistically be called a king of the Jews. Jephethah also was elected by the elders of Gilead to become commander-in-chief and king of the Israelites during a war-time crisis, and was even ratified by a general assembly of the people when they were later attacked by the king of Ammon, but he never was given a permanent position by a meeting of tribal elders, and therefore did not actually initiate a royal system of government.[63]

That the Israelites desired to form a monarchy for defensive military reasons is not surprising, since vesting the authority of one's country in the hands of a powerful warrior was standard practice during the Late Bronze Age. In addition, Moses had told them when they were about to cross the Jordan River into the Promised Land that they should pick a king that would rule over them, as long as it was from within their own ranks, and not a foreigner.[64] Moses added a cautionary note, however, warning them that there was an inherent danger in such a move, and that they should not allow the future monarch to amass many wives, or silver and gold to excess, "lest his heart go astray."[65] These recommendations would prove particularly salient during the rule of King Solomon, whose wealth was legendary, and whose faith was shaken by the pagan nature of his many wives.[66] In order to point the Israelite king in the right direction, Moses recommended that once he was crowned, he should keep a copy of the Mosaic laws at his side, and read the contents every day to remind him of the Primacy of the Lord.[67]

The book of *Judges* explains that the time for the Israelites to appoint a king became imperative after a number of years, for under the legal system of the tribal government, justice became chaotic, and "everyone did as he pleased."[68] Without

---

60 Zevit, The Religions of Ancient Israel: A Synthesis of Parallactic Approaches, 616.

61 Judg 8:22-23. Amit, "Judges," 529.

62 Judg 9:6.

63 Judg 11:5-11.

64 Deut 17:14-15.

65 Deut 17:16-17. Tigay, <u>Deuteronomy</u>, 167.

66 Solomon was the son of king David and Bathsheba (Bathshua), the daughter of Eliam (Ammiel), who had previously been married to Uriah the Hittite, a member of David's army. 2 Sam 5:14; 1 Chron 3:5. Although this might suggest she was a pagan, Bathsheba was actually the daughter of Eliam, one of The Thirty, the top-ranking officers of David's army. 2 Sam 11:3; 23:13, 34.

67 Deut 17:18-19.

68 Judg 21:25. Amit, "Judges," 557. See e.g., Judg 18:1; 19:1.

a strong leader who could cut across the petty desires of divided tribes, the security of the country was at risk, and in order to modify things for the better, the people came to the prophet Samuel (c. 1070-1000 BCE), who was the last of the great Judges, and asked for a change that would put the young nation into modern times. "Appoint a king for us, to govern us like all other nations," they pleaded, but Samuel was initially reluctant to accede to their demands.[69] He told the people that their idea was not a good one, for a king would oppress and exploit them. He gave a long list of likely disasters that would follow vestment of such authority in one man: their sons would be drafted into military service and be forced to do slave labor in the royal fields; their daughters would be compelled to work for the king; and the best of their fields, as well as a tenth of their harvest and flocks, would be taken and distributed among the king's friends. In short, Samuel told them that this decision would cause them to shed "bitter tears."[70]

The people refused to listen to his warning, however, and said that they wanted a king to govern them and lead them into battle like the neighboring countries who, by all accounts, were doing quite well. The Philistines had settled along the southern coastal plain of Canaan at the time, and were threatening the very existence of the Israelite state. Samuel asked God what he should do, and God told him that He would sent a man from the land of Benjamin to be anointed king. The next day, Saul came to meet him, and the Lord told Samuel that Saul was the man to rule My people. Saul was tall and handsome, the son of a rich, influential man from the tribe of Benjamin. He looked the part of a monarch, so Samuel acquiesced and called a convocation of all the tribal leaders at Mizpah, where Saul was chosen as king.[71]

Under the accepted chronology, Saul ruled from 1020-1006 BCE, although it is uncertain how old he was when he became king, or how long he actually reigned.[72] Some modern biblical scholars have even questioned whether Saul reigned at all, and whether the entire Israelite Monarchy was a fictional contrivance, as I discussed in chapter 5, but I am not going to accept these claims in this book, and will follow the majority of historians who accept that the Israelite Monarchy was a real event. According to the biblical text, Saul did not initially disappoint the Israelites, although he also did not exactly follow the precepts of Moses on how a king should act. This was evident when he conducted sacrifices by himself, without waiting for Samuel to arrive, despite the fact that the king was not

---

69 1 Sam 8:5. Bar-Efrat, "First Samuel," 574.

70 1 Sam 8:18. The Living Bible, 233.

71 1 Sam 10:17, 20.

72 1 Sam 11:15. Comay, The Hebrew Kings, 16. The chronologies for the Hebrew monarchies varies between one and ten years, depending on the sources consulted, and in this book I will use the chronology of Cogan and Tadmor, as cited in Hill & Walton, A Survey of the Old Testament, 232-233.

authorized to perform such a holy task.[73] The Bible does not mention any actual acts of apostasy during his reign, however, nor is there any evidence of impious worship during the reign of his successor King David.

The piety of the United Monarchy began to fall apart during the reign of King Solomon, however, who followed his father David on the throne, and instituted many acts of royal apostasy. Solomon disregarded Moses' advice, and married many foreign princesses from nations where idols were worshiped, including Moab, Ammon, Edom, Sidon, Egypt, and the Hittites, accumulating over seven hundred wives and three hundred concubines in his marital fervor.[74] These women "turned his heart away from the Lord, especially in his old age,"[75] and caused him to give homage to Asherah (goddess of the Sidonians),[76] Milcom (head of the pantheon of the Ammonites),[77] Chemosh (god of Moab),[78] and Molech (god of the Ammonites).[79] He built temples where he and his wives could worship these gods, and participate in their pagan cults. Professor Ziony Zevit, from the University of Judaism in Los Angeles, has attempted to downplay these references with respect to King Solomon himself, noting that nothing in the biblical text indicated that these shrines were places of Israelite cultic activity, and may have only been built as places for Solomon's wives to worship their native

---

73 1 Sam 13:6. When Samuel arrived near the end, he was furious and called Saul a fool for having disobeyed the commandment of God. 1 Sam 13:13. King David later offered sacrifices and performed blessings upon the people, without any untoward comments or effects. 2 Sam 6:13, 17-18.

74 1 Kgs 11:3.

75 1 Kgs 11:3-4. The Living Bible, 292. The reign of Solomon has been described as religious syncretism - the amalgamation of alien cultural elements with Israel's native traditions. Anderson, Understanding the Old Testament, 223.

76 Asherah was not only a goddess of the Canaanites, but also a moon-goddess, who the Greeks called Aphrodite. Keil & Delitzsch, Commentary on the Old Testament, III.170. The Egyptians referred to Asherah as Qudshu, and equated her with the goddesses Astarte and Anat. Dever, Did God Have a Wife? Archaeology and Folk Religion in Ancient Israel, 177. Astarte is mentioned in the Bible at 1 Sam 31:10; 1 Kgs 11:5, 33; 2 Kgs 23:13.

77 The prophet Jeremiah declared that the end of the Ammonites would come because Milcom (Milkom) dispossessed Gad. Jer 49:1. In the book of *Zephaniah*, the god is referred to as Malcam. Zeph 1:5.

78 Jeremiah also warned that Moab would be shamed because of Chemosh, just as Israel was shamed because of the temple King Jeroboam I erected at Beth-el. Jer 48:7, 12. Sweeney, "Jeremiah," 1021.

79 1 Kgs 1:5-7. According to Jeremiah, the people of Judah deserved contempt for their abominations to the Lord, including the charge that they built shrines of Topheth in the Valley of Ben-hinnom to burn their sons and daughters in the fire. Jer 7:31; 19:2, 5-6. This region ran along the southwest borders of the city of Jerusalem, and was an area known for the sacrifice of children to the pagan gods Baal and Molech. Sweeney, "Jeremiah," 940. See e.g., 2 Kgs 23:10; 2 Chron 28:3; 33:6; Isa 30:33; Jer 19:11-14.

gods.[80] Allowance of such iconic activity to persist on Holy Land, however, was still an apostasy, and the Lord was so incensed by Solomon's activities that He warned the king that if he, or his people, did not desist from idol-worship and follow His laws, He would take away the Temple and the land which He had given his Chosen People.[81] According to the prophet Ahijah from Shiloh, YHWH planned to tear ten tribes away from Solomon's kingdom, and give them to Jeroboam I (931-911 BCE) to rule over as the king of Israel, for his illicit worship of Asherah (the goddess of the Sidonians), Chemosh (the god of Moab), and Milcom (the god of the Ammonites).[82] Solomon must have overheard and believed these forecasts, for he attempted to prevent his being punished in this manner by killing Jeroboam I, failing in his attempt when Jeroboam fled to King Shishak, who is identified with Pharaoh Shoshenq I (945-924 BCE), the founder of the Twenty-Second Dynasty in Egypt.[83] Jeroboam I remained under the protection of Shishak until Solomon's death, when the United Monarchy finally dissolved, dividing the United Monarchy into the Divided Monarchies of Judah, under the rule of Rehoboam (931-915 BCE), the son of Solomon and the Ammonite Naamah,[84] and Israel, under Jeroboam I.[85]

Although the Bible singled out Solomon for his acts of pagan worship during the United Monarchy, no such distinction was necessary during the Divided Monarchy, as monarchs from both kingdoms continued to promote the adoration of gods other than YHWH, eventually resulting in both Israel and Judah being punished by Exile from the Promised Land. The reign of Jeroboam I in Israel was particularly abhorrent, as he made two golden calf-idols for the people to worship in the cities of Beth-el and Dan, in an attempt to prevent their returning to Jerusalem to pay homage to YHWH in the Solomonic Temple. These images, clearly remindful of the golden calf-idol which was constructed at the foot of Mt. Sinai, were a direct violation of the Third Commandment, and archaeologic evidence from this period suggests that the majority of the population then sought the welfare of God through the purchase of a multitude of images, with virtually every excavation site in Israel containing metallic and ceramic representations of

80 Zevit, The Religions of Ancient Israel: A Synthesis of Parallactic Approaches, 458.

81 1 Kgs 9:6-8. This threat would have certainly made Solomon economically insecure, given the fact that the construction of the First Temple used up one hundred thousand talents of gold, according to the Chronicler. 1 Chron 22:14. This is an immense amount, weighing 3,750 tons and worth about $45 billion at today's prices. The United States Central Bank gold reserve is about 9,000 tons. Walton, Matthews, & Chavalas, The IVP Bible Background Commentary: Old Testament, 417.

82 1 Kgs 11:3, 35, 37.

83 1 Kgs 11:40. Zevit, "First Kings," 700.

84 1 Kgs 14:21.

85 1 Kgs 11:40.

both male and female deities. Jeroboam I encouraged this activity by telling his constituents that the idols were their god, "who brought you up from the land of Egypt,"[86] ignoring the fact that it was this same attitude and show of iconic worship that initiated the campaign of parricidal retribution against the Hebrews who refused to follow the edicts of the Mosaic Code. His descendants on the throne of Israel continued to worship idols, being mentioned fourteen times directly, and twelve indirectly, by the Deuteronomist for their guilty acts.[87]

Eventually, the kingdom of Israel was sent into Exile in 724 BCE by Assyria, scattering the ten tribes which had formed the country to unknown regions, creating the myth of the Lost Tribes of Israel, which continues to fascinate biblical scholars today. At the same time the kings of Israel and their constituents were abandoning the precepts of Yahwism, the people of Judah also began to sin under Rehoboam by building shrines and idols "on every high hill and under every leafy tree."[88] Perhaps because He had already warned King Solomon of the dangers of such illicit activity, YHWH wasted no time in abandoning His protection of the Judahites, allowing King Shishak of Egypt to attack Jerusalem, and ransack the Temple, stealing all of the gold shields Solomon had made. This drastic punishment did not alter the impiety of the royal house, however, as Rehoboam's son Abijam (Abijah) (915-912 BCE) continued to encourage the practice of idol-worship. Abijam's son Asa (912-871 BCE) digressed from these sins, removing the idols from the shrines,[89] but although these actions were said to please the Lord, the Judahites returned to heretical activity under succeeding kings. Hezekiah (715-687 BCE) also instituted reforms by removing the shrines on the hills, breaking down the obelisks, and knocking down the idols of Asherah, which had existed for centuries in his land.[90] Once again, however, his reforms were temporary, as his son Manasseh (698-642 BCE), and his grandson Amon (641-640 BCE), rebuilt the high places, worshiping other gods and consigning their sons to the fire.

As the kingdom of Judah neared its final demise, signs appeared which warned the Judahites to change their evil ways or face the wrath of God. In 622 BCE, during the reign of King Josiah (639-609 BCE), repairs were made to the Temple in Jerusalem, and it was during this construction that a "book of the Law" was discovered by the high priest Hilkiah, proving that the regulations of the Mosaic Code were firmly based on a factual source.[91] This treatise has been identified with the biblical book of *Deuteronomy*, and Josiah reacted by purging the worship

86 1 Kgs 12:28. Zevit, "First Kings," 702.
87 Zevit, The Religions of Ancient Israel: A Synthesis of Parallactic Approaches, 454.
88 1 Kgs 14:23. Zevit, "First Kings," 706.
89 1 Kgs 15:14; 2 Chron 14:2, 4; 15:17.
90 2 Kgs 18:4; 2 Chron 31:2.
91 2 Kgs 22:8.

of foreign gods in the country, attempting to return his country to the mandates of the Mosaic Code. He ordered the priests and guards of the Temple to destroy all the equipment used to worship Baal and Asherah, killing the heathen priests and destroying the idols. According to the Bible, Josiah's actions excelled all other kings in Judah or Israel for a record of obedience to God, but his successors once again did not obey the edicts of God, causing the prophet Jeremiah to warn that the apostasy of the Judahites was even more wicked than the Israelites, who had been sent into Exile by the Assyrians.[92] Instead of changing their sinful ways, the people of Judah pursued the same policies with greater abandon, and Ezekial, a priest in the Temple at Jerusalem, berated them in 529 BCE for offering their sons to be burned to ashes before idols made of wood and stone.[93] Ezekiel warned the people that YHWH would judge them as He did during the Exodus, when an entire generation of Hebrews were forced to die off in the wilderness, without ever stepping foot on the Promised Land. His words proved true in 587 BCE, when King Nebuchadrezzar II (605-562 BCE) of Babylon destroyed the people of Judah, sending them into an extended Exile which lasted fifty years.[94] When the Jews were finally allowed to return to Palestine, the true foundation of a monotheistic Jewish religion was firmly established, and from that time forward, Jews refrained from idol-worship and became the model for modern Judaism which is accepted today as the world's first monotheistic faith.

It should be emphasized that the history of the Jewish nation's process of conversion from repetitive apostasy to final obedience of their monotheistic faith took almost a millennium to complete, and it is therefore no wonder that the dissident Hebrews during the Exodus refused to forgo the faith of their ancestors, just because Moses told them that YHWH demanded they change their methods of showing homage and faith. Conversion to a monotheistic creed went against all the teachings of the Late Bronze and Iron Age religions, as well as the belief in ancestral worship, and the symbol of One Almighty God would have to be forged in a furnace with a flickering flame before emerging as the dominant religious belief of our modern world.

B.   Nomenclature

Evidence of patriarchal and post-Mosaic polytheism is not only evident in the stories of apostasy in the Bible, it is also apparent in the manner in which the Hebrews referred to God throughout their travels in the Promised Land. There were three primary appellations of God in the Old Testament: YHWH, Elohim, and Adonai. Biblical scholars have found within the etymology of each

92 2 Kgs 23:25; Jer 3:11.

93 Ezek 20:31-32.

94 Throughout the Bible, the Babylonian king's name is generally spelled as "Nebuchadnezzar."

of these designations evidence that the Hebrews evolved from an earlier worship of Canaanite pagan deities to the adoration of One Almighty God alone. Since my thesis claims that the dissident Hebrews fled the Exodus to remain loyal to the polytheistic beliefs of their ancestors, I will discuss each of these terms in greater detail.

1. YHWH

The name which is most frequently used in the Old Testament to refer to God is the Tetragrammaton YHWH (JHWH, YHVH, JHVH), a word which is written only with consonants, representing God as the "Revealer of the Torah." It appears almost 7,000 times in the Old Testament, 700 times in the book of *Psalms* alone.[95]   During High Holiday services, and in daily Torah study, the name was never pronounced by the reader, a habit based on the commandments in Exod 20:7 that "you shall not take the name of YHWH your God in vain," and in Lev 22:32 that "you shall not profane my holy name."[96] In the Dead Sea Scrolls, which date from 150 BCE-70 CE, the Essene sect held that if an individual ever pronounced the name, "even though frivolously, or as a result of shock, or for any other reason, while reading the Book or praying," he was immediately dismissed from the sect and refused readmission forever.[97] Gradually, this restriction of saying the Tetragrammaton out loud was eased, and the word "Jehovah," or "Yahweh," was chosen as a reasonable alternative pronunciation, combining the consonants of YHWH with the vowels of the word Adonai.[98]

There are two traditions about the time when YHWH was first used: the "J" tradition holds that YHWH appeared as the God of Israel in the pre-Mosaic era;[99] while the "E" and "P" traditions hold that God's statement to Moses that He appeared to the Patriarchs as El Shaddai, but was now to be known as YHWH, is an accurate reflection of its origination.[100] This latter passage took place when

95 Lockyer, All the Divine Names and Titles in the Bible, 18.

96 Trimm, "Nazarenes and the Name of YHWH," 1-2. The name was allowed to be pronounced by the priests in the Temple when blessing the people. "Names of God," 6.

97 Vermes, The Dead Sea Scrolls in English, 5.

98 Pixley, On Exodus, A Liberation Perspective, 69; "Names of God," 2. The more accurate pronunciation is Yahweh, with Jehovah provided by the Masoretes, who read the vowels of Adonay into YHWH. Kaiser, "Exodus," 323.

99 God used the Tetragrammaton in speaking to Abraham (Gen 15:7) and Jacob (Gen 28:13). The name was also used by angels (Gen 16:11; 18:14; 19:13), by the Patriarchs themselves (Gen 14:22; 15:2, 8; 16:2, 5; 22:14; 24:27, 31, 40, 44, 48; 26:22; 27:7, 27; 28:31; 29:32; 30:24, 30; 32:10; 33:35; 49:18), and even by Gentiles (Gen 24:3, 31; 26:28; 30:27; 31:49). Kaplan, the Living Torah: The Five Books of Moses and the Haftarot, 281.

100 Anderson, Understanding the Old Testament, 58-59.

God appeared to Moses at the burning bush and told him that His name was *"Ehyeh-Asher-Ehyeh,"* which literally means "I am who I am, or I will be who I will be."[101] YHWH clarified that He was the same God Who had earlier appeared to Abraham, Isaac and Jacob as "El-Shaddai," even though He did not use the name YHWH at that time.[102]

If the use of the name YHWH by the Hebrews in the Bible did not appear until the time of Moses and the Exodus, the question then arises as to whether it was a new name, devised by the Hebrews solely to refer to their new monotheistic God, or whether the name was already in existence in parts of Canaan from an earlier date, and was incorporated into the image of the Hebrew God.[103] The earliest extant recording of the name YWHW in an extra-biblical text appears in an Egyptian toponym list in southern Palestine from the time of Amenhotep III (1382-1344 BCE), where it referenced a place called *Yhw*, associated with nomadic Shasu tribes.[104] The Shasu are known to have resided in Edom and Midian, near the "mountain of God," where Moses first faced God at the burning bush. This has raised the possibility that the early poetry of Israel used the name because of the familiarity of the Israelites with the locus of YHWH in that location. Donald B. Redford, Professor of Near Eastern Studies at the University of Toronto, has argued that Yahwism actually originated among these Shasu nomads, thereby dating the Exodus to the thirteenth, rather than the fifteenth, century BCE, and determining that the name did not originate with Moses.[105] The name does not appear again in the extant historical record until the Inscription of Mesha, king of Moab in the ninth century BCE, when it is clearly identified with the Israelites, but it is not known whether the name was reflective of the Shasu inscription.[106] If the Exodus took place in the fifteenth century BCE, however, then the name of YHWH could have been generated by Moses, and then later taken up by the Shasu inhabitants of the region, including Hebrews who took part in the Conquest of the Promised Land. The dissident Hebrews who fled the Exodus would then have been aware of the YHWH designation, but would have maintained their faith in the gods of Abraham, Isaac, and Jacob, rather than YHWH alone.

Another favored theory about the origin of the name YHWH, similar to that opined by Redford, is that it referred to one of the Kenite gods in Midian, where

---

101 Exod 6:2-3. Exodus, The Torah, A Modern Commentary II, 40.

102 The name El Shaddai appears six times in the patriarchal narrative (Gen 17:1; 28:3; 35:11; 43:14; 46:3; 49:3). In the book of Job it appears thirty times. Kaiser, "Exodus," 340.

103 The name of YHWH appeared in the book of *Genesis* for the first time, after Seth named his son Enosh, and it was noted that men began to invoke YHWH by name, but this was an era well before the birth of Abraham. Gen 4:26. Sarna, Genesis, 40.

104 Miller, The Religion of Ancient Israel, 1.

105 Redford, Egypt, Canaan, and Israel in Ancient Times, 273, 275-280.

106 The Oxford Illustrated History of the Bible, 9-10.

Moses fled after killing an Egyptian, the so-called "Kenite hypothesis."[107] Under this proposal, Moses married the daughter of Jethro, a Kenite priest who worshiped a god named YHWH, and during the forty years Moses spent in Midian before being called by God to Egypt, he became particularly devoted to his father-in-law's faith. When he encountered God in the form of the burning bush while tending sheep in the region, he identified the deity with YHWH, and decided to restrict the homage of the Hebrews to that One God alone. This theory does not favor any particular Exodus date, since the Kenites have not been identified with the name YHWH in any archaeologic remains from a specific era.

Both of these hypotheses have some support in the biblical academic community, but the most favored theory of origin is the one which holds that YHWH was originally a cultic name of El, one of the primary pagan gods, and that with time the Israelites at Shiloh, Shechem, and Jerusalem restricted their worship to YHWH alone, thereby setting aside the other El deities.[108] Yahwism, under this theory, "originated in the worship of tutelary clan deities identified with the high god El of Amorite and Canaanite religion, modified by images and practices from the mythology of Baal," such as fire, light, smoke, cloud, thunder and quaking.[109] Mark S. Smith, Skirball Professor of Bible and Ancient Near Eastern Studies at New York University, points out that this thesis is supported by the fact that the name of Israel clearly derives from the name of the god El, and that Deut 32:8-9 casts YHWH as one of the sons of El, here called Most High (*Elyon*), an indication that YHWH was given Israel as his portion.[110] I will discuss this proposal in more detail in the following section, but, once again, this concept does not favor any particular Exodus date.

2. Elohim

Elohim is the first word used to refer to God in the Bible, appearing as the third word in the opening line of the book of *Genesis*. It is second only to the word YHWH as the most frequently used designation for God in the Old Testament, appearing 2,570 times.[111] The Muslim faith particularly related to this designation, naming their God "*Allah*," which is *Elohim* in Arabic, bypassing the designation

---

107 Parke-Taylor, Yahweh: The Divine Name in the Bible, 22-31.

108 Arnold, "Religion in Ancient Israel," 394. El was the chief deity of the West Semitic pantheon, and was succeeded, according to the *Enuma Elish* conflict myth, by Baal, the storm-god, who defeated Yam, the sea-god, and Mot, the underworld-god. Arnold & Beyer, <u>Readings From the Ancient Near East</u>, 50.

109 Younger, "Religion in Ancient Israel," 401.

110 Smith, The Early History of God: Yahweh and the Other Deities in Ancient Israel, 7-8.

111 Brown, Driver, & Briggs, A Hebrew and English Lexicon of the Old Testament, 43a.

of YHWH, which became the most Holy Name for God in the Jewish religion. Because the word appears in a plural form in many sections of the Bible, with the singular form occurring only in poetry and late prose, a number of scholars have interpreted the usage of Elohim to mean that there were multiple gods during the patriarchal generation. This could explain why the appellation "El" was combined with many different sanctuaries or altars during that era, including *El-Shaddai* (God Almighty),[112] *El-Khai* (the Living God),[113] *El-Roi* (The Beholding God) at Beer-lahai-roi,[114] *El-Olam* (the Abiding God) at Beer-sheba,[115] *El-Bethel* (God of Bethel) at Luz,[116] *El-Elohe-Israel* (El, God of Israel),[117] and *El-Elyon* (the Most High God) at Jerusalem.[118] Some scholars have hypothesized that El may have actually been the original God of the Hebrews, since the name of Israel does not contain the divine element of YHWH, but rather El's name.[119]

Because the name Elohim is derived from the term El (pleural *'elim*), most biblical scholars have concluded that the appellation originated from Semites

112 This name is used when YHWH first appeared to Abraham and opened His message with the declaration "I am the Almighty God." Gen 17:1. It is used eight times in the Torah, with *Shaddai* occurring alone thirty-one times in the book of *Job*, and nine times in other sections. Ibid., 13. The Hebrew word "shadad," from which Shaddai is supposed to be derived, means "to overpower," or "to lay waste," which would imply "overpowering strength." "Names of God," 4. Feminists interpretations of the Bible have translated *Shaddai* as "breast," making God the "Great Mother." Kedar, "Va-era: The Many Names of God," 128, 132.

113 This name is sometimes combined with El- Shaddai.

114 This name only appears during Hagar's flight from Sarah's persecution. Gen 16:13. Lockyer, All the Divine Names and Titles in the Bible, 10.

115 God is referred to as *El Olam* in two sections of the Bible: Gen 21:33 and Isa 40:28. Plaut, Genesis, The Torah: A Modern Commentary, 198. It implies an Everlasting God, or God of Eternity. Lockyer, All the Divine Names and Titles in the Bible, 11.

116 Gen 31:13, 35:7.

117 This was the name Jacob gave to the altar which he erected on the piece of land where he pitched his tent before Shechem. Gen 33:20. This phrase would seem to indicate that El was the proper name for the God of Jacob. When Moses first asked the Pharaoh to let the Hebrews leave for a festival to worship God in the Wilderness, this designation as the God of Israel is used. Exod 5:1.

118 Many English Bibles refer to God as "the most high God," but the Canaanites also referred to their most high god as El Elyon, and the Canaanite king Melchizedek of the city of Salem, later renamed Jerusalem, was the priest of El Elyon. Benson, The Origins of Christianity and the Bible, A Critical Scholarly Investigation of the Sources of Christianity and the Bible, 67. The term appears four times in the book *Genesis (Gen 14:18-22)*, once in the book of *Numbers (Num 24:16)*, once in *Deuteronomy (Deut 32:8)*, twenty times in *Psalms*, twice in *Lamentations*, and twelve times in *Daniel*. Lockyer, All the Divine Names and Titles in the Bible, 9.

119 Smith, The Origins of Biblical Monotheism; Israel's Polytheistic Background and the Ugaritic Texts, 142.

who lived in Canaan before the arrival of Abraham. Wayne Pitard, Professor of the Hebrew Bible and Ancient Near East Religions at the University of Illinois, believed that this indicated that the Judaic traditions preserved "the memory that the ancestors of Israel worshiped the god El as their patron deity, and that the beginnings of the worship of Yahweh in early Israel were perceived as a break from the older tradition."[120] Albrecht Alt believed that *El-Bethel* became identified with the God of Jacob, *El-Olam* the Fear of Isaac, and the local God of the sanctuary of Mamre became identifiable with the God of Abraham.[121] Once again, the transition could have taken place at any time, and the sequence does not favor an Exodus in any particular era, since the Patriarchs are generally dated to the Middle Bronze Age, when numerous Semitic tribes roamed the ancient Near East, worshiping El, along with many other Canaanite gods. The dissident Hebrews would have been well-acquainted with the term, and included it as part of their reference to ancient family deities.

3. Adonai

A third name for God in the Old Testament is *Adonai*, a title that many scholars believe was the source for the name of the god *Adonis* among the Phoenicians and the Classical Greeks.[122] Adonai was often compounded with YHWH as a translation of the title of "Lord," with YHWH being distinguished by the use of capital letters, and Adonai having only the A in capital letters, in order to show preference for the term YHWH. Before the custom of not pronouncing the word YHWH was eased, the name Adonai was often substituted for YHWH when the Torah was read in the synagogue. Eventually, the vowels of Adonai were inserted into the name YHWH, in order to formulate the title of "Jehovah," as discussed above. Rabbinic tradition differentiated the reasoning for the names Adonai and Elohim by representing Adonai as the quality of mercy associated with the nature of God, while Elohim represented the quality of justice.[123] Orthodox Jews often restrict the use of the word Adonai ("Lord") to worship in the synagogue, and call God *Hashem* (*Hassem*, "the Name") as a euphemism in everyday conversation.[124]

The exact derivation of the name Adonai is not known, but the root "Adon" is linguistically similar to *Aten*, the name of the sun-god which Pharaoh Amenhotep IV (Akhenaten) (1352-1336 BCE) attempted to raise to the level of monotheistic

120 Pitard, "Before Israel: Syria-Palestine in the Bronze Age," 74.
121 Saggs, "Pre-Exilic Jewry,"41.
122 Lockyer, All the Divine Names and Titles in the Bible, 15.
123 The Classic Midrash: Tannaitic Commentaries on the Bible, 143. Before the twentieth century CE, the two names were sometimes combined as *Adoshem*.
124 "Names of God in Judaism," 3-4.

worship in Egypt. [125] As discussed in chapter 2, there is active debate over whether Amenhotep IV may have become enamored of Aten by hearing of Moses' arguments for the power of YHWH, or whether Moses may have been raised in the royal court of Amenhotep IV, and then resurrected the sun-god image after he fled Egypt for Midian, eventually returning to lead the Hebrews out of their enslaved state. Whether the derivation of the word "Adonai" could have been related to the name of the Egyptian god "Aten" is a question which has been raised by proponents who believe that Moses and Amenhotep IV developed monotheism in some type of cooperative effort, as discussed in Chapters 2 and 6, but the general consensus among biblical scholars is that the two names are not related.

C. Greek Polytheism

In many ways, our understanding of how a polytheistic faith functions is derived from the writings of the Greek poets, playwrights, and philosophers, who parlayed the pantheon of Greek gods into an animate procession of deities who both controlled the destiny of human beings, and interacted with them on an intimate, anthropomorphic basis. The gods would take sides in human disputes, as seen in Homer's *Iliad*, where Hera favored the Trojans and Athena the Greeks, and Aeschylus' *Orestia*, where Apollo argued that the murder of a husband and king demanded expiation, and the Erinyes demanded expiation for a matricide committed by Orestes, leaving Athena to cast a tie-breaking vote when the human jury could not come to a majority decision. The Roman Empire was so enthralled with Greek mythology that they accepted the entire Greek pantheon into their own religious hierarchy, changing the names of the gods into appellations with Latin derivations, but maintaining their essential characteristics. The Greek deities were more than vague supernatural beings to whom the populace was obliged to show proper homage and obedience, they were a network of divine personages who eliminated the rigid barrier which characterized the relationship of mortals and gods in many other polytheistic religions, including those found in Canaan and Ugarit during the Late Bronze Age. Many Greek heroic warriors had their favorite god or goddess who protected them in times of need, as evidenced by Odysseus' claim that Athena was always watching over him. This closeness was never to be taken for granted, however, for although the gods might enter into a true friendship with a person, it was not a bond between equals, and if any man or woman behaved in an inappropriate manner, as defined by the requirements of the god in question, they paid a penalty that could be extreme, and without mercy. The gods had to be obeyed no matter what was demanded, a requirement that Orestes used as a defense when he claimed that Apollo had directed him to kill his

---

125 The ancient Kemetic letter "T" is equivalent to the Hebrew letter "D".

mother Clytemnestra for the murder of his father Agamemnon.[126] If a particular god presented you with a clear and necessary task, you had to perform the deed or suffer intense consequences, a situation very reminiscent of the directive which Abraham received about the need to sacrifice his son, Isaac.

The fundamentals of this relationship between humans and gods was taught to the Greeks in numerous literary tales, beginning first and foremost with the heroic poems of Homer. Not only were the *Iliad* and the *Odyssey* the first literary texts committed to writing in the Western World, they functioned as a Bible of Greek religious behavior, providing examples of appropriate actions, just as the Torah provided commandments to those who followed the Judaic faith. Ancient Greece did not have a formal Church liturgy which set regulations about proper worship of the gods, but each city-state paid attention to the lessons of their ancestors, and rules of appropriate conduct were codified, carrying possible death sentences for those who were found guilty of violation, as was seen with the famous trial of Socrates, who was put to death for his impious behavior and teachings.[127] Impiety was not only a capital crime among the Hebrews during the Exodus, it was something which the Classical Greeks took to heart as well, and enforcement of proper homage was a vital part of protecting the welfare of the entire community from retribution by the gods. Even the Greek philosophers who began to break with the automatic assumption that the gods created the Universe, and began to search instead for natural explanations, nevertheless continued to pay homage to the *theoi* in their speculations about the higher powers, which they believed were instrumental in forming the world we live in.[128]

Although the Greeks pictured the entire world as being under the control of a variety of gods, they did set one deity above the others in both importance and strength – Zeus, a god whose Indo-European name indicates an origin that predated the Classical Age. Zeus was already one of the primary gods in Mycenae, representing the Sky Father and having one of the months named after him, but he did not become the dominant god in the Greek pantheon until after the time of Homer. His superior strength and power was dramatically evident

---

126 Euripides, "Orestes," 285-288, 129. Orestes claimed later that "it was he who commanded my mother's murder." Ibid., 416, 136. See, e.g., 592-595, 146. His defense was that "we obey the gods – whoever the gods may be." Ibid., 418, 136.

127 The charges brought against Socrates was that he "does wrong by not acknowledging the gods the city acknowledges, and introducing other, new powers. He also does wrong by corrupting the young." Parker, "Law and Religion," 67. Protagoras (c. 490-420 BCE), the Sophist with whom Socrates contended, was not killed, but his books were burned and he was banished from Athens for declaring that he could not ascertain whether the gods existed or did not. Graham, <u>The Texts of Early Greek Philosophy: The Complete Fragments and Selected Testimonies of the Major Presocratics, Part II</u>, 697.

128 Stenudd, Cosmos of the Ancients: The Greek Philosophers on Myth and Cosmology, 17.

in his role as the Weather God, hurling his mighty thunderbolts against mortals and gods alike from the top of the mountains where the storm clouds gathered.[129] This characterization was very similar to the biblical representation of YHWH appearing as a huge cloud in the midst of a terrific thunder and lightning storm during the theophany on Mt. Sinai, and in the sky during the parting of the Reed Sea.[130] The labeling of Zeus as the cloud-gatherer throughout the *Iliad* by Homer is also akin to king Solomon's declaration that "The Lord has chosen to abide in a thick cloud," which was the reason the First Temple was constructed to properly supply an appropriate abode.[131]

The resemblance between Zeus and YHWH not only included the imagery of the weather, but also the might of a warrior who could assure victory or defeat by a manifestation of his will. Zeus was the strongest of the Greek gods, and quickly challenged any other deity who showed disobedience to his commands, knowing full-well that they would have to eventually submit to his awesome powers. YHWH similarly brought His people through the Exodus into the Promised Land as a mighty war-God, and Moses told the Hebrews during the Exodus how "the Lord will battle for you," a fact that was clearly shown when the Reed Sea parted and then closed over and drowned the Egyptian military which had followed the Hebrews after the Exodus.[132] Moses repeated this forecast before the Hebrews crossed over into the Promised Land, emphasizing to the congregation that they need not fear the Canaanites for "the Lord your God, who goes before you, will fight for you, just as He did for you in Egypt before your very eyes."[133] For both the Hebrews and the Greeks, war was a battle not ultimately won by human prowess or the force of arms, but by the "free exercise

---

129 The Canaanite Baal is also depicted as grasping a handful of thunderbolts in many ancient Near Eastern myths. Walton, Matthews, & Chavalas, The IVP Bible Background Commentary: Old Testament, 352.

130 Exod 14:19-20; 19:16-19. The Prophets also utilized this description when Jeremiah warned the people of Judah that the anger of the Lord goes forth in the fury of a whirling storm (Jer 23:19), and when Ezekiel told how YHWH demonstrated His power in thunder, lightning, and rain (Ezek 1:3-4). Although some scholars, such as Mark S. Smith, Skirball Professor of Bible and Ancient Near Eastern Studies at New York University, have postulated a similarity between YHWH and Baal, based on the characterization of Baal as a storm-god, and the fact that YHWH inherited some of the names of Baal's cosmic enemies, such as Leviathan, Sea, Death, and Tannin, I find the resemblance between YHWH and Zeus to be much greater. Smith, The Origins of Biblical Monotheism: Israel's Polytheistic Background and the Ugaritic Texts, 168.

131 1 Kgs 8:12. Zevit, "First Kings," 690.

132 Exod 14:14. Sarna, Exodus, 72.

133 Deut 1:30. Tigay, Deuteronomy, 17. In the "Song at the Sea," YHWH was referred to as "the Warrior," whose right hand "shatters the foe!" Exod 15:3, 6. Sarna, Exodus, 77-78.

of God's will."[134]

This affinity between the portrayals of YHWH and Zeus was noted by number of Jewish commentators during the Hellenistic Age (323-100 BCE), when Palestine was brought under the control of the successors of Alexander the Great (356-323 BCE). In the fictional *Aristeas to Philocrates* (*The Letter of Aristeas*), a Jewish work from the first or second century BCE, the narrator, who called himself Aristeas, pointed out to King Ptolemy II that the God Who guided his kingdom was the same God which the Jews worshiped, suggesting a possible consanguinity between the ancient Hebrews and Greeks.[135] Philo of Alexandria (20 BCE-50 CE), the well-known Hellenistic Jewish philosopher who particularly favored Greek intellectual precepts, also commented on the resemblance, noting that both the Jews and the Greeks saw their primary God as "He through whom all things are endowed with life and come into being."[136] Although Philo found similitude between the Greek and Jewish philosophic tenets, he did not claim that their ancestry was the same.

The awareness by many ancient Jews of an analogy between YHWH and Zeus suggests the possibility that the Classical Greeks may have been influenced by the Jews when they elevated Zeus to a position of power above the other gods in the Greek pantheon. In support of this proposition is evidence that other Hebrew terms were also included as names for a number of Greek gods. The names of Adonai and Jehovah were directly incorporated into the Greek words for Lord, a result which would not be expected from casual contact alone.[137] The term Aidoneus frequently was used to refer to Hades, the god of the underworld;[138] while El-Elyon, or the most high God, was used to express Zeus, and El-Shaddai became the word for "Almighty" in Greek, often used to denote the god Hermes.[139] While it is possible that the Greeks were introduced to these concepts by other Eastern cultures, such as the Phoenicians, I believe it is much more reasonable to ascribe the assimilation to the dissident Hebrews, given the nature of other contributions which have been discussed throughout this book.

Sarah P. Morris, Professor of Classics and Archaeology at the University of California, Los Angeles, has pointed out another analogy between the biblical tales and Greek Gods, by noting how the talents of the Greek god Hephaestus, known for his construction of the Shield of Achilles in *The Iliad*, is reminiscent

---

134 Ibid., 78.

135 Aristeas to Philocrates, 113.

136 Wolfson, Philo, I.15.

137 Ibid., I.12.

138 In the "Hymn to Demeter," from the *Homeric Hymns*, the opening lines invoked the goddess of grain: "And now let me sing Demeter, that awesome goddess, with her beautiful hair, her and her daughter with slender feet, whom Aidoneus carried away. The Homeric Hymns, 91.

139 Graves, The Greek Myths: 1, 24.14, 95.

of the talent which YHWH endowed upon Bezalel, of the tribe of Judah, and Oholiab, of the tribe of Dan, to construct the Tent of Meeting and Ark of the Covenant, as detailed in the book of *Exodus*.[140] Rather than suggest any connection between the two, however, Morris ascribed Ugaritic and Mycenaean sources as representing a Near Eastern origin for stories of Daidalos, a mortal cult figure who was competitive with Hephaestus in epic poetry.[141]

Many classicists have ascribed the development of the Greek gods to other eastern sources, rather than the Hebrews. Charles Penglase, Lecturer at the University of Newcastle, Australia, in particular pointed out the likely origin of the Greek gods in Hesiod's *Theogony*, and the *Homeric Hymns*, from Mesopotamian sources, particularly from Babylon.[142] According to Penglase, this is especially evident in the resemblance between Aphrodite and the Mesopotamian goddess Ishtar.[143] Similar correspondence was found between Pandora and Prometheus with those of the god Enki, and Okeanos and his wife Tethys with Apsu and Tiamat.[144] Penglase argues that there are two periods of contact between Mesopotamia and Greece, primarily in trade and cultural contacts, and that was in the late Mycenaean times of the thirteenth and fourteenth centuries BCE, when the Greeks established settlements in cities like Tarsus and northwest Syria, and from 850 BCE onwards, when Greece was especially open to Near Eastern cultures.[145] While these contacts are similar to those proposed for the Phoenicians, I again will emphasize that they do not explain the type of close assimilation which I have proposed for the immigration of dissident Hebrews from the Exodus, and re not likely to have influenced the Greeks in the manner in which the Hebrews would have provided with the wide array of biblical lore.

D. Discussion

The origins of Jewish monotheism began on Mt. Sinai, when God handed Moses the Ten Commandments, the second of which proclaimed that "you shall have no other gods beside Me."[146] This mandate also included a prohibition against idol-worship, something which had been a vital part of every prior religious faith practiced in the ancient Near East. That the directive to forgo the worship of all other gods fell upon suspect ears during the Exodus is readily apparent from the actions of the Hebrews who remained in the camp when Moses ascended

---

140 Exod 31:1-11. Morris, Daidalos and the Origins of Greek Art, 97.

141 Ibid., 99.

142 Penglase, Greek Myths and Mesopotamia: Parallels and Influence in the Homeric Hymns and Hesiod, 1-2.

143 Ibid., 3.

144 Ibid., 3-4.

145 Ibid., 5.

146 Exod 20:2; Deut 5:7. Sarna, <u>Exodus</u>, 109.

Mt. Sinai, and immediately set about to build a golden calf-idol once Moses was absent for an extended period of time. Most of the congregation continued to question the authority of YHWH, refusing to cross into the Promised Land at Kadesh-barnea when ordered to do so by Moses after a foray of spies had warned of impregnable hostile forces in the region. Their apostasy so infuriated God that He decided to allow the entire generation of adults to die off before He would allow the next generation to cross the Jordan River.

As noted earlier in this chapter, this reluctance to accept the monotheistic tenets of the Mosaic Code was not confined to the first generation of adults to leave Egypt, however, as the generation which crossed into the Promised Land quickly began to worship the likes of Baal, El and Asherah during the period of the Judges, as well as during the United and Divided Monarchies. A steadfast unity of worship to YHWH alone did not take place until the return of the Jews from the Babylonian Exile (587-538 BCE), when YHWH banished His Chosen People from Palestine as punishment for their evil ways. This extensive period of time required to thoroughly change Judaism from a polytheistic to a monotheistic faith makes it clear that many dissident Hebrews during the Exodus were simply not ready to toss aside the teachings of their ancestors and modify their religious beliefs.

Once Moses started to kill any Hebrew who refused to follow the edicts of the Mosaic Code, I believe many of these dissidents emigrated to the distant shore of Mycenae, carrying with them their unique traditions, which were later incorporated into the Old Testament, and into aspects of Classical Greek culture as well.

Clearly, one of these legacies was the emphasis on the overpowering might of YHWH. Even though the dissident Hebrews were not willing to restrict their devotion to YHWH alone, especially with the added restriction of idol-worship, they were definitely impressed with the way in which YHWH was able to protect them during the intensive trials and tribulations which arose during the Sinai wandering. The stories they told fit quite nicely with the developing Greek religious mystique.

Although the early Greeks accepted that a variety of deities were important to the welfare of the community, by the time of Homer, Zeus had clearly risen above the other gods, portrayed in a manner similar to that of a general leading an army into battle. Zeus stood at the head of the pantheon of gods on Mt. Olympus, and, in my opinion, his rise to the exalted position was fueled by the stories of YHWH, Whose exploits allowed the enslaved Hebrews to break the yoke of the mightiest nation on earth.

As I will show in the conclusion to this book, the Eastern influences which have been attributed to the evolving Greek culture did not come from Phoenician or Egyptian sources, but rather came from Hebrew immigrants who fled the Exodus from Egypt after Moses ordered parricidal punishments for all those who disobeyed his Mosaic Code. The Phoenicians may have transported the Hebrews to Mycenae, but they had little to do with making the early Greeks aware of the value of the mighty Hebrew monotheistic God.

Chapter 12
SACRIFICE & CELEBRATIONS

I n the previous chapter, I discussed how the pre-Mosaic worship of ancestral gods was similar to the polytheistic faith that was prevalent throughout the Mediterranean Basin in the Late Bronze Age (1600-1200 BCE), and how the attempt by Moses to restrict homage to YHWH alone may have caused a rebellion among the congregants of the Exodus. When the dissident Hebrews traveled to Mycenae, they brought tales of a mighty God called YHWH, Who had aided their survival in the wilderness of Sinai. This characterization, in my opinion, was the impetus for the Greeks to place Zeus in a position of dominance over the other gods on Mt. Olympus. In this chapter, I am going to continue my comparison of Greek and Jewish religious practices, in order to support my claim that much of the Greek religious practice was influenced by the dissident Hebrews who arrived in Mycenae before the Trojan War.

A. Sacrifice

Although the word sacrifice is generally intended today to refer to an act of self-deprivation, the ancients saw sacrifice as a vital religious rite, which expressed reverence and thanksgiving to a god in the hope of warding off disaster, or obtaining favors. The word itself is derived from the ancient Roman *sacrificium*, which meant "to make something holy," and almost every society during the Late Bronze Age performed sacrifices, including the Greeks and Hebrews.[1] While most of the sacrificial acts were similar in the manner of their performance throughout the ancient Near East, there are certain details which suggest the possibility that the Greeks became intimately familiar with the practice through the assimilation of knowledge brought to them by dissident Hebrew immigrants.

1. Hebrews

While Judaism set aside the practice of sacrifice shortly after the fall of the Third Temple built by Herod the Great in 20 BCE, the ancient Hebrew religion was characterized by the offerings of animals and grain as an integral part of their worship to the Lord from the moment God notified Abraham that his descendants would become the Chosen People. This pattern carried on the biblical tradition which emphasized from the very start of human existence that sacrifice had to be made in a proper manner to God or no expiation would result. Such a mandate

---

1 Yerkes, Sacrifice in Greek and Roman Religions and Early Judaism, 17.

was evident when God showed a preference to the offering of Abel over that given by his brother Cain. Abel had brought the unblemished firstlings of the flock, while Cain only brought some of the fruit of the ground, implying that the gifts cost him next to nothing.[2] The obvious implication of this determination was that when one made an offering to the Lord, it had to be something of value, and not an item superfluous to wealth or happiness. Cain was so angered by the Lord's snub that he killed Abel in a jealous rage, and one wonders if he had any reason to have know his offering was substandard, given the fact that there is nothing in the Bible to suggest that any instructions were heretofore given by the Lord. Whether Cain had been educated in this regard by his father Adam or not, there is no question that future generations of Hebrews were forewarned by this tale, and when the Torah was finally compiled, an entire book (*Leviticus*) detailed exactly how the sacrifices were to be carried out.

The next episode of sacrifice mentioned in the Bible was that performed by Noah, who built an altar after departing the ark, in order to offer some of the clean animals and birds to God in appreciation for his family being saved. The Bible explained that "as Yahweh smelled the soothing odor, He said to Himself, 'Never again will I doom the world because of man.'"[3] The Rules in the Temple Scroll of the Dead Sea Scrolls emphasized this olfactory aspect of the sacrifice, making it clear that the offering of fire provided a "soothing odor before YHWH."[4] Abraham followed this same pattern of gratitude soon after he made a covenant with God, celebrating the honor he was given with an offering of a three year-old heifer, a three year-old she-goat, a three year-old ram, a turtledove, and a young bird.[5] Without describing how the offering was to be carried out, YHWH made it clear to Moses and the Hebrews that they were to give Him the firstborn among their sons, explaining later that the firstborn male of the flocks were to be sacrificed, while their own sons were to be redeemed.[6]

Although the aroma of burning the animal was likely the most propitious aspect of the Hebrew sacrifice, the expiation which accompanied the spilling of blood in the midst of the Holy Presence was also a major part of the Hebrew ritual. There are no references to the sprinkling of blood during any of the patriarchal sacrifices, but when Moses sacrificed at the altar built at the foot of Mt. Sinai following the delivery of the Mosaic Code by YHWH, the blood of the sacrificial animals was drawn into basins, and one-half was splashed against the altar.[7] To confirm

---

2 Gen 4:3-4.

3 Gen 8:21. Sarna, <u>Genesis</u>, 59.

4 Vermes, The Complete Dead Sea Scrolls in English, 195.

5 Gen 15:9.

6 Exod 13:2, 13, 15; 22:28-29; 34:19-20; Num 3:12-13; 8:17-18; 18:15. YHWH would later take the Levites to serve His needs in place of all the firstborn children. Num 3:11-13; 8:13-18.

7 Exod 24:6.

and seal the covenant which God had made with the congregation, Moses then threw the remaining blood from the basins toward the people, thereby investing them with the sanctity of the blood-ritual.[8] Not only was an individual sinner cleansed by this blood-atonement, but the whole conclave was purified as well. This magical intense use of blood as a conduit for the grace of God may be one reason why Theophrastus (372-287 BCE), the disciple of Aristotle, concluded that the Jews "were the first to institute sacrifices both of other living beings and of themselves," despite the fact that sacrifice of animals, and even human beings, dated back to the Paleolithic era.[9] Since the Greeks also practiced the blood-ritual, as will be discussed later in this chapter, it is likely that this methodology was introduced on the Greek mainland by the dissident Hebrews, although the Hebrews may have initiated the practice after encountering the rite among Arabs in neighboring lands.[10]

The biblical rules for how sacrificial worship was to be carried out appeared primarily in the book of *Leviticus*, where all sacrifices were put in the hands of the priests at select sites only. When God gave instructions for the building of the Tabernacle following the Exodus from Egypt, He selected Aaron and his sons to serve as priests, and to be responsible for the performance of sacrifices. Although the tribe of Levi was to perform important tasks in the sanctuary, neither they, nor the general populace, was given any role in the sacrificial process, which was left entirely to the priestly caste.[11] This restoration of sacrifice to a specialized priestly caste was a strict modification from what took place in many other ancient cultures, including the Greeks, where all commoners could perform sacrifices to appease deities and ask for divine assistance. Beginning with the era of the Exodus, and continuing into the period of the Conquest, Judges, and United and Divided Monarchies, it was only the priest who could offer an animal to God. Once the

---

8 Exod 24:8. Blood was seen as the seat of life, and the splashing of blood on the altar represented the sacred return of life back to the Deity, Who was responsible for the giving of life in the first place. Because life belonged to God alone, the consumption of blood by humans was strictly forbidden, a ban which led to the Kosher method of butchering. Sarna, Exodus, 152. See, e.g., Gen 9:4; Lev 3:17; 7:26; 17:10-12, 14.

9 Davies, Human Sacrifice, 32. Theophrastus (372-287 BCE) was the first to claim that the Jews practiced human, as well as animal, sacrifice. Bar-Kochva, The Image of the Jews in Greek Literature: The Hellenistic Period, 32. It is believed that Theophrastus' reference may have been to the story of the Akeda. Stern, Greek and Latin Authors on Jews and Judaism, 10-12.

10 The blood rite, with a double sprinkling first on the altar and then on the audience, was similar to the practice of ancient Arabs in neighboring lands. de Vaux, The Early History of Israel, 447.

11 Num 18:1. Leviticus, 227. This rule was sacrosanct, and God warned that "the Levites must be careful not to touch any of the sacred articles or the altar, lest I destroy both them and you." Num 18:3. The Living Bible, 129.

First Temple was constructed, the Torah restricted sacrifice to the altar at that location, and did not allow for similar structures to be placed anywhere else in the land, although, as discussed in the previous chapter, this particular regulation was not followed in the land of Israel throughout the era of the Divided Monarchy.[12]

It is generally accepted that the pre-Mosaic patriarchal heads of Hebrew families were allowed to take part in the sacrificial process, and the restrictive rules set forth by Moses to limit the task to the priests alone must have created much dissension during the Exodus, as many Elders felt that their authority to have communion with God through the sacrificial process was being undermined. Not only was homage to the gods of their ancestors forbidden, but the ability of an individual family to safeguard their future welfare through an act of sacrifice was being declared an apostasy. Many Hebrews, in my opinion, would have found it impossible to cede the practice which had been taught to them by their ancestors, once again choosing instead to migrate to Mycenae, rather than face parricidal retribution by Moses, and angry reprisals from unsatisfied deities. In Mycenae, as would carry over into ancient Greece, the head of every family was allowed to sacrifice for himself, and so the family and clan could have felt secure in their devotional practices.

Six types of sacrifices were outlined in the book of *Leviticus*, falling into three general categories: (1) "Gift-offerings," which were meant to present something to the Lord as a token of love and reverence through the burning of a whole animal ("burnt-offering," *olah)*, a non-animal gift ("cereal-offering," *twotot*), or a sacrifice of well-being (*zevach*); (2) "Fellowship-offerings," which kept communion with God by burning part of an animal and consuming the rest in a fellowship meal ("peace-offering," *shelamim*, or "thank-offering," *todah*);[13] and (3) "Cleansing-offerings," or "Purification-offerings," which were intended to remove sin through either a "sin-offering" (*hatta't*), intended to appease sins against God, a "guilt-offering" (*asam*), intended to compensate a neighbor for a wrong, or a "consecration-offering" (*milu'im*), which was offered on behalf of the priests. When Moses anointed Aaron and his sons, and conducted the first burnt-offering with a bull and a ram, a second ram was then offered as an installation-offering, placing some of its blood on the priests right ear lobe, right thumb, and right big toe.[14] Priests were consecrated to serve God by the giving of a sin-offering, a burnt-offering, and a peace-offering.[15] When thousands of

12 Lev 17:3-9; Deut 12:4-7.

13 The part offered to Yahweh, usually the fat around the intestines, the kidneys, and the liver, was burnt upon the altar, while the remainder was eaten by the persons offering the sacrifice, including the priest. de Vaux, Ancient Israel, Its Life and Institutions, 417-418. The fat could not be eaten, because it belonged to God as His share alone. Lev 3:16-17. Levine, Leviticus, 17.

14 Lev 8:22-24.

15 Exod 29:10-21.

sacrifices were offered, it was usually given in the form of the fellowship offering (*sifra*), also known as repayment offering or perfection offering, which was partly eaten.

Burning either all or part of animals and fowl as an offering to God was not an invention of the Hebrews, having been part of the worship service in Ugarit (*srp)* and Samaria for centuries, but we know more of the Hebrew process because of the detailed descriptions in the Bible. When the animal was offered on the altar, it was often prepared as an holocaust, with the entire animal entirely destroyed by fire except for the hide, which was then given to the officiating priest as compensation for his services. Because none of the meat was consumed, the sacrifice was seen as a "gift offering par excellence," providing a clear show of appreciation to God for all of His divine assistance. Two yearling lambs were to be given as a burnt-offering every day, along with a meal-offering, one in the morning and one at twilight throughout the generations.[16] On certain special occasions, the animals had to be males without blemish, but if the offender was too poor to afford an animal,[17] he was allowed to offer either two turtledoves or two pigeons, one for a sin-offering and the other for a burnt-offering. If even this was too expensive, he had to bring a tenth of an ephah of choice flour without oil or frankincense.[18] As seen with the sacrifices of Cain and Abel, the gift had to show some evidence of hardship in order to not be a superfluous show of respect, but allowances were made to assure that the loss would not be unfairly detrimental to the welfare of the family.

The actual slaughtering of the animal did not have to be performed by the priests, but they were given the sole responsibility of handling the sprinkling of blood. According to tradition, the blood was received in bowls as it spilled from the animals throat at a slaughterhouse, and was then brought to the altar where a priest dashed the fluid against two opposite corners so that it spattered on all four sides.[19] The Kohen sons of Aaron then sprinkled the blood on the walls which surrounded the altar seven times. It was the blood which made the atonement for the congregation and the individual soul. Sacrificial birds were not slaughtered in this manner, but rather were left whole, a symbol which the rabbis theorized

---

16 Exod 29:38-39.

17 Lev 1:3, 10, 14; Num 28-29. During the Divided Monarchy, the people were often guilty of providing animals that were either blind or lame as a sacrifice, and the prophet Malachi warned that such animals would not even be accepted by the provincial governors, let alone the Lord. Mal 1:6-9.

18 Lev 5:7, 11. An ephah was about two thirds of a bushel of grain, weighing thirty to fifty pounds, and representing about a month's worth of the grain ration usually allotted to male workers. Walton, Matthews, & Chavalas, The IVP Bible Background Commentary: Old Testament, 279.

19 Lev 4:4-7. Leviticus, 11.

indicated that the state of Israel would live forever.[20]

The grain-offering (*minha*) provided an opportunity for even the poorest Israelite to make a freewill- offering, and was usually made of semolina flour or grits, olive oil, and aromatic spices. It could be directly placed on the altar as a token, or be burnt as an offering, and part of the meal was usually offered to the priests for consumption. No meal-offering was allowed to be made with leaven, remindful of the restrictions which characterized the Passover celebration, although some of the cakes that were used in the thanksgiving sacrifice, and offered on the Feast of Weeks, were spared this constraint. Meal-offerings of this type were part of the ritual of all ancient peoples, and special "offering tables" made of stone have been uncovered in Egypt from as early as the Fifth Dynasty (middle of the third millennium BCE).

Purification-offerings included the giving of sin-offerings, which were required to atone for a number of sins against God, such as touching unclean things and failing to properly purify, uttering oaths which were unfulfilled, or failing to come forward with important testimony in a public matter. They were only efficacious if the offense was unwitting, and did not apply to defiant acts or premeditated crimes, which would bring upon the offender the penalty of *karet*, involving banishment or death. The reasoning behind this rule was that the law did not permit one to do a deliberate wrong and then square the account with a sacrifice, since "the sacrifice of the wicked is an abomination to the Lord."[21] An intentional sin could only be atoned through repentance, whereby the sinner confronted his misdeeds, acknowledged them, and sincerely resolved to change.[22] If the transgression was committed by a priest, or by the whole community, the sin-offering required that a bull, the largest of all sacrificial animals, be slaughtered in the interior of the Tabernacle, while if the offense was only committed by a lay individual, the type of animal used depended upon the social status of the perpetrator.

Another type of purification-offering was the guilt-offering , a compensatory sacrifice that generally required a ram without blemish to be offered, although recompense could be attained by paying an equivalent amount of silver by sanctuary weight. If the guilt involved a theft, there had to be restitution of the principal amount plus a penalty of one-fifth, in addition to a confession in order to achieve atonement. The procedural details for the performance of a sin-offering and guilt-offering were the same.

If the offerings were intended to provide atonement for the entire community, the sacrificial process could become quite immense, involving a large part of the Israelite population. When King Solomon dedicated the First Temple, for example, the celebration was so great that 22,000 oxen and 120,000 sheep were

---

20 Leviticus, 69.
21 Prov 15:8. Leviticus, 27.
22 Scherman, The Chumash, 555, 638-639.

slaughtered, an event which surely provided an impressive display to the entire population.[23]   With the destruction of the Third Temple in 70 CE, the use of sacrifice to show appreciation to the Lord ceased to be an important aspect of Jewish worship, and as a substitute, Rabbinic Judaism emphasized the faithful maintenance of the ordinances of the Torah. The study of Mosaic Law became a hallowed art, and allowed individual practitioners the ability to honor God on a daily basis. According to the Menahoth Tractate, from the *Babylonian Talmud*: "Whosoever occupies himself with the study of the laws of the sin-offering is as though he were offering a sin-offering, and whosoever occupies himself with the study of the laws of the guilt-offering is as though he were offering a guilt-offering."[24]

This evolution from sacrifice to piety as a means to show respect to God was presaged by the Prophets who forewarned the people that they could not expiate their sins against God by the sacrificial process. Amos (c. 750 BCE) explained that the Lord hated hypocrisy, and would "not accept your burnt offerings and thank offerings" if you continued to disobey the precepts of the Mosaic Code.[25] Isaiah added that the Lord had become sick of their sacrifices: "Who wants your sacrifices when you have no sorrow for your sins?,"[26] and Hosea warned that the Lord does not "want your sacrifices – I want your love; I don't want your offerings – I want you to know Me."[27] Micah cautioned that if you offered God thousands of rams and ten thousands of rivers of olive oil, He would not be satisfied and would not forgive your sins.[28] Even royalty could not rely on sacrifice to expiate impious behavior, as when Samuel reminded King Saul that he could not depend on offering the best sheep and oxen to the Lord to expiate his sin, for "obedience is far better than sacrifice."[29] It would take many centuries before Rabbinic Judaism displaced the displacement of the sacrificial process, however, and both the Hebrews and Greeks during the Late Bronze and Iron Ages continued to place great emphasis on showing homage to God, or the gods, throughout the process of sacrificial immolation.

2. Greeks

Greek religion similarly held that proper homage to a variety of gods was necessary to ensure that the populace would be free from divine retribution.[30] It

23 1 Kgs 8:63; 2 Chron 7:5.
24 "Menathoth," Babylonian Talmud, 110a, 681.
25 Amos 5:21-22. The Living Bible, 703.
26 Isa 1:11-12. Ibid., 534.
27 Hos 6:6. Ibid., 693.
28 Mic 6:7.
29 1 Sam 15:21-22.
30 In the *Iliad* by Homer, the aged Phoinix told how the immortals "can be moved;

was sacrifice, rather than faith or fidelity to a particular belief, which guided the Greek *theos*, and the deities were extremely dangerous if they were not acknowledged and placated by appropriate offerings. When a Greek city was threatened by external forces, the people turned to the gods for divine assistance, as evidenced by Aeschylus (525-426 BCE) in his play *The Seven Against Thebes*, where the chorus chanted:

Hear us, you gods perfect in power; hear us, sovereign gods and goddesses, protectors of our country's bulwarks: do not betray our city thus in the labour of battle to enemies of alien mind ... Remember the offerings of this people, and remembering, deliver us![31]

Although this requirement was primarily satisfied by the slaughter of a domestic animal, we have already seen how the offering could rise to the level of a human being, when Agamemnon was forced to sacrifice his daughter in order to appease Artemis, thereby allowing the Greek fleet at Aulis to sail away and begin the Trojan War. This reliance on sacrifice would last throughout the history of the ancient Greek civilization, defining them as pagan adherents until the emergence of Christianity in the third century CE.

The similarity to the Hebrew ritualistic methodology went beyond mere use of animal offerings, as noted by Walter Burkert, Emeritus Professor of Classics at the University of Zurich, who concluded that "the combination of food offering, libation, and burning of parts of the slaughtered animal on an altar connects Old Testament and Greek Sacrificial practice."[32] Despite the distinctly anthropomorphic element of pleasure associated with the odor of a burnt-offering, the Bible and the Greeks did not suggest that God fed on any of the sacrifice, as was common among the Mesopotamian traditions.[33] Unlike the Hebrews, the performance of sacrifice in Greece was not in the hands of a priestly caste, as individual citizens, including housewives and slaves, were able to offer an animal on the altar to seek assistance from the gods. This resulted in the sacrifice becoming a festive occasion for the whole community, with each participant taking some

---

their virtue and honour and strength are greater than ours are, and yet with sacrifices and offerings for endearment, with libations and with savor men turn back even the immortals in supplication, when any man does wrong and transgresses. Homer, The Iliad, 9.497-501, 211.

31 Aeschylus, The Seven Against Thebes, 174-181, 93. The war of the "Seven Against Thebes" is usually accepted as an actual event of the Late Bronze Age, taking place a generation before the Trojan War. Burkert, The Orientalizing Revolution: Near Eastern Influence on Greek Culture in the Early Archaic Age, 106.

32 Burkert, Greek Religion, 51.

33 Alter, The Five Books of Moses, 48. The Babylonians, Hittites, and Egyptians all viewed their sacrifices as somehow providing food for the gods. Pagolu, The Religion of the Patriarchs, 35, 37, 40. The Hebrews never described an actual consumption of food by YHWH, but the Greeks believed that the gods fed on ambrosia and nectar.

small part in communal action. A priesthood did eventually develop in order to ensure that everything was done in proper order, but it was not given the level of importance which was attained in post-Mosaic Judaism.

This ability of the Greek patriarch to maintain his authority in the sacrificial process was very similar, in my opinion, to what concerned the dissident Hebrews who I believe fled the Exodus and traveled to Mycenae before the Trojan War. The restriction of the sacrificial process to the priestly caste was one of the regulations imposed by Moses in the Mosaic Code, which the dissidents, in my opinion, rebelled against. Before that period of time, each individual family was responsible for offering gratitude to the gods, as discussed in the previous chapter, and the dissident Hebrews maintained this practice when they fled the parricidal punishments ordered by Moses. When they became integrated into Mycenaean society, their system of worship would have been seen as compatible with the ritualistic techniques of the early Greeks, allowing an easy assimilation of the Hebraic methods into the developing Greek custom, to the point of even influencing the manner in which the sacrifices were carried out.

As with the Hebrews, at the heart of Greek ritual observance was animal sacrifice. Although there were some "bloodless" sacrifices of corn, cakes, and fruit, animals were the preferred offering, and the commonest rite in Greek religions was the *thusia*, or Olympian sacrifice, an offering which began with a portion of the animal flesh being ceremonially burnt on an altar, followed by a common meal of what remained.[34] It was often called the "fire rite," or the "smoke rite," with reference to the force of the fire, which in Greek mythology had been stolen by Prometheus from Zeus, and then given to mankind at the dawn of human evolution. A description of the *thusia* is present in the opening book of the *Iliad*, where a feast is prepared by Chryses in thanksgiving for the return of his daughter. After an initial prayer, grains of barley were scattered and the animal was sacrificed and thigh pieces burnt in offering to the gods, followed by the eating of the animal along with libations of wine.[35] Like the Hebrew offering, sacrifice was seen as a "gift to the gods," a combination of sharing that closely resembled the Hebrew "fellowship-offering," and was not generally found among the Canaanite rituals.[36] In the sacrifices which were offered to heroes, the funerary or oath sacrifices, or the sacrifices performed before battle, the victims were burned entirely.

The most common animal to be sacrificed was the sheep, but the most noble animal was the ox, especially the bull. The sacrifice of poultry was also common,

---

34 Yerkes, <u>Sacrifice in Greek and Roman Religions and Early Judaism</u>, 93. The bones, gall bladder, and fat were burned on the altar as an offering to the gods. Hughes, <u>Human Sacrifice in Ancient Greece</u>, 4.

35 Homer, <u>The Iliad</u>, I.447-473. The process is repeated at II.422-423.

36 de Vaux, Ancient Israel, Its Life and Institutions, 440.

although it was unusual for birds such as geese and pigeons to be used in an offering. As with the biblical practice, the animal chosen had to be perfect, and there was ample spreading of blood on the altar (*haimassesthai*). In Sparta, when the animal was sacrificed, blood would be sprinkled on the altar, as was described in the book of *Leviticus*, even when the sacrificial animal was a human being.[37] To stain the altar with blood was considered a pious duty, and a bloody altar, or *haimassesthai*, was considered a characteristic of the sacrificial act. Since the Hebrews were generally seen in ancient times as the initiators of this particular facet of the sacrificial process, it is likely that the practice was suggested to the Greeks by the dissident immigrants from the Exodus. The animal was then skinned and butchered, and the inner organs, especially the heart and liver, were the first to be roasted on the fire. Unlike the biblical traditions, tasting the entrails became the privilege and duty of the innermost circle of participants. The Greeks did not perform a holocaust sacrifice as often as the Jews, except in the cult of the dead, when a corpse was totally burnt on a funeral pyre, but the smoke which traveled up to the heavens was again believed to please the olfactory senses of the gods.[38] Libations, or the pouring of wine on the altar, also regularly accompanied the rituals, an act that was very common during the Late Bronze Age. Libations which were poured on the earth were destined for the dead, and for the gods who dwelled in the earth, and was the method by which Odysseus conjured up the dead in the *Odyssey*, pouring three libations into an offering pit, first with a honey drink, and then with wine, followed by water, and then strew white barley over the ground.[39] The use of wine was also common in the Jewish rituals, although it was primarily given center stage in various parts of the family celebratory process, rather than during the priestly sacrifice itself.

In addition to these sacrificial similarities, the Greeks purified murderers from blood guilt by utilizing the blood of a piglet which was poured over the head of the man, as first depicted by Aeschylus with Orestes. Although Burkert attempts to trace this origin to Mesopotamia,[40] I believe it is part of the Hebrew ritual, first promulgated by Moses, and then passed to the priestly caste, as described above.

B. Celebrations

Another indication that there may have been interaction between the ancient Hebrews and Greeks was the resemblance between certain celebrations carried

---

37 Spiegel, The Last Trial: On the Legends and Lore of the Command to Abraham to Offer Isaac as a Sacrifice: The Akedah, 64.

38 I Burkert, <u>Greek Religion</u>, 56, 59, 63.

39 Homer, <u>The Odyssey</u>, 10.518-526.

40 Burkert, The Orientalizing Revolution: Near Eastern Influence on Greek Culture in the Early Archaic Age, 55-60.

out by both societies, particularly the Hebrew Festival of Tabernacles and the Greek rites of Dionysus. In the Bible, Moses was told by the Lord that there were to be five annual festivals when the people of Israel were to assemble and worship the Lord. These included the Passover of the Lord (*Pesach*); the Festival of Unleavened Bread (*Chag Hamatzot*); the Festival of First Fruits (*Bikkurim*, also known as the Festival of the First Wheat); the Festival of Pentecost (*Shavu'ot*), also known as the Festival of Weeks, or Feast of Weeks; the Festival of Trumpets (*Yom Teruah*), when the shofar was sounded; the Day of Atonement (*Yom Kippur*); and the Festival of Tabernacles (*Sukkoth*), also known as the Feast of Tents, Feast of Booths, or Feast of Ingathering.[41] The Festival of Weeks, the Festival of the First Wheat, and the Harvest Festival were particularly important as all the men and boys of Israel were to appear before the Lord on each of these occasions.[42]

The Festival of Tabernacles was the most important, and most crowded, occasion for rejoicing in biblical times, whereby came its name *zeman simhatenu*, "the time of our rejoicing."[43] Josephus referred to it as "the holiest and the greatest of Hebrew feasts."[44] It was to be observed for seven days, seven weeks after the harvest began, when the grain was threshed and the grapes pressed. Because the Hebrews uncharacteristically spent so much time celebrating during this week-long festival, decorating themselves and their surroundings with vine and ivy tendrils and imbibing large amounts of wine, a number of ancient commentators pointed out that their festivities were very similar to the rites of Dionysus, a joyous celebration of the harvest which first appeared in Greece about 1000 BCE.[45] Dionysus was the son of Zeus and Semele, and was born from the thigh of his father, where he was concealed until the time of his birth, after his mother died from seeing the face of Zeus. He was also known as Bacchus, which is believed to be a Semitic loan-word meaning wailing, and some scholars have suggested that this may explain why the women of Israel bewailed Tammuz, an ancient nature deity who was worshiped in Babylonia.[46] Because Dionysus was a bastard son of her husband, Hera was angered at his birth, and attempted to kill him and drive him mad. To escape her retribution, the young god wandered all over the world, spreading the vine-cult over Europe, Asia, and North Africa, accompanied by his tutor Silenus and a wild army of Satyrs and Maenads, whose weapons were ivy-twined staffs called a *thyrsus*. Although he represented the force of life in all growing things, animal and vegetable, he became particularly regarded as the

---

41 Lev 23:1-34. The reference to the Festival of Tabernacles being a Feast of Booths came from the practice of dwelling in booths, or bowers, made of branches and foliage during the seven-day festival. Lev 23:42-43. Tigay, Deuteronomy, 469.

42 Exod 23:17; 34:23.

43 Ibid., 158.

44 de Vaux, Ancient Israel, Its Life and Institutions, 495.

45 Stapleton, The Illustrated Dictionary of Greek and Roman Mythology, 69.

46 Ezek 8:14. Burkert, Greek Religion, 163.

god of the vine, and his celebrations made free use of this intoxicating beverage. His worship in Greece dates to Mycenaean times, and perhaps even earlier to Minoan times, and the Dionysian cults of the seventh and sixth centuries BCE were revivals, and not new creations.

There were at least four types of Greek festivals which celebrated the attributes of Dionysus: the Anthesteria festival in the Ionic-Attic area, which was directly concerned with wine-drinking; the Agrionia festival in the Dorian and Aeolic area, which involved a women's uprising with madness and cannibalistic fantasies; the Greek Country Dionysia, which was the original rite from which the Lenaia and the City Dionysia were derived, consisting of a procession of wine and vines, followed by a he-goat and basket of raisins which were used to crown the phallus; and the Great Dionysia, which was introduced in Athens in the sixth century BCE and was celebrated with a procession of ships.[47]

Plutarch (45-125 CE), the Greek historian, biographer, and essayist, was intrigued by the similarity between the Jewish and Greek festivals, noting that the Festival of Tabernacles was celebrated at the height of the grape vintage, when the Jews set out tables of all sorts of fruit under tents and huts, plaited with vines and ivy, while the Greek festival of Bacchus was a sort of "Procession of Branches," or "Thyrsus Procession," in which the celebrants entered the temple carrying a thyrsus.[48] Plutarch implied that the Jews were aware of this resemblance, and that they testified to a "connection with Dionysus when they keep the Sabbath by inviting each other to drink and to enjoy wine."[49] He went on to describe how the High Priest of the Jews "leads the procession at their festival wearing a mitre and clad in a gold-embroidered fawnskin, a robe reaching to the ankles, and buskins, with many bells attached to his clothes and ringing below him as he walks," pointing out a resemblance not only in the method of revelry to the Greeks, but also in the manner of priestly dress.[50] By his descriptions, it is clear that Plutarch believed that the Jews had likely copied their festival from the Greeks, following the usual Greek pattern of ascribing their own culture as the instigator, rather than follower, of most civilized practices.

The Roman historian Tacitus (55-117 CE), who was a contemporary of Plutarch, also observed how the Jewish priestly garb resembled the Dionysian costumes. In *The History*, he described how they "made use of fifes and cymbals: they were crowned with wreaths of ivy and a vine wrought in gold was seen in their temple."[51] It is not clear if Tacitus ascribed the origin of one to the other, but the tone of his description suggests that he also saw the Greek practice as the

---

47 Parke, Festivals of the Athenians, 101; Burkert, Greek Religion, 163.

48 Plutarch, "Table-Talk IV," Question 6, 2.671D, <u>Moralia</u>, 363.

49 Ibid., 363-365.

50 Ibid., 363.

51 Tacitus, <u>The History</u>, V.V, 289.

primal event. Once again, we have a situation where a likely Hebrew influence on the early Greek culture is ignored, and the Greeks are given credit for an influence I don't think they deserve.

This similitude between the two festivals was not mentioned by other ancient authorities, but in modern times, Erwin Goodenough (1893-1965 CE), the late Yale Psychologist of Religion, declared that the Jews often performed dance routines in various ceremonies while wearing laurel crowns and offering libations of water and wine, which were similar to the Bacchanalian rites.[52] Goodenough described how bread often appeared in Jewish figures, depicted as round objects or baskets of loaves, while similar objects were frequently represented in Dionysiac scenes as well. He noted that wine was the primary symbol of Dionysus, and also a prominent symbolic element for the Jews during this festival, particularly by the time of the Maccabees (167-160 BCE), when Greek influence among the Jews had reached its peak.[53] Goodenough did not comment on how the relationship came about, but Robert Graves (1895-1985 CE), the English poet, novelist, and critic, concluded that "the rites of the Jews were founded in honour of Dionysus."[54]

One aspect of connecting the rites of Dionysus with ancient Hebrew sacrifices also includes the similarity of satyrs, who are half-human and half-goat, with the goat-demons in the book of *Leviticus*, who the people were said to be sacrificing to in the fields, and were to cease by bringing their offerings to the priests instead.[55] The Hebrew word *sair* is identical with the word for he-goat, and has suggested to some scholars that the Greek word satyr is a derivative.[56] The annual sin-offering on the Day of Atonement involved the offering of two goats – one to be sacrificed for the Lord, and the other to be set free into the desert as a scapegoat.[57] This latter goat was designated in ancient times as "for Azalel," considered to be an evil supernatural being, and during the days of the First Temple in Jerusalem, the goat was pushed off a cliff into the rugged rocks of the desert in Judea known as Azazel.[58] This was a symbolic representation of the sending back the people's sins and evil consequences to the spirit of desolation and ruin. While it maybe simply coincidental that these two events were similar in terminology, it remains an intriguing possibility that their origins are based in similar celebrations..

Although Goodenough and Graves accepted a similarity between the Festival of Tabernacles and the Bacchus rites, most modern scholars continue to explain

---

52 Goodenough, "The Problem of Method/Symbols From Jewish Cult," 184.

53 Ibid., 100.

54 Graves, The White Goddess, 335.

55 Lev 17:7. It was in this section that the Israelites were told that sacrifice was to be restricted to the Tent of Meeting, and eventually to the First Temple in Jerusalem.

56 Harris, "Leviticus," 595.

57 Lev 16:8-10.

58 "Azazel," 1-3.

away the similitude as simply being due to coincidence, rather than cause and effect, once again ignoring any possible relationship between the ancient Hebrews and Greeks. Roland de Vaux (1903-1971 CE), the former Director of the Ecole Biblique et Archeologique in Jerusalem (Dominican Biblical School), typified this stance by observing that there is no basis to conclude that the similitude was a purposeful deed, despite the fact that some writers had suggested that the relationship was real.[59] How de Vaux and others came to this conclusion is not clear, but I believe it is once again reflective of the general scholastic view which ignores Hebrew contributions to Greek civilization, and argues that the numerous concordances pointed out throughout this book support the contention that the Greeks were aware of the Hebrew festival, leading to the development of similar unique characteristics, which were then recognized by Plutarch and Tacitus. The only question is whether it is possible that the interaction took place during the Hellenistic Age, rather than being derived from the dissident Hebrews migrating to Mycenae before the Trojan War. Although the Festival of Tabernacles is clearly discussed in the Torah, the celebration is not described in any detail, for the revelry did not appear until much later, when the Dionysian rites were already a commonplace event. Because I believe that the Hebrew sacrificial process was transported to the Mycenaeans by the dissident Hebrews who fled the Exodus, I favor that the concept of the Festival of Tabernacles was initiated at that time, although it is possible that the biblical descriptions were flavored by the compilers awareness of Dionysian rites, which had begun to appear during Hellenistic times.

---

59 de Vaux, Ancient Israel, Its Life and Institutions, 500.

FLOOD MYTHOLOGY

T he legend of a great Flood, sent by an angry god to destroy the world as punishment for the evil nature of mankind, is a common tale found in the folklore of many ancient societies. Lloyd Bailey, Professor of Religion at Mount Olive College, collected 302 texts which told of a great deluge destroying the world, including multiple stories from Mesopotamia, Egypt, Greece, and Syro-Palestine.[1] Because few legends "spring out of nothing," the shear number of stories of a flood has led researchers to investigate the archaeologic record for signs of such an event, and possible evidence has been found in the bed of the Black Sea, where remains of freshwater molluscs are contained in an older silt level, indicating that the Black Sea may have once been a freshwater lake which was altered when the Ice Age began to melt c. 5600 BCE, causing the Mediterranean Sea to spill over the Bosporus Strait into the lake.[2] Whether these ancient tales were responsive to memories of a factual or fictional event is not likely to ever be answered with certainty, but what really matters is that most ancient societies sought to describe the event as having been due to the actions of a Deity, and the question then arises as to which one came first, and whether they developed independently or in unison.

Although modern religions tend to accentuate the more passive and beneficial attributes of Divine Beings, ancient people often portrayed their deities as a jealous breed, who had to be obeyed and appeased or severe punishment would be meted out to individuals, as well as to entire populations. Gods were not gentle souls who readily accepted views not identical with their own; they fought with rival gods in order to dominate their realm, and their anger was often directed at human beings who, despite being their favorite mortal part of creation, were frequently destroyed because they did not behave in an appropriate manner. The methods of execution were quite varied, but when large numbers of people had to be annihilated for a particularly detestable behavior, the choice of a Flood to bring about widespread devastation was a customary tale. Although the basic storyline appears quite similar among these many diverse cultures, the Jewish and Greek traditions are remarkably alike, and I am going to argue in this chapter that this is due to the Greeks having been introduced to the legend by dissident Hebrews who migrated to Mycenae before the Trojan War. I will analyze the story of the biblical Flood, and compare its details to earlier Mesopotamian sources, in order to show that the Hebrews were likely introduced to the concept by their Near

---

1 Bailey, Noah, The Person and the Story in History and Tradition, 6.
2 Wilson, <u>The Bible Is History</u>, 20-21.

Eastern neighbors, but that the Greeks then followed the Hebrew model when they developed their own particular fable.

A. The Story of Noah

The biblical story of Noah and the Great Flood is generally ascribed by literary criticism to the "J" and "P" traditions, with most scholars proposing that the basic plot was initially borrowed from a Babylonian tradition, which told of an earlier calamity that almost wiped out mankind. There are four major literary accounts of this Flood in the ancient Near East record, including the Sumerian account of the story of Ziusudra, appearing in accounts from c. 2300 BCE, clearly before the era of the Patriarchs;[3] the eleventh tablet of the Akkadian text of the *Epic of Gilgamesh*, an historical king of Uruk (c. 2500 BCE), which described how Utnapishtim and his family survived a Flood that killed all of the world's inhabitants;[4] the *Atrahasis Epic*, which is believed to be the parent version of the Gilgamesh epic, dating to the first half of the second millennium BCE, close to the era of the Patriarchs; and the account of Berossus, a Babylonian priest of Marduk from the third century BCE, who included a saga of a Flood in his history of Babylon, *Babyloniaca*, c. 280-270 BCE, near the time when the Hebrew Bible was being collated.[5] The name of the surviving mortal differed in each of these versions, with Ziusudra appearing in the *Sumerian Flood Story*, Utnapishtim in the *Epic of Gilgamesh*, Atrahasis in the *Atrahasis Epic*, and Xisuthros, the tenth king of Babylon, in the *Babyloniaca* of Berossus.

The resemblance of the plots in all of these fables suggests that the stories may have been inspired by a single historic event, although there is no consensus on when such an occurrence may have taken place. Archaeologic studies in Mesopotamia have shown evidence of massive flooding by periodic rainfalls which inundated the flat alluvial valley between the Tigris and Euphrates Rivers before the Early Bronze Age (3000-2000 BCE), and it is possible that the memory of that event was repeated in oral traditions for centuries before being recorded in

---

3 This legend is also known as the *Eridu Genesis* or *Sumerian Flood Story*. Schmidt, "Flood Narratives of Ancient Western Asia," 2339. Ziusudra is a god-fearing king who in the Sumerian king list is supposed to have ruled over Sumer from his capital city Shuruppak. Kramer, "The Deluge," "Sumerian Myths and Epic Tales," 42.

4 The Sumerian King-list assigned Gilgamesh to the First Dynasty of Uruk, and allowed him a reign of 126 years, between 2700-2500 BCE. He was said to be two-thirds god and one-third man, and possessed inexhaustible energy and strength, performing heroic deeds very much in the manner of Heracles. Heidel, The Gilgamesh Epic and Old Testament Parallels, 3, 11.

5 Berossus wrote the *Babyloniaca* as a new national tradition in response to the treatment of Babylonian history by the older Greek historians, and utilized texts that had been preserved in Babylon over a very long period of time as his primary sources. Van Seters, Prologue to History: The Yahwist as Historian in Genesis, 67.

a permanent format. The Euphrates River repeatedly shifted its bed over the course of this era, with one particularly severe flood dated to around 3000 BCE, a chronology that would fit the timeline of the Babylonian legends quite well. Although layers of waterlaid silt found deep below the surface at sites such as Ur, Kish and Shuruppak have led some archaeologists to claim that the destruction was the result of a Great Flood, similar to the biblical Deluge, most scholars believe that the findings are due to local inundations over different eras, downplaying the likelihood that an actual Flood like that described in the Bible left its mark in the historical record.

While any of the early Mesopotamian tales could have been the model for the biblical story, it is the *Epic of Gilgamesh* which has received the most attention, since it has survived in a remarkably complete form, and is from a civilization which most biblical scholars believe provided other material for the biblical compilers. As I describe the details of the biblical account, I will therefore provide equivalent information from the Gilgamesh legend as well, in order to highlight areas which are either similar or different from the biblical text. In this way, I hope to show that while the biblical story may have been influenced by the Gilgamesh text, the Greek Flood mythology seems to be more in line with the biblical account, which made significant changes.

The biblical story of the Flood is told in the book of *Genesis* 6-9, and begins with God viewing the contemporaneous generation with disdain, regretting His decision to create mankind because the progeny which evolved from the sexual union between evil beings from the spirit world and mortal human women were so distasteful and impious. In His infinite mercy, He searched for some type of solution which could possibly save humanity from being totally destroyed, and after a long deliberation, He finally decided to give the human race one hundred and twenty more years to mend their evil ways or face annihilation. After the allotted time had passed, God once again looked down upon His creation, but did not see enough improvement to satisfy His anger. He therefore decided to remove all mankind from the face of the earth by sending a Flood which would destroy all living beings, man and animal alike. During His preparations for the disaster, God noted the presence of one righteous (*tsaddik*) and blameless (*tamim*) man on earth, who had always tried to conduct his affairs according to His will.[6] This pious soul was Noah, and in His infinite mercy, God decided to save Noah from the holocaust, as well as his wife and three sons Shem, Ham, and Japheth (Yefeth), along with their wives, and a pair of every bird, animal and reptile.[7]

6 Gen 6:8-10; 7:1. Sarna, Genesis, 50. Many authors have pointed out that God referred to Noah as the most righteous of his generation, indicating that he was not righteous in absolute terms, but rather was the best his generation had to offer.

7 Japheth was actually the eldest son, but rabbinic scholars (Sanhedrin 69b) claim that Shem was mentioned first because Scripture enumerated them according to wisdom, rather than age. The Semites, including the Hebrews, were descended from Shem. Scherman,

In the Mesopotamian tales, there was evidence of a similar type of divine mercy, although concern was not uniform among all the gods. In the *Eridu Genesis* (columns III-VI), the *Atrahasis Epic* (tablet III), and the *Gilgamesh Epic* (tablet XI), the god Enlil was distraught about the noise of mankind, rather than immoral behavior, and he decided to destroy humanity in order to achieve some peace and quiet. He had no intentions of sparing any human being from his anger, but another god, Enki (Ea), the god of wisdom and civilization, was sympathetic to humankind, and warned Utnapishti (Atrahasis), to build an ark, which kept him alive as the rains came for seven days before he landed on Mount Nisi (Nisir). This particular concern for human welfare was unique to Enki's general description, and it showed how a polytheistic faith was able to segregate out the benefactors to mankind, so that special homage could be paid to those specific gods. The legend, however, was not intended to warn mankind to behave in a moral, pious manner, but rather to show how the power of the gods was all-encompassing, and worthy of reverence and respect.

To survive the Deluge which YHWH had planned for the world, Noah was directed to build an ark (*tevah*) that measured 300 x 50 x 30 cubits.[8] By most modern estimations of the size of a cubit, this resulted in a vessel that was about 450 x 75 x 45 feet in size, displacing 43,000 tons, somewhat smaller than the size of the ocean liner *Titanic*, which was 825 x 93 feet, with a displacement of 46,000 tons.[9] Most biblical readers do not imagine an ark this size, but while of considerable dimensions, the biblical ship was about one-third the size of Utnapishtim's vessel, which was a gigantic cube, 200 x 200 x 200 feet, displacing over 200,000 tons.[10] The description of the biblical ship was much more sea-worthy in design than that in the *Epic of Gilgamesh*, and even used techniques of shipbuilding that were widely available in ancient times, including the use of gopher wood, and the covering of both the inside and outside of the vessel with pitch.[11] If the biblical

---

The Chudash, 31.

8 Gen 6:15. Tradition sources vary on how long it took Noah to build the ark, ranging from 52-120 years. Rappoport, Ancient Israel, Myths and Legends, 209-210. The ark was a three-storied ship, having a window and a door, and Talmudic comment varies on how many rooms were included, varying from 330-900 cells. Patai, The Children of Noah: Jewish Seafaring in Ancient Times, 7-8.

9 Rehwinkel, The Flood: In the Light of the Bible, Geology, and Archaeology, 59.

10 The Illustrated Family Encyclopedia of the Living Bible, I.31. The vessel described by Berossus was 1,000 yards long, and 400 yards wide. Patai, The Children of Noah: Jewish Seafaring in Ancient Times, 5.

11 Gen 6:14. Sarna, Genesis, 52. The exact nature of the construction material is still not known today. Some scholars have interpreted the term "gopher wood" to mean either cedar or cypress wood, since gopher means a common tree in Hebrew. Sailhamer, "Genesis," 83; Genesis, The Old Testament Study Bible, 63. Utnapishtim and Atrahasis also used pitch to caulk their respective ships. Matthews & Benjamin, Old Testament

compilers took the basic storyline of the Flood from the ancient Babylonian text, the construction of the ark likely came from factual contemporary information, rather than legendary heresay.[12] While the description thereby seems more sound from an engineering standpoint, it should be remembered that the vessel did not have to be actually sail on the waters, since there would be no shore to sail to, but simply be able to float until the waters abated.

Once the ark was completed, Noah was commanded to enter with his entire family, including his wife Naamah, the daughter of Enosh, his three sons and their wives, and all the animals, one week before the rain began to fall.[13] The delineation of how many animals were taken on board differs in various sections, with the "J" source stating that there were seven pairs of clean animals admitted, and only one pair of each unclean animal, because sacrifices of clean animals would have to take place before procreation could occur.[14] In the "P" source, however, only one pair of every animal was admitted, because the rules for sacrifice were not yet laid out, so there was no need to differentiate the nature of clean and unclean.[15] Noah did not apparently ask for clemency for his contemporaries, as did Abraham when he heard of God's plan to destroy the cities of Sodom and Gomorrah, although tradition holds that it was Noah who transmitted God's warning to the populace to change their evil ways before the rain began to fall.

The Flood took place when Noah was 600 years old, with a torrential rain that began as "all the wellsprings of the great deepburst and the casements of the heavens were opened."[16] The rain fell for forty days and nights (Gen 7:12), an interval corresponding to the forty years the Hebrews had to wander in the wilderness before God allowed them to enter the Promised Land, followed by a period of one hundred and ten days (Gen 7:24), when the waters remained covering the earth. This was followed by another seventy-four days to let the waters gradually decrease (Gen 8:5), and then forty days more before Noah sent out a raven to see if dry land had appeared. (Gen 8:6-7). When the raven

---

Parallels: Laws and Stories From the Ancient Near East, 24.

12 The relations between the length, width, and height of the ark was 30:5:3, a ratio which might be observed in war galleys at any seaport in ancient times, although none of the ships reached the size of Noah's ark. Patai, The Children of Noah: Jewish Seafaring in Ancient Times, 4-5.

13 Although Noah's wife is never named in the biblical text, Naamah is her name according to biblical legend. Spitzer, "Noach: Mrs. Noah," 53. Estimates of the total number of species which were saved by being brought aboard the ark have ranged from 17,600-35,000. This, of course, did not require the protection of fish, which were impervious to the flood waters. Whitcomb, Jr., & Morris, The Genesis Flood, The Biblical Record and Its Scientific Implications, 65-69.

14 Gen 7:2, 14-16.

15 Gen 6:19-20. Frazer, Folklore in the Old Testament, 61.

16 Gen 7:11. Alter, The Five Books of Moses, 44.

returned to the ship, Noah sent out a dove three times, one week apart (Gen 8:8, 10, 12), and then another 86 days passed before Noah finally left the ark (Gen 8:13), giving a total of 285 days from the start of the rain until the time of disembarkation. As the water slowly receded, the ark which carried Noah and his family ultimately landed on top of Mt. Ararat, a sight which is still unidentified today, although many theories abound on its precise location.[17] The choice of Mt. Ararat as the landing place is also seen in the Hurrian flood legend, which has led some scholars to support the possibility that the deluge may have occurred at the end of the Ice Age, c. 5600 BCE, when the Mediterranean Sea is thought to have spread over the Bosporus into what was then a freshwater Black Sea lake, as discussed earlier.[18]

The extended period of time which Noah spent on the waters is much more impressive than the *Epic of Gilgamesh*, where the rain lasted for only seven days, an interval that does not seem adequate for such a destructive Deluge. Once again, this is consistent with the Bible's attempt to tell a tale that did not require a great leap of faith to accept the fact that YHWH had intended to destroy all of humanity, except for His select chosen few. Even though the duration of the rain was much shorter, the ship which saved Utanapishtim landed in a similar area as Noah's ark, finally coming to rest on Mount Nisir, near the mountains of Ararat.

The fact that Noah opened the window of the ark, and sent out a raven to see if there was any dry land on which the ship could alight, is again consistent with contemporary knowledge about seafaring techniques, where ancient mariners frequently took birds aboard their ships, in order to determine their proximity to land. Ravens were recognized as carrion-eaters, able to feed on the carcasses of dead animals, so if the raven did not return, then it was likely that there was a food supply on dry ground in the nearby vicinity. Since the raven flew back and forth in the biblical tale, but constantly remained near the ark, it indicated that the flood had not yet dropped to a level where dry land appeared. Seven days later, Noah released a dove, which was a valley-bird that fed off the foliage of trees which would rise above the water. When it also returned without evidence of finding anything to eat, Noah knew that the waters had not yet receded to a safe level. Seven days later, he released the dove again, and this time the bird returned with an olive leaf, indicating that the waters had begun to subside to a level where

---

17 Gen 8:4. The Living Bible, 6. Ararat is known as Urartu in Assyrian inscriptions, and is believed to be part of a mountain range in present-day Armenia, between the River Araxes and Lake Van, near the origins of the Tigris and Euphrates rivers. Sarna, Genesis, 57. The *Book of Jubilees* claimed that the ark came to rest on Mount Lubar, one of the Ararat mountains in Armenia. Views of the Biblical World, I The Law, 33. In the Koran, the ark rested upon Mt. Judi (Gudi, Kudi), part of the great mountain mass of the Ararat plateau. Sur 11.3.44. Ali, The Meaning of the Holy Qur'an, 522.

18 Wilson, The Bible Is History, 22.

the branches of trees appeared.[19] Noah waited another seven days to allow for further seepage into the ground, and then sent the dove out again, but this time the bird did not return, a sign that the earth was finally dry.

This use of birds to determine the presence of dry land was also utilized in the *Epic of Gilgamesh*, where Utnapishtim opened a window and sent out a dove, then a swallow, and finally a raven, which did not return, indicating that the flood waters had finally receded and it was safe to land.[20] The fact that both tales utilized methodology well-known to sailors at the time clearly indicates the desire of both authors to make the story as believable as possible to their intended audience. Ronald Hendel, the Norma and Sam Dabby Professor of Hebrew Bible and Jewish Studies at the University of California, and editor-in-chief of *The Oxford Hebrew Bible*, points out that neither story required the use of birds to tell the waters had abated, since both legends had the ship land on top of a mountain, allowing for full view of the surrounding domain, but "the sending of the birds is a colorful motif that slows down the action – thereby creating suspense – and vividly depicts the passage of time."[21] This decision of both authors to use the description of the birds in such a similar manner strongly suggests, in my opinion, that there was an awareness of the subsequent author of the prior account, and the known timeline would strongly suggest that the biblical tale followed that from Babylonia.

Unlike the Mesopotamian stories, where the hero left the ship as soon as the vessel landed, Noah waited for God to tell him to disembark, since it was clear that the entire event was being orchestrated by a divine plan. Once Noah stepped on dry ground, he built an altar to the Lord and sacrificed burnt-offerings in order to show appreciation for his survival.[22] God was pleased with the sweet aroma, and promised Noah that He would never curse all of humanity again, and that the earth would never be totally destroyed. In a similar fashion, Utnapishtim set up seven kettles with sweet cane, cedar, and myrtle in order to please the gods with sweet savor, but no direct communication with a god took place. As discussed in chapter 12, sacrifice to the gods was an important element of all ancient civilizations, and the actions of the survivors of the Flood to show their gratitude to the gods fit the standard model of pious behavior.

---

19 The choice of an olive tree reflects the fact that olive trees are difficult to kill, and a freshly plucked shoot shows Noah that recovery has begun. The olive is also a symbol of new life and fertility to come after the Flood. Walton, Matthews, & Chavalas, The IVP Bible Background Commentary: Old Testament, 38.

20 Ibid. Berossus stated that there were three separate dispatches of birds, but did not give details of which birds were involved. Sarna, Genesis, 57.

21 Hendel, The Book of *Genesis*: a Biography, 28.

22 Gen 8:20-21. The sacrifice and the building of the altar appear only in the "J" source, as the priestly tradition would not allow for a sacrifice by a layman, or outside the temple in Jerusalem. Frazer, Folklore in the Old Testament, 61-62.

The Bible used this occasion to emphasize the unique relationship between mankind and God, ratifying the Lord's promise to make a sacred covenant (*berit*) with the human race for the first time in the biblical text.[23] To remind Noah's descendants of this solemn pact, God placed a rainbow in the sky after a rainstorm, a sign of His pledge to never again wash away mankind.[24] This promise did not mean that God was satisfied with the nature of man, however, for He explained that "man's heart is evil from his youth," thereby initiating the concept of original sin.[25] God also commanded Noah to be fruitful and multiply, in order to repopulate the planet. It was Noah's descendants who, like Adam's progeny, would become the generation of the entire human race, unlike the Gilgamesh epic, where Utnapishtim, after being granted immortality along with his wife, was removed from human society. The Bible was doing more than simply extolling the powerful nature of God, it was explaining the unique relationship that the Hebrews would inherit by becoming the descendants of Abraham, God's next favored human being, ten generations later. The Mesopotamian tales did not use this event to claim that a close bond was created between Utnapishtim and the gods.

The Bible went on to use God's covenant with Noah to explain other attributes of the human civilization which evolved from Noah's ancestry. The first was that the Lord gave Noah and his descendants permission to eat animal flesh, a right which had not been granted to Adam. This bequest was restricted by the prohibition against the ingestion of blood, however, for blood represented the soul of man and was therefore forbidden to be eaten.[26] In addition, Noah was allowed to become a "tiller of the soil," once again an improvement over Adam's fate, which decreed that the earth would only produce thorns and thistles during the lifetime of Adam and his descendants.[27] Man would now be able to cultivate the earth, and provide not only an abundant food supply, but also a soporific beverage to appease his troubled soul.

All would not be well, however, for almost immediately, Noah planted a vineyard and when the harvest was completed, he "drank of the wine and became

---

23 Gen 6:18. Sarna, Genesis, 53.

24 Gen 9:12-17. Scherman, The Chudash, 42-43. The rainbow appears in ancient Babylonian, Arab and Indian legends as a symbol of the heavenly host, often appearing in the sky after victory over their foes. The Illustrated Family Encyclopedia of the Living Bible, I.34.

25 Gen 8:21. Scherman, The Chudash, 41.

26 The sanctity of blood is apparent in God's commandment that "whoever sheds the blood of man, by man shall his blood be shed; for in the image of God He made man," a passage which has been used by advocates who claim that the use of capital punishment is forbidden by the biblical text. Gen 9:6. Scherman, The Chudash, 41.

27 Gen 9:20. Ibid., 65.

drunk."[28] While lying naked in his tent in a stupor following this event, Noah was seen by his middle son, Ham, who did not cover this father's disgrace. Shem and Japheth then entered the room and took a garment to cover their father, walking backwards with their faces turned away so as not to witness Noah's nakedness.[29] Ham was punished for his inconsiderate behavior by having his son Canaan be cursed by Noah to forever become a slave to his cousins' families. This extreme punishment is believed to reflect the use of the phrase in biblical times which implies that to *see* nakedness means to have sex, which in this case would be homosexual rape, while to *uncover* nakedness means to have sexual relations with the wife, which would imply that Ham had incest with his mother. In either case, the passage clearly placed an atrocity upon Ham, and thereby on the Canaanites, whose territory the Hebrews would inherit when they took control of the Promised Land.

The Bible then completed the story of the Deluge by explaining the heritage of the world's population in the Table of Nations, which told how the lands of Shem's descendants would eventually embrace the area stretching from the Iranian mountains into northern Mesopotamia, Syria and the Arabian Peninsula; the Japhethites would populate the areas of Anatolia, the Greek mainland, and the islands of the eastern Mediterranean; and the Hamites, whose descendants were cursed by Noah to be the slaves of his brothers, would comprise the extensive areas of the river civilizations of the Nile and the Euphrates, as well as some parts of southern Arabia. The total number of nations delineated by the passage was seventy, a number that was topologically important in the biblical world, generally used to convey the notion of the totality of the human race.[30] We will see in the next section how the Greek legend also used the Flood to describe the heritage of the Classical Greek civilization, while the Mesopotamian stories were not intended to be part of a larger epic tale.

---

28 Gen 9:21. Sarna, Genesis, 65. The earliest evidence of wine-making comes from neolithic Iran, in the Zagros region, where archaeologists have discovered a jar with a residue of wine from the second half of the sixth millennium BCE. Walton, Matthews, & Chavalas, The IVP Bible Background Commentary: Old Testament, 39.

29 Gen 9:21-26. The book of *Leviticus* forbade one from uncovering the nakedness of anyone of his own flesh, which generally implied a family member. Lev 18:6. Schwartz, "Leviticus," 250. The shame of Noah resembles the shame of nakedness which Adam and Eve experienced after eating the forbidden apple from the tree of the knowledge of good and evil.

30 Ibid., 69. The household of Jacob that went down to Egypt was also comprised of seventy souls, while the representative body of the entire community of Israel in the wilderness consisted of seventy elders. Gen 46:27; Exod 1:5; 24:9; Num 11:24.

B. The Story of Deucalion

The Greek legend of a great Flood is preserved in the *Bibliotheca*, a work that has often been attributed to Apollodorus of Athens (second century BCE), but more likely was written by his contemporary, Pseudo-Apollodorus.[31] Reference to the story can be found as early as the fifth century BCE, in both the Greek historian Hellanicus (fl. fifth century BCE), and the lyric poet Pindar (522-443 BCE), so the exact date of origin is uncertain. This timeline is either later than, or contemporary with, the postulated manuscripts of the Documentary Hypothesis, and many scholars believe that the Greeks may have received the story of Noah from early copies of the Torah, rather than from oral legends that found their way into Greece from a myriad of Eastern sources. In my opinion, however, the genesis is more likely part of the multitude of Old Testament tales that were transmitted by the migration of dissident Hebrews who fled the parricidal reprisals of Moses.

To try and determine if the biblical tale, rather than Mesopotamian manuscripts, was the more likely source for the Greek story, it is necessary to compare the two legends and analyze which elements favor one derivation over the other. An important part of this examination is the role which the inciting god played. In the Greek version of the myth, Zeus decided that the present race of man was not worthy of survival because they acted in an immoral manner, a decision that was very similar to that of the Hebrews. Greek mythology held that there were Four Ages of Man: the Golden Age, or the Age of Cronos, before the reign of Zeus, where men lived alongside the gods; the Silver Age, where men were less noble and neglected to worship the gods, leading to their eventual destruction; the Age of Brass, where men were terrible and strong, but fought with each other and perished by their own hands; and finally the Iron Age, which was the era in existence at the time of the flood. Zeus found that mortal humans during the Iron Age were evil in their behavior to other men, and that they did not properly give homage to the gods, so they deserved to suffer the same fate of their unworthy ancestors. This concern of Zeus with the moral activity of men, rather than with the mundane annoyance of their day-to-day activity, is more suggestive of an Hebraic origin than Mesopotamian, since the Bible made it clear that the cause of the Flood was the impious activity of the human race, rather than irritating conduct, which was the precipitating event in the Mesopotamian sources.

Zeus was especially upset over the actions of the barbarous Arcadian King Lycaon (Lynceus), the son of Pelasgus who was feared throughout the land. Lycaon was the first man to civilize Arcadia, and even though he instituted the worship of Zeus Lycaeus in his own land, he angered Zeus by sacrificing a boy to him, rather than a bull or a ram. In anger, Zeus had him changed into a bloodthirsty wolf. The sons of Lycaon continued to commit innumerable crimes,

---

31 Schmidt, "Flood Narratives of Ancient Western Asia," 2344.

so Zeus decided to destroy all mankind in retribution. Initially, he planned to burn the world into ashes by hurling his devastating thunderbolts, setting the world ablaze. But this tactic worried Zeus for the flames might burn heaven as well, so he then decided to send a Flood to destroy mankind instead. Just as Noah was the only righteous man worth saving in the Hebrew Old Testament legend, Zeus discerned that Deucalion, the king of Phthia, and son of Prometheus, and his wife, Pyrrha, the daughter of Spimetheus and Pandora, were better than any of the other human beings, and deserved to survive the Deluge. He therefore had them float safely with their son Hellen in a wooden chest, and when the waters abated after nine days of rain, the vessel landed on top of Mt. Parnassus, near Delphi.[32] Deucalion showed his appreciation by sacrificing to Zeus, once again following the pattern of Noah. Like both the biblical and Mesopotamian tales, Deucalion was reassured by a dove sent on an exploratory flight that there was dry land nearby, a consistency which does not favor any particular source to the story. In some versions of the myth, Deucalion was said to have brought the invention of wine to Greece, just as Noah was the one to invent viniculture in the Bible, although the Greeks mostly suppressed this generative part of the story in favor of the god Dionysus, who became the celebrated deity of wine.

While the Greeks accentuated the disappointment of Zeus with the moral behavior of the human race as the reason for the Flood, they did not spend much detail on the description of the vessel, or on the survival of the animal kingdom, focusing instead on the role of Zeus as the primary god who determined the fate of all human beings, a trait which closely approximated the monotheistic stance of YHWH. Zeus' decision to save Deucalion, and have him begin a new generation of humans, was similar to the role of Noah, although in true Greek xenophobia fashion, the only future descendants mentioned were those of the Greek race. The son of Deucalion and Pyrrha, the survivors of the flood in Greek mythology, fathered Dorus, Aeolus and Xuthus, the latter then fathering Ion and Achaeus, leading to the major subdivisions of the Hellenes: the Dorians, Aeolians, Ionians and Achaeans. To the Greeks, their own progeny were the only ones worthy of mention, but the identification of the Flood as the event which brought about the identity of the Greek population is a sequence which closely follows that of the Bible.

C. Discussion

While it seems clear that the similarities between the biblical and Mesopotamian tales indicate a likely transference from the more ancient Near-eastern source to the biblical compilers, the question of where the Greeks may have obtained

---

32 Other versions claim that they landed on Mount Othrys in Thessaly, or Mount Aetna in Sicily, as well as other locations. Guthrie, In the Beginning: Some Greek Views on the Origins of Life and the Early State of Man, 25.

their information about a Deluge which destroyed mankind has never been fully answered. That the Greeks utilized one of the Eastern myths in the evolution of many of their own traditions is widely accepted, but who transmitted this data, and from what region of the ancient Near East, is still uncertain.

I believe that a comparison of the details of the various Flood myths supports the proposition that the story was initiated in Greece, along with many other legends and practices, by the dissident Hebrews who fled the Exodus and traveled to Mycenae before the Trojan War. The basis for my premise rests upon the fact that both the biblical and Greek tales blamed the evil nature of man for the necessity to destroy humankind, resulting in the survival of one righteous family which then provided a generating seed for the evolution of their respective populations. This sequence differs greatly from the Mesopotamian tales, which punished annoying behavior by humans, rather than impiety, and used the story to fictionalize the anthropomorphic behavior of their deities, rather than use the event to explain the origin of their civilization. In addition, YHWH and Zeus are the only Gods to take part in the great Deluge, despite the fact that the Greeks, like the Mesopotamians, believed in a polytheistic pantheon of deities. As discussed in chapter 11, I believe that this primary role of Zeus in the Flood legend was a byproduct of the supreme position which the Hebrews gave to YHWH, eventually resulting in Zeus playing a dominant role in the hierarchy of the gods, almost rising to the level of a monotheistic force. Although the dissident Hebrews refused to cede the existence of other gods, as demanded by the Mosaic Code, they still were impressed enough by the feats of YHWH to portray Him as a mighty War-God, with weapons which included lightning and thunder-bolts, and the Greeks transposed the story of the biblical Flood to involve Zeus alone as the god who determined the structure of their contemporary society.

Chapter 14

HEBRAIC INFLUENCES ON GREEK PHILOSOPHY

Ancient and modern scholars have uniformly recognized that Greek philosophy set the framework for the development of Western intellectual thought. The word "philosophy" in Greek literally means "love of wisdom," and it was during the Greek Archaic Age (850-480 BCE), the dynamic era of Greek intellectual advancement between the time of Homer and the Persian Wars, that men first began to inquire into the first principles and causes of things, including the formation of the world itself. Although the use of the word "archaic" today has generally come to mean something which is primitive or antiquated, it was applied to this magnificent period in ancient Greece because it truly can be seen as the start of an intellectual revolution, particularly in the field of philosophy, where rational investigation into "cosmogony," from the Greek words *kosmos* meaning "order," and *genesis*, meaning "birth," first began. Unlike the cosmogonies associated with theology, which generally ascribe the generating force to a deity, the opinions of a philosopher required that there be a rational basis for the theory, and not merely the description of a myth. Homer and Hesiod discussed how the world was created by gods in a mystical process unamenable to scholarly debate, but the Greek philosophers put forth hypotheses which could be scientifically argued and tested. As noted by W. K. C. Guthrie (1906-1981 CE), the former Laurence Professor of Ancient Philosophy in the University of Cambridge, "with the Greeks we stand at the beginning of rational thought in Europe."[1]

The first Greek philosopher whose name and teachings survived the test of time is Thales (c. 624-546 BCE), who postulated that the world was fundamentally made of water, thereby placing the question of the formation of the universe on a platform that could be tested. Thales, and his fellow Milesians Anaximander (610-546 BCE) and Anaximenes (585-528 BCE), gave birth to the twin studies of philosophy and science, and scholars ever since have acclaimed their introduction of "a new kind of wisdom to the world."[2] While I agree with the basic premise

---

1 Guthrie, A History of Greek Philosophy, Volume I, The Earlier Presocratics and the Pythagoreans, 1.

2 Graham, <u>The Texts of Early Greek Philosophy: The Complete Fragments and Selected Testimonies of the Major Presocratics, Part I</u>, 1. While the Greeks are accredited with the institution of philosophical thought, they are clearly not the first people to record philosophical maxims. That credit goes to the Egyptian vizier Ptahhotep, whose maxims

of all of these assessments, we must remember that no original Greek manuscript, in the hand of the actual author, has survived intact, meaning that we must rely on reports that are extant in authors who lived centuries later. While this is not necessarily an extreme detriment to reasonable interpretations of what the early Greek philosophers may have proposed, it does leave open a window of interpretation to the sources they turned to, and it is this aspect which I want to expound upon in this chapter.

It is important to remember that the early Greek philosophers, generally referred to as the Presocratics because they lived before the time of Socrates, did not develop their innovations in a vacuum of intellectual endeavors. While they are generally credited with being the first to apply rational thought to scientific principles by historians of the Western World, it is clear that much investigation into similar matters was being conducted throughout the civilized world, beginning with the Babylonians and Egyptians.

We know that Herodotus made contact with Egyptian priests during the writing of his magisterial *The History*, and I believe that he and other early Greek scholars crossed the Mediterranean Sea to study with these Near-Eastern sources. During these travels, I believe that they also encountered beliefs that were being distributed throughout these same regions by Hebrew prophets, and were made aware of circulating copies of the Documentary Sources that were being compiled into the Hebrew Bible at the time.[3] Greek pottery has been found in Samaria from as early as the eighth century BCE, indicating commercial ties between the two countries, and struggles between Athens and the Persian empire in the fourth century BCE would have called the attention of the Athenians to the land of Israel. This is made more credible by Herodotus mentioning Ashkelon (I.105.2-4) and Cadytis (presumably Gaza) (3.3.1-2) in his fifth century BCE *The History*.[4]

Although many Jews were exiled from Jerusalem during the Babylonian Exile, Jewish communities were established in many of the key cities in Egypt and Babylonia, and many of the Jews who had risen to high status were allowed to practice their religion freely. The books of the Prophets were written during the times of Homer, while the *Chronicles* reflect the period of the great Athenian dramatists. This coexistence led Othniel Margalith to conclude that the presence

---

were discovered on a bit of frayed papyrus from 2500 BCE. Holliday, <u>The Dawn of Literature</u>, 6-7.

3 That translations of the Hebrew parchments into Greek or Aramaic may have existed prior to the standard translation into the Septuagint during the reign of Ptolemy II is suggested by the *Letter of Aristeas*, where Demetrius of Phalerus, the king's librarian who was appointed with the task of preparing an approved copy of the Torah for the Library at Alexandria, apparently suggested that a new text be prepared for others "have been transcribed somewhat carelessly and not as they should be." "Letter of Aristeas," 30, <u>The Old Testament Pseudepigrapha</u>, vol. 2, 14.

4 Feldman, Jew & Gentile in the Ancient World, 3.

of Greek words in the Bible is likely due to the fact that the bulk of the *Pentateuch* and Prophets was written before the return from the Babylonian Exile, and the most likely source of these inclusions is an interaction between the two groups of authors.[5] Following the Conquest of Judah by the Babylonians, many of the Hebrews fled to Egypt before they were deported during the Exile. In the late seventh and early sixth centuries BCE, Judaean clay pottery has been found in a number of sites in the Egyptian Delta indicating the presence of a resident Judaean trading and refugee diaspora. When Alexander conquered Egypt, and the Macedonian dynasty was set up by Ptolemy I Soter in 305 BCE, Jewish emigration to the region increased greatly.[6]

Hebraic teachings, whether encountered in Egypt, Canaan, or Babylon, would have certainly interested the Greek philosophers who were searching for knowledge from other cultures, for, as Arnaldo Momigliano (1908-1987 CE), former Professor of Ancient History at the University of London, has proposed, "when Jews were discovered at the end of the fourth century BC, they appeared, of course, as a new variety of Brahmins or magi."[7] Plato, in particular, would have likely been very impressed with the ancient writings of the Hebrews, and the reliability of their wisdom having been handed down for hundreds of years, since he had Critias relate a story near the start of *Timaeus* of how an Egyptian priest had chided Solon, the wisest of the Seven Sages, for thinking that the Greeks were learned when their civilization had been frequently destroyed by numerous natural disasters, so that they were more like children than learned men, since they did not have a tradition based on a long recorded history.[8]

Clearchus of Soli (fourth century BCE) in a dialogue on *Sleep*, wrote that Aristotle considered the Jews the descendants of the Indian philosophers called Kalanoi, an impression also stated by Megasthenes (third century BCE), another indication that their teachings were equivalent to those of other respected cultures.[9] In addition, Hecataeus of Abdera (fourth century BCE) presented the

---

5 Margalith, The Sea Peoples in the Bible, 14-15.

6 Barclay, Jews in the Mediterranean Diaspora: From Alexander to Trajan (323 BCE-117 CE), 20. *The Letter of Aristeas* claimed that Ptolemy I moved up to 100,000 Jews from Judah into Egypt. Ibid., 21. This included not only soldiers and slaves, but a large number of economic migrants. Ibid., 22.

7 Momigliano, Essays on Ancient and Modern Judaism, 17.

8 Zeyl, "Timaeus," 22-24. Herodotus noted how Hecataeus had once proudly claimed in Thebes that he was able to trace his ancestry back sixteen generations to a god, and an Egyptian priest had shown Herodotus a visual recording of a family tree that had gone back for 345 generations, and never claimed descent from a god. Herodotus, The History, 2.143, 194.

9 Momigliano, Essays on Ancient and Modern Judaism, 17. In his work *Indica*, Megasthenes stated that the ancients' opinions concerning nature could be found among philosophers outside Greece, among them the Indian Brahamans, and others in Syria

banishment of the Hyksos from Egypt as an expulsion of foreigners, part of whom were led by Moses to Palestine, where he founded the Temple of Jerusalem and promulgated laws in "the great tradition of philosopher-leaders."[10] The accounts of Theophrastus (372-387 BCE), Hermippus of Smyrna (third century BCE), and Megasthenes (c. 350-290 BCE) also referred to the Jews as philosopher-priests.[11] This continual reference to the wisdom of the Hebrews would have made it natural for traveling Greek scholars to study their work when they visited Babylon and Egypt, where the Hebrews were then residing.

In addition to wanting to learn the Hebraic concepts about cosmology and allied precepts about law and the social order, the Greek intellectuals would have been interested in what the prophets were saying about foreign nations which also affected the lives of the Greeks, such as the Egyptians, Babylonians, Assyrians, and Phoenicians. Although the prophets primarily directed their frightening oracles to the citizens of Israel and Judah, their addresses were given publicly, and available to all who wanted to listen, especially since many of the speeches were translated into Aramaic, the tongue which was till used by many of the Hebrew citizens.[12] Such tirades could be found in *Ezekiel* 25-32, *Isaiah* 13-23, *Jeremiah* 46-51, and *Amos* 1-2. The Greeks during this era were very much a regional power, and the Greek philosophers all held important governmental positions, which would have required that they become aware of the teaching and actions of their contemporary neighbors.

As I mentioned, the Greek intellectuals did not have to learn the Hebrew language to study foreign texts, or listen to the tirades of the Hebrew prophets, for portions of the Old Testament, as well as speeches to the public, were often translated into Aramaic in order to aid interested Hebrews in comprehending the lessons therein. Momigliano has emphasized that "the Jews of the postexilic period spoke Aramaic and therefore were able to read the gentile literature in this international language of the Persian Empire.[13] In addition, from 586-331 BCE, the Jews had been deported to Assyria and Babylon, and during this time, many of the Jews adopted the Aramaic language, which was the official language (*lingua franca*) of Babylon at the time.[14]

---

called Jews. Feldman, Jew & Gentile in the Ancient World, 7-8.

10 Ibid., 18.

11 Bar-Kochva, The Image of the Jews in Greek Literature: The Hellenistic Period, 7. Some authors even went so far as to claim that Greek philosophy did actually originate from Judaism, referring to it as "the theft" of Jewish wisdom by the Greeks. Ibid., 8.

12 Aramaic gradually replaced both the Phoenician and Hebrew languages throughout Syria and Palestine, and was utilized by Christians, Jews, and pagans. Healey, The Early Alphabet, 11-12. Ezra is generally credited with having introduced the Aramaic script during the return of the Babylonian Exile. Ibid., 32.

13 Momigliano, The Classical Foundations of Modern Historiography, 12.

14 Benson, The Origins of Christianity and the Bible, A Critical Scholarly Investigation

In the synagogues, when the Hebrew Old Testament was read aloud, a meturgeman (professional interpreter) would translate it orally into Aramaic and try to reproduce the original text. Because there were no vowels in Hebrew, however, the results were sporadic and undirected.[15] While written versions of these translations became more common after the destruction of the Second Temple in 70 CE, it is likely that versions existed during the time of the Presocratic philosophers, and that the traveling Greek philosophers and authors would have had access to the manuscripts as well. This is particularly important, for Babylonian literature was also translated into Aramaic, explaining why the Babylonian *Talmud* shows a great deal of Aramaic influence, while the Jerusalem *Talmud* shows primarily Greek influence.[16] Traveling Greek scholars would therefore have access to both Jewish and Babylonian writings through the available Aramaic translations, and, in my opinion as I will discuss throughout this chapter, they showed evidence of being influenced by what they read and heard. Although Tertullian (160-220 CE), the Christian apologist who is referred to as the father of Latin Christianity, famously queried "What has Athens to do with Jerusalem," attempting to show that the teachings of Scripture and philosophy were incompatible, I believe his fundamental assessment is flawed, given the availability of these Aramaic translations.[17]

Not only would the Greeks have been intrigued with the position put forth by the Hebrews, but much of the Hellenistic (323-100 BCE) Jewish population was also comfortable with the teachings of Greek philosophy, finding a similarity between the tenets proposed by both their ancestors and contemporary Greek teachers. The Hellenic Jews found it easy to merge their religious beliefs with the writings of the Greek philosophers because they saw elements that were very close to the precepts which they ascribed to Moses in the pages of their Torah, a synergy which I believe the Greek philosophers would have also seen. Although scholars have often noted an Eastern influence throughout much of Greek culture, they have generally argued that it was the Phoenicians, or other Eastern mystics, who provided this direction.[18] The Hebrews, however, are a more likely

---

of the Sources of Christianity and the Bible, 9.

15 Ibid. This was apparent in the book of Sirach (Ecclesiasticus), where a translator in 132 BCE was concerned that some phrases were rendered imperfectly "for what was originally expressed in Hebrew does not have exactly the same sense when translated into another language." Ibid., 10. For the purposes of the Greek philosophers, an exact translation was not important.

16 Geller, "The Survival of Babylonian Wissenschaft in Later Tradition," 2.

17 Tertullian, De Prescriptione Haereticorum, 7.9

18 Although most ancient and modern historians accepted an Eastern influence on early Greek philosophical thought, some historians of philosophy, like Frederick Copleston (1907-1994 CE), the former Professor Emeritus of Philosophy in the University of London, decried such a proposal, claiming that the Greek philosophers and writers

source, given the fact that there was a genetic consanguinity between the two civilizations, as discussed earlier in this book. Although there is no clear evidence that the Greeks actually knew Jewish historians directly before this period of time, there is indisputable evidence that both the Greeks and the Jewish historians were in contact with the Persians, and the Byzantine scholar Photius (c. 815-897 CE), in his summary of Diodorus' (first century BCE) Book XL, attributes to Hecataeus of Miletus (c. 550-475 BCE) a description of Jewish religion that, if authentic, would indicate that Hecataeus "knew something of the Sacred Books of the Jews at the end of the sixth century BCE."[19] This is at the very start of Greek philosophic and theatric evolution, and Hecataeus would have been a salient lynchpin for providing information from the Persians to both the Greeks and Hebrews, since he traveled in the Persian Empire as a Persian subject during the period of Persian rule in Judah (536-336 BCE).[20]

Clement of Alexandria, the second century CE Athenian who converted to Christianity, pointed out similarities between the Greeks and the Judeo-Christians, and claimed that the Greeks drew their great ideas from the Old Testament.[21] Bezalel Bar-Kochva, Professor of the History of the Jews in the Ancient World at Tel Aviv University, points out that the Jews in the Hellenistic Age were seen as a group of philosophers similar to the Brahmans, and this may very well explain why the early Greek philosophers looked to study their treatises, along others in Egypt and Babylon.[22] Although the eminent British philosopher Bertrand Russell (1872-1970 CE) claimed that the Milesian Greek school "was brought into existence by the contact of the Greek mind with Babylonia and Egypt," I think it more likely that the teachings of the Torah had a major influence as well.[23]

I should point out at this juncture that my contention that the Greek scholars were influenced by Hebraic and biblical thought applies only to the individuals themselves, and to their resultant writings and teachings, and not to the Classical Greek culture itself. The willingness of the Greeks to travel throughout the ancient Near East during the Archaic Age is well-attested, as I will describe throughout this chapter, and it is through this interaction that they became interested in Hebrew

---

knew nothing of the teachings in Egypt and Babylon, and that the Oriental-origin theory was an imagination of Alexandrian writers. Copleston, A History of Philosophy, Volume I Greece and Rome, 14. Copleston argued that "Science and Thought, as distinct from mere practical calculation and astrological lore, were the result of the Greek genius and were due neither to the Egyptians nor to the Babylonians." Ibid., 16.

19 Momigliano, The Classical Foundations of Modern Historiography, 9.

20 Ibid.

21 Bar-Kochva, The Image of the Jews in Greek Literature: The Hellenistic Period, 142.

22 Ibid., 158.

23 Russell, A History of Western Philosophy, 28.

legendary material. One need only look at the journey of Herodotus (490-420 BCE), the generally accepted "father of history," who traveled widely to gather material for his book, to realize that many of the philosophers that preceded him took a similar trip. Such excursions were not costly, and Herodotus visited many sites along the main caravan route from Palestine to Egypt, including Thasos, Tyre, Heliopolis, Buto, and other places in Egypt, as well as Gaza and Babylon.[24] That he may have encountered Jews during his travels is suggested by the fact that his mention of the circumcised Syrians in Palestine is, according to Josephus, an actual reference to the Hebrew custom.[25] Herodotus was a contemporary of the Jewish Prophets Ezra, Joel and Obadiah, as well as the Greek tragedists, and the philosophers Anaxagoras and Leucippus.

Sara Mandell, Professor of Interdisciplinary Arts and Sciences at the University of South Florida, and David Noel Freedman (1922-2008), former holder of the chair of Hebrew Biblical Studies at the University of California, San Diego, have noted that there are remarkable similarities between Herodotus' *History*, and the Primary History of Ezra, who is credited as the editor who divided the Old Testament into the parts which became the *Pentateuch* and the Prophetic were "too numerous to be either accidental or merely characteristic of a shared genre."[26] They went on to suggest that there may have been shared knowledge between the two men that led to this similarity, and that this particularly was evident in the fact that both the Jewish Primary History, and the writings of Herodotus and the Greek tragic playwrights "paid attention to the relationship of a man or a state to the divine."[27] They further opined that "if one of them had access to the other's work, it would have been Herodotus who had access to Primary History as both re-divided and received by Ezra," since Herodotus knew Aramaic, or would have had access to a translation, and was a contemporary of Ezra.[28] While this hypothesis is not a generally accepted premise among historians, it points out that an Hebraic influence is consistent with what is known about the two ancient cultures, and that further investigation into the relationship between the Hebrew prophets and the Greek scholars is necessary in order to study how the two cultures may have closely intermingled.

---

24 Myres, Herodotus: Father of History, 5-7.

25 Feldman, <u>Jew & Gentile in the Ancient World</u>, 4. This opinion would be bolstered by the statement of Theophrastus that the Jews were a part of the Syrians. Ibid., 7.

26 Mandell & Freedman, The Relationship Between Herodotus' *History* and Primary History, ix.

27 Ibid., 143.

28 Ibid., 175. After Ezra instituted the reading of the Torah to the public at the beginning of the Second Temple era, c. 445 BCE, a group of Levites would stand at his side in order to expound the full significance of the text, making it possible for those who did speak Aramaic to fully comprehend the message. Steinsaltz, <u>The Essential Talmud</u>, 14.

Later in this chapter I will give detailed citations about where the important Greek philosophers traveled and were alleged to have learned the teachings of former and contemporary colleagues throughout the world. I will also analyze the writings of the tragedists, and show where they were likely influenced by Hebrew motifs.

A. Cosmogony in Hesiod

Although the exact date of the writings of Homer and Hesiod, the first two examples of extant Greek written treatises, is not known, Homer is believed to have lived in the ninth century BCE, and Hesiod in the eighth century BCE. While Homer is generally accorded the title of being the first author in the Western World, the first written texts of his work that have survived date to the second century BCE, although there is evidence that written texts were widely available in the sixth century BCE.[29] It is clear that his books were used to instruct the youth of Greek throughout the Classical Age, and his influence on all of Greek culture is immense. His reputation as one of the greatest authors of all time led Professor John Sutherland, Modern English Professor of Literature at University College London, in 2008 to extol Homer and the Bible by noting that "was there ever a more heady literary cocktail than these two ... it's literary nuclear fusion."[30]

But Homer's importance is due to his two epic poems, *The Iliad* and *The Odyssey*, being used as the compendium of early Greek legendary thought about the Trojan War, and the relationship between gods and men, with little necessity to supplement or modify those basic facts. Homer was not commenting on the appropriateness of those events, he was recording history with a masterful recollection that painted a landscape with such beautiful strokes that readers still marvel at the brilliance today.

The Oxford classical scholar Sir Cecil Maurice Bowra (1898-1971 CE) may have pointed out that "when we speak of the poet or poets of the Homeric poems, we must always remember that any passage or phrase may well be inherited from other poets before them," but it would be impossible, in my opinion, to try and point to any particular source as influencing the greatest writer of all time.[31]

Hesiod, on the other hand, is generally seen as the major source for ancient Greek mythology, and while much of his work involved simple descriptions of the gods and Greek heroes, he was the first to record a cosmogony, which resembled that found in the book of *Genesis* so closely, that I believe it is likely that Hesiod used the knowledge he gained from Hebraic sources to write the *Theogony*. If Hesiod indeed lived during the eighth century BCE, he would have been contemporary with the events which took place during the Assyrian Conquest

29 Edwards, <u>Homer, Poet of the *Iliad*</u>, 23, 26-27.
30 Classics of British Literature, Part 1, The Teaching Company, 2008.
31 Bowra, "Composition," 39.

of Israel in 722 BCE. Hosea, the first of the Hebrew prophets to commit his prophecies to writing, and Amos, who originally was a shepherd, began their work during the reign of Jeroboam II in Israel, and Uzziah in Judah, and therefore would have been very accessible to Hesiod if he traveled at all out of Greece.

Pagan worship had a resurgence during this era, and the prophets Hosea and Amos waged a war of vocal condemnation. As Hosea said of the rule in Israel: "They have made kings, but not with My sanction."[32] Micah added that YHWH will destroy Samaria and "tumble her stones into the valley and lay her foundations bare."[33]   Anarchy reigned in the royal residence as Shallum assassinated Zechariah, and Menahem then killed Shallum. Menahem's son Pekahiah was later assassinated by his chariot commander, Pekah, who tried to put together an alliance to resist Assyrian subjugation. As the prophet Hosea warned: "there is no honesty and no goodness and no obedience to God in the land."[34] Pekah was eventually assassinated by Hoshea, who was prepared to submit to Assyria's Tiglath-pileser III (745-727 BCE), but then, after the death of the Assyrian king, when Shalmaneser V (727-722 BCE) rose to power, Israel fell in 722 BCE. The prophecies of the fall of Israel would have been seen by Hesiod as evidence of the power of the gods, especially the power of the One Almighty God, YHWH, and we will see how his conception of the beginning of the world, in my opinion, was influenced by the book of *Genesis*.

In addition to the prophets, Hesiod would have begun to have access to circulating manuscripts prepared by the authors of the Documentary Hypothesis treatises, as discussed in chapter 4. That theory, developed by Julius Wellhausen (1844-1918 CE), a German biblical scholar from the University of Greifswald, remains viable with modifications today, and considers that the final edition of the Torah was written in four stages: a history by the Jahwist (J), who used *Jahweh* for the name of God throughout the book of *Genesis*, written in the tenth century BCE, during the rule of King Solomon (970-930 BCE), or shortly thereafter in the ninth century BCE; a history by the Elohist (E), using *Elohim* as the name of God, written in the eighth and ninth century BCE; a history by the Deuteronomist (D), found primarily in the book of *Deuteronomy*, written in the seventh and sixth centuries BCE, during the Josianic reforms; and a history by the Priestly (P) source, which added material related to worship and genealogical lists, written in the fifth century BCE. The various sources were then combined into larger units by theologians whose efforts labeled them as Redactors (R), and the final fusion of the various sources into the Torah to some time during the post-exilic period, c. 450 BCE, close to one thousand years after the Exodus. During Ezra's rearrangement, the Primary History was created, and this would include a timeline whereby the First Bible was compiled c. 560 BCE, the Second

---

32 Hos 8:4. Zvi, "Hosea," 1155.
33 Mic 16. Zvi, "Micah," 1206.
34 Hos 4:1. Zvi, "Hosea," 1149.

Bible c. 518 BCE by Redactors, and finally, Ezra's Bible, or the Third Bible, c. 430 BCE.[35]

This timetable means that early manuscripts of the eventual biblical sources were available to scholars during the earliest inception of Greek philosophical thought, including the era of Homer and Hesiod, as well as the Presocratic philosophers. It is even possible that some of these may have been already translated into Greek before the legitimate translation of the Septuagint, which is supposed to have taken place sometime around 250 BCE. This is suggested by the passage in Josephus, where he had access to the letter which Demetrius sent to Ptolemy II Philadelphos (283-246 BCE) asking for assistance to obtain a new translation of the Hebrew Bible for the Library at Alexandria, for they are written in Hebrew, and are unintelligible in that tongue. He added that "it hath also happened to them, that they have been transcribed more carelessly than they should have been," an indication that translations may have been made by others who were not careful enough to assure their validity, and not of the caliber to be included in the Alexandrian collection.[36] This does not mean, however, that the early Greek philosophers who traveled to Egypt and Babylon would not have access to these early manuscripts, and learned of the Old Testament tales either through Greek translations, or with the aid of interpreters. According to Professor William Albright, considerable copying was done in Egypt in the post-exilic times, making the availability to interested scholars more likely.[37]

All of this prevalence of Hebraic material, I believe, affected Hesiod's understanding of cosmogony. Where Homer sought to expound on the heroic feats of the Trojan War, and therefore restricted himself to standard ancient Greek legendary material, Hesiod set out in the *Theogony* to explain the origin of the gods and the cosmos, stepping outside the realm of oral history.[38] In his discussion of Creation, Hesiod's words and concepts are extraordinarily analogous

---

35 Mandell & Freedman, The Relationship Between Herodotus' *History* and Primary History, 84-86, 89.

36 Josephus, "Antiquities of the Jews, The Complete Works of Josephus, XIII. II.4, 247. He also claimed, however, that the scribes accurately reproduced the ancient writings, and "no one has been so bold as either to add anything to them or take anything from them, or to make any change in them." Josephus, "Against Apion," The Complete Works of Josephus, I.8, 609.

37 Albright, Yahweh and the Gods of Canaan, 28-29.

38 Although Homer did not discuss a cosmogony, per se, Aristotle pointed out that he did make Ocean and Tethys the parents of creation (Homer, Iliad, 14.201, 299), and also described the oath of the gods as being by water (Homer, Iliad, 2.755, 96; 14.271, 301; 15.37, 310), thereby possibly referring to water as the first principle. Ross, "Metaphysica," I.983b30-35, 694. This would also be consistent with the book of *Genesis*, as well as the postulate of Thales, where water was the primary element of Creation, as will be discussed shortly.

to the opening chapters of the book of *Genesis* in the Bible. The comparison goes beyond the simple decision to relate a creation myth, which characterized most of the world civilizations, but is remarkable in the fact that Hesiod's story of creation emphasized that the world as we know it was formed out of a void known as the Chaos, which is remarkably close to that which was being circulated by the story of Creation in the Bible. Was this simply a serendipitous occurrence, or did Hesiod utilize the Hebraic model, given the fact that circulating copies of the Torah would have been available during his lifetime, and even publically discussed by the prophets?

According to Hesiod, before all else, there came into being the Chaos or Gaping Chasm, which was then followed by Earth (Gaia) and Love (Eros), thereby constituting "the triad of Powers whose genesis precedes and introduces the entire process of cosmogonic organization."[39] For the Greeks, Chaos did not mean a confused mass or mixture, but rather an abyss, or yawning gulf. Although Hesiod described a progression from chaos to order in the poem, he never offered an explanation of how or why the event took place. That Hesiod intended to indicate spontaneous generation of these elements, rather than the effect of an outside force or deity, is suggested by the fact that he used the verb *genet'*, which means "it occurred" or "there was."[40] The problem with calling it a void, and failing to then explain why or how it was changed, however, is that it leaves open the question of how "chaos" was formed in the first place, and the philosophers which followed all agreed that such a proposal was impossible. Plato explained this matter further when he described how the framer of the universe did not create it out of nothing, but rather took what existed "in discordant and disorderly motion – and brought it from a state of disorder to one of order, because he believed that order was in every way better than disorder."[41] Hesiod was content with having the gods follow the formation of Chaos, but we will see shortly that the Hebraic myth accepted that Chaos coexisted with YHWH from the very start. Where, then, did Hesiod get his conception of this primordial Chaos in the first place? Based upon a chronological basis of inception, the possibilities include the early documentary manuscripts of the Old Testament, and the Creation myths that were circulating from Babylonia, Egypt, and India.

I am not the first to suggest that the Bible was the source of Hesiod's cosmogony, for Philo of Alexandria (20 BCE-50 CE), the first century CE Jewish philosopher and theologian who admired the works of Plato, suggested that Plato's belief that the world was created and indestructible was drawn from Hesiod's claim that the

---

39 Hesiod, Theogony, 116-120, cited by Bonnefoy, Greek and Egyptian Mythologies, 69.

40 O'Brien, & Major, In The Beginning: Creation Myths from Ancient Mesopotamia, Israel and Greece, 63.

41 Zeyl, "Timaeus," 30a, 1236.

universe arose out of Chaos.[42] He then reminded his readers that many years before Hesiod, Moses had said the same thing.[43] Philo, like Josephus, attempted "to prove to the Greeks the conformity of all that was best in their philosophy with the teachings of the Bible."[44] Philo was the first Jewish commentator to try and harmonize the Hebrew and Greek heritages, and he did this by trying to show, by the allegorical method of interpreting Scripture, that the Bible taught many of the ideas familiar to the Greeks. One of his examples was explaining the eviction of Hagar by Abraham as an example of showing that the ideal man, represented by Abraham, has to send away his lust for material possessions or bodily pleasures, represented by Hagar, in order to follow the way of the mind.[45] His views did not reach sympathetic ears, however, at least among the Jews, and much of his writing was ignored until the Middle Ages.

The Bible presents the most likely source of inspiration to Hesiod, when one closely examines all of the other options. The biblical Creation Epic is contained at the opening of the book of *Genesis*, which in Hebrew is known as *Bereshit* ("in the beginning"), a name which would have intrigued the Presocratic philosophers who were searching for an answer to the same question.

At the very start of the book of *Genesis*, the action of Creation begins, and we are told that at that moment, the earth had not yet been formed and there was a condition that has variously been described as a void, which the ancients described as Chaos.[46] This description is incredibly close to that of Hesiod, but the biblical story of Creation was a variant of myths which were popular throughout the ancient Near East, and so it is necessary to consider Mesopotamian sources, as well. William Foxwell Albright (1891-1971 CE), the former Professor of Semitic Languages at Johns Hopkins University, considers the account of Creation in *Genesis* 1 as following the ancient Sumerian cosmogenic pattern which was kept in Akkadian translation, but not in the North-west Semitic texts.[47] The German Old Testament scholar Georg Fohrer (1915-2002 CE) also believed that this mythological material was borrowed by Israel, mostly from Mesopotamia and Canaan, and then transformed by incorporation into the Yahwistic monotheism.[48]

The Creation myths from the Sumerian texts, which date back to the third millennium BCE, however, describe a triad of great gods, made up of An, En-lil, and En-ki, but they do not discuss the actual Creation of the Universe, as

---

42 Philo, "On the Eternity of the World," <u>The Works of Philo</u>, V.17, 708-709.
43 Ibid., V.19, 709.
44 Lewy, "Introduction," 14.
45 Jacobs, Jewish Ethics, Philosophy and Mysticism, 54.
46 Levenson, "Genesis," Gen 1:1-2, 13.
47 Albright, Yahweh and the Gods of Canaan, 91-92.
48 Fohrer, Introduction to the Old Testament, 87-88.

we see in Hesiod and the book of *Genesis*.[49] The closest the Sumerians come to an actual cosmogony is describing Nammu, the goddess of the sea, as "the mother who gave birth to heaven and earth," an indication that the universe arose from a watery mass, which was a common theme in ancient cosmogonies.[50] The Babylonian *Enuma Elish* ("When on high") is a creation myth that is believed to date to the early part of the second millennium BCE, and gives a similar picture of the primacy of water as the earliest stage of the universe being watery chaos with three intermingled elements: Apsu, who represents the fresh (sweet) waters; Tiamat, who represents the salt waters of the sea or primeval waters; and Mummu, who cannot as yet be identified with certainty, but may represent cloud-banks and mist.[51] The three elements, not labeled as gods, "mingled chaotically," and resulted in the creation of other gods.[52] The "Eridu Creation Story," which is another mythological poem from Mesopotamia from the sixth century BCE, also said that in the beginning "all lands were sea," but did not define a true cosmogony.[53] Berossus, a Babylonian priest of Marduk from the third century BCE, included an account of Creation in his history of Babylon, *Babyloniaca*, c. 280-270 BCE, near the time when the Hebrew Bible was being collated, and in his account of Creation, there was a time when dark, wet chaos was ruled over by the sea goddess Omorka, who was similar to the primordial Tiamat.[54]

The primacy of water is an important element in all of these Mesopotamian stories, and may explain why water was so prominent in the biblical story of Creation, but the Bible places the cosmogony in a more direct sequence, consistent with a scientific premise, rather than interposing the involvement of multiple gods. It is a short step from the generative power of a single Deity, to the generative power of a primary Moving Source, even though it leaves open to question how that primary element was formed in the first place. Hesiod and the subsequent Greek philosophers were able to easily add their own rational interpretations of the process by analyzing the Hebrew story of Creation without the interposition of a theologic element. Thales, in particular, follows the biblical, rather than the Babylonian, approach by postulating water as the primary element of the Universe, and I will discuss other aspects of his contribution shortly.

---

49 Eliade, A History of Religious Ideas, Volume 1, From the Stone Age to the Eleusinian Mysteries, 57.

50 Quoting from the Tablets of Sumer. Gaster, <u>Myth, Legend, and Custom in the Old Testament</u>, 3.

51 T. Jacobsen in *Before Philosophy*, as quoted by Guthrie, <u>A History of Greek Philosophy, Volume I, The Earlier Presocratics and the Pythagoreans</u>, 59. Some translations label Tiamat and Mummu as a single entity, Mummu-Tiamat. Speiser, "The Creation Epic," 61.

52 Graves & Patai, Hebrew Myths, the Book of Genesis, 23.

53 Gaster, Myth, Legend, and Custom in the Old Testament, 3.

54 Sproul, Primal Myths: Creating the World, 121.

While Near-Eastern sources have frequently been seen as important contributors to both the ancient Hebrews and Greeks, fables from ancient India have generally been ignored. Analyzing the tenets of Indian cosmogony, however, reveals some interesting comparisons, and since the Indian philosophies were referenced in some of the Greek works, it is possible that some of their concepts were influential to the evolution of Greek cosmologic thought.

The *Rig-Veda* was the first of the sacred books of Hinduism, believed to have been composed between 2000-900 BCE, early enough to have predated both the Hebrew and Greek texts, but contemporary with the Mycenaean civilization. Prajapati (the Golden Embryo, or Brahama) in Hinduism was said to have been born from the primordial waters, and was envisioned as the life-force of all the gods.[55] Vishnu also was said to have extracted the earth from a watery abyss, joining almost all of the other ancient sources in the emphasis on water as the generating substance.[56] It seems possible that this was an important element in both the writing of the *Genesis* account, and also the subsequent decision of Thales to choose water as the primary element, but contact between the Hebrews, Greeks, and Indian philosophers was quite limited, and in my opinion the Indian material did not play a great role in formulating the biblical design.

In summary, the cosmogony of the Hebrews resembled many contemporary beliefs, particularly with reference to the primacy of water as the initial generative source, and so it is difficult to prove that their texts and prophetic speeches were the very ones which directly influenced the early Greek thinkers. The biblical tale is directed specifically to the origin of the Universe, however, and there is a clear similitude between their views, with a timetable that strongly supports the thesis that the Hebrews were the primary source for the Greeks. In this view, I follow the writing of Aristobulus, a mid-second-century BCE Jewish Hellenistic author active in the Alexandrian court during the reign of Ptolemy VI Philometor, who claimed that Homer and Hesiod "learned from the Torah of the Jews about the holiness of the seventh day,"[57] and that Pythagoras, Plato, and other ancient poets like Orpheus and Aratus, had acquired knowledge from the *Pentateuch*.[58]

As I continue to analyze the philosophers and playwrights who followed Homer and Hesiod, I will point out how this train of similarity follows a repetitive pattern, indicating support for my contention that much of Greek philosophical thought sprang from concepts contained in the documents which led to the compilation of the Hebrew Bible.

---

55 Rig-Veda X.cxxi. Sproul, Primal Myths: Creating the World, 179, 181.

56 Gaster, Myth, Legend, and Custom in the Old Testament, 3.

57 Quoting passages from Clement and Eusebius. Bar-Kochva, The Image of the Jews in Greek Literature: The Hellenistic Period, 199.

58 Momigliano, Essays on Ancient and Modern Judaism, 19.

B. The Presocratic Philosophers

While modern historians have generally credited the Greeks with the development of Western philosophical thought, little is known about how that remarkable transition took place. Sparse extant material has survived to the present day, none of it from the early Presocratics, leaving scholars with only snippets of information about what these philosophers actually taught and wrote.[59] It is known that many of the Greek Archaic Age intellectuals traveled throughout the civilized world, reading the academic texts of their contemporaries in other lands, but exactly who these sources were, and what materials were reviewed, is not known. The Royal Library of Alexandria, in Alexandria, Egypt, flourished from the third century BCE until it was burned during the Roman conquest of Egypt in 30 BCE, and since it is credited with being the first institution to collect all of the world's knowledge, it is obvious that manuscripts were available to scholars during that era, but because all of the books contained in the library were destroyed, and most have not been found intact in other public and private collections, it is not possible to determine exactly what materials were actually present to review.[60] I believe, however, that comparing what is known about their revolutionary views from commentaries supplied by later authors, with the teachings of the Old Testament and Hebrew prophets will provide a reasonable basis for concluding that the Hebrew lore provided much of the rationale for the views of the ancient Greek philosophers, historians, and playwrights.

It is probably not insignificant that the beginnings of Greek philosophy did not begin on the Greek mainland, but rather with the Milesian Presocratic exponents – Thales, Anaximander and Anaximenes – who were citizens of Miletus, an Ionian city on the west coast of Asia Minor (modern day Turkey), close to ancient Persia and the "full current of Oriental thought."[61] These pioneers were living during the time in 546 BCE when Ionia was taken over by Cyrus the Great (c. 600-529 BCE), becoming part of the Persian (Achaemenid) Empire. This is

---

59 Diogenes Laertius, of whose life almost nothing is known, is our most prolific source of the Presocratic philosophers, and in his *Lives of the Eminent Philosophers*, he makes 1,186 explicit references to 365 books by about 250 authors, almost all of them no longer extant. Stenudd, <u>Cosmos of the Ancients: The Greek Philosophers on Myth and Cosmology</u>, 18.

60 This magnificent resource for compiling all of the world's knowledge was founded by Ptolemy I Soter (305-283 BCE), and his son Ptolemy II Philadelphos (283-246 BCE) was reputed to have added 200,000 volumes to the collection, with the total eventually reaching 700,000 tomes. Tarn, "Ptolemy II," 253. Although many of these books were available in other locations, being able to have access to all in one site surely attracted many visitors at the time.

61 A. T. Olmstead (1880-1945 CE) in *History of the Persian Empire*, as quoted by Guthrie, <u>A History of Greek Philosophy, Volume I, The Earlier Presocratics and the Pythagoreans</u>, 31.

the very same man who freed the Jews from their Babylonian Exile in 538 BCE, and enabled them to return to Jerusalem and rebuild the Second Temple. We therefore have a remarkable synergistic era, when both the Hebrews and Greeks began to expand their intellectual growth. The fact that the biblical compilers and early Greek historians were writing during the same historical era provides, in my opinion, a plausible explanation as to why there are so many similarities between their compositions, particularly between the Deuteronomistic histories, and the orations in Herodotus (490-420 BCE) and Thucydides (460-400 BCE), who followed shortly upon the heels of the Milesian philosophers. Many scholars have noted this chronologic similitude, but the general opinion, is that the Jews took their model from the Greeks. Once again, I believe this conclusion is based upon the general bias of Western historians toward the advancements put forth by the ancient Greeks, and I will attempt to show here that it was the Greeks who borrowed from the Hebrews, rather than vice versa.

The Deuteronomist History (DtrH), as first suggested by Martin Noth, is believed to have included the books of *Deuteronomy, Joshua, Judges, Samuel and Kings*, and was written a few decades after the Babylonian Exile in 587 BCE.[62] It is likely that copies of early compilations of these books were available for other scholars to study, and this may very well have influenced the early Greek philosophers, who were known to have traveled widely in their search for knowledge. Many commentators have pointed out the similarity between Herodotus and the DtrH, and given the fact that Herodotus was known to have traveled in this region before writing his book, he likely spoke with Hebrew priests in the same manner he did with the Egyptian clergy. A Milesian garrison occupied the first Greek settlement in Egypt at Daphnae, established by Psammetichus I (665-610 BCE) in 665 BCE, and the book of *Jeremiah* indicates that the prophet and other Jewish refugees spent time there while taking refuge from king Nebuchadrezzar II (605-562 BCE).[63] If Thales visited Egypt, it is very likely that he would have spent some time in that location, and he could have spoken with Hebrew priests who would have explained the biblical story of Creation and the primacy of water.

The mobility and freedom of the Jews opened up new avenues of dissemination of knowledge of Hebrew texts, even though the completed Torah was not yet translated into a Greek text. Translations into Aramaic, as discussed earlier, were readily available, and so the Greeks would have easily been able to familiarize themselves with the context. Herodotus acknowledged that the Egyptians and Babylonians provided the essentials of mathematics, geometry and astronomical calculations to the Greeks, and I believe there is no reason to deny the importance

---

62 Nielsen, The Tragedy in History: Herodotus and the Deuteronomistic History, 18, 86.

63 Jer 43:5. Russell, A History of Western Philosophy, 25.

of Hebrew contributions as well.[64] Guthrie may be correct when he credits the Greeks with taking the practical information provided by the Orientals, and elevating it into a system of explaining the world-at-large by advancing the understanding "from percepts to concepts," but the Hebraic explanation of the role of the Almighty God, the "One" unifying force, in my opinion, was also vital in this cross-cultural transformation.[65]

The importance of Thales in this regard is that he was the man credited with being the first to deserve the label of philosopher by Aristotle, who made a distinction between those who described the world in terms of myth, or *theologi*, such as the priests from Egypt and Babylon, and those who sought to describe natural causes, or *physiologi*, with Thales being the founder of this latter kind of philosophy.[66] Modern philosophers have agreed with his assessment, crediting Thales for attempting to look for a Unity, or first principle, in the diversity of the many. But while this may have been unique to the Greek thinkers at the time, given the polytheistic nature of their theologic concepts, it is clear that the ancient Hebrews taught that the Universe had been brought forth from Chaos, or a watery chasm, by the force of a single entity – YHWH – for centuries before. While the first line of the Bible is "in the beginning God created heaven and earth," it is followed by the explanation that God's spirit, as He was performing this task, "moved on the water's surface," and the creation of the Heaven and the Earth, was divided by the water above and below.[67] In essence then, water was present when God set out to create the Universe, and it therefore was the primary element to all who read the earliest writings that were eventually compiled into the biblical text.

We do not know precisely what Thales exactly said about the underlying substance of the world, since none of his writings have ever been discovered, but Aristotle recorded that he believed that the principle of all things was water, upon which the earth floats.[68] Aristotle believed Thales came to this belief because the nature of moist things is water, and the seeds of all things have a moist nature, but Thales' judgment is remarkably similar to the opening lines of the book of *Genesis*, and, in my opinion, his concept of water being the primary element came from his learning of this legend, and then attempting to find a scientific, rather than a theologic, premise for the explanation. Thales did not accept that God

---

64 Herodotus, The History, 2.109, 175.

65 Guthrie, A History of Greek Philosophy, Volume I, The Earlier Presocratics and the Pythagoreans, 38.

66 Aristotle, Metaphysics, A983b20, 17. From a chronologic standpoint, it appears that Hippo may have been in line for this accolade, but Aristotle did not consider him worthy "because of the shallowness of his *thought*." Ibid., 984a5, 17.

67 Gen 1:1-2. Kaplan, The Living Torah: The Five Books of Moses and the Haftarot, 3.

68 Aristotle, Metaphysics, A983b20-21, 17.

alone was responsible for the formation of the Universe, but he did follow its genesis from the element of water. Although other religions, as discussed above, also promoted the primogenitor status of water, the most available source for discussing this premise would have been the circulating documents of the early biblical compilers.

Thales, and the philosophers who followed, attempted to take the cosmogonies found in religious texts and provide them with explanations that were based in scientific principles. As Guthrie pointed out, "the perennial fascination exercised by the Milesians lies just in this, that their ideas form a bridge between the two world of myth and reason."[69] Their new understanding of the world consisted of the substitution of natural for mythological causes. They did this by searching for a primary substance to explain the origin of things, and then explaining diversity by finding more or less of it in a given space – a monistic view of reality.

It is easy to see where Thales may have been introduced to the biblical transcripts in Babylon at the time. He was known to have traveled widely and learned much from both the Egyptians and Babylonians.[70]

Daniel W. Graham, Professor of Philosophy at Brigham Young University, says Thales went beyond the teachings of his contemporaries, however, and formulated a theory about the origin of the world which sought to expand upon the fanciful myths of his predecessors.[71] This created, as put forth by Aristotle, the "divine science," which holds that God is the first principle cause of all things, and I believe this facet of his cosmogony was taken from the biblical material.[72] Like so many other supposed influences on Greek culture that have ignored the role played by the Hebrews, most authors have ascribed the influence on Thales' explanation of the world to have come by "variegated traditional background of earlier Greek quasi-mythological cosmogonical versions, but also by a specific cosmological idea derived directly, perhaps, from further east."[73] The "further

---

69 Guthrie, A History of Greek Philosophy, Volume I, The Earlier Presocratics and the Pythagoreans, 70.

70 There is an "unchallenged tradition" that he visited Egypt, and some have suggested his theory of water being the *arche* of all things was of Babylonian origin. Guthrie, <u>A History of Greek Philosophy, Volume I, The Earlier Presocratics and the Pythagoreans</u>, 58. Egyptian priests claimed that Thales and Homer both learned from Egypt that water was the origin of all things, basing this view on the generative powers of the Nile River. Ibid., 58-59. Josephus claimed that all agreed that Pherecydes the Syrian, Pythagoras (c. 570-490 BCE), and Thales all learned what they knew from the Egyptians and Chaldeans. Josephus, "Against Apion," <u>The Complete Works of Josephus</u>, I.2, 608.

71 Graham, The Texts of Early Greek Philosophy: The Complete Fragments and Selected Testimonies of the Major Presocratics, Part I, 17.

72 Ross, "Metaphysica," I.983a8-10, 693.

73 Kirk & Raven, The Presocratic Philosophers: A Critical History with a Selection of Texts, 89.

east," in my opinion, was the information contained in the early biblical manuscripts, rather than from Egypt or Babylon, teachings, as is often asserted. Whether Thales may have also had some Hebrew genetic material floating around his brain, making him more conducive to the biblical story, given the fact that his ancestors had been derived from these Hebrew dissidents who fled the Exodus, can never be known, with certainty, although Herodotus claimed that his family was Phoenician, despite the fact that the majority of historians view him "as a genuine Milesian of distinguished family."[74]

The next philosopher of note was Anaximander, who was said to have been the pupil of Thales. He also traveled widely and was purported by Strabo (63 BCE-21 CE) to have been the first author to publish a map of the earth. Unlike Thales, Anaximander did publish some books, although none have survived extant. According to the Neoplatonist Simplicius (490-560 CE), he named the *arche* "the boundless" (*apeiron*, unlimited), explaining that "things perish into those things out of which they have their being."[75] He did not try to define the nature of this original substance, unlike Thales and many of the other early cosmologists who followed, or postulate that one of the four elements (air, water, fire, earth) changed into each other, but rather described the elements as "a separation of the opposites caused by the eternal motion."[76] Although Anaximander is credited with carrying on the tradition of rational thought which formed the basis of Greek philosophy, there is nothing about his life that suggests a contact with Hebraic teaching.

Anaximenes is believed to have been a pupil and successor of Anaximander, but rather than follow his refusal to characterize the nature of the Universe in the attributes of a single element, he proposed that air was the *arche* of all things. We will never know the exact reasons for his decision, as once again there are no extant original writings, but it is generally thought that he attempted to find a natural explanation of why and how things arose by a separation of what had previously been mingled, and he saw this in the natural process of rarefaction and condensation. Simplicius explained that he believed air was both indefinite in character, but determinate, and that it became fire when fully rarefied, and then wind, cloud, and water when first condensed, and finally earth and stones when further condensed.[77] Like Anaximander, Anaximenes attempted to add a rational basis for the presence of the universe with arguments that failed to

---

74 Guthrie, A History of Greek Philosophy, Volume I, The Earlier Presocratics and the Pythagoreans, 50.

75 Quoted by Guthrie, A History of Greek Philosophy, Volume I, The Earlier Presocratics and the Pythagoreans, 76.

76 Ibid., 74.

77 Simplicius, *Physics* 149.28-150.4, as cited by Graham, The Texts of Early Greek Philosophy: The Complete Fragments and Selected Testimonies of the Major Presocratics, Part I, 77.

clearly identify the underlying structure, given the impossible task of proving their assertions with the limited means of investigation available. All the Milesian philosophers tried to describe the basic element of the Universe without explaining how the *arche* came about in the first place, thereby mimicking the actions of a god, without applying the term deity to their process. Their attempt to try and explain the Universe by some rational analysis was admirable, but it failed because as Philo noted in his treatise "On the Creation" (*De Officio Mundi*), the Greek philosophers had admired the world itself rather than the Creator, thereby not recognizing the important principle of nature that all existing things must have an active cause.[78] As might be expected, the Presocratic argument for a Unity in the world could never be proven, and so the philosophical schools which followed were free to expand their arguments in other directions.

The next Presocratic philosopher of note is Xenophanes of Colophon (c. 570–475 BCE), the man generally accredited as being the founder of the Eleatic school, which followed up on the initial success of the Milesians, although his theories are best seen as following the Ionian tradition started in Miletus. His cosmology held that things are composed of earth and water, which vary in quantity during periods of flooding and drying out. Although most historians see the Milesians as identifying the divine with the basic reality of their systems, Xenophanes actually posited a transcendent God, thereby laying the foundation for Greek rational theology.[79] He appears to have believed in the Unity of One God, as evident in his extant verse which states that "God is one, greatest among gods and men, in no way like mortals either in body or in mind."[80] This latter conclusion was in response to the portrayal of the gods as immoral in Homer, and Xenophanes strongly argued that no mortal could know the entire truth about the gods.[81] His verse "from earth come all things, all things end in earth,"[82] very much resembles the biblical line of man being born of dust and returning to dust, although many scholars wrongly consider this to be his reference to earth being the *arche* instead of water or air.[83] In either case, by emphasizing the role of the earth in the genesis

---

78 "On the Creation," II.7-8, in The Works of Philo, 3. Like Pythagoras, Philo believed in the importance of numbers, explaining that the world was made in six days because six, by the laws of natures, is the most productive, and the most perfect, number. Ibid., III.13, 4.

79 Ibid., 96.

80 Guthrie, A History of Greek Philosophy, Volume I, The Earlier Presocratics and the Pythagoreans, 374. Aristotle says he was the first to posit a unity. Aristotle, "Metaphysics," The Basic Works of Aristotle, I.5.986b22, 699.

81 Nielsen, The Tragedy in History: Herodotus and the Deuteronomistic History, 23.

82 Fr. 27, Guthrie, A History of Greek Philosophy, Volume I, The Earlier Presocratics and the Pythagoreans, 383.

83 Ibid., 384. Aristotle, however, noted twice that no prior philosopher posited earth as an *arche*. See *Metaphysics* A989a5 and *De Anima* 405b8. Ibid., 385.

of the world, and in proposing the necessity of a god as the generating force, Xenophanes is clearly showing, in my opinion, an influence of biblical thought that certainly came, in my opinion, from his exposure to manuscripts or prophetic speeches. Xenophanes likely had access to Hebraic publications from the fact that by the time of his adult life, the Jews were resettled in Jerusalem, and early biblical texts would have been readily available for him to study. Aristotle explained that Xenophanes argued that there can only be one god, for if there were many, he could not longer be mightiest and best of all, and therefore not have the attributes of a god.[84] I believe, however, that the unity of god was more likely an acceptance of Mosaic monotheism.

Heraclitus (c. 535-475 BCE), a contemporary of Xenophanes, has been the subject of conflicting interpretations over the years, primarily due to the obscure nature of his writings, and therefore provides a difficult model to search for an Hebraic influence, although I believe his views share some common ground. Ancient interpretations, almost without exception, saw his theory "as confused and incoherent," but Diogenes Laertiusa (third century CE) nevertheless said that his treatise was so influential that it produced a school of followers known as Heracliteans.[85] According to Diogenes, "he inquired of himself, and learned everything from himself," and so doing, he generally disagreed with the writing of other philosophers.[86] This is not surprising, since the era of the Presocratics was a time when philosophers were just beginning to set the framework for schools of thought, but it is evident that he must have read the opinions of his contemporaries, or at least heard of them from others, to disagree with their tenets, and his own views suggest that he also read some of the early biblical texts. This can be seen in his argument that there was "first and foremost a Logos," which he said determined the course of all that comes to pass.[87] What he exactly meant by the use of this word has been open to controversy, for at the time a Logos could refer to a story or narrative, whether true or fictitious, a reputation, a conversation with oneself, the notion of cause or reason, or a general principle or rule, to name a few. According to Guthrie, however, he appears to have used the word to refer both to human thought, and to the governing principle of the Universe, reflecting the basis for a "divine force which brings rational order into the Universe."[88] Once again, there was an awareness that the world could not

84 Aristotle, "On Melissus, Xenophanes, Gorgias," 977a14-b20 as cited in Graham, The Texts of Early Greek Philosophy: The Complete Fragments and Selected Testimonies of the Major Presocratics, Part I, 113.

85 Graham, The Texts of Early Greek Philosophy: The Complete Fragments and Selected Testimonies of the Major Presocratics, Part I, 135, 141.

86 Diogenes, "Heraclitus," <u>Lives of Eminent Philosophers</u>, vol. II, IX.5, 413.

87 Guthrie, A History of Greek Philosophy, Volume I, The Earlier Presocratics and the Pythagoreans, 419.

88 Ibid., 429.

just appear by itself, and that some principle of generation, similar to the role of YHWH in the Bible, is by necessity a required ingredient.

Parmenides (early fifth century BCE) put the evolution of Presocratic philosophy into a different direction with his writings about the One Being and the Way of Truth, and while we do not know much about his teaching from extant manuscripts, his reputation and influence among the Classical Greeks was clearly profound. He was born in Elea, and is therefore sometimes referred to as the real founder of the Eleatic School, although this title is also ascribed to Xenophanes, as well. Only 154 lines of his famous poem have survived extant, but it seems evident that where Heraclitus and the Pythagoreans strove to accentuate contradictions, Parmenides would tolerate no such conception. He tried desperately to find a unified answer to the nature of the Universe, and did not accept that something could come into being from nothing, an axiom *Ex nihilo nihil fit* that Aristotle wrote was the opinion of all natural philosophers.[89] He added, however, that "thus it must be completely or not at all," a belief that clearly was against the creation of the universe out of a void, but not out of a watery Chaos.[90] How the Chaos was first formed, however, was still open to question. It is not possible to know what the details of his cosmogony were, as very little of that section of the poem has survived, and the comments of later philosophers to this aspect of his teachings were few and far between. The same is true for his descriptions of the soul, and so Parmenides, who clearly was important to the evolution of his contemporaries, can add little to our ability to detect an influence of biblical teachings in the evolving Greek arena of philosophical thought.

The next philosopher of note I want to discuss is Empedocles (484-424 BCE), a contemporary of the great Greek dramatists, Sophocles and Euripides, and the philosopher whose name is identified as one of the first philosophers to merge the concept of nature with the gods. Empedocles accepted the premise of Parmenides that nothing can come out of nothing, and what exists cannot perish, so the sum of being is constant. But where Parmenides still found that reality was a unity, Empedocles held, according to Aristotle, that the four basic elements of nature – fire, water, earth and air – were equivalent to gods and formed the roots of all things. In this system, the god Zeus was fire, Hera was earth, Aidoneus was air, and Nestis was water.[91]

Aristotle believed that Empedocles was the originator of this concept, although the ancient Hindus certainly discerned in the world these same four material elements, beginning with water, at a much earlier time.[92] Empedocles then further

---

89 Copleston, A History of Philosophy, Volume I Greece and Rome, 29.

90 Quoting Simplicius and Sextus. Graham, The Texts of Early Greek Philosophy: The Complete Fragments and Selected Testimonies of the Major Presocratics, Part I, 217.

91 Diogenes, "Empedocles," <u>Lives of Eminent Philosophers</u>, vol. II, VIII.76, 391.

92 Ross, "Metaphysica," I.984a9, 694.

divided the four elements into two categories, with fire by itself, and earth, air and water as a second entity, which under the influence of friendship came together as one. Homer had also divided the control of the universe into management by four gods, with the heavens falling to the lot of Zeus, the sea to Poseiden, the misty darkness to Hades, and the earth which was held in common by all of them, and so Empedocles, in some ways, can be seen as reverting from the monotheistic teachings of his philosophic predecessors, and reverting to the classic teachings of ancient Greek polytheism.[93] The doctrine of the four elements was supported by Aristotle, and his tremendous authority extended beyond the Middle Ages. In addition, Philo of Alexandria, who combined Hellenistic Jewish theology with Platonic thought, characterized the ten plagues which Moses brought down upon the Egyptians as having the four elements of the universe, earth, water, air, and fire, brought into a state of hostility against Egypt by the command of God.[94]

Contemporary with Empedocles was Anaxagoras, who is usually described as the philosophical heir of Anaximenes. He wrote only one book, the *Physica*, in which he set forth his views on the first principles and the origin of the cosmos. A copy of this work was available to Simplicius in the sixth century CE, although only fragments survive today. Like Empedocles, he agreed that coming-into-being and perishing were impossible, but that mixture and separation did take place in a manner of generation and extinction. According to Diogenes Laertius, his principle was that "all things were together, then Mind (*Nous*) came and set them in order."[95] While not being equated with God, the Mind was infinite and independent, and is the "finest and purest of all things, and has all judgment of everything and greatest power."[96] It set everything in order, including the revolution of the universe which separated the hot from the cold, the bright from the dark, the dry from the wet. While this may not be an exact description of YHWH, and the Creation story in the book of *Genesis*, it comes awfully close, and, in my opinion, shows the most clear effect which the reading of the early biblical texts had on the evolution of Greek philosophical thought. Saint Augustine, who studied philosophy before his conversion to Christianity, considered Anaxagoras to have imbued the Mind with a divine essence, and it becomes increasingly clear why Plato, who carried on this same line of thought, was so popular among both the Hellenistic Jews and the Christians who followed.[97]

---

93 Homer, Iliad, 15.187-193, 314.

94 Philo, "On the Life of Moses, I," The Works of Philo, XVII.96, 468.

95 Diogenes, "Anaxagoras," Lives of Eminent Philosophers, vol. I, II.6, 137. Aristotle labeled this as "Intelligence," and credits Hermotimus of Clazomenae with having made the statements earlier. Aristotle, Metaphysics, A984b19, 18.

96 Guthrie, A History of Greek Philosophy, Volume II, The Presocratic Tradition From Parmenides to Democritus, 273.

97 Augustine, The City of God, VIII.2, 245. What is particularly important, is that Anaxagoras, who was the first philosopher to arrive in Athens in 480 BCE, had written

In summary, the Presocratics clearly saw the world as emanating from a monistic element, and although they never specifically attributed the generative power to the function of a god, their theories were consistent with a generative force that acted in a like manner to YHWH, as depicted in the book of *Genesis*, except that the concept of a God was not invoked. I believe that this concept was suggested to them by early manuscripts of the book of *Genesis*, and that these treatises were read by Hesiod and the Milesian Presocratic philosophers, who then proceeded to try and explain Creation by a natural, rather than theologic, basis. Without believing in the role of YHWH as a monotheistic God, the inquisitive Greek mind looked for a non-theistic explanation for the One, and in so doing followed the pattern which led to the evolution from Hesiod to the Socratic era.

Before moving on to the writings of Pythagoras, I want to briefly mention the Atomists of the fifth century BCE, Leucippus and his pupil Democritus, who were concurrent with the end of the Presocratic philosophers, and then followed later by Epicurus and Lucretius. I am not going to dwell on their theories, as their views are the true beginning of what today is known as the atomic theory, a scientific premise that does not concern itself with the presence of a divine authority, or a cosmogony similar to that put forth in the book of *Genesis*.

Under the Atomist view, the universe is made up of atoms and empty space, and the plurality of infinite atoms which make up matter move in the void, while their combination then causes coming-to-be, and their separation leads to dissolution. They generate matter by coming together and interlocking, but the actual atoms are imperishable, infinite, unchangeable, and indivisible, and of microscopic size. What they left out of their equation, however, was the question of where these atoms came from, and why. Did the Atomists know of the theory of creation in the book of *Genesis*? If they did, did they purposely not address this issue, choosing instead to concentrate on the physics of matter, rather than the cosmogony of the world? I am unable to add any further hypothesis to answering these questions, but for the sake of this book, I will not claim that the Old Testament writings added inspiration to the theories of these remarkable men.

C. Pythagoras

St. Augustine divided the two early schools of philosophy in ancient Greece, before the rise of Plato and Aristotle, as coming from the Ionic school, founded by Thales, and the Italic school, founded by Pythagoras.[98]

Pythagoras is one of the most remarkable men in all of ancient Greece, both for the breadth of his knowledge and teaching, and also for the effect he had

a book, not extant, by the title of *Ta Physika* ("The Nature of Things"), which discussed cosmogony, and, if my beliefs are correct, could have introduced the concepts of Hebrew teaching in Greek, rather than Aramaic or Hebrew texts. Herrington, Aeschylus, 25.

98 Augustine, The City of God, VIII.2, 244.

on the evolution of Greek intellectual thought. Although Pythagoras never committed his views to writing, his teachings were memorialized in the school of men and women he fostered over the next two centuries. His reputation among his followers reached the level of veneration, more in tune with a religious sect than a philosophical school, and despite the supposed ban on discussing the details of the master's teaching, his doctrines became well known to others outside of his community, and their recollections provide much information about his deepest held beliefs. Whether the doctrines were truly from "the word of the Master," or were instead invented by those who followed, like the memory of Socrates in the dialogues of Plato, is not important, for we are more concerned with how he was remembered, then how he actually lived.

Like most of the early Greek intellectuals, Pythagoras, who was born c. 570 BCE and a contemporary of Anaximenes, strove to gather all of the information about the physical world by studying what others knew about it through travels to Babylon and Egypt. As Porphyry said, "the ancient Egyptians excelled in geometry, the Phoenicians in numbers and proportions, and the Chaldeans in astronomical theorems, divine rites, and worship of the gods," and Pythagoras actively sought out their knowledge.[99] Even while growing up in Samos, he made frequent trips across the strait to study with Thales and Anaximander in Miletus.[100]

Diogenes Laertius asserted that he was so eager for knowledge that he had himself initiated into all the mysteries and rites not only of Greece, but also of foreign countries.[101] He often sailed to Sidon in Phoenicia, and joined the descendants of Mochus, the prophet and natural philosopher, and was said to have been initiated into all of the sacred rites of the mysteries in Phoenicia and Syria, as well.[102] The time Pythagoras was said to have studied in Babylon was after the Jews were freed from the Babylonian Exile in 538 BCE, shortly before Pythagoras left his land of birth, at a time when the Bible was being actively formulated into its present form.[103] Iamblichus even reports that Pythagoras was seen on the crest of Mt. Carmel in Israel, which was believed to be the holiest of mountains.[104] This means that Pythagoras would have had access to their manuscripts and prophesies, and since he treated his philosophic tenets as a strict way-of-life, more similar to a religious faith than an academic endeavor, he would have listened avidly to their

---

99 Ferguson, The Music of Pythagoras, 18. Iamblichus claimed he spent twenty-two years in Egypt and twelve years in Babylon. Iamblichus, On the Pythagorean Way of Life, 4.19, 45.

100 Ferguson, The Music of Pythagoras, 17.

101 Diogenes, "Pythagoras," Lives of Eminent Philosophers, vol. II, VIII.3, 323.

102 Iamblichus, On the Pythagorean Way of Life, 3.14, 41.

103 Ferguson, The Music of Pythagoras, 24, 26.

104 Iamblichus, On the Pythagorean Way of Life, 3.15, 43. Ezekiel defeated the 450 prophets of Baal, and the 400 prophets of Asherah on Mt. Carmel. 1 Kgs 18:19ff.

pronouncements, especially the concept of an Almighty God being the One and Only God, given the fact that numbers retained a mystical significance for the Pythagoreans. He eventually left his homeland of Samos to escape the tyranny of Polycrates, and migrated to Croton c. 532 BCE, the leading Achaean colony in South Italy, where he founded his school. According to Iamblichus of Chalcis (260-330 CE), he went to Italy for "men well disposed towards learning were to be found in the greatest abundance" there.[105] He was then forty years old, and would live in Croton for the next thirty years.

That Pythagoras was indeed influenced by the words of the *Torah* is not a new revelation, but is a concept that was expressed by a number of ancient authors. Josephus, the first century CE Jewish historian, in *Against Apion*, stated that Pythagoras "did not only know our doctrines, but was in very great measure a follower and admirer of them."[106] He further concluded that "he took a great many of the laws of the Jews into his own philosophy."[107] In coming to this conclusion, Josephus seems to have relied, in part, on Hermippus of Smyrna, a late third-century BCE Alexandrian scholar and biographer, who wrote a biography of Pythagoras. While many have claimed that Josephus was simply attempting to highlight the affinity between the Jews and the Greeks to promote his own prominent position in Greece, others have also noted a resemblance between the two philosophies, supporting the premise that Pythagoras showed evidence of Hebraic teachings.

Aristobulus, a mid-second-century BCE Jewish Hellenistic author active in the Alexandrian court during the reign of Ptolemy VI Philometor, claimed in *Commentaries on the Torah of Moses*, that Pythagoras transferred many of the Jewish ideas to his belief system.[108] He added that Socrates, Plato and Pythagoras all learned from the Torah of Moses "the concept of the voice of God."[109] Similar contacts of Pythagoras with Jewish thought are alleged by the ancient Greek author Antonius Diogenes, at the end of the first century CE, and the Christian author Origen, in the third century CE.[110]

Today, few academicians find enough evidence to suggest that Pythagoras actually incorporated Hebraic teachings, an attitude typified by Professor Bezalel Bar-Kochva, from Tel Aviv University, who suggested that the link between

---

105 Ferguson, The Music of Pythagoras, 32.

106 Josephus, "Against Apion," The Complete Works of Josephus, I.22, 614.

107 Ibid. Origen's *Contra Celsum* (1.15) made a similar claim that Pythagoras brought his own philosophy from the Jews to the Greeks. Bar-Kochva, The Image of the Jews in Greek Literature: The Hellenistic Period, 200.

108 Josephus was aware of the writings of Aristobulus, but did not mention his work. Bar-Kochva, The Image of the Jews in Greek Literature: The Hellenistic Period, 197-198.

109 Ibid., 199.

110 Feldman, Jew & Gentile in the Ancient World, 9.

Pythagorean doctrine and Judaism was made by Hellenistic Jews because they were aware that Pythagoras had already been portrayed in the classical period as borrowing from various sources, such as the Egyptians and Babylonians.[111] Rather than ascribe a true influence based on inspiration for much of early Greek philosophy, Bar-Kochva claimed that the Jews were simply trying to improve their image and status. This conclusion, however, fails to take into account many congruencies between the two philosophies, as I will now discuss.

First and foremost, as I have already pointed out, the concept of an Almighty God being the One and Only God was especially intriguing to Pythagoras, given the fact that numbers retained a mystical significance for the Pythagoreans. Pythagoras saw numerology as being responsible for the "harmony" in the Universe, the divine principle that governed the structure of the whole world.[112] Numbers not only explained the physical world, but also symbolized moral qualities and other abstractions. Each numeral represented a particular meaning, such as justice for the number four, and marriage for five. The number three was the determinate for the universe in their system, according to Aristotle, since there was a beginning, middle, and end, forming a triad.[113] Because the number ten was felt to be a perfect number, and only nine planets were visible in the sky, Pythagoras invented the "counter-earth" as a tenth planet, assuring that the design of the universe would fit his sublime theme.[114]

But the number one was the most important numeral, since Pythagoras believed that everything springs from the number one, which is the basis for then determining all the other numbers. One is the generating principle because it is seen as being composed of both odd and even numbers, and is therefore unlimited and constitutes the whole universe.[115] The Platonist Theo, as quoted by Francis Cornford (1874-1943 CE), the English classical scholar and poet, described the monad as "the principle of all things and the highest of all principles ... that out of which come all things but which itself comes out of nothing, indivisible and potentially all things."[116] It is clear that this description could have been taken almost verbatim from the book of *Genesis*, eliminating simply the reference to the One as God Almighty. When Pythagoras heard about the monotheistic explanation of the Torah, he certainly would have been intrigued enough to study

111 Bar-Kochva, The Image of the Jews in Greek Literature: The Hellenistic Period, 198-199.

112 Ibid., 213.

113 Stocks, "On the Heavens," I.268a10-12, 447.

114 Citing Aristotle *Metaphysics* 986a1-13, Graham, The Texts of Early Greek Philosophy: The Complete Fragments and Selected Testimonies of the Major Presocratics, Part I, 499.

115 Aristotle, Metaphysics, A986a17-21, 21.

116 Guthrie, A History of Greek Philosophy, Volume I, The Earlier Presocratics and the Pythagoreans, 244.

what was being said. This strong inclination to monism would be continued by both the Platonists and Neopythagoreans.[117]

Philosophy for Pythagoras and his followers also closely followed the precepts of a religion for, as Guthrie concluded, it "had to be first and foremost the basis for a way of life: more than that, for a way of eternal salvation."[118] This extreme devotion to a rigid adherence of a code of behavior was very similar to the mandates of the Mosaic Code, and included a rigid adherence to not only devotion to a God, or to a philosophic principle, but also to dietary restrictions and habits of communal living and sharing. Aristoxenus (fourth century BCE) said of Pythagoras and his followers:

Every distinction they lay down as to what should be done or not done aims at conformity with the divine. This is their starting-point; their whole life is ordered with a view to following God, and it is the governing principle of their philosophy.[119]

While this mode of life characterized some ancient Hebrews, it very much resembled the ancient Essene Hebrew sect, which was prominent at the end of the second millennium BCE, and recorded its rules of conduct in the Dead Sea Scrolls (200 BCE–100 CE).[120] While all orthodox Jews followed this same credo of life to some degree, the Essenes were particularly adamant about their devotion to the teachings of God. Like the Pythagoreans, the Essenes of Qumran put all their possessions into one common stock, renounced the world, abstained from public sacrifices, had a solemn initiation, prohibited taking oaths, wore white garments, paid special honor to the sun, used a calendar which originated with the Pythagoreans, and made use of numerology.[121] Josephus noted that the Essenes lived the same kind of life as the Pythagoreans, but he did not elaborate on the details.[122] It is likely, however, that their long list of dietary taboos, including the abstaining from eating beans, highlighted the similarity in the two sects.[123]

---

117 Ibid., 244.

118 Ibid., 182.

119 Ibid., 199.

120 Both Josephus (Antiq. XVIII.I.5) and Philo (Every Good Man is Free 75) claimed that the Essenes numbered more than 4,000, and both compared them to the Pythagoreans. Dillon, "The Essenes in Greek Sources: Some Reflections," 125-127.

121 Benson, The Origins of Christianity and the Bible, A Critical Scholarly Investigation of the Sources of Christianity and the Bible, 135-136.

122 Josephus, "Antiquities of the Jews," The Complete Works of Josephus, XV.X.4, 333.

123 Guthrie, A History of Greek Philosophy, Volume I, The Earlier Presocratics and the Pythagoreans, 183.

D. Plato to Aristotle

As discussed above, it is clear that both the Presocratics and Pythagoras show evidence of exposure to Hebraic ideology, but it is with Plato and Aristotle that the shift from pure speculation on the materialism of monism shifts back to a more monotheistic theologic tone that suggests a biblical influence. In the words of William Rowe, Emeritus Professor of Philosophy at Purdue University, the cosmological argument for the presence of a God as the initiator of the universe, "can be traced to the writings of the Greek philosophers, Plato and Aristotle."[124] With the teaching of Socrates, man replaced the universe as the focus of interest, but the primacy of a generating God in Greek philosophy begins with the writings of Plato, the most respected philosopher in the Western World.[125] Plato was born in Athens c. 427 BCE, a time when the city was becoming a cultural and political metropolis after emerging successfully from the Persian Wars. The era of his birth was marked by widespread social unrest, as a highly lethal epidemic gripped the city from 430-427 BCE, and the first phase of the Peloponnesian War (431-421 BCE) had just begun. Plato was disheartened about political life after his elderly friend Socrates was convicted and put to death, and so he turned to philosophy, because, as he wrote in one of his letters, it alone can show "what is right in public or private affairs."[126]

Plato traveled widely for ten years after the death of Socrates in 399 BCE, including trips to Megara, Egypt, Italy and Sicily before returning home to found his Academy in Athens.[127] It is believed that he also visited the Land of Israel, since the orator Demosthenes (384-322 BCE), and the orator Isaeus (c. 420-350 BCE), both implied that Athenians inhabited Acre during the fourth century BCE, providing access to information about their Jewish neighbors.[128] His

---

124 William Rowe, "An Examination of the Cosmological Argument," as cited in Pojman & Rea, Philosophy of Religion, An Anthology, 24. A cosmological argument begins with a posteriori assumptions that the universe exists, and that something must have therefore created it. Such a being is God. Today, scientists generally explain the origin of the universe as a result of the "Big Bang" theory, whereby the universe was created *ex nihilo* about fifteen billion years ago, but for many, this answer cries out for a transcendent cause. William Lane Craig and J. P. Moreland, "The *Kalam* Cosmological Argument," as cited Ibid., 34.

125 Alfred North Whitehead (1861-1947 CE), the noted English mathematician and philosopher, famously noted that "the safest general characterization of the European philosophical tradition is that it consists of a series of footnotes to Plato." The Great Thinkers on Plato, ix.

126 Crombie, An Examination of Plato's Doctrines, I. Plato on Man and Society, 3.

127 Ibid., 7. According to St. Augustine, he traveled extensively "going to every place famed for the cultivation of any science of which he could make himself master." From Chapter VIII, *City of God*, as quoted by The Great Thinkers on Plato, 20.

128 Feldman, Jew & Gentile in the Ancient World, 4.

teaching that the world had to come into being, and not have always existed, since it is visible, tangible, and corporeal, and that it therefore must have had some cause, since nothing can otherwise arise spontaneously, "introduced, for the first time in Greek philosophy, the alternative scheme of creation by a divine artificer, according to which the world is like a work of art designed with a purpose."[129] He went on to explain that god placed "water and air between fire and earth," in proper proportions, leading Neoplatonists , according to Benjamin Jowett (1817-1893 CE), the influential English scholar and theologian, to believe that Plato "was inspired by the Holy Ghost, or had received his wisdom from Moses."[130]

I bring this comparison up because the conclusion of many of the ancient followers of Plato fit quite nicely with my view that Plato, in fact, did take much of Moses' teaching to heart. Plato's cosmogony held that the universe, or cosmos, was created by the craftsman "modeled after that which is changeless and is grasped by a rational account."[131] According to Plato, the God who framed the Universe was good, and desired that it "become as much like himself as was possible."[132] He took all that was visible "in discordant and disorderly motion - and brought it from a state of disorder to one of order, because he believed that order was in every way better than disorder."[133] That Plato was not thinking of a monotheistic God, however, is evident in his explanation that the Father who had begotten the universe set it up as "a shrine for the everlasting gods."[134] He went on to spell out that after the universe was created, the gods were formed and spread throughout the whole heaven to be a true adornment for the whole.[135] What is not certain, however, is whether these statements were necessary for Plato's philosophical beliefs, or his health and welfare, living in a country where his mentor Socrates was put to death for his impious teachings.

Plato's concept of God (the Father) as active cause for the formation of the universe was very appealing to Jews during the Hellenistic Age, and may explain why so many of the Jews at that time became enamored of all things Greek. This is evidenced by the writings of Philo of Alexandria, the first century CE Jewish philosopher and theologian, who is generally categorized as belonging to the Middle Platonic school of thought. Philo acclaimed Moses as reaching the very summit of philosophy by noting that "it is indispensable that in all existing things there must be an active cause, and a passive subject," and the active cause,

---

129 Pelikan, What Has Athens To Do With Jerusalem?: *Timaeus* and *Genesis* in Counterpoint, 23; Zeyl, "Timaeus," 27c, 1234-35.

130 Ibid.; 32b, 1237; Pelikan, What Has Athens To Do With Jerusalem?: *Timaeus* and *Genesis* in Counterpoint, 24.

131 Zeyl, "Timaeus," 29a, 1235.

132 Ibid., 29e, 1236.

133 Ibid., 30a, 1236.

134 Ibid., 37c, 1241.

135 Ibid., 339e-40b, 1243.

of course, was God.[136]

Another similarity between Plato and the Hellenistic Jews is the concept of resurrection, and it is possible that this concept also came from some of the teachings of the Prophets. According to Plato, death was the departure of the soul from the body.[137] He maintained that the souls after death do not return for 10,000 years, and after judgement go to expiate their sins in places of punishment beneath the earth, unless their previous life in human form has earned them the right to be borne aloft by justice to a region of the heavens.[138] Depending on how well or how poorly they have lived their life, they will spend their time in either Acheron or Tartarus, being purged of their sins, or if the enormity of their sins is deemed incurable, they will be cast into Tartarus for all eternity.[139] At the time Plato expounded this view of the soul being able to leave the body and continue its existence was not part of Judaism, which held that the spirt of the deceased Jews expired at the time of their death, and at the resurrection. But Ezekiel had put forth a view of resurrection with his comments that after death, God declared that "I am going to open your graves and lift you out of the graves," and "I will put My breath into you and you shall live again," an indication that it was God alone Who would resurrect not only the body, but the soul.[140] It is generally believed that Plato got his conception of reincarnation from Pythagoras, who got it, according to Diogenes Laertius, from the Egyptians, but the teaching of Ezekial, who also promoted the biblical theory of cosmogony, would have supported this same understanding.[141]

Numenius of Apamea (second century CE), a Neopythagorean and forerunner of Neoplatonism, went one step further in noting allegiance to Hebrew thought by calling Plato "the Attic speaking Moses," who greatly acclaimed the law of Moses.[142] Fragments of his works were preserved by Origen, Theodoret (c. 393-457 CE), and Eusebius (c. 260-340 CE), and his influence on Plotinus (205-270 CE) and the Neoplatonists who followed may have been one reason St. Augustine was initially influenced by Platonic readings before turning to the New Testament leading up to his conversion.[143] In his *Confessions*, Augustine told how he "found

---

136 Philo, "On the Creation," The Works of Philo, II.8, 3.

137 Grube, "Phaedo," 64C, 56.

138 Nehamas & Woodruff, "Phaedrus," 249A-B, 526-527.

139 Grube, "Phaedo," 113-114C, 96-97.

140 Ezek 37:12, 14. Sweeney, "Ezekiel," 1114.

141 Benson, The Origins of Christianity and the Bible, A Critical Scholarly Investigation of the Sources of Christianity and the Bible, 170.

142 Bar-Kochva, The Image of the Jews in Greek Literature: The Hellenistic Period, 158.

143 He held that Plato shone with a glory that far excelled all the other Greek philosophers. Augustine, The City of God, VIII.4, 247. The term Neoplatonist was applied to the doctrines of Plotinus who was often seen as merely a continuation of the

that all the truth I had read in the Platonists were stated there together with the commendation of your grace."[144] Of all the philosophers, "none came nearer to us than the Platonists," because he believed they recognized the true God as the author of all things.[145] He noted that some have surmised that when Plato traveled to Egypt, he may have heard the prophet Jeremiah, or read the prophetic scriptures, but he put this possibility aside because he was born a hundred years after Jeremiah, and seventy years before the Septuagint was written.[146] He nevertheless noted that Plato in the *Timaeus* said that God first united earth and fire when the world was created, a passage very similar to *Genesis* declaration that in the beginning God created heaven and earth.[147] And when the Spirit of God moved over the waters, he hypothesized that Plato may have seen this as a reference to air and water, thereby placing a discussion of the four elements of the world put forth by the Presocratics directly into the biblical text.[148]

Aristotle, as well, seems to have taken biblical themes to heart in many of his writings. In his *Metaphysics*, for example, he concluded that all of the theories which posited matter as having one nature were erroneous, for they were only positing the elements of bodies, and not of incorporeal things, such as motion.[149] They did not explain where the elements themselves were generated, and those who then tried to explain the cause of things in ideas rather than matter turned to the concept of Forms, which continued to ignore the cause of motion, or the knowledge of other things.[150] He argued that "even if the Forms do exist, still no thing which participates in something is generated unless there is a mover," thereby emphasizing the importance of a generating God, or force.[151] While one would not expect Aristotle, the man who truly began the scientific inquiry into the natural world, to expound belief in a Deity as the composer of the Universe, it is clear that his disagreement with all of the prior philosophic concepts of cosmogony were based on their failure to explain the concept of something arising out of nothing. Aristotle discussed the Intellect as God, and explained that there were certain difficulties as to how He could exist as such.[152]

Aristotle's argument about the possible existence of God has puzzled scholars

---

philosophy of Plato, although he added much to the belief in urging one to follow a path which leads "to mystic union with the One, the supreme principle of all things." Great Thinkers on Plato, xix.

144 Augustine, Confessions, VII.xxi.27, 130-131.
145 Augustine, The City of God, VIII.5, 248-49.
146 Ibid., VIII.11, 255-56.
147 Ibid., VIII.11, 256.
148 Ibid., VIII.11, 256.
149 Aristotle, Metaphysics, A987b23-26, 24.
150 Ibid., A991a11-13, 30.
151 Ibid., A991b5, 21.
152 Ibid., L1074b15-1075a10, 209-210.

for years, and I am not here to try and clarify his stance in the small amount of space I have allotted to Aristotle in this book, but it seem clear to me that he believed it was beyond his capability to try and prove the existence of a God by reason, rather than by faith. When he described how others thought of God, he sounded quite Jewish: "We say that God is a living being which is eternal and the best; so life and continuous duration and eternity belong to God, for this is God."[153] Aristotle defined the Universe as being a system made up of heaven and earth and the natural things contained therein, but he was aware that others defined it as the "ordering and arrangement of all things, preserved by and through God."[154] He went on to say that "God is in very truth the preserver and creator of all that is in any way being brought to perfection in this universe," and that He dwells on the topmost crest of the whole heaven.[155] He does not use the pleural form here, which would have been compatible with the polytheistic belief that existed in Greece at that time, but continues to use the singular annunciation which I believe stems from the influence of the Torah manuscripts. He went on to say that God "in might is most powerful, in beauty most fair, in life immortal, in virtue supreme; for, though he is invisible to all mortal nature, yet is he seen in his very works."[156]

That Aristotle may have gotten his information about the Bible through discussions, rather than reading translated texts, is suggested by the fact that he did indeed converse with Jews, as stated in a reference from Clearchus of Soli (fourth century BCE), a scholar of Aristotle, who mentioned in his first book, *On Sleep*, that Aristotle related to him a conversation he had with a Jews about "wonder and philosophy."[157] He went on to explain that the Jews at the time were derived from Indian philosophers, and the discussion they had "communicated to us more information than he received from us."[158] These complimentary statements of Clearcus are the sole surviving testimony of a conversation between a Jew and a Greek philosopher of the classical period, and some scholars have maintained that the meeting was a figment of his imagination.[159] If the event is true, however, it may very well explain why Aristotle held that the heavens and the world of nature all depend upon the first mover, and God is that actuality, referring to a single God alone.[160] Although most scholars dismiss it as unhistorical, the comments

---

153 Ibid., L1072b30, 205.
154 Forster, "On the Universe," 391b10, 627.
155 Ibid., 397b20-26, 635.
156 Ibid., 399b20, 637.
157 Josephus, "Against Apion," The Complete Works of Josephus, I.22, 615.
158 Ibid.
159 Feldman, Jew & Gentile in the Ancient World, 5. Aristotle's writings do not mention Jews specifically, although there is a reference to a bitter and salty lake in Palestine, which could represent the Dead Sea. Ibid., 6.
160 Aristotle, "Metaphysica," XII.1072b.10-26, 880.

have been frequently cited as evidence that Greek authors at the beginning of the Hellenistic Age expressed great admiration for the wisdom of the Jews.[161]

Following the first verified contact between Aristotle and the Jews, more information began to appear from other Greek philosophers. Hecataeus of Abdera was active shortly after the deaths of Plato and Aristotle, and perhaps because he was contemporary with Alexander the Great in his youth, and later was associated with Ptolemy I Soter, he composed an entire book concerning the Jews, which Josephus claimed to have read.[162] It is one of the most detailed surviving accounts on Jews and Judaism in ancient Greek and Roman literature, and served as a source of information on Jews which later authors drew upon.[163] According to most sources, the material was part of his major ethnographic work, *Aegyptiaca*, rather than a separate treatise. Josephus claims that in the book he read, Hecataeus asserts that the High Priest Hezekiah went with Ptolemy to Egypt, after the defeat of Demetrius at Gaza.[164] He added that Hezekiah was able to explain all the circumstances of his people, for everything was committed to writing. This would certainly indicate that the Greek philosophers in the generations before would have had access to similar information, even if it would have required the use of a translator.[165]

Hecataeus also described the Jewish excursus from Egypt, most of which is preserved in the fortieth book of Diodorus, and the *Bibliotheca* of Photius, the ninth-century CE patriarch of Constantinople.[166] He stated that there was an exodus of a group of foreigners from Egypt during a pestilence, with one group led by Moses, and the others by Danaus and Cadmus.[167] This simultaneous origin

---

161 Bar-Kochva, The Image of the Jews in Greek Literature: The Hellenistic Period, 40.

162 Josephus, "Against Apion," The Complete Works of Josephus, I.22, 615.

163 Bar-Kochva, The Image of the Jews in Greek Literature: The Hellenistic Period, 90. Many books were written on the Jews by other authors who applied the name Hecataeus to their work, hoping that their readers would not realize it was a forgery. Ibid., 91. This includes works entitled *On the Jews*, and *On Abraham and the Egyptians*. Ibid., 92-93.

164 Ibid. The High Priest at the time was actually Onias I (c. 320-290 BCE), who was succeeded by his son Simon I.

165 That some authors of that era attempted to read the Hebrew texts is apparent from Josephus' mention of Demetrius Phalereus, the elder Philo, and Eupolemus having missed the truth about the Jews in their books, "for it was not in their power to understand our writings with the utmost accuracy." Josephus, "Against Apion," The Complete Works of Josephus, I.23, 617.

166 Ibid., 99. The statement of Diodorus ends with the assertion that the account is what Hecataeus of Miletus narrated, it is long been accepted that this was an error of a copyist, and it should read Hecataeus of Abdera. Ibid., 105.

167 A minority of the inhabitants, "the most outstanding and active," were headed by Danaus and Cadmus and landed on the coasts of Greece, while the vast majority turned to nearby Judaea under Moses. Ibid., 116.

of both the Jews and the ancient Greeks arising out of Egypt during the Exodus is very similar to my theory, except that Hecataeus does not presume that Danaus and Cadmus were Hebrews, while I believe their origin is based on the influx of dissident Hebrews who fled the Exodus and then traveled to Mycenae, raising the possibility that they may actually have been of Hebraic lineage. Hecataeus claimed that Moses founded Hierosolyma (Jerusalem), and established the Temple, and the twelve-tribe system.[168]

In summary, I believe that a close reading of the evolution of Greek philosophical thought from Thales to the time of Alexander the Great, indicates that their attempt to find a unity in the Universe resulted in a form of Monism similar to, if not identical with, the description of YHWH throughout the Old Testament. It was non-theistic in nature, but clearly invoked the conceptual involvement of a monotheistic deity. That early biblical texts and the speeches of Hebrew prophets were available to the Greek philosophers who traveled to Babylon and Egypt, providing a basis for understanding how the Greeks had contact with biblical theology. In my opinion, the Greeks were intrigued with the clarity of the Hebrew explanation for the formation of the Universe, and my belief that dissident Hebrews left the Exodus and traveled to Greece before the Trojan War adds a genetic attachment of Hebrew patriarchal thought to the developing Greek mind. Following the tenets set forth by Plato and Aristotle, Greek philosophy began to evolve into schools of thought such as those of the Stoics, Epicureans and Sceptics, and since their development was now primarily generated from disagreements with the major Greek teachings which preceded, I believe the influence of the Hebrew texts were less important, and will therefore end my discussion of the subsequent Greek philosophical thought at this time, and move on to a discussion of the Greek playwrights.

E. Greek Playwrights

Semidramatic rituals were common in many ancient cultures, but the true use of drama to tell stories on the stage began with the ancient Greeks. Most critics believe that tragedy originated with the dithyramb, a passionate poem or speech similar to a Bacchanalian song, that was popular in the seventh century BCE by poets such as Archilochos (c. 680-645 BCE), Arion (c. 620 BCE), and Stesichorus (c. 632-536 BCE).[169] Only fragments of the works of these men

---

168 Ibid., 101, 117. We now know that Moses did not found Jerusalem, and did not establish the First Temple. Attributing such feats to Moses follows the foundation literature (*ktsis*) that was widespread in Greek culture in the seventh and sixth centuries BCE. The legendary founder of a city was often held responsible for many of the features and customs for which the place was later famous. Ibid., 121.

169 Aylen, The Greek Theater, 51-52. The earliest mention of dithyramb is found in a fragment of Archilochus of Paros, from the first half of the seventh century BCE, where it

survive, but it appears that they were sung to the accompaniment of a lyre, in a fashion similar to the *Psalms*, attributed to David in the Old Testament by tradition, although there is no credible historical grounding to this belief. This connection of Greek tragedy with the dithyrambs, which were composed by many of the early Greek poets, is very important, for it is taking place simultaneously with the distribution of the Hebrew Psalms throughout Jerusalem following the return from the Babylonian Exile in 538 BCE. The dates of the composition of the *Psalms* are not known, with many thought to be dated to the centuries before the First Commonwealth (c. 996-586 BCE), and others following the return from the Babylonian Exile.[170] This would place the performance of some of the Psalms in an earlier era than the Greek poets, although the compilation of the Book of *Psalms* was likely in the fifth century BCE, about the time the dithyrambs were becoming popular. While it is possible that the Psalms played a role in the eventual development of theater art in ancient Greece, there is not enough extant evidence to reasonably suggest such a connection.

It is clear, however, that the Greeks took the level of the production of tragic theater to a stage not otherwise achieved in the ancient world. According to Aristotle, the purpose of tragedy was to use characters to portray an action that would demonstrate the chief quality of life: happiness and misery in the same production.[171] The plot was the primary purpose, and the characters secondary, and for this reason, it was easy for the Greek tragedists to use their own particular mythologic and historical personages in order to put forth their reinterpretation of the essence of life. The difference between the historian and the poet was that the historian "describes the thing that has been, and the other a kind of thing that might be."[172] Perhaps for this reason, the extant plays which we have from the fifth century BCE in Greece are all based on traditional myths except one, the *Persians*, by Aeschylus, which was produced in 472 BCE after the victory over the Persian fleet at Salamis in 480 BCE, following the destruction of Athens by Xeres I (486-465 BCE). Aeschylus had fought with the Greek forces at both Marathon and Salamis, and so it is easy to see why he sought to include a current event in his repertoire of material available for presentation on the stage.

For all of their concern upon how mortal human beings acted upon the stage of life, the Greek playwrights were still primarily concerned, as was Herodotus, with "man's relationship to the gods and with the inexorable effect of fate on men and nations," depicting the gods as acting in history directly and indirectly through their oracles.[173] This, of course, is identical to how the Old Testament

---

is said to be "the fair song of Lord Dionysus." Pickard-Cambridge, <u>Dithyramb, Tragedy and Comedy</u>, 1.

170 Alter, The Book of Psalms, xv.

171 Aristotle, <u>The Basic Works of Aristotle</u>, "Poetics," 5.1450a15-25, 1461.

172 Ibid., 9.1451b4-5, 1464.

173 Mandell & Freedman, The Relationship Between Herodotus' *History* and Primary

Primary History was written, although the number of gods involved was obviously different. I therefore think it is a valid undertaking to carefully peruse the Greek texts to discover what relationship may have existed between the two bodies of work. While it is the Greek philosophers who I believe were influenced most by their introduction to ancient Hebrew text of the Old Testament, the change in theology from Homer to the Greek playwrights also provides evidence that discussions of YHWH began to modify the image of the gods, particularly Zeus. In Homer, Zeus was the most powerful of the gods, but the depiction of all of the gods was anthropomorphic, with attributes, despite their power and position, closely resembling those of human beings.

The era in which the great Greek tragedists practiced begins c. 534 BCE, when the Great Dionysia was founded in Athens during the reign of Pisistratus (Peisistratos, c. 605-527 BCE), a few decades after the flowering of Greek philosophical thought with Thales. An integral part of this early Greek drama was the presentation of a moral message conveyed in the action of the characters and chorus on stage. The theater was more than a place of pure entertainment, it was a living classroom where actors portrayed important lessons of life, aimed at educating the public on acceptable modes of behavior. Aristotle, in his work *Poetics*, pointed out that a tragic play was one in which a catharsis, or change of feeling within a character, occurred in such a way that the spectator underwent a similar change "through a course of events involving pity and fear."[174] The outpouring of emotion by an actor on stage was intended to allow the audience to purge or purify themselves by watching actions which were descriptive of universal, rather than particular, points of truth. The lesson of Greek drama was to search for truth which all men could follow: it would set examples for parents to use in the education of their children and the management of their own lives. Aristotle cautioned that this meant the tragic hero must have his good fortune shift to bad because of some unintentional mistake, rather than villainy, and that the tragedy was best revealed by plays which described a few noble houses: Alcmeon, Oedipus, Orestes, Meleager, Thyestes and Telephus.[175]

In interpreting the texts of the extant Greek plays in order to point out passages which I believe are representative of Hebraic influence, I realize I am relying on select translations, which may not be agreed upon by all translators. It is a general axiom that translation is an art, and any one interpretation is not definitive. It therefore is not possible to choose any one rendering as "correct," and fault may be found with any particular quotation I choose to utilize in my comparison. I made every effort to read multiple translations of every line I have quoted, however, and

History, 69.

174 Gerald F. Else, <u>Aristotle's Poetics: The Argument</u> (Cambridge: Harvard University Press, 1957), 221, 226-7.

175 Aristotle, <u>Poetics</u>, 53a12-16, 20, 376.

I believe I have given a fair rendering which will stand up to scholarly criticism.

1. Aeschylus

The first Greek tragedist I will discuss is Aeschylus (525-456 BCE), who is generally known as the "father of tragedy," although he was preceded by the semi-legendary Thespis of Icaria (sixth century BCE), who was the first actor to appear on the stage. Partly because of his talent, and partly because his *The Persians*, produced in 472 BCE, is the earliest extant Greek play, any discussion of ancient Greek theater must begin with the work of Aeschylus. That Aeschylus would have incorporated the teachings of other authors is apparent in the fact that he was quite curious about many things, having been initiated into the Eleusinian Mysteries, and later prosecuted for revealing some of its secrets, which was forbidden. If he believed that truth was apparent in any non-Greek system of beliefs, he would have transmitted that information through one of the legends he discussed.

Only seven of the ninety plays written by Aeschylus survive, but a fragment of one of his lost plays, *Heliades* ("The Daughters of the Sun"), shows how he began to view Zeus in ways quite suggestive of YHWH: "Zeus is air, and Zeus is earth, and Zeus is sky – Zeus is all things, and all beyond the all!"[176] This image continues in *The Suppliants*, which was produced in 470 BCE, where Zeus is said to be the "King of kings, among the blest most blest, of sovereign powers most sovereign."[177] The power of Zeus is even seemingly equal to that of the Hebrew God, for "when by the nod of Zeus it is decreed that a thing be accomplished, the event falls firm on its feet."[178] And like YHWH, Whose anger must be feared, the anger of Zeus must be heeded for he "avenges and fulfils, which none can fight against.[179] But with this fearsome image, Zeus is also compared to YHWH as the one "who establishes Right by immemorial law."[180] Like YHWH, Zeus is also given credit for agricultural abundance: "May Zeus make their soil fertile to yield its dues of fruit and each crop in its season."[181] And finally, just as is directed in the Ten Commandments, "for the law of reverence to parents – this duty is written third in the laws of Justice, whom all must honor."[182] This type of description clearly reflects a view of Zeus as more than one of many Olympian deities, and begins to resemble the homage which the Hebrews paid to their monotheistic God.

---

176 Herington, <u>Aeschylus</u>, 7.
177 Aeschylus, "The Suppliants," 523, 70.
178 Ibid., 91-93, 57. "If Zeus be for us, all will have a happy end." Ibid., 210, 60.
179 Ibid., 647-648, 73-74.
180 Ibid., 674, 74.
181 Ibid., 687-89, 75.
182 Ibid., 708-710, 75.

But I will deal with only the extant plays of Aeschylus in this book, and will analyze them in chronologic order. *The Persians* was the first extant play of Aeschylus that we have, and was produced in 472 BCE, eight years after the victory of the Athenians over the Persians at Salamis. It is the only contemporary historical play of Aeschylus, and it opens with the Persians not yet aware of their overwhelming defeat, and worrying about "the flower of Asian youth" that left home and were serving in Greece.[183] The Dowager Queen Atossa, wife of the late king Darius, and mother of the present King Xeres, is soon brought the news of the slaughter which the Greeks inflicted upon both the navy and the army of the Persians, as Xeres himself witnessed from afar. It should be remembered that Xeres is the grandson of Cyrus the Great, who had allowed the Jews to return to Jerusalem in 538 BCE, and so it is likely that Aeschylus was well aware of the family connections. Aeschylus has the grieving Queen mourn her loss with dignity by pouring libations to the gods below, and summoning the shade of her husband Darius to help them understand how to save their land. The only advice Darius can give is to tell the Persians never to try and fight Greece again, for you cannot win as the land itself fights on their side.[184] He adds that Xeres was foolish to try and overpower the immortal gods, and Atossa explains that he only did it because of his desire to match the glory won by his father. The desire of a son to attain the honor accorded his father was also a theme in the story of Absalom and King David, and the prophecy that disasters will follow disobedience to the edicts of the gods was something that could have come straight out of the warnings of the Hebrew prophets who had warned Israel and Judah of their forthcoming destruction for disobeying the commandments of YWHW in the century before. Since the play deals specifically with the valorous defeat of the Persians by an undermanned Greek force, I will not attempt to project a further biblical influence.

In *The Suppliants*, from 1470 BCE, we have a retelling of the Danaus and Aegyptus story, which I discussed earlier when outlining the legendary founding of Argos by Danaus. The Chorus at the beginning of the play is standing in a grove where there are images of the gods Zeus, Apollo, Poseidon and Hermes, and they explain that "there is an altar of refuge from destruction, where reverence for the gods will keep them safe."[185] This use of a god's temple as a shelter to keep fugitives from being slain is found throughout Greek literature, but it is not clear from where this concept developed. I suggest that the refuge associated with a sanctuary is very similar to its function in the Old Testament, where Moses in the book of *Numbers* was commanded by YHWH to construct six cities of refuge

183 Aeschylus, "The Persians," 9, 122.
184 Ibid., 794, 144.
185 Aeschylus, "The Suppliants," 84-85, 57. "An altar is stronger than a fortress." Ibid., 190, 59. "Zeus protects the suppliant." Ibid., 477, 68.

for the Levites, in order to allow those who killed unintentionally to be kept safe from family vengeance until they could be given a fair trial.[186] Those who committed murder intentionally were put to death without being given refuge, but the protection associated with a sanctuary could very well have been suggested by the Hebrew scriptures.[187]

The third play of Aeschylus, produced in 467 BCE, was *Seven Against Thebes*, the third part of a trilogy about the Theban legend of Laius, king of Thebes, who is primarily known for being the ill-fated father of Oedipus, whose story I will discuss later when I analyze the famous trilogy by Sophocles. Eteocles, son of Oedipus, is presently the king of Thebes, and his brother, Polyneices, is leading an invading force to retake the city from Eteocles. Eteocles chooses six of his most ardent warriors to help him defend the seven gates of the city, and it turns out that in his defense of the seventh gate, he will have to fight his own brother Polyneices, who he had exiled and now wants revenge.

This battle of brother versus brother is very reminiscent of many biblical tales, including Cain and Abel, and Isaac and Jacob, and a soldier warns the king that such a battle could result in brother-murdering, which would be an horrific act with dangerous ramifications for "not through an age of time could that pollution fade."[188] Eteocles ignores his warning, as well as that of the Chorus, responding that "when the gods send destruction there is no escape."[189] As I discussed above, the Greek playwrights would have been well aware of the fate of the Hebrews during the Babylonian Exile, and of the warnings of the Hebrew prophets about the fated destruction of Israel and Judah for failing to heed the commandments of their God, YHWH. Seeing the clear evidence of prophecies of doom affecting an entire contemporary population would have certainly strengthened the belief of the Greeks in the power of the gods.

Sophocles and Euripides also dealt with this theme, and I will discuss their versions here before continuing on with the plays of Aeschylus, since the story of brother-conflict is so prevalent in both Greek drama and the Bible. In *Antigone* by Sophocles, which was written c. 442 BCE, the action takes place the day after the battle for Thebes, when Eteocles and Polyneices had killed each other in mortal combat. Creon has buried Eteocles with honor, but forbidden the burial of Polyneices, which Antigone promises to defy, holding true to the sanctity of affording a proper burial which was a constant theme in Greek literature, dating back to the *Iliad* by Homer. When Antigone asks Ismene to help her bury their brother, Ismene answers that she cannot, and wants the Spirits of the Dead to

---

186 Num 35:6. See e.g., Josh 20:3-6.. In Deut 19:2-4, the number of cities was three.

187 Exod 21:12-13.

188 Aeschylus, "Seven Against Thebes," 679-680, 108.   Zerah and Perez also struggled to be first born in the womb of Tamar. Gen 38:28-29.

189 Ibid., 719, 109.

understand she is not free, but "must obey whoever's in charge."[190] Antigone says she'll do it herself, "go ahead, please yourself – defy laws the gods expect us to honor."[191] This dedication to proper burial of a loved one was also highlighted in the Bible when Moses paused during the rushed Exodus following the death of the firstborn children in Egypt to collect the bones of Joseph in order to carry them back to the Promised Land for a proper burial. It follow the important trait of ancestral worship, which is so prevalent in both the Hebrew and Greek traditions.

Euripides' version of the legend, *The Phoenician Women* (*The Phoenissae*), was probably presented in 409 BCE, and then added to by fourth century BCE producers. This version of the story has Jocasta, the mother of the two brothers, try to have them settle their disagreements without resorting to mortal combat. When Polyneices enters and speaks to Jocasta, he explains that he came to retake his old town, because "men honor property above all else; it has the greatest power in all human life."[192] Eteocles then enters the stage, and the mother asks them to look at each other, face to face, and try to forget old wrongs, something which Jacob and Esau must have also done when they met upon Jacob's return home with his wives and children. Polyneices is first to speak, and says if he is allowed his turn to rule the land, he will forfeit it again when his time is up, as they first agreed to, but if not, will consider it an unjust offense to heaven. Eteocles answers not he decides not from justice, but from might, and that he will not give the kingship up, for "it's cowardice to let the big thing go and settle for the smaller," and shameful if he does it after a show of force.[193] Jocasta tells Eteocles that Injustice is the worst goddess, and that it is better to honor Equality. "Men do not really own their private goods;" she argues, "we simply care for things which are the gods'; and when they will, they take them back again."[194] She tells Polyneices, however, that taking the city by force would ruin his reputation, or lead to his death, so his approach is faulty, as well. Unlike the biblical reunion of Jacob and Esau, the attempt at reconciliation fails, and the two brothers part in order to prepare for war. Although the approach each playwright took to the issue of brotherly parricide is quite varied, it is clear that the Greeks saw fate and concern for valorous conduct to be more important than following the commandment of a god.

The next play assigned to Aeschylus, *Prometheus Bound*, is still of uncertain lineage and date. It deals with the nature of the Olympian gods, rather than with human affairs, and particularly with the fate of Prometheus, who had taken

---

190 Sophocles, "Antigone," 80, 633.
191 Ibid., 93-94, 634.
192 Euripides, "The Phoenician Women," 440, 88.
193 Ibid., 509-10, 90.
194 Ibid., 555-57, 92.

such pity on the helplessness of man that he gave them the precious gift of fire, in violation of Zeus' ordinance which had sought to destroy the race of man and replace them with other beings. For punishment, Zeus commanded that Prometheus be chained to a rock for a thousand years. It is believed to have been the first play in a trilogy, but we do not get a chance to see much of the nature of Zeus in this play because he does not appear on stage. Although Zeus is referred to as the Father, a term which resembles that applied to YHWH, there is little in this play to suggest biblical influence, and I will not discuss it further.

This brings us to the trilogy of the *Orestia*, which is believed by most scholars to be Aeschylus' masterpiece. It won first prize in 458 BCE, and because it is extant, we have the opportunity to carefully analyze the entire nature of the legend of the House of Atreus, which formed the basis of much of Greek drama over the next few centuries. It is not known from where this story first came, but the legend told how Atreus and Thyestes, son of Pelops, became enemies, and how Thyestes wronged Atreus's wife, causing Atreus, in response, to slay Thyestes' children and serve them to him in a ghastly fashion for dinner. Certainly a more horrible tale could not be imagined, and Aeschylus does not spend much time on that generation of family life, but concentrates on the children of Atreus, Agamemnon and Menelaus, who became the heroes of the Trojan War. In dissecting out these incredibly moving plays, I believe we can find vestiges of ancient Hebrew stories which Aeschylus encountered throughout his life, and perhaps utilized in expounding the details of parricidal vengeance.

The first play, *Agamemnon*, begins with the arrival home of Agamemnon following the victorious conclusion of the Trojan War. The Watchman, waiting for signs of Agamemnon's return, prays to Apollo to not let the winds die down in Troy and force a second sacrifice, referring to the one of Iphigenia, "for the terror returns like sickness to lurk in the house; the secret anger remembers the child that shall be avenged."[195] The very opening, therefore, sets the stage for what Agamemnon will suffer as a result of having sacrificed his daughter, and highlights the fact that even though many ancient cultures did not punish infanticide as a crime, they also did not ever condone it as an acceptable act of obedience to a god's command, except for the ancient Hebrews and Greeks. Aeschylus tells how on that fateful day when Agamemnon was told he had to sacrifice his daughter, he knew how wrong it was for a father to shed the blood of his daughter, "but when necessity's yoke was put upon him he changed, and from the heart the breath came bitter and sacrilegious, utterly infidel, to warp a will now to be stopped at nothing."[196] Like Abraham, whose dedication to his deed caused the angel to have to call his name out twice before the knife plunged down, Agamemnon rose to his task, and showed the strength which was required of a commanding

---

195 Aeschylus, "Agamemnon," 154-155, 39.
196 Ibid., 218-20, 41.

general preparing his army for war. "Her supplications and her cries of father were nothing, nor the child's lamentation to kings passioned for battle," and for me, this exposition of Agamemnon's actions indicates an awareness of options which were evident in the story of Abraham, and provides the true basis for why Aeschylus felt the need to extend the story into a trilogy, turning the event into a moral lesson for generations to come.[197]

Aeschylus, from the very start of the play, shows how Clytemnestra has been infuriated by the sacrifice of her daughter, and the Chorus adds incriminations against Agamemnon's returning in glory by warning that:

The vaunt of high glory is bitterness; for God's thunderbolts crash on the towering mountains. Let me attain no envied wealth, let me not plunder cities, neither be taken in turn, and face life in the power of another.[198]

That this admonition refers to Agamemnon and the Greeks is highlighted by the Herald who then appears and explains how we can now boast of our fame and glory for the victory over Troy. Clytemnestra then tells how she, as well, sat at home while the warriors were away for ten years, and "made sacrifice," using a play on words to highlight her husband's crime.[199] The continuous use of the same words to describe the actions of both Clytemnestra and Agamemnon force the audience to understand the suffering which she has gone through, although the memory of her actions once the play has ended will leave little sympathy in the hearts of the Classical Greeks. This attitude is perhaps due to Clytemnestra's obvious deceit in telling the Herald to remind Agamemnon that she has remained "as true as on the day he left her," and "with no man else have I known delight."[200] This claim is patently false, as she has taken a lover during Agamemnon's absence, thereby making her affirmation a duplicitous lie.

When Agamemnon finally arrives on stage, he appears with Cassandra, the prophetess daughter of Priam who he has taken home as a prize. Clytemnestra then appears and explains how glad she is to finally welcome him home, and has her handmaidens spread a crimson carpet for him to walk on, obviously reflecting not only a royal welcome, but a reflection of the blood of the warriors that have lost their lives in the war, as well as the sacrifice of their daughter, and her future plans to slay him in revenge. Agamemnon says not to treat him like a god, but reverence him as a man, and "call that man only blest who has in sweet tranquility brought his life to close."[201] This masterful use of double entendre is a specialty of Aeschylus, and he is at his very best when dealing on stage with the planned murder of Agamemnon.

---

197 Ibid., 228-30, 41.
198 Ibid., 468-74, 49.
199 Ibid., 594, 53.
200 Ibid., 606-611, 53.
201 Ibid., 928-29, 63.

Cassandra then portends to the Chorus the death of Agamemnon and herself at the hands of Clytemnestra, "the woman-lioness, who goes to bed with the wolf, when her proud lion ranges far away."[202] She courageously portends that they will not remain unavenged, for the son will come to slay his mother to retaliate for his father's death. After she enters the house, the voice of Agamemnon being stabbed is heard, and when the door opens again, the bodies of Agamemnon and Cassandra are shown, with Clytemnestra standing over them. Clytemnestra is proud of her actions and tells how "he filled our cup with evil things unspeakable and now himself come home has drunk it to the dregs."[203] Because he slaughtered his own child, her killing him has driven Justice to fulfillment. "With the sword he struck, with the sword he paid for his own act."[204] We do not know if the same blade was used in the killing of both Agamemnon and Iphigenia, as Clytemnestra suggests, but there is no question that Aeschylus is tying the two acts together. At the end of the play, Clytemnestra tells Aegisthus that "you and I have the power; we two shall bring good order to our house at least."[205]

I have spent an excessive period of time on outlining the play of *Agamemnon*, for I believe the incredible detail given to this topic by Aeschylus is evidence of his comparing the difference between the treatment of the act afforded by the biblical authors, and the myth that was handed down from his own ancestors. Aeschylus must have known, in my opinion, how similar this legend of an infanticidal act was to the story of Abraham and Isaac, and despite the completion of the sacrificial act in the Greek version, I believe the influence of the biblical tale is clearly evident. I will complete my discussion of the trilogy with the final two plays, and in my analysis I will point out the aspects which further touch upon messages from the Old Testament.

The next play in the trilogy is *The Libation Bearers (The Choephori)*, and it opens with Orestes, the son of Agamemnon, appearing at his father's tomb and finding his sister Electra paying tribute with libations, and saying how she is now living as a slave in her own house. She adds that Orestes is an outcast from his great properties, while Clytemnestra and Aegisthus live in high style as rulers of the land. Electra prays for Orestes to return and avenge them, and Orestes then comes forth from where he had been keeping himself hidden from view. The storyline of children being deprived of their inheritance by power-hungry relatives is not uncommon in both the biblical text during the period of the Divided Monarchy, and in the royal records of many ancient near Eastern civilizations, and the mention of the Chorus that "the spirit of Right cries out aloud and extracts atonement due: blood stroke for the stroke of blood shall be

---

202 Ibid., 1258-59, 75.
203 Ibid., 1397-98, 80.
204 Ibid., 1528-29, 85.
205 Ibid., 1672-73, 90.

paid," is quite mindful of the blood-vengeance that had to be paid among many societies, including the ancient Hebrews.[206] In tribal societies which lacked a strong central authority, it was the responsibility of the kinship group to be the primary defender of its members, and the Hebrews were no different, requiring that a person who killed one of the clan members would himself be killed in order to "redeem" the blood of the slain member.[207] Such retaliation, however, would not generally extend to innocent relatives. When Tamar, the daughter of King David was raped by her half-brother Amnon, her brother Absalom killed him, and all of his allies, to avenge Tamar's outrage, but did not extend the carnage to innocent people.[208] In this play, Orestes will kill both Aegisthus and Clytemnestra, and at the end tell how he had was right to kill his mother, and he should not be charged with wrong-doing, advice which will prove not to carry any guarantee of safe-passage.[209]

In the final play, *The Eumenides*, Orestes is hounded by the Furies for his matricide, and Apollo tells him at the outset how he will stand by him against the Furies, for "it was I who made you strike your mother down."[210] Aeschylus does not intend to have Orestes carry the burden for this family killing, and involves the gods in order to show how an action of this type will always carry conflicting choices, similar to the choices which both Abraham and Agamemnon faced when directed to perform their infanticidal sacrifices.

While Apollo is speaking, the Furies are sleeping, and Orestes is able to get away, but the ghost of Clytemnestra comes and chides the Furies awake. She is now demanding payment for her own dishonor, and the Furies tell Apollo that he is wrong to shelter Orestes for his matricide, since the killing of a husband is not the shedding of kindred blood, and therefore not equal to what Orestes did.[211] This is a very interesting argument, and it reminds us that the Ten Commandments demand that we honor our mother and father, but does not make any reference to our spouse. Eventually a trial is held in Athens, where Athena calls a jury of twelve citizens to determine the fate of Orestes. Orestes' defense is simple: he killed his mother out of vengeance for the death of his father, and he was told by Apollo that pains would come if he failed to act against the guilty ones.[212] How can he be charged with a crime when he was ordered to act by a god? Once again, we must remember that it was a god, either directly with Abraham, or indirectly through the advice of a seer in touch with a god with

206 Aeschylus, "The Libation Bearers," 310-13, 104.
207 2 Sam 3:27-30. Tigay, "Exodus," 153.
208 2 Sam 13:1-29.
209 Aeschylus, "The Libation Bearers," 1027-31, 130.
210 Aeschylus, "The Eumenides," 84, 137.
211 Ibid., 212, 142. "The man she killed was not of blood congenital." Ibid., 605, 156.
212 Ibid., 464-67, 151.

Agamemnon, who ordered the sacrifice to take place. The Furies argue that if such a matricide goes unpunished, Justice will not be done, and "parents will await the deathstroke at their children's hands."[213] One only needs to remember the rebellion of Absalom against his father King David to realize how critical this argument was at the time.

During the trial, Apollo supports Orestes before the jury, and takes blame for ordering him to act. He adds that he only prophecies through the will of Zeus, thereby evoking the approval of the head deity in the performance of justice.[214] This argument certainly is reflective of the willingness of Abraham to follow YHWH's directive to kill his son Isaac, even though the act itself was aborted at the last second. He then turns the argument made by the Furies around, by stating that the mother is not the parent of her child, "but only nurse of the new-planted seed that grows ... the parent is he who mounts."[215] This explanation of the primacy of the male over the female, even in the act of procreation, was generally accepted by all civilizations of the ancient world, although in Judaism, the Bible was seen as defining the child of a Hebrew (Jewish) mother as being a Jew, and not the father's heritage. Apollo then points to Athena as evidence of the ability to have only a father and not a mother, given the birth of Athena directly from Zeus' head. While this may have evoked a smile on the face of the audience, I do not believe it was intended to indicate current physiologic thought. The sanctity of motherhood was well-accepted in Greek mythology, even if the woman was generally relegated to a subservient role in the family and state.

The jury is divided on the outcome, leaving Athena to cast the deciding vote, and she votes for Orestes, stating her heart is always on the father's side.[216] The Furies are infuriated at this outcome, and threaten to "let loose on the land the vindictive poison dripping deadly out of my heart upon the ground."[217] This anger of gods in the polytheistic system is reflected by the Hebrew prophets in the anger of YHWH over the failure of the Hebrew people to follow His commandments on how to live. Athena convinces them not to take their anger out against the land of Athens, but to turn the battles of men "outward hard against the man who has fallen horribly in love with high renown."[218]

This trilogy concludes the doomed generations of the House of Atreus, and, in my opinion, the tragic concept may very well have been introduced by the traditions of the dissident Hebrews, for in the Torah, God warned the Hebrews not to worship other gods or idols or guilt would fall upon the children, up to

---

213 Ibid., 497-98, 152.
214 Ibid., 615-20, 157.
215 Ibid., 659-60, 158.
216 Ibid., 738, 161.
217 Ibid., 811-13, 164.
218 Ibid., 864-65, 165.

the third and fourth generation.[219] Later Israelite civil and criminal law did not incorporate this legal principle, and instead restricted punishment to the agent alone,[220] but the Hebrews who participated in the Exodus were not subject to the modifications of the post-exilic rabbis, and their view of Justice was very similar to that espoused on the Greek stage. Aeschylus, in the presentation of the fateful lives which followed the crime of Atreus, presents a clear expose of why one's children should not be fated to suffer for the evils of their ancestors, and yet throughout the era of the destruction of Israel and Judah, we see the Hebrew prophets continually warn on how the present generation was suffering, in part, for the apostasy which their parents performed.

2. Sophocles

The next major Greek dramatist was Sophocles, but only seven of his original one hundred twenty-three plays have survived. Once again, we can only lament the loss of these priceless works of art, but continue to marvel at the legacy that has been left by the few which escaped destruction. Sophocles won his first victory in the competitions of tragedy in 468 BCE, sixteen years after Aeschylus first obtained victory in 484 BCE. Athens had become a wealthy city by then, and their victories over the Persians in 490 BCE at Marathon, and 480 BCE at Salamis, encouraged philosophers and scientists alike to flock there from Ionia. In Jerusalem, the Hebrews had returned from the Babylonian Exile, and the words of Ezra were being spread throughout the region following his return to Jerusalem in 458 BCE, allowing traveling Greek intellectuals ready access to the Old Testament tales. We have already discussed the play *Antigone*, and I will now analyze his other productions to show where there are probable influences from the Bible.

Ajax (Aias) is probably the earliest of Sophocles' extant plays, being produced sometime between 450-430 BCE. Ajax was the greatest Greek warrior after Achilles at Troy, and when Agamemnon and Menelaus awarded the armor of Achilles to Odysseus, Ajax set out to kill them in anger, and was deluded by Athena into slaughtering sheep and goats, believing they were his comrades. When Ajax came to his senses, he eventually committed suicide in shame. A forerunner to the big galoot in American gangster movies, Ajax has little of the hero motif surrounding his personna, and his brute strength alone could not compete with the cunning deceit of Odysseus. Although in some ways the contest for the prize of Achilles' armor between Ajax and Odysseus resembles the competition for the primogeniture birthright between Jacob and Esau in the Bible, there is little else in this play to suggest a biblical influence, and so I will not dwell on the details

219 Deut 5:9.
220 Levinson, "Deuteronomy," 377.

of the action.

Oedipus the King, Sophocles' masterpiece, is believed to have been produced between 429-425 BCE, and in this play we begin to see some influx of Old Testament teaching. Most critics see the play as a declaration of the Greek belief that one's fate in life was bound up with a *daimon*, a divinity that presided over one's destiny. With every step in the legend which is told, Oedipus attempts to do the right thing, but his *daimon* appears to steer him straight to the one fate he so desperately tried to avoid. The belief that the Fates or the gods, and not an individual's own decision, determines what will happen in your life is very remindful of the disasters which befell Job. The book of *Job*, is believed to have been written in the sixth century BCE, and Ezekiel is said to have expounded on the righteousness of Job, so it is possible that Sophocles would have had access to the disasters which befell Job at the hands of God, rather than as a result of his own wrongdoing.

The play opens in front of the royal palace at Thebes, where a delegation comes to Oedipus, who now is ruler of the land, to ask how the plague which spreads over the city can be lifted. "We need *now* the great power men everywhere know you possess," they say, referring to his ability to solve the riddle of the Sphinx when he first appeared in Thebes.[221] Oedipus does not know the answer to the problem, but tells how he sent his brother-in-law Creon to Delphi to ask the oracle what was wrong, and he will soon return. Creon then appears and divulges that the oracle said we harbor something incurable, and must purge it by banishing a man or killing him. "It's blood-kin murder that bring this storm on our city," he explains, and the man who killed the former king Laius must be punished or the plague will remain.[222] Once again, as we saw in the trial of Orestes, fratricide is an especially grievous crime, and it highlights how unusual it was for the ancient Greeks and Hebrews to be the only two civilizations to extol a story of infanticide by a respected ancestor in their lore.

Oedipus responds with a willingness to act against the culprit, using a double entendre that would make Euripides proud: "I pray this, too: if he's found at my hearth, inside my house, and I know he's there, may the curses I aimed at others punish me."[223] He tells how Laius had no luck fathering children, and so he would fight for Laius "as I would for my own father," not realizing that, in fact, Laius was his biologic father.[224] The Chorus suggests that the aid of the seer Tiresias be sought, and when Oedipus agrees, Tiresias comes and surprises him with the news that he is the cause of the plague that poisons the land, and "you

---

221 Sophocles, "Oedipus the King," 48-49, 399. When Oedipus first arrived,, he was asked what walks on four legs when young, two legs when an adult, and three legs when older, with the answer being a man.

222 Ibid., 113-14, 129.

223 Ibid., 301-03, 411.

224 Ibid., 320, 411.

have been living unaware in the most hideous intimacy with your nearest and most loving kin," meaning, of course, that he has been sleeping with his own mother.[225]

The incredible intricacies of this plot are truly remarkable, and one wonders if this entire trilogy was truly the imagination of Sophocles alone, or whether it was preceded by other authors whose works have not survived. Either way, the stories define the modern conception of Freud's Oedipus Complex, where a man is believed to have an inherent rivalry with his father for the love of his mother, but I believe that Sophocles went one step further and actually believed that the mother of Oedipus, Jocasta, was aware that Oedipus was her son, and chose to marry him anyway, as I will explain further with quotations from the text. The basis for my view is that when Oedipus was exposed at birth, an iron bar was put through his ankles, causing a deformity which I do not believe she could have ever forgotten. It is not possible, in my opinion, that during their first encounter in bed, she would not have realized that this was the son she long ago abandoned, especially since she also saw a visual resemblance between Oedipus and her husband, as I will discuss shortly. Freud, in my opinion, would have better named the love between a mother and her son the Jocasta Complex, rather than the Oedipal Complex, but I will leave that discussion for another time.

Oedipus is not only surprised, but offended by the explanation of Tiresias, and claims that Creon hired him to overtake the throne. Tiresias, who is blind, answers Oedipus, who will be blind at the end of the play, "I will tell you what your eyes don't see: what evil you are steeped in."[226] When Tiresias leaves, Oedipus repeats the charge of treason against Creon to his face, threatening his life, and Jocasta, hearing of the argument, tells Oedipus she can prove that no man has mastered prophecy, for when she and Laius were married, a prophet told him that he was destined to die at the hands of a son born to them, and yet Laius was killed by foreign bandits at a place where three roads meet. She adds that when their child was three days old, Laius pinned its ankles together and left it exposed, so Apollo failed to have Laius die at the hands of his son. Oedipus' heart starts to race when he hears these details, remembering that location as where he had slain the old man. He asks for further details about the junction where Laius was killed, and when it happened. Jocasta tells how Laius was about your age, tall, with some gray salting his hair, and "he looked then not very different from you now."[227] Oedipus then explains what is frightening him, as Polybus was his father, and Merope his mother, but at a banquet, a drunk told him he was not their real child, so he went to Delphi and was told "I would be my mother's lover," and murder my father. I therefore fled from the house, and when I approached a

---

225 Ibid., 440-41, 418.
226 Ibid., 598-99, 510.
227 Ibid., 860, 442.

junction like you just described, I killed an old man who crowded me off the road.[228] The audience by now is engrossed with the scene opening up on stage, masterfully presented by Sophocles with visual evidence of the horror about to unfold on the faces of the participants. As Oedipus comes to realize that Tiresias was correct in his pronouncement, he declares that his whole nature is evil, for "I make love to his wife with hands repulsive from her husband's blood."[229] Jocasta tells him not to rush to judgement until he hears what an eyewitness to the murder has to say.

The Chorus, anticipating what will happen next, tells how if prophecies cannot show us the way, then we will no longer to be able to honor Delphi as untouchable. They also question whether the gods can truly hold power if they can allow such horrible things to happen, once again citing the accepted belief that the gods control human behavior. These events, of course, are mimicking the attitude of the majority of people in Jerusalem who were ignoring the warnings of the Hebrew Prophets, refusing to believe that such men could truly know the workings of God. A messenger then arrives and seems to confirm this belief, for he states that Polybus is dead, and it was not at the hands of Oedipus, thereby proving the earlier prophecy false. Jocasta then tells Oedipus not to worry any longer, for "chance rules our lives," and not prophecy.[230] She also shows her awareness of what Freud had concluded, by stating that "in their dreams, before now, many men have slept with their mothers," not spelling out further whether this was known from her own dreams, which I believe is the real explanation.[231] The messenger, however, continues his story and admits to Oedipus that he could not have been the true son of Polybus, since I had found you exposed in the woods, and brought you to him to raise, and your ankles were pinned.[232] The messenger then finalizes the connection by saying that a shepherd who worked for Laius was the one who gave the infant to him. Jocasta, instead of showing interest in what is being told, tells Oedipus not to listen and to ignore his words: "If you care about your life, give up your search," and "let my pain be enough!"[233] If there ever was evidence of self-indictment in the words of a defendant, the response of Jocasta is clearly that of one who was aware of the identity of her only son. Oedipus says I must have the truth, and Jocasta runs into the palace. When the herdsman is brought in, he explains that the child was given to him by Jocasta, because she heard of the prophecy and was afraid Laius would kill the

---

228 Sophocles, "Oedipus the King," 910-30, 445. In *Oedipus at Colonus*, he explains how the men he fought would have killed him, so "before the law my hands are clean." Sophocles, "Oedipus at Kolonos," 599-600, 543.

229 Sophocles, "Oedipus the King," 946-47, 446.

230 Ibid., 1119, 455.

231 Ibid., 1123-24, 455.

232 Oedipus shows that there were signs of this by saying "from birth I've carried the shame of those scars." Ibid., 1178, 460.

233 Ibid., 1215-16, 462.

child, so there was no question of her not knowing of the exposure event. News is then brought that Jocasta has killed herself, proof-positive evidence that she knew what was happening all along. Screaming out that his eyes will never see the evil that he has caused, Oedipus pulls the pins he had taken from his mother's dress, and plunges them into his eyes.

The story of Oedipus is certainly one of the most famous of all the Greek tragic legends, and while it stands alone in its tale of love between a mother and her son, it has roots in similar types of legends which I described about the desire of Potiphar's wife for Joseph, and the wife of Theseus for her step-son Hippolytus. Other biblical stories, such as Jacob sleeping with Jacob's concubine, and Absalom sleeping with David's wives, all point to suggestive relationships which may have been gathered and eventually coalesced into the Oedipal saga that has so vibrantly characterized the pinnacle of Greek tragedy. Although the Greek version stands out as the true epitome of incestual love, and Sophocles' play as the most masterful extant version of this illicit behavior, the biblical material, in my opinion, helped the Greek playwrights refine their art with descriptions of human behavior that included the love of a mother for her son.

The follow up to the events of this horrific day of realization are portrayed by Sophocles in *Oedipus at Colonus*, the date of which is uncertain, but is believed to have been produced in 401 BCE. The play discusses the end of Oedipus' life, but has few other biblical connections, and I will not discuss the details any further. The date of *The Women of Trachis* (*The Trachiniae*) is uncertain, but it is thought to have been written between 450-430 BCE. At the time Sophocles wrote the play, Heracles was a widely worshiped cult figure, with a reputation as a savior and benefactor of humankind. There are elements of the strength of Samson in the exploits of Heracles, but nothing to reach the level which this demigod attained, even though some similarities reverberate in Sophocles' production. I will also not discuss the details of this play any further.

Another play which carried on the Orestes tradition is *Electra*, the date of which is uncertain, although it likely was produced 420-410 BCE. Since by now, the tale of Orestes has been dealt with by many playwrights, I do not feel the version by Sophocles shows any direct biblical influence, and will not present the details.

The *Philoctetes* was presented in 409 BCE, when Sophocles was eighty-seven years old. Both Aeschylus and Euripides rendered the story, but their plays are no longer extant. The story revolves around Philoctetes, who has been abandoned on the desolate island of Lemnos by the Greeks under Odysseus ten years previously because of a festering foot wound. The Greeks cannot take Troy without his bow, which was given to him by Heracles, but he refuses to return. Odysseus must now assure that the man returns to Troy with them so the war can be won. It offers some insight into the similarity of the wiles possessed by both Odysseus and

Jacob. Odysseus opens the play on the island telling Neoptolemos how they had to leave Philoctetes behind because of the stench, and the constant screaming which interfered with the sacrifices. He sends Neoptolemus to find him to then try and convince him that he also hates the Greeks, and wants revenge. Neoptolemus is bothered by this subterfuge, and wants to try and convince him with a rational argument, but Odysseus answers that at your age, I was the same, "but now I've learned it's words that move people, not deeds."[234] Odysseus, of course, like Jacob, was known for his masterful cunning, although he also had all the strength and valor for which Greek heroes were famous.

When they finally find Philoctetes, Neoptolemus follows Odysseus' advice, and pretends he doesn't know who he is, and that he is angry at the leaders of the Greek force because they humiliated him. When he then says he has to leave, Philoctetes begs to be taken with, and Neoptolemus agrees to his rescue. Odysseus then shows up and they plan to return to the ship with only the bow, leaving Philoctetes behind. Neoptolemus feels ashamed by the ruse as they head toward the ship, and wants to return the bow, but Odysseus forbids the action. Neoptolemus goes anyway and is unable to convince Philoctetes to come with them to Troy, but Heracles appears and tells Philoctetes his true fame will come as the Greeks with his aid defeat Troy. In true Hollywood fashion, Philoctetes finally agrees to go to Troy.

3. Euripides

Euripides was the last of the renowned tragedists, having won his first victory in 441 BCE. The famous Sophist Protagoras was said to have read from his acclaimed book, *On the Gods*, at the house of Euripides, an indication that the reputation of Euripides was respected throughout the Athenian populace. Despite these accolades, Euripides was not as popular as his predecessors Aeschylus and Sophocles, and he was often attacked with biting farce by Aristophanes, the noted comic playwright.[235] Although modern critics often see Euripides as sympathetic to the cause of women, the ancients usually described him as a woman-hater.[236] Seventeen or eighteen of his ninety-five plays have survived intact, with *Rhesus* being contested as to its true authorship.

The first of Euripides' plays was *Alcestis*, presented in 438 BCE as the fourth play of a tetralogy which has not survived extant. It tells the story of Admetus, king of Thessaly, who had been destined to die early, and his devoted wife, Alcestis,

---

234 Sophocles, "Philoktetes," 110-11, 197.

235 Aristophanes also parodied Socrates in *The Clouds*, but Plato showed Socrates and Aristophanes as friends in the *Symposium*. Plato, Complete Works, "Symposium," 223C-D, 505.

236 Murray, Euripides and His Age, 18.

the daughter of Pelias, agreed to be a substitute and die in his place. Phrynichus (early fifth century BCE) had written an earlier version of the story, which has been lost. Alcestis is depicted with full honors, in this play, and her willingness to give up her life for her husband is remindful of the willingness of Isaac to be sacrificed by his father Abraham, and that of Iphigenia as well, to forfeit their own lives, if necessary, as indicative of the subservience of the lesser to the greater in both the ancient Hebrew and Greek societies.[237] As I discussed in Chapter 9, I believe the fable of Abraham and Isaac is what influenced the Greeks to initiate the legend of the sacrifice of Iphigenia by Agamemnon, but it appears that the Greeks alone took this devotion of a child to a father to the next step by including the willingness of a wife to die in order to spare the life of her husband.

While this first extant play of Euripides seems not to fulfill his reputation as one of the three great dramatists of Classical Greece, his next tragedy, *The Medea*, is one of the greatest, and most sinister, play in all of ancient Greek tragedy. Produced in 431 BCE, it tells the story of Medea, a woman who was depicted with all of the evil traits which the ancient world found to warn men of the dangers of the power of the opposite sex. Not only were women seen as abusing their power of sensuality in the conquest of men, but their ambition and desire for revenge were dangerous obstacles which even the most potent hero could fail to overcome. Medea was a barbarian princess from Colchis, at the eastern extremity of the Black Sea, and a sorceress, who was the daughter of King Aeetes, who owned the golden fleece which Jason and the Argonauts came to steal. She fell in love with Jason and helped him to obtain the prize and escape, even though she had to murder her own brother to succeed. They settled in Iolcus, and had two children, but were later exiled to Corinth, where Jason abandoned Medea to marry the daughter of Creon, the king of the land. The play opens with Medea's nurse ruing that Medea and Jason ever met, now that Jason has abandoned Medea and her children, to take a royal wife. Medea is wasting away in tears, and turning away from her children, and she is afraid something dreadful might happen, "for her heart is violent."[238]

In Greek tragedy, omens are often true forebodings of things to come, a condition which is apparent in the Old Testament, as well. Medea then appears and laments how she is lost in sufferings so great, "I wish I might die."[239] This comment makes clear the option of suicide that Medea might consider, and makes her eventual decision even more grotesque. The nurse tells the children to run inside, and keep well out of sight, a warning which the audience would clearly understand, knowing the legend which preceded the play. Medea then

---

237 "Could any woman show that she loves her husband more than herself better than by consent to die for him?" Euripides, "Alcestis," 154, 14.

238 Euripides, "The Medea," 38, 60.

239 Ibid., 97, 62.

foretells the entire play by saying "I hate you, children of a hateful mother," and then curses them and Jason with the final request of "let the whole house crash."[240] With plays about the house of Atreus and the family of Agamemnon fresh in their minds, the Greek audience was well aware of what this line meant.

The nurse points out the role of the gods in this scenario, and how "god indeed, when in anger, brings greater ruin to great men's houses."[241] This type of punishment was also being warned about throughout Israel and Judah in the centuries before by the Hebrew prophets who wailed of how the Hebrews would be decimated because of their impiety and failure to heed the commandments of YHWH.

Euripides compares Medea to a lioness guarding her cubs, but in real life it is the male lion, and not the mother, who will destroy the children of another male, in order to put the lioness back in heart to produce his own offspring. Whether it be because of the vindictiveness of a god, or the jealousy of a woman, the blood of innocent victims would have to once again flow free.

Very much sounding like Clytemnestra, Medea then bemoans the fate of women who are forced to keep their eyes on only their husband, while the man can do what he pleases. In addition, she had to give up her home, and her homeland, to follow her husband, and now she is left alone so he can bed the daughter of a king. King Creon then enters to tell Medea that she is being expelled from the land because he fears for the life of his daughter, whom Jason has sought to marry. Medea pleads to be allowed to stay, assuring him that her anger is not directed at him or his daughter, but he refuses. She then asks to be allowed to stay only for one day, in order to plan where to go. She plays on his love of his own children by saying she has no problem going into exile, but "it is the children being in trouble that I mind."[242] The mastery of Euripides' choice of words to admit that the children are in trouble, without suggesting that it is from her that the danger exists, would surely convey a chill through the spines of those watching this performance. Creon says he knows he is making a mistake, but agrees to her request. It is not recorded if anyone in the audience stood up and yelled "NO!" at the stage.

I am not going to give more detail about what happens next, except to say that Medea considers the various ways she can kill all three of her enemies – Creon, his daughter, and Jason – but she decides to make a poisoned dress and diadem as a gift for the bride-to-be, and all who touched it would die. She also decides that she will kill her own children, for their loss will make Jason grieve even more intensely. It should be remembered that when Hagar left Abraham's house, she was so despondent that she was ready to expose Ishmael to death, but was stopped

240 Ibid., 114, 63.
241 Ibid., 130, 63.
242 Ibid., 347, 71.

by an Angel who told her that the boy would one day become great. The killing of one's child as an act of mercy, rather than abandoning them to be left alone in the world, was a common occurrence in the ancient world, and was reflected in the Bible as occurring during times of famine, although at times the biblical incentive was cannibalism rather than compassion.[243] That her concern is not for her children alone, however, is evident in her answer to the Chorus' asking if she has the heart to kill her own flesh and blood: "Yes, for this is the best way to wound my husband."[244] Hell hath no fury like a woman scorned, Shakespeare famously wrote, and at the end of the play, she murders her children with a sword, and then explains to Jason what she has done as she is drawn away from the top of the house in a chariot drawn by dragons, carrying the bodies of the children with her.

The stories of how wives react when they are scorned by their husbands is reflective of the attitude which the ancient Greek and Hebrew societies placed on the image and role of women. In the Bible, polygamy was acceptable up to the time of the return from the Babylonian Exile. Stories of the biblical women were not always complementary, but they never were seen as directly threatening the lives of their husbands. In general, they were subservient partners, who sought means to gain the affection of the husbands without causing harm to real or potential competitors. The portrayal of Clytemnestra, Medea, and the wife of Heracles, on the other hand, tells a different story. Although Greek playwrights did not suggest that the moral code of monogamy should be abandoned, they definitely highlighted the dangers of jealousy, which caused the death of many a hero who thought of bedding another concubine or wife. Did the biblical stories convince the Greek tragedists that monogamy was the preferable way to go? We are lacking too many extant plays to make a decision in this question, but it is clear that the actions of many of the Greek wives was indicative of the dangers associated with jealousy ignited by sexual exploits outside the marriage bond.

The next play, *Hippolytus*, was produced in 428 BCE, and was the second version of the script, the first of which did not survive, probably because it was not received with favor. I have previously discussed the legend of Hippolytus in comparison to the story of Joseph and the wife of Potiphar, since it involves an attempt by Phaedra, the wife of Theseus and the stepmother of Hippolytus, who was the illegitimate son of Theseus and an Amazon Queen, to sexually entice the young man into who's home she married. When he refused her advances, she falsely claimed he tried to rape her, as did the wife of Potiphar against Joseph, thereby forcing a punishment, which involved jail time for Joseph, but death for Hippolytus. In Euripides' version of the tale, Aphrodite (Cypris) opens the play with an explanation for why she decided to reek such havoc on Hippolytus. She

---

243 Lev 26:29; Deut 28:53, 56-57; 2 Kgs 6:28; Jer 19:6, 9; Ezek 5:10.
244 Euripides, "The Medea," 817, 87.

tells how she exalted men who gave her honor, but Hippolytus was the only man who blasphemed her, and refused the bed of love or marriage, choosing instead to honor the Maiden Goddess Artemis, with whom he reveled in the hunt of wild things. In many ways, this detestation was remindful of the commandment of YHWH to put procreation between man and woman as one of the essential duties of all men. Failing to couple and produce children was an impious act, and although punishment for this deficit was not outlined in the biblical text, the Greek legend took a more violent turn. Aphrodite decides to punish Hippolytus by making Phaedra fall in love with him, knowing that Phaedra will die from the rejection of her advances in the process, but "her suffering does not weigh in the scale so much that I should let my enemies go untouched."[245]

This anthropomorphic quality for revenge of the Greek gods is remindful of the story of Job in the Old Testament, where the Divine Adversary, indicative of the Devil, convinces God that Job is only faithful because of all the benefits he has received.[246] It is also something which the playwrights would have heard from the rantings of the Hebrew prophets who warned of YHWH's decision to destroy Judea and Jerusalem for the apostasy being committed in the land.

Hippolytus first appears in the play laying a garland on the altar of Artemis, and noting how he can only hear her words but "may not see God face to face," a condition identical to that warned about in the Hebrew Bible.[247] His servant cautions him that it is dangerous to only honor one god, and not another like that of Aphrodite who stands before his gate, but Hippolytus explains that "men make their choice: one man honors one God, and one another."[248] While the polytheistic Greeks were careful to try and honor all the gods to some degree, they obviously had their favorites, and this play warned of the dangers which accompanied the exaggeration of favoritism to the degree which was necessitated by those with monotheistic tendencies.

The Epode of the Chorus then seems to soften the usual Greek approach to the dangers of women in love, and notes Phaedra's misery as stemming from the fact that "unhappy is the compound of woman's nature; the torturing misery of helplessness, the helplessness of childbirth and its madness are linked to it for ever."[249] The reason for Phaedra's distress is not yet known to those on stage, but we soon find out that she is starving herself to death for the love of Hippolytus, and her nurse is so distressed by the immoral admission that she wants to kill herself. She returns to her senses, however, and tells Phaedra that her plight is not uncommon, and that she must find some way to turn her sickness into

---

245 Euripides, "Hippolytus," 47-48, 165.

246 Job 1:8-11.

247 Euripides, "Hippolytus," 87, 166. God told Moses that "you cannot see My face, for man many not see Me and live." Exod 33:20. The Jewish Study Bible, 188.

248 Euripides, "Hippolytus," 103, 167.

249 Ibid., 161-64, 170.

health again. She says she has some magic potions which will help her. When Hippolytus returns, however, the nurse betrays Phaedra's secret to him, and he is incensed and damns the whole female race, wishing that men "might have lived in houses free of the taint of women's presence."[250] Phaedra overhears all of this, and hangs herself, choosing a "good name rather than life."[251] Theseus returns and finds a letter she had left for him, which says that Hippolytus has raped her. He then turns toward the sea and prays to Poseidon to kill his son, an infanticidal act not commanded by a god, but evoked out of anger. Hippolytus appears and swears he is a virgin and did not do what he is accused of, but Theseus does not believe him and banishes him at once. A messenger then returns with the news that as Hippolytus was fleeing, Poseidon heard Theseus' prayers and sent waves on the shore, causing the horses to bolt and drag the young man, killing him on the rocks. At the end, Artemis tells Theseus that "you have murdered a son, you have broken nature's laws."[252] She adds, however, that all was caused by the anger of Aphrodite, which is the settled custom of the gods, and your ignorance acquits you. The ghost of Hippolytus also enters to absolve his father of guilt. Euripides, in my opinion, has incorporated the biblical proscriptions to accept the necessity of procreation – be fruitful and multiply – as well as the infanticidal motif of a father killing his son, in highlighting the basic message of this particular legendary text. It is evident how expansive the Greek stage became in portraying simple moral storylines, first compiled in the biblical text, and then amplified by the imagination and literary artistry of the talented Greek playwrights.

Hecuba is believed to have been produced in 425 BCE, and was extremely popular and often quoted in ancient times. Hecuba was the wife of King Priam of Troy, and her nineteen children included the hero-warrior Hector, the abductor of Helen, Paris, and the prophetess who was brought home by Agamemnon, Cassandra. She also appears in *The Trojan Women* by Euripides, where she becomes the slave of Odysseus, so it is clear that Euripides found her position as matriarch of the Trojan royal house very intriguing. Her tragic life bears little relationship to the matriarchs in the Bible, however, and so I will not discuss this play in detail.

The date of *Andromache* is uncertain, but it probably was written between 430-424 BCE. Andromache is the widow of the Trojan hero Hector, and after the fall of Troy she was allotted as a slave to Neoptolemus (Pyrrhus), the son of Achilles and Deidamia. The war had been a truly tragic ordeal for Andromache, forcing her to witness the death of her husband at the hand of Achilles, and the demise of her infant son Astyanax, who was hurled from the highest tower in Troy, dashed to

250 Ibid., 623-24, 189. "I'll hate you women, hate and hate and hate you, and never have enough of hating." Ibid., 664, 190.
251 Ibid., 774, 195.
252 Ibid., 1287, 214.

death by the rocks below. She now was living with Neoptolemus in the Thessalian plains of Phthia, near the city of Pharsalus, and had since given birth to a son, which had resulted in her being cruelly persecuted by the wife of Neoptolemus, Hermione, the daughter of Menelaus and Helen, in a manner resembling the treatment of Hagar by Sarah. Like Sarah, Hermione had remained barren, and because Andromache was able to conceive, indicating that the fault did not lie with Neoptolemus, she claimed Andromache had been giving her potions, and she wanted her eliminated. To protect her son while Neoptolemus was off at Delphi, Andromache had secretly put him in another's keeping, and as the play opened, she was at the altar of Thetis, protecting her own life in the process. Like Hecuba, her life does not resemble biblical tales, except for this use of a sanctuary to provide a safe-haven, and I will not analyze this play further.

The date of *The Heracleidae* (*The Children of Heracles*) is uncertain, but the plot revolves around the hatred of the powerful Eurystheus, King of Argos, for his cousin Heracles, and offers little evidence of biblical influence, so I will not discuss it in detail. *The Suppliants* (*The Suppliant Women*) is believed to have first been acted in 420 BCE, and deals with the same legend of *Seven Against Thebes*, and the inhumanity of war. In the play, Aethra, the mother of Theseus, king of Athens, is at Eleusis, near Athens, praying to Demeter for the seven women who have come as suppliants for the loss of their seven noble sons who commanded the attack on the gates of Thebes under the directive of Adrastus, king of Argos, who led the expedition in an attempt to claim a share of Oedipus' inheritance for his son-in-law Polynices. They are being refused the right to bury their son's bodies, and are asking her to seek help for them from her son: "To mourn the dead brings honor to those who live," they say, once again voicing the ancient concerns over the sanctity associated with a proper burial."[253] Theseus asks them on what ground the refusal to bury is made, since the request is sacred and follows the laws of war, and Adrastus answers that there are no reasonable grounds, and the rulers of Thebes are only bad winners. Without the aid of Athens, they are not able to press their case. Theseus tells how he believes that the good outweighs the bad in human life, "and I praise the god who set our life in order."[254] He then list the benefits the god provides, which mimic those found in the Bible: human intelligence and language, nourishment from the land, and seers who help tell the future. But you flouted the gods in pursuing your attacks, he adds, and so "take what comes: wrestle with fate alone, and let me be."[255] Aethra tells him that the power which holds men together "is noble preservation of the laws," and it would be wrong to not allow these women the right to bury their sons.[256] Theseus agrees

---

253 Euripides, "The Suppliant Women," 78, 59.
254 Ibid., 201, 66.
255 Ibid., 248-49, 67.
256 Ibid., 313, 70.

that the Greeks look to him to punish wickedness, and so he will go and free the dead. He adds, "I think it wrong that a child should not return his parents' care," echoing the words of the fifth commandment.[257]

The necessity to afford proper burial of the dead shows up repeatedly in Greek drama, and while the tradition is not attributable to Hebrew practices alone, the teachings of the Bible would have been consistent with Greek practice, as seen with Moses' concern over the return of Joseph's bone to his homeland when the Exodus began. When a herald comes from Thebes asking to speak to the master of the land, Theseus tells him "this city is free, and ruled by no one man," the people reign.[258] The herald answers with words which reflect the view of Plato in his favored philosopher-king rule that the people are no right judge of arguments, for they are swayed to much by puffed-up speech: "when a wretch, a nothing, obtains respect and power from the people by talk, his betters sicken at the sight."[259] Theseus responds that nothing is worse than an absolute ruler, for "with written laws, people of small resources and the rich both have the same recourse to justice."[260] This treatise on political science would play equally well in both Athens and Jerusalem. The herald warns Theseus to banish Adrastus from his land, and to leave the city of Thebes alone, or face war. Theseus answers that all Greece is concerned when anyone tries to strip the dead of their due. The sides cannot agree and the stage is set for war, in which Theseus is victorious. Many more men die in battle, however, and when Adrastus hears the news of the victory, he responds, "If you lose money you can get it back, but no one recovers this expense; a human life."[261]

This play holds particular importance in my theory of Hebraic influence on the Greek playwrights, as it presents a standard Greek social norm – the sanctity of the burial rite – with a reason that follows the standard Hebraic explanation of the sanctity of the God-given laws. The Torah and the Ten Commandments were the basis of the entire system of Hebrew laws, and the Greeks would follow this same path in forming the first democracy on earth, based upon a fundamental faith in the legal system which gave all Greek citizens equality and the guarantee of legal redress for wrongs committed either by individuals or the state. Euripides clearly believed in this concept, and his language is very reminiscent of that which permeated the biblical text.

The Trojan Women was produced in 415 BCE, soon after the siege and capture of the island of Melos by the Athenians. It again deals with the theme of captives of the Trojan War, similar to *Hecuba* and *Andromache*, and opens shortly after the

257 Ibid., 361-62, 71.
258 Ibid., 405, 73.
259 Ibid., 423-25, 73.
260 Ibid., 432-33, 74.
261 Ibid., 775-76, 86.

capture of Troy when all the men have been killed. As before there is no biblical influence to be identified. Another play with an infanticidal theme is *Heracles*, the date of which is uncertain, although it seems to have been written c. 420 BCE. In this play, Hera causes madness to be inflicted on Heracles, who then proceeds to kill his own children, believing they are the sons of Eurystheus, who had imposed the terrible Twelve Labours upon him. When Theseus later tries to comfort him once he comes to his senses by saying that "fate exempts no man; all men are flawed, and so the gods, unless the poets lie,"[262] Heracles disagrees, using the biblical adage that "if god is truly god, he is perfect, lacking nothing."[263] This eulogy seems to me to be a direct response of a Greek thinker attempting to collate the multiple stories of infanticide which pervade Greek mythology, with the story of Abraham and Isaac, and the entire warnings of YHWH throughout the Bible to not perform the impious sacrificial killings of children that characterized the pagan religions.

For the Greeks, having the gods play the scapegoat for the unimaginable actions of men was an easy excuse, but the ancient Hebrews were forced to explain such actions in a manner consistent with the anger and beneficence of YHWH alone, which may explain why Isaac was spared, while Iphigenia was allowed to die. Euripides, however, is not content with placing the blame for our actions on the gods, and searches for more rational explanations, which are based on the moral frailty of Man, rather than divine intercession.

Iphigenia in Tauris is believed to have been composed c. 420 BCE, with some dating the play between 414-410 BCE. In this play, Euripides attempts to provide and alternate interpretation of the sacrifice of Iphigenia by Agamemnon, more in line with the ending of the attempted sacrifice of Isaac by Abraham. As the play opens, Iphigenia is the High Priestess in the Temple of Artemis Tauris, and tells how people believe she was sacrificed by her father, Agamemnon, but Artemis rescued her and substituted a deer to bleed on the altar, a clear reference to the biblical story. The plot again involves her being reunited with Orestes, and is extremely contrived, but I believe it reflects an attempt by Euripides to do everything he can with his position of authority as one of the renowned tragedists of ancient Greece to modify the image of Greek mythology, making some of the legends more consistent with the moral presented by Abraham and Isaac, then of the original Agamemnon and Iphigenia tradition. Since we do not have the entire list of the plays written by the Greek tragedists extant, it is difficult to prove such a theory, but it is easy to see why the literary giants of the era would strive to have their civilization remembered more for the brave and moral actions of their heroes, than for ghastly remembrances of parricide and infanticide.

Ion is generally categorized as one of the later works of Euripides, believed

---

262 Ibid., 1333-35, 110.
263 Ibid., 1345-46, 111.

to have been written sometime between 420-410 BCE. It deals with Ion, a young man who had been born to Creusa, the daughter of Erechtheus, the autochthonous king of Athens, who was seduced by Apollo and gave birth to a son, who she exposed because of fear of her parents. Unknown to her, Apollo had Hermes bring the child to Delphi, where he was raised by the prophetess, and now lived in service of the god. The Greeks practiced exposure throughout their entire early history, and a Greek father could legally expose any unwanted child as early as 600 BCE, as evidenced by the rulings of Solon (c. 638-558 BCE), the Athenian statesman and law-giver.[264] There is little else in this play to reflect biblical tradition.

Helen, which was produced in 412 BCE, also follows a variant of the standard Greek legend, whereby Helen never actually went to Troy, but only a phantom-image was sent, a suggestion first made by Hesiod, and recorded by Stesichorus, the sixth century BCE Greek lyricist and successor to Hesiod.[265] Herodotus claimed he heard from the priests of Hephaestus in Memphis, Egypt, that Helen and Paris fled together, but the winds forced them ashore on the Egyptian coast, and Proteus, King of Egypt, confiscated Helen and kept her safe until Menelaus could retrieve her.[266] Much like the standard biblical text being reinvented by rabbis, and collected in the Talmud, the Greek playwrights continued to reflect on their oral legends, and modify them when necessary to maintain a history more consistent with their changing mores. The servant tells how the workings of God are hard to predict:

"He moves the pieces and they come somehow into a kind of order. Some have bad luck while others, scatheless, meet their evil and go down in turn. None can hold fortune still and make it last.[267]

Euripides, however, takes the opportunity to warn that prophecy is full of lies: "There never was any good in burning things on fires nor in the voices of fowl."[268] The art was invented for making money, and the "best prophet is common sense, our native wit."[269] While reflecting, perhaps, on the type of prophecy which was going on in Jerusalem at the time, it does not appear that this opinion of Euripides was held by the general public, given the fact that the Delphic Pythia was renowned throughout the civilized world at the time. The Chorus, while agreeing with his advice, still notes that "if you have the gods for friends you have

---

264 Milner, Hardness of Heart, Hardness of Life: The Stain of Human Infanticide, 129. The Greek father could expose his infant child whether it was legitimate or not, as opposed to the Roman patriarch who only had control over his legitimate offspring. Ibid.

265 Euripides, "Helen," 261.

266 Herodotus, The History, 2.112-16, 117-18.

267 Euripides, "Helen," 712-15, 221.

268 Ibid., 746-47, 222.

269 Ibid., 757, 222.

a better thing than prophecy in your house."[270]

Electra was produced in 413 BCE, about the same time as *Helen*, and takes place in Argos after the end of the Trojan War, when Agamemnon had been killed by Clytemnestra, leaving Aegisthus as king of the land. Orestes was saved by Agamemnon's servant from being killed by Aegisthus, and was given to Stophius to bring up in the land of Phocis, while Electra stayed at home, pursued by suitors. Aegisthus was afraid that Electra could bear sons who would take vengeance for his actions, raising the scepter of fear I discussed earlier, and therefore kept her hidden in the house, away from the princes of the land, eventually giving her to a poor local farmer to marry, who opens the play and tells how she is still a virgin. While this play again reflects the retelling of a popular fable for interested Greek audiences, there is little evidence of biblical influence, and so I will not describe the action in detail. We now begin to enter the final few years of Euripides' life, and the plots of the tragedies continue to reflect an input from biblical themes. *Orestes* was produced in 408 BCE, and takes place six days after Orestes had murdered his mother. We have seen the theme of this play many times before on the Greek stage, with most quite respectful and understanding of Orestes' anger directed at his mothers's assassination of his father, but in this play we begin to see some investigation into how Clytemnestra's action may have been justified. In discussing how his mother has affected the life of Orestes, Euripides shows, in my opinion, some influence of biblical teaching.

The play opens with Orestes asleep, and Electra arising to speak the prologue. She tells how there are terrible mortal tortures, like those inflicted on Tantalus who must tremble with a rock hanging overhead; or Thyestes who was fed his own children by his brother Atreus. She then adds Orestes to this list, for he murdered his mother after being persuaded by a god, and admits that she and his friend Pylades have tried to help. He lies here now, wasted by a raging fever and whirled on to madness, pursued by the Eumenides, hounding him with terror. For six days he has not tasted food or wet his lips or bathed, while the people of Argos have posted a decree declaring us matricides and outlaws, forbidding anyone to speak to us or give us shelter. Today, an assembly decides whether we shall live or die. In this short space of fifty lines, Euripides has painted a picture with words and starkness that must have had an incredible effect on the audience, who had seen portrayals of this story many times before, but none, I am sure, quite so terrifying.

The agony of Orestes is summarized by the chorus in its description of "Just the act, crime unjust ... Right and wrong confounded in a single act."[271]

While the Bible does not spend time in detailing the agony which Abraham must have gone through in his own deliberations after being asked by YHWH to

---

270 Ibid., 759-60, 222.
271 Ibid., 193-94, 123.

sacrifice Isaac, I believe that Euripides pondered his reaction at length, and was impressed by how Abraham remained steadfast in following his orders, which were given directly by God without the intercession of a seer. While he was willing to sacrifice his son, however, his action was forestalled, indicating the need to realize that a true deity would never require a believer to perform such an impious act. This is most evident in Electra's compassionate admission:

> O Mother, mother who gave me birth, who killed and was killed, you slew your husband, you killed your children too. By your death we died. We are the living dead. You are dust and ashes, while I, a living ghost, dead to this sunlit world, stalk with withered life, childless, unmarried, crying my sorrow, lost, alone in the endless night.[272]

When Menelaus enters the stage and sees the condition Orestes is in, he asks what sickness is responsible, and Orestes says "I call it conscience," the certain knowledge of wrong, which makes me sick from remorse.[273] He then tells Menelaus that the court verdict was death by stoning, and asks Menelaus to rescue him. At that moment, Tyndareus, the father of Helen and Clytemnestra, enters and is sickened by the sight of Orestes, asking Menelaus how he could talk to him. He says that when he found out about his father's murder, he should have dragged Clytemnestra to court, and taken legal action, not murder. Our ancestors proscribed banishment and not murder. This opinion is very much in keeping with the letter of the law in Athens, but it bypasses the argument of both Abraham and Orestes that they were simply following the bidding of a God (god). He turns on Orestes, calling him monster and says these fits of madness are the price you pay for your act as "heaven itself has made you mad."[274] Orestes responds angrily, stating that he had no choice for his mother had taken a lover and killed his father, and I had every right in the world to kill her. "I should not invoke the gods when defending myself on a charge of murder, but *in god's name, in the name of heaven,* what was I supposed to do?"[275] "Apollo, the one god whose every oracle and word mankind obeys blindly" commanded me to murder my mother, what could I do?[276] His argument goes nowhere, and Tyndareus walks away, wishing for his death. The ending of the play is quite haphazard and confused, with many critics relegating the play to "howling spiritual lunacy."[277] While I agree that the play as a whole is quite unsatisfactory, I find Euripides concern for dealing with the issues confronting Orestes to be superb, and indicative of how taken he must

---

272 Ibid., 194-207, 123-24.
273 Ibid., 395, 134.
274 Ibid., 532-33, 143.
275 Ibid., 578-79, 146.
276 Ibid., 592-96, 146.
277 Ibid., 106.

have been in trying to compare the tales of Abraham and Isaac, and Agamemnon and Iphigenia, and in the end to try and find a way to explain away the Greek resolution which seemed to only result in a disservice to the very gods they were taught to worship.

The next play, *Iphigenia in Aulis*, follows a similar path. It was produced, together with the *Bacchae* and the *Alcmaeon*, in 405 BCE, a few months after Euripides' death. The play takes place in Aulis, where the Greek armada lies dormant in the waters because the winds had died down. At the very start of the play, Agamemnon portends the problem he will soon face by telling an old man who says that those with honors have glory in their lives that "high honors are sweet to a man's heart, but ever they stand close to the brink of grief."[278] The old man responds that it is fated that you be glad and you will be sad, but whether you like it or not, "what the gods will comes true."[279] This declaration, in my opinion, is meant to confirm that when Abraham was told by YHWH that he must sacrifice Isaac, he believed that the commandment would come true, just as Agamemnon would soon do when told that he must sacrifice his daughter, as well, but that YHWH had also told Abraham that his future was to be generated through the seed of Isaac, an indication that Isaac would live and not have to die. The old man then tells Agamemnon that he has watched him write and then tear up a letter over and over again, crying all the time, and asks what is wrong. Agamemnon relates how all the Greek suitors of Helen followed her father's order to sign a pact that they would defend each other before he allowed Helen to marry. She then chose Menelaus, and when she was kidnapped by Paris, Menelaus called on their oath, and they are now set to sail to Troy to avenge the honor of Greece. I was appointed commander-in-chief, he continues, but the prophet Calchas has said that the winds will not arise unless I sacrifice my daughter, Iphigenia, and so I made a proclamation to dismiss the army, for "I would never have the cruel brutality to kill my own daughter!"[280] This response indicates to me that Euripides was aware that it was Calchas who made the declaration, and not God, and although the prophet was well-respected and honored, even revered, Agamemnon had no intention to follow his suggestion. Menelaus was very upset, however, and so Agamemnon explains he was writing a letter to his wife asking Iphigenia to be sent in order to be married to Achilles. He decides, however, to ask the man to take the letter to Clytemnestra at once, and reads the letter which says do not send Iphigenia here, for we must wait another season. When the old man asks whether Achilles will be upset, and finds out it was only a ruse to bring his daughter here, he tells Agamemnon he "dared

---

278 Euripides, "Iphigenia in Aulis," 22-23, 218.
279 Ibid., 34, 219.
280 Ibid., 96, 220.

a deed of horror."[281] Agamemnon then tells him to run with haste and intercept the coming of Iphigenia, and send her back home with this letter.

What are we to make of this modification of the legend which Euripides is so desperately trying to make? I think it is clear that Euripides is very disturbed by the comparison of the two infanticidal tales, and is attempting to rationalize the necessity of Iphigenia's death by highlighting the fact that the request for the sacrifice did not come directly from the god (God). This allows for human intervention to be the cause of the catastrophe, and legitimizes the retribution which Clytemnestra too, and subsequently the blame which fell upon Orestes as well.

With *The Bacchae*, which was composed sometime after 405 BCE, we find a comparison of contemporary Greek customs with those discussed in the Bible, although this awareness may not have been evident to Euripides. What is of interest here is not the violent events which take place on stage, but rather the infatuation of the Greeks with the god Dionysus, and its possible relationship to information that came from the ancient Hebrews, as the ancient Hebrew Festival of Tabernacles was the most important, and most crowded, occasion for rejoicing in Israel in biblical times. Josephus referred to it as "the holiest and the greatest of Hebrew feasts."[282] It was to be observed for seven days, seven weeks after the harvest began, when the grain was threshed and the grapes pressed.[283] Because the Hebrews uncharacteristically spent so much time celebrating during this week-long festival, decorating themselves and their surroundings with vine and ivy tendrils and imbibing large amounts of wine, a number of ancient commentators pointed out that their festivities were very similar to the rites of Dionysus, a joyous celebration of the harvest which first appeared in Greece about 1000 BCE.[284] The name Bacchus is believed to be a Semitic loan-word meaning wailing, and some scholars have suggested that this may explain why the women of Israel bewailed Tammuz, an ancient nature deity who was worshiped in Babylonia.[285] Although Bacchus represented the force of life in all growing things, animal and vegetable,

281 Ibid., 137, 222.

282 de Vaux, Ancient Israel, Its Life and Institutions, 495. The importance of the Feast of Tabernacles was recognized by Moses who direct the Hebrews to read the laws he had delivered at the end of every seven years during the festival. Deut 31:10-11.

283 Exod 23:16; 34:22; Lev 23:33, 39; Deut 16:9-10, 13. Miller, The Religion of Ancient Israel, 84. In the book of *Leviticus* it is called the Festival of Pentecost and begins fifty days after the Festival of First Fruits. Lev 23:15.

284 Stapleton, The Illustrated Dictionary of Greek and Roman Mythology, 69.

285 Ezek 8:14. Burkert, Greek Religion, 163. Tammuz was a Mesopotamian god, revered by the Babylonians and Assyrians, and the Babylonian month of Tammuz became the fourth month in the Jewish calendar. Benson, The Origins of Christianity and the Bible, A Critical Scholarly Investigation of the Sources of Christianity and the Bible, 102-103.

he became particularly regarded as the god of the vine, and his celebrations made free use of this intoxicating beverage. His worship in Greece dates to Mycenaean times, and perhaps even earlier to Minoan times, and the Dionysian cults of the seventh and sixth centuries BCE were revivals, and not new creations.[286]

The *Rhesus* is a literary problem with neither its date or authorship certain. It is a dramatization of the so-called *Doloneia*, the tenth book of the *Iliad*, and there is little to my contention that Euripides utilized biblical information in his plays, so I will also not discuss this play in detail. *The Cyclops* is the final play attributed to Euripides, and like *Rhesus*, there is little evidence of Hebraic influence. It is the only complete satyr-play extant, but its date is uncertain. It is a farce, but is generally considered to be written about a serious issue of civilized brutality.

F. The Hebrew Prophets

In the preceding sections, I have detailed why I believe the Greek philosophers and playwrights were influenced by biblical teachings, primarily gathered by circulating manuscripts that were prevalent in Babylonia and Egypt following the return from the Babylonian Exile. In this section I now want to focus my analysis on what the Hebrew prophets were saying, both before and after the Babylonian Exile, to likely have influenced the traveling Greek intellectuals, based upon their books that were eventually collected in the Old Testament. Prophets (*nabi*) were well-accepted as important communicators with God in the Bible, although divination and diviners, as practiced in other pagan countries, were condemned throughout the Old Testament. During the Exodus, when the Lord told Moses at Taberah to gather seventy of the elders in order for Him to endow them with spirit to aid in his burden of managing the complaints of the congregation, Joshua complained that two men, Eldad and Medad, were declaring prophecies in the camp. Moses was not offended by this action, and told Joshua "would that all the Lord's people were prophets," despite the fact that the biblical text clearly indicated that Moses jealously guarded his primary status as spokesman for the Lord.[287] The prophets were an extremely important source of information about biblical teachings in the centuries following the Conquest of the Promised Land, and Abraham Joshua Heschel (1907-1972 CE) said it best when he described the prophet as "a man who feels fiercely ... God has thrust a burden upon his soul, and he is bowed and stunned at man's fierce greed."[288] The manner of the prophet was intended to intensify responsibility, and "his words are often slashing, even horrid – designed to shock rather than to edify."[289] Their manner has been described as encompassing a "forthteller" of the will of God, rather than

---

286 Pickard-Cambridge, <u>Dithyramb, Tragedy and Comedy</u>, 129.
287 Num 11:29. Fox, "Numbers," 308.
288 Heschel, The Prophets: An Introduction, 5.
289 Ibid., 7.

as a "foreteller" of future events, but it is clear that their words as recorded in the Old Testament were clearly directed at warning the rulers and population of Israel and Judah of future destruction if they did not change their ways.[290] They were horrified by the impious behavior of the population in Judah and Israel, and threatened destruction for both countries as a punishment from God. This behavior was reflective of the belief that suffering was the natural and inevitable result of rebellion, "retribution for insubordination to divine authority."[291]

Readers of the Bible today often react with neutrality at the words of the prophets, knowing that the kingdoms of Israel and Judah would eventually be overrun, but that the devastation would be temporary, and the Babylonian Exile would eventually end, resulting in a condensation of the Jewish population into an obedient congregation that would stand the test of time. We understand that the historical text attempts to explain how and why the ancient Hebrews were punished for not following the commandments of YHWH, but this information does not necessarily inform us as to why the contemporary audience failed to heed the warnings they were given. In my opinion, the traveling Greek scholars who were searching for wisdom would have heard these tirades on the streets, and been impressed with the message, especially when the forecast of doom was proven true in the overthrow and Exile of the Hebrew population. This was an era when people believed that deities did appear on earth and affect what happened to mankind, and watching the retribution take place before their very eyes would have been clear evidence of the wrath, and the reality, of the Jewish Deity. In addition, the Greeks were extremely interested in the art of rhetoric during this era, as witnessed by the popularity of the Sophists during the time of Socrates, and many commentators have characterized the prophets as mastering the art of persuasive speech in attempting to turn their audience away from their disobedience of God's law.[292] It would be particularly interesting to imagine how Plato, who vilified the empty eloquence of the Sophist practitioners, would have reacted to the purposeful speech of the Hebrew prophets, who were the forerunners of the fiery preachers who characterized much of the religious fervor in the centuries which followed.

We know that the words of the prophets were spread throughout the population by either oral or written transmission, for in the book of *Jeremiah* it is noted that the elders in Judah rose in defense of Jeremiah, who was arrested for claiming that Jerusalem would be destroyed, by stating that the prophet Micah, who prophesied one hundred years earlier, had also claimed that the city would

---

290 McFadden, "Micah and the Problem of Continuities and Discontinuities in Prophecy," 131-132.

291 Heschel, Heavenly Torah: As Refracted Through the Generations, 127.

292 Baker, "Israelite Prophets and Prophecy," 280.

fall.[293] Susan Niditch, Samuel Green Professor of Religion at Amherst College, has demonstrated that writing became an increasingly important resource from the late monarchies of the eighth century BCE onward, when the Greek philosophers were beginning their inquiries discussed above, and so it is likely that the words of the prophets would have been available to traveling scholars by one means or the other.[294]

The question about what the Greek philosophers may have thought about these rantings when they encountered them in their travels and studies is an issue which has never, in my opinion, been satisfactorily investigated. Hermann Cohen (1842-1918 CE), one of the most important Jewish philosophers of the nineteenth century, said that "Plato and the prophets are the two most important sources of modern culture,"[295] but no one has satisfactorily examined the possible close relationship that may have existed between these two pillars of Western thought. In fact, Leo Strauss (1899-1973 CE), a German-Jewish political philosopher who focused his research on Plato and Aristotle, believed that "Cohen has brought out very well the antagonism between Plato and the prophets," thereby supporting a view which I have vigorously challenged throughout this book that a chasm existed between the ancient Hebrews and the Classical Greeks.[296] That Strauss would have this belief is strange, for he also contended that "Western man became what he is and is what he is through the coming together of biblical faith and Greek thought."[297] And just as Plato taught that the unexamined life is not befitting human beings, the ancient Hebrews taught that life without study of the Torah was not worthwhile. Little did Strauss realize, however, that the "coming together" was an actual personal encounter, and, in my opinion, that the Greeks listened intently to the adages they read and heard.

The primary question which needs to be answered is which of the two groups of thinkers came to the idea first, and who may have learned from whom. I have no doubt that all of the Greek philosophers encountered stories about these Hebrew prophets, if not hearing speeches by them personally, since they lived at the very same time, in the very same area where the Greeks traveled to during their

---

293 Jer 26:17-18. This is an example of a direct oral expression of transmission to a written text, while the use of formulas or "stock phrases" have been mentioned as an indirect sign of transmission. Kofoed, <u>Text and History: Historiography and the Study of the Biblical Text</u>, 80-81. Kofoed adds that "there is no reason to doubt that literary works existed in Israel *to some extent* as early as the 10th century B.C.E." Ibid., 88. Alan Ralph Millard, Professor Emeritus of Hebrew and Ancient Semitic Languages at the University of Liverpool, goes even further and argues that books "were not so scarce" at that time, and literary texts were likely to have been found in some Israelite homes. Ibid., 86-87.

294 Niditch, Oral World and Written Word: Ancient Israelite Literature, 39.

295 Strauss, "On Socrates and the Prophets," 225.

296 Ibid., 226.

297 Strauss, "The Beginning of the Bible and Its Greek Counterparts," 23.

quest for knowledge. Palestine was clearly along the well-traveled road between these two centers of ancient wisdom, and it is known that prophets practiced in Jerusalem from as early as the period of the Monarchy as "a gregarious folk, living and working in groups or communities."[298] This is referenced in the Bible after Samuel anointed Saul king and told him to travel to Gilgal. Samuel explained that at the Hill of God (Gibeah of God) Saul would meet a band of prophets coming down from the shrine, playing instruments and speaking in ecstasy, and that he should speak in ecstasy with them, which he eventually did.[299] When Saul sent three separate messengers to David at Naioth in Ramah, they also found a similar band of prophets speaking in ecstasy. The prophet Elisha, much more than Elijah, was also associated with a prophetic community where he lived, and it is believed that the enclave was under his direction.[300] When Ahab, the king of Israel, planned to march upon Ramoth-gilead for battle, he first gathered four hundred prophets to ask for advice, an indication that there were many such seers available at short notice.[301] Finally, when Jezebel was persecuting the prophets, Obadiah hid a hundred of them in caves and fed them, despite the presence of a famine.[302] All of these passages clearly indicate that there were many available prophets in the land to satisfy the questions of the Greek philosophers searching for truth among all the known religions. Gerhard von Rad (1901-1971 CE), the respected Professor of Old Testament at the University of Heidelberg, believed that they were the "last representatives of pure, uncontaminated Jahwism and its divine law,"[303] and so it is likely that if any written material were available, it would have been contained in their environs.

If the Greeks visited any of the Jewish shrines they would have certainly encountered some of the prophets, since "it has never been doubted that the prophets liked to pay visits to sanctuaries."[304] There is little archaeologic evidence of libraries in ancient Israel, as opposed to those found throughout Mesopotamia, so if the Greek philosophers wanted to gather information, about the Hebrews they likely would have looked to the prophets, both as a source of knowledge, and

---

298 Smith, The Prophets and Their Times, 2.

299 1 Sam 10:5, 10.

300 2 Kgs 6:1. Zevit, "Second Kings," 737. Before Elijah was taken up to heaven, a group of prophets came to Elisha to notify him of the event. 2 Kgs 2:3. When Elisha accompanied Elijah to the Jordan River, where he would be swept up to heaven by a chariot of fire, fifty prophets accompanied them. Wiesel, <u>Five Biblical Prophets,</u> 34. Elisha later fed some of the prophets when there was a famine at Gilgal. 2 Kgs 4:38. It seems that they lived together in settlements, and that their standards of eating and housing were "miserable in the extreme." von Rad, <u>Old Testament Theology,</u> vol. II, 26.

301 1 Kgs 22:6.

302 1 Kgs 18:4.

303 Ibid.

304 Ibid., 51.

as a source of access to written texts. We know from the New Testament that until John the Baptist began to preach, "the laws of Moses and the messages of the prophets were your guides."[305] The general view is that the "writing prophets" were seen as members of a radical wing which were independent of the official cult, while the traveling group of prophets were seen as authorised spokesmen of the whole body of the people.[306] Rabbis were not yet a prominent sect in this period of time, and the prophets would have likely been more accessible than the priests who were in charge of managing the First and Second Temple.

The prophets were also known as seers, and when someone wanted to inquire how to properly worship YHWH, they went to a prophet, much as the Greeks did with the Delphic oracle. With the fall of Jerusalem in 586 BCE, and the resultant Exile of the Jews to Babylon, the Greek philosophers who traveled to Babylon and Egypt did not even have to stop in the states of Israel and Judah to interact with Hebrew prophets, but could have encountered them, along with many other wise sages, in the Babylonian empire. Although the kingdom of Judah fell with the sack of Jerusalem, Judaism and the Jewish nation survived, and even flourished, among the exiles who brought with them the copies of their sacred texts. Once in Babylon, they enjoyed a comparatively normal existence, and were granted tracts of land upon which to build houses and gardens.[307]

When Cyrus the Great, the king of the Persians, defeated the Babylonian army at Opis in 539 BCE, he allowed the Jews to return to their homeland in 538 BCE, and access to the Hebrew prophets, and their writings, would have been greatly expanded. That the Greek philosophers would have respected these prophets is evident from Homer's *Odyssey*, where Melanthios explained that not all foreigners were looked on as barbarians, and one would certainly call in "an artisan with skill to serve the realm, a healer, or a prophet, or a builder, or one whose harp and song might give us joy."[308] We should therefore look to the writings of the Hebrew prophets to learn of what the philosophers may have heard. That many of the writings were likely available to the early Greek philosophers is evident from the fact that Sargon II (722-705 BCE) established the library at Nineveh during the era when the Assyrian Empire was at its greatest extent, and it is believed that it contained tablets inscribed in several languages, including the Hebrew Epic of Creation and the Epic of Gilgamesh.

We do not have other extant information about what the early prophets in Israel spoke about, except for the citations which are present in the Bible, but the Major and Minor prophets who have books associated with them have left

305 Luke 16:16. The Living Bible, 824.

306 von Rad, Old Testament Theology, vol. II, 52.

307 Minkin, The Shaping of the Modern Mind: The Life and Thought of the Great Jewish Philosophers, 47.

308 Homer, The Odyssey, 17.365-368, 323.

us much information, and it is with these individuals that I want to discuss what it is that the traveling Greek scholars would have likely learned about Hebraic theology, and how it affected the developing Greek philosophical thought. One thing which is consistent among all of these men is their claim that there is only one God who must be served by all mankind. Such a radical monotheistic thought should have fit nicely with the concepts of the Greek philosophers, who, despite their apparent acceptance of polytheism in their writings, they were searching for universals in life which would apply to all mankind, and appeared to be quite comfortable with the Monism espoused by these men, as well as admiring the warnings of the prophets against mixed marriages, as this was consistent with the Greek concept that all non-Greeks were barbarian. The prophets were attempting to eliminate mixed marriages in Judea at the same time the decree of 451-450 BCE in Athens deprived inhabitants of citizenship unless they were able to prove their dual Athenian parentage.[309] Purity of race was something which all ancient societies strived for, but the ancient Hebrews and Greeks were especially concerned, since their societies were so open to the intrusion of foreign elements.

I will begin my discussion in chronologic order of the lives of the Prophets with Amos, who lived around the time Homer and Hesiod's great epic poems were thought to be written, c. 750 BCE, before the era when Socrates and Plato were living in Athens.[310] Amos was likely part of the band of prophets that roamed both Israel and Judah in the eighth century BCE, and their message of the power and authority of the monotheistic YHWH would have reached the ears of not only the Hebrew population, but the Greeks as well. Israel was enjoying a period of prosperity during this era, but Amos' prophecy of destruction would prove true as the country was eventually overrun, and the capital of Samaria captured, by Assyria in 722 BCE. At the time Amos was preaching, however, Tiglath-pileser III's threat to Israel was not yet solidified into the dangerous onslaught that would be evident during the era of Hosea.

It is easy to understand why the fledgling Presocratic philosophers, beginning with Thales, who lived a century later, may have been interested in the words of Amos, for his imagery of the power of YHWH clearly resembled that of Zeus. His warnings of how God would send fire down on the fortresses of Damascus, Gaza, Ashdod, Ekron, Tyre, Edom and Moab, just to name a few, including Judah and Jerusalem for their transgressions against His commandments, were similar to the retribution of the Greek gods against those they disliked in the works of Homer.[311]

---

309 Momigliano, The Classical Foundations of Modern Historiography, 17.

310 The prophecies of the early prophets like Amos and Hosea are believed to have been preserved by an oral tradition until the exilic period (587-539 BCE), when they were then committed to writing. Nielsen, Oral Tradition, 14.

311 Amos 1:1-2:5.

The power of the Lord also extended to natural disasters, like drought, blight, mildew and locusts, something which the Greeks clearly attributed to their gods as well.[312] In addition, Amos did not limit the authority of YHWH to just the Hebrews as the Chosen People, for although He brought the Hebrews out of Egypt, He also brought the Philistines from Caphtor and the Arameans (Syrians) from Kir.[313] As for the causes of cosmogony, Amos reminded his audience how YHWH built heaven and earth, and was responsible for earthquakes, floods and even a solar eclipse.[314] His exhortation to "hate evil and love good, and establish justice in the gate," could have been taken straight from the tomes of Plato.[315] He also foreshadowed Plato by telling how YHWH wanted the people to "let justice well up like water, righteousness like an unfailing stream," rather than desire festivals and sacrifices.[316] Plato's insistence on the necessity to understand that the Good is identified with the One, and that knowledge of this comes from divine inspiration, is closely allied with these warnings of Amos. The unique similarity of the cosmogony in the book of *Genesis,* and the claim of Thales that water was the generative element of the Universe, also suggests that Thales' view may have been taken directly from the biblical text. As the Greek philosophers molded their views of nature and reality into a monistic concept to the formation of the Universe, the words of Amos, in my opinion, resounded in their ears.

A few years later, c. 740 BCE, Hosea similarly prophesied about the primacy of the ethical law. Like Amos, his comments would have aroused the curiosity of the Greek philosophers with statements such as the cause of the Lord's anger is that "there is no honesty and no goodness and no obedience to God in the land."[317] While the piety of the Greek philosophers has been questioned by many scholars, given their enthusiasm to look for natural explanations of the world rather than theologic, we must remember that this is still the region where Athens put Socrates to death for his refusal to follow the edicts of the state religions. Hosea's charge to the priests and king that "right conduct is your responsibility," is very reminiscent of the Greek insistence on valor and reputation above all else, and this requirement to behave in a judicious manner would have been seen as consistent with the Greek ethos.[318] What is clearly not consistent with Greek teaching, however, is Hosea's declaration that God desires goodness, not sacrifice, and obedience to God, rather than burnt offerings.[319] While conduct does represent the ultimate ideal of the Greek heroic figure, the works of Homer

---

312 Amos 4:7-9.
313 Amos 9:7.
314 Amos 8:8; 9:5-6.
315 Amos 5:15. Zvi, "Amos," 1186.
316 Amos 5:24. Ibid., 1187.
317 Hosea 4:1. Zvi, "Hosea," 1149.
318 Hosea 5:1. Ibid., 1151.
319 Hosea 6:6.

clearly show their dedication to the rite of sacrifice, and it is likely that the Greek scholars would have shaken their heads at Hosea's ignorance of the requirement of proper sacrifice. His use of agricultural similes, however, would have likely found favor, such as his admonition for "you have plowed wickedness, you have reaped iniquity," and you shall now eat the fruits of your treachery.[320]

Between 740-700 BCE, the century before Thales was born, Micah and Isaiah also spread their warnings of severe punishments for apostasy throughout the land, although it is unclear which one was actually first. Micah, whose writings are among the most obscure in the Bible, is best known for his advice "to do justly, and to love mercy, and to walk humbly with thy God."[321] Sounding very much like his two earlier contemporaries, Micah would have continued the stream of belief in showing homage to YHWH by your actions, a theme which Plato and Aristotle would eventually highlight as well. That the early Greek philosophers would have taken notice of Micah seems likely to his me in his use of descriptions rampant throughout Homer's *Iliad*. He was the first prophet to actually predict the destruction of Jerusalem, and he castigated the rulers of Israel who have "devoured My people's flesh; you have flayed the skin off them, and their flesh off their bones ... And after tearing their skins off them, and their flesh off their bones, and breaking their bones to bits, you have cut it up as into a pot, like meat in a cauldron."[322] We do not know precisely what the Greek philosophers thought of the attributes of the Sibyls that were widely respected in ancient Greece, as evident by the state reliance on the words of the Oracle at Delphi, but Micah's declaration that the Lord withdrew His contact with the other prophets, but "I am filled with strength by the spirit of the Lord, and with judgment and courage, to declare to Jacob his transgressions and to Israel his sin," would have certainly attracted the attention of the Greek populace.[323] And after reading the dismay of the Greek warriors in the *Iliad*, and their desire to return home and be reunited with their families, they also would have understood the meaning of his promise that following the path of the Lord would allow the nations to "beat their swords into plowshares and their spears into pruning hooks," a desire greatly hoped for by the Greek families who were forced to live apart from their husbands, fathers, and brothers during the ten years of the Trojan War.[324]

When we come to Isaiah, perhaps the most controversial of all the Hebrew prophets, we encounter a controversy about whether the book ascribed to him was actually spoken by one, two, or three people, whose prophecies were collected by

320 Hosea 10:13. Ibid., 1160.
321 Micah 6:8. Podhoretz, The Prophets: Who They Were, What They Are, 158. This passage is cited more than any other prophetic text in rabbinic literature, and more haftarot are taken from it than from any other prophetic book. Sommer, "Isaiah," 780.
322 Micah 3:3. Ziv, "Micah," 1209-10.
323 Micah 3:8. Ziv, "Micah," 1210.
324 Micah 4:3. Ibid., 1211.

scribes and placed into a single scroll. This debate does not really affect my thesis that the words of Isaiah affected the beliefs of the Greek philosophers, since my concern is only with availability of oral or written texts about what the prophet said, rather than who actually said it. Biblical scholars who analyze the text from a variety of methods believe that the First Isaiah of Jerusalem wrote the first thirty-nine of the sixty-six chapters of the book c. 740-700 BCE, while the second, known as Deutero-Isaiah (Second Isaiah), wrote in the sixth century BCE, and the third, Trito-Isaiah, was probably a group of prophets who composed the final ten chapters of the book after the Babylonian Exile had ended, at the end of the sixth century BCE. The differentiation comes about because the historical conditions, and the style of the speeches, in the books are quite different, with Judah defending itself against the Assyrian Empire in First Isaiah, while in Deutero-Isaiah the Judeans are in Exile, and during Trito-Isaiah, the Exile had ended. Be that as it may, the book of *Isaiah* is widely held to be the supreme example of prophetic literature in the Hebrew Bible, and its influence was carried over into the revisions of the coming of the messiah by the followers of Jesus Christ.[325]

Isaiah's message is clear to all people from the very outset of the book, and would have struck a sympathetic chord among the Greeks: "I reared children and brought them up – and they have rebelled against Me! An ox knows its owner, an ass its master's crib: Israel does not know, My people take no thought."[326] And if the rest of the world had not yet been aware of, or reminded of, one of the most important images of the Torah, outside of the Akeda and the delivery of the Ten Commandments on Mt. Sinai, then Isaiah let it be known that Judah and Israel were at least left some survivors by YHWH, unlike the cities of Sodom and Gomorrah, which were demolished without a vestigial survivorship.[327] Isaiah also sounded very much like the Greek seers who explained tragedies which befell the country as being due to the anger of the gods. He warned how the earth would be stripped bare by the Lord, and its inhabitants scattered, because "they transgressed teachings, violated laws, broke the ancient covenant."[328] Once again, however, Isaiah continued the diatribe against the use of sacrifices, which would certainly have been offensive to many of the Greeks.[329] That the concept of beating swords into plowshares, and spears into pruning hooks, was something that was discussed in the public arena seems obvious by Isaiah's use of the same

---

325 Podhoretz, The Prophets: Who They Were, What They Are, 183-84. It is cited more than any other prophetic text in rabbinic literature, and more haftarot are taken from it than from any other prophetic book. Sommer, "Isaiah," 780.

326 Isa 1:2-3. Sommer, "Isaiah," 784.

327 Isa 1:9. See e.g., Isa 13:19.

328 Isa 24:1, 5. Ibid., 829.

329 Isa 1:11-16.

imagery as that of Micah.[330]

Isaiah is also likely to have interested the Greek scholars because he went beyond the words of the Torah in describing Sheol as a true underground where souls went for retribution, an identification similar to that described by Homer as the destination where Odysseus traveled to in the *Odyssey*. The Torah never really described the concept of Sheol, but Isaiah clearly noted how "Sheol has opened wide its gullet and parted its jaws in a measureless gape; and down into it shall go that splendor and tumult, that din and revelry."[331] He later told how the king of Babylon would be overtaken by the Jews who had been exiled and returned, and how Sheol would greet his coming by "rousing for you the shades of all the earth's chieftains, raising from their thrones all the kings of nations," and "worms are to be your bed, maggots your blanket!"[332] This imagery was very popular among Greek authors, and Isaiah's description would have appeared as a place identical to their own conception of the underground. Although the Greeks portrayed the Kingdom of the Dead as the place where heroes went, as well as those less worthy, it is noteworthy that when Odysseus met Achilles there, and told him that he was fortunate to have died a hero, Achilles answered that "better, I say, to break sod as a farm hand for some poor country man, on iron rations, than lord it over all the exhausted dead."[333] Greeks who had read Homer's works as a major part of their education would have found the words of Isaiah to be complementary.

The Greek philosophers would also have clearly understood the meaning of monotheism in Isaiah's succinct passage: "I am the first and I am the last, and there is no god but Me."[334] Once again, however, his explanation that the makers of idols are serving no purpose, for all they do is make representations that are made of metal or wood, and then bow down and worship the idol as if it was some god, would not have been greeted as a valid conclusion.[335] "Foolishness!" Isaiah explained, he bows down to an idol of wood, and pursues ashes; but rather he should say, "the thing in my hand is a fraud!"[336] The Greeks would have answered that such remarks are not the words of a wise man, but a fool. As for cosmogony, they also would have agreed with YHWH's boasting of having been the Creator of heaven and earth, and of mankind as well.[337] How could one argue with his

---

330 Isa 2:4.

331 Isa 5:14. Sommer, "Isaiah," 794.

332 Isa 14:9-11. Ibid., 812. See e.g., Isa 14:15.

333 Homer, The Odyssey, 11.86-88, 201.

334 Isa 44:6. Sommer, "Isaiah," 872. See e.g., Isa 45:5-6; 14, 18, 21-22; 46:9; 47:8, 10.

335 "Those who fabricate idols, all are shamed and disgraced." Isa 45:16. Ibid., 876. See e.g., Isa 46:6-8.

336 Isa 44:20. Ibid., 874.

337 "It was I who made the earth and created man upon it; My own hands stretched out the heavens, and I marshaled all their host." Isa 45:12. Ibid., 876.

Maker; "shall the clay say to the potter, 'What are you doing?'"[338] It is clear that the Christians found the book of Isaiah to be a wellspring of knowledge, and, in my opinion, the Greek philosophers would have done the same.

The book of *Isaiah* also provides us with evidence that the words of the prophets were written down, although it is unclear how, and to what degree, they were distributed.[339] This documentation makes it even more plausible that the traveling Greek scholars who may have missed hearing the tirades of the prophets first-hand would have been able to still study their declarations by this means. It is possible that Isaiah may have influenced Aesop (c. 620-564 BCE) in this manner, the contemporary author known for his fables where animals speak and have human characteristics. Isaiah prophesied in a messianic tale of how a perfect Davidic king will reign in Jerusalem, and the wolf shall dwell with the lamb, the leopard will lie down with the kid, the cow and bear shall graze and the lion, like the ox, shall eat straw while a babe shall play over a viper's hole.[340] Using animals to preference human morality fits quite nicely with the message of the Hebrew prophets, and Aesop, more than any other ancient fabulist, made the methodology a popular art-form.

The next category of Hebrew prophets from the seventh century BCE would have been alive when Thales began his travels to gather the wisdom of the world. This includes the pre-exilic writings of Zephaniah, Nahum, Habakkuk, and Jeremiah, who began his prophecy in the pre-exilic period, but continued into the Exile itself. Zephaniah foretold the destruction of Judah, but there is little else that likely drew the attention of the Greek philosophers. While Nahum evokes images of YHWH which more closely resemble Zeus, there also is little else of interest in his speech of interest to the Greeks.[341] Habakkuk may have incited some interest, since he specifically mentioned how YHWH was raising up the Chaldeans (Babylon) to invade other countries and amass captives like sand.[342] As discussed above, it is believed that many of the Greek philosophers traveled to Babylon as part of their education to the knowledge of the world, and while not contemporary necessarily with Habakkuk, his prophecies would have interested them, if only for an awareness of their personal safety. That his words were likely available to be read as easily as the modern daily news in our own era is apparent in his statement that the Lord told him to write his prophecy down and "inscribe it clearly on tablets, so that it can be read easily."[343] This again is supportive of the ready availability of the prophetic texts to traveling Greek philosophers. As I have

---

338 Isa 45:9. Ibid., 875.

339 Isa 8:1; 30:8.

340 Isa 11:6-8.

341 Nahum tells how God travels in whirlwind and storm with clouds at his feet, and makes the mountains quake and the seas dry up. Nahum 1:3-5.

342 Hab 1:6-9.

343 Hab 2:2. Ziv, "Habakkuk," 1229.

discussed earlier in this chapter, the dissemination of these messages was often accompanied by their translation into Aramaic, a language used in international commerce, and understood by Greek intellectuals.

With Jeremiah, however, we enter a period when the publication of the Torah documents is even more apparent, making access to Greek scholars readily available. King Josiah ascended to the throne of Judah in 640 BCE and instituted a great campaign of religious reform. As part of his efforts, repairs were made to the First Temple, and the Book of *Deuteronomy* was discovered hidden away in a recess. The king had the book read publically, and any traveling philosopher who desired to learn about the teachings of the Hebrews would have had easy access to the details through this process. If Thales was born c. 624 BCE, as is generally believed, he would have been traveling to Babylon and Egypt during this same period of time. Since Jeremiah was called to his prophetic ministry in 626 BCE, Thales would have had access not only to the readings of the Deuteronomy scroll, but also to the speeches of Jeremiah in person.

Jeremiah's book contains many references which would have intrigued the early Presocratic philosophers, and it is likely that they would have wanted to hear what he said, since he was a priest at Anathoth, in the territory of Benjamin, in addition to being a prophet.[344] Like Habakkuk, Jeremiah relates that the Lord told him to write in a scroll all the words which He had spoken to him.[345] Thales would have particularly been interested in Jeremiah's description of the role of YHWH in the creation of the world:

> *He made the earth by his might,*
> *Established the world by His wisdom,*
> *And by His understanding stretched out the skies.*
> *When He makes His voice heard,*
> *There is a rumbling of water in the skies;*
> *He makes vapors rise from the end of the earth,*
> *He makes lightning for the rain,*
> *And brings forth wind from His treasuries.*[346]

There is no mention of Chaos being the first principle in this passage, but the concept of searching for the generation of the Universe among the four elements

---

344 Jer 1:1.

345 Jer 30:2. This request was repeated when Jeremiah told Baruch to write down on a scroll all that the Lord had told him, and to then read it aloud to all the people in the House of the Lord on a fast day. Jer 36:2, 5-6, 8-10, 18. King Jehoiakim burned the scroll after hearing its contents, which claimed that the king of Babylon would come and destroy the land, but the Lord then instructed Jeremiah to prepare another identical scroll. Jer 36:27-29, 32. See e.g., Jer 45:1.

346 Jer. 10:12-13. Sweeney, "Jeremiah," 947.

of the earth, and particularly that of water, stimulated through the power of the One, clearly shows forth, and, in my opinion, influenced the thought of Thales.

The other prophets of the sixth century BCE include Ezekiel, Obadiah, and second Isaiah, and particularly important is Ezekiel (c. 622-570 BCE), who is considered, along with Isaiah and Jeremiah, one of the three Hebrew Major Prophets. Like Jeremiah, Ezekiel was a priest who was exiled to Babylon,[347] but it seems that he died there and did not return to Jerusalem. During his stay in Babylon, however, he evidently was a very respected member of the exile community, for he tells at the start of one of his visions how he was sitting at home in 592 BCE with the elders of Judah in attendance.[348] Although many scholars consider the book to have been written by a group of scholars, rather than one man, I will treat the writings as if they were put forth by a single author, as I did for Isaiah. Of particular importance is that some have claimed that Ezekiel was actually Nazaratus Assyrius, a teacher of Pythagoras.[349] This identification may refer to the fact that Pythagoras, along with other early Greek philosophers, actually met with Ezekiel during his trip to Babylon. Once again, I emphasize the availability of the Hebrew writings and prophets to traveling Greek scholars, and the desire of the Greeks to educate themselves on the wisdom of other cultures, thereby becoming interested in the monotheistic principles contained therein.

Once again, Ezekiel tells about a written scroll, although this time he relates how the Lord handed him a written scroll which was inscribed on the front and back with lamentations, dirges, and woes.[350] Instead of reading it, Ezekiel was instructed to eat it, thereby imbibing him with the exact words from God. And to ensure that Ezekiel would obey His command to preach to the House of Israel, YHWH told him that his own life would be forfeited if he did not warn the wicked of their misgivings. These are extremely strong words, not seen in any of the other prophetic books, and it may help explain the intensity of Ezekiel's warnings. He was also instructed to perform symbolic actions such as lying on his left side for three hundred and ninety days to reflect the punishment which will be inflicted on Israel, and forty days on his right side to reflect the punishment on Judah, each day reflecting a year of punishment to come. To indicate the misery of the people to be exiled, he was also to eat barley cakes baked on human excrement, which was eventually changed to cow dung.

These actions were certainly intended to gather attention by outrageous behavior, but we have already seen in the preceding section on Greek drama that the Greeks were not adverse to stories that shocked the public. While the

347 Ezek 1:3. He was deported in 598 or 597 BCE, after the first siege of Jerusalem.
348 Ezek 8:1. See e.g., Ezek 14:1.
349 Sweeney, "Ezekiel," 1.
350 Ezek 2:9-10.

philosophers may not have been overly interested in Ezekiel's strange personna, I believe the playwrights would have taken notice, and tried to study the actions of Ezekiel, and prophets like him. Ezekiel told how God was so angry with the disobedience of those living in Israel and Judah that He would do things He had never done before, and would never do again, such as causing parents to eat their children, and children to eat their parents.[351] As I discussed earlier, this warning very much resembled the sins of the house of Atreus, where Atreus served up the children of Thyestes for him to eat in a ghastly dinner. In addition, Ezekiel claimed that one-third would die of pestilence or famine, one-third would die by the sword, and one-third would be scattered in every direction. Coming from the very God who had supposedly made these inhabitants the Chosen People, such rhetoric must have made the inquiring Greek scholars wonder about the entire process. The only saving grace was that YHWH told how He would save a remnant who would loathe themselves for all their abominable deeds which brought such retribution. After castigating the Israelites for their acts of adultery, bloodshed, wantonness and widespread idolatry, and describing in vivid detail how their ranks would be decimated and cities leveled to the ground, Ezekiel told how God would repopulate the land once the people had been cleansed of their iniquities, "and they shall know that I am the Lord."[352] At the very end of the book, Ezekiel had a vision on Yom Kippur, 573-572 BCE, of the restored Temple in Jerusalem. There are no recordings that any of the Greek philosophers ever actually visited the Temple, and were struck by the images which Ezekiel forecast, but I again submit that since it is clear that many of them visited Babylon when the Hebrews were residing there during the Babylonian Exile, and then traveled to Egypt which is on a direct line from Babylon through the city of Jerusalem, and so it is almost certain that the inquisitive minds of the Archaic Age of Greece sought information from the Hebrew prophets who were so active at the very same time.

Obadiah may have also attracted the attention of the Greek philosophers, since he was said to have been a convert to Judaism, and therefore offered some insight into the reasons for foregoing a polytheistic faith, and switching to monotheism. We are limited in our knowledge of what he may have said during his years of prophetic activity, however, since his book is the shortest one in the Bible, containing only 291 Hebrew words. I therefore will not attempt to analyze his possible contribution to the developing Greek philosophical evolution, and move on to the post-exilic prophets, including Joel, Haggai, Zechariah, Malachi, and third Isaiah.

Most scholars date the book of Joel to the start of the Persian Period (539-333 BCE), which would place him in the era of Socrates and Plato. Joel's message

---

351 Ezek 5:9-10.
352 Ezek 36:33, 38. Sweeney, "Ezekiel," 1113.

may have intrigued Plato, who was often involved with politics, since he forecast an invasion of locusts, grubs, cutters, and hoppers that would ravage the land.[353] These hoards were interpreted to represent the nations of Babylonia, Persia, Greece and Rome, thereby interesting those with political interests, something which characterized Plato above any of the other Greek philosophers.[354] Rather than prepare the inhabitants for disaster, Joel exhorted them to "turn back to the Lord your God, for He is gracious and compassionate, slow to anger, abounding in kindness, and renouncing punishment."[355] This is a far cry from the angry retribution inflicted by YHWH as detailed by the prior prophets, and is clearly in contrast to the gods portrayed in the Greek epic poems as well, but when Joel castigated the Phoenicians for having stolen the treasures of Judah, and proclaimed to the neighboring nations to beat your plowshares into swords, and your pruning hooks into spears, he was using an imagery that was reminiscent of the Greek soldiers desire during the Trojan War, as well as passages brought forth by Isa 2:4, Joel 4:10, Micah 4:3, and Jer 51:11.

The next two prophets, Haggai and Zechariah, both lived during the early years of Darius I (reigned 522-486 BCE), which is about eighteen years after Cyrus the Great conquered Babylon and allowed the Hebrews to return to Jerusalem and build the Second Temple in 538 BCE. Both prophets are mentioned in the book of *Ezra*, which I will discuss shortly.[356] This was obviously an extremely ecstatic time for the Hebrew population, given the fact that they were allowed to return to their homeland and rebuild the Second Temple, but it was up to the prophets to guide them toward their recovery with proper piety and appreciation. Haggai encouraged Zerubbabel, the governor of Judah, and the high priest Joshua to be strong and begin the Second Temple construction. Zechariah cautioned that they should not be like their fathers who did not obey the Lord, but rather they should turn back from their evil ways, for the Lord will choose Jerusalem again. Zechariah also used imagery which would have been familiar to the Greeks, when he had a vision of four chariots coming from the mountains with the first led by horses of bay color, the second of black color, the third of white color, and the fourth dappled. An angel told him that these were the four winds of heaven coming out after presenting themselves to the Lord of the earth, an image which resembled the gods of the four winds in Greek mythology, Boreas (north), Notus (south), Zephryrus (west), and Eurus (east).[357] Following up on the moral tone of these new pronouncements, the Lord said to "execute true justice; deal loyally and compassionately with one another."[358] And to remind those who were

---

353 Joel 1:4.
354 Ziv, "Joel," 1168.
355 Joel 2:13. Ibid., 1170-1171.
356 Ezra 5:1-2; 6:14.
357 Zec 6:1-7.
358 Zec 7:9. Ziv, "Zechariah," 1256.

listening, Zechariah noted that this was "the utterance of the Lord, Who stretched out the skies and made firm the earth, and created man's breath within him," a cosmogony which would have drawn Plato's interest. Given his monotheistic bent, as discussed earlier.[359]

The twelve minor prophets end with the book of Malachi which is set in the period when the Second Temple was rebuilt. This impressive structure must have been a favored sight on the list of contemporary tourist guides, and it is likely that the traveling Greek philosophers would have made a pilgrimage there while visiting Babylon or Egypt. By tradition, Malachi was considered as the last of the prophets. The Lord told Malachi that His name was honored among the other nations three times in the very first chapter, but He had not given due honor by the Israelite people. Malachi asked "Have we not all one Father? Did not one God create us?"[360] While it has been debated whether this refers to all of mankind, or just the Israelites, those hearing or reading the text would have certainly considered the unity of this statement, which fits nicely with the Greek philosophical search for unity in the world, although not with the Athenian elitism which saw all non-Greeks as simply barbarians. The land of Israel and Judah was now resurrected in the city of Jerusalem, and rededicated by the presence of a magnificent temple, which made it an impressive site, and the words of the prophets would have surely attracted the attention of the Greek philosophers.

Following the books of the Minor Prophets, we have the books of Ezra and Nehemiah, two important leaders in the reconstruction of both the Second Temple, and the structure of Jewish religious practice in Jerusalem, after Cyrus the Great freed them from their Exile in Babylon. These two men were primarily responsible for modifying the Jewish faith as it was detailed in the Mosaic Code, and clarifying how modern Jews were to act in accordance with the dictates of YHWH, so that an Exile would never again be a necessary punishment. Ezra, also known as Ezra the Scribe, is particularly important, since he was not only a priest, but is held to be the author of the *Chronicles*. The books of *Ezra* and *Nehemiah* are considered to be written as a continuation of *Chronicles*. Ezra is believed to have arrived in Jerusalem in 458 BCE, and Nehemiah, who was governor of Judah, was sent to Jerusalem to rebuild the city in 445 BCE, serving under both Artaxeres I (465-424 BCE) and Darius II (423-405 BCE).[361] Since Plato was born c. 427 BCE, this would place both men being in Jerusalem during the life of Socrates.

Because he is the one who brought the Torah to the returning exiles, and read and interpreted it publicly, Ezra is sometimes called the second Moses.[362] After Ezra instituted the reading of the Torah to the public at the beginning of

---

359 Zec 11:17. Ibid., 1263.
360 Mal 2:10. Ziv, "Malachi," 1271.
361 Najman, "Ezra," 1666-1667.
362 Ibid., 1669.

the Second Temple era, a group of Levites would stand at his side in order to expound the full significance of the text, making it possible for those who did speak Aramaic, like the Greek philosophers, to fully comprehend the message.[363] Some authors have also claimed that Herodotus was aware of Ezra's writings, since he knew the Aramaic language, although this possibility has been criticized by others.

Ezra begins his book with a quotation from Cyrus the Great who said that "The Lord God of Heaven has given me all the kingdoms of the earth and has charged me with building Him a house in Jerusalem, which is in Judah."[364] Since Cyrus was Persian, these words must have piqued the interest of the Greek philosophers, and I believe they would have certainly wanted to hear more about this monotheistic deity who so impressed the foreign king. To assist the Hebrews in building their Temple, Cyrus released treasure that had been taken away from Jerusalem by Nebuchadnezzar, including a total of 5,400 gold and silver vessels. The number of people who returned from Exile was listed as 42,360, along with 7,337 servants, and 200 male and female singers.[365] To assure their safe passage, Cyrus sent an escort of one thousand mounted soldiers. This impressive migration would have certainly made Jerusalem an extremely congested, but exciting, place to visit for some time.

The laying of the foundation of the Second Temple was associated with joyous celebrations, and a Mardi Gras type atmosphere appears to have been prevalent. The Greeks were known for their extensive travels, and while there are no extant records about this particular city at that time, I believe we can find vestiges of the visits in the philosophical positions that were adopted. The non-Hebrew residents of the city were apparently not in favor of the Temple construction, and wrote to King Artaxeres (not defined as I or II) who agreed to have the rebuilding stopped. This halt lasted until the second year of the reign of King Darius.

Work was started again after the prophets Haggai and Zechariah prophesied of the divine command for the task, and Darius found a record of the letter which King Cyrus had issued commanding that the Temple be rebuilt. Upon completion, one hundred bulls, two hundred rams, four hundred lambs, and twelve goats were sacrificed as a purification offering. Ezra was then sent to Jerusalem by King Artaxeres, along with gifts of silver and gold. When he arrived, however, he found that the people had begun to worship the local gods, as well as marry foreigners, which was forbidden by the Mosaic Law. He rent his clothes and tore out his hair, and confessed to God of his sorrow for their actions, since YHWH had allowed a remnant of the Exiled people to be saved, and they did not respond with proper behavior and respect. He called a meeting of all of the returning

---

363 Steinsaltz, The Essential Talmud, 14.
364 Ezra 1:2. Najman, "Ezra," 1671.
365 Ezra 2:64-65.

Israelites and made them swear to follow the Mosaic Law.[366]

The book of *Ezra* ends at this point, but the story is then taken up by Nehemiah. What is especially important about what happens next, is that seven months after his arrival in Jerusalem, the entire population assembled in the square "and they asked Ezra the scribe to bring the scroll of the Teaching of Moses with which the Lord had charged Israel."[367] Ezra complied, stood on a wooden tower, and read from the entire scroll. That the message would have been understood by all those gathered around, including interested foreigners, is evident by the statement that the text was transcribed and given sense in order to be sure they understood the reading.[368] This meant that Greeks, as well, would likely be able to understand the words, since they were often conversant with the common languages of the era. In addition, the people began to gather in order to study the words of the Teaching. This would have allowed for multiple sites for the Greek philosophers to find information on what the Torah said. One sad sidelight to the rebuilding of the Second Temple is that the Samaritans had come to Zerubbabel asking to be allowed to take part in the reconstruction, but were denied. The rejection brought about a deep and lasting division between the two groups that was never healed.[369]

The prophets, then, were the transmitters of the Law of Moses up to the time when Ezra introduced the written words of God. Once the Bible was completed, the dissemination of biblical teaching was taken over by the men of the "Great Synagogue," said to number one hundred and twenty members. The rabbis and

---

366 One of the primary changes demanded was that the citizens become divorced from their miscegenating with foreign women. Ezra 10:10-44; Neh 10:30. At about the same time, Athens was making it a condition of citizenship that mothers and fathers both be Athenian citizens. Halpern, "Ezra's Reform and Bilateral Citizenship in Athens and the Mediterranean World," 44. This law, promulgated by Pericles in the late 450s BCE, may very well have been suggested to the Athenian ruler by the actions of Ezra to purify the population of Jerusalem to return to the mandates of the Mosaic Code following the rebuilding of the Second Temple.

367 Neh 8:1. Najman, "Nehemiah," 1699.

368 Neh 8:8. The reading of the law is commonly said to have taken place in the autumn of 445 BCE. Moore, <u>Judaism in the First Centuries of the Christian Era: The Age of the Tannaim</u>, vol. I, 5.

369 Minkin, <u>The Shaping of the Modern Mind: The Life and Thought of the Great Jewish Philosophers</u>, 54. Samaria had historically been part of David's kingdom, and after the death of Solomon it became the separate kingdom of Israel. The Judeans had their center in Jerusalem, and the Samaritans on Mount Gerizim by the city of Shechem. Each group claimed to be the true people of Israel, and the irreparable split was prompted by the building of the Second Temple. The schism was so great that the Samaritans took over only the *Pentateuch* for their holy Bible, and rejected the Prophets and the rest of the Jewish Scriptures. Moore, <u>Judaism in the First Centuries of the Christian Era: The Age of the Tannaim</u>, vol. I, 27.

scribes completed the collection of sacred books, by adding the words and stories of the prophets, and from that point forward, the written text, including the eventual completion of the Mishnah and Talmud would provide material for all scholars to study. By now, the Greek philosophers were into the era of Plato and Aristotle, and the primary influence of biblical monotheistic thought would have been widely displayed to all interested scholars.

G. Discussion

The task of analyzing the evolution of Greek philosophical thought is difficult, and I don't pretend to have accomplished the feat in the space of one chapter. It is clear, however, that it did not grow independently, isolated from the teachings of the adjacent centers in Egypt and Babylon, and so any analysis must take into account the advancements that were being made in nearby civilizations. Most historians agree that the ancient Near East was an important contributor to ancient Greek teachings, but few concur with me that most of this influence came from the Hebraic sources of the Old Testament.

The Chinese and Indian civilizations were geographically distant from the Western World, making contact on a regular basis difficult, and even though some of that philosophy found its way onto the Greek mainland, most of the influence was from the Near East. The Greeks were constantly in contact with the scholars from Egypt and Mesopotamia, and the early philosophers, playwrights and historians traveled frequently to the region to study with their sages, and learn their holy texts. My concept that the Greeks saw the readings of the early Old Testament as a model for their own philosophical thought is not new, even if it has fallen out of favor in modern times. *The Tripartite Tractate*, which is part of the Nag Hammadi Scriptures from the second or third century CE, goes so far as to claim that the Hebrews were the model which the Greeks used for "everything they thought."[370] I am not prepared to go that far, but in many ways this conclusion makes great sense, since the very crux of the start of Greek philosophical thought with the Presocratic philosophers was the search for the one *arche* which would provide a rational explanation for the state of reality. Despite a uniform belief in a polytheistic system of gods, the Greek intellectuals did not look to mythologic explanations for the working of the universe, and the Hebrew teaching that the power of YHWH, the one and only God and Creator of the Universe, clearly showed forth in all of their attempts to identify the One as the reason for our existence on earth.

I will reiterate some of my reasons for this belief in the Conclusion which follows, but I once again want to emphasize my contention that much of this interaction which took place during the beginning of the Classical Greek era

---

370 Thomassen, "The Tripartite Tractate," 89.

was initiated, in my opinion, by the transference of Hebraic though into the developing Greek mind by dissident Hebrews who left the Exodus and fled to Mycenae before the Trojan War, in order to escape the parricidal punishments inflicted by Moses on all who would not forgo the faith of their ancestors.

Chapter 15

CONCLUSION

hile the Western World has acknowledged its debt to the Classical Greeks (500-323 BCE) for much of its present-day standard of political thought and intellectual endeavors, the origin of that remarkable civilization remains masked in mystery. Historians have generally acknowledged that the first inhabitants on the Greek mainland who could truly be called "Greek" were the Mycenaeans, a wealthy, militaristic society, whose leader, King Agamemnon, directed the Greek army in the famed Trojan War, c. 1183 BCE. Although this event has never been proven to have taken place in extant archaeologic records, and is therefore, like the story of the Exodus in the Bible, considered by many to be a fictional tale, it is nevertheless a fact that the Mycenaeans did exist at the time the war was presumed to have taken place, and the city of Troy was a location proven by archaeologic ruins to have suffered some type of destruction.

Mycenae flowered during the fifteenth century BCE, becoming the major force in the Aegean region following the destruction of the palaces on the island of Crete, but despite its prominent position as the most powerful Greek force in the Trojan War, according to *The Iliad* by Homer, the Mycenaean civilization disappeared from the geopolitical scene following the victorious end to the conflict, and Greece entered a prolonged Dark Age (1000-850 BCE), finally emerging with the fundamentals of a democratic society during the ensuing Archaic Age (850-500 BCE).

It is generally accepted that the Classical Greek culture which followed gave rise to an explosion of intellectual advancements in the Arts and Sciences, but where these remarkable savants learned to expand the limits of their universe has never been satisfactorily answered. It is not even known with certainty from where the initial immigrants who founded the Mycenaean culture came, but Greek legend held that Danaus fled Egypt with his seventy daughters in the fifteenth century BCE, and founded the city of Argos, while Cadmus emigrated shortly thereafter and established Thebes. If this story was based on a valid oral tradition, this would align the founding of Greece with the Early Date of the Exodus, which is also believed to have taken place in the fifteenth century BCE, although others have suggested dates somewhat later. As I have detailed throughout this book, the Exodus was a critical turning point in modifying the religious principles of the Patriarchs into the monotheistic commandments of the Mosaic Law, but Moses was forced to resort to parricidal punishments in order to force the Hebrews to worship only one God – YHWH. In so doing, it is my belief that the dissident Hebrews who did not want to modify their ancestral faith into monotheism demanded by Moses fled to Mycenae, where they prospered during the years before the Trojan War, adding their remembrances of the stories from the patriarchal oral tradition which eventually resulted in the writing of the Bible, to the traditions which were already inherent among the Mycenaean populace. This is the very reason, in my opinion, why there are so many similarities between the legends of the Hebrew Bible and Classical Greek writing and lore.

I will detail these analogies shortly, but I want to point out that there is more than mere congruity of fictional storylines to suggest an interaction between the ancient Hebrews and Greeks.

Modern historians do not generally trust legendary material, and have often turned to linguistic evidence to suggest that the Greeks originated from the Indo-European realm, based upon the fact that the Classical Greek alphabet belongs to the Indo-European superfamily of languages.[1] While this linkage may indeed connect the early immigrants to regions north and west of Greece, it does little to identify the exact location where the early Greek ancestors resided before they migrated to the Greek mainland. It also fails to explain how the Classical Greek language and culture came to incorporate Eastern characteristics, an assimilation that is agreed upon by most scholars.

The Phoenicians have often been credited with introducing the Eastern concepts to Greece, as I will discuss shortly, but this explanation is far-fetched, in my opinion, since the Phoenicians never settled in Greece at any time during their existence, and there is no evidence to indicate that they ever hired themselves out as mercenaries or slaves to the ruling Greek Monarchy.

Martin Bernal, Professor of Government and Near Eastern Studies at Cornell University, has modified the thesis of Phoenician influence in Greece by claiming in his book *Black Athena* that there was "massive cultural borrowing" by the Greeks from the Hyksos, a group of Semitic- and Egyptian-speaking dynasts who ruled Egypt during the Second Intermediate Period (1786-1550 BCE).[2] According to Bernal, it was the black Egyptians who truly inaugurated the early Greek evolution, and his claim that there was a racist basis for historians refusing to accept this derivation, has evoked widespread debate in many academic circles.

As I have previously discussed, I do not accept Bernal's thesis that the emigrants to Greece were native black Egyptians, but there is one ancient culture that would readily explain both the legendary rule of Danaus and Cadmus, as well as the Eastern influence on the Classical Greek language, while maintaining a consistent timeline of historicity with societies known to have flourished during the Late Bronze Age (1600-1200 BCE). That population is the pre-Mosaic generation of Hebrews who left their indentured status in Egypt during the Exodus, and

---

1 Myres, Who Were the Greeks?, 101.
2 Bernal, <u>Black Athena</u>, II.410.

wandered for forty years in the Wilderness of Sinai before crossing the Jordan River into the Promised Land. Although some biblical scholars question whether the Exodus ever took place, pointing out the lack of any archaeologic proof of the event, I stand with the majority who may question the details as outlined in the biblical text, but still believe the post-patriarchal Hebrews were enslaved in Egypt and then departed en-masse for the Promised Land.

This integration of pre-Mosaic Hebrews into Mycenae before the Trojan War would not only provide a reason why there are many Eastern influences in ancient Greece, but also would answer why there are a multitude of similarities between the writings of Homer and the Old Testament. As I discussed in Chapter 4, the general consensus among biblical scholars is that the Torah was not written by Moses, but by a group of authors known as "J" for the use of the Yahwistic name for God, "E" for the use of the Elohistic name for God, "P" for the priestly caste, and "D" for the Deuteronomist. Their individual treatises were then collated by redactors ("R") in a process that has become known as the "Documentary Hypothesis." The "J" source is believed to have created many of the popular stories in the books of *Genesis* and *Exodus*, and his tales are so enthralling that Peter Ellis referred to the author as "the Hebrew Homer."[3] If a group of Hebrews left the Exodus before the passage into the Promised Land because they refused to change their religious beliefs into monotheism, which went against the teachings of their ancestors, and found their lives therefore threatened by the parricidal punishments of Moses for such obstinance, they likely would have brought with them stories of their heritage which were assimilated into the evolving Greek culture, just as the descendants of those who remained with Moses developed oral legends which later were integrated into the Torah by the biblical compilers.

There has been a trend in modern times to try and denigrate the historical accuracy of the Bible, both because there has not been much archaeologic verification of the stories contained therein, and also because it is said to have been written to promote the rights of the Israelites to claim ownership of the Promised Land, rather than to present an unbiased historical fact.

Norman K. Gottwald, Professor of Old Testament Emeritus at New York Theological Seminary, claimed that the writers of the Bible "were not moved by the same notions of 'objective' historiography that characterize the humanistic discipline of historical writing."[4] This view, in my opinion, is flawed because you cannot claim that the monarchic historians were only content "to record

---

3 Friedman, The Hidden Book in the Bible, 6. Harold Bloom, Sterling Professor of the Humanities at Yale University, considers "J" to be a "writer more inescapable than Shakespeare and more pervasive in our consciousness than Freud," and his "only cultural rival would be an unlikely compound of Homer and Plato." Bloom, "Introduction," 2.

4 Gottwald, The Tribes of Yahweh: A Sociology of the Religion of Liberated Israel, 1250-1050 BCE, 27.

the meaning-bearing accounts of Israel's beginnings,"[5] when there is an entire collection of legendary information that characterizes the improper behavior of the Hebrews, adding much valuable information about the historicity of the early Israelite society. Gottwald accepts that "the early biblical accounts are based on presumably good memory," but throws their value aside because of their cultic-ideological intent, while at the same time insisting that form criticism and tradition history "have fully validated their fundamental insight into the immense multilevel cultural and historical complexity of the traditions."[6] You cannot throw the baby out with the bath water, and then claim that refilling the tub with fresh water reincarnates life.

The discovery of the Dead Sea Scrolls has provided texts of the Bible that were written one thousand years earlier than any previously discovered manuscripts, and in the years which have followed the proof of their existence, just before the modern state of Israel was mandated, enormous information about the very actuality of the ancient Hebrews continues to provide information on exactly how the Jewish nation evolved, lending support to the likely validity of the Old Testament itself.

In addition to downplaying the reliability of the historicity of the biblical text because of a presumed bias of the authors, a lack of non-biblical texts which are synchronized with the events is often pointed out as a reason to question the premonarchic Israelite history. This critique is rapidly becoming less reliable, however, as archaeologic finds have continued to uncover a cache of material from the Early and Late Bronze Ages. From the Amarna Letters to the cache of material found in Mesopotamia, the ability to validate the lifestyles of contemporary peoples, without actually having any of them actually referred to as Hebrews or Israelites, is clearly evidence of reasonableness of descriptions in the Bible, if not proof that the events were identical in nature.

Biblical scholars like Gottwald are willing to allow for leeway in writing from a sociologic, rather than an historical, perspective for "the historian strives for fuller detail than does the sociologist," who can "survive on less historical detail than the historian, provided it is of the sort that facilitates understanding of the social system from some clearly articulated analytic perspective."[7] I beg to differ here, as it is clear that modern historians of the Late Bronze Age must always suffer from a lack of detail, given the paucity of material available, but that does not negate the possibility of placing enough reliance on comparative analysis in order to make acceptable conclusions on what effect one contemporary civilization

---

5 Ibid., 27.

6 Ibid., 29. Although Gottwald admits that the traditions could contain actual memories of Yahwistic prehistory, he clearly favors, like most biblical scholars, that they "are retrojections into prehistory of traditions drawn from a later Israelite experience." Ibid., 34.

7 Ibid., 31.

might have had on another. I believe that Gottwald answers this question with his own conclusion:

In history and in sociology, as in all disciplined human efforts to know, the aim of the inquiry determines whether we feel informed and how fully we feel informed. Only when we know the question are we able to say if a given datum or theory is an "answer."[8]

When we ask the question about who provided the early Greeks with information that seems to have been derived from Eastern sources, I think the answer is clear: it was the ancient Hebrews.

My thesis in this book depends upon two interpretations of what happened during the 400-year enslavement of the Hebrews in Egypt, and their experience during the Exodus, both of which I believe are quite reasonable. The first is that all the members of the congregation who left Egypt would have had the same recollections of their patriarchal ancestors, taught to them by their parents as a faithful remembrance of their Hebrew heritage. While we cannot know with certainty how the Hebrews worshiped their gods in Egypt, there is no reason to doubt it was in a polytheistic manner, based upon the problems which Moses faced in attempting to force obedience to the monotheism of his new Mosaic Code. Since the legends of the patriarchs which were recorded in the Torah reveal vestiges of this pattern of worship, there is no reason why the dissidents who left the Exodus would not have had a similar veneration. The second is that not all of the congregants submitted to Moses' attempt to change their religious devotion from a polytheistic format to a monotheistic belief, as evidenced by the number of Hebrews killed for impious acts, beginning with the construction of the golden-calf idol. Not only did this disobedience take place throughout the Exodus, it continued during the years of the Conquest and Monarchy, and did not become a standard practice until the return of the Babylonian Exile in 537 BCE. Postulating, therefore, that some of the Hebrews during the Exodus may have decided to leave and travel to Mycenae, is not a strange conclusion, and makes perfect sense, given the fact that Moses had never been part of their community before suddenly appearing with his magical rod and message from YHWH that they were to now follow Moses to the Promised Land. The initial announcement was exciting, but once the trials of the wilderness were realized, and the notice given that none of them were ever going to actually be allowed to enter the Promised Land, there would have been no reason for them to stay with Moses unless they truly believed he was a savior sent by God.

When the dissident Hebrews left and traveled to Mycenae, they would have remembered the tales of the Patriarchs, and the power and might of YHWH as a warrior god capable of miraculous undertakings when they settled in their new-found land. Although this thesis fails to identify who the first founders of

8 Ibid.

Mycenae were, and where they came from, it provides a clear explanation for how the Classical Greek society evolved from their Mycenaean ancestors with a strong infusion of Eastern concepts, a question which has heretofore been enmeshed in mystery and misunderstanding.

I am not the first person to postulate a possible ancestral relationship between the Israelites and the Greeks, as the postulate was put into concrete form during the Hellenistic Age (323-100 BCE), when a number of commentators claimed that there were familial ties between the two ancient cultures.

In *1 Maccabees*, a deuterocanonical book of the Bible written by a Jewish author c. 100 BCE, Areus (308-265 BCE), the king of Sparta (Lacedaemon), wrote to Onias, the Jewish High Priest, and related how "the Spartans are said to be brothers of the Jews, descendants of the family of Abraham."[9] In *2 Maccabees*, from the same era, the Jewish High Priest Jason was said to have sought refuge in Sparta when he was expelled from his own country because of the supposed racial kinship of Sparta to the people of Israel.[10] Josephus, the prominent Jewish historian from the first century CE, accepted this blood-relationship, noting that the Greek philosopher, geographer and historian Alexander Polyhistor (fl. 100-40 BCE) claimed that the Greek God Heracles married a granddaughter of Abraham.[11] He also called attention to a seal on the letter which was four-square and had an eagle with a dragon in its claws, an emblem which represented the tribe of Dan.[12] These reminiscences do not prove that the ancestral relationship is real, but they do point out that the Hellenistic Jews not only desired to claim an ancestral relationship to the Greeks, they found contemporary evidence within their own records to prove the kinship.

Greek authors, as well, found a relationship between their ancestors and the Jews. Diodorus of Sicily (first century BC), in his *Library of History*, claimed that Danaus and Cadmus led colonists from Egypt during a pestilence and settled the oldest city of Greece, Argos, and that emigrants from that location under Moses then founded the nation of the Jews in Judea, and the city of Jerusalem.[13] This was the reason why, Diodorus concluded, that "it is a long-established institution among these two peoples to circumcise their male children, the custom having been brought over from Egypt."[14] As I discussed earlier, the legend of Danaus and Cadmus being the founders of Greece was widely accepted in much of the ancient world, and many other authors also tied Moses in with the supposed migration.

9 I Macc 12:21. Agus, The Meaning of Jewish History, I.121.

10 II Macc 5:9.

11 Josephus, "Antiquities of the Jews," The Complete Works of Josephus, I.15.1, 38.

12 Ibid., XII.4.10, 256.

13 Meyers, "Biblical Archaeology: The Date of the Exodus According to Ancient Writers," 12.

14 Diodorus, The Library of History, I.28.2-3, 91.

Modern scholars have totally ignored these ancient claims of consanguinity, charging that the references were simply an attempt by the Hellenized Jews to identify themselves with the Classical Greek mystique. Despite superficial similarities between the two cultures, the general consensus has been that there was no direct connection between the ancient Hebrew and Mycenaean civilizations. This belief that the ancient Hebrews were isolated from the rest of society was noted in the Bible when the seer Baalam pointed out to king Balak, after he was hired to curse the Hebrews, that they are "a people that dwells apart, not reckoned among the nations."[15] Even Cyrus Gordon, Professor Emeritus of Mediterranean Studies at Brandeis University, who has championed the theory that Greece and Israel both owed their origin to the Ugaritic culture of the Late Bronze Age, categorically denied that their social development was due to any interaction between the two ancient cultures.

The English Zionist Norman Bentwich (1883-1971 CE), former Attorney General of Palestine, also noted that both the Jews and Greeks were an aloof people, thinking of all foreigners as barbarians and reluctant to allow them admission to their closed society, but their resemblance was a chance event, for they always lived "in disparate spheres, each nation unconscious of the other's existence."[16] Whatever similarity was present between the two ancient peoples was serendipitous, and not due to any cause-and-effect influence, according to most modern historians.

I believe that this total disregard for an Hebraic contribution to the Classical Greek culture is an erroneous position, inconsistent with a multitude of similarities which, in my opinion, can only be reasonably explained by some direct interaction having taken place between the two societies during the Late Bronze Age, before the Trojan War. This contact almost certainly took place at the time of the Exodus, when Moses attempted to force the Hebrews to give up the polytheistic practices of their ancestors or face the punishment of death for their apostasy. Over 40,000 of the participants were killed according to the biblical text, and many others, unwilling to change, but in fear for their lives, in my opinion fled the control of Moses and traveled to Ugarit, where they boarded Phoenician vessels to Mycenae.[17]

---

15 Num 23:9. Fox, "Numbers," 331.

16 Bentwich, Hellenism, 27.

17 After returning from the top of Mt. Sinai with the Ten Commandments and finding the Hebrews worshiping the golden calf-idol, Moses ordered 3,000 men killed. Exod 32:28. In response to the rebellion of Korah, a plague was sent to kill his impudent supporters, and in the conflagration which followed, 14,700 people died. Num 16:49. After the orgy at Acacia, Moses ordered those who worshiped Baal to be executed, and 24,000 people died. Num 25:9. This total of almost 42,000 does not include the unnumbered people who died when God sent venomous snakes as punishment when they complained about the lack of food and water on their way to Edom (Num 21:6), the ones killed by a plague at Kibroth-hattaavah (Num 11:33-34), or the objectors who were burned in a fire sent by

Such a migration is not only possible, it provides the best explanation we have to date for multiple categories of evidence, both legendary and archaeologic, which indicate an Hebraic contribution to the Classical Greek society. Although many historians have had no problem accepting the supposition that the Phoenician language was the primary source of Semitic additions to the Greek alphabet, no one has suggested that the Hebrews may have instead been responsible for the contribution, despite the fact that the ancient Hebrew and Phoenician languages were very similar, both evolving from the Canaanite lexicon in the early Iron Age (1200-587 BCE).

The primary reason most scholars have ignored the Hebrews as generating the Semitic elements found in Greece is the fact that there is such a clear distinction between modern Judaic monotheistic principles, and those found in Greek polytheism. These discrepancies, however, are the result of the evolution of the Israelite society from post-Mosaic Jews, a culture which completely modified the faith of the patriarchal generation. The pre-Mosaic Hebrews, on the other hand, were very similar to the Mycenaeans, maintaining a strong belief in polytheistic religious tenets, and a staunch loyalty to the practices of their ancestors. This deep-felt commitment to the faith of their fathers was the primary reason for a rift in the Exodus community when Moses attempted to reform the Jews into a monotheistic faith. It should be remembered that at the very start of the Exodus, before the Hebrews who were enslaved in Egypt for generations had any introduction to the power of YHWH, a search for the sacred bones of Joseph was made in order to follow his request, sworn to by an oath of his brothers, that his body be taken back to Canaan by his descendants. As noted by Rabbi Maimonides (1135-1204 CE), the preeminent medieval Jewish philosopher and scholar, it is contrary to "discontinue everything to which he has been accustomed," and although this comment was intended to explain why God retained the ancient rite of sacrifice in the Torah, it is applicable to the reasons why the Hebrews were reluctant to follow the radical changes in the Mosaic Law.[18]

These dissident Hebrews were the same congregants who the Bible referred to as "stiff-necked," and resistant to the regulations imposed by Moses, causing YHWH to react with consternation and disappointment over their failure to obey His commands. They constantly complained to Moses about his harsh regulations, and even threatened his life at times if he did not desist from his autocratic reformations. The fact remains, however, that they were only "stiff-necked" to Moses' interpretation of what God commanded, requirements which modified their centuries-old tradition of polytheistic worship, and thereby seemed to be the words of a false prophet, rather than a true man of God. They believed that their ancestors had properly followed the directives of the gods, including

---

God at Taberah (Num 11:1-3).

18 Maimonides, <u>The Guide For the Perplexed</u>, III.XXXII, 322-323.

those of YHWH, and that the reason their prayers to be freed from the Egyptian bondage had finally been answered was because of the pious nature of their parent's faith. YHWH had told Isaac that He would bless him and his descendants, "because Abraham obeyed me and kept my requirements, my commands, my decrees and my laws."[19] Although the Bible claimed that YHWH was upset with their failure to obey the new demands made by Moses to modify these practices, this was a history written by the post-Mosaic victors of the reformation, and not the dissident Hebrews who had remained loyal, in their interpretation of their ancestor's actions, to the religion of the Patriarchs. God's promise to Abraham did not depend upon the modifications made by Moses.

As pointed out by Bernhard W. Anderson (1916-2007 CE), Professor of Old Testament Theology Emeritus of Princeton Theological Seminary, many of the pre-Mosaic Hebrews believed strongly in the gods of the land of Canaan:

"These people probably did not intend to turn away from the God of the Exodus and the Sinai covenant. Rather, they meant to serve YHWH and Baal side by side or to identify YHWH with Baal."[20]

When Abraham crossed the border of Mesopotamia into Canaan, he built altars to YHWH which were later prohibited by the Mosaic Code. When Jacob returned to the land of Canaan from Haran, after marrying Leah and Rachel and raising his family for fourteen years, Rachel stole her brother's household idols (*teraphim*) to bring along, a clear indication that his extended family did not follow the precepts of the Mosaic Code. Jacob himself showed that he had continued to have faith in the polytheistic nature of the gods when he rested on his way to Haran after fleeing Esau's wrath over the loss of his father's deathbed blessing, and dreamt of a ladder rising to heaven at Beth-el. He made a vow to God at that time that if He would remain with him and protect him then "the Lord shall be my God."[21] This promise clearly indicated that Jacob had not yet decided to give exclusive allegiance to YHWH, and had accepted the importance of other family deities.

The allegiance to Baal lasted into the era of the monarchy, as evidenced by the fact that Saul named one of his sons Ishbaal (Ish-Bosheth, "man of Baal," 1 Sam 14:49, 2 Sam 2:8; 1 Chon 8:33, 9,39), and his son Jonathan named his own son Mephibaal (Mephibosheth, Meribbaal, "Baal is an advocate," 2 Sm 4:4; 1 Chron 8:34, 9:40), while King David had a son named Beeliada (Eliada, "an open idol," 2 Sam 5:16; 1 Chron 3:8, 14:7). In the words of Eugene Merrill, Professor of Old Testament Studies at Dallas Theological Seminary, covenant infidelity affected the people "from the leaders on down," who quickly began "to

19 Gen 26:5. Sailhamer, "Genesis," 184.
20 Anderson, Understanding the Old Testament, 175.
21 Gen 28:21. Sarna, <u>Genesis</u>, 200.

embrace syncretism and outright paganism."[22] The two religions were not seen as contradictory, but when Moses began his parricidal campaign to weed out anyone who did not accept YHWH as the one and only God, based upon the demand that Israel was to have no other gods before YHWH (Exod 20:3, 34:14), the battle for survival began in earnest, and those Hebrews who wanted to remain loyal to their ancestors had to leave, since it was clear their lives were in danger. During the rebellion of Korah, Dathan and Abiram openly complained to Moses that "you brought us up from the land flowing with milk and honey to kill us in the wilderness."[23] Jeremiah would later explain that the transgressions led to YHWH deciding that a new covenant would be made with Israel and Judah after the Babylonian Exile that "will not be like the covenant I made with their fathers," since they broke the prior covenant by failing to follow the requirements set forth in the Ten Commandments.[24] It is evident, therefore, that patriarchal worship of God clearly resembled that of the polytheistic Semites throughout Canaan, even though it showed evidence of YHWH beginning to attain a level of prominence resembling that of Zeus in the Greek pantheon. It seems reasonable to conclude, therefore, that the generations which descended from the twelve sons of Jacob would have continued the practices of their ancestors during their years in Egypt, rather than follow foreign rites which characterized the veneration of Egyptian gods, even if the Bible does not describe how they actually behaved.

The reluctance to follow the demands of Moses is readily understandable if we put ourselves in the minds of the Hebrew congregants at the time of the Exodus. When Moses suddenly appeared to lead them out of Egypt, he had been known to them first as an Egyptian prince who was part of the Egyptian royal house, and then as a refugee who returned from a forty-year absence in the land of Midian, where he had married the daughter of a Midian priest. He had no obvious Hebrew training, no position as a respectable Hebrew elder, and no Semitic identity, except for his lineage as Aaron's long-lost brother. Despite the fact that his magical powers supported his claim to have intimacy with the Hebrew gods, he was a stranger whose checkered past belied his declaration that he was chosen by the god of Abraham, Isaac, and Jacob to save the Hebrews from their long-suffering enslaved state. At the Reed Sea, when the Egyptian army suddenly appeared hell-bent on their destruction, some of the Hebrews even had second thoughts about whether they should have followed Moses out of Egypt in the first place. As the army neared their position on the waters edge, many of them prayed for a return to Egypt, where at least their lives, and the lives of their children, were not endangered by a foreign armed force. After Moses

---

22 Merrill, <u>Kingdom of Priests: A History of Old Testament Israel</u>, 242. Under this concept of syncretism, Baal and YHWH were different aspects of one divine power.

23 Num 16:13. Friedman, <u>Commentary on the Torah</u>, 482.

24 Jer 31:31-32. Sweeney, "Jeremiah," 991.

miraculously parted the Reed Sea and destroyed the Pharaoh's army, however, they quickly put their concerns aside, and once again agreed to follow his lead. But Moses had set himself up as the sole leader of the conclave, ruling over them with autocratic authority that did not accept any input from other heads of the community. His mannerisms were not consistent with the normal workings of Semitic tribes during the Late Bronze Age, where the destiny of the tribe was put in the hands of a Council of Elders, rather than in the control of a single despotic member. No one man was allowed to rule over the others, as was seen with the monarchies of the Levantine city-states during the Late Bronze Age, and now Moses was telling the congregation that their entire history was to be overturned, and no discussion or meetings were held to receive input from other respected members.

Moses had argued that he was the only one entitled to make decisions for the Hebrews because he was the only one in direct contact with the God that appeared to Abraham and designated his descendants as the Chosen People. He warned the congregation that if they did not want to suffer the same fate as the Egyptians who succumbed to the disasters of the Ten Plagues, they had better follow the letter of the law he had laid down during their travels in the wilderness. This may have worked before the theophany on Mt. Sinai, when the restrictions were primarily administrative and did not pertain to the details of religious worship, but following his attempt to restrict reverence to YHWH alone, dissension and dissatisfaction rapidly spread among the people, and the result was a sudden annulment of their contractual oath to follow the Mosaic Code.

Two events confirm the ill-will which gradually developed over Moses' authoritarian command. The first was with his own brother and sister, Aaron and Miriam, who complained about their lack of involvement in the Exodus, and were eventually castigated, and punished, by God. The other event was the dissatisfaction of important Hebrew leaders during the rebellion of Korah.

That the people often reacted with uncertainty over Moses' demands shows the strength of their prior training in the polytheistic worship of their ancestors. The fact that Aaron immediately agreed to the demands of the congregation to build an idol to worship suggests that his faith in the Mosaic Code may have also been shaken by Moses' absence. God had chosen him to act as Moses' spokesman when Moses wavered at the burning bush, but we have no evidence that Aaron had any leadership experience or qualities which would allow him to stand up to the demands now being made. He relented to their request, asking the people to bring him all of their golden earrings in order to provide appropriate material to make the idol in the form of a golden calf. When the image was completed, the people showed their pent-up relief and exclaimed "this is your god, O Israel, who brought you out of the land of Egypt."[25] Quickly thereafter, burnt-offerings were brought to the altar, and a wild party and feast ensued. When Moses returned to the camp with the two tablets containing the Ten Commandments etched by the hand of God, he found the people dancing around the golden calf-idol, celebrating in pagan, impious ways. He became so enraged that he threw the tablets to the ground, shattering the hallowed words of God into little pieces. To punish the revelers for their heretical sins, he ordered the idol to be melted down and then ground into a powder for the people to drink. He then called the Levites to his side, and ordered them to kill the culpable evil doers: "even your brothers, friends and neighbors," emphasizing that family bonds were to offer no protection from retribution of the Lord.[26]

These violent actions indicate that Moses had decided to cleanse the congregation of their illegal ancestral practices by killing all the men who had disobeyed his orders, rather than attempt to encourage them to accept the Almighty Unity of YHWH through the process of education and reform. This was the first instance where one Jew had actually killed another in the biblical text, for although Abraham had attempted to sacrifice Isaac, and the brothers of Joseph had hoped to eliminate their sibling through an act of murder, no actual physical harm had ever ensued. Moses may have previously been reluctant to have Hebrew blood on his hands, but after the meeting with God on Mt. Sinai, his attitude had radically changed. He knew that he need not worry if he eliminated those who seemed to be the most resistant to change, since God Himself had threatened to exterminate all the Hebrews for their rebellious behavior. Rashi (Rabbi Shelomo Yitzchaki 1040-1105 CE), considered by many to be the greatest of all biblical commentators, justified Moses' action by noting that one of the crimes for which capital punishment was authorized was sacrificing to a god other than the YHWH.[27] But while this rationalization carried an element of truth, the extent of the parricide which Moses began was more akin to a commission of genocide, than to corporeal punishment alone. Over the years, Moses would become more of a Marauder than a Messiah to the Hebrews who wished to remain loyal to the teachings of their mothers and fathers, and in time it became obvious that the malcontents would have to leave the congregation if they hoped to continue their practice of a polytheistic faith.

Despite the threat of capital punishment for disobedience, Moses found that

---

25 Exod 32:8. Ibid., 204. When Jeroboam I was made king of Israel, he worried that the people would return to Jerusalem, and the rule of King Rehoboam of Judah, so he constructed two golden calves, one at Bethel and one at Dan, and told the people that "this is your god, O Israel, who brought you up from the land of Egypt!" the same phrase used by the people at Mt. Sinai. 1 Kgs 12:28. Zevit, "First Kings," 702.

26 Exod 32:27. The Living Bible, 78.

27 Exodus, The Torah, A Modern Commentary II, 373.

the dissidents did not give up easily, for as Maimonides (Rambam, 1135-1204 CE), the preeminent medieval Jewish philosopher, later explained in *The Guide for the Perplexed*, "it is contrary to man's nature that he should suddenly abandon all the different kinds of Divine service and the different customs in which he had been brought up."[28] Although it is generally recognized that the kinship bonds which "give unity and cohesion to the lineage and family in tribal societies become attenuated" as those societies move to a confederation of tribes,[29] the Hebrews had not yet reached this level of cooperation during the Exodus, and many were simply not willing to change their beliefs in their long-held family traditions just because it was demanded by Moses. It would take almost 1,000 years before the Judaic faith was accepted by the entire community following the return from the Babylonian Exile (587-538 BCE), where the Jews were forced to return to the land where they first were born, but Moses' resolve to force an immediate change was uncompromisingly steadfast at the time, and he continued to punish all those Hebrews who disobeyed his orders with a sentence of death. Three thousand Hebrews were executed on that day when the golden calf-idol was destroyed, and when Moses returned to the mountain top to receive another set of the Ten Commandments, YHWH reinforced the appropriate nature of Moses' punitive action by sending a plague upon the people as further punishment for worshiping a false idol, raising the death total above 3,000.[30] God also told Moses that He would no longer travel in their midst as He drove out their enemies from the Promised Land, for they were such a stiff-necked people that He might decide to suddenly destroy them if He remained nearby. These actions transformed Moses from a military leader in charge of the migration of a group of enslaved Hebrews to freedom into a High Priest and King with the authority to inflict capital punishment upon all who disobeyed his commands. The Mosaic Code was now the ultimate Law of the land, and all adherents would have to worship the One and Only Almighty God if they wanted to remain part of the orthodox Hebrew faith.

The Hebrews had been raised to worship family gods in a way which included iconic adoration, and when Moses set forth the first four Commandments outlining the aniconic worship of One God alone, the Hebrews who had followed him out of Egypt must have been shocked to hear the enormity of their task. Their confusion would have been compounded by the words of the Fifth Commandment, one of only two Commandments that positively demanded a

---

28 Maimonides, The Guide for the Perplexed, 32, 324.

29 Cross, From Epic to Canon: History and Literature in Ancient Israel, 7.

30 Exod 32:35. The nature of the scourge, and the exact number of congregants killed, was never fully disclosed in the biblical text. According to the Talmud, those who had been warned not to serve the idol, and did so anyway, were slain by the Levites, while those who had not been warned, died in the plague. Seder Moed 66b.26-28, 35. Scherman, The Chumash, 498.

specific type of behavior. This edict ordered them to honor their mothers and fathers, a mandate that should have been easy to follow, since they had practiced this type of homage for centuries. But how were they to honor their parents when the first four Commandments ordered them to forgo the iconic worship of the family gods which these very same progenitors had taught them diligently to observe? Although modern readers may find the Ten Commandments to be a logical and consistent summary of the basic tenets of a monotheistic religion, the pre-Mosaic Hebrews must have been confused by this irrational dilemma, leaving them at odds with the very man who had so impressively brought the mighty Pharaoh to his knees. Their entire religious faith was being destroyed and replaced by contrary demands which surely left them thunderstruck and bewildered.

While many of the Hebrews surely were surely distraught over the loss of their brethren, they likely remained with the Exodus, at first relying on their knowledge of the tradition of the last words of Joseph that "God will surely come and get you, and bring you out of this land of Egypt and take you back to the land he promised to the descendants of Abraham, Isaac and Jacob."[31] This forecast changed, however, after the episode of the spies at Kadesh-barnea, however, when God had told Moses that the enclave was ready to enter the Promised Land, and Moses sent twelve men to scout the region and assess the dangers. On their return, the men talked of giant warriors and fortified cities, so frightening the gathering that they refused to follow God's directive, despite the pleas of Joshua and Caleb, who were part of the surveillance team. God was so enraged that He forbade any of the adults from ever entering the Promised Land, forcing them to wander in the wilderness for forty years while the entire adult population died off. Only their children would inherit the divine gift of everlasting freedom. At first, many of the Hebrews may have been satisfied with this dispossession, but as time passed, and the killings continued, it would have taken a saint to both change their religious beliefs, and realize that they would never be able to witness the reaping of any benefit.

Mutiny against this proclamation was not completely quenched by the parricidal punishments, however, and the next break from Moses' tyrannical rule occurred when Korah accused Moses of illegally restricting the chain-of-command to his decision-making alone. Korah had the backing of a number of other respected leaders in the conclave, but Moses refused to give in to any of his demands, and in the carnage which followed, another 14,000 Hebrews were killed.[32] This rebellion not only involved the rank and file members of the Exodus, as did the golden calf-idol incident, but rather the upper echelon of men, including some who probably sat on the Council of Elders. The loss of so many prominent members of the community at one time must have shown the survivors that the

---

31 Gen 50:24. <u>The Living Bible</u>, 47.
32 Num 16:35, 49.

parricidal punishments of Moses spared no one who questioned his authority. Since this was not a matter of overt impiety against God, but rather about having a say in the administration of the entire congregation, it was clear that Moses would not tolerate any questioning of his authority and dictatorial control. Those Hebrews who still felt obliged to follow the teachings of their ancestors must have now realized that they could not safely remain with the Exodus congregation, and plans for an emigration likely began following this catastrophic event.

The importance of this event has often been overlooked in modern times, as has the confrontation between Moses and his siblings, Aaron and Miriam, when Miriam was struck with leprosy at Hazeroth for daring to criticize Moses about his marriage to a Cushite woman, and his refusing to share leadership with his brother and sister. Over the centuries, Moses has become such a revered figure in the evolution of the Judaic faith, that the extent of disagreement with his edicts has been ignored by most biblical scholars. When the Torah is read in its entirety, the primal position of Moses as God's choice to lead the Hebrews out of Egypt into the Promised Land is crystal clear, but at the time, many of the Exodus participants were not ready to anoint him as a savior, despite his success, including his own siblings. It should not be surprising, therefore, that following his parricidal reprisals, many survivors must have questioned their agreement to follow him out of bondage.

The final proof of Moses' intent to kill all idol-worshipers came as the forty-year trial of wandering in the wilderness began to wind down. When the Hebrews neared the Jordan River for their eventual passage into the Promised Land, they encamped at Acacia, where celebrations, including homage to the god Baal, took place with some of the local Moabite inhabitants. YWHW was so infuriated by this expansive show of apostasy, that he ordered Moses to execute all the tribal leaders who had taken part in the festivities. By the time the carnage was completed, another twenty-four thousand Hebrews were killed.[33] These slayings not only were directed at the original generation who had left Egypt, but also at younger members who were now old enough to know better than to act with the kind of impiety that had forbade their parents being able to enter the Promised Land. If any Hebrews were still loyal to the teachings of their ancestors, it was obvious they now had to flee for their lives. The Hebrews who remained with Moses may have been "hammered into a national unit" by their exclusive patriarchal faith and allegiance to only one God, but the solidarity of that commitment would nevertheless prove to be a superficial facade that would take centuries of time to harden into the unity of faith that characterizes the modern Judaic religion.[34]

Once the dissidents fled the Exodus congregation, they had to decide where

---

33 Num 25:9.

34 Hawkes & Woolley, History of Mankind I. Prehistory and the Beginnings of Civilization, 745.

to go, and may have received assistance and advice from distant relatives who had long ago settled in the land of Palestine, rather than follow Jacob into Egypt. Much of central Palestine was populated by partly settled Hebrew clans, and it is likely that these distant cousins would have sympathized with the plight of the dissident Hebrews, since their religious beliefs were the same, having not been modified by the monotheistic demands of Moses. It would be dangerous to remain in Palestine once the Mosaic Hebrews invaded their territory, and when their brethren heard of the atrocities that were being committed by Moses, many may have decided to join the migration, since they could possibly be in as much danger as the ones who had just fled Moses' parricidal retributions. The success of the Exodus congregation against indigenous kings near the end of the Exodus would have been forefront in their consideration, and so finding a distant place to live would have been the likely choice.

The newly expanded dissident Hebrew force would have then likely moved northward out of Palestine toward Ugarit, the international port of departure in Syria for merchants from all corners of the world. Ugarit was a multilingual city, and was known to provide goods and transportation to the entire Mediterranean Basin. If you wanted to travel by sea to a distant land from the Fertile Crescent during the Late Bronze Age, and did not have private means to do so, you went to Ugarit, much as Americans who wanted to travel by boat to Europe went to New York in our modern era. That their passage was not noted by contemporary records is not surprising, for their travels to Ugarit would not have been recognized as unique, but rather as simply another movement of a category of Canaanites known as Habiru, rather than as a people specifically designated as Hebrew. Texts from Ugarit and Alalakh during the Late Bronze Age indicate that Habiru tribes were scattered throughout northern Syria, providing service to the local kings in return for land and rations. Escaped slaves often found asylum with the Habiru, even though the practice was forbidden by many contemporary treaties. There were no distinctive facial features to distinguish the Hebrews from these other Semitic groups, such as the Palestinians, Phoenicians, Moabites, Akkadians or Edomites, and so it is understandable that their activities would have been seen as one generalized movement, rather than as a specific agenda, even if their intentions were entirely unrelated. This would also explain why there is no record of the Exodus of the larger group of Hebrews under Moses in extra-biblical sources at that time. Mobile people leave very little evidence of their existence in the archaeologic record, and depend on their own oral traditions to immortalize their existence. Since Egyptian hieroglyphics are our primary source for the historical register during the Late Bronze Age, one would not expect much attention to have been paid to the Hebrew Exodus, which would have been embarrassing to the Egyptian regime.

Once in Ugarit, the dissident Hebrews would have likely booked passage to Mycenae, planning to work as mercenary soldiers, craftsmen, or even slaves.[35] Knowledge of the Mycenaean civilization was quite widespread in the Levant during the Late Bronze Age, primarily due to their widespread economic activities following the fall of the Cretan palace society. The Mycenaeans were expanding their economy, both abroad and at home, and the Hebrews would have been aware of what opportunities this afforded. Ships during the Late Bronze Age had a capacious storage deck, indicating that they were primarily intended for cargo transport, and the passage would have been similar to that of the Philistines who arrived in Canaan by sea from Crete. Travel to Mycenae would not have been difficult, as it has been estimated that 100 penteconter ships could have transported 5,000 people and hundreds of tons of cargo during those transits.[36] If prolonged stops were not made along the way, the trip took about five days, so that provisions would not have to be very great. In addition, the valuables which the Hebrews took from the Egyptians at the time of the Exodus would have provided a means to pay for the necessary transport.

The choice of Mycenae would have been natural, given the fact that the ancient Greeks were characterized by family loyalty, which placed the father at the head of the family, ruling over his children, women and slaves by authority that was, according to Aristotle, the "natural" way.[37] The patriarchal families, like most of the ancient Greeks, were very paternalistic, and the loyalty and reverence they showed their ancestors was the basis for the Fifth Commandment, which directed that one should honor thy mother and father. As part of this loyalty, the pre-Mosaic Hebrews also had a family god, who "was a personal and social god who provided protection and guidance for the family as well as the blessings of fertility and the continuity of life," and the people relied on this deity to support them through their troubled times.[38] This formula would have created no problem in Mycenae, for the Mycenaeans readily accepted new ideas and made them part of their own religious creed when they encountered new cultures, especially when

---

35 Slavery was not then the horrible condition it later became associated with, and slaves were generally protected and provided with regular shelter, food and clothing. Albright, Yahweh and the Gods of Canaan, 85.

36 Barako, "One if by Sea ... Two if By Land, How Did the Philistines Get to Canaan? One: By Sea," 64.

37 Aristotle noted that this patriarchal rule was agreed to by Homer, who said that "each man has power of law over children and wives." Aristotle, The Politics, I.2, 27. The ancient Hebrew family, or beth 'ab ("the house of the father"), like the Greeks was an extended family of relatives and slaves ruled over by a patriarch. Miller & Hayes, A History of Ancient Israel and Judah, 2nd edition, 85.

38 Miller, The Religion of Ancient Israel, 63.

the underlying tenets were compatible with their own.

The experience of the Hebrews, both in survival and combat prowess, and their knowledge of the Levantine geography, would have been eagerly welcomed by the Mycenaean rulers, who were beginning to expand their authority to regions throughout the Levant. The Hebrews were experienced workers who had traveled for years in the Levant, and their advice on the conditions of the hinterland would have been invaluable. During this era, the militias of most countries were filled by professional men who were paid to fight. By the late thirteenth century BCE, many of the kings preferred to buy the services of men for a longer period of time, often offering land in return for their services. Although there is little concrete evidence on how the Aegean world gathered their forces, Robert Drews, Professor of Classics and History at Vanderbilt University, concluded that prior to the Catastrophe which sent the Greek mainland into a prolonged Dark Age, "the Mycenaean palaces might have depended almost entirely on 'foreign' professionals for their infantry forces."[39] Drews believed that many of these men came from the mountains beyond Boeotia, but I judge that the dissident Hebrews would have provided a more likely source, since they came from a society that "depended for security entirely on a militia."[40] The Hebrews, like the Habiru in the Levant, were experienced in hostile combat, and would have provided the Mycenaeans an opportunity to reduce their need to use their own populace by conscription. In return, the Hebrews would have been given a chance to obtain a secure way-of-life for their extended families in a land where their religious beliefs would not have been seen as an heretical threat. Diodorus of Sicily noted that Moses had prepared the Hebrews during the Exodus for warfare, "and required the young men to cultivate manliness, steadfastness, and, generally, the endurance of every hardship."[41] They were perfectly fit for service in what would proved to be a ten year siege outside the walls of Troy.

This postulated passage of dissident Hebrews to Mycenae would explain better than any other theory to date why there were so many apparent links between Egypt and Mycenae during this period of time, since the Hebrews would have been very knowledgeable of Egyptian customs, and possessed many valuable objects made of gold and silver taken from the Egyptians the night before the Exodus began. Mycenaean remains attest to the use of gold masks for burial, and metal-inlay techniques which were commonly used in Egypt at the time of the Hyksos expulsion (c. 1550 BCE), and the reason for this widespread influence is not clear. Martin Bernal has argued that the findings indicate that the Hyksos

39 Drews, The End of the Bronze Age, 155.

40 Ibid., 173. When the Hebrews left Egypt, they traveled in military formation, "troop by troop," rather than in the manner of an enslaved throng. Tigay, "Exodus," 116.

41 Diodorus, *Historical Library*, XL.3.6, quoted in Bar-Kochva, Pseudo-Hecataeus, "On the Jews": Legitimizing the Jewish Diaspora, 20.

actually infiltrated Mycenae during their tenure in Egypt, but few scholars accept this premise, and while it is possible that the artifacts came from Greek mercenaries serving in Egypt, such a prolific effect is not likely to have occurred from transitory contact alone. The Hebrews, on the other hand, would have had an extensive knowledge of Egyptian engineering and construction skills through their years of forced labor as slaves, and when they arrived on the mainland, they would have provided the information and goods which Bernal ascribed to the Hyksos invaders. Although the artifacts which have been uncovered are Egyptian in nature, I believe it was the Hebrews who brought them to Mycenae who are responsible for what has remained in the archaeologic record.

Strong evidence that such a migration did in fact take place is provided by the Greek legend which told how the initial founders of Greece were people who had been forced to leave the land of Egypt, and travel to the Greek mainland, where they conquered the weaker indigenous inhabitants. According to Hecataeus of Abdera (fourth century BCE), an early Greek historian who wrote *Aegyptiaca*, this move was necessitated by a pestilence in Egypt, which the people ascribed to the gods being angered by the presence of foreigners in their country. To pacify the gods and resolve their troubles, the Egyptians ousted the aliens, who then left en-masse, led by Danaus and Cadmus. Danaus took his seventy daughters and colonized Argos, while Cadmus settled in Greece, and founded the city of Thebes. Although this explanation ascribes the eviction as having emanated from the Egyptians, the tale is very similar to the one presented in the Torah.

This version of the legend was held by other ancient authors, including Diodorus of Sicily, a Greek historian who wrote the well-known *Library of History* in the first century BCE. Diodorus explained that during this process "the most outstanding and active among them banded together and, as some say, were cast ashore in Greece, and certain other regions; their leaders were notable men, chief among them being Danaus and Cadmus."[42] In addition to the founding of important centers in Greece, Hecataeus added that a larger colony headed by Moses also left Egypt and migrated to the land of Judea, where Moses founded the city of Jerusalem and divided the Jews into twelve tribes. Hecataeus did not supply a chronological framework for these events, but subsequent authors, such as the Egyptian historian Charemon (first century CE), the Egyptian priest Ptolemy of Mendes (first century CE), and the Roman historian Tacitus, provided estimates which placed the event in the fifteenth century BCE, the era when I believe the Exodus took place.

In many ways, this tradition is virtually identical to my theory of dissident Hebrew migration, since Danaus and Cadmus would thereby become identified as being part of the initial Exodus congregation, and then splitting from the others who were led by Moses across the Jordan River into the Promised Land.

---

42 Diodorus of Sicily, The Library of History, 40.3.2, 281.

The two men would have left with the dissident Hebrews and traveled to the Greek mainland, where they founded cities which later became identified as the earliest Greek ancestors. They may have actually been the leaders of the dissident Hebrews, and their initial membership in the Hebrew Exodus congregation would explain the concept which arose during Hellenistic times that there was an hereditary link between the Israelites and ancient Greeks. That Danaus was in fact a member of the tribe of Dan, thereby explaining the similarity of their names, is an important aspect of this proposal, and I will return to this argument later, after I first summarize other salient comparisons between the Patriarchs and the legends of the Classical Greeks.

Most historians over the centuries have supported the concept that these legends are due to a Phoenician influence, which was a direct result of their involvement in trade throughout the Mediterranean Basin during the Late Bronze Age. Michael Astour, Professor at Southern Illinois University, advanced the case for Phoenician presence in Mycenae by identifying their presence as Western Semites in several parts of Mycenaean Greece and their colonies, including the Danaans of Argolis, the Cadmeians of Boeotia, and the islands of Thera, Cos, and Rhodes. He concluded that "the entire Mycenaean civilization was essentially a peripheral culture of the Ancient East, its westernmost extension."[43] This characterization, in my opinion, provides far too much authority to the Phoenicians, who may have traveled throughout these areas in their capacity as purveyors of trade, but they did not populate the land and intermingle with the Mycenaeans in a manner that explains a transference of their cultural characteristics. It is rather the Hebrews, and not the sailors who transported them, who should be given credit for much of what the majority of historians ascribe to the Phoenicians.

The most dramatic and obvious congruence between the legends of the Patriarchs and those of the Homeric Greeks is the singular use of infanticide to teach a parable about maintaining faith and loyalty to an overriding entity which was more important than any human life, even the life of your child. In the case of the Jews, this involved obedience to the dictates of the Almighty God, while for the Greeks it was the importance of the State above the individual. Abraham's willingness to sacrifice his son Isaac when ordered to do so by YHWH, and the agonized decision of Agamemnon to support the honor of Greece by sacrificing his daughter Iphigenia to the goddess Artemis, are remarkably alike, especially in light of the fact that no other culture in all of human civilization ever raised this act of compliance to the level requiring an infanticidal act. It is not possible, in my opinion, that these two stories developed independently of each other, given the fact that their origins are dated to the same historical era. Abraham is believed to have lived in the early Middle Bronze Age (2000-1600 BCE), but the legends of

---

43 Astour, Hellenosemitica: An Ethnic and Cultural Study in West Semitic Impact on Mycenaean Greece, 357-358.

the Patriarchs were developed following the Exodus from Egypt, during the Late Bronze Age, an era just before the Trojan War, which is generally believed to have taken place c. 1183 BCE. The origins of the oral traditions of both the Bible and the Trojan War are therefore contemporaneous. In addition to the sources of both stories being developed in the same era, the commitment to writing also took place around the same period of time, with the stories of Homer dating to the ninth or eighth century BCE, and the early documentary sources of the Bible to a similar period of time. While it cannot be determined with certainty which legend influenced the writing of the other, I believe that my postulated migration of dissident Hebrews from the Exodus to Mycenae favors the proposition that the tale of Abraham and Isaac was brought to Mycenae by the Hebrews, and there took root to eventually surface as the fable of Agamemnon and Iphigenia.

This concept of cross-fertilization is supported by many other similarities between the tales of the Patriarchs and the Homeric Greeks, particularly with the personalities of Jacob, the third Patriarch and father of the twelve sons for whom the Hebrew tribes are named, and Odysseus, the great hero whose prolonged travel home after the end of the Trojan War formed the basis for the *Odyssey* by Homer. Each of these heroes utilized cunning and strength to achieve their desired ends, and their attributes were particularly highlighted by each society. Jacob was able to obtain the privileged status of being Isaac's firstborn son by forcing his elder twin brother Esau to transfer his birthright in order to obtain food after he came home famished from a long day of hunting in the field. He compounded this mordacious ruse at the deathbed of his father by wearing a lambskin to mimic the hairy feel of his brother's skin, allowing him to illegitimately receive the blind Jacob's blessing. His wiles continued later in life when he cheated his brother-in-law Laban out of a flock of sheep by causing the pure white sheep to give birth to spotted progeny, which he then claimed as his own. Jacob's extraordinary strength was evident when he wrestled with the Angel of the Lord at Peniel, and when he moved a heavy stone covering a well by himself, displaying what Robert Alter, Hebrew scholar and literary critic, called an "Homeric" feat of strength.[44]

Odysseus, like Jacob, also stood for the concept of victory at all costs, resulting in his reputation for being cunning and devious in order to obtain his desired ends. Hecuba, the wife of Hector, voiced this well-deserved trait when she referred to him as "that vile, that slippery man, right's enemy, brute, murderous beast, that mouth of lies and treachery, that makes void faith in things promised and that which was beloved turns to hate."[45] It was Odysseus who suggested that the Greeks build a wooden model of a horse filled with warriors, the so-called Trojan Horse, in order to fool the residents of Troy into believing that the Greek force had accepted defeat in their attempt to overtake the city after a ten-year siege.

---

44 Gen 29:10. Alter, <u>Genesis</u>, 152.
45 Euripides, "The Trojan Women," 88-90, 130.

The plan cleverly allowed the Greeks to enter the impenetrable walled-city of Troy and lay the inhabitants to waste, ending the war which had so decimated their ranks. Odysseus was adept at fooling not only men, but also the immortals, as witnessed by his victory over Circe and Polyphemus in Homer's the *Odyssey*. Although his strength did not surpass that of other Greek heroes, like Achilles, Ajax, or the mighty Heracles, he was clearly more powerful than most mortal men, as witnessed by his ability to string his own bow when he returned home from the Trojan War, and shoot an arrow through twelve axe-heads, a feat which none of the suitors of Penelope were able to do.

In addition to the similarity of their personalities, the prolonged period of servitude which Jacob spent in Haran before being allowed to marry Leah and Rachel closely resembled the twenty years Odysseus was away from his beloved Penelope, ten years fighting the Trojan War, as chronicled in the *Iliad*, and ten years returning home, only to find his wife besieged by suitors, as detailed in the *Odyssey*. Both stories described a migration which was not completed until the protagonist – Odysseus or Jacob – reached home, and this congruence led William G. Pollard (1911-1989 CE), physicist and Anglican priest, to refer to the biblical tales as the "Hebrew Iliad" and the "Hebrew Odyssey."[46]

There are also many other literary cross-references between the two cultures which suggest an acceptance of biblical traditions by various sources of Greek mythology. The story of the three strangers who forecast the future birth of Isaac to Abraham at Mamre is one such example. When Abraham was ninety-nine years old, three men appeared and told him that despite his and Sarah's advanced age, the Lord had decided to grant them a son. The men were in reality three Angels of the Lord, sent by YHWH to forecast the destruction of Sodom and Gomorrah. A similar granting of a son to a childless elderly couple was also seen in the Greek legend of Orion. In that tale, Hyrieus had worked so hard and long that he and his wife Tamagra were never able to bear offspring. They were rewarded by the gods Zeus, Poseidon and Hermes with a son Orion, who was killed by the gods later in life for claiming that he was the greatest of hunters. The unique combination of three Angels or gods granting the birth of a son to a childless elderly couple is quite unusual, and suggests that some transference of the myth may have taken place from one culture to the other. Once again, the earlier dating of the biblical legends implies that it was the Hebrews who originated the myth.

In like manner, the turning of Lot's wife into a pillar of salt when she turned

---

46 Pollard, The Hebrew Iliad, The History of the Rise of Israel Under Saul and David," 8. Telemachus is an infant when Odysseus leaves for the Trojan War, is eleven years old when the suitors take over his household, and is twenty years old at the start of the *Odyssey*, bewailing his treatment by the suitors until Athena appears and tells him to stop bemoaning his fate and do something about it.

back to see the cities of Sodom and Gomorrah burn to the ground provides a parallel with the Greek myth of Orpheus and Eurydice. Orpheus, the legendary musician and poet who is considered as the "father of poetry," was renowned for the beauty of his verse and music, which was so powerful that he could cast a spell over wild beasts with the sound of his lyre. When his wife died, he was so distraught that he descended into Hades to try and retrieve her home, despite the fact that no living person was allowed to cross the River Styx into the underworld. Hades was so taken with Orpheus' grief that he promised that he could lead his wife back into the upper world if he did not turn back to look at her. At first, Orpheus was able to obey this command, but before long he could not contain his desires, and when he turned back to see her beautiful face, she slipped away into the oblivion of the darkness for all eternity. While the story of Orpheus reflected disobedience on his own part, and Lot's grief was due to an error by his wife, the loss of a beloved mate because of an inability to keep one's gaze directed forward when warned to do so by a divine agent is another unusual theme, suggesting the possibility that the ancient Greek culture was introduced to the story by dissident Hebrews who traveled to Mycenae before the Trojan War.

The biblical story of Dinah is also very reminiscent of the Greek "Helen of Troy" motif, where vengeance against the distant Trojans was carried out by the Greeks after Paris abducted Helen, the wife of King Menelaus. Dinah, the only daughter of Jacob, was visiting the neighboring women of Shechem, when she was assaulted by prince Shechem, the son of Hamor who had sold Jacob the land on which they presently lived. This violation was apparently precipitated by the young man's love for Dinah, and after the attack Shechem asked his father to obtain Dinah as his wife. Despite the honorable intentions of the suitor, Simeon and Levi, two of Dinah's brothers, were outraged by the atrocity, and planned to revenge the defilement of their sister in a manner similar to the Greek revenge for the abduction of Helen. When Hamor arrived to formally present the marriage proposal, Jacob's sons answered that it was not possible for Dinah to marry someone who was not circumcised. Hamor accepted the requisition, perhaps as a sign of displeasure with how Dinah was taken, and ordered all the men in town to immediately undergo the operation. When the men were disabled by pain on the third day following the procedure, Simeon and Levi entered the town and killed every male inhabitant. The other brothers then ravaged the town and took all their children, wives, and goods as booty.

Another plot found in the legends of both societies was the incest committed by Reuben, when he lay with Bilhah, the handmaid of Rachel, shortly after Rachel died giving birth to Benjamin.[47] While this act may have been Reuben's way to publicize his firstborn's right during his father's lifetime, a maneuver typical among rulers during the Bronze Age, such sexual contact was culturally

---

47 Gen 35:22.

forbidden by the Hebrews at the time, and Jacob responded in his final Testament by disenfranchising Reuben from his priority position as firstborn son, and transferring his birthright to Joseph, his favorite son and firstborn of Rachel.[48] In the *Iliad*, a similar punishment was inflicted upon Phoinix, who lay with the mistress of his father Amyntor after his mother asked him to avenge the dishonor which had befallen her. When Amyntor heard of Phoinx's action, he cursed him and invoked the Fates to prevent his ever bearing a son.[49]

Even the story of Jephthah making a promise to the Lord that if He would assure his victory over the Ammonites, he would sacrifice the first thing he saw upon returning home bears a resemblance to Greek mythology. Jephthah had been appointed to lead the fighting men of Gilead against the Ammonites, and after a victorious campaign he returned home expecting to see his dog exit his house, but instead it was his only daughter. Jephthah eventually offered her as a burnt-sacrifice, but unlike Abraham, the Lord did not interrupt the carnage. In Greek legend, Idomoneus, the son of Deucalion and suitor of Helen, was caught in a storm at sea following the Trojan War and vowed to Poseidon that if he arrived home safely, he would sacrifice the first creature he saw. It turned out to be his young son, and in most versions of the story, he carried out the act and was eventually exiled from his homeland in Crete.

The final literary theme which was highlighted by both the Hebrews and the Greeks involved the attraction of Potiphar's wife for Joseph, and the Greek legend of Hippolytus. In the Bible, Potiphar's wife was sexually attracted to Joseph, and made numerous unsuccessful attempts to seduce him. One day she coaxed him into her boudoir, and when he still refused to succumb to her advances, she grabbed his coat and screamed that he had tried to rape her.[50] Joseph was thrown into prison at once, but the story had a happy ending, for it eventually resulted in Joseph being called upon to interpret the Pharaoh's dream, whereby he was rewarded by being named vizier of all Egypt. The Greek tale, on the other hand, had a tragic ending, typical of most of the Classical Greek legends, for when Theseus, the father of Hippolytus, heard of the false accusation of his wife Phaedra that Hippolytus had attempted to rape her, he prayed that Hippolytus not "live to behold another sun's bright rays."[51] As a result, Hippolytus was dragged to death when his chariot overturned as he attempted to flee his stepmother's wrath. The Hellenized Jews of Alexandria were very taken with this Greek tale, and *The Testament of Joseph*, a Hebrew work belonging to the class called *Pseudepigrapha*, incorporated the Hippolytus theme into a retelling of the Joseph encounter with

---

48 Gen 49:3-4; 1 Chron 5:1. The prohibitions against incest appear at Lev 18:6-18; 20:11-12; Deut 27:20, 22-23.
49 Homer, The Iliad, IX.447-457.
50 Gen 39:13-15.
51 Seneca, Phaedra, IV.I, 661.

Potiphar's wife, not realizing that the Greek tale, in my opinion, owed its origin to the original Hebrew legend. A similar Greek legend is found in the tale of Bellerophon, the son of Glaucus, who was so handsome that Anteia, the wife of king Proteus (Proitos), fell in love with him and then falsely blamed him with attempted rape when he spurned her advances.

Another aspect of Hebrew influence on the Classical Greeks, in my opinion, is the effect which the biblical story of Creation had on the development of Greek philosophy. While this contribution has been totally ignored by the entire philosophic community, I find it incredibly more than coincidence that the label of water as the first primary element of the earth by Thales of Miletus (c. 624-546 BCE), who is generally considered to be the first rational Greek philosopher, is exactly the same substance which the Bible says was present in the void when God created the Universe. Everyone is aware that the first line of the Bible is "in the beginning God created heaven and earth."[52] What is often forgotten, however, is that God's spirit, as He was performing this task, "moved on the water's surface," and the creation of the Heaven and the Earth, was divided by the water above and below.[53] This primacy of water is highlighted by the decision of God to destroy the civilization He created when He was disappointed by the decadence that was rampant during the era of Noah by returning the physical cosmos to a watery Chaos that was present at the creation of the Universe. In essence then, water was present when God set out to create the Universe, and it therefore was the primary element to all who read the earliest writings that were eventually compiled into the biblical text. Since the Documentary Hypothesis, as discussed in Chapter 4, presupposes that oral traditions were used to record what is contained in the book of *Genesis*, these very same concepts would have been known to the dissident Hebrews who fled the Exodus and traveled to Mycenae before the Trojan War.

Some of these stories may then have been carried on and eventually collated into the first writings of the early Greeks, particularly those of Thales, who was known to have traveled widely and learned much from both the Egyptians and Babylonians. A man whose quest for knowledge was this great would certainly read the available Jewish writings as well, acquainting himself with all the theories concerning the origin of the Universe before pronouncing that, in the words of Aristotle, "the 'principle' of all things is water," upon which the earth floats.[54] Although Aristotle attributed Thales' conclusion to the necessity of water to maintenance of life, the judgment is remarkably similar to the opening lines of the book of *Genesis*, and while I don't mean to say that Thales took his theory

---

52 Gen 1:1. Kaplan, The Living Torah: The Five Books of Moses and the Haftarot, 3.

53 Gen 1:2. Ibid.

54 Kirk & Raven, The Presocratic Philosophers: A Critical History with a Selection of Texts, 88. This passage is found in his Metaphysics, A.983b6ff.

directly out of some early biblical text, I believe that he was impressed with the theory, and further modified it into his cosmogony, just like he was impressed with the Babylonian arithmetic and studies of planetary movements, so as to be able to predict the eclipse in 585 BCE. Like so many other supposed influences on Greek culture that have ignored the role played by the Hebrews, most authors have ascribed the influence on Thales' explanation of the world to have come by "variegated traditional background of earlier Greek quasi-mythological cosmogonical versions, but also by a specific cosmological idea derived directly, perhaps, from further east."[55] The "further east," in my opinion, was the writings of the progeny of the dissident Hebrew migrants, rather than from Egypt or Babylon, as is often asserted. Whether Thales may have also had some Hebrew genetic material floating around his brain, making him more conducive to the biblical story, can never be known, although Herodotus claimed that his family was Phoenician, despite the fact that the majority of historians view him "as a genuine Milesian of distinguished family."[56]

Pythagoras is another Greek philosopher with strong ties to the Hebrew prophets, particularly Ezekiel. Some have claimed that Ezekiel was actually Nazaratus Assyrius, a teacher of Pythagoras. This identification may refer to the fact that Pythagoras, along with other early Greek philosophers, actually met with Ezekiel during his trip to Babylon. Recent studies have indicated that books in Israel were not so scarce from the ninth century BCE forward, and Jens Bruun, from the Copenhagen Lutheran School of Theology, believes that "there is no reason to doubt that literary works existed in Israel *to some extent* as early as the 10th century B.C.E."[57] While this supports the probability that Greek philosophers traveling to the Levant could easily have been introduced to the concepts, both oral and written, which were eventually incorporated into the Hebrew Bible, it also makes it likely that such material could have been incorporated by the documentary sources in a manner similar to the transmission of the Gilgamesh Epic through multiple sources over a thousand years in a reasonably similar fashion.

Other Greek philosophers, as well, seem to have taken lessons from the prophets, despite the claim by Hermann Cohen (1842-1918 CE), one of the most important Jewish philosophers of the nineteenth century, there was antagonism between Plato and the prophets. Leo Strauss (1899-1973 CE), a German-Jewish political philosopher who focused his research on Plato and Aristotle found unity

55 Kirk & Raven, The Presocratic Philosophers: A Critical History with a Selection of Texts, 89.

56 Guthrie, A History of Greek Philosophy, Volume I, The Earlier Presocratics and the Pythagoreans, 50. Guthrie even noted that Thales may have subconsciously been influenced by the society in which he was born and bred, noting that the country in which he lived was familiar with both Babylonian and Egyptian ideas, civilizations where water played a preponderant part of their mythology. Ibid., 58.

57 Kofoed, Text and History: Historiography and the Study of the Biblical Text, 88.

between Socrates and the prophets, in that both have a divine mission, and are concerned with justice or righteousness. The primary question I then have to ask is which of the two thinkers came to the idea first, and who may have learned from whom. I have no doubt that all of the Greek philosophers encountered stories about these prophets, if not hearing speeches by them personally, since they lived at the very same time, in the very same area where the Greeks traveled to during their quest for knowledge. We know that Aristotle considered that God was "a living being, eternal, most good," but did he consider that God would partake in human events, as depicted by Homer?[58] I believe it is more likely that the monotheistic teachings of the Torah, and the warnings of what would befall the people if they did not follow the commandments of YHWH by the prophets, directly influenced Greek philosophy, and explains why the evolution of thought took the path it did.

A final effect of the biblical themes on Greek literature can be seen in the fact that all of Greek tragedy, in the words of H. D. F. Kitto (1897-1982 CE), the late professor of Greek at Bristol University who concentrated his studies on the subject, is "concerned with the serious aspect of human existence in which law prevails, in which offence will incur disaster, in which the very nature of things will have the last word."[59] Divine governance is taken for granted by both the playwrights, and the populace, and such importance to following the dictates of God is something which clearly is at the forefront of the entire Old Testament, and the warnings espoused by the prophets who were spreading their words during the same era of Sophocles, Euripides, and Aeschylus. I have discussed the many themes which I believe these authors expanded upon in the preceding chapter, and will not detail them again here, but to look to other Eastern sources, rather than the Hebrews, for the germination of these themes is nothing short of anti-Semitic favoritism.

In addition to legendary material, there are other aspects of Mycenaean culture which have been credited to the Phoenicians or Egyptian, but are much more likely, in my opinion, to have been derived from the dissident Hebrews, such as the construction of the Cyclopean walls in the archaeologic ruins of Mycenae. As discussed above, Greek legend held that Danaus and Cadmus migrated from Egypt to the Greek mainland, and since the followers of Cadmus were said by the ancients to be Phoenicians, historians have generally accepted that the Phoenicians were the ones to give their alphabet to the Greeks. The Phoenician and ancient Hebrew languages were very similar, however, both developing from the Canaanite tongue during the end of the Late Bronze Age, so it is not possible to distinguish which source was the more important by linguistic analysis alone. In fact, the Greek names for *alpha* and *delta* reflect Aramaic pronunciation, rather

---

58 Aristotle, "Metaphysics," <u>The Basic Works of Aristotle</u>, XII.7.1072b.28-30, 880.
59 Kitto, "The *Odyssey*: The Exclusion of Surprise," 16.

than Phoenician, but most scholars suggest a Phoenician contribution because the Arameans were not known as seafarers, and this would require an overland transmission across Asia Minor. Since my postulate of Hebrew migration provides a reasonable basis to place the Hebrews on the Greek mainland when the Greek language was evolving, I believe that a Hebrew contribution is a much more reasonable assumption than claiming that the Phoenicians, who never spent a prolonged period of time on the Greek mainland, provided an infusion of Semitic words, simply through contacts from their maritime trade activities. As pointed out by David O'Connor, Lila Acheson Wallace Professor of Ancient Egyptian Art in the Institute of Fine Arts of New York University, "trading contacts are, on the whole, not good mechanisms for transmitting cultural modes likely to affect substantially the political and religious ethos and structure of either trading partner."[60] If the Hebrews became enmeshed in Mycenaean society for centuries of time, it is likely that components of their language would have been incorporated into the evolving Greek tongue, thereby explaining the Semitic influence as coming from indigenous, rather than extraneous, sources.

The same reasoning holds true for the claim that the Mycenaean's use of Cyclopean construction techniques came from a Phoenician influence. Three techniques of construction have been excavated in Mycenae, one of which has been termed Cyclopean, because the walls were built with of huge blocks of roughly shaped limestone, often measuring seven feet long and four feet thick, packed together with small stones and yellow clay in the interstices. Since the ancients believed that super-human strength was necessary to move these stones, they claimed that the walls were built by the Cyclopes, legendary giants imported from Lykia. The Greek historian and mythographer Apollodorus (second century BCE), and the Greek geographer Pausanias (second century CE), both delegated the building of the walls to the Cyclopes,[61] while Euripides (c. 480-406 BCE), in *Iphigenia in Aulis*, referred to Argos as the "city of Cyclops," because of the presence of these structures.[62] The other two methods were also conglomerates of large blocks, including one that was well-dressed with a hammer and regularly coursed, and another that was fitted together with great art. The construction of these protective walls showed "familiarity and skill in handling and dressing large masses of stone," as many of the stones weighed as much as five tons.[63]

A number of theories have been proposed to explain how the early Greeks were able to carry out this process, without resorting to the aid of mythical creatures sent by sympathetic gods. Heinrich Schliemann (1822-1890 CE), the

---

60 O'Connor "Egypt and Greece, The Bronze Age Evidence," 60.

61 Pausanias claimed that the Cyclopes made the walls at Tiryns for Proetus. Pausanias, Description of Greece, 2.16.5; 2.25.8.

62 Euripides, "Iphigenia in Aulis," 266, 226.

63 Wace, Mycenae: An Archaeological History and Guide, 49, 110.

German businessman who first uncovered the remains of the capital of Mycenae in the nineteenth century CE, postulated that "as the Phoenicians managed their import, it is possible that this whole decorative style came through that nation to Greece."[64] Schliemann relied on the fact that the Phoenicians were credited with supplying many words of Semitic origin to the earliest forms of the Greek language, and because they were also the ones to transport goods by ship throughout the Mediterranean Basin, he reasoned that they would have assisted in the building of the gigantic walls of Tiryns, as well as other prehistoric walls throughout Greece. The Phoenicians were never known for their masonry or construction skills, however, and I find it highly unlikely that they were responsible for either the transference of knowledge, or the supply of large amounts of skilled labor, simply because they manned the supply ships. The Hebrews, on the other hand, were very experienced in these manufacturing techniques from their years of working in Egypt as slaves. Although the Torah primarily referred to construction with bricks at the time of the Exodus, there was also much utilization of stone up to that period of time. The construction of the Cyclopean walls in Mycenae and Tiryns took place around 1340 BCE, with the Lion Gate following around 1250 BCE. If the Exodus took place in either the fifteenth or the fourteenth century BCE, as I believe it did, the Hebrews could have easily provided the Mycenaeans with a means by which the walls could have been constructed. The Phoenicians may have been the ones to transport Hebrew artisans to Mycenae, but they were not an integral part of the engineering process themselves.

A final category of Hebraic influence in Greece is the amphictyony method of government, which I believe was suggested to the Greeks by the format of the union of twelve Hebrew tribes. As I discussed in chapter 10, no one knows precisely how the Greeks developed the amphictyony configuration, with the Greek philosopher Plato (427-347 BCE) adjudging that the ideal state always had its city, citizens and property divided into twelve parts. Plato did not explain his reasoning for this conclusion, and may have simply been accepting the fact that his hallowed Greek ancestors were basing their original formulation on knowledge of universal perfection which was unique to the Greek mind. Because the Hebrew and Greek political systems both were comprised of twelve members, however, twentieth century CE biblical scholars often accepted that the Hebrew tribal system was a form of an amphictyony, without commenting on any possible collusion between the two ancient societies. As summarized by Martin Noth (1902-1968 CE), Professor of the Old Testament at the University of Bonn, the

---

64 Schliemann, Tiryns, The Prehistoric Palace of the Kings of Tiryns, xlix. Schliemann may have been simply reiterating the view of Josephus, who claimed that the Egyptian influence in early Greece came about through the Phoenicians, who carried wares from the southern Mediterranean shore to the Greek mainland. Josephus, "Against Apion," Complete Works of Josephus, I.12, 610.

confederacy of Hebrew tribes clearly qualified as an amphictyony because they centered their worship of YHWH in a particular city, which changed on a rotating basis.[65] This characterization has recently fallen out of acceptance, however, and most scholars now favor the view that the two systems were unrelated, and find no value in attempting to compare their attributes. I find this attitude condescending to the possibility of Hebraic contribution to ancient Greek culture, and believe that the resemblance is more than incidental. Once a migration of dissident Hebrews to Mycenae is understood as a likely event, it becomes the likely source for the concept of an amphictyony which evolved in Greece during the Archaic Age, when Greece was awakening from the doldrums of their prolonged Dark Age. To deny that the similitude is allied, when there are so many other facets of Greek culture that are arguably derived from the Hebrews, is simply refusing to see the forest for the trees.

Where do all of these arguments leave us with respect to answering the most likely origin of the Classical Greek culture? Can we point to all of these legendary, linguistic, and cultural similarities as proof that the Semitic influence in Classical Greece came from a group of dissident Hebrews who fled the Exodus in fear for their lives before the Trojan War? Certainly not. But as Walter Burkert aptly advised when he first postulated a strong Oriental influence in ancient Greece, if the evidence does not provide "incontrovertible evidence of cultural transfer, the establishment of similarities will still be of value."[66] If we accept that there was a Semitic contribution to Greek culture, which is generally conceded by almost every historian today, and also agree that there are numerous parallels between the Bible and the writings of Homer, which is also a well-accepted analogy, then I believe that the most likely explanation of these relationships is that a group of dissident Hebrews fled the Exodus in fear for their lives after Moses began a series of parricidal reprisals against all Hebrews who refused to modify their ancestral polytheistic beliefs, and traveled to Mycenae before the Trojan War. Despite the fact that most historians credit the Phoenicians with providing this information, in my opinion they do not fulfill the criteria of having a close and intricate long-lasting relationship with the early Greeks to explain why the inclusion took place. No other Semitic culture has ever been shown to have a historicity which would explain a prolonged appearance on the Greek mainland during the Late Bronze and Early Iron Ages, with enough contact to explain why the early Greeks incorporated their traditions.

This proposal would also support the legends of Danaus and Cadmus, without raising the contention of Martin Bernal, Professor of Government and Near

---

65 Gottwald, The Tribes of Yahweh: A Sociology of the Religion of Liberated Israel, 1250-1050 BCE, 346.

66 Burkert, The Orientalizing Revolution: Near Eastern Influence on Greek Culture in the Early Archaic Age, 8.

Eastern Studies at Cornell University, that the ancient myth indicates that the Greeks owed their origin to dark-skinned Egyptians, rather than white-skinned Indo-Europeans, since the two men came from Egypt, a country where the population was dark-skinned. Bernal has argued that racial bias among nineteenth century CE historians kept this explanation from receiving serious consideration, but there are many aspects of Classical Greek culture which could never be resolved by postulating an indigenous Egyptian ancestry, while a contribution by the pre-Mosaic Hebrews is an entirely consistent thesis. While Danaus and Cadmus were indeed the founders of the first cities in ancient Greece, they were not indigenous Egyptians, but rather enslaved Hebrews who took part in the Exodus led by Moses.

As to identifying which part of the Hebrew tribal system made up the majority of the dissident Hebrew contingent, I believe it is likely that many of the malcontents belonged to the tribe of Dan, thereby explaining the origin of the name of Danaus, the legendary founder of Argos. The name "Dan" also resembles the term "Danaan," one of the appellations Homer applied to the Greek force during the Trojan War. As discussed above, the legendary dates of the Exodus and the arrival of Danaus in Greece, along with the claim of Hecataeus that Moses left Egypt at the same time of Danaus, suggests that Danaus was actually one of the leaders of the dissident Hebrews who then traveled to the Greek mainland along with Cadmus. This postulate that the legend of Danaus was derived from a member of the tribe of Dan is supported by the fact that of all the Hebrew tribes, Dan showed the most attributes which would fit with a group of dissident Hebrews rallying against the changes demanded by Moses. The tribe of Dan has generally been regarded by rabbinical sources as the black sheep of the house of David, and has been associated with evil deeds which went against the regulations of the Mosaic Code. In one biblical story, a Danite blasphemer, whose mother had married an Egyptian, was stoned to death for cursing God.[67] Such stories, along with the fact that the genealogies of *Chronicles* ignored the tribe altogether, has suggested that there was intermingling of the Danites and their neighbors which was not favored by the biblical chroniclers.

If many of the Danites did indeed leave the Exodus with the dissident Hebrews because they disagreed with the mandates of Moses to forgo the faith of their ancestors, it would explain their inability to control the region allotted to them by Joshua after the Conquest of the Promised Land. When Joshua gave each tribe their apportioned land in Palestine, Dan was the last tribe to receive their share. The land they inherited in the western hills of the Benjamin-Judean territory, however, was not well suited for agriculture, and was still under a strong Canaanite rule, which resisted Danite control. Although each of the other Hebrew tribes prospered within their designated regions, the Danites were not able to capture

---

67 Lev 24:11, 23.

any of the cities under their jurisdiction, and therefore were not able to successfully settle in the Valley of Aijalon and in the Shephelah. They therefore decided to search for another location, and moved northward to Laish (*Lasham*), which they renamed Dan after overpowering the indigenous population. This city is located thirty miles southeast of Sidon, on the northeastern border of Palestine, and the route the Danites took to reach that region would have been similar to the one I believe the dissident Hebrews took on their way to Ugarit.

The manner in which the Bible described the move of the Danites is consistent with their later description as blasphemers, a trait which would have been shared by the dissident Hebrews. As they first prepared for their move from their allotted territory, the Danite leaders asked one of the priests of Micah if their trip would be successful, a faith in divination that was prohibited by the Mosaic code. They then stole images of God from Micah, and set them up for idol-worship in their new homeland so they would not have to travel to Shiloh to participate in the approved worship of the other Hebrews. This practice would have been punished by death if the precepts of the Ten Commandments were enforced. While this type of faith was vilified by Moses, the Mycenaeans would have seen the practice as consistent with their own religious beliefs, since Classical Greek mythology strongly accepted the value of oracles, even elevating the priestess at Delphi to the level of a deity.

A final piece of supportive evidence for the Danites being part of the dissident Hebrew migration has to do with their possible relationship to one of the tribes of the People of the Sea, a group of marauders who were making violent incursions in the Levant during the thirteenth century BCE. These invaders derived their name from the belief that they arrived in ships from distant regions, including Mycenae, and then traveled inland to attack Egypt and regions throughout the ancient Near East. The Philistines were part of this invasion force, coming from their native Crete to populate the coastal regions of Palestine. In the Bible, the Song of Deborah told how the tribe of Dan remained with the ships, rather than fighting with their fellow tribes against King Jabin of Canaan. No reason was given for their action, although the battle took place during the period of time the Danites were beginning to reconnoiter the land to the north, suggesting that the Danites may have already decided to break their relationship with the rest of the Hebrew congregation. Many scholars have been puzzled by this reference to the sea, since there is no other evidence to indicate that the Danites engaged in any type of maritime activity. Yigael Yadin, head of the Institute of Archaeology of the Hebrew University in Jerusalem, however, has proposed that when the Danites first settled in their allotted land, they undertook the occupation of seamen, and it was through this labor that they became identified with the Danai (Danuna), who were members of the People of the Sea, eventually becoming known as the

Danaans.[68] As discussed above, this possibility is supported by the likelihood that the name of the Danaans was derived from the name of Dan.

That the dissident Hebrews may have fought alongside the Danunu is consistent with hieroglyphic accounts of the fighting that occurred between Egypt and the People of the Sea in the fifth year of the reign of Pharaoh Merneptah (1213-1203 BCE). Egypt repelled an attack of Libyan forces in that battle, and in the memorial stele which commemorated the victory there is mention of a tribe known as the Akawasha, who are believed to represent the Achaean or Mycenaean Greeks. The Achaeans are portrayed in the Merneptah stele as having no foreskins (*qrn.t*), requiring that their hands, as with the Sardana and Turusa, were collected as carnal trophies on the battlefield, something which was not consistent with the Achaean practice. This finding is "absolutely out of keeping with everything that we know about the Greeks," and has left scholars wondering about the identity of the warriors.[69] Michael Astour, Professor at Southern Illinois University, in his book *Hellenosemitca: An Ethnic and Cultural Study in West Semitic Impact on Mycenaean Greece*, made note of this fact and emphasized its importance in supporting his proposition that the Phoenicians were the source of Semitic influence in Greece during the Late Bronze Age.[70]

Circumcision was a common practice among the Hebrews, however, and if they fought alongside the Achaeans, they could easily have been depicted in this manner. Since the dissident Hebrews would have become part of the military force of the Greeks following their arrival in Mycenae, they would not have been segregated out as a separate tribal element by the Egyptians, and would have been portrayed alongside their compatriots. This could very well explain why some of the warriors in the Egyptian records were pictured as being circumcised. Once again, I believe that the Phoenicians are given credit for an influence that is more likely to have come from a group of dissident Hebrews who left the Exodus and traveled to Mycenae before the Trojan War.

Another tribe that may have traveled with the Danites to Mycenae, or at least have been sympathetic to their disparate views, is the tribe of Simeon, which showed the most dramatic decrease in the numbers of men between the first and last census taken of the Hebrews. After the theophany at Mt. Sinai, the tribe of Simeon numbered 59,300, while just before passage into the Promised Land, their numbers had plummeted to 22,200, a total of 37,100 men, which is remarkably close to the listing of over 41,000 Hebrews who were killed by Moses in the biblical text because of their heretical behavior.[71] This number

68 Yadin, "'And Dan, Why Did He Remain In Ships!' (Judges 5:17)", 306-307.

69 Barnett, "The Sea Peoples," 367.

70 Astour, Hellenosemitica: An Ethnic and Cultural Study in West Semitic Impact on Mycenaean Greece, 356.

71 Num 1:23; 26:14.

made the Simeons the smallest of the Hebrew tribes, outside the tribe of Levi, who numbered 22,000 in the first census, and 23,000 at the end of the Exodus. It is perhaps for this reason that when land was allotted to the various tribes in the Promised Land, Simeon only received a portion within the area given to the tribe of Judah. Since none of the other tribes showed a similar percentage fall in numbers, it is possible that many of the dissidents who were killed for their refusal to follow the edicts of the Mosaic Code were members of the tribe of Simeon.[72] This would explain why the only tribe not mentioned by Moses in his blessing in the book of *Deuteronomy* was the tribe of Simeon.

If my proposal of dissident Hebrew migration to Mycenae before the Trojan War is correct, the Exodus would have most likely taken place during the fifteenth or fourteenth century BCE, rather than the thirteenth century BCE, which is favored by most biblical scholars. For the dissident Hebrews to become an integral part of the Mycenaean civilization, important enough to have aspects of their own culture incorporated into that of their adoptive country, there had to be enough time for the Hebrews to be seen as a vital part of the Greek population. This would have come about both because of their value as mercenaries in the Mycenaean military, and as workmen on construction projects at home. If the Trojan War took place c. 1183 BCE, as most historians believe, an Exodus in the thirteenth century BCE is simply not a long enough period to support such an all-encompassing assimilation of legends, language, and cultural characteristics. A fifteenth or fourteenth century BCE Exodus, however, would fit this scenario quite well, and would also correlate much of the historicity of the Bible with appropriate timelines, placing the Patriarchs in the Middle Bronze Age, and the Egyptian Pharaohs in eras which are consistent with the biblical references.

Ahmose I (1539-1514 BCE), under a fifteenth century BCE Exodus timeline, would then be identified as the Pharaoh "who did not know Joseph," since he was the one who expelled the Semitic Hyksos rulers from his country, thereby fitting the description of a ruler who hated and feared the Hebrews so much that he would order all of the newborn Hebrew male children to be killed. If the Hebrews remained in Egypt to work as slaves, an excessive proliferation of their population growth would put the country at risk. Eliminating the Hebrew male newborns would protect Egypt from an uprising in the future, without depleting the man-power needed to maintain the Egyptian economy while the military was away pursing the Hyksos deep into the Palestine hinterland. Thutmose III (1479-1425 BCE) would then be the Pharaoh of the Exodus eighty years later, providing an explanation as to why there was still not a larger contingency of military forces at home to prevent the Exodus from taking place, since he was

---

72 Other tribes which were reduced in number to a lesser extent were the tribes of Gad (11%)(Num 1:25; 26:18), Ephraim (20%)(Num 1:33; 26:37), Naphtali (15%)(Num 1:43; 26:50), and Reuben (6%)(Num 1:20; 26:5).

away from Egypt for so many years, conquering areas of the Levant to expand the boundaries of Egyptian authority. It is also possible that Amenhotep III would have been the Pharaoh of the Exodus, since this would provide an explanation why his son, Amenhotep IV, became enamored by the sun-god Aten, given the terrifying power of YHWH which was demonstrated during the Ten Plagues which were inflicted upon the Egyptian people. If the elder son of Amenhotep III led the chariot force which later followed the fleeing Hebrews to the Reed Sea, his untimely death would explain why Amenhotep IV later became Pharaoh.[73]

After forty years of wandering in the Sinai wilderness, the post-Mosaic Hebrews would have then emerged into Canaan in the fourteenth century BCE, when the Amarna letters made frequent references to the Habiru creating problems in the region. Their Conquest of the Promised Land would not have incited a significant Egyptian reaction, since Amenhotep IV(1352-1336 BCE), who was on the throne at the time, ignored politics in this region in order to concentrate his efforts at home on raising the sun-god Aten to the level of a monotheistic deity. His actions may have actually been fostered by discussion with Moses, who had earlier been present in the Egyptian royal court before being forced to flee into exile in the land of Midian. Contemporary chroniclers would have seen the Hebrews as simply a faction of the Habiru population, providing ample reason to explain why the Exodus congregation was not specifically recorded in the historical annals of the era. A conquest during this era would also explain why there was a lack of letters from Jericho, Gibeon, Bethel, and Hebron, which would have been captured by the Hebrews, while letters from Jerusalem, Megiddo, Ashkelon, Gezer, and Acco continued to reach the Pharaoh requesting aid to help them defend against the Habiru, and Hebrew, threat.[74]

While all of these arguments do not prove that Achilles was a Jew, as I queried in the title to this book, they clearly provide the best explanation to date as to why there are so many similarities between the two ancient cultures, and why the Classical Greeks included Semitic and Eastern influences in their evolving language and mythology. I believe I have shown that this deduction is a distinct possibility, and have traveled that fine line between making a probability our of possibility, and making a possibility into an irrelevancy. Moses may have completely remodeled the patriarchal faith into an epitome of monotheism, but the pre-Mosaic Hebrews played a major role in the formulation of the Classical Greek society, providing our modern Western World with many principles that were expanded upon by the philosophers and playwrights of that remarkable era. Michael Astour, Professor at Southern Illinois University, was correct, in my opinion, in his claim that "Hellenism became the epilogue of the Oriental

---

73 I discuss this reasoning in my novel *Tainted Hands*.

74 Stiebing, Out of the Desert? Archaeology and the Exodus/Conquest Narratives, 42.

civilizations, but Semitism was the prologue of Greek civilization."[75] I believe, however, that the Semites involved were the ancient Hebrews who had remained loyal to their patriarchal roots, rather than to the monotheistic mandates of their self-proclaimed messiah, Moses. Douglas A. Knight, Professor of Hebrew Bible and Jewish Studies at Vanderbilt University, concluded that "the ultimate test of an historical hypothesis is its ability to account for the evidence better than any other explanation,"[76] and I believe that under this definition, Achilles was a Jew.

---

75 Astour, Hellenosemitica: An Ethnic and Cultural Study in West Semitic Impact on Mycenaean Greece, 361.

76 Knight, "Introduction: Tradition and Theology," 4.

BIBLIOGRAPHY

Books

AAbramaovitch, Henry Hanoch, The First Father Abraham: The Psychology and Culture of a Spiritual Revolutionary, Lanham, MD: University Press of American, Inc., 2010.

Aeschylus, Orestia, transl. Richmond Lattimore, Chicago: University of Chicago Press, 1953.

Aeschylus, Prometheus Bound, The Suppliants, Seven Against Thebes, The Persians, transl. Philip Vellacott, Middlesex: Penguin Books, 1961.

Agus, Jacob B., The Meaning of Jewish History, London: Abelard-Schuman, 1963.

Ahlstrom, Gosta W., The History of Ancient Palestine, Minneapolis: Fortress Press, 1993.

Albertz, Rainer, Israel in Exile: The History and Literature of the Sixth Century B.C.E., transl. David Green, Atlanta: Society of Biblical Literature, 2003.

Albo, Joseph, Sefer Ha-`Ikkarim, Book of Principles, transl. Isaac Husik, Philadelphia: The Jewish Publication Society of America, 1929.

Albright, William Foxwell, Yahweh and the Gods of Canaan, Winona Lake, IN: Eisenbrauns, 1990.

Aldred, Cyril, The Egyptians, London: Thames and Hudson, 1984.

Aldred, Cyril, Akhenaten, King of Egypt, London: Thames and Hudson, 1988.

'Ali, 'Abdullah Yusuf, The Meaning of the Holy Qur'an, Beltsville, MD: Amana Publications, 2001.

Alt, Albrecht, Essays on Old Testament History and Religion, transl. R. A. Wilson, Sheffield: JSOT Press, 1989.

Alter, Robert, Genesis, New York: W. W. Norton & Company, 1996.

Alter, Robert, The Five Books of Moses, New York: W. W. Norton & Company, 2004.

Alter, Robert, The Book of Psalms, New York: W. W. Norton & Company, 2007.

Anatolia: Cauldron of Cultures, Alexandria, VA: Time-Life Books, 1995.

Ancient Israel, A Short History from Abraham to the Roman Destruction of the Temple, edit. Hershel Shanks, Washington, D. C.: Biblical Archaeology Society, 1988.

Ancient Israel: The Old Testament in Its Social Context, edit. Philip F. Esler, London: SCM Press, 2005.

Ancient Near Eastern Texts Relating to the Old Testament, Third Edition with Supplement, Edit. James B. Pritchard, Princeton: Princeton University Press, 1969.

Anderson, Bernhard W., Understanding the Old Testament, Fifth Edition, Upper Saddle River, NJ: Pearson Prentice Hall, 2007.

The Ante-Nicene Fathers, Translations of the Writings of the Fathers Down to A.D. 325, Volume VI, Fathers of the Third Century: Gregory Thaumaturgus, Dionysius the Great, Julius Africanus, Anatolius and Minor Writers, Methodius, Arnobius, edit. Alexander Roberts & James Donaldson, Grand Rapids: MI, Wm. B. Eerdmans Publishing Company, 1951.

Aristotle, The Basic Works of Aristotle, edit. Richard McKeon, New York: The Modern Library, 2001.

Aristotle, The Complete Works of Aristotle, edit Jonathan Barnes, Volume One, Princeton, NJ: Princeton University Press, 1984.

Aristotle, The Complete Works of Aristotle, edit Jonathan Barnes, Volume Two, Princeton, NJ: Princeton University Press, 1984.

Aristotle, Metaphysics, transl. Hippocrates G. Apostle, Bloomington, IN, Indiana University Press, 1966.

Aristotle, The Politics, transl. Benjamin Jowett, New York: Modern Library, 1943.

Aristeas to Philocrates, transl. Moses Hadas, New York: KTAV Publishing House, Inc., 1951.

Arnold Bill T., & Beyer Bryan E., Readings From the Ancient Near East, Grand Rapids: Baker Academic, 2002.

Arrian, The Anabasis of Alexander, transl. Edward J. Chinnock, The Greek Historians, edit. Francis R. B. Godolphin, New York: Random House, Volume II, 1942.

Asimov, Isaac, Asimov's Guide to the Bible, Volume One: The Old Testament, Garden City, NY: Doubleday & Company, Inc. 1968.

Assmann, Jan, Moses the Egyptian: the Memory of Egypt in Western Monotheism, Cambridge: Harvard University Press, 1997.

Astour, Michael C, Hellenosemitica: An Ethnic and Cultural Study in West Semitic Impact on Mycenaean Greece, Leiden: E. J. Brill, 1967.

Augustine, Saint, The City of God, transl. Marcus Dods, New York: The Modern Library, 1993.

Augustine, Saint, Confessions, transl. Henry Chadwick, Oxford: Oxford University Press, 1992.

Aylen, Leo, The Greek Theater, Cranbury, NJ: Associated University Presses, 1985.

B Back to the Sources, Reading the Classic Jewish Texts, edit. Barry W. Holtz, New York: Touchstone Books, 1992.

Bailey, Lloyd R., Noah, The Person and the Story in History and Tradition, Columbia: University of South Carolina Press, 1989.

Barclay, John M. G., Jews in the Mediterranean Diaspora: From Alexander to Trajan (323 BCE-117 CE), Edinburgh: T & T Clark, 1996.

Bar-Kochva, Bezalel, Pseudo-Hecataeus, "On the Jews": Legitimizing the Jewish Diaspora, Berkeley: University of California Press, 1996.

Bar-Kochva, Bezalel, The Image of the Jews in Greek Literature: The Hellenistic Period, Berkeley: University of California Press, 2010.

Barthell, Edward E. Jr., Gods and Goddesses of Ancient Greece, Coral Gables: University of Miami Press, 1971.

Bartlett, John R., Jews in the Hellenistic World, Cambridge: Cambridge University Press, 1985.

Beckman, Gary, Hittite Diplomatic Texts, Atlanta: Scholars Press, 1996.

Benson, Andrew D., The Origins of Christianity and the Bible, A Critical Scholarly Investigation of the Sources of Christianity and the Bible, Clovis, CA: Prudential Publishing Company, 2003.

Bentwich, Norman, Hellenism, Philadelphia: The Jewish Publication Society of America, 1919.

Berlinerblau, Jacques, Heresy in the University: The *Black Athena* Controversy and the Responsibilities of American Intellectuals, New Brunswick, NJ: Rutgers University Press, 1999.

Bernal, Martin, Black Athena, New Brunswick, NJ: Rutgers University Press, 1987.

Bernal, Martin, Black Athena Writes Back, Durham: Duke University Press, 2001.

Beyerlin, Walter, Origins and History of the Oldest Sinaitic Traditions, transl. S. Rudman, Oxford: Basil Blackwell, 1965

Beyond Babylon: Art, Trade, and Diplomacy in the Second Millennium B.C., edit. Joan Aruz, Kim Benzel, & Jean M. Evans, New Haven: Yale University Press, 2008.

The Bible, Modern Critical Views, edit. Harold Bloom, New York: Chelsea House Publishers, 1987.

Bierbrier, Morris, The Tomb-Builders of the Pharaohs, New York: Charles Scribner's Sons, 1982.

Bierlein, J. F., Parallel Myths, New York: The Ballantine Publishing Group, 1994.

Bimson, John J., Redating the Exodus and Conquest, Journal for the Study of the Old Testament, Supplement Series 5, Sheffield: England, 1978.

Bonnefoy, Yves, Greek and Egyptian Mythologies, transl. Wendy Doniger, Chicago: The University of Chicago Press, 1992.

Book of Mormon, Salt Lake City: The Church of Jesus Christ of Latter-Day Saints, 1990.

Boswell, John, The Kindness of Strangers, New York: Vintage Books, 1988.

Botsford, George Willis & Robinson, Charles Alexander Jr., Hellenic History, New York: The Macmillan Company, 1956.

Bouscaren, T. Lincoln & Ellis, Adam C., Canon Law: A Text & Commentary, Milwaukee: Bruce Publishing Co., 1949.

Bowra, C. M., The Greek Experience, New York: The New American Library, 1957.

Boyce, Mary, Textual Sources for the Study of Zoroastrianism, Chicago: The University of Chicago Press, 1984.

Breasted, James Henry, Ancient Records of Egypt; Historical Documents from the Earliest Times to the Persian Conquest, Collected, Chicago: The University of Chicago of Chicago Press, 1906.

Bright, John, A History of Israel, Fourth Edition, Louisville: Westminster John Knox Press, 2000.

Broad, William, J., The Oracle: The Lost Secrets and Hidden Message of Ancient Delphi, New York: The Penguin Press, 2006.

Brown, F., Driver, S. R., & Briggs, C. A., A Hebrew and English Lexicon of the Old Testament, Oxford: Clarendon Press, 1906.

Brown, John Paisman, Ancient Israel and Ancient Greece: Religion, Politics, and Culture, Minneapolis: Augsburg Fortress, 2003.

Brueggemann, Walter, An Introduction to the Old Testament: The Canon and Christian Imagination, Louisville: Westminster John Knox Press, 2003.

Buber, Martin, Moses: The Revelation and the Covenant, Atlantic Highlands, NJ: Humanities Press International, Inc., 1988.

Buber, Martin, On the Bible: Eighteen Studies, edit. Nahum N. Glatzer, New York: Schocken Books, 1968.

Budge, E. A. Wallis, The Gods of the Egyptians, Volume 1, New York: Dover Publications, Inc., 1969.

Burckhardt, Jacob, The Greeks and Greek Civilization, transl. Sheila Stern, edit. Oswyn Murray, New York: St. Martin's Press, 1998.

Burkert, Walter, Greek Religion, transl. John Raffan, Cambridge: Harvard University Press, 1985.

Burkert, Walter, The Orientalizing Revolution: Near Eastern Influence on Greek Culture in the Early Archaic Age, transl. by Margaret E. Pinder and Walter Burkert, Cambridge, MA: Harvard University Press, 1992.

Burnett, Joel S., A Reassessment of Biblical Elohim, Atlanta: Society of Biblical Literature, 2001.

Calvin, John, Commentaries on the First Book of Moses Called Genesis, Grand Rapids: Wm. B. Eerdmans Publishing Company, Volume 2, 1963.

Campbell, Antony F., & O'Brien, Mark A., Sources of the Pentateuch: Texts, Introductions, Annotations, Minneapolis: Fortress Press, 1993.

Campbell, Anthony F., & O'Brien, Mark A., Unfolding the Deuteronomistic History: Origins, Upgrades, Present Text, Minneapolis: Fortress Press, 2000.

Capt, E. Raymond, Missing Links Discovered in Assyrian Tablets, Muskogee, OK: Artisan Sales, 1985.

Casson, Lionel, Daily Life in Ancient Egypt, New York: American Heritage Publishing Co., Inc., 1975.

Casson, Lionel, The Ancient Mariners, Princeton: Princeton University Press, 1991.

Chadwick, John, The Mycenaean World, Cambridge: Cambridge University Press, 1976.

Cicero, The Nature of the Gods, transl. P. G. Walsh, Oxford: Oxford University Press, 1998.

The Classic Midrash: Tannaitic Commentaries on the Bible, transl. Reuven Hammer, New York: Paulist Press, 1995.

Clayton, Peter A., Chronicle of the Pharaohs, London: Thames and Hudson Ltd., 1994.

Clement of Alexandria, Writings, transl. William Wilson, Edinburgh: T. & T. Clark, 1847.

Clement of Rome, Epistles, transl. James A Kleist, Westminster, MD: The Newman Bookshop, 1946.

Coats, George W., Rebellion in the Wilderness: The Murmuring Motif in the Wilderness Traditions of the Old Testament Nashville: Abingdon Press, 1968.

Cohen, Shaye J. D., From the Maccabees to the Mishnah, Philadelphia: The Westminster Press, 1987.

Collins, John J., Between Athens and Jerusalem, Jewish Identity in the Hellenistic Diaspora, Grand Rapids: William B. Eerdmans Publishing Company, 2000.

Collins, John J., The Scepter and the Star: The Messiahs of the Dead Sea Scrolls and Other Ancient Literature," New York: Doubleday, 1995.

Comay, Joan, The Hebrew Kings, New York: William Morrow and Company, Inc., 1977.

A Companion to Greek and Roman Historiography, Volume I edit. John Marincola, Oxford: Blackwell Publishing Ltd, 2007.

A Companion to Homer, edit. Alan J. B. Wace & Frank H. Stubbings, London: Macmillan & Co Ltd, 1962.

Coogan, Michael David, Stories From Ancient Canaan, Philadelphia: The Westminster Press, 1978.

Coogan, Michael D., The Old Testament: A Historical and Literary Introduction to the Hebrew Scriptures, New York: Oxford University Press, 2006.

Cook, Stephen L., The Social Roots of Biblical Yahwism, Atlanta: Society of Biblical Literature, 2004.

Copleston, Frederick, A History of Philosophy, Volume I Greece and Rome, Mahwah, NJ: Paulist Press, 1946.

Cosmas Indiopleustes, Christian Topography, transl. J. W. McCrindle, Forgotten Books, 2008.

Cotterell, Arthur, The Minoan World, New York, Charles Scribner's Sons, 1980.

Courville, Donovan, The Exodus Problem and Its Ramifications, Volume I-II, Loma Linda, CA: Challenge Books, 1971.

Craigie, Peter C., Ugarit and the Old Testament, Grand Rapids: William B. Eerdmans Publishing Company, 1983.

Crawford, Harriet, <u>Sumer and the Sumerians</u>, Cambridge: Cambridge University Press, 1991.

Crombie, I. M., An Examination of Plato's Doctrines, I. Plato on Man and Society, London: Routledge & Kegan Paul, 1962.

Cross, Frank Moore, Canaanite Myth and Hebrew Epic: Essays in the History of the Religion of Israel, Cambridge: Harvard University Press, 1997.

Cross, Frank Moore, <u>From Epic to Canon: History and Literature in Ancient Israel</u>, Baltimore: The Johns Hopkins University Press, 1998.

Currid, John D., <u>Ancient Egypt and the Old Testament</u>, Grand Rapids: Baker Books, 1997.

Daiches, David, <u>Moses: The Man and His Vision</u>, New York: Praeger Publishers, Inc., 1975.

Darwin, Charles, <u>The Descent of Man</u>, Chicago: Encyclopedia Britannica Great Books, 1971.

David, Rosalie, <u>Handbook to Life in Ancient Egypt</u>, New York: Facts on File, Inc., 1998.

Davies, John A., A Royal Priesthood: Literary and Intertextual Perspectives on an Image of Israel in Exodus 19.6, London: T & T Clark International, 2004.

Davies, Nigel, <u>Human Sacrifice</u>, New York: William Morrow & Company, Inc., 1981.

Davis, John J., Moses and the Gods of Egypt, Grand Rapids: Baker Book House, 1971.

de Breffny, Brian, The Synagogue, New York: Macmillan Publishing Co., Inc., 1978

De Geus, C. H. J., The Tribes of Israel, Assen, The Netherlands: Van Gorcum, 1976.

The Dead Sea Scrolls, transl. Geza Vermes, New York: The Heritage Press, 1962.

The Dead Sea Scrolls Bible: The Oldest Known Bible Translated for the First Time into English, transl. Martin Abegg, Jr., Peter Flint, & Eugene Ulrich, New York: HarperSanFrancisco, 1999.

<u>Deuteronomy</u>, <u>The Anchor Bible</u>, transl. Moshe Weinfeld, NY: Doubleday, 1991.

<u>Deuteronomy</u>, <u>The Torah, A Modern Commentary V</u>, commentary by W. Gunther Plaut, New York: Union of American Hebrew Congregations, 1983.

de Vaux, Roland, <u>Ancient Israel, Its Life and Institutions</u>, transl. John McHugh, New York: McGraw-Hill Book Company, Inc., 1961.

de Vaux, Roland, <u>The Early History of Israel</u>, transl. David Smith, Philadelphia: The Westminster Press, 1978.

Dever, William G., What Did The Biblical Writers Know and When Did They Know It?: What Archaeology Can Tell Us About the Reality of Ancient Israel, Grand Rapids: William B. Eerdmans Publishing Company, 2001.

Dever, William G., <u>Who Were the Early Israelites and Where Did They Come From?</u>, Grand Rapids: William B. Eerdmans Publishing Company, 2003.

Dever, William G., <u>Did God Have A Wife? Archaeology and Folk Religion in Ancient Israel</u>, Grand Rapids: William B. Eerdmans Publishing Company, 2005.

Dillon, Matthew & Garland, Lynda, Ancient Greece, Social & Historical Documents from Archaic Times to the Death of Socrates (c.800-399 B.C.), London: Routledge, 1994.

Diodorus of Sicily, <u>The Library of History</u>, transl. C. H. Oldfather, London: William Heinemann, Ltd., 1933.

Diogenes Laertius, <u>Lives of Eminent Philosophers</u>, Volume I, transl. R. D. Hicks, London: William Heinemann, Ltd., 1972.

Diogenes Laertius, <u>Lives of Eminent Philosophers</u>, Volume II, transl. R. D. Hicks, London: William Heinemann, Ltd., 1979.

Diop, Cheikh Anta, <u>The African Origin of Civilization: Myth or Reality</u>, transl. Mercer Cook, Chicago: Lawrence Hill Books, 1974.

Diop, Cheikh Anta, <u>Civilization or Barbarism: An Authentic Anthropology</u>, transl. Yaa-Lengi Meema Ngemi, Brooklyn: Lawrence Hill Books, 1991.

Dothan, Trude, <u>The Philistines and Their Material Culture</u>, Jerusalem: Israel Exploration Society, 1982.

Dothan, Trude, & Dothan, Moshe, <u>People of the Sea, The Search for the Philistines</u>, New York: Macmillan Publishing Company, 1992.

Drews, Robert, <u>The Coming of the Greeks</u>, Princeton: Princeton University Press, 1988.

Drews, Robert, <u>The End of the Bronze Age</u>, Princeton: Princeton University Press, 1993.

Drummond, William, <u>Oedipus Judaicus: Allegory in the Old Testament</u>, London: Bracken Books, reprinted 1986.

Duncker, Max, <u>History of Greece: From the Earliest Times to the End of the Persian War</u>, transl. S. F. Alleyne, London: Richard Bentley & Son, 1883.

Durando, Furio, <u>Ancient Greece: The Dawn of The Western World</u>, New York: Barnes & Noble Books, 2004.

Duruy, Victor, History of Greece, and of the Greek People, From the Earliest Times to the Roman Conquest, transl. M. M. Ripley, Boston: Estes and Lauriat, 1890.

Edwards, Mark W., <u>Homer, Poet of the *Iliad*</u>, Baltimore: The Johns Hopkins University Press, 1987.

Egypt, Israel, and the Ancient Mediterranean World: Studies in Honor of Donald B. Redford, edit. Gary N. Knoppers & Antoine Hirsch, Leiden: Brill, 2004.

Ehrenberg, Victor, <u>The Greek State</u>, New York: Barnes & Noble, Inc., 1960.

Eliade, Mircea, <u>Cosmos and History: The Myth of the Eternal Return</u>, New York: Harper Torchbooks, 1954.

Eliade, Mircea, <u>A History of Religious Ideas, Volume 1, From the Stone Age to the Eleusinian Mysteries</u>, transl. Willard R. Trask, Chicago: The University of Chicago Press, 1978.

Ellis, Peter F., The Yahwist: The Bible's First Theologian, Collegeville, MN: The Liturgical Press, 1968.

Essential Papers on Israel and the Ancient Near East, edit. Frederick E. Greenspahn, New York: New York University Press, 1991.

Euripides, Euripides I, edit. David Grene and Richmond Lattimore, Chicago: The University of Chicago Press, 1955.

Euripides, Euripides II, edit. David Grene & Richmond Latimore, Chicago: The University of Chicago Press, 1956.

Euripides, Euripides III, edit. David Grene & Richmond Lattimore, Chicago: The University of Chicago Press, 1958.

Euripides, Euripides IV, edit. David Grene & Richmond Lattimore, Chicago: The University of Chicago Press, 1958.

Euripides, Euripides V, edit. David Grene & Richmond Lattimore, Chicago: The University of Chicago Press, 1959.

Eusebius, Preparation for the Gospel, transl. Edwin Hamilton Gifford, Grand Rapids: Baker House Books, 1981.

Exodus, The Torah, A Modern Commentary II, commentary by W. Gunther Plaut, transl. Jewish Publication Society, New York: Union of American Congregations, 1974

Exodus 1-18, transl. William H. C. Propp, The Anchor Bible, New York: Doubleday, 1998.

The Expositor's Bible Commentary, Genesis, Exodus, Leviticus, Numbers, Volume 2, edit. Frank Gaebelein, Grand Rapids: Zondervan, 1990.

F The Face of Old Testament Studies: A Survey of Contemporary Approaches, edit. David W. Baker & Bill T. Arnold, Grand Rapids: Baker Books, 1999.

Feldman, Louis H., Jew & Gentile in the Ancient World, Princeton: Princeton University Press, 1993.

Ferguson, Kitty, The Music of , New York: Walker & Company, 2008.

Fields, Nic, Troy c. 1700-1250 BC, Oxford: Osprey Publishing Ltd., 2004

Fine, John V. A., The Ancient Greeks, A Critical History, Cambridge, Harvard University Press, 1983.

Finegan, Jack, Handbook of Biblical Chronology, Peabody, MA: Hendrickson Publishers, 1998.

Finkelstein, Israel, The Archaeology of the Israelite Settlement, Part I: The Results of Excavations and Surveys, Jerusalem: Israel Exploration Society, 1988.

Finkelstein, Israel & Mazar, Amihai, The Quest for the Historical Israel: Debating Archaeology and the History of Early Israel, edit. Brian B. Schmidt, Atlanta: Society of Biblical Literature, 2007.

Finkelstein, Israel & Silberman, Neil Asher, The Bible Unearthed: Archaeology's New

Vision of Ancient Israel and the Origin of its Sacred Texts, New York: The Free Press, 2001.

Firestone, Reuven, Journeys in Holy Lands: The Evolution of the Abraham-Ishmael Legends in Islamic Exegesis, Albany: State University of New York Press, 1990.

Fishbane, Michael, Biblical Interpretation in Ancient Israel, Oxford: Clarendon Press, 1985.

Fitton, J. Lesley, The Discovery of the Greek Bronze Age, Cambridge: Harvard University Press, 1996.

Flaceliere, Robert, Greek Oracles, transl. Douglas Garman, New York: W. W. Norton & Company, Inc., 1965.

Fletcher, Joann, Chronicle of a Pharaoh: The Intimate Life of Amenhotep III, New York: Oxford University Press, 2000.

Fohrer, Georg, Introduction to the Old Testament, transl. David E. Green, Nashville: Abingdon Press, 1968.

Forsdyke, John, Greece Before Homer, New York: W. W. Norton & Company, Inc., 1964.

Frazer, James G., Folklore in the Old Testament, New York: Avenel Books, 1988.

Freedman, David Noel, The Nine Commandments: Uncovering a Hidden Pattern of Crime and Punishment in the Hebrew Bible, New York: Doubleday, 2000.

Freeman, Charles, Egypt, Greece and Rome: Civilizations of the Ancient Mediterranean, 2nd edition, Oxford: Oxford University Press, 2004.

Freud, Sigmund, Moses and Monotheism, transl. Katherine Jones, New York: Vintage Books, 1955.

Freund, Richard A., Digging Through the Bible: Modern Archaeology and the Ancient Bible, Lanham, MD: Rowman & Littlefield Publishers, Inc., 2009.

Friedman, Richard Elliott, The Hidden Book in the Bible, New York: HarperCollins, 1998.

Friedman, Richard Elliott, Commentary on the Torah, New York: HarperSanFrancisco, 2001.

Friedman, Richard Elliott, The Bible With Sources Revealed, New York: HarperSanFrancisco, 2003.

The Future of Biblical Archaeology: Reassessing Methodologies and Assumptions, edit. James K. Hoffmeier and Alan Millard, Grand Rapids: William B Eerdmans Publishing Company, 2004.

G Gabriel, Richard A., The Military History of Ancient Israel, Westport, CT: Praeger, 2003.

Gardiner, Alan, Egypt of the Pharaohs, London: Oxford University Press, 1964.

Gaster, Theodor H., Myth, Legend, and Custom in the Old Testament, New York: Harper & Row, 1969.

Gelb, Norman, Kings of the Jews: Exploring the Origins of the Jewish Nation, Philadelphia: The Jewish Publication Society, 2010

Genesis, edit. Harold Bloom, New York: Chelsea House Publishers, 1986.

Genesis, The Anchor Bible, edit. E. A. Speiser, Garden City, NY: Doubleday & Company, Inc., 1964.

Genesis, The Old Testament Study Bible, edit. Thoralf Gilbrant, Springfield, MO: World Library Press Inc., 1994.

Genesis, The Torah, A Modern Commentary II, commentary by W. Gunther Plaut, transl. Jewish Publication Society, New York: Union of American Congregations, 1974.

Gillies, John, The History of Ancient Greece, Its Colonies and Conquests, From the Earliest Accounts Till the Division of the Macedonian Empire in the East: Including The History of Literature, Philosophy, and the Fine Arts, Philadelphia: Joseph Marot, 1829.

Ginzberg, Louis, Legends of the Bible, Philadelphia: The Jewish Publication Society of America, 1956.

Ginzberg, Louis, Legends of the Jews, transl. Henrietta Szold, Volumes 1-5, Baltimore: The Johns Hopkins University Press, 1998.

Gispen, W. H., Bible Student's Commentary - Exodus, transl. Ed van der Maas, Grand Rapids: Zondervan Publishing House, 1982.

Godbey, Allen H., The Lost Tribes - A Myth, Suggestions Toward Rewriting Hebrew History, New York: KTAV Publishing House, Inc., 1974.

Goldin, Judah, The Song at the Sea, New Haven: Yale University Press, 1971.

Goodenough, Erwin R., Jewish Symbols in the Greco-Roman Period, New York: Pantheon Books, Bollingen Series XXXVII, 1958.

Gordon, Cyrus, H., Before the Bible: The Common Background of Greek and Hebrew Civilizations, New York: Harper & Row, 1962.

Gordon, Cyrus, H., The Common Background of Greek and Hebrew Civilizations, New York: W. W. Norton & Company, Inc., 1965.

Gordon, Cyrus, Ugarit and Minoan Crete, New York: W. W. Norton & Company, Inc., 1966.

Gordon, Cyrus H., Homer and the Bible: The Origin and Character of East Mediterranean Literature, Ventnor, NJ: Ventnor Publishers, 1967.

Gordon, Cyrus H. & Rendsburg, Gary A., The Bible and the Ancient Near East, New York: W. W. Norton & Company, 1997.

Gottwald, Norman K., The Hebrew Bible–A Socio-Literary Introduction, Philadelphia: Fortress Press, 1985.

Gottwald, Norman K., The Tribes of Yahweh: A Sociology of the Religion of Liberated Israel, 1250-1050 BCE, Maryknoll, New York: Orbis Books, 1979.

Graham, Daniel, W., The Texts of Early Greek Philosophy: The Complete Fragments and Selected Testimonies of the Major Presocratics, Part I, Cambridge: Cambridge University Press, 2010.

Graham, Daniel, W., The Texts of Early Greek Philosophy: The Complete Fragments and Selected Testimonies of the Major Presocratics, Part II, Cambridge: Cambridge University Press, 2010.

Grant, Michael, The Ancient Mediterranean, London: Weidenfeld and Nicolson, 1969.

Grant, Michael, The Rise of the Greeks, New York: Charles Scribner's Sons, 1988.

Graves, Robert, The Greek Myths: 1, Baltimore: Penguin Books, 1955.

Graves, Robert, The Greek Myths: 2, London: Penguin Books, 1955.

Graves, Robert, The White Goddess, New York: The Noonday Press, 1998.

Graves, Robert, & Patai, Raphael, Hebrew Myths, the Book of Genesis, Garden City, New York: Doubleday & Company, Inc., 1964.

Great Events of Bible Times, Garden City, New York: Doubleday & Company, Inc., 1987.

The Great Thinkers on Plato, edit. Barry Gross, New York: Capricorn Books, 1969.

Greek and Latin Authors on Jews and Judaism, Volume One: From Herodotus to Plutarch, edit. Menahem Stern, Jerusalem: The Israel Academy of Sciences and Humanities, 1976.

Green, Arthur, EHYEH: A Kabbalah for Tomorrow, Woodstock, VT: Jewish Lights Publishing, 2003.

Greenberg, Moshe, The Hab/piru, New Haven: American Oriental Society, 1955.

Greenberg, Moshe, Understanding Exodus, New York: Behrman House, Inc., 1969.

Grimal, Nicolas, A History of Ancient Egypt, transl. Ian Shaw, Oxford: Blackwell, 1992.

Grollenberg, L. H., Atlas of the Bible, transl. Joyce M. H. Reid & H. H. Rowley, London: Thomas Nelson and Sons, Ltd., 1956.

Gruen, Erich S., Heritage and Hellenism: The Reinvention of Jewish Tradition, Berkeley: The University of California Press, 1998.

In the, W. K. C., A History of Greek Philosophy, Volume I, The Earlier Presocratics and the Pythagoreans, London: Cambridge University Press, 1962.

Guthrie, W. K. C., A History of Greek Philosophy, Volume II, The Presocratic Tradition From Parmenides to Democritus, London: Cambridge University Press, 1965.

Guthrie, W. K. C., In the Beginning: Some Greek Views on the Origins of Life and the Early State of Man, Ithaca, NY: Cornell University Press, 1957.

H Hadas, Moses, A History of Greek Literature, New York: Columbia University Press, 1950.

Hadas, Moses, Hellenistic Culture, Morningside Heights, New York: Columbia University Press, 1959.

Haldar, Alfred, Who Were the Amorites?, Leiden: E. J. Brill, 1971.

Hall, Jonathan M., A History of the Archaic Greek World, ca. 1200-479 BCE, Oxford: Blackwell Publishing Ltd., 2007.

Halpern, Baruch, The First Historians: The Hebrew Bible and History, San Francisco: Harper & Row, 1988.

Hamilton, Edith, Mythology, New York: Mentor Book, 1955.

The Harper Atlas of the Bible, edit. James B. Pritchard, New York: Harper & Row, 1987.

Harrison, R. K., Numbers, An Exegetical Commentary, Grand Rapids: Baker Book House, 1992.

Hawkes, Jacquetta & Woolley, Sir Leonard, History of Mankind I. Prehistory and the Beginnings of Civilization, New York: Harper & Row, 1963.

Hayes, William C., The Scepter of Egypt, Part II: The Hyksos Period and the New Kingdom (1675-1080 B.C.), New York: The Metropolitan Museum of Art, 1959.

Haywood, John, Historical Atlas of the Ancient World, Oxfordshire: Andromeda Oxford Ltd., 1998.

Healey, John F., The Early Alphabet, Berkeley: University of California Press, 1990.

The Hebrew Bible in Literary Criticism, compiled and edit. by Alex Preminger & Edward L. Greenstein, New York: Unger Publishing Company, 1986.

Heidel, Alexander, The Gilgamesh Epic and Old Testament Parallels, Chicago: The University of Chicago Press, 1949.

The Heirs of Assyria: Proceeding of the Opening Symposium of the Assyrian and Babylonian Intellectual Heritage Project Held in Tvarminne, Finland, October 8-11, 1998, edit. Sannaa Aro & R. M. Whiting, Helsinki: The Neo-Assyrian Text Corpus Project, 2000.

Heltzer, Michael, The Rural Community in Ancient Ugarit, Wiesbaden: Ludwig Reichert Verlag, 1976.

Hendel, Ronald, Remembering Abraham: Culture, Memory, and History in the Hebrew Bible, Oxford: Oxford University Press, 2005.

Hendel, Ronald, The Book of Genesis: a Biography, Princeton, Princeton University Press, 2013.

Henry, Matthew, Commentary, edit. Leslie F. Church, Grand Rapids: Zondervan, 1961.

Herington, John, Aeschylus, New Haven: Yale University Press, 1986.

Herodotus, The History, transl. David Grene, Chicago: The University of Chicago Press, 1987.

Heschel, Abraham Joshua, Heavenly Torah: As Refracted Through the Generations, edit. and transl. Gordon Tucker with Leonard Levin, New York: Continuum, 2010.

Heschel, Abraham J., The Prophets: An Introduction, New York: Harper Torchbooks, 1962.

Hesiod, Theogony, Works and Days, Shield, transl. Apostolos N. Athanassakis, Baltimore: The Johns Hopkins University Press, 1983.

Hill, Andrew E., & Walton, John H., A Survey of the Old Testament, Grand Rapids: Zondervan, 2000.

Hindson, Edward E., The Philistines and the Old Testament, Grand Rapids: Baker Book House, 1971.

Hippolytus, The Extant Works and Fragments of Hippolytus, transl. S. D. F. Salmond, LaVergne, TN: Kessinger Publishing, 2010.

Hoffman, Joel M., In the Beginning: A Short History of the Hebrew Language, New York: New York University Press, 2004.

Hoffmeier, James K., Israel in Egypt, The Evidence for the Authenticity of the Exodus Tradition, New York: Oxford University Press, 1996.

Hoffmeier, James K., Ancient Israel in Sinai, The Evidence for the Authenticity of the Wilderness Tradition, New York: Oxford University Press, 2005.

Holliday, Carl, The Dawn of Literature, New York: Frederick Ungar Publishing Co., 1962.

Homer, The Iliad, transl. Richmond Lattimore, Chicago: University of Chicago Press, 1951.

Homer, The Odyssey, transl. Robert Fitzgerald, Garden City, NY: Anchor Books, 1963.

Homer: A Collection of Critical Essays, edit. George Steiner and Robert Fagles, Englewood Cliffs, NJ: Prentice-Hall, Inc., 1962.

The Homeric Hymns, transl. Charles Boer, Chicago: The Swallow Press, Inc., 1970.

Homer's the Iliad, edit. Harold Bloom, New York: Chelsea House Publishers, 1987.

Homer's the Odyssey, edit. Harold Bloom, New York: Chelsea House Publishers, 1988.

Hornung, Erik, Akhenaten and the Religion of Light, transl. David Lorton, Ithaca: Cornell University Press, 1999.

Hughes, Dennis D., Human Sacrifice in Ancient Greece, Routledge: London, 1991.

Hughes, Jeremy, Secrets of the Times, Myth and History in Biblical Chronology, Sheffield: JSOT Press, 1990.

Huxley, G. L., The Early Ionians, New York: Barnes & Noble Books, 1972.

Iamblichus, On the Pythagorean Way of Life, transl. John Dillon and Jackson Hershbell, Atlanta: Scholars Press, 1991.

The Illustrated Atlas of Jewish Civilization, edit. Josephine Bacon, London: Quantum Books Ltd, 2006.

Isbell, Charles David, The Function of Exodus Motifs in Biblical Narratives: Theological Didactic Drama, Lewiston, NY: The Edwin Mellen Press, 2002.

Isserlin, B. S. J., The Israelites, Minneapolis: Fortress Press, 2001.

Jacobs, Louis, Jewish Ethics, Philosophy and Mysticism, New York: Behrman House, Inc., 1969.

Jaeger, Walter, Padeia: The Ideals of Greek Culture, Volume I, Archaic Greece, the Mind of Athens, New York: Oxford University Press, 1945.

Jamieson, Robert, Fausset, A. R., & Brown, David, <u>Commentary Critical and Explanatory on the Whole Bible</u>, Grand Rapids: Zondervan Publishing House, 1871.

<u>Jesus and the Dead Sea Scrolls</u>, edit. James H. Charlesworth, New York: Doubleday, 1992.

<u>The Jewish Encyclopedia</u>, edit. Isidore Singer, New York: Funk and Wagnalls Company, 1916.

<u>The Jewish Study Bible</u>, The Jewish Publication Society Tanakh Translation, edit. Adele Berlin & Marc Zvi Brettler, Oxford: Oxford University Press, 2004.

<u>The Jewish World: History and Culture of the Jewish People</u>, edit. Elie Kedourie, New York: Harry N. Abrams, Inc., 1979.

<u>Jews in the Hellenistic and Roman Cities</u>, edit. John R. Bartlett, New York: Routledge, 2002.

Jidejian, Nina, <u>Sidon Through the Ages</u>, Beirut: Dar El-Machreq Publishers, 1971.

Johnson, Paul, <u>Civilizations of the Holy Land</u>, New York: Atheneum, 1979.

Johnson, Paul, <u>The Civilization of Ancient Egypt</u>, New York: HarperCollins, 1999.

Jones, Allen H., <u>Bronze Age Civilization, The Philistines and the Danites</u>, Washington, D.C.: Public Affairs Press, 1975.

Jones, Floyd Nolen, <u>The Chronology of the Old Testament</u>, Green Forest, AR: Master Books, 2005.

Joseph and Potiphar's Wife in World Literature: An Anthology of the Story of the Chaste Youth and the Lustful Stepmother, edit. John D. Yohannan, New York: New Directions, 1968.

Josephus, <u>The Complete Works of Josephus</u>, transl. William Whitson, Grand Rapids: Kregel Publications, 1960.

<u>The JPS Torah Commentary: Exodus</u>, Philadelphia: The Jewish Publication Society, 1991.

<u>Judges</u>, transl. Robert G. Boling, <u>The Anchor Bible</u>, Garden City: Doubleday & Company, Inc., 1969.

K<u>The Kabbalistic Bible: Exodus: Technology for the Soul</u>, edit. Yehuda Berg, Los Angeles: Kabbalah Publishing, 2009.

Kaiser, Walter C. Jr., <u>The Old Testament Documents: Are they Reliable & Relevant?</u>, Downers Grove, IL: InterVarsity Press, 2001.

Kaplan, Rabbi Aryeh, <u>The Living Torah: The Five Books of Moses and the Haftarot</u>, New York: Maznaim Publishing Corporation, 1981.

Keel, Othmar & Uehlinger, Christoph, <u>Gods, Goddesses, and Images of God in Ancient Israel</u>, transl. Thomas H. Trapp, Minneapolis: Fortress Press, 1998.

Keil, C. F. & Delitzsch, F., <u>Commentary on the Old Testament</u>, Grand Rapids: William B. Eerdmans Publishing Company, 1976.

Keller, Werner, The Bible as History, 2nd Revised Edition, transl William Neil & B. H. Rasmussen, revised by Joachim Rehork, New York: William Morrow and Company, Inc., 1981.

Kenyon, Kathleen, Royal Cities of the Old Testament, New York: Schocken Books, 1971.

Kierkegaard, Soren, Fear and Trembling, transl. Walter Lowrie, Princeton: Princeton University Press, 1954.

Kierkegaard, Soren, Fear and Trembling and The Sickness Unto Death, transl. Walter Lowrie, Garden City: Doubleday & Company, 1954.

The King James Study Bible, Nashville: Thomas Nelson Publishers, 1988.

Kirk, G. S., Homer & the Oral Tradition, Cambridge: Cambridge University Press, 1976.

Kirk, G. S. & Raven, J.E., The Presocratic Philosophers: A Critical History with a Selection of Texts, London: Cambridge University Press, 1960.

Kirsch, Jonathan, Moses, New York: Ballantine Books, 1998.

Kishlansky, Mark, Geary, Patrick, & O'Brien, Patricia, Civilization in the West, New York: HarperCollins Publishers, Inc., 1991.

Kitchen, K. A., Pharaoh Triumphant, The Life and Times of Ramesses II, Warminster: Aris & Phillips Ltd., 1982.

Kitchen, K. A., On the Reliability of the Old Testament, Grand Rapids: William B. Eerdmans Publishing Company, 2003.

Kitto, H. D. F., The Greeks, Baltimore: Penguin Books, 1968.

Klassen, Frank R., The Chronology of the Bible, Nashville: Regal Publishers, Inc., 1975.

Klinghoffer, David, The Discovery of God: Abraham and the Birth of Monotheism, New York: Doubleday, 2003.

Knapp, A. Bernard, The History and Culture of Ancient Western Asia and Egypt, Belmont, CA: Wadsworth Publishing Company, 1988.

Knapp, A. Bernard, Society and Polity at Bronze Age Pella: An *Annales* Perspective, Sheffield: Sheffield Academic Press, 1993.

Kofoed, Jens Bruun, Text and History: Historiography and the Study of the Biblical Text, Winona Lake, IN: Eisenbrauns, 2005.

Kuenen, A., The Religion of Israel to the Fall of the Jewish State, transl. Alfred Heath May, London: Williams and Norgate, 1883.

Kugel, James L., In Potiphar's House, The Interpretive Life of Biblical Texts, Cambridge: Harvard University Press, 1994.

Kugel, James L., The Bible As It Was, Cambridge: Belknap Press, 1997.

Kuhrt, Amelie, The Ancient Near East c. 3000-330 BC, Volume I, Routledge History of the Ancient World, gen. edit., Fergus Millar, London: Routledge, 1997.

LaCocque, Andre, <u>Daniel in His Time</u>, Columbia, SC: University of South Carolina Press, 1988.

Launderville Dale, Piety and Politics: the Dynamics of Royal Authority in Homeric Greece, Biblical Israel, and Old Babylonian Mesopotamia, Grand Rapids: William B. Eerdmans Publishing Company, 2003.

Lefkowitz, Mary, Not Out of Africa: How Afrocentrism Became an Excuse to Teach Myth as History, New York: BasicBooks, 1996.

Lehmann, Johannes, <u>The Hittites, People of a Thousand Gods</u>, transl. J. Maxwell Brownjohn, New York: The Viking Press, 1977.

Leick, Gwendolyn, <u>Mesopotamia: The Invention of the City</u>, London: Penguin Books, 2002.

Lemche, Niels Peter, <u>The Canaanites and Their Land</u>, Sheffield: Sheffield Academic Press Ltd, 1991.

Lemche, Niels Peter, <u>The Israelites in History and Tradition</u>, Louisville: Westminster John Knox Press, 1998.

Lerner, Gerda, <u>The Creation of Patriarchy</u>, New York: Oxford University Press, 1986.

<u>Letters of Maimonides</u>, transl. and edit. Leon D. Stitskin, New York: Yeshiva University Press, 1982.

Levenson, Jon D., The Death and Resurrection of the Beloved Son: The Transformation of Child Sacrifice in Judaism and Christianity, New Haven: Yale University Press, 1993.

Levenson, Jon D., <u>Sinai and Zion: An Entry into the Jewish Bible</u>, Minneapolis: Winston Press, 1985.

Leveque, Pierre, <u>The Greek Adventure</u>, transl. Miriam Kochan, Cleveland: The World Publishing Company, 1968.

Levi, Peter, <u>Atlas of the Greek World</u>, New York: Facts on File Publications, 1980.

Levine, Baruch A., <u>Leviticus, The JPS Commentary</u>, Philadelphia: The Jewish Publication Society, 1989.

Levine, Lee I., <u>The Ancient Synagogue: The First Thousand Years</u>, New Haven: Yale University Press, 2000.

<u>Leviticus</u>, commentary by Bernard J. Bamberger, <u>The Torah, A Modern Commentary III</u>, transl. Jewish Publication Society, New York: Union of American Hebrew Congregations, 1979.

Lichtheim, Miriam, <u>Ancient Egyptian Literature, Volume I: The Old and Middle Kingdoms</u>, Berkeley: University of California Press, 1973.

Lichtheim, Miriam, <u>Ancient Egyptian Literature, Volume II: The New Kingdom</u>, Berkeley: University of California Press, 1976.

Lind, Millard C., <u>Yahweh is a Warrior</u>, Scottdale, PA: Herald Press, 1980.

Lipinski, Edward, <u>On the Skirts of Canaan in the Iron Age: Historical and Topographical Research</u>, Belgium: Peeters Publishers & Faculty of Oriental Studies, 2006.

The Living Bible, Wheaton, IL: Tyndale House Publishers, 1971.

Livingston, G. Herbert, The Pentateuch in Its Cultural Environment, Grand Rapids: Baker Book House, 1974.

Lockyer, Herbert, All the Divine Names and Titles in the Bible, Grand Rapids: Zondervan Publishing House, 1975.

Lods, Adolphe, Israel, From Its Beginnings to the Middle of the Eight Century, transl. S. H. Hooke, New York, Alfred A. Knopf, 1962.

Luban, Marianne, The Exodus Chronicles: Beliefs, Legends & Rumors from Antiquity Regarding the Exodus of the Jews from Egypt, Second Edition, Ogden, UT: Pacific Moon Publications, 2008.

Luther, Martin, Commentary on Genesis, transl. J. Theodore Mueller, Grand Rapids: Zondervan Publishing House, 1958.

M I Maccabees, transl. Jonathan A. Goldstein, The Anchor Bible, Garden City, NY: Doubleday & Company, Inc., 1976.

II Maccabees, transl. Jonathan A. Goldstein, The Anchor Bible, Garden City, NY: Doubleday & Company, Inc., 1983.

Macqueen, J. G., The Hittites, and Their Contemporaries in Asia Minor, Boulder, CO: Westview Press, 1975.

Maimonides, The Commandments, Volume 2, The Negative Commandments, transl. Charles B. Chavel, New York: The Soncino Press, Ltd., 1967

Maimonides, Moses, The Guide For the Perplexed, transl., M. Friedlander, New York: Dover Publications, Inc., 1956.

Malamat, Abraham, Mari and the Early Israelite Experience - The Schweich Lectures 1984, Oxford: The Oxford University Press, 1989.

Mandell, Sara & Freedman, David Noel, The Relationship Between Herodotus' *History* and Primary History, Atlanta: Scholars Press, 1993.

Manetho, transl. W. G. Waddell, Cambridge: Harvard University Press, 1940.

Manley, Bill, The Penguin Historical Atlas of Ancient Egypt, London: Penguin Books, Ltd., 1996.

Mann, Thomas W., The Book of the Torah: The Narrative Integrity of the Pentateuch, Louisville: Westminster John Knox Press, 1988.

Margalith, Othniel, The Sea Peoples in the Bible, Weisbaden: Harrassowitz, 1994.

Martin, Thomas R., Ancient Greece, From Prehistoric to Hellenistic Times, New Haven: Yale University Press, 1996.

Matthews, Victor H., A Brief History of Ancient Israel, Louisville: Westminster John Knox Press, 2002.

Matthews, Victor H. & Benjamin, Don C., Old Testament Parallels: Laws and Stories From the Ancient Near East, New York: Paulist Press, 1991.

Matthews, Victor H. & Benjamin, Don C., <u>Old Testament Parallels: Laws and Stories From the Ancient Near East</u>, Third Edition, New York: Paulist Press, 2006.

Matthews, Victor Harold, <u>Pastoral Nomadism in the Mari Kingdom (ca. 1830-1760 B.C.)</u>, Cambridge, MA: American Schools of Oriental Research, 1978.

McCarty, Nick, <u>Troy: The Myth and Reality Behind the Epic Legend</u>, New York: Barnes & Noble Books, 2004.

McInerney, Jeremy, <u>Ancient Greek Civilization</u>, Chantilly, VA: The Teaching Company, 1998.

Meek, Theophile James, <u>Hebrew Origins</u>, New York: Harper, 1960.

<u>Menahoth</u>, transl. Eli Cashdan, <u>The Babylonian Talmud</u>, edit. I. Epstein, London: The Soncino Press, 1948.

Mendenhall, George E., <u>Ancient Israel's Faith and History, An Introduction to the Bible in Context</u>, Louisville, Kentucky: Westminster John Knox Press, 2001.

Mendenhall, George E., <u>The Tenth Generation: The Origins of the Biblical Tradition</u>, Baltimore: The Johns Hopkins University Press, 1973.

Merrill, Eugene H., <u>An Historical Survey of the Old Testament</u>, Grand Rapids: Baker Book House, 1991.

Merrill, Eugene H., <u>Kingdom of Priests: A History of Old Testament Israel</u>, Grand Rapids: Baker Academic, 2008.

Mertz, Barbara, Temples, Tombs & Hieroglyphs: A Popular History of Ancient Egypt, New York: HarperCollins, 2007.

<u>Mesopotamia and the Bible</u>, edit. Mark W. Chavalas & K. Lawson Younger, Jr., Grand Rapids: Baker Academic, 2002.

Mikra: Text, Translation, Reading & Interpretation of the Hebrew Bible in Ancient Judaism & Early Christianity, edit. Martin Jan Mulder, exec. edit Harry Sysling, Peabody, MA: Hendrickson Publishers, Inc., 2004.

Milgrom, Jacob, <u>Numbers, The JPS Torah Commentary</u>, edit. Nahum M. Sarna, Philadelphia: The Jewish Publication Society, 1990.

Miller, J. Maxwell & Hayes, John H., <u>A History of Ancient Israel and Judah</u>, Philadelphia: Westminster Press, 1986.

Miller, J. Maxwell & Hayes, John H., <u>A History of Ancient Israel and Judah</u>, 2nd Edition, Louisville: Westminster John Knox Press, 2006.

Miller, Patrick D., <u>The Religion of Ancient Israel</u>, Louisville: Westminster John Knox Press, 2000.

Miller, Robert D. II, Chieftains of the Highland Clans: A History of Israel in the 12th and 11th Centuries BC, Grand Rapids: William B. Eerdmans Publishing Company, 2005.

Miller, Stephen M., & Huber, Robert V., <u>The Bible: A History</u>, Intercourse, PA: Good Books, 2004.

Milner, Larry S., <u>Hardness of Heart/Hardness of Life: The Stain of Human Infanticide</u>, Lanham, MD: University Press of America, Inc., 2000.

Milner, Larry S., Was Achilles a Jew? Hebraic Contributions to Greek Civilization, New York: Xlibris, 2008.

Milton, John, <u>Paradise Lost</u>, edit. Alastair Fowler, London: Longman, 1971.

Minkin, Jacob S., The Shaping of the Modern Mind: The Life and Thought of the Great Jewish Philosophers, New York: Thomas Yoseloff, 1963.

The Missing Books of the Bible, Volume 1, Owings Mill, MD: Halo Press, 1996.

Mitford, William, <u>The History of Greece, Volume I</u>, Elibron Classics Replica Edition, 2007.

Momigliano, Arnaldo, <u>The Classical Foundations of Modern Historiography</u>, Berkeley: University of California Press, 1990.

Momigliano, Arnaldo, <u>Essays on Ancient and Modern Judaism</u>, transl. Maura Masella-Gayley, Chicago: The University of Chicago Press, 1994.

Montet, Pierre, <u>Lives of the Pharaohs</u>, transl. George Weidenfeld & Nicolson Ltd, Cleveland: The World Publishing Company, 1968.

Montet, Pierre, <u>Everyday Life in Egypt</u>, transl. A. R. Maxwell-Hyslop & Margaret S. Drower, Philadelphia: University of Pennsylvania Press, 1981.

Moore, George Foot, <u>Judaism in the First Centuries of the Christian Era: The Age of the Tannaim</u>, Volume I, Cambridge: Harvard University Press, 1966.

Morenz, Siegfried, <u>Egyptian Religion</u>, transl. Ann E. Keep, Ithaca, NY: Cornell University Press, 1960.

Morris, Sarah P., <u>Daidalos and the Origins of Greek Art</u>, Princeton: Princeton University Press, 1992.

Morrison, James, <u>A Companion to Homer's Odyssey</u>, Westport, CN: Greenwood Press, 2003.

Moscati, Sabatino, <u>The World of the Phoenicians</u>, transl. Alastair Hamilton, New York: Frederick A. Praeger, 1968.

Murray, Gilbert, <u>Euripides and His Age</u>, London: Oxford University Press, 1946.

Murray, Margaret A., <u>The Splendour That Was Egypt</u>, London: Sidgwick and Jackson, 1963.

Mylonas, George E., <u>Mycenae & The Mycenaean Age</u>, Princeton: Princeton University Press, 1966.

Myres, John L., <u>Herodotus: Father of History</u>, Oxford: Clarendon Press, 1953.

Myres, John Linton, <u>Who Were the Greeks?</u>, New York: Biblio and Tannen, 1967.

N <u>The Nag Hammadi Scriptures</u>, edit. Marvin Meyer, New York: HarperOne, 2007.

<u>The New Interpreters Bible</u>, Volume I, Nashville: Abington Press, 1994.

Nibbi, Alessandra, <u>The Sea Peoples and Egypt</u>, Park Ridge, NJ: Noyes Press, 1975.

Nicholson, Ernest, The Pentateuch in the Twentieth Century: The Legacy of Julius Wellhausen, Oxford: Oxford University Press, 1998.

Niditch, Susan, <u>Oral World and Written Word: Ancient Israelite Literature</u>, Louisville: Westminster John Knox Press, 1996.

Nielsen, Eduard, <u>Oral Tradition</u>, London: SCM Press Ltd, 1954.

Nielsen, Flemming A. J., <u>The Tragedy in History: Herodotus and the Deuteronomistic History</u>, Sheffield: Sheffield Academic Press, 1997.

Noth, Martin, <u>The History of Israel</u>, transl. P. R. Ackroyd, New York: Harper & Row, 1960.

Noth, Martin, <u>Exodus, A Commentary</u>, Philadelphia: The Westminster Press, 1962.

Noth, Martin, <u>Numbers, A Commentary</u>, transl. James D. Martin, Philadelphia: The Westminster Press, 1968.

<u>Numbers, The Torah, A Modern Commentary IV</u>, commentary W. Gunther Plaut, transl. Jewish Publication Society, New York: Union of American Hebrew Congregations, 1979.

OOakes, Lorna & Gahlin, Lucia, <u>Ancient Egypt</u>, London: Hermes House, 2002.

O'Brien, Joan & Major, Wilfred, In The Beginning: Creation Myths from Ancient Mesopotamia, Israel and Greece, Chico, CA: Scholars Press,1982.

<u>The Old Testament Pseudepigrapha</u>, Volume 1, edit. James H. Charlesworth, New York: Doubleday, 1983.

<u>The Old Testament Pseudepigrapha</u>, Volume 2, edit. James H. Charlesworth, New York: Doubleday, 1985.

Origen, <u>The Fathers of the Church</u>, transl. Ronald Heine, Washington, D.C.: The Catholic University of America Press, 1981.

Osman, Ahmed, The Hebrew Pharaohs of Egypt: The Secret Lineage of the Patriarch Joseph, Rochester, VT: Bear & Company, 2003.

Osman, Ahmed, Moses and Akhenaten: the Secret History of Egypt at the Time of the Exodus, Rochester, VT: Bear & Company, 2002.

Osman, Ahmed, The Lost City of the Exodus: The Archaeological Evidence Behind the Journey Out of Egypt, Rochester, VT:Bear & Company, 2014.

<u>The Other Bible</u>, edit. Willis Barnstone, San Francisco: HarperSanFrancisco, 1984.

Ovid, <u>Metamorphoses</u>, transl. Rolfe Humphries, Bloomington: Indiana University Press, 1955.

<u>The Oxford Bible Commentary</u>, edit. John Barton & John Muddiman, Oxford: Oxford University Press, 2001.

<u>The Oxford Encyclopedia of Archaeology in the Near East</u>, Volumes 1-5, edit. Eric M. Meyers, New York: Oxford University Press, 1997.

<u>The Oxford History of Ancient Egypt</u>, edit. Ian Shaw, Oxford: Oxford University Press, 2000.

The Oxford History of the Biblical World, edit. Michael D. Coogan, Oxford: Oxford University Press, 1998.

The Oxford Illustrated History of the Bible, edit. Michael D. Coogan, Oxford: Oxford University Press, 1998.

The Oxford Illustrated History of the Bible, edit John Rogerson, Oxford: Oxford University Press, 2001.

P Pagolu, Augustine, The Religion of the Patriarchs, Journal for the Study of the Old Testament, Suppl. 277, Sheffield: Sheffield Academic Press, 1998.

Pangborn, Cyrus R., Zoroastrianism: A Beleaguered Faith, New York: Advent Books, 1983.

Parke-Taylor, G. H., Yahweh: The Divine Name in the Bible, Waterloo, ON: Wilfrid Laurier University Press, 1975.

Patai, Raphael, The Children of Noah: Jewish Seafaring in Ancient Times, Princeton: Princeton University Press, 1998.

Pausanias, Description of Greece, transl. W. H. S. Jones, Cambridge: Harvard University Press, 1969.

Pelikan, Jaroslav, What Has Athens To Do With Jerusalem?: *Timaeus* and *Genesis* in Counterpoint, Ann Arbor: The University of Michigan Press, 1997.

Penglase, Charles, Greek Myths and Mesopotamia: Parallels and Influence in the Homeric Hymns and Hesiod, London: Routledge, 1994.

Peoples of the Old Testament World, edit. Alfred J. Hoerth, Gerald L. Mattingly, Edwin M. Yamauchi, Grand Rapids: Baker Books, 1998.

Petrie, W. M. Flinders, Syria and Egypt from the Tell El Amarna Letters, Chicago: Ares Publishers Inc., 1978.

Petter, Donna Lee, The Book of Ezekiel and Mesopotamian City Laments, Fribourg, Switzerland: Vandenhoech & Ruprecht Gottingen, 2011.

Pfeiffer, Charles F., Egypt and the Exodus, Grand Rapids: Baker Book House, 1964.

Philo, On Abraham, The Works of Philo, transl. C. D. Yonge, Peabody, MA: Hendrickson Publishers, 1993.

Philo, The Works of Philo, transl. C. D. Yonge, Peabody, MA: Hendrickson Publishers, 1993.

Philo of Byblos, The Phoenician History, transl. Harold W. Attridge & Robert A. Oden, Jr., Washington, D.C.: The Catholic Biblical Association of America, 1981.

The Phoenicians, edit. Sabatino Moscati, New York: Rizzoli International Publications, Inc., 1999.

Pillot, Gilbert, The Secret Code of the Odyssey, transl. Francis E. Albert, London: Abelard-Schuman, 1972.

Pixley, George V., On Exodus, A Liberation Perspective, transl. Robert R. Barr, Maryknoll, New York: Orbis Books, 1987.

Plato, The Laws of Plato, transl. Thomas L. Pangle, Chicago: The University of Chicago Press, 1980.

Plato, Phaedrus and Letters VII and VIII, transl. Walter Hamilton, Middlesex, England, Penguin Books, 1973.

Plato Complete Works, edit. John M. Cooper, Indianapolis, IN: Hackett Publishing Company, 1997.

Plaut, W. Gunther, Genesis, The Torah: A Modern Commentary, New York: Union of American Hebrew Congregations, 1974.

Plaut, W. Gunther, Numbers, The Torah: A Modern Commentary, New York: Union of American Hebrew Congregations, 1979.

Pliny (Gaius Plinius Secundus), Natural History, Cambridge: Harvard University Press, 1969.

Plutarch, Moralia, transl. W. C. Helmbold, London: William Heinemann, Ltd., 1927.

Plutarch, Lives, transl. Bernadotte Perrin, Cambridge: Harvard University Press, 1967.

Plutarch, The Age of Alexander, transl. Ian Scott-Kilvert, Middlesex: Penguin Books, 1973.

Podhoretz, Norman, The Prophets: Who They Were, What They Are, New York: The Free Press, 2002.

Pojman, Louis P. & Rea, Michael, Philosophy of Religion, An Anthology, Belmont, CA: Thomson Wadsworth, 2008.

Polano, Hymen, The Talmud, reprinted San Bernardino, CA: Forgotten Books, 2014.

Pollard, William G., The Hebrew Iliad, The History of the Rise of Israel Under Saul and David, transl. Robert H. Pfeiffer, New York: Harper & Brothers, 1957.

Porter, J. R., The Illustrated Guide to the Bible, New York: Oxford University Press, 1995.

Powell, Barry B., Homer, Oxford: Blackwell Publishing, 2004.

Provan, Iain, Long, V. Philips, & Longman III, Tremper, A Biblical History of Israel, Louisville: Westminster John Knox Press, 2003.

Purcell, H. D., Cyprus, New York: Frederick A. Praeger, 1968.

Q Qumran and the History of the Biblical Text, edit. Frank Moore Cross & Shemaryahu Talmon, Cambridge, MA: Harvard University Press, 1975.

R Rappoport, Angelo S., Ancient Israel, Myths and Legends, London: The Mystic Press, 1987.

Rashi, Pentateuch With Targum Onkelos, Haphtaroth and Rashi's Commentary, Deuteronomy, transl. M. Rosenbaum & A. M. Silbermann, New York: Hebrew Publishing Company.

Rashi, <u>Pentateuch With Targum Onkelos, Haphtaroth and Rashi's Commentary, Exodus</u>, transl. M. Rosenbaum & A. M. Silbermann, New York: Hebrew Publishing Company.

Rashi, <u>Pentateuch With Targum Onkelos, Haphtaroth and Rashi's Commentary, Genesis</u>, transl. M. Rosenbaum & A. M. Silbermann, New York: Hebrew Publishing Company.

Rashi, <u>Pentateuch With Targum Onkelos, Haphtaroth and Rashi's Commentary, Numbers</u>, transl. M. Rosenbaum & A. M. Silbermann, New York: Hebrew Publishing Company.

Rast, Walter E, <u>Tradition History and the Old Testament</u>, Philadelphia: Fortress Press, 1972.

<u>Reading the Past: Ancient Writing From Cuneiform to the Alphabet</u>, Introduced by J. T. Hooker, Berkeley: University of California Press, 1990.

Redford, Donald B., <u>History and Chronology of the Eighteenth Dynasty of Egypt</u>, Toronto: University of Toronto Press, 1967.

Redford, Donald B., <u>Akhenaten, The Heretic King</u>, Princeton: Princeton University Press, 1984.

Redford, Donald B., <u>Egypt, Canaan, and Israel in Ancient Times</u>, Princeton: Princeton University Press, 1992.

Reeves, Nicholas, <u>Ancient Egypt: The Great Discoveries</u>, New York: Thames & Hudson, 2000.

Reeves, Nicholas, <u>Akhenaten, Egypt's False Prophet</u>, New York: Thames & Hudson, 2001.

Rehwinkel, Alfred M., <u>The Flood: In the Light of the Bible, Geology, and Archaeology</u>, St. Louis: Concordia Publishing House, 1951.

<u>Religion in Ancient Egypt: Gods, Myths, and Personal Practice</u>, edit. Byron E. Shafer, Ithaca: Cornell University Press, 1991.

<u>Religious Diversity in Ancient Israel and Judah</u>, edit. Francesca Atavrakopoulou and John Barton, London, T & T Clark International, 2010.

Religious Foundations of Western Civilization: Judaism, Christianity, and Islam, edit. Jacob Neusner, Nashville, Abingdon Press, 2006.

Roaf, Michael, Cultural Atlas of Mesopotamia and the Ancient Near East, New York: Facts On File, Inc., 1990.

Robbins, Manuel, Collapse of the Bronze Age, The Story of Greece, Troy, Israel, Egypt and the People of the Sea, Lincoln, NE: Authors Choice Press, 2001.

Robertson, C. C., <u>On the Track of the Exodus</u>, Thousand Oaks, CA: Artisan Sales, 1990.

Robertson, Joseph, The Parian Chronicle: Or the Chronicle of the Arundelian Marbles; With a Dissertation Concerning Its Authenticity, London: J. Walter, 1788, Reprint, Kessinger Publishing, 2009.

Rogerson, John, <u>Chronicle of the Old Testament Kings</u>, London: Thames and Hudson, Ltd., 1999.

Rohl, David M., A Test of Time, The Bible - From Myth to History, London: Century Ltd., 1995.

Rohl, David M., <u>Pharaohs and Kings, A Biblical Quest</u>, New York: Crown Publishers, Inc., 1995.

Romer, Thomas, The So-Called Deuteronomistic History: A Sociological, Historical and Literary Introduction, London: T & T Clark, 2007.

Rouse, W. H. D., <u>Gods, Heroes and Men of Ancient Greece</u>, New York: The New American Library of World Literature Inc., 1957.

Roux, Georges, <u>Ancient Iraq</u>, London: Penguin Books, 1966.

Rowley, H. H., Worship in Ancient Israel, Its Forms and Meaning, London: S.P.C.K., 1967.

Russell, Bertrand, <u>A History of Western Philosophy</u>, New York: Simon and Schuster, 1945.

Russell, D. S., <u>The Jews from Alexander to Herod</u>, Oxford, Oxford University Press, 1967.

SSaggs, H. W. F., <u>Civilization Before Greece and Rome</u>, New Haven: Yale University Press, 1989.

Samuel, Alan E., <u>The Mycenaeans in History</u>, Englewood Cliffs, NJ: Prentice-Hall, Inc., 1966.

Sandars, N. K., The Sea Peoples: Warriors of the Ancient Mediterranean 1250-1150 B.C., London, Thames and Hudson, 1978.

Sanders, Stephen H., Israel and the Pharaohs: Israel, Egypt, and Canaan in the Bible and Near Eastern Texts, Sonora, CA: Arone Publications, 2002.

<u>Sappho, Poems & Fragments</u>, transl. Josephine Balmer, Secaucus, NJ: Meadowland Books, 1984.

Sarna, Nahum M., <u>Understanding Genesis</u>, New York: The Jewish Theological Seminary of America, 1966.

Sarna, Nahum M., <u>Genesis, The JPS Torah Commentary</u>, edit. Nahum M. Sarna, Philadelphia: The Jewish Publication Society, 1989.

Sarna, Nahum M., <u>Exodus, The JPS Torah Commentary</u>, edit. Nahum M. Sarna, Philadelphia: The Jewish Publication Society, 1991.

Sarna, Nahum M., <u>Exploring Exodus, The Origins of Biblical Israel</u>, New York: Schocken Books, 1996.

Schedl, Claus, History of the Old Testament I. The Ancient Orient and Ancient Biblical History, Staten Island, NY: Society of St. Paul, 1973.

Schedl, Claus, <u>History of the Old Testament II. God's People of the Covenant</u>, Staten Island, NY: Society of St. Paul, 1973.

Scherman, Nosson, <u>The Chumash</u>, The Stone Edition, Brooklyn: Mesorah Publications, Ltd., 2000.

Schliemann, Henry, Mycenae; A Narrative of Researches and Discoveries at Mycenae and Tiryns, London: John Murray, 1878.

Schliemann, Heinrich, <u>Tiryns, The Prehistoric Palace of the Kings of Tiryns</u>, 1885, New York: Arno Press, 1976.

Schmidt, Werner H., <u>The Faith of the Old Testament</u>, transl. John Sturdy, Philadelphia: The Westminster Press, 1983.

Schultz, Joseph P. & Spatz, Lois, <u>Sinai & Olympus, A Comparative Study</u>, Lanham, MD: University Press of America, Inc., 1995.

Schwab, Gustav, <u>Gods & Heroes: Myths & Epics of Ancient Greece</u>, transl. Olga Marx & Ernst Morwitz, New York: Pantheon Books Inc., 1946.

Schwantes, Siegfried J., <u>A Short History of the Ancient Near East</u>, Grand Rapids: Baker Book House, 1965.

<u>Scripture in Context II: More Essays on the Comparative Method</u>, edit. William W. Hallo, James c. Moyer, & Leo G. Perdue, Winona Lake, IN: Eisenbrauns, 1983.

Sealey, Raphael, <u>A History of the Greek City States ca. 700-338 B.C.</u>, Berkeley: University of California Press, 1976.

<u>The Second Book of Maccabees</u>, edit. Solomon Zeitlin, transl. Sidney Tedesche, New York: Harper & Brothers, 1954.

Sedlar, Jean W. <u>India and the Greek World: A Study in the Transmission of Culture</u>, Totowa, NJ: Rowman & Littlefield Publishers, Inc., 1980.

Segal, Jerome M., Joseph's Bones: Understanding the Struggle Between God and Mankind in the Bible, New York: Riverhead Books, 2007.

Seneca, <u>Agamemnon</u>, <u>The Complete Roman Drama</u>, Volume II, transl. Frank Justus Miller, edit. George E. Duckworth, New York: Random House, 1942.

Seneca, <u>Phaedra</u>, <u>Four Tragedies and Octavia</u>, transl. E. F. Watling, Middlesex: Penguin Books, 1966.

Seneca, <u>Thyestes</u>, <u>Four Tragedies and Octavia</u>, transl. E. F. Watling, Middlesex: Penguin Books, 1966.

Seters, John von, <u>The Hyksos: A New Investigation</u>, New Haven: Yale University Press, 1966.

Shelley, Percy Bysshe, <u>Selected Poetry and Prose</u>, edit. Kenneth Neill Cameron, New York: Rinehart & Co., Inc., 1978.

Simons, J., The Geographical and Topographical Texts of the Old Testament, Leiden: E. J. Brill, 1959.

Slack, Walter, White Athena: The Afrocentrist Theft of Greek Civilization, New York: iUniverse, Inc., 2006.

Smick, Elmer B., <u>Archaeology of the Jordan Valley</u>, Grand Rapids: Baker Book House, 1973.

Smith, J. M. Powis, <u>The Prophets and Their Times</u>, Revised Edistion by William A. Irwin, Chicago: The University of Chicago Press, 1941.

Smith, Mark S., <u>The Early History of God: Yahweh and the Other Deities in Ancient Israel</u>, Grand Rapids, MI: William B. Eerdmans Publishing Company, 2002.

Smith, Mark S., The Origins of Biblical Monotheism; Israel's Polytheistic Background and the Ugaritic Texts, Oxford: Oxford University Press, 2001.

Soggin, J. Alberto, A History of Ancient Israel, transl. John Bowden, Philadelphia: The Westminster Press, 1984.

Soggin, J. Alberto, Israel in the Biblical Period: Institutions, Festivals, Ceremonies, Rituals, Edinburgh: T & T Clark, 2001.

Sophocles, The Complete Plays of Sophocles, Robert Bagg and James Scully, New York: HarperCollins Publishers, 2011.

Sparks, Kenton L., Ethnicity and Identity in Ancient Israel: Prolegomena to the Study of Ethnic Sentiments and Their Expression in the Hebrew Bible, Winona Lake, IN: Eisenbrauns, 1998.

Spiegel, Shalom, The Last Trial: On the Legends and Lore of the Command to Abraham to Offer Isaac as a Sacrifice: The Akedah, transl. Judah Goldin, Woodstock, VT: Jewish Lights Publishing, 1993.

Sproul, Barbara C., Primal Myths: Creating the World, New York: Harper & Row, 1979.

Stapleton, Michael, The Illustrated Dictionary of Greek and Roman Mythology, New York: Peter Bedrick Books, 1986.

Starr, Chester G., The Origins of Greek Civilization, 1100-650 B.C., New York: Alfred A. Knopf, 1961.

Starr, Chester G., A History of the Ancient World, New York: Oxford University Press, 1992.

Steinsaltz, Adin, The Essential Talmud, Northvale, NJ: Jason Aronson Inc., 1992.

Stenudd, Stefan, Cosmos of the Ancients: The Greek Philosophers on Myth and Cosmology, North Charleston, SC: BookSurge, LLC, 2007.

Stern, Menahem, Greek and Latin Authors on Jews and Judaism, Volume One, From Herodotus to Plutarch, Jerusalem: The Israel Academy of Sciences and Humanities, 1976.

Stewart, Ted T., Solving the Exodus Mystery, Volume I: Discovery of the True Pharaohs of Joseph, Moses and the Exodus, Lubbock, TX: Biblemart.Com, 2003.

Stiebing, William H. Jr., Out of the Desert?: Archaeology and the Exodus/Conquest Narratives, Buffalo: Prometheus Books, 1989.

Strabo, The Geography, transl. Horace Leonard Jones, Cambridge: Harvard University Press, 1960.

Strauss, Barry, The Trojan War: A New History, New York: Simon & Schuster, 2006.

T Tacitus, The History, transl. Arthur Murphy, New York: J. M. Dent & Sons, Ltd., 1932.

The Tale of Sinuhe and Other Ancient Egyptian Poems, 1940-1640 B.C., transl. R. B. Parkinson, Oxford: Oxford University Press, 1998.

Taylor, J. Glen, <u>Yahweh and the Sun: Biblical and Archaeological Evidence for Sun Worship in Ancient Israel</u>, Journal for the Study of the Old Testament, suppl 111, London: Sheffield Academic Press, 1993.

Taylour, Lord William, <u>The Mycenaeans</u>, New York: Frederick A. Praeger, 1964.

Tertullian, <u>Apologetical Works, the Fathers of the Church</u>, transl. Rudolph Arbesmann, Emily Joseph Daly, & Edwin A. Quain, Washington, D.C.: The Catholic University of America Press, 1950.

Tetlow, Elisabeth Meier, Women, Crime, and Punishment in Ancient Law and Society, Volume 1, The Ancient Near East, New York: Continuum, 2004.

Tetlow, Elisabeth Meier, Women, Crime, and Punishment in Ancient Law and Society, Volume 2, Ancient Greece, New York: Continuum, 2005.

Thompson, Thomas L., The Mythic Past, Biblical Archaeology and the Myth of Israel, London: Basic Books, 1999.

Thompson, Thomas L., The Historicity of the Patriarchal Narratives, The Quest for the Historical Abraham, Harrisburg: Trinity Press International, 2002.

<u>Three Jewish Philosophers</u>, New York: Atheneum, 1976.

Thucydides, <u>The Peloponnesian War</u>, transl. Rex Warner, New York: Penguin Books, 1954.

Tidball, Derek, <u>The Illustrated Survey of the Bible</u>, Minneapolis: Bethany House Publishers, 2001.

Tigay, Jeffrey H., <u>Deuteronomy, The JPS Torah Commentary</u>, edit. Nahum M. Sarna, Philadelphia: The Jewish Publication Society, 1996.

<u>The Torah, A Modern Commentary</u>, W. Gunther Plaut & Bernard J. Bamberger, New York: The Union of American Hebrew Congregations, 1981.

<u>Tradition and Theology in the Old Testament</u>, edit. Douglas A. Knight, Atlanta: Society of Biblical Literature, 2007.

Trumbull, H. Clay, <u>Kadesh-Barnea, Its Importance and Probable Site</u>, New York: Charles Scribner's Sons, 1884.

Tubb, Jonathan N., <u>Peoples of the Past: Canaanites</u>, Norman: University of Oklahoma Press, 1998.

Tullock, John H., <u>The Old Testament Story</u>, Upper Saddle River, NJ: Prentice Hall, 1996.

<u>Twentieth Century Interpretations of the Odyssey</u>, edit. Howard W. Clarke, Englewood Cliffs, NJ, Prentice-Hall, Inc., 1983.

<u>Twentieth Century Interpretations of the Odyssey</u>, edit. Michael J. O'Brien, Englewood Cliffs, NJ, Prentice-Hall, Inc., 1968.

Tyldesley, Joyce, <u>Hatchepsut: The Female Pharaoh</u>, London: Penguin Books, 1998.

Tyldesley, Joyce, <u>Nefertiti: Egypt's Sun Queen</u>, London: Penguin Books, 1998.

Tyldesley, Joyce, <u>Ramesses: Egypt's Greatest Pharaoh</u>, London: Penguin Books, 2000.

U Ulrich, Eugene, The Dead Sea Scrolls and the Origins of the Bible, Grand Rapids: William B. Eerdmans Publishing Company, 1999.

Understanding the Dead Sea Scrolls,: A Reader from the *Biblical Archaeology Review*, edit. Hershel Shanks, New York: Random House, 1992.

V Van Dam, Cornelis, The Urim and Thummim: A Means of Revelation in Ancient Israel, Winona Lake: Eisenbrauns, 1997.

Van De Mieroop, Marc, A History of the Ancient Near East, ca. 3000-323 BC, Oxford: Blackwell Publishing, 2004.

VanderKam, James & Flint, Peter, The Meaning of the Dead Sea Scrolls: Their Significance for Understanding the Bible, Judaism, Jesus, and Christianity, New York: HarperSanFrancisco, 2002.

Van Seters, John, The Hyksos, A New Investigation, New Haven: Yale University Press, 1966.

Van Seters, John, Prologue to History: The Yahwist as Historian in Genesis, Louisville: Westminster/John Knox Press, 1992.

Van Seters, John, In Search of History: Historiography in the Ancient World and the Origins of Biblical History, Winona Lake, IN: Eisenbrauns, 1997.

Velikovsky, Immanuel, Ages in Chaos, Garden City, NY: Doubleday & Company, Inc., 1952.

Velikovsky, Immanuel, Peoples of the Sea, Garden City, NY: Doubleday & Company, Inc., 1977.

Verbrugghe, Gerald P. & Wickersham, John M., Berossos and Manetho, Introduced and Translated, Ann Arbor: The University of Michigan Press, 2000.

Vercoutter, The Search for Ancient Egypt, transl. Ruth Sharman, New York: Harry N. Abrams, Inc., 1992.

Vermes, Geza, The Dead Sea Scrolls in English, London: Penguin Books, 1995.

Vermeule, Emily, Greece in the Bronze Age, Chicago: The University of Chicago Press, 1964.

Vernant, Jean-Pierre, The Origins of Greek Thought, Ithaca, NY: Cornell University Press, 1982.

Vernant, Jean-Pierre, The Universe, the Gods, and Men: Ancient Greek Myths, transl. Linda Asher, New York: HarperCollins Publishers, 2001.

Veyne, Paul, Did the Greeks Believe in Their Myths? An Essay on the Constitutive Imagination, transl. Paula Wissing, Chicago: The University of Chicago Press, 1988.

Views of the Biblical World, I The Law, Chicago: Jordan Publications, Inc., 1959.

von Rad, Gerhard, Old Testament Theology, Volume I, The Theology of Israel's Historical Traditions, transl. D. M. G. Stalker, Louisville: Westminster John Knox Press, 1962.

von Rad, Gerhard, <u>Old Testament Theology</u>, Volume II, The Theology of Israel's Prophetic Traditions, transl. D. M. G. Stalker, Louisville: Westminster John Knox Press, 1965.

von Rad, Gerhard, <u>From Genesis to Chronicles</u>, transl. E. W. Trueman Dicken, edit. K. C. Hanson, Minneapolis: Fortress Press, 2005.

W.Wace, Alan J. B., <u>Mycenae: An Archaeological History and Guide</u>, New York: Biblio and Tannen, 1964.

Walton, John H., <u>Ancient Israelite Literature In Its Cultural Context</u>, Grand Rapids: Zondervan Publishing House, 1990.

Walton, John H., Ancient Near Eastern Thought and the Old Testament: Introducing the Conceptual World of the Hebrew Bible, Grand Rapids, MI: Baker Academic, 2006.

Walton, John H., Matthews, Victor H., & Chavalas, Mark W., <u>The IVP Bible Background Commentary: Old Testament</u>, Downers Grove, IL: InterVarsity Press, 2000.

Watterson, Barbara, <u>The Egyptians</u>, Oxford: Blackwell Publishers, Ltd, 1997.

Watterson, Barbara, <u>The Gods of Ancient Egypt</u>, New York: Facts on File Publications, 1984.

Weinreich, Beatrice Silverman, <u>Yiddish Folktales</u>, transl. Leonard Wolf, New York: Pantheon Books, 1988.

Weippert, Manfred, <u>The Settlement of the Israelite Tribes in Palestine</u>, London: SCM Press, Ltd., 1971.

Wellhausen, Julius, <u>Prolegomena to the History of Ancient Israel</u>, New York: Meridian Books, 1957.

Wesselius, Jan-Wim, <u>The Origin of the History of Israel: Herodotus's</u> *Histories* <u>as Blueprint for the First Books of the Bible</u>, Journal for the Study of the Old Testament, Suppl. 345, London: Sheffield Academic Press, 2002.

Westenholz, Joan Goodnick, <u>Legends of the Kings of Akkadia, The Texts</u>, Winona Lake, IN: Eisenbrauns, 1997.

Whitcomb, Jr., John C., & Morris, Henry M., <u>The Genesis Flood, The Biblical Record and Its Scientific Implications</u>, Philadelphia: The Presbyterian and Reformed Publishing Company, 1961.

Whitelam, Keith W., The Invention of Ancient Israel: The Silencing of Palestinian History, London: Routledge, 1996.

Wiesel, Elie, <u>Five Biblical Prophets</u>, Notre Dame: University of Notre Dame Press, 1981.

Wiesel, Elie, <u>Messengers of God</u>, transl. Marion Wiesel, New York: Random House, 1976.

Willetts, R. F., <u>Everyday Life in Ancient Crete</u>, London: B. T. Batsford, Ltd., 1969.

Willoughby, Harold R., Pagan Regeneration: A Study of Mystery Initiations in the Graeco Roman World, Chicago: The University of Chicago Press, 1929.

Wilson, Ian, The Exodus Enigma, London: Weidenfeld and Nicolson, 1985.

Wilson, Ian The Bible Is History, London: Weidenfeld and Nicolson, 1999.

Wilson, John A., The Culture of Ancient Egypt, Chicago: The University of Chicago Press, 1951.

Wise, Michael, Abegg, Martin Jr., & Cook, Edward, The Dead Sea Scrolls: A New Translation, New York: HarperOne, 2005.

Wolfson, Harry Austryn, Philo, Cambridge: Harvard University Press, 1948.

The Women's Torah Commentary: New Insights from Women Rabbis on the 54 Weekly Torah Portions, edit. Elyze Goldstein, Woodstock, VT: Jewish Lights Publishing, 2000.

The Works of Philo, transl. C. D. Yonge, Peabody, MA, Hendrickson Publishers, Inc., 1993.

Wood, Michael, In Search of the Trojan War, New York: Facts on File Publications, 1985.

Y Yamauchi, Edwin, Greece and Babylon: Early Contacts Between the Aegean and the Near East, Grand Rapids, MI: Baker Book House, 1967.

Yerkes, Royden Keith, Sacrifice in Greek and Roman Religions and Early Judaism, New York: Charles Scribner's Sons, 1952.

Z Zevit, Zionly, The Religions of Ancient Israel: A Synthesis of Parallactic Approaches, London: Continuum, 2001.

Zondervan NIV Matthew Henry Commentary, edit. Leslie F. Church, Grand Rapids: Zondervan Publishing House, 1992.

Zornberg, Avivah Gottlieb, Genesis: The Beginning of Desire, Philadelphia: The Jewish Publication Society, 1995.

Articles

A Adler, Jonathan, "Dating the Exodus: A New Perspective," Jewish Bible Quarterly 23 (1995):44-51.

Aeschylus, "Agamemnon," transl. Richard Lattimore, Orestia, Chicago: University of Chicago Press, 1953, 33-90.

Aeschylus, "The Eumenides," transl. Richard Lattimore, Orestia, Chicago: University of Chicago Press, 1953, 133-171.

Aeschylus, "The Libation Bearers," transl. Richard Lattimore, Orestia, Chicago: University of Chicago Press, 1953, 91-132.

Aeschylus, "The Persians," transl. Philip Vellacott, Prometheus Bound, The Suppliants, Seven Against Thebes, The Persians, Middlesex: Penguin Books, 1961, 122-152.

Aeschylus, "Prometheus Bound," transl. Philip Vellacott, Prometheus Bound, The Suppliants, Seven Against Thebes, The Persians, Middlesex: Penguin Books, 1961, 20-53.

Aeschylus, "The Seven Against Thebes," transl. Richard Lattimore, Orestia, Chicago: University of Chicago Press, 1953, 88-121.

Aeschylus, "The Suppliants," transl. Philip Vellacott, Prometheus Bound, The Suppliants, Seven Against Thebes, The Persians, Middlesex: Penguin Books, 1961.

Ahituv, Shmuel, "Sources for the Study of the Egyptian-Canaanite Border Administration," Israel Exploration Journal 46 (1996):219-224.

Albright, W. F., "Syria, the Philistines, and Phoenicia," The Cambridge Ancient History, Volume II, Part 2, History of the Middle East and the Aegean Region, edit. I. E. S. Edwards, C. J. Gadd, N. G. L. Hammond & E. Sollberger, Cambridge: Cambridge University Press, 1975, 507-536.

Alleman, Herbert C., "The Book of Genesis," Old Testament Commentary, edit. Herbert C. Alleman & Elmer E. Flack, Philadelphia: Fortress Press, 1948, 171-206.

Alleman, Herbert C. & Flack, Elmer E., "The Book of Exodus," Old Testament Commentary, edit. Herbert C. Alleman & Elmer E. Flack, Philadelphia: Fortress Press, 1948, 207-244.

Allen, Ronald B., "Numbers," The Expositor's Bible Commentary, edit. Frank E. Gaebelein, Grand Rapids: Zondervan Publishing House, Volume 2, 1990, 657-1008.

Alt, Albrecht, "The God of the Fathers," Essays on Old Testament History and Religion, transl. R. A. Wilson, Garden City, NY: Anchor Books, 1968, 1-100.

Alter, Robert, "Sacred History and the Beginnings of Prose Fiction," The Bible, Modern Critical Views, edit. Harold Bloom, New York: Chelsea House Publishers, 1987, 21-44.

Amit, Yairah, "Judges," The Jewish Study Bible, The Jewish Publication Society Tanakh

Translation, edit. Adele Berlin & Marc Zvi Brettler, Oxford: Oxford University Press, 2004, 508-557.

"Amphictyonic League: Encyclopedia Beta," <http://experts.about.com/e/a/am/Amphictyonic_League.htm>, (7/7/06), 1-2.

Anderson, Carl A., "The Book of Numbers," Old Testament Commentary, edit. Herbert C. Alleman & Elmer E. Flack, Philadelphia: Fortress Press, 1948, 268-299.

Arnold, Bill T., "Religion in Ancient Israel," The Face of Old Testament Studies, A Survey of Contemporary Approaches, edit. David W. Baker & Bill T. Arnold, Grand Rapids: Baker Books, 1999, 391-420.

Astour, Michael C., "Place Names," Ras Shamra Parallels: The Texts from Ugarit and the Hebrew Bible, edit. Loren R. Fisher, Rome: Pontificium Institutum Biblicum, 1975, 251-369.

Astour, Michael, "Ugarit and the Great Powers," Ugarit in Retrospect, edit. Gordon Douglas Young, Winona Lake, Indiana: Eisenbrauns, 1981, 3-29.

Averbeck, Richard E., "Sumer, the Bible, and Comparative Method: Historiography and Temple Building," Mesopotamia and the Bible, edit. Mark W. Chavalas & K. Lawson Younger, Jr., Grand Rapids: Baker Academic, 2002, 88-125.

"Azazel," <http://en.wikipedia.org/wiki/Azael>(10/27/09), 1-7.

B Baker, David W., "Israelite Prophets and Prophecy," The Face of Old Testament Studies: A Survey of Contemporary Approaches, edit. David W. Baker & Bill T. Arnold, Grand Rapids: Baker Books, 1999, 266-294.

Barako, Tristan, "One if By Sea ... Two if By Land, How did the Philistines Get to Canaan? One: By Sea," Biblical Archaeology Review 29 (2003):26-33, 64-66.

Bar-Efrat, Shimon, "First Samuel," The Jewish Study Bible, The Jewish Publication Society Tanakh Translation, edit. Adele Berlin & Marc Zvi Brettler, Oxford: Oxford University Press, 2004, 558-618.

Barnett, R. D., "The Sea Peoples," The Cambridge Ancient History, Volume II, Part 2, History of the Middle East and the Aegean Region, edit. I. E. S. Edwards, C. J. Gadd, N. G. L. Hammond & E. Sollberger, Cambridge: Cambridge University Press, 1975, 359-378.

Barstad, Hans M., "Deuteronomists, Persians, Greeks, and the Dating of the Israelite Tradition," Did Moses Speak Attic: Jewish Historiography and Scripture in the Hellenistic Period, edit. Lester L. Grabbe, Journal for the Study of the Old Testament, Suppl. 317, Sheffield: Sheffield Academic Press, 2001, 47-77.

Bass, George, F., "Sea and River Craft in the Ancient Near East," Civilizations of the Ancient Near East, edit. Jack M. Sasson, New York: Charles Scribner's Sons, Volume III, 1995, 1421-1431.

Beitzel, Barry J., "The *Via Maris* in Literary and Cartographic Sources," Biblical Archaeologist 54 (1991):64-75.

Berlin, Adele & Brettler, Marc Zvi, "Psalms," The Jewish Study Bible, The Jewish

Publication Society Tanakh Translation, edit. Adele Berlin & Marc Zvi Brettler, Oxford: Oxford University Press, 2004, 1280-1446.

Bietak, Manfried, "Israelites Found in Egypt," Biblical Archaeology Review 29 (2003):40-49, 82-83.

Bloom, Harold, "Introduction," Genesis, edit. Harold Bloom, New York: Chelsea House Publishers, 1986, 1-10.

Bloom, Harold, "Introduction," Homer's the Iliad, edit. Harold Bloom, New York: Chelsea House Publishers, 1987, 1-10.

Bodine, Walter R., "Sumerians," Peoples of the Old Testament World, edit. Alfred J. Hoerth, Gerald L. Mattingly, Edwin M. Yamauchi, Grand Rapids: Baker Books, 1998. 19-42.

Bowra, Sir Maurice, "Composition," A Companion to Homer, edit. Alan J. B. Wace & Frank H. Stubbings, London: Macmillan & Co Ltd, 1962, 38-74.

Bratcher, Dennis, "The Date of the Exodus: The Historical Study of Scripture," http://www.cresourcei.org/exodusdate.html>(10/15/04), 1-16.

Brawer, A. J., "A. The Land of Israel - From 'the Brook of Egypt' to the Litani. 2. Morphology," At the Dawn of Civilization, A. Background of Biblical History, edit. E. A. Speiser, The World History of the Jewish People, edit. B. Netanyahu, Israel: Jewish History Publications, 1961, 10-27.

C Callaway, Joseph A., "The Settlement in Canaan, The Period of the Judges," Ancient Israel, A Short History From Abraham to the Roman Destruction of the Temple, edit. Hershel Shanks, Englewood Cliffs, NJ: Prentice Hall, 1988, 53-84.

Carson, T., "Numbers," The International Bible Commentary, With the New International Version, edit. F. F. Bruce, Grand Rapids, Marshall Pickering/Zondervan, 1986, 214-255.

Catling, H. W., "Cyprus in the Late Bronze Age," The Cambridge Ancient History, Volume II, Part 2, History of the Middle East and the Aegean Region, edit. I. E. S. Edwards, C. J. Gadd, N. G. L. Hammond & E. Sollberger, Cambridge: Cambridge University Press, 1975, 808-823.

Chadwick, John, "The Linear Scripts and the Tablets as Historical Documents (b) the Linear B Tablets as Historical Documents," The Cambridge Ancient History, Volume II, Part 1, History of the Middle East and the Aegean Region, edit. I. E. S. Edwards, C. J. Gadd, N. G. L. Hammond & E. Sollberger, Cambridge: Cambridge University Press, 1975, 609-626.

Chambers, Henry E., "Ancient Amphictyonies, Sic Et Non," Scripture in Context II: More Essays on the Comparative Method, edit. William W. Hallo, James C. Moyer, & Leo G. Perdue, Winona Lake, IN: Eisenbrauns, 1983, 39-59.

Chavalas, Mark W. & Adamthwaite, Murray R., "Archaeologic Light on the Old Testament," The Face of Old Testament Studies: A Survey of Contemporary Approaches, edit. David W. Baker & Bill T. Arnold, Grand Rapids, MI: Baker

Academic, 1999, 59-96.

Choi, Baek Sung, "Exodus: How Big was the Population?" <u>Jewish Bible Quarterly</u> 24 (1996):115-118.

Coleman, John E., "Did Egypt Shape the Glory that was Greece?" <u>Black Athena Revisited</u>, edit. Mary R. Lefkowitz & Guy MacLean Rogers, Chapel Hill, NC: The University of North Carolina Press, 280-302, 1996.

Cook, B.F., "Greek Inscriptions," <u>Reading the Past: Ancient Writing From Cuneiform to the Alphabet</u>, Introduced by J. T. Hooker, Berkeley: University of California Press, 1990, 259-320.

Coote, Robert B., "Social Organization in the Biblical Israels," <u>Ancient Israel: The Old Testament in Its Social Context</u>, edit. Philip F. Esler, London: SCM Press, 2005, 35-49.

Cooper, Alan, "Divine Names and Epithets in the Ugaritic Texts," <u>Ras Shamra Parallels: The Texts from Ugarit and the Hebrew Bible</u>, edit. Stan Rummel, Rome: Pontificium Institutum Biblicum, 1981, 335-500.

Crawshaw, Steve, "Found: The World's Wickedest City," The Independent, Sunday, 7 January 1996, <http://www.independent.co.uk/news/world/found-the-worlds-wickedest-city-1322799.html> (2/18/2005), 1-3.

Cross, Frank Moore, "Newly Found Inscriptions in Old Canaanite and Early Phoenician Scripts," <u>Bulletin of the American Schools of Oriental Research</u> 238 (1980):1-20.

D   Davies, W.V., "Egyptian Hieroglyphs," <u>Reading the Past: Ancient Writing From Cuneiform to the Alphabet</u>, Introduced by J. T. Hooker, Berkeley: University of California Press, 1990, 75-136.

de la Torre, Walter Reinhold Warttig Mattfeld y, "Dating the Exodus, The Hyksos Expulsion of 1540/1530 BCE?", http://www.bibleorigins.net/Exodus1540BCHyksos.html> (10/1/04), 1-19.

de Meester, E.J., "Saul, David and Solomon and the Amarna Period," <http://home.worldonline.nl/meester7/ engarmarna.html> (8/5/03), 1-6.

Demsky, Aaron, "Writing in Ancient Israel and Early Judaism, Part One: The Biblical Period," <u>Mikra: Text, Translation, Reading & Interpretation of the Hebrew Bible in Ancient Judaism & Early Christianity</u>, edit. Martin Jan Mulder, exec. edit. Harry Sysling, Peabody, MA: Hendrickson Publishers, Inc., 2004, 2-20.

Desborough, V. R. d'A., "The End of the Mycenaean Civilization and the Dark Age (a) The Archaeological Background," <u>The Cambridge Ancient History</u>, Volume II, Part 2, <u>History of the Middle East and the Aegean Region</u>, edit. I. E. S. Edwards, C. J. Gadd, N. G. L. Hammond & E. Sollberger, Cambridge: Cambridge University Press, 1975, 658-677.

de Vaux, Roland, "Was There an Israelite Amphictyony?" <u>The Biblical Archaeology Review</u> 3 (1977):40-47.

Dever, William G., "How to Tell a Canaanite From an Israelite," <u>The Rise of Ancient</u>

Israel, Symposium at the Smithsonian Institution, October 26, 1991, Washington, D.C.: Biblical Archaeology Society, 1992, 26-61.

Dever, William G, "Archaeology and the History of Israel," The Blackwell Companion to the Hebrew Bible, edit. Leo G. Perdue, Oxford: Blackwell Publishing, Ltd., 2005, 119-127.

Dillon, John, "The Essenes in Greek Sources: Some Reflections," Jews in the Hellenistic and Roman Cities, edit. John R. Bartlett, New York: Routledge, 2002, 117-128.

Dods, Marcus, "The Book of Genesis," The Expositor's Bible, edit. W. Robertson Nicoll, Grand Rapids: Wm. B. Eerdmans Publishing Co., Volume I, 1940, 1-116.

Doig, Kenneth F., "The 1552 Exodus," <http://www.doig.net/OT_Chronology.htm> (02/14/2004) 1-11.

E Euripides, "Alcestis," transl. Richmond Lattimore, Euripides, Euripides I, edit. David Grene and Richmond Lattimore, Chicago: The University of Chicago Press, 1955, 1-54.

Euripides, "Andromache," transl. John Frederick Nims, Euripides, Euripides III, edit. David Grene & Richmond Lattimore, Chicago: The University of Chicago Press, 1958, 69-120.

Euripides, "The Bacchae," transl. William Arrowsmith, Euripides, Euripides V, edit. David Grene & Richmond Latimore, Chicago: The University of Chicago Press, 1959, 141-220.

Euripides, "The Cyclops," transl. William Arrowsmith, Euripides, Euripides II, edit. David Grene & Richmond Latimore, Chicago: The University of Chicago Press, 1956, 1-42.

Euripides, "Electra," transl. Emily Townsend Vermeule, Euripides, Euripides V, edit. David Grene & Richmond Latimore, Chicago: The University of Chicago Press, 1959, 1-66.

Euripides, "Hecuba," transl. William Arrowsmith, Euripides, Euripides III, edit. David Grene & Richmond Lattimore, Chicago: The University of Chicago Press, 1958, 1-68.

Euripides, "Helen," transl. Richmond Lattimore, Euripides, Euripides II, edit. David Grene & Richmond Latimore, Chicago: The University of Chicago Press, 1956, 189-264.

Euripides, "The Heracleidae," transl. Ralph Gladstone, Euripides, Euripides I, edit. David Grene and Richmond Lattimore, Chicago: The University of Chicago Press, 1955, 109-156.

Euripides, "Heracles," transl. William Arrowsmith, Euripides, Euripides II, edit. David Grene & Richmond Latimore, Chicago: The University of Chicago Press, 1956, 43-116.

Euripides, "Hippolytus," transl. David Grene, Euripides, Euripides I, edit. David Grene and Richmond Lattimore, Chicago: The University of Chicago Press, 1955, 157-221.

Euripides, "Ion," transl. Ronald Frederick Willetts, Euripides, <u>Euripides III</u>, edit. David Grene & Richmond Lattimore, Chicago: The University of Chicago Press, 1958, 177-255.

Euripides, "Iphigenia in Aulis," transl. Charles R. Walker, Euripides, <u>Euripides IV</u>, edit. David Grene & Richmond Lattimore, Chicago: The University of Chicago Press, 1958, 209-307.

Euripides, "Iphigenia in Tauris," transl. Witter Bynner, Euripides, <u>Euripides II</u>, edit. David Grene & Richmond Latimore, Chicago: The University of Chicago Press, 1956, 117-188.

Euripides, "The Medea," transl. Rex Warner, Euripides, <u>Euripides I</u>, edit. David Grene and Richmond Lattimore, Chicago: The University of Chicago Press, 1955, 55-108

Euripides, "Orestes," transl. William Arrowsmith, Euripides, <u>Euripides IV</u>, edit. David Grene & Richmond Lattimore, Chicago: The University of Chicago Press, 1958, 105-208.

Euripides, "The Phoenician Women," transl. Elizabeth Wyckoff, Euripides, <u>Euripides V</u>, edit. David Grene & Richmond Latimore, Chicago: The University of Chicago Press, 1959, 67-140.

Euripides, "Rhesus," transl. Richmond Lattimore, Euripides, <u>Euripides IV</u>, edit. David Grene & Richmond Lattimore, Chicago: The University of Chicago Press, 1958, 1-50.

Euripides, "The Suppliant Women," transl. Frank William Jones, Euripides, <u>Euripides IV</u>, edit. David Grene & Richmond Lattimore, Chicago: The University of Chicago Press, 1958.51-104.

Euripides, "The Trojan Women," transl. Richmond Lattimore, Euripides, <u>Euripides III</u>, edit. David Grene & Richmond Lattimore, Chicago: The University of Chicago Press, 1958, 121-176.

Evans, Jean M., "The Mitanni State," <u>Beyond Babylon: Art, Trade, and Diplomacy in the Second Millennium B.C.</u>, edit. Joan Aruz, Kim Benzel, & Jean M Evans, New Haven: Yale University Press, 2008, 194-196.

F Feldman, Louis H., "Homer and the Near East: The Rise of the Greek Genius," <u>Biblical Archaeologist</u> 59 (Jan 1996):13-21.

Finkelstein, Israel, "Digging for the Truth: Archaeology and the Bible," Israel Finkelstein & Amihai Mazar, <u>The Quest for the Historical Israel: Debating Archaeology and the History of Early Israel</u>, edit. Brian B. Schmidt, Atlanta: Society of Biblical Literature, 2007, 9-20.

Finkelstein, Israel, "Patriarchs, Exodus, Conquest: Fact or Fiction?" Israel Finkelstein & Amihai Mazar, <u>The Quest for the Historical Israel: Debating Archaeology and the History of Early Israel</u>, edit. Brian B. Schmidt, Atlanta: Society of Biblical Literature, 2007, 41-55.

Finkelstein, Israel, "When and How Did the Israelites Emerge?" Israel Finkelstein &

Amihai Mazar, <u>The Quest for the Historical Israel: Debating Archaeology and the History of Early Israel</u>, edit. Brian B. Schmidt, Atlanta: Society of Biblical Literature, 2007, 73-83.

Forster, E. S., "On the Universe," Aristotle, <u>The Complete Works of Aristotle</u>, edit Jonathan Barnes, Volume One, Princeton, NJ: Princeton University Press, 1984, 626-640.

Fox, Nili S., "Numbers," <u>The Jewish Study Bible</u>, The Jewish Publication Society Tanakh Translation, edit. Adele Berlin & Marc Zvi Brettler, Oxford: Oxford University Press, 2004, 281-355.

G Geller, M. J., "The Survival of Babylonian Wissenschaft in Later Tradition," The Heirs of Assyria: Proceeding of the Opening Symposium of the Assyrian and Babylonian Intellectual Heritage Project Held in Tvarminne, Finland, October 8-11, 1998, edit. Sannaa Aro & R. M. Whiting, Helsinki: The Neo-Assyrian Text Corpus Project, 2000, 1-6.

Geller, Stephen A., "The Religion of the Bible," <u>The Jewish Study Bible</u>, The Jewish Publication Society Tanakh Translation, edit. Adele Berlin & Marc Zvi Brettler, Oxford: Oxford University Press, 2004, 2021-2040.

Georgiev, V. I., "The Arrival of the Greeks in Greece: the Linguistic Evidence," <u>Bronze Age Migrations in the Aegean</u>, edit. R. A. Crossland & Ann Birchall, Park Ridge, NJ: Noyes Press, 1974. 243-256.

Goldenberg, Robert, "Talmud," <u>Back to the Sources, Reading the Classic Jewish Texts</u>, edit. Barry W. Holtz, New York: Touchstone Books, 1992, 129-176.

Goodenough, Erwin R., "The Problem of Method/Symbols From Jewish Cult," <u>Jewish Symbols in the Greco-Roman Period</u>, New York: Pantheon Books, Volume IV, 1958.

Gordon, Cyrus H., "Recovering Canaan and Ancient Israel," <u>Civilizations of the Ancient Near East</u>, edit. Jack M. Sasson, New York: Charles Scribner's Sons, Volume IV, 1995, 2779-2789.

Greenberg, M., "HAB/PIRU and Hebrews," <u>Patriarchs</u>, Volume II, edit. Benjamin Mazar, <u>The World History of the Jewish People</u>, First Series: Ancient Times, gen. edit. Benjamin Mazar, Israel: Jewish History Publications, 1970, 188-200.

Greenspahn, Frederick E., "Primogeniture in Ancient Israel," <u>"Go to the Land I Will Show You", Studies in Honor of Dwight W. Young</u>, edit. Joseph E. Coleson & Victor H. Matthews, Winona Lake, IN: Eisenbrauns, 1996, 69-79.

Grube, G. M. A., "Phaedo," <u>Plato Complete Works</u>, edit. John M. Cooper, Indianapolis, IN: Hackett Publishing Company, 1997, 49-100.

Grube, G. M. A. & Reeve, C. D. C., "Republic," <u>Plato Complete Works</u>, edit. John M. Cooper, Indianapolis, IN: Hackett Publishing Company, 1997, 971-1223.

Guthrie, K. C., "The Religion and Mythology of the Greeks," <u>The Cambridge Ancient History</u>, Volume II, Part 2, <u>History of the Middle East and the Aegean Region</u>, edit.

I. E. S. Edwards, C. J. Gadd, N. G. L. Hammond & E. Sollberger, Cambridge: Cambridge University Press, 1975, 851-905.

H Hakimian, Suzy, "Byblos," Beyond Babylon: Art, Trade, and Diplomacy in the Second Millennium B.C., edit. Joan Aruz, Kim Benzel, & Jean M Evans, New Haven: Yale University Press, 2008, 49-60.

Hallo, William, "Again the Abecedaries," Sefer Moshe: the Moshe Weinfeld Jubilee Volume: Studies in the Bible and the Ancient Near East, Qumran, and post-Biblical Judaism, edit. Chaim Cohen, Avi Hurvitz, & Shalom M. Paul, Winona Lake, IN: Eisenbrauns, 2004, 285-302.

Halpern, Baruch, "The Exodus From Egypt: Myth or Reality?," The Rise of Ancient Israel, Symposium at the Smithsonian Institution, October 26, 1991, Washington, D.C.: Biblical Archaeology Society, 1992, 87-117.

Halpern, Baruch, "Ezra's Reform and Bilateral Citizenship in Athens and the Mediterranean World," Egypt, Israel, and the Ancient Mediterranean World: Studies in Honor of Donald B. Redford, edit. Gary N. Knoppers & Antoine Hirsch, Leiden: Brill, 2004, 439-453.

Harris, R. Laird, "Leviticus," The Expositor's Bible Commentary, Genesis, Exodus, Leviticus, Numbers, Volume 2, edit. Frank Gaebelein, Zondervan: Grand Rapids, 1990, 501-654.

Hawass, Zahi, Gad, Yehia Z, Ismail, Somaia, Khairat, Rabab, Fathalla, Dina, Hasan, Naglaa, Ahmed, Amal, Elleithy, Hisham, Ball, Markus, Gaballah, Fawzi, Wasef, Sally, Fateen, Mohamed, Amer, Hany, Gostner, Paul, Selim, Ashraf, Zink, Albert, and Pusch, Carsten M, "Ancestry and Pathology in King Tutankhamun's Family," JAMA, 303(2010):638-647.

Healey, John F., "The Early Alphabet," Reading the Past: Ancient Writing From Cuneiform to the Alphabet, Introduced by J. T. Hooker, Berkeley: University of California Press, 1990, 197-258.

Henderson, Michael L. C., "Sermons From the Pulpit: Beyond All Reason," http://users. ren.com/exetercongchurch/Serm_06-30-02.htm, (8/3/05), 1-4.

Hesiod, "Works and Days," Theogony, Works and Days, Shield, transl. Apostolos N. Athanassakis, Baltimore: The Johns Hopkins University Press, 1983, 110-176.

Hess, Richard S., "Early Israel in Canaan: A Survey of Recent Evidence and Interpretation," Palestine Exploration Quarterly 125 (1993):125-142.

Hoffmeier, James K., "Exodus," Baker Commentary on the Bible, edit. Walter A Elwell, Grand Rapids: Baker Books, 1989, 38-63.

Houston, Walter, "Exodus," The Oxford Bible Commentary, edit. John Barton and John Muddiman, Oxford: Oxford University Press, 2001, 67-91.

Howard Jr., David M., "Philistines," Peoples of the Old Testament World, edit. Alfred J. Hoerth, Gerald L. Mattingly, Edwin M. Yamauchi, Grand Rapids: Baker Books, 1998, 231-250.

Huehnergard, John, & Hackett, Jo Ann, "The Hebrew and Aramaic Languages," The Biblical World, edit. John Barton, London: Routledge, 2002, Volume 2, 3-24.

Humphreys, Colin J., "The Number of People in the Exodus From Egypt: Decoding Mathematically the Very Large Numbers in Numbers I and XXVI," Vetus Testamentum 48 (1998):196-213.

Humphreys, Colin J., "The Numbers in the Exodus From Egypt: A Further Appraisal," Vetus Testamentum 50 (2000):323-328.

Hutchinson, Richard Wyatt, "The Decadence of Minoan Crete: The Mycenaean Empire," The Rise and Fall of Civilizations: Modern Archaeological Approaches to Ancient Cultures, edit. C. C. Lamberg-Karlovsky & Jeremy A. Sablof, Menlo Park, California: Cummings Publishing Company, 1974, 412-423.

I Izre'el, Shlomo, "The Amarna Letters From Canaan," Civilizations of the Ancient Near East, edit. Jack M. Sasson, New York: Charles Scribner's Sons, Volume IV, 1995, 2411-2419.

J Jasanoff, Jay H. & Nussbaum, Alan, "Word Games: The Linguistic Evidence in Black Athena," Black Athena Revisited, edit. Mary R. Lefkowitz & Guy MacLean Rogers, Chapel Hill: The University of North Carolina Press, 1996, 177-205.

Johnston, Ian, "Trojan War," 1996, <http://webhome.crk.umn.edu/~sneet/WesCiv/TrojanWar.htm> (5/11/03), 1-7.

K Kaiser, Walter C. Jr., "Exodus," The Expositor's Bible Commentary, edit. Frank E. Gaebelein, Grand Rapids: Zondervan Publishing House, Volume 2, 1990, 287-497.

Kedar, Karyn D., "Va-era: The Many Names of God," The Women's Torah Commentary: New Insights from Women Rabbis on the 54 Weekly Torah Portions, edit. Elyze Goldstein, Woodstock, VT: Jewish Lights Publishing, 2000, 127-132.

Kedourie, Elie, "Introduction," The Jewish World: History and Culture of the Jewish People, edit. Elie Kedourie, New York: Harry N. Abrams, Inc., 1979, 7-11.

Kempinski, Aharon, "Jacob in History," Biblical Archaeology Review 14 (1988):42-47.

Kempinski, Aharon, "The Middle Bronze Age," The Archaeology of Ancient Israel, edit. Amnon Ben-Tor, New Haven: Yale University Press, 1992, 159-210.

Kenyon, Kathleen M., "Palestine in the Middle Bronze Age," The Cambridge Ancient History, Volume II, Part 1, History of the Middle East and the Aegean Region, edit. I. E. S. Edwards, C. J. Gadd, N. G. L. Hammond & E. Sollberger, Cambridge: Cambridge University Press, 1975, 526-556.

Kitto, H. D. F., "The Odyssey: The Exclusion of Surprise," Homer's the Odyssey, edit. Harold Bloom, New York: Chelsea House Publishers, 1988, 5-34.

Knapp, A. Bernard, "Bronze Age Mediterranean Island Cultures and the Ancient Near East, Part 2," Biblical Archaeologist 55 (1992):112-128.

Knapp, A. Bernard, "Island Cultures: Crete, Thera, Cyprus, Rhodes, and Sardinia," Civilizations of the Ancient Near East, edit. Jack M. Sasson, New York: Charles Scribner's Sons, Volume III, 1995, 1433-1449.

Knight, Douglas A., "Introduction: Tradition and Theology," Tradition and Theology in the Old Testament, edit. Douglas A. Knight, Atlanta: Society of Biblical Literature, 2007, 1-8.

Kramer, S. N., "Sumerian Myths and Epic Tales," Ancient Near Eastern Texts Relating to the Old Testament, Third Edition with Supplement, Edit. James B. Pritchard, Princeton: Princeton University Press, 1969, 37-59.

Kuhl, J. J., Orion, "The Tale of Orion, Canis Major, Canis Minor, Lepus and Scorpio," Tales of the Immortal Night, 2003, <http://www.business-esolutions.com/starmyths/myths/orion.htm> (6/18/03), 1-7.

L Larsen, Mogens Trolle, "The Middle Bronze Age," Beyond Babylon: Art, Trade, and Diplomacy in the Second Millennium B.C., edit. Joan Aruz, Kim Benzel, & Jean M Evans, New Haven: Yale University Press, 2008, 12-17.

Lefkowitz, Mary R., "Ancient History, Modern Myths," Black Athena Revisited, edit. Mary R. Lefkowitz & Guy MacLean Rogers, Chapel Hill: The University of North Carolina Press, 3-23, 1996.

Lemche, N. P., "The Greek 'Amphictyony' - Could it be a Prototype for the Israelite Society in the Period of the Judges?" Journal for the Study of the Old Testament 4 (1977):48-59.

Levenson, Jon D., "Genesis," The Jewish Study Bible, The Jewish Publication Society Tanakh Translation, edit. Adele Berlin & Marc Zvi Brettler, Oxford: Oxford University Press, 2004, 8-101.

Levinson, Bernard M., "Deuteronomy," The Jewish Study Bible, The Jewish Publication Society Tanakh Translation, edit. Adele Berlin & Marc Zvi Brettler, Oxford: Oxford University Press, 2004, 356-450.

Lewy, Hans, "Introduction," Philo: Selections, edited by Hans Lewy, in Three Jewish Philosophers, Atheneum, New York, 1976, 7-25.

M Malamat, Abraham, "Let My People go and Go and Go and Go," Biblical Archaeology Review 24 (1998): 62-66.

Marblestone, Howard, "A `Mediterranean Synthesis'," Biblical Archaeologist 59 (1996): 22-30.

Marcus, David, "Akkadian," Beyond Babel: A Handbook for Biblical Hebrew and Related Languages, edit. John Kaltner & Steven L. McKenzie, Atlanta: Society of Biblical Literature, 2002, 19-41.

Marinatos, Spyridon, "The First `Mycenaeans' in Greece," <u>Bronze Age Migrations in the Aegean</u>, edit. R. A. Crossland & Ann Birchall, Park Ridge, NJ: Noyes Press, 1974, 107-114.

Mariottini, Claude F., "Ur and Haran, Abraham's Background," <u>Biblical Illustrator</u> 24 (1997):50-53.

Marks, John H., "The Book of Genesis," <u>The Interpreter's One-Volume Commentary on the Bible</u>, edit. Charles M. Laymon, Nashville: Abingdon Press, 1971, 1-32.

Mazar, B., "The Historical Development," Part One: Canaan in the Egyptian New Kingdom Period, <u>Judges</u>, Volume III, edit. Benjamin Mazar, <u>The World History of the Jewish People</u>, First Series: Ancient Times, gen. edit. Benjamin Mazar, Israel: Jewish History Publications, 1971, 3-22.

Mazar, B., "The Exodus and the Conquest," Part Two: Beginnings of the Nation, <u>Judges</u>, Volume III, edit. Benjamin Mazar, <u>The World History of the Jewish People</u>, First Series: Ancient Times, gen. edit. Benjamin Mazar, Israel: Jewish History Publications, 1971, 69-93.

McCarter, P. Kyle Jr., "The Patriarchal Age," revised by Ronald S. Hendel, <u>Ancient Israel, From Abraham to the Roman Destruction of the Temple</u>, edit. Hershel Shanks, Washington, D. C.: Biblical Archaeology Society, 1999, 1-31.

McFadden, W. Robert, "Micah and the Problem of Continuities and Discontinuities in Prophecy," <u>Scripture in Context II: More Essays on the Comparative Method</u>, edit. William W. Hallo, James c. Moyer, & Leo G. Perdue, Winona Lake, IN: Eisenbrauns, 1983, 127-146.

McGing, Brian, "Population and Proselytism: How Many Jews Were There in the Ancient World?" <u>Jews in the Hellenistic and Roman Cities</u>, edit. John R. Bartlett, New York: Routledge, 2002, 88-106.

"The Merneptah Stela: Israel Enters History," <u>Biblical Archaeology Review</u> 23 (1997):30.

Meyers, Carol, "Early Israel and the Rise of the Israelite Monarchy," <u>The Blackwell Companion to the Hebrew Bible</u>, edit. Leo G. Perdue, Oxford: Blackwell Publishing, Ltd., 2005, 61-87.

Meyers, Carol, "Joshua," <u>The Jewish Study Bible</u>, The Jewish Publication Society Tanakh Translation, edit. Adele Berlin & Marc Zvi Brettler, Oxford: Oxford University Press, 2004, 462-507.

Meyers, Stephen C., "Biblical Archaeology: The Date of the Exodus According to Ancient Writers," <http://www.bibleandscience.com/archaeology/exodusdate.htm> (10/15/04), 1-24.

Milner, Larry S., "Punishment for the Crime of Infanticide: A Historical Overview," <u>The Journal of Graduate Liberal Studies</u> IV (1998):15-27.

Mondriaan, Marlene E., "Yahweh and the Origin of Yahwism: A Critical Evaluation," <u>Old Testament Essays</u> 17(2004):580-594.

"Mythical Chronology," <http://homepage.mac.com/cparada/GML/MythicalChronology.html>(10/24/09), 1-6.

N Najman, Hindy, "Ezra," <u>The Jewish Study Bible</u>, The Jewish Publication Society Tanakh Translation, edit. Adele Berlin & Marc Zvi Brettler, Oxford: Oxford University Press, 2004, 1666-1687.

Najman, Hindy, "Nehemiah," <u>The Jewish Study Bible</u>, The Jewish Publication Society Tanakh Translation, edit. Adele Berlin & Marc Zvi Brettler, Oxford: Oxford University Press, 2004, 1688-1711.

"Names of God," Executive Committee of the Editorial Board, <http://www.Jewish Encyclopedia.com>(11/20/03), 1-10.

"Names of God in Judaism," Wikipedia, the Free Encyclopedia, http://en.wikipedia.org/ wiki/Adonai>(11/25/06), 1-12.

Nehamas, Alexander & Woodruff, Paul, "Phaedrus," <u>Plato Complete Works</u>, edit. John M. Cooper, Indianapolis, IN: Hackett Publishing Company, 1997, 506-556.

Newgrosh, Bernard, Rohl, David M., & van der Veen, Peter G., "The el-Amarna Letters and Israelite History," <http://www.nunki.net/isis/jacf6article1.htm>(8/5/03), 1-27.

Newgrosh, Bernard, Rohl, David M., & van der Veen, Peter G., "The el-Amarna Letters and Israelite History (I)," http://www.ouviroevento.hpg.ig.com.br/textos/ arqueologiaehist/theelamarnaletters.htm>(2/9/2005, 1-46.

O O'Connor, David, "Egypt and Greece: The Bronze Age Evidence," <u>Black Athena Revisited</u>, edit. Mary R. Lefkowitz & Guy MacLean Rogers, Chapel Hill, The University of North Carolina Press, 49-61, 1996.

O'Connor, David, "Egypt, the Levant, and the Aegean from the Hyksos Period to the Rise of the New Kingdom," <u>Beyond Babylon: Art, Trade, and Diplomacy in the Second Millennium B.C.</u>, edit. Joan Aruz, Kim Benzel, & Jean M Evans, New Haven: Yale University Press, 2008, 108-112.

Oded, B., "Where is the 'Myth of the Empty Land' to be Found: History Versus Myth," <u>Judah and the Judeans in the Neo-Babylonian Period</u>, edit. Oded Lipschits & Joseph Blenkinsopp, Winona Lake: Eisenbrauns, 2003, 55-74.

P Parada, Carlos, "The Trojan War," 1997. <http://homepage.mac.com/cparada/ GML/TrojanWar.html>(5/11/03), 1-22.

Parada, Carlos, "Troy," 1997. <http://homepage.mac.com/cparada/GML/TrojanWar. html>(5/11/03), 1-9.

Parker, Robert, "Law and Religion," <u>The Cambridge Companion to Ancient Greek Law</u>, edit. Michael Gagarin & David Cohen, Cambridge: Cambridge University Press, 2005, 61-81.

Pitard, Wayne T., "Before Israel, Syria-Palestine in the Bronze Age," <u>The Oxford History of the Biblical World</u>, edit. Michael D. Coogan, Oxford: Oxford University Press, 1998, 25-57.

Plutarch, "Alexander," The Age of Alexander, transl. Ian Scott-Kilvert, Middlesex: Penguin Books, 1973, 252-334.

Plutarch, "Dion," The Age of Alexander, transl. Ian Scott-Kilvert, Middlesex: Penguin Books, 1973, 104-150.

"Prehistoric Archaeology of the Aegean: Lesson 27: Troy VII and the Historicity of the Trojan War," <http:// projects.dartmouth.edu/history/bronze-age/chrono.html> (5/20/03), 1-11.

Propp, William H. C., "Jewish Origins," The Archaeology of Ancient Judea and Palestine, edit. Ariel Lewin, Los Angeles: Getty Publications, 2005, 8-11.

Pulak, Cemal, "The Uluburun Shipwreck and Late Bronze Age Trade," Beyond Babylon: Art, Trade, and Diplomacy in the Second Millennium B.C., edit. Joan Aruz, Kim Benzel, & Jean M Evans, New Haven: Yale University Press, 2008, 289-305.

R Rahtjen, Bruce Donald, "Philistine and Hebrew Amphictyonies," Journal of Near Eastern Studies 24 (1965):100-104.

Ridpath, Ian, "Orion the Hunter," <http://www.arash.macunlimited.net/ianrid/startales/orion> (6/18/03), 1-4.

Ross, W. D., "Metaphysics," Aristotle, The Complete Works of Aristotle, edit Jonathan Barnes, Volume Two, Princeton, NJ: Princeton University Press, 1984, 1552-1728.

Ryan, William Burke, "Child Murder in Its Sanitary and Social Bearings," Sanitary Review and Journal of Public Health, London (1858): 4.

S Saggs, H. W. F.," Pre-Exilic Jewry," The Jewish World: History and Culture of the Jewish People, edit. Elie Kedourie, New York: Harry N. Abrams, 1979, 37-51.

Sailhamer, John H., "Genesis," The Expositor's Bible Commentary, Genesis, Exodus, Leviticus, Numbers, Volume 2, edit. Frank E. Gaebelein, Zondervan: Grand Rapids, 1990, 1-284.

Sanderson, Judith E., "Ancient Texts and Versions of the Old Testament," The New Interpreters Bible, Volume I, Nashville: Abington Press, 1994, 292-304.

"Santorini," Wikipedia, the Free Encyclopedia, <http:en.wikipedia.org/wiki/thera#Dating_the_volcanic-eruption> (9/25/05, 1.

Sarna, Nahum M., "Israel in Egypt, the Egyptian Sojourn and the Exodus," Ancient Israel, A Short History from Abraham to the Roman Destruction of the Temple, edit. Hershel Shanks, Washington, D.C.: Biblical Archaeology Society, 1988, 31-52.

Saunders, Trevor J., "Laws," Plato Complete Works, edit. John M. Cooper, Indianapolis, IN: Hackett Publishing Company, 1997, 1318-1616.

Schmidt, Brian B., "Flood Narratives of Ancient Western Asia," Civilizations of the Ancient Near East, edit. Jack M. Sasson, New York: Charles Scribner's Sons, Volume IV, 1995, 2337-2351.

Schoville, Keith N., "Canaanites and Amorites," <u>Peoples of the Old Testament World</u>, edit. Alfred J. Hoerth, Gerald L. Mattingly, Edwin M. Yamauchi, Grand Rapids: Baker Books, 1998, 157-182.

Schwartz, Baruch J., "Leviticus," <u>The Jewish Study Bible</u>, The Jewish Publication Society Tanakh Translation, edit. Adele Berlin & Marc Zvi Brettler, Oxford: Oxford University Press, 2004, 203-280.

"Second Temple of Jerusalem," <http://en.wikipedia.org/wiki/Second_Temple_of_ Jerusalem,> (3/23/20) 1-2.

Setterfield, "Creation and Catastrophe Chronology," <http://www.setterfield.org/ scriptchron.htm> (1/30/04) 1-25.

Shaw, Ian, "Introduction: Chronologies and Cultural Change in Egypt," <u>The Oxford History of Ancient Egypt</u>, Oxford: Oxford University Press, 2000, 1-16.

Smend, "Tradition and History: A Complex Relation," <u>Tradition and Theology in the Old Testament</u>, edit. Douglas A. Knight, Atlanta: Society of Biblical Literature, 2007, 49-68.

Sommer, Benjamin D., "Isaiah," <u>The Jewish Study Bible</u>, The Jewish Publication Society Tanakh Translation, edit. Adele Berlin & Marc Zvi Brettler, Oxford: Oxford University Press, 2004, 780-916.

Sophocles, "Aias," <u>The Complete Plays of Sophocles</u>, Robert Bagg and James Scully, New York: HarperCollins Publishers, 2011, 3-98.

Sophocles, "Antigone," <u>The Complete Plays of Sophocles</u>, Robert Bagg and James Scully, New York: HarperCollins Publishers, 2011, 619-706.

Sophocles, "Elektra," <u>The Complete Plays of Sophocles</u>, Robert Bagg and James Scully, New York: HarperCollins Publishers, 2011, 285-388.

Sophocles, "Oedipus at Kolonus," <u>The Complete Plays of Sophocles</u>, Robert Bagg and James Scully, New York: HarperCollins Publishers, 2011, 495-619.

Sophocles, "Oedipus the King," <u>The Complete Plays of Sophocles</u>, Robert Bagg and James Scully, New York: HarperCollins Publishers, 2011, 389-494.

Sophocles, "Philoktetes," <u>The Complete Plays of Sophocles</u>, Robert Bagg and James Scully, New York: HarperCollins Publishers, 2011, 183-284.

Sophocles, "Women of Trakhis," <u>The Complete Plays of Sophocles</u>, Robert Bagg and James Scully, New York: HarperCollins Publishers, 2011, 99-182.

Speiser, E. A., "The Patriarchs and Their Social Background," <u>Patriarchs</u>, Volume II, edit. Benjamin Mazar, <u>The World History of the Jewish People</u>, First Series: Ancient Times, gen. edit. Benjamin Mazar, Israel: Jewish History Publications, 1961, 160-168.

Speiser, E. A., "The Creation Epic," <u>Ancient Near Eastern Texts Relating to the Old Testament</u>, Third Edition with Supplement, Edit. James B. Pritchard, Princeton: Princeton University Press, 1969, 60-72.

Spitzer, Julie Ringold, "Noach: Mrs. Noah," <u>The Women's Torah Commentary: New Insights from Women Rabbis on the 54 Weekly Torah Portions</u>, edit. Elyze Goldstein, Woodstock, VT: Jewish Lights Publishing, 2000, 53-56.

Stager, Lawrence E., "Forging an Identity: The Emergence of Ancient Israel," The Oxford History of the Biblical World, edit. Michael D. Coogan, Oxford: Oxford University Press, 1998, 123-176.

Stager, Lawrence E. & Wolff, Samuel R., "Child Sacrifice at Carthage; Religious Rite or Population Control?" Biblical Archaeology Review 10 (1984): 31-51.

Sterling, Gregory E., "The Jewish Appropriation of Hellenistic Historiography," A Companion to Greek and Roman Historiography, Volume I, edit. John Marincola, Oxford: Blackwell Publishing Ltd, 2007, 231-243

Stiebing, William H., Jr., "Climate and Collapse - Did the Weather Make Israel's Emergence Possible?" Bible Review 10 (August 1994):18-27.

Stocks, J. L., "On the Heavens," Aristotle, The Complete Works of Aristotle, edit Jonathan Barnes, Volume One, Princeton, NJ: Princeton University Press, 1984, 447-511.

Strauss, "The Beginning of the Bible and Its Greek Counterparts," Genesis, edit. Harold Bloom, New York: Chelsea House Publishers, 1986, 23-42.

Strauss, Leo, "On Socrates and the Prophets," The Bible, Modern Critical Views, edit. Harold Bloom, New York: Chelsea House Publishers, 1987, 225-232.

Stubbings, Frank, "The Rise of Mycenaean Civilization," The Cambridge Ancient History, Volume II, Part 1, History of the Middle East and the Aegean Region, edit. I. E. S. Edwards, C. J. Gadd, N. G. L. Hammond & E. Sollberger, Cambridge: Cambridge University Press, 1975, 627-658.

Sweeney, Marvin A., "Ezekiel," The Jewish Study Bible, The Jewish Publication Society Tanakh Translation, edit. Adele Berlin & Marc Zvi Brettler, Oxford: Oxford University Press, 2004, 1042-1138.

Sweeney, Marvin A., "Jeremiah," The Jewish Study Bible, The Jewish Publication Society Tanakh Translation, edit. Adele Berlin & Marc Zvi Brettler, Oxford: Oxford University Press, 2004, 917-1041.

T Tadmor, H., "Chronology of the Ancient Near East in the Second Millennium BCE," Patriarchs, Volume II, edit. Benjamin Mazar, The World History of the Jewish People, First Series: Ancient Times, gen. edit. Benjamin Mazar, Israel: Jewish History Publications, 1970, 61-101.

Tarn, W. W., "Ptolemy II," The Journal of Egyptian Archaeology 14 (1928):246-260.

Thomassen, Einar, "The Tripartite Tractate," The Nag Hammadi Scriptures, edit. Marvin Meyer, New York: HarperOne, 2007, 57-102.

"The True Date of the Exodus," <http://www.christianhospitality.org/exodus.htm> (10/15/04) 1-68.

Tigay, Jeffrey H., "Exodus," The Jewish Study Bible, The Jewish Publication Society Tanakh Translation, edit. Adele Berlin & Marc Zvi Brettler, Oxford: Oxford University Press, 2004, 102-202.

Trimm, James, "Nazarenes and the Name of YHWH," <http://www.nazarene.net/_halacha/Name.htm> (6/6/03), 1-7.

Tritle, Lawrence A., "*Black Athena*, Vision or Dream of Greek Origins?" Black Athena Revisited, edit. Mary R. Lefkowitz & Guy MacLean Rogers, Chapel Hill: The University of North Carolina Press, 1996, 303-330.

U   "Ugarit and the Bible," <http://www.theology.edu/ugarbib.htm> (5/20/03), 1-6.

V   van der Horst, Pieter W., "The Interpretation of the Bible by the Minor Hellenistic Jewish Authors," Mikra: Text, Translation, Reading & Interpretation of the Hebrew Bible in Ancient Judaism & Early Christianity, edit. Martin Jan Mulder, exec. edit. Harry Sysling, Peabody, MA: Hendrickson Publishers, Inc., 2004, 519-546.

Vercoutter, Jean, "The Second Intermediate Period and the Hyksos Invasion of Egypt," The Near East: The Early Civilizations, edit. Jean Bottero, Elena Cassin & Jean Vercoutter, New York: Delacorte Press, 1967, 383-418.

Vinson, Steve, "Ships in the Ancient Mediterranean," Biblical Archaeologist 53 (1990):13-18.

W   Wachsmann, Shelley, "A Complex Migration: Did the Philistines Get to Canaan by Land or by Sea?" Biblical Archaeology Review 29 (2003):22-64.

Wenham, Gordon J., "The Akedah: A Paradigm of Sacrifice," Pomegranates and Golden Bells: Studies in Biblical, Jewish, and Near Eastern Ritual, Law, and Literature in Honor of Jacob Milgrom, edit. David P. Wright, David Noel Freedman, & Avi Hurvitz, Winona Lake, IN: Eisenbrauns, 1995, 93-102.

Wente, Edward F., & Van Siclen, Charles C., "A Chronology of the New Kingdom," Studies in Ancient Oriental Civilization, Chicago: The Oriental Institute, 1976, 217-261.

Whybray, R. N., "Genesis," The Oxford Bible Commentary, edit. John Barton and John Muddiman, Oxford: Oxford University Press, 2001, 38-66.

Wilson, J. A., "Egypt - The Kingdom of the 'Two Lands' 1. First Things," At the Dawn of Civilization, A. Background of Biblical History, edit. E. A. Speiser, The World History of the Jewish People, gen. edit. B. Netanyahu, Israel, Jewish History Publications, 1964, 267-276.

Wilson, J. A., "Egypt - The Kingdom of the 'Two Lands' 4. The Challenges to Power," At the Dawn of Civilization, A. Background of Biblical History, edit. E. A. Speiser, The World History of the Jewish People, gen. edit. B. Netanyahu, Israel, Jewish History Publications, 1964, 315-328.

Wilson, "Egyptian Myths, Tales, and Mortuary Texts," Ancient Near Eastern Texts Relating to the Old Testament, Third Edition with Supplement, Edit. James B. Pritchard, Princeton: Princeton University Press, 1969, 3-36.

Wilson, John A., "The Story of Sinuhe," The Ancient Near East, Volume I, An Anthology of Texts and Pictures, edit. James B. Pritchard, Princeton: Princeton University Press, 1973, 5-11.

Wilson, John A., "The Journey of Wen-Amon to Phoenicia," The Ancient Near East, Volume I, An Anthology of Texts and Pictures, edit. James B. Pritchard, Princeton: Princeton University Press, 1973, 16-24.

Wilson, John A., "The Expulsion of the Hyksos," The Ancient Near East, Volume I, An Anthology of Texts and Pictures, edit. James B. Pritchard, Princeton: Princeton University Press, 1973, 173-175.

Wood, Bryant G., "Debunking 'The Exodus Decoded'," <http://www.biblearchaeology.org/post/2006/09/demunking-the-exodus-decoded.aspx> (9/20/2006), 1-21.

Worschech, Udo, "Egypt and Moab," Biblical Archaeologist 60 (1997):229-236.

Y Yadin, Y., "Warfare in the Second Millennium BCE," Patriarchs, Volume II, edit. Benjamin Mazar, The World History of the Jewish People, First Series: Ancient Times, gen. edit. Benjamin Mazar, Israel: Jewish History Publications, 1970, 127-159.

Yadin, Yigael, "'And Dan, Why Did He Remain In Ships!' (Judges 5:17)", Essential Papers on Israel and the Ancient Near East, edit. Frederick E. Greenspahn, New York: New York University Press, 1991, 294-310.

Yasur-Landau, Assaf, "One if By Sea ... Two if By Land, How did the Philistines Get to Canaan? Two: by Land" Biblical Archaeology Review 29 (2003):34-39, 66-67.

Younger, Jr., K. Lawson, "Early Israel in Recent Biblical Scholarship," The Face of Old Testament Studies, A Survey of Contemporary Approaches, edit. David W. Baker & Bill T. Arnold, Grand Rapids: Baker Books, 1999, 176-206.

Yurco, Frank J., "Merneptah's Canaanite Campaign and Israel's Origins," Exodus: The Egyptian Evidence, edit. Ernest S. Frerichs & Leonard H. Lesko, Winona Lake, IN: Eisenbrauns, 1997, 27-56.

Yurco, Frank J., "Black Athena: An Egyptian Review," Black Athena Revisited, edit. Mary R. Lefkowitz & Guy MacLean Rogers, Chapel Hill: The University of North Carolina Press, 1996, 62-100.

Z Zevit, Ziony, "First Kings," The Jewish Study Bible, The Jewish Publication Society Tanakh Translation, edit. Adele Berlin & Marc Zvi Brettler, Oxford: Oxford University Press, 2004, 668-725.

Zevit, Ziony, "Second Kings," The Jewish Study Bible, The Jewish Publication Society Tanakh Translation, edit. Adele Berlin & Marc Zvi Brettler, Oxford: Oxford University Press, 2004, 726-779.

Zeyl, Donald J., "Timaeus," Plato Complete Works, edit. John M. Cooper, Indianapolis, IN: Hackett Publishing Company, 1997, 1224-1291.

Zvi, Ehud Ben, "Amos," The Jewish Study Bible, The Jewish Publication Society Tanakh Translation, edit. Adele Berlin & Marc Zvi Brettler, Oxford: Oxford University Press, 2004, 1176-1192.

Zvi, Ehud Ben, "Habakkuk," The Jewish Study Bible, The Jewish Publication Society Tanakh Translation, edit. Adele Berlin & Marc Zvi Brettler, Oxford: Oxford University Press, 2004, 1226-1233.

Zvi, Ehud Ben, "Hosea," The Jewish Study Bible, The Jewish Publication Society Tanakh Translation, edit. Adele Berlin & Marc Zvi Brettler, Oxford: Oxford University Press, 2004, 1143-1165.

Zvi, Ehud Ben, "Joel," The Jewish Study Bible, The Jewish Publication Society Tanakh Translation, edit. Adele Berlin & Marc Zvi Brettler, Oxford: Oxford University Press, 2004, 1166-1175.

Zvi, Ehud Ben, "Malachi," The Jewish Study Bible, The Jewish Publication Society Tanakh Translation, edit. Adele Berlin & Marc Zvi Brettler, Oxford: Oxford University Press, 2004, 1268-1274.

Zvi, Ehud Ben, "Micah," The Jewish Study Bible, The Jewish Publication Society Tanakh Translation, edit. Adele Berlin & Marc Zvi Brettler, Oxford: Oxford University Press, 2004, 1205-1218.

Zvi, Ehud Ben, "Zechariah," The Jewish Study Bible, The Jewish Publication Society Tanakh Translation, edit. Adele Berlin & Marc Zvi Brettler, Oxford: Oxford University Press, 2004, 1249-1267.

INDEX